Prioritarianism in Practice

Prioritarianism is an ethical theory that gives extra weight to the well-being of the worse off. In contrast, dominant policy-evaluation methodologies, such as benefit-cost analysis, cost-effectiveness analysis, and utilitarianism, ignore or downplay issues of fair distribution. Based on a research group founded by the editors, this important book is the first to show how prioritarianism can be used to assess governmental policies and evaluate societal conditions. This book uses prioritarianism as a methodology to evaluate governmental policy across a variety of policy domains: taxation, health policy, risk regulation, education, climate policy, and the COVID-19 pandemic. It also demonstrates how prioritarianism improves on GDP as an indicator of a society's progress over time. Edited by two senior figures in the field with contributions from some of the world's leading economists, this volume bridges the gap from the theory of prioritarianism to its practical application.

MATTHEW D. ADLER is Richard A. Horvitz Professor of Law and Professor of Economics, Philosophy, and Public Policy at Duke University. He is the author of *Measuring Social Welfare* (2019) and *Well-Being and Fair Distribution: Beyond Cost-Benefit Analysis* (2012).

OLE F. NORHEIM is Professor of Medical Ethics at University of Bergen and Adjunct Professor of Global Health at Harvard T.H. Chan School of Public Health.

Prioritarianism in Practice

Edited by

MATTHEW D. ADLER
Duke University

OLE F. NORHEIM
University of Bergen

CAMBRIDGE
UNIVERSITY PRESS

CAMBRIDGE
UNIVERSITY PRESS

Shaftesbury Road, Cambridge CB2 8EA, United Kingdom

One Liberty Plaza, 20th Floor, New York, NY 10006, USA

477 Williamstown Road, Port Melbourne, VIC 3207, Australia

314–321, 3rd Floor, Plot 3, Splendor Forum, Jasola District Centre, New Delhi – 110025, India

103 Penang Road, #05–06/07, Visioncrest Commercial, Singapore 238467

Cambridge University Press is part of Cambridge University Press & Assessment, a department of the University of Cambridge.

We share the University's mission to contribute to society through the pursuit of education, learning and research at the highest international levels of excellence.

www.cambridge.org
Information on this title: www.cambridge.org/9781108703604

DOI: 10.1017/9781108691734

First published 2022
First paperback edition 2024

A catalogue record for this publication is available from the British Library

Library of Congress Cataloging-in-Publication data
Names: Adler, Matthew D., editor. | Norheim, Ole Frithjof, editor.
Title: Prioritarianism in practice / edited by Matthew D. Adler, Duke University, North Carolina, Ole F. Norheim, Universitetet i Bergen, Norway.
Description: Cambridge, United Kingdom ; New York, NY : Cambridge University Press, 2022. | Includes bibliographical references and index.
Identifiers: LCCN 2021045508 (print) | LCCN 2021045509 (ebook) | ISBN 9781108480932 (hardback) | ISBN 9781108703604 (paperback) | ISBN 9781108691734 (epub)
Subjects: LCSH: Social indicators. | Economic indicators. | Quality of life. | BISAC: POLITICAL SCIENCE / Public Policy / Economic Policy
Classification: LCC HN25 .P74 2022 (print) | LCC HN25 (ebook) | DDC 301–dc23
LC record available at https://lccn.loc.gov/2021045508
LC ebook record available at https://lccn.loc.gov/2021045509

ISBN 978-1-108-48093-2 Hardback
ISBN 978-1-108-70360-4 Paperback

Contents

Figures

Tables

List of Contributors

MATTHEW D. ADLER is Richard A. Horvitz Professor of Law and Professor of Economics, Philosophy, and Public Policy, Duke University.

DAVID E. BLOOM is Clarence James Gamble Professor of Economics and Demography, Harvard T. H. Chan School of Public Health.

PAOLO BRUNORI is Assistant Professorial Research Fellow, International Inequality Institute, London School of Economics.

RICHARD COOKSON is Professor, Centre for Health Economics, University of York.

KOEN DECANCQ is Associate Research Professor, Herman Deleeck Centre for Social Policy, University of Antwerp.

MADDALENA FERRANNA is Research Associate, Harvard T. H. Chan School of Public Health.

FRANCISCO H. G. FERREIRA is Amartya Sen Professor of Inequality Studies, London School of Economics.

MARC FLEURBAEY is Senior Researcher and Professor, CNRS and Paris School of Economics.

JAMES K. HAMMITT is Professor of Economics and Decision Sciences, Harvard University, and Associate, Toulouse School of Economics.

OLE F. NORHEIM is Professor of Medical Ethics, University of Bergen, and Adjunct Professor of Global Health, Harvard T. H. Chan School of Public Health.

ERWIN OOGHE is Professor of Economics, KU Leuven and Research Fellow at ZEW, Mannheim and CESifo, Munich.

VITO PERAGINE is Professor of Economics, University of Bari.

ERIK SCHOKKAERT is Professor of Economics (emeritus), KU Leuven.

JP SEVILLA is Research Associate, Harvard T. H. Chan School of Public Health.

IEVA SKARDA is Postdoctoral Research Fellow, Centre for Health Economics, University of York.

BENOÎT TARROUX is Professor of Economics, University Lumière Lyon 2 and GATE-Lyon-Saint-Etienne.

NICOLAS TREICH is Researcher, University Toulouse Capitole, Toulouse School of Economics, INRAE.

MATTI TUOMALA is Professor of Economics (emeritus), Tampere University.

MATTHEW WEINZIERL is Joseph and Jacqueline Elbling Professor of Business Administration, Harvard Business School.

1 Introduction

Prioritarianism in Practice

MATTHEW D. ADLER AND
OLE F. NORHEIM*

1.1 Prioritarianism

"Prioritarianism" is a framework for ethical assessment that gives extra weight to the well-being of the worse off. Unlike utilitarianism, which uses a simple summation of well-being, prioritarianism adds up *transformed* well-being numbers: well-being numbers inputted into a concave transformation function.[1] Assume that Andre is worse off than Beatrice. We can increase Andre's well-being by an increment Δw, or increase Beatrice's well-being by the same increment Δw. Utilitarianism is indifferent between these two options. Prioritarianism prefers the first: giving Δw to the worse-off one (Andre) yields a larger ethical improvement than giving Δw to the better-off one (Beatrice).

* *Acknowledgments.* Adler thanks David Levi and Kerry Abrams who, as successive deans of Duke Law School, provided generous financial support for conferences held at Duke Law in connection with this volume. He thanks Carol Abken, Leanna Doty, and Victoria Zellefrow for providing administrative support for these conferences and all other aspects of the "Prioritarianism in Practice" Research Network, and Wick Shreve of the Duke Law Library for research advice and assistance. Norheim thanks the Bill & Melinda Gates Foundation (INV-010174) and the Trond Mohn Foundation (BFS2019TMT02) for financial support to organize the Bergen conference in 2019.

A number of scholars who are not volume authors participated in *Prioritarianism in Practice* conferences, and the volume benefitted from their insights. We thank Mathias Barra, Alexander Cappelen, Jacob Goldin, Ori Heffetz, Anders Herlitz, Miles Kimball, Jeremy Lauer, Paolo Piacquadio, Carl Tollef Solberg, and Bertil Tungodden. Finally, we are grateful to our editor Philip Good, and to everyone else who worked on *Prioritarianism in Practice* at Cambridge University Press and Straive – including Denise Bannerman, Jessica Norman, Sindhuja Sethuraman, and Erika Walsh – for bringing this volume to publication.

[1] To be more precise: the prioritarian transformation function is strictly increasing and strictly concave. Throughout the chapter, we use "concave" in reference to this transformation function as shorthand for strictly increasing and strictly concave.

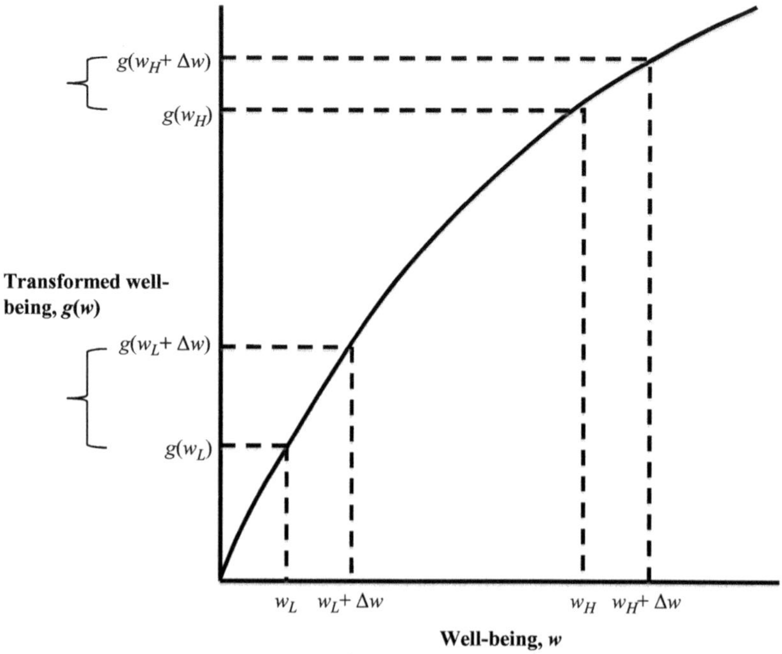

Figure 1.1 Well-being numbers inputted into a concave transformation function

Note: Andre is at lower well-being level w_L and Beatrice at higher well-being w_H. The increase in well-being from w_L to $w_L + \Delta w$ produces a bigger increase in transformed well-being than the increase in well-being from w_H to $w_H + \Delta w$.

(*Source*: Figure 1.1 in Matthew D. Adler, *Measuring Social Welfare* (2019), reproduced with permission of Oxford University Press)

See Figure 1.1, illustrating that the prioritarian rule of summing concavely transformed well-being has the effect of giving priority to the worse off.

Utilitarianism has had sweeping influence in academic scholarship (in philosophy, economics, law, public health, and other fields), and in governmental practice, for centuries. (For historical sources on utilitarianism, see Eggleston and Miller [2014]. For contemporary defenses, see, e.g., Brandt [1979], Broome [1991], Goodin [1995], Harsanyi [1977], Singer [2011].) Prioritarianism is a much newer idea. In ethics, prioritarianism is most closely associated with the philosopher Derek

Parfit. Parfit's 1991 Lindley Lecture triggered an intensive philosophical examination of prioritarianism, continuing to the present[2] (Parfit 2000, publishing his 1991 lecture). Although Parfit was not in fact the first philosopher to discuss prioritarianism, it *is* certainly true that wide philosophical investigation and debate about prioritarianism only began with Parfit's work. In short: this is a relatively new idea in ethics, much newer than utilitarianism.

Although the term "prioritarianism" is a piece of philosophical vocabulary that is uncommon in economics, the underlying idea – summing a concave transformation of well-being, and thereby according extra weight to the worse off – has figured in welfare economics since the 1970s. At that time, the concept of the "social welfare function" (SWF) began to play a more central role in several economic literatures: theoretical welfare economics, optimal tax theory, and the measurement of inequality. A variety of types of SWFs have been examined by these literatures, including prioritarian SWFs.[3]

The SWF methodology, in a nutshell, converts each possible outcome of governmental policy choice into a list ("vector") of well-being numbers – measuring the well-being of the individuals in the population of ethical concern. A given outcome is some possible combination of welfare-relevant characteristics (income, health, leisure, happiness, etc.) for each person in the population. Let x be a possible outcome, y a different possible outcome, and so forth. If there are N individuals in the population, then x corresponds to the well-being vector $(w_1(x), w_2(x), \ldots w_N(x))$ – with $w_1(x)$ denoting the well-being number of individual 1 in x, $w_2(x)$ the well-being number of individual 2 in x, and so forth. Similarly, outcome y corresponds to the well-being vector $(w_1(y), w_2(y), \ldots w_N(y))$. The SWF is a rule for ranking well-being vectors and, thereby, the corresponding outcomes. Many different such rules are possible, including the utilitarian SWF, prioritarian SWFs, and others.

In short, the concept of prioritarianism, if not the term "prioritarianism," has figured in various SWF-related economic literatures for

2 The philosophical literature on prioritarianism is discussed and cited below, in Section 1.2.1.

3 The literature on SWFs is discussed and cited below, in Section 1.2.2, and in Chapter 2.

the last 50 years. Still, in economics as in ethics, this is a much newer idea than utilitarianism. Further, although a variety of economic concepts and tools have had a large impact on governmental practice, prioritarianism has not (yet) had this influence.

This chapter is the introductory chapter in a volume entitled *Prioritarianism in Practice*. The aim of the volume is to study and showcase the use of prioritarianism as a methodology for evaluating governmental policy, across a variety of policy domains: taxation, health policy, risk regulation, education, climate policy, and the COVID-19 pandemic (a global catastrophe, urgently requiring wise governmental policy, that occurred while the volume was being drafted). The volume also examines prioritarianism as an indicator of social condition (as an alternative to GDP, currently the dominant social-condition metric).

Prioritarianism in Practice is the first book to study the *application* of prioritarianism as a policy-assessment framework. It grows out of an international research network which we founded. The participants in this network are now chapter authors in this volume.

Why study prioritarianism? After all, there are *many* competitors to utilitarianism, including but hardly limited to prioritarianism.

The answer is that prioritarianism retains most of the attractive characteristics of utilitarianism, but drops one feature that many have found problematic: utilitarianism's indifference to the distribution of well-being.[4]

First, prioritarianism, like utilitarianism, is a species of welfare consequentialism. An ethical view is *consequentialist* if it evaluates choices in light of the possible outcomes of those choices. Outcomes are ranked from best to worst; and it is this goodness ranking of outcomes that drives ethical assessment. An ethical view is, more specifically, *welfare* consequentialist if the goodness ranking of outcomes hinges on individuals' well-being. The SWF methodology, in turn, is just a formal procedure for implementing welfare consequentialism.

For those who endorse welfare consequentialism as the appropriate architecture for ethical assessment and, specifically, the assessment of

[4] The normative case for prioritarianism, summarized in the next several paragraphs, is presented in much greater detail in Chapter 2.

governmental policies, the fact that prioritarianism – like utilitarianism – has this structure is a welcome feature of prioritarianism.[5]

Further, both the utilitarian SWF and prioritarian SWFs are "score-based"; in each case, the SWF operates by assigning a numerical score to a given vector and then ranking vectors in the order of these scores.[6] (The utilitarian score is just the sum of well-being; the prioritarian score is the sum of concavely transformed well-being.) By contrast, for example, the "leximin" SWF – roughly corresponding to John Rawls' notion of "maximin" (Rawls 1999) – employs an algorithm for ranking well-being vectors that cannot be summarized by a numerical score.[7]

Score-based SWFs are especially tractable – a virtue for policy assessment – and can readily be generalized to policy choice under uncertainty. If we conceptualize a governmental policy as a probability distribution across outcomes, then the utilitarian SWF can be used to rank policies by assigning each policy its expected score (namely, the expected sum of well-being). The prioritarian SWF can be applied under uncertainty in an analogous way (now, policies are ranked according to the expected sum of concavely transformed well-being).[8]

Prioritarianism shares yet another desirable feature with utilitarianism: it is *separable*. If a group of individuals is unaffected by policy choice – whichever policy might be chosen, the well-being of individuals within the group doesn't change – then utilitarian assessment can

[5] One important critique of welfare consequentialism is that it fails to take account of individual responsibility. How to refine prioritarianism so as to incorporate individual responsibility is the topic of Chapter 11. A different critique is that welfare consequentialism ignores deontological constraints and other non-consequentialist factors. For those who believe that ethics is a hybrid of consequentialism and non-consequentialist factors, prioritarian policy analysis can still be seen as capturing one *part* of ethical assessment, namely the consequentialist component (Adler 2019, pp. 24–27).

[6] We use the term "SWF" to mean what is, strictly, a social welfare ordering: a rule for ranking well-being vectors. Some (not all) such rules can be represented by a real-valued function $S(\cdot)$, such that: vector $\mathbf{w}$ is at least as good as vector $\mathbf{v}$ if and only if $S(\mathbf{w}) \geq S(\mathbf{v})$. In our terminology, these SWFs are "score-based."

[7] Leximin orders two well-being vectors according to the levels of the worst-off individuals in each; if the worst-off individuals are equally well off in the two vectors, according to the levels of the second-worst-off individuals; and so forth.

[8] This formula (the expected sum of concavely transformed well-being) is one methodology for applying prioritarianism under uncertainty, so-called "ex post prioritarianism" (EPP). Chapter 2, Section 2.7, discusses both EPP and other possible formulas.

simply ignore the individuals.[9] The utilitarian comparison of policies is wholly determined by the well-being of *affected* individuals. The same is true of prioritarianism. Separability, like the feature of being score-based, increases the tractability of both utilitarianism and prioritarianism.

The critical *difference* between the two approaches is that prioritarianism embodies a concern for the distribution of well-being that is absent from utilitarianism. The utilitarian SWF is such that: if total well-being is greater in outcome y than outcome x, y is better than x regardless of how well-being is distributed in the two outcomes. In particular, imagine that Cedric is better off than Dahlia in x. Cedric's well-being in y increases by Δw^*, while Dahlia's decreases by Δw. As long as the increment to Cedric's well-being is larger than the loss to Dahlia (that is, as long as $\Delta w^* > \Delta w$), then utilitarianism ranks y better than x *regardless* of the well-being levels of the two individuals, and regardless of the magnitudes of Δw^* and Δw (even if Cedric's gain is only slightly more than Dahlia's loss). This is problematic. By contrast, prioritarianism may well prefer x; whether it does depends upon the well-being levels of the two individuals, the comparative magnitudes of Cedric's gain and Dahlia's loss, and the concave transformation function.

Further, prioritarianism is quite flexible regarding the degree of ethical priority to the well-being of the worse off. Here, a contrast not only with utilitarianism, but also leximin, is instructive. The utilitarian SWF is a specific such rule (a specific rule for ranking well-being vectors), as is the leximin SWF. The utilitarian SWF gives zero priority to the worse off; the leximin SWF gives absolute priority to the worse off. Prioritarianism is an entire *family* of SWFs; the choice of concave transformation function determines a particular such rule. A more concave function means that, as between two individuals at two given well-being levels, the worse-off one has a greater degree of priority. The prioritarian, by means of her choice of transformation function, can specify whatever degree of priority for the worse off she judges

[9] To be more precise, the utilitarian SWF and prioritarian SWFs both satisfy an axiom of Separability with respect to the ranking of well-being vectors. Further, they both can be applied under uncertainty in a manner that satisfies an analogous axiom with respect to policies. Only SWFs that satisfy Separability with respect to the vector ranking can be separable with respect to policies. See Chapter 2, Section 2.4.

reasonable – approaching utilitarianism at one extreme and the absolute priority of leximin at the other.

In the remainder of this introductory chapter to *Prioritarianism in Practice*, we do the following. First, we briefly survey existing scholarship on prioritarianism in philosophy, economics, and public health (the main academic literatures in which prioritarianism has, to date, played a role), so as to give the reader a sense of the intellectual backdrop for the volume. Second, we provide an overview of the volume.

1.2 Scholarship on Prioritarianism: A Brief Survey

1.2.1 Philosophy

As mentioned, it was Derek Parfit's 1991 Lindley Lecture that triggered widespread philosophical attention to prioritarianism[10] (Parfit 2000, publishing his 1991 lecture). There is now a substantial body of work in academic philosophy on the topic.

In the lecture, Parfit introduces prioritarianism – contrasting it with egalitarianism – with reference to a hypothetical case previously described by the philosopher Thomas Nagel in his article, "Equality" (Nagel 1979). Nagel imagines that he has two children, the first who is healthy and the second who has a serious health condition and is worse off than the first; and that he faces a choice between moving to a city or a suburb. In the city, the second child would have access to treatment for her condition, and so she would be somewhat better off than in the suburb. In the suburb, the first child would flourish, so much so that the difference for him between moving to the suburb and moving to the city is larger than the benefit the second child would reap from moving to the city.

Parfit uses well-being numbers to present Nagel's case. The first child would be at well-being level 20 in the city, and would gain 5 units moving to the suburb. The second child, who would be worse off than the first regardless of where the family lives, would be at level 9 in the suburb and 10 in the city. See Table 1.1 (from Parfit [2000, p. 83]).

[10] There is some philosophical work on the concept of prioritarianism (not using that term) that slightly predates Parfit. See McKerlie (1984); Temkin (1983); Weirich (1983).

Table 1.1. *Nagel's two-child case, as presented by Parfit*

	First child	Second child
Move to the city	20	10
Move to the suburb	25	9

Utilitarianism recommends moving to the suburb: the sum total of the children's well-being is greater in the suburb (34) than the city (30). Nagel, discussing the case, writes that the decision to move instead to the city would be an "egalitarian" decision (Nagel 1979, p. 124). Parfit suggests that the rationale for moving to the city *might* be egalitarian, but it might instead be prioritarian. The aim of the Lindley Lecture is to differentiate these two distinct species of non-utilitarian reasoning.

Parfit observes that the most plausible version of egalitarianism is *pluralist*. Egalitarians endorse "The Principle of Equality": "It is in itself bad if some people are worse off than others" (Parfit 2000, p. 84). But they also should endorse "The Principle of Utility": "It is in itself better if people are better off" (ibid.). An egalitarian who endorsed only the first principle, not the second, would see no difference between everyone being equally well off at a low level of well-being, and everyone being equally well off at a high level of well-being.

Within the space of pluralist egalitarianism, Parfit differentiates between "strong" and "moderate" egalitarians. Strong pluralist egalitarians believe that the "Principle of Equality" may outweigh the "Principle of Utility" even in cases where the more equal outcome is worse for some and better for none. As between an outcome in which everyone is at well-being level w, and a second outcome in which some are at w and others are better off than w, the strong pluralist egalitarian *might* choose the first outcome. By contrast, moderate pluralist egalitarians accept that, in such a case, the two principles always balance against each other so as to favor the second outcome. In the language of welfare economics, moderate pluralist egalitarians accept the Pareto axiom: if some are better off in outcome x than y, and none are worse off, then x is better than y.[11]

[11] "Pareto" is used in Chapter 2 to mean the combination of two axioms: Strong Pareto (if some are better off in one outcome as compared to a second, and none are worse off, then the first outcome is better), and Pareto Indifference (if each

In the two-child case, the Pareto axiom does not come into play: the first child is better off in the suburb, the second in the city. A moderate pluralist egalitarian who gives little weight to equality will recommend the suburb; if she gives more weight to equality, she will recommend the city.

A distinct rationale for moving to the city, Parfit observes, is prioritarianism. Actually, Parfit doesn't use the term "prioritarianism." Instead he speaks of "the Priority View" or "prioritarians." Philosophical nomenclature thereafter shifted slightly, with "prioritarianism" becoming the standard name for what the Lindley Lecture denotes the "Priority View."

Parfit characterizes prioritarianism ("the Priority View") as follows: "Benefitting people matters more the worse off these people are." He continues:

> For Utilitarians, the moral importance of each benefit depends only on how great this benefit would be. For *Prioritarians*, it also depends on how well off the person is to whom this benefit comes. We should not give equal weight to equal benefits, whoever receives them. Benefits to the worse off should be given more weight. (Ibid., p. 101)

Depending on how it assigns moral weights to well-being gains at various levels, prioritarianism may recommend moving to the city in the two-child case. It may conclude that the moral impact of a well-being improvement for the second child from level 9 to level 10 is greater than the moral impact of a well-being improvement for the first child from level 20 to level 25.

The crucial difference between egalitarianism and prioritarianism, according to Parfit, is that egalitarians care about "relativities" while prioritarians do not.

> [O]n the Priority View, we do not believe in equality. We do not think it in itself bad, or unjust, that some people are worse off than others. This claim can be misunderstood. We do of course think it bad that some people are

person is just as well off in one outcome as a second, then the two outcomes are equally good). For purposes of Parfit's discussion of egalitarianism and prioritarianism, the relevant part of the Pareto axiom combination is Strong Pareto: moderate pluralist egalitarians and prioritarians accept, while strong pluralist egalitarians reject, the Strong Pareto axiom. In this chapter, therefore, we use "Pareto" as shorthand for "Strong Pareto."

worse off. But what is bad is not that these people are worse off than *others*. It is rather that they are worse off than *they* might have been.

Consider next the central claim of the Priority View: benefits to the worse off matter more.... In this view, if I am worse off than you, benefits to me are more important. Is this *because* I am worse off than you? In one sense, yes. But this has nothing to do with my relation to you.

It may help to use this analogy. People at higher altitudes find it harder to breathe. Is this because they are higher up than other people? In one sense, yes. But they would find it just as hard to breathe even if there were no other people who were lower down. In the same way, on the Priority View, benefits to the worse off matter more, but that is only because these people are at a lower *absolute* level. It is irrelevant that these people are worse off *than others*....

The chief difference is, then, this. Egalitarians are concerned with *relativities*: with how each person's level compares with the level of other people. In the Priority View, we are concerned only with people's absolute levels. (Ibid., p. 104)

Parfit does not use axioms to describe prioritarianism. However, his discussion of the difference between prioritarianism and egalitarianism can readily be translated into axiomatic language. The Separability axiom says: the ranking of any two outcomes is invariant to the well-being levels of individuals who are equally well off in both. More precisely: Let x and y be two outcomes such that some individuals are not equally well off in the two (these individuals are "affected" as between x and y); and other individuals *are* equally well off in the two (these individuals are "unaffected" as between x and y). Further, let x^* and y^* be two other outcomes which are related to x and y as follows: each individual who is affected as between x and y is at the same well-being level in x^* as she is in x, and the same well-being level in y^* as she is in y (thus also affected as between x^* and y^*); and each individual who is unaffected as between x and y is unaffected as between x^* and y^* (although perhaps at a different well-being level in the x^*/y^* pair than the x/y pair). In other words, the x^*/y^* pair is the same as the x/y pair with respect to everyone's well-being *except* for the well-being levels of the unaffected. Separability requires that, for any two such outcome pairs, the x^*/y^* ranking must be the same as the x/y ranking.[12]

A prioritarian outcome ranking satisfies Separability, while an egalitarian outcome ranking does not. Separability is a parsimonious

[12] See Chapter 2, Table 2.4.

axiomatic expression of Parfit's statement that prioritarians, unlike egalitarians, are unconcerned with "relativities."

Parfit's discussion also points to two further axioms that are satisfied by prioritarianism: the Pareto axiom (if some are better off in x than y and none are worse off, than x is better than y); and the Pigou-Dalton axiom (a pure transfer of well-being from someone better off, to someone worse off, that shrinks the gap between them and affects no one else, is a moral improvement). He writes that the "Priority View ... contains the idea that benefits are good" (this statement suggests that prioritarians would endorse the Pareto axiom), and that it "merely adds that benefits matter more the worse off the people are who receive them" (which suggests that prioritarians would endorse the Pigou-Dalton axiom, as does Parfit's observation that utilitarians believe in the diminishing marginal utility of resources, while prioritarians believe in the "diminishing marginal moral importance" of well-being itself) (ibid., pp. 103–105).

The axiom cluster Pareto, Pigou-Dalton, and Separability serves neatly to demarcate between utilitarianism, moderate egalitarianism, and prioritarianism. Prioritarianism satisfies all three. Utilitarianism satisfies Pareto and Separability but not Pigou-Dalton. While strong egalitarians reject Pareto, moderate egalitarians endorse Pareto. They also may endorse Pigou-Dalton;[13] but they reject Separability. Parfit's chief aim in the Lindley Lecture was to show that there is a place in moral reasoning for a view that denies utilitarianism, yet also is not egalitarian. Indeed, he shows that there is a place in *Paretian* moral reasoning for utilitarianism, egalitarianism, and a distinctive approach, prioritarianism. The axiomatic approach allows us clearly to see this. Within the space of Paretian moral views (those that satisfy the Pareto axiom), there is a subspace containing those that also satisfy both Pigou-Dalton and Separability. Prioritarianism, but neither utilitarianism nor egalitarianism, falls within this subspace.

It has become quite common in the contemporary philosophical literature on prioritarianism to describe it in the terms used at the very beginning of the chapter: as the sum of a concave transformation of well-being. This is, in effect, to describe prioritarianism as an SWF: as a rule for ranking well-being vectors, and thereby for ranking outcomes

[13] See Adler (2019, pp. 95–106), differentiating within the space of non-utilitarian ethical views between those that do, and those that do not, satisfy Pigou-Dalton.

on the assumption that each outcome corresponds to a vector. The Lindley Lecture itself does not do so. In fact, to get from the axiom cluster Pareto, Pigou-Dalton and Separability, to the prioritarian SWF, we need a number of additional assumptions: that well-being is measurable, that the outcome ranking is complete, and that axioms of Anonymity and Continuity are also satisfied. See Chapter 2.

The corpus of philosophical work on prioritarianism triggered by Parfit's contribution is, now, quite rich and complex, and can hardly be surveyed in detail in this chapter. (For surveys of this literature, see Adler [2012, chapter 5]; Adler and Holtug [2019]; Holtug [2010, 2017]; Otsuka and Voorhoeve [2018].) We have been understanding prioritarianism as a species of welfare consequentialism, and indeed this is also Parfit's understanding of it in the Lindley Lecture. One avenue of research pursued in the philosophical literature since Parfit has been to investigate the possibility of "deontic" prioritarianism, i.e., *non-consequentialist* ethical views that are in some sense prioritarian (Nebel 2017; Williams 2012). However, this volume, like much of the literature on policy assessment, works within welfare consequentialism; and deontic prioritarianism (although certainly worth exploring) will not play a role here.

Among contemporary ethicists working within welfare consequentialism, three major lines of critique of prioritarianism can be described. First, some philosophers reject prioritarianism in favor of utilitarianism (Broome 1991; Greaves 2015; McCarthy 2008). One important argument pressed by philosophers in this group is that utilitarianism has important advantages over prioritarianism – and indeed over all non-utilitarian approaches – under uncertainty. Consider the ranking, not of a set of outcomes, but instead of a set of choices each understood as a probability distribution across outcomes. A variety of plausible axioms govern this set-up, including the ex ante Pareto axiom. While all prioritarians endorse the Pareto axiom (an axiom concerning the outcome ranking), a dilemma arises with respect to the ex ante Pareto axiom. Prioritarians must either reject the ex ante Pareto axiom or a very plausible Dominance axiom.[14] Prioritarianism can be specified for conditions of uncertainty; but however thus specified, it cannot satisfy both ex ante Pareto and Dominance. By contrast,

[14] Dominance requires that if one policy produces a better outcome than a second policy in every state of nature, then the first policy must be ranked better.

utilitarianism under uncertainty satisfies both of these axioms. See Chapter 2.

A second line of response to prioritarianism is egalitarian. Parfit, recall, writes: "[O]n the Priority View, we do not believe in equality. We do not think it in itself bad, or unjust, that some are worse off than others" (Parfit 2000, p. 104). Egalitarians have pressed the case that we *should* care about the relative well-being of different individuals in the population. For example, Larry Temkin has argued that "comparative fairness" is an important moral consideration: it is unfair that one person is worse off than others, at least absent responsibility for this disparity on the part of the worse-off one (Temkin 1993, 2003a, 2003b). Thus, in comparing any two outcomes, x and y, we should take account of the full distribution of well-being in x and the full distribution in y – that is, how each person in x compares to everyone else in x, and how each person in y compares to everyone else in y, including in these comparisons both those individuals affected as between the two outcomes and unaffected individuals. In short, Temkin defends the moral relevance of "comparative fairness" and, in so doing, rejects Separability.[15]

Third, some philosophers have criticized prioritarianism from a standpoint that is neither utilitarian nor egalitarian. The leading example is Roger Crisp, who has defended a view known as "sufficientism" (Crisp 2003). Sufficientism is a complicated view, which incorporates a well-being threshold. It is prioritarian in evaluating well-being transfers between those below the threshold; gives absolute priority to those below the threshold, as against those above; but is utilitarian in evaluating transfers between those above the threshold. The intuition here, which Crisp presses, is that the choice between improving the well-being of a rich person by Δw and improving the well-being of a super-rich person by Δw is a matter of moral indifference.

In the face of these critiques, a significant number of philosophers have defended prioritarianism (see Adler and Holtug [2019, note 1], citing proponents). Prioritarians can argue that utilitarianism's wholesale indifference to transfers of well-being from better-off to worse-off persons is deeply problematic. Violations of ex ante Pareto are a price

[15] Michael Otsuka and Alex Voorhoeve (2009, 2018) are also prominent egalitarian critics of prioritarianism.

worth paying (or so prioritarians can contend) for the sake of satisfying the Pigou-Dalton axiom. As against egalitarians, it can be argued that prioritarianism embodies a concern for equity – in the shape of Pigou-Dalton – while also retaining the pragmatic benefits of Separability. Finally, sufficientists can be challenged to specify the well-being threshold that plays a pivotal role in their theory; and the absence of equity concerns above that threshold can reasonably be disputed as well.

The intensive philosophical debate about prioritarianism initiated by Parfit's writings shows it to be a plausible view worth sustained consideration. Although prioritarianism is not immune from challenge, neither is it *dominated* by utilitarianism, egalitarianism, or sufficientism. Prioritarianism as an ethical theory has, we believe, survived the process of rigorous academic scrutiny. It has shown itself to be a serious contender now worth systematically exploring in a more applied manner, as the basis for policy assessment – what this volume attempts to do.

1.2.2 Economics

The distinguished scholar John Broome, both a philosopher and an economist, notes that, as of 1991 (when Parfit delivered the Lindley Lecture and Broome published his book, *Weighing Goods*), "prioritarianism was well established amongst economics, but was only just being discovered by philosophers" (Broome 2015, p. 219).

As already mentioned, the term "prioritarianism" was certainly *not* well established in economics as of the Lindley Lecture, and is little used by economists even now. What was established was the prioritarian SWF. Beginning around 1970, the concept of the SWF began to play a key role in various economic literatures: in particular, theoretical welfare economics, optimal tax theory, and the measurement of inequality. The prioritarian SWF (the sum of concavely transformed well-being) emerged as one possibility among others.

The concept of the SWF dates from a 1938 article by Abram Bergson and was adopted by Paul Samuelson in his influential 1947 work, *Foundations of Economic Analysis*. However, further development of the concept was interrupted by Kenneth Arrow's groundbreaking 1951 study of social choice, *Social Choice and Individual Values*. In 1970, Amartya Sen's *Collective Choice and Social Welfare* re-energized the SWF concept, and it has since then flourished as a foundational construct in theoretical welfare economics.

The setup of Arrow's analysis is this: each individual in the population has an individual ranking of the possible outcomes, and the social ranking wholly depends upon this profile of individual rankings. No other information is allowed. "In particular, the very formulation of the problem rules out the use of *interpersonal comparisons* of well-being or utility. Classical social decision rules such as utilitarianism, or any other rule which allows for trade-offs between the utilities experienced by different individuals, simply cannot be expressed" in the Arrow setup (Bossert and Weymark 2004, p. 1100).

In *Collective Choice and Social Welfare*, Sen enriches the Arrow setup by supposing that the social ranking of outcomes depends upon individuals' well-being numbers rather than individuals' preference orderings. Specifically, he supposes that there is a functional relation from a given well-being measure $w(\cdot)$ to an outcome ranking (Sen 1970 pp. 118–130). Under some basic, quite plausible assumptions, this functional relation takes the form of an SWF (as we are using that term). A given well-being measure $w(\cdot)$ maps each outcome x onto the well-being vector $(w_1(x), \ldots, w_N(x))$, with $w_i(x)$ the well-being number of individual i in x according to well-being measure $w(\cdot)$. There is a rule for ranking these vectors – the SWF – and the outcomes are ranked correspondingly.[16]

Collective Choice and Social Welfare has inspired a rich and continuing theoretical literature regarding SWFs. (For surveys of this literature, see Blackorby, Bossert and Donaldson [2002; 2005, chapters 2–4]; Boadway and Bruce [1984, chapter 5]; Bossert and Weymark [2004]; d'Aspremont and Gevers [2002]; Mongin and d'Aspremont [1998]; Weymark [2016].) A core aim of this literature is to provide axiomatic characterizations of SWFs. An axiom is a constraint on the ranking of well-being vectors.

The literature, by virtue of its axiomatic focus, is not limited to utilitarianism. We start with a wholly generic conception of the SWF – *any* rule for ranking well-being vectors – and ask how various

[16] We are using the term SWF to mean a rule for ranking well-being vectors. See above, note 6. The so-called "welfarism theorem" establishes the conditions under which the functional relation Sen describes takes the form of an SWF. See Chapter 2, note 57.

axiom combinations serve to narrow down the possibilities. Some axiom combinations *will* lead us to the utilitarian SWF, but others will preclude utilitarianism, or allow both the utilitarian SWF and other rules. Prioritarian SWFs, or particular species of prioritarian SWFs (not using that term!), show up repeatedly in this axiomatic literature. Chapter 2 in this volume, building from the axiomatic literature, uses the four axioms Pareto, Anonymity, Separability, and Continuity to characterize a "generalized utilitarian" class of SWFs including both the utilitarian SWF and prioritarian SWFs. Prioritarian SWFs are the unique subclass of generalized utilitarian SWFs that satisfy not only the four axioms just mentioned but also the Pigou-Dalton axiom.

Economists working in this literature often assume that the well-being measure $w(.)$ is based upon individuals' utility functions – a utility function being a mathematical construct that tracks individual preferences. $w_i(x) = u_i(x)$, with $u_i(x)$ the number assigned to x by individual i's utility function $u_i(\cdot)$, and which is such that: if i prefers x to y, $u_i(x) > u_i(y)$ and if i is indifferent between x and y, $u_i(x) = u_i(y)$. However, the SWF construct is more generic. The theory of well-being underlying $w(\cdot)$ might be a preference-based theory of well-being, but it need not be. In contemporary scholarship regarding well-being, it is a contested question how an individual's well-being relates to her preferences. Although some authors in this volume do adopt a preference view of well-being, that premise is not universal here. See Chapter 3.

Let us now turn to the second body of economic scholarship in which the SWF concept plays a key role: namely, optimal tax theory. In 1971, James Mirrlees published his article, "An Exploration in the Theory of Optimum Income Taxation," which led to the contemporary literature on optimal tax theory and eventually earned Mirrlees the Nobel Prize. The Mirrleesian setup supposes that individuals trade their labor for income; the income a given individual earns from an hour of labor depends upon her productivity, reflected in her wage rate. Individuals' productivities are unobservable by government, but their incomes are observable. An individual's utility depends upon her income (which she consumes) and her leisure (the amount of time left over after laboring). Government sets tax rates on income so as to maximize the value of its SWF – taking account of the fact that each individual will respond to a given tax schedule by choosing between the various income/leisure combinations available to her (given her wage rate) so as to maximize her own utility.

This setup, and variations on it, has been the foundation for a half-century of optimal tax scholarship since 1971. The place of prioritarian SWFs in optimal tax theory is discussed in Chapter 4 of this volume. Although most analyses in this literature do use a utilitarian SWF, prioritarian SWFs also figure in this literature – and indeed do so from the very beginning, in Mirrlees' 1971 article. As the authors of Chapter 4 (Tuomala and Weinzierl) explain, the general expression for the SWF adopted by Mirrlees (1971) is an additive SWF that admits of both utilitarian and prioritarian specifications. In his numerical analyses, Mirrlees specifically works with an SWF that is the sum of $g(u_i)$, with $g(u_i) = -\frac{1}{\beta}e^{-\beta u_i}$, u_i the utility of individual i, for $\beta > 0$ (a prioritarian SWF); and $g(u_i) = u_i$ for $\beta = 0$ (the utilitarian SWF).[17]

Finally, prioritarian SWFs have an important place in the economic literature on inequality measurement. One strand in this literature (as reviewed, e.g., in Lambert 2001) seeks to derive an inequality metric from an SWF. A seminal contribution of this sort, and one that brings prioritarian SWFs into play, is Anthony Atkinson's 1970 article, "On the measurement of inequality."

Atkinson supposes that the SWF is defined on the distribution of individual incomes. Let y_i be the income of individual i. Atkinson supposes that the SWF is score-based, additive and symmetric in individual incomes. If $\mathbf{y} = (y_1, y_2, \ldots, y_N)$ is a distribution of incomes to N individuals, then the SWF assigns score $S(\mathbf{y})$ to this distribution, with $S(\mathbf{y})$ the sum of some function $f(\cdot)$ of individual income: $S(\mathbf{y}) = \sum_{i=1}^{N} f(y_i)$.[18] Atkinson then defines an inequality metric corresponding to this SWF, using the notion of an "equally distributed equivalent." For a given distribution of income $\mathbf{y}$, let y_{EDE} be the level of income which – if had by all N individuals – would yield the same level of social welfare as $\mathbf{y}$. Then the degree of inequality corresponding

[17] Mirrlees expresses the SWF as an integral, but to simplify we instead express it as a summation. We have swapped his "$G(\cdot)$" for "$g(\cdot)$," which is the symbol generally used in this volume for the prioritarian transformation function.

[18] Atkinson, like Mirrlees, expresses the SWF as an integral, but again we simplify by expressing it as a summation. We also substitute the more generic symbol "$f(\cdot)$" for Atkinson's "$U(\cdot)$." Atkinson assumes that $f(\cdot)$ is strictly increasing and weakly concave.

to **y**, Atkinson proposes, can be quantified as $1 - y_{EDE}/\mu(\mathbf{y})$, with $\mu(\mathbf{y})$ the mean income in **y**.

Adding the assumption that the inequality metric should be invariant to proportional rescalings of income (multiplication by a positive constant), Atkinson narrows down the functional form of the SWF. It must take the form $S(\mathbf{y}) = \sum_{i=1}^{N} \frac{y_i^{1-\gamma}}{1-\gamma}$, $\gamma \geq 0$.[19] The corresponding inequality metric is what is now known as the Atkinson inequality metric.

The restrictive assumption of an income-based SWF is not essential to Atkinson's inquiry. This assumption is restrictive because an individual's well-being depends upon more than her income. As in theoretical welfare economics and the optimal tax literature, the inputs to the SWF should be seen as well-being numbers, rather than incomes – which become one input into well-being. Atkinson's analysis immediately translates to this more general setup. With **w** a well-being vector, the SWFs described by Atkinson take the form $S(\mathbf{w}) = \sum_{i=1}^{N} \frac{w_i^{1-\gamma}}{1-\gamma}$, $\gamma \geq 0$. Such SWFs are referred to in this volume as Atkinson SWFs; they are also known in the literature as iso-elastic or constant-elasticity-of-substitution SWFs. Atkinson SWFs with $\gamma > 0$ are a class of prioritarian SWFs; γ is the degree of priority for the worse off. An Atkinson SWF with $\gamma = 0$ is just the utilitarian SWF.

Serge-Christophe Kolm wrote about the relation between inequality metrics and SWFs shortly before Atkinson (Kolm 1969).[20] Kolm's chapter, like Atkinson's article, is now seen as a foundational work in inequality measurement. Prioritarian SWFs figure in this chapter, as they do in the Atkinson analysis. In particular, Kolm discusses SWFs of the form $S(\mathbf{w}) = -\sum_{i=1}^{N} e^{-\beta w_i}$,[21] which become prioritarian with $\beta > 0$ and are now often termed Kolm-Pollak SWFs.[22]

[19] In the special case of $\gamma = 1$, $S(\mathbf{y}) = \sum_{i=1}^{N} \log(y_i)$.

[20] Atkinson was not aware of this work until after his article had been accepted for publication. See Atkinson (1970, p. 262).

[21] This is the same SWF mentioned above with reference to Mirrlees, except that Mirrlees multiplies the SWF by a factor (1/β) – which makes no difference to the ranking of well-being vectors.

[22] "Pollak" is in reference to Pollak (1971), who also discusses this functional form.

The reader may well find it puzzling to learn that prioritarian SWFs play a role in the literature on inequality measurement. After all, philosophers differentiate between prioritarianism and egalitarianism. That distinction is the central thrust of Parfit's Lindley Lecture, as we have seen. So how can a prioritarian SWF

Although our brief survey has focused on theoretical welfare economics, optimal tax theory, and inequality measurement – since these are literatures in which the SWF concept has been central for decades – it should also be noted that this concept is currently yet more widespread in economics. (For example, it has become a key part of the economic literature on climate change.) The reader interested to locate scholarship in economics that employs a prioritarian SWF, outside the three literatures just described, should consult the policy chapters in this volume – which cite extant research on prioritarianism.

1.2.3 Health Policy

In the health sector, methods for measuring health and health outcomes are fairly well developed and health interventions and policies are often assessed though economic evaluations before they are introduced and covered by health insurance or public funds. The dominant method for economic evaluation is cost-effectiveness analysis, sometimes called cost per QALY[23] analysis (Drummond et al. 1987).

A special concern for the worse off in terms of health – sometimes defined in terms of lifetime health and sometimes in terms of remaining future health – has been identified as important in addition to the standard objective of health maximization (Fleurbaey and Schokkaert 2009; Johri and Norheim 2012; Ottersen 2013; Dolan et al. 2005; Sassi et al. 2001).

Prioritarianism applied to health is typically understood in a restricted sense, as a way to rank social states according to a subset

correspond to an inequality metric? For example, Atkinson SWFs are a type of prioritarian SWF (as mentioned), and yet link up with the Atkinson inequality metric. How does this happen?

The answer requires close attention to the different meanings of "egalitarian." Prioritarianism is distinct from egalitarianism, as per Parfit, in that prioritarianism does not attend to "relativities." Using the SWF formalism, Parfit's distinction is best captured as a distinction between SWFs that satisfy (prioritarian) or fail to satisfy (egalitarian) Separability. An inequality metric is a formal economic tool that quantifies the degree of inequality in a distribution of some item (income, well-being). Various SWFs have corresponding inequality metrics; failing Separability is not a necessary condition for having one; and so it turns out that prioritarian SWFs, notwithstanding the fact that they satisfy Separability, do have corresponding inequality metrics. See Chapter 2, Section 2.10.

23 QALY is an acronym for "quality adjusted life year."

of well-being: distributions of expected lifetime health (longevity and morbidity) by disease group or socioeconomic status (Norheim et al. 2021). Such evaluations take information about the baseline level of health and increments in health from this baseline into account (for some early studies and theoretical contributions, see Anand et al. 2001; Asaria et al. 2016; Asaria et al. 2015; Hernæs et al. 2017; Johansson and Norheim 2011; Norheim 2013; Norheim et al. 2020). Taking health as the measure of well-being, distributions can then be summarized by prioritarian SWFs, and the impact on the distribution of well-being from alternative health policies can be evaluated.

One reason for restricting information to health only, in this literature, is practical or institutional. The policy questions relevant for priority setting, e.g., the relative rank of new expensive drugs, are typically formulated in terms of health-, not well-being-impact. The health sector (with its limited budget) is responsible for improving health, not well-being. Prioritarian SWFs have been presented as alternatives to cost-effectiveness analysis in health, and are therefore only concerned about total health and its distribution.

Cookson and colleagues have proposed a broader category of economic evaluations – distributional cost-effectiveness analysis (DCEA) – that may include health prioritarian approaches, but also includes other ways of evaluating distributions of health and non-health outcomes (Cookson et al. 2021). They describe two ways of using CEA to address distributional concerns: (1) equity impact analysis, which quantifies the distribution of costs and effects by equity-relevant variables such as socioeconomic status, location, ethnicity, sex, and severity of illness; and (2) equity trade-off analysis, which quantifies trade-offs between improving total health and assigning higher weights to health gains for the least advantaged (poorest with least health). Hitherto DCEA has tended to use either direct equity weights or rank-dependent equity weights (Bleichrodt et al. 2004), but analysis based on Kolm-Pollak or Atkinson prioritarian SWFs is also recommended (Norheim et al. 2021).

Another strand of this literature presents the social welfare function approach as an alternative to benefit-cost analysis using the value per statistical life (VSL). This approach is broader and sees both health (often mortality reduction), and income or consumption as components of well-being (Adler et al. 2014; Adler et al. 2021). These studies find that the way in which VSL ranks risk-reduction measures is insensitive to the Pigou-Dalton transfer principle and differs from both utilitarian and prioritarian frameworks.

Theoretical and empirical applications have been developed, independently, by using equivalent income as a measure of well-being (Fleurbaey et al. 2013; Samson et al. 2018). Compared to traditional cost-effectiveness analysis in health technology assessment, they show that it is feasible to go beyond a narrow evaluation of health outcomes in a richer welfare framework that includes both health and income, that takes account of the distinction between an ex ante and an ex post evaluation approach, and that captures distributional effects in a broader institutional setting, including how health services are financed.

In the policy context, some recommendations and guidelines have been inspired by prioritarianism applied to health. There may be insufficient resources or time available to design and undertake a full distributional cost-effectiveness analysis of a new health technology involving detailed modeling of all distributional consequences. It may, however, still be possible to provide a useful indication of the likely health equity impacts of decisions.

One approach is to conduct a partial DCEA that just compares how badly-off program recipients are in terms of baseline health compared with the wider population served by the decision-making organization (the "baseline health comparison" approach). If program recipients are worse off than non-recipients, then this provides a simple indication that the program may tend to improve health for the worse off. This approach has been used to inform priority setting decisions in low-income countries, and in health technology reimbursement decisions in Norway and the Netherlands, by assessing baseline health of program recipients and making a judgment about severity of illness compared with non-recipients (Ottersen et al. 2016; van de Wetering et al. 2013). This approach has important limitations, however, and makes no attempt to provide a distributional breakdown of all effects and costs.

The World Health Organization and the World Bank have championed cost-effectiveness as a key criterion for global and national priority setting (WHO 2020; World Bank 1993). In 2014, the World Health Organization's Consultative Group on Equity and Universal Health Coverage (UHC) published the report *Making Fair Choices on the Path to UHC* (WHO 2014). This work was part of the response to more than 70 low- and middle-income countries that had requested policy support and technical advice for UHC reform from the WHO. The consultative group included ethicists, philosophers, economists, health-policy experts, and clinical doctors, spanning 13 nationalities. This helped the group address fundamental ethical issues and difficult trade-offs when defining an essential health benefit package.

The report identified a growing consensus that the aims of the health system should be to promote health maximization, fair distribution, and protection against poverty and financial risk. From these guiding principles, the consultative group recommended three criteria for priority setting: cost-effectiveness, priority to the worse off, and financial risk protection. This was, fundamentally, a novel approach in the WHO context where cost-effectiveness had been the key criterion for priority setting. Priority to the worse off was given a prominent place in these new recommendations. The justification was prioritarian: priority to the worse off is important because benefitting them matters more than those who are better off. WHO also recommended to adopt a population perspective and focus not merely on those *currently* worse off but also on the people who are expected to be worse off over their lifetime. The worse off were defined as: (a) those with the most severe, large individual disease burden, and (b) the poorest or otherwise disadvantaged. Since the most cost-effective services do not always benefit the worse off, services targeting the worse off should be assigned extra value.

Although no formal policy evaluation framework was developed, the principle of prioritarianism was recognized, and this may be encouraging for the further development of methods in this area.

1.3 This Volume

This volume is a systematic study of prioritarianism as a methodology for policy analysis and for measuring social condition. The theory of prioritarianism has been the topic of intensive investigation for decades, now, in philosophy and welfare economics, as surveyed in Section 1.2. Much less studied has been the *application* of prioritarianism to problems of governmental policy. This is what the current volume, *Prioritarianism in Practice* aspires to do – and in a reasonably comprehensive fashion.

Although prioritarianism in the philosophical literature is sometimes discussed as a type of ethical view with certain features, and not as an

SWF – recall that this is Parfit's approach in the Lindley Lecture – the present volume is oriented around prioritarian *SWFs*: around the family of SWFs that take the form of summing concavely transformed well-being. It is the SWF framework that rigorously operationalizes prioritarianism as a tool for policy assessment. For reasons rehearsed in Chapter 2, contributors generally focus more specifically on two quite tractable subclasses of prioritarian SWFs: Atkinson SWFs and Kolm-Pollak SWFs.

At the heart of the volume are six chapters analyzing prioritarianism in various policy domains – taxation (Chapter 4), health policy (Chapter 6), risk regulation (Chapter 7), climate policy (Chapter 8), education (Chapter 9), and the COVID-19 pandemic (Chapter 12) – and one examining prioritarianism as an indicator of social condition (Chapter 5). These chapters both review existing work on applications of prioritarianism within the policy domain (such as exists), and report on new research. Many of the analyses described in these chapters are new.

The chapters generally apply prioritarianism in tandem with utilitarianism. This is done both because of utilitarianism's dominance in ethical thought, and because the normative case for prioritarianism proceeds by way of comparison to utilitarianism. It shares many of utilitarianism's attractive features, but adds the further feature of an extra concern for the well-being of the worse off. It is therefore important to see how this difference translates into a difference in policy advice.

Some chapters also compare the prioritarian methodology to dominant non-SWF tools within the domain, specifically benefit-cost analysis (BCA) or cost-effectiveness analysis (CEA).

These application chapters are firmly buttressed by three theory chapters: Chapters 2, 3, and 11. Chapter 2 systematically presents the theory of prioritarian SWFs. Chapter 3 discusses the construction of the well-being measure $w(\cdot)$ that is the linchpin for prioritarian as well as other SWFs. Chapter 11 integrates prioritarianism into the theory literature on equality of opportunity. Finally, Chapter 10 is a rich empirical chapter reviewing empirical research on ethical preferences.

What follows are brief chapter summaries.

Chapter 2, "Theory of Prioritarianism," reviews the SWF framework and provides a detailed discussion of the specific features of prioritarian SWFs as distinct from others. The chapter describes the major types of SWFs. It discusses the axiomatic characterization of SWFs, via axioms that have been mentioned in this Introduction: Pareto, Anonymity, Separability, Continuity and Pigou-Dalton. Prioritarian SWFs, and only these, satisfy all five axioms. The chapter reviews the major methodologies for applying prioritarianism under conditions of uncertainty: "ex post" prioritarianism (EPP), "ex ante" prioritarianism (EAP), and expected equally-distributed-equivalent prioritarianism (EEDEP). It analyzes the two major subfamilies of prioritarian SWFs, namely Atkinson SWFs and Kolm-Pollak SWFs. Chapter 2 also discusses interpersonal well-being comparisons: all SWFs require some such comparisons, and prioritarian SWFs require well-being difference as well as level comparisons. Alongside its formal analysis of prioritarianism, the chapter offers a normative defense of prioritarianism.

Chapter 3, "Well-Being Measurement," provides theoretical foundations for the construction of a well-being measure $w(\cdot)$ that contains both intra- and interpersonal well-being information, concerning both well-being levels and well-being differences. The dominant theory of well-being in economics is preference-based: a given individual is better off in x than y if and only if that individual prefers x to y (in light of her actual preferences or, perhaps, her well-informed and otherwise "laundered" preferences). To account for the dependence of well-being on preferences, Chapter 3 conceptualizes the well-being measure as operating on individual "histories" – with a "history" being a combination of a possible bundle of individual attributes and a preference. $w(\cdot) = w(a, R)$, with (a, R) a history containing attribute bundle a and preference R. This is a very general and flexible setup. Preference-based well-being measures satisfy the Deference Principle: $w(a, R) \geq w(a^*, R)$ if and only if preference R is such as to weakly prefer a to a^*. Chapter 3 reviews the two major approaches in the literature to constructing a preference-based well-being measure: the "equivalence approach" (the widely used equivalent-income well-being measure is one specific version of the equivalence approach), and measuring well-being with von Neumann/Morgenstern (vNM) utilities. However, the setup here also allows for non-preference-based well-being measures – such as a $w(\cdot)$ grounded in an objective good/"capability"-based account of well-being – since well-being numbers can be assigned to histories without satisfying the Deference Principle.

Chapter 4, "Prioritarianism and Optimal Taxation," discusses the use of a prioritarian SWF to set tax policy – in particular, to design income taxes. The chapter works within the literature on optimal taxation that grows out of the work of James Mirrlees (1971), noted above. The difficult design problem at the heart of the income tax system is how to advance government's revenue-raising and distributional goals while taking account of the disincentive effects of higher tax rates. The Mirrleesian setup seeks to tackle this design problem. In the setup, the policy objective is to maximize an additive SWF (in the terminology of this volume, a generalized-utilitarian SWF), which can be either utilitarian or prioritarian, subject to a revenue constraint. An individual's utility depends upon her consumption and her leisure. The policymaker chooses a schedule of income tax rates so as to maximize the SWF; each individual, in turn, maximizes her utility by trading labor for income, in light of her productivity (wage rate) and the income tax schedule. This framework yields an analytic expression for optimal marginal income tax rates. Chapter 4 discusses how the functional form of the SWF (utilitarian or prioritarian) figures into the analytic expression. The chapter then reports an extensive series of simulations, with optimal income tax schedules that depend upon: the distribution of individual productivities; the shape of individual preferences; whether the SWF is utilitarian or, alternatively, prioritarian (Atkinson or Kolm-Pollak) with various degrees of priority for the worse off; and government's exogenous revenue requirements. These simulations tend to find that the shift from utilitarianism to prioritarianism (even at the lower end of the range of priorities considered) yields significant differences in optimal marginal tax rates. Finally, the chapter reports on "inverse optimum" research, which examines the implicit social objective reflected in actual tax laws.

Chapter 5, "Prioritarianism and Measuring Social Progress," discusses how prioritarianism can be used as a way to move "beyond GDP" as the indicator of a society's condition. The limitations of GDP (gross domestic product) have been much discussed; it equals the total market value of final goods and services produced in a country in a given time period, ignoring both non-market goods and the distribution of income. SWFs provide a much richer framework for assessing societal condition. The well-being measure $w(\cdot)$ can take as its argument any type of individual attribute (not merely marketed goods and services); a utilitarian SWF is sensitive to the distribution of income;

a prioritarian SWF is sensitive to the distribution of well-being itself. Chapter 5 focuses, specifically, on the use of utilitarian and prioritarian SWFs as a measure of social *progress* (change in social condition over time). The chapter sets out an analytic framework that meshes with a utilitarian, Atkinson, or Kolm-Pollak SWF; and that expresses social progress in terms of the absolute or percentage change in well-being at different percentiles of the well-being distribution (a growth-incidence curve). The chapter then surveys existing scholarship in economics using SWFs to measure social progress. This literature review illustrates the flexibility of the methodology with respect to the nature of well-being; it covers a variety of well-being measures, including income alone, objective goods, happiness, and preference-based measures. Finally, Chapter 5 uses a detailed longitudinal dataset for one country (Russia for the period 1995–2005) as an empirical illustration. This exercise not only illustrates the use of utilitarian and prioritarian SWFs as metrics of social change during a tumultuous period in Russia's history, but also showcases the two leading preference-based well-being measures analyzed in Chapter 2, namely the equivalence approach and vNM utilities.

Chapter 6, "Prioritarianism and Health Policy," focuses on the assessment of health policy via a prioritarian or utilitarian SWF in tandem with a measure of individual lifetime well-being that takes account not merely of an individual's longevity and her health across the lifespan, but also non-health components of well-being (in particular, income). Although there is an existing SWF-based literature on health policy, scholarship here generally ignores well-being attributes other than longevity and health. Because income is a major determinant of well-being, and because the costs of health policies are ultimately borne by individuals in the form of reduced income, a fuller SWF-based analysis should consider lifespan, health, *and* income as inputs into the well-being measure $w(\cdot)$. Chapter 6 shows, in detail, how this can be done. It analyzes two different ways to construct a lifetime well-being measure, both versions of the equivalence approach discussed in Chapter 2: the equivalent-life metric and the equivalent-income metric. (For a given life-history described as a temporal profile of income and health states across some lifespan, the equivalent life is the lifespan which would be equally good if combined with a reference profile of income and health; and the equivalent income is the income which would be equally good if combined with a reference lifespan and health profile.) Finally, Chapter 6 combines these measures with a utilitarian SWF and an Atkinson prioritarian SWF – the latter applied under uncertainty using both the EAP and EPP formulations – in a simulation model of the choice of health policy. The choice between out-of-pocket payment and public funding of cancer treatment in a low-income country is assessed using this SWF-based approach as compared with the standard health-policy-analytic methodologies, namely BCA and CEA.

Chapter 7, "Prioritarianism and Fatality Risk Regulation," discusses SWF-based evaluation of policies that reduce fatality risks (which is the main aim or at least a significant benefit of numerous types of governmental policies, including anti-pollution laws, workplace safety codes, food safety regulation, the regulation of the transportation sector, natural-disaster planning, and others). BCA – which evaluates policies by converting well-being effects into monetary equivalents and summing up these equivalents – is a widely used methodology for assessing risk-reduction policies. The so-called value per statistical life (VSL) is the linchpin concept here. VSL_i is, in effect, a conversion factor that takes a small risk reduction for individual *i* and translates that reduction into a monetary equivalent. The counterpart concept for the SWF is the "social value of risk reduction" (SVRR_i), namely the increase in social welfare per unit of risk reduction to individual *i*. The authors of Chapter 7 (Hammitt and Treich), along with other authors in this volume (Adler and Ferranna), have published a number of works developing the SVRR concept and comparing it to VSL. Chapter 7 reviews this scholarship and also reports on new contributions by the chapter authors. The work generally uses a utilitarian SWF and a prioritarian SWF applied in accordance with EPP or EAP. A headline finding is that BCA using VSL gives a significantly different picture of the comparative social value of risk reduction (as between individuals of different ages or incomes) than both the utilitarian and the prioritarian SVRRs. Substantial differences between utilitarianism and prioritarianism also emerge. Utilitarianism is considerably less biased toward the rich than BCA, but still prefers to allocate a unit of risk reduction to a higher-income than a lower-income individual; prioritarianism with a sufficient degree of concavity in the transformation function will neutralize or reverse this preference. Prioritarianism gives extra weight to risk reduction for the young, beyond the utilitarian preference.

Chapter 8, "Prioritarianism and Climate Change," compares utilitarian and prioritarian assessments of climate policy. The SWF framework is well established in the economics literature on climate change. However, prioritarianism has to date played little role. Instead, the dominant SWF is a *discounted* utilitarian SWF: the sum of the utility of present and future generations, with utility a function of individual consumption, and with consumption utility adjusted by a time-discount factor that is a decreasing function of time (so as to down-weight the utility of a later-in-time generation relative to that of an earlier generation). A central concept for climate policy is the so-called social cost of carbon (SCC), which expresses the harms of carbon emissions to the well-being of future generations in terms of an equivalent consumption loss for the present. The discounted-utilitarian SWF just described is used to calculate the SCC. Chapter 8 compares this discounted-utilitarian SCC to the SCC as calculated by a non-discounted-prioritarian SWF: one that sums the consumption utility of present and future generations, plugged into a prioritarian transformation function $g(\cdot)$, and without a time-discount factor. In a deterministic setting, assuming economic growth, later generations have greater consumption than earlier ones; they are better off than the present, and increasing the priority for the worse off (the concavity of the transformation function) will tend to lower the prioritarian SCC – just as increasing the utilitarian time-discount factor will tend to lower the discounted-utilitarian SCC. Matters become more complicated when uncertainty[24] is introduced; there is now some chance of a climate catastrophe, in virtue of which the future will be worse off than the present. Chapter 8 considers how prioritarianism applied with EAP, EPP, and EEDEP compare to expected discounted utilitarianism in calculating the SCC under uncertainty.

Chapter 9, "Prioritarianism and Education," examines what prioritarianism recommends with respect to the allocation of educational resources. The chapter first reviews existing academic literatures that evaluate or seek to design educational policies. A desire to equalize educational attainments or opportunities is evident in these literatures, but they diverge in how they conceptualize equality – in terms of

[24] We use the term "uncertainty" generically to mean the absence of certainty, including the case of well-defined probabilities; chapter 8 refers to this as the case of "risk."

realized attainments or, rather, opportunities; and in terms of students' long-run economic attainments as a function of education, ability, and social background or, rather, in terms of educational attainment.[25] Chapter 9 argues that the appropriate "currency" for a prioritarian SWF, at least at the level of primary education, and at least with respect to resource-allocation choices made within each school, should be students' educational attainment. An opportunity rather than attainment metric presupposes some degree of individual responsibility for low attainment, but young students lack such responsibility; and a classroom teacher should not be asked to shift his effort away from a low-performing student simply because that student comes from a more privileged background (and thus has greater expected economic attainment). The heart of the chapter is a detailed formal model, whereby a school team uses a utilitarian, prioritarian, or Rawlsian (leximin) SWF to decide how to allocate resources among students of differing abilities and social backgrounds, and over two stages of primary education. The model's assumptions – regarding the interaction of class resources, ability, and background to produce educational attainment – are grounded in empirical findings from the literature on educational policy. Chapter 9 finds significant differences between the utilitarian, prioritarian, and Rawlsian allocations. The chapter then discusses possible extensions of the model: to address policy choices by an educational minister (allocating resources among schools) rather than a school team (allocating resources among students within a school); to address non-primary rather than primary education; to cover policy tools other than resource allocation; and in other ways.

Chapter 10 is entitled "Empirical Research on Ethical Preferences: How Popular is Prioritarianism?" This chapter plays a unique role in the *Prioritarianism in Practice* volume. While most chapters consider the policy implications of prioritarianism in various domains, and others elaborate theoretical underpinnings, Chapter 10 reviews the survey and experimental literature, with the aim of determining what this literature shows regarding popular support for prioritarianism. The focus of the chapter is surveys and lab experiments that seek to

[25] Chapter 9 uses the term "outcome," but because "outcome" is used here to mean a social outcome rather than the outcome for a particular individual, we substitute the term "attainment."

ascertain individuals' ethical preferences (their impartial preferences, as opposed to self-regarding preferences, or preferences that combine altruism or envy with self-interest). Ethical preferences can be elicited by prompting survey respondents or experimental participants to take the perspective of the social planner, or to imagine themselves making choices for a society under a veil of ignorance (without knowledge of what specific position they occupy in that society). The chapter pays closest attention to surveys or experiments that test support for the axioms of prioritarianism, or that seek to calibrate the degree of priority for the worse off in a prioritarian SWF. To be sure, prioritarianism is a normative theory, and its normative force does not hinge on popular acceptance. Still, as the chapter argues, empirical research on ethical preferences will be relevant to the would-be prioritarian policymaker for two reasons: as evidence of political feasibility, and as input into the policymaker's own reflective equilibrium. The chapter does not find broad empirical support for the Pigou-Dalton axiom, which is the axiom that differentiates utilitarianism from prioritarianism.[26] This finding needn't undercut a policymaker's own commitment to prioritarianism, or lead her to conclude that a particular prioritarian policy intervention is infeasible – but it is certainly an important empirical result.

Chapter 11 engages the topic of "Prioritarianism and Equality of Opportunity." Within the structure of welfare consequentialism, equity considerations are expressed in terms of the distribution of well-being. Whether outcome x is more or less equitable than y depends upon how well-being is allocated among the population in the two outcomes. This reveals an important normative limitation of welfare consequentialism, and of the SWF framework as an implementation thereof: namely that they fail to differentiate between (1) inequality in well-being that arises in virtue of characteristics beyond individuals' control, and (2) inequality for which the individuals concerned are partly responsible. This critique of welfare consequentialism has been pressed by the philosophical literature on "luck egalitarianism" (Lippert-Rasmussen 2016) and, within economics, by a substantial body of formal and empirical work under the rubric of "Equality of Opportunity" (EOp) (Ferreira and Peragine 2016). The EOp setup characterizes individuals in terms of "circumstances" and "effort" as

[26] See Chapter 2.

well as well-being (or a measurable proxy for well-being, such as income). The animating ideas of EOp theory are, first, a "Principle of Compensation" (differences in circumstances beyond the control of the individuals warrant compensation, as they generate unfair inequalities in well-being) and, second, a "Principle of Reward" (efforts should be rewarded, and the resulting inequalities in well-being should be preserved). The key axioms of prioritarianism (in particular Anonymity and Pigou-Dalton) are inconsistent with these principles. The analytic work undertaken by Chapter 11, therefore, is to systematically examine how Pigou-Dalton and Anonymity might be modified so as to cohere with various specific versions of the compensation and reward principles; and to characterize the opportunity-adjusted prioritarian SWFs and dominance criteria that arise from this merger of prioritarianism and the EOp setup. The analytic tools developed in Chapter 11 are then illustrated in an empirical exercise using South African data.

Although incorporating considerations of individual responsibility may not be appropriate for every policy domain (see the arguments on this topic in Chapter 9, regarding primary education), there is a plausible normative case for doing so in many domains. Indeed, one of the findings of the empirical literature on ethical preferences, reviewed in Chapter 10, is that survey respondents generally wish to compensate for income differentials that result from brute luck, but not those that result from differential effort. The theoretical work on opportunity-adjusted prioritarianism in Chapter 11, therefore, can be seen as a stepping stone to future applied work.

The final chapter in *Prioritarianism in Practice* – Chapter 12, "Prioritarianism and the COVID-19 pandemic"—was added to the project once it became clear that the COVID-19 pandemic would be one of the major policy challenges of our time. The chapter shows how prioritarianism can be employed as a tool to guide the types of policy choices that were thrust onto governments by the pandemic. Two such choices were especially salient. First, governments had to weigh the fatality-risk-reduction benefit of social distancing measures, against the economic costs. Second, as vaccines became available, allocation rules – specifying which groups would come first in receiving vaccination – needed to be developed. Both types of policy choices are closely studied by Chapter 12. The chapter was drafted during 2020, while the pandemic was still raging, and thus is intended not to provide a definitive after-the-fact review of the virus' features or of policy interventions, but rather to illustrate the applicability of prioritarianism in guiding responses to this catastrophe.

The core of Chapter 12 is a simulation model, calibrated to data available as of the drafting date, in which the population is divided into two age groups, young (under 65) and old (65+), each with five income quintiles. Being infected by COVID-19 increases the risk of both the young and the old of dying prematurely, but dramatically more so for older individuals. Lifetime well-being for a given lifespan is calculated as a function of longevity and income each year alive, using the vNM approach. (Methodologically, therefore, Chapter 12 nicely complements Chapter 6, which as mentioned builds its measure of lifetime well-being using the equivalence approach). Chapter 12 compares the recommendations of a utilitarian SWF, prioritarianism (EAP and EPP) and BCA with respect to social distancing policy and vaccine allocation. Social distancing is studied by determining the maximum one-year reduction in GDP that each methodology is willing to bear in return for eliminating the virus. Because richer individuals are willing to pay more for risk reduction, BCA prefers a more stringent lockdown than the SWF methodologies; moreover, those methodologies are sensitive to the distribution of lockdown costs (especially so prioritarianism), while BCA is not. With respect to vaccine allocation, the social value of vaccinating a particular age-income group depends on vaccine efficacy, the group's infection fatality rate, and the social value of reducing the group's fatality risk.

References

Adler, M.D. (2012). *Well-Being and Fair Distribution: Beyond Cost-Benefit Analysis*. New York: Oxford University Press.

(2019). *Measuring Social Welfare: An Introduction*. New York: Oxford University Press.

Adler, M.D., Ferranna, M., Hammitt, J.K., and Treich, N. (2021). "Fair innings? The utilitarian and prioritarian value of risk reduction over a whole lifetime." *Journal of Health Economics*, 75: 102412.

Adler, M.D., Hammitt, J.K., and Treich, N. (2014). "The social value of mortality risk reduction: VSL versus the social welfare function approach." *Journal of Health Economics*, 35: 82–93.

Adler, M.D., and Holtug, N. (2019). "Prioritarianism: A response to critics." *Politics, Philosophy & Economics*, 18: 101–144.

Anand, S., Diderichsen, F., Evans, T., Shkolnikov, V.M., and Wirth, M. (2001). "Measuring disparities in health: methods and indicators." In T. Evans, M. Whitehead, F. Diderichsen, A. Bhuiya, and M. Wirth, eds., *Challenging Inequities in Health: From Ethics to Action.* Oxford: Oxford University Press, pp. 49–67.

Arrow, K.J. (1951). *Social Choice and Individual Values.* New York: Wiley.

Asaria, M., Griffin, S., and Cookson, R. (2016). "Distributional cost-effectiveness analysis: A tutorial." *Medical Decision Making*, 36: 8–19.

Asaria, M., Griffin, S., Cookson, R., Whyte, S., and Tappenden, P. (2015). "Distributional cost-effectiveness analysis of health care programmes—a methodological case study of the UK bowel cancer screening programme." *Health Economics*, 24: 742–754.

Atkinson, A.B. (1970). "On the measurement of inequality." *Journal of Economic Theory*, 2: 244–263.

Bergson, A. (1938). "A reformulation of certain aspects of welfare economics." *The Quarterly Journal of Economics*, 52: 310–334.

Blackorby, C., Bossert, W. and Donaldson, D. (2002). "Utilitarianism and the theory of justice." In K.J. Arrow, A.K. Sen, and K. Suzumura, eds., *Handbook of Social Choice and Welfare*, vol. 1. Amsterdam: Elsevier, pp. 543–596.

(2005). *Population Issues in Social Choice Theory, Welfare Economics, and Ethics.* Cambridge: Cambridge University Press.

Bleichrodt, H., Diecidue, E., and Quiggin, J. (2004). "Equity weights in the allocation of health care: The rank-dependent QALY model." *Journal of Health Economics*, 23: 157–171.

Boadway, R., and Bruce, N. (1984). *Welfare Economics.* Oxford: Basil Blackwell.

Bossert, W., and Weymark, J.A. (2004). "Utility in social choice." In S. Barberà, P.J. Hammond, and C. Seidl, eds., *Handbook of Utility Theory*, vol. 2 (*Extensions*). Boston: Kluwer Academic, pp. 1099–1177.

Brandt, R.B. (1979). *A Theory of the Good and the Right.* Oxford: Oxford University Press.

Broome, J. (1991). *Weighing Goods: Equality, Uncertainty, and Time.* Oxford: Basil Blackwell.

(2015). "Equality versus priority: A useful distinction." *Economics and Philosophy*, 31: 219–228.

Cookson, R., Griffin, S., Norheim, O.F., and Culyer, A.J., eds. (2021). *Distributional Cost-Effectiveness Analysis: Quantifying Health Equity Impacts and Trade-Offs.* Oxford: Oxford University Press.

Crisp, R. (2003). "Equality, priority, and compassion." *Ethics*, 113: 745–763.

d'Aspremont, C., and Gevers, L. (2002). "Social welfare functionals and interpersonal comparability." In K.J. Arrow, A.K. Sen and

K. Suzumura, eds., *Handbook of Social Choice and Welfare*, vol. 1. Amsterdam: Elsevier, pp. 459–541.

Dolan, P., Shaw, R., Tsuchiya, A., and Williams, A. (2005). "QALY maximisation and people's preferences: A methodological review of the literature." *Health Economics*, 14: 197–208.

Drummond, M.F., Stoddart, G.L., and Torrance, G.W. (1987). *Methods for the Economic Evaluation of Health Care Programmes*. Oxford: Oxford University Press.

Eggleston, B., and Miller, D.E., eds. (2014). *The Cambridge Companion to Utilitarianism*. Cambridge: Cambridge University Press.

Ferreira, F.H.G., and Peragine, V. (2016). "Individual responsibility and equality of opportunity." In M.D. Adler and M. Fleurbaey, eds., *The Oxford Handbook of Well-Being and Public Policy*. New York: Oxford University Press, pp. 746–784.

Fleurbaey, M., Luchini, S., Muller, C., and Schokkaert, E. (2013). "Equivalent income and fair evaluation of health care." *Health Economics*, 22: 711–729.

Fleurbaey, M., and Schokkaert, E. (2009). "Unfair inequalities in health and health care." *Journal of Health Economics*, 28: 73–90.

Goodin, R.E. (1995). *Utilitarianism as a Public Philosophy*. Cambridge: Cambridge University Press.

Greaves, H. (2015). "Antiprioritarianism." *Utilitas*, 27: 1–42.

Harsanyi, J.C. (1977). *Rational Behavior and Bargaining Equilibrium in Games and Social Situations*. Cambridge: Cambridge University Press.

Hernæs, U.J.V., Johansson, K.A., Ottersen, T., and Norheim, O.F. (2017). "Distribution-weighted cost-effectiveness analysis using lifetime health loss." *PharmacoEconomics*, 35: 965–974.

Holtug, N. (2010). *Persons, Interests, and Justice*. Oxford: Oxford University Press.

(2017). "Prioritarianism." *Oxford Research Encyclopedia of Politics*, http://dx.doi.org/10.1093/acrefore/9780190228637.013.232.

Johansson, K.A., and Norheim, O.F. (2011). "Problems with prioritization: Exploring ethical solutions to inequalities in HIV care." *American Journal of Bioethics*, 11: 32–40.

Johri, M., and Norheim, O.F. (2012). "Can cost-effectiveness analysis integrate concerns for equity? Systematic review." *International Journal of Technology Assessment in Health Care*, 28: 125–132.

Kolm, S.-C. (1969). "The optimal production of social justice." In J. Margolis and H. Guitton, eds., *Public Economics*. London: Macmillan, pp. 145–200.

Lambert, P.J. (2001). *The Distribution and Redistribution of Income*, 3rd ed. Manchester: Manchester University Press.

Lippert-Rasmussen, K. (2016). *Luck Egalitarianism*. London: Bloomsbury Academic.

McCarthy, D. (2008). "Utilitarianism and prioritarianism II." *Economics and Philosophy*, 24: 1–33.

McKerlie, D. (1984). "Egalitarianism." *Dialogue*, 23: 223–237.

Mirrlees, J.A. (1971). "An exploration in the theory of optimum income taxation." *Review of Economic Studies*, 38: 175–208.

Mongin, P. and d'Aspremont, C. (1998). "Utility theory and ethics." In S. Barberà, P.J. Hammond, and C. Seidl, eds., *Handbook of Utility Theory*, vol. 1 (*Principles*). Dordrecht: Kluwer Academic, pp. 371–481.

Nagel, T. (1979). "Equality." In T. Nagel, ed., *Mortal Questions*. Cambridge: Cambridge University Press, pp. 106–127.

Nebel, J.M. (2017). "Priority, not equality, for possible people." *Ethics*, 127: 896–911.

Norheim, O.F. (2013). "Atkinson's index applied to health: Can measures of economic inequality help us understand trade-offs in health care priority setting?" In N. Eyal, S. Hurst, O.F. Norheim, and D. Wikler, eds., *Inequalities in Health: Concepts, Measures, and Ethics*. New York: Oxford University Press, pp. 214–231.

Norheim, O.F., Asaria, M., Johansson, K.A., Ottersen, T., and Tsuchiya, A. (2021). "Level-dependent equity weights." In R. Cookson, S. Griffin, O.F. Norheim and A.J. Culyer, eds., *Distributional Cost-Effectiveness Analysis: Quantifying Health Equity Impacts and Trade-Offs*. Oxford: Oxford University Press, pp. 253–274.

Norheim, O.F., Ottersen, T., Tolla, M.T., Memirie, S.T., and Johansson, K.A. (2020). "Incorporating distributional concerns into practical tools for priority-setting." In O.F. Norheim, E.J. Emanuel and J. Millum, eds., *Global Health Priority-Setting: Beyond Cost-Effectiveness*. New York: Oxford University Press, pp. 181–203.

Otsuka, M., and Voorhoeve, A. (2009). "Why it matters that some are worse off than others: An argument against the priority view." *Philosophy and Public Affairs*, 37: 171–199.

Otsuka, M., and Voorhoeve, A. (2018). "Equality versus priority." In S. Olsaretti, ed., *The Oxford Handbook of Distributive Justice*. Oxford: Oxford University Press, pp. 65–85.

Ottersen, T. (2013). "Lifetime QALY prioritarianism in priority setting." *Journal of Medical Ethics*, 39: 175–180.

et al. (2016). "A new proposal for priority setting in Norway: Open and fair." *Health Policy*, 120: 246–251.

Parfit, D. (2000). "Equality or priority?" In M. Clayton and A. Williams, eds., *The Ideal of Equality*. Houndmills: Palgrave, pp. 81–125. Delivered as the Lindley Lecture at the University of Kansas in 1991.

Pollak, R. (1971). "Additive utility functions and linear Engel curves." *Review of Economic Studies*, 38: 401–414.

Rawls, J. (1999). *A Theory of Justice*, rev. ed. Cambridge, MA: Harvard University Press. First published in 1971.

Samson, A.L., et al. (2018). "Fairness in cost-benefit analysis: A methodology for health technology assessment." *Health Economics*, 27: 102–114.

Samuelson, P.A. (1947). *Foundations of Economic Analysis*. Cambridge, MA: Harvard University Press.

Sassi, F., Archard, L., and Le Grand, J. (2001). "Equity and the economic evaluation of healthcare." *Health Technology Assessment*, 5: 1–138.

Sen, A.K. (1970). *Collective Choice and Social Welfare*. San Francisco: Holden-Day.

Singer, P. (2011). *Practical Ethics*. New York: Cambridge University Press, 3rd ed.

Temkin, L.S. (1983). *Inequality*. Ph.D. Thesis, Princeton University.

(1993). *Inequality*. New York: Oxford University Press.

(2003a). "Egalitarianism defended." *Ethics*, 113: 764–782.

(2003b). "Equality, priority or what?" *Economics and Philosophy*, 19: 61–87.

Weirich, P. (1983). "Utility tempered with equality." *Nous*, 17: 423–439.

van de Wetering, E.J., Stolk, E.A., van Exel, N.J.A., and Brouwer, W.B.F. (2013). "Balancing equity and efficiency in the Dutch basic benefits package using the principle of proportional shortfall." *European Journal of Health Economics*, 14: 107–115.

Weymark, J.A. (2016). "Social welfare functions." In M.D. Adler and M. Fleurbaey, eds., *The Oxford Handbook of Well-Being and Public Policy*. New York: Oxford University Press, pp. 126–159.

Williams, A. (2012). "The priority view bites the dust?" *Utilitas*, 24: 315–331.

WHO (2014). *Making Fair Choices on the Path to Universal Health Coverage*. Final report of the WHO Consultative Group on Equity and Universal Health Coverage. Geneva: World Health Organization.

(2020). Cost-effectiveness and strategic planning (WHO-CHOICE). Available at www.who.int/choice/cost-effectiveness/en/ (accessed February 26, 2020).

World Bank (1993). *World Development Report 1993: Investing in Health*. Oxford: Published for the World Bank, Oxford University Press.

2 *Theory of Prioritarianism*

MATTHEW D. ADLER*

2.1 Introduction

This chapter is the second chapter in *Prioritarianism in Practice*. See Adler and Norheim, Chapter 1, for an overview of the book. In a nutshell, *Prioritarianism in Practice* aspires to advance our understanding of prioritarianism as a policy-assessment tool. The book does so by considering the application of prioritarianism to a variety of policy domains, including taxation (Tuomala and Weinzierl, Chapter 4); health care (Cookson, Norheim, and Skarda, Chapter 6); fatality risk regulation (Hammitt and Treich, Chapter 7); climate change (Ferranna and Fleurbaey, Chapter 8); education (Ooghe, Chapter 9); and the Covid-19 pandemic (Ferranna, Sevilla, and Bloom, Chapter 12). Prioritarianism can also be used as a methodology for assessing societal condition, analogous to GDP (Decancq and Schokkaert, Chapter 5). For all these applications, it is relevant to know whether individuals' ethical preferences are in fact prioritarian and – if so – what degree of priority is given to the worse off (Schokkaert and Tarroux, Chapter 10).

The intention of *this* chapter is to provide theoretical foundations for the *Prioritarianism in Practice* enterprise by reviewing the theory of prioritarianism in some detail. The chapter interlocks with Chapter 3 (Adler and Decancq), which covers one major theoretical problem not addressed here – namely, how to construct an interpersonally comparable well-being measure.[1] Chapter 11 (Brunori, Ferreira and Peragine) is also an important theory chapter; it considers how to modify

* Thanks to Francisco Ferreira, Erwin Ooghe, Ole Norheim, Paolo Piacquadio, and to participants in the *Prioritarianism in Practice* book conferences at Duke University and University of Bergen, for their comments.

[1] This chapter does address a range of issues regarding well-being, as the reader will see; but it "hands off" the problem of constructing an interpersonally comparable well-being measure to Chapter 3.

prioritarianism so as to be sensitive not only to the pattern of individual well-being, but also to considerations of individual responsibility.

Utilitarianism makes overall well-being the master criterion for ethics. One outcome is ethically better than a second if and only if (iff) the sum total of individual well-being in the first outcome is larger. Utilitarianism is, of course, very well entrenched both in philosophy and in economics. It dates back hundreds of years to the writings of Jeremy Bentham; has inspired generations of philosophical scholarship; and also lies behind much of the literature in normative (welfare) economics (Blackorby, Bossert, and Donaldson, 2002; Brandt, 1979; Broome, 1991; Eggleston and Miller, 2014; Hare, 1981; Harsanyi, 1977; Mongin and d'Aspremont, 1998; Sen and Williams, 1982; Singer, 2011; Smart and Williams, 1973).

Prioritarianism is a newer entry to the history of ethical thought. It ranks outcomes according to the pattern of well-being, but so as to give *priority* (hence the term "prioritarianism") to individuals at lower well-being levels. (As will be discussed below, this is accomplished by summing *transformed* well-being numbers – more precisely, well-being numbers plugged into a strictly increasing and strictly concave transformation function.) Prioritarianism was introduced to philosophy at the end of the twentieth century, and to economics a few decades earlier. In philosophy, prioritarianism is most closely associated with Derek Parfit – who described the view in a lecture given in 1991, calling it the "priority view," which in turn morphed into the term "prioritarianism," now canonical among philosophers. (Parfit's 1991 lecture was published in Parfit [2000].)[2] For overviews of the philosophical literature on prioritarianism, see Adler (2012, chapter 5); Adler and Holtug (2019); Holtug (2010, 2017); Otsuka and Voorhoeve (2018). On the history of prioritarianism (not using that term) in economics, see Adler and Norheim, Chapter 1, this volume.

Utilitarianism and prioritarianism are both species of *welfare consequentialism* (Adler, 2012, chapter 1). According to consequentialism, there is an ethical ranking of outcomes; and the ethical ranking of choices in any given choice set (the set of choices available to some decisionmaker, at a given point in time) is determined by the ranking of

[2] Philosophers frequently credit Parfit with the invention of prioritarianism, although in fact there is work by a few other philosophers on the concept of prioritarianism (not using that term) that slightly predates Parfit's (McKerlie, 1984; Temkin, 1983; Weirich, 1983).

outcomes.[3] *Welfare* consequentialism constrains the outcome ranking so as to depend upon individual well-being. Formally, this is accomplished via the Pareto Indifference axiom: If two outcomes, x and y, are such that each person is equally well off in x as she is in y, then x and y are equally ethically good. Both utilitarianism and prioritarianism satisfy this axiom.

The social welfare function (SWF) framework is a systematic decision procedure for implementing welfare consequentialism. Governmental decisionmakers who wish to operationalize prioritarianism can most rigorously do so by means of the SWF framework: by employing a prioritarian SWF. This book, *Prioritarianism in Practice*, therefore operates within the SWF framework. It examines the use of prioritarian *SWFs* as a policy-assessment methodology.

In turn, therefore, the present chapter will set forth the theory of prioritarianism via the SWF framework.[4] The chapter's aims are both explicative and argumentative: to explain how prioritarianism is formalized as an SWF; and to present arguments in defense of a prioritarian SWF rather than alternative functional forms.[5]

Although the topic of the chapter is "Theory of Prioritarianism," utilitarianism is also discussed in considerable depth. Prioritarianism has many similarities to utilitarianism; yet, in certain critical respects, the two are different. One gains a clearer understanding of prioritarianism by seeing it how it both relates to, and innovates upon, the dominant approach within ethics and welfare economics, namely utilitarianism.

[3] "Outcomes," here, might be understood as possible worlds, or alternatively as cognitively tractable models of possible worlds. This chapter takes the latter position. See Section 2.2.1.

[4] This chapter focuses on the SWF framework as a decision procedure. However, as already suggested, we might employ prioritarianism not merely as a policy-assessment methodology (that is, as guidance to governmental officials in making policy choices), but also as a tool for evaluating societal condition. This application of the SWF framework is covered in Decancq and Schokkaert, Chapter 5, this volume.

[5] The chapter presents straight normative (ethical) arguments in favor of prioritarianism. These arguments are certainly contestable, and in particular reach conclusions that may not be well reflected in citizens' ethical preferences. See Schokkaert and Tarroux, Chapter 10, this volume. How the policymaker should take account of these dual inputs into decision – the ethical arguments presented to her by academics or others who engage her in ethical deliberation, and information about citizens' ethical preferences – is a complicated topic not addressed here (Adler 2019, chapter 6).

More precisely, both the utilitarian SWF and prioritarian SWFs fall within a broader class of SWFs: generalized-utilitarian SWFs. The argument offered by the chapter in defense of prioritarianism will have a two-part structure: first, a defense of generalized-utilitarian SWFs over competitors (Section 2.4); and second, within the generalized-utilitarian class of SWFs, a defense of prioritarianism over utilitarianism (Section 2.8).

Section 2.2 provides an overview of the SWF framework. This framework revolves around three critical formal tools: a well-being measure $w(\cdot)$, for converting outcomes into lists ("vectors") of well-being numbers; an SWF, which is a rule for ranking these well-being vectors, abbreviated as $\succcurlyeq$; and a procedure for applying the SWF under uncertainty. It presents formulas for the most widely used SWFs, including the utilitarian SWF, prioritarian SWFs, and others (the leximin SWF, rank-weighted SWFs, and sufficientist SWFs). Utilitarianism is a specific SWF (the simple sum of well-being numbers), while prioritarianism is a family of SWFs (defined by all possible strictly increasing and strictly concave transformation functions).

Section 2.3 discusses the axiomatic characterization of SWFs. The major axioms useful in demarcating the space of SWFs are: Pareto (meaning the combination of Pareto Indifference and Strong Pareto), Anonymity, Continuity, Separability, and Pigou-Dalton. The first two are generally accepted by welfare-consequentialists and, indeed, are satisfied by all major SWFs; this is not true of the remaining three axioms. Generalized-utilitarian SWFs satisfy Pareto, Anonymity, Continuity and Separability. Pigou-Dalton, an equity axiom, is *not* satisfied by the utilitarian SWF, but *is* satisfied by prioritarian SWFs.

Section 2.4 offers a defense of the generalized-utilitarian class of SWFs. Section 2.5 addresses well-being. The SWF framework requires interpersonally comparable well-being numbers. This part of the chapter explains why.

Section 2.6 takes on a question sometimes raised about prioritarianism, namely: is prioritarianism truly distinct from utilitarianism? The answer is "yes." In a nutshell: the outcome ranking that results from a prioritarian SWF in combination with a given well-being measure $w(\cdot)$ can be mimicked by conjoining the utilitarian SWF with a different well-being measure $w^*(\cdot)$. But utilitarianism and prioritarianism are distinct *relative to* any particular well-being measure $w(\cdot)$. If $w(\cdot)$ is the *correct* well-being measure – correct in the sense of capturing our judgments about intra- and interpersonal comparisons of well-being levels and differences – then $w^*(\cdot)$ is not.

Section 2.7 discusses the application of prioritarianism and utilitarianism under uncertainty. This topic has great practical relevance (human policymakers operate under uncertainty), but also theoretical import. Utilitarianism under uncertainty satisfies the ex ante Pareto axiom, while prioritarianism under uncertainty runs afoul of that axiom. (To be precise: prioritarianism under uncertainty is unable to satisfy both the ex ante Pareto axiom and a Dominance axiom that captures the essence of consequentialism under uncertainty.)

Section 2.8 engages the normative debate between utilitarianism and prioritarianism.

Section 2.9 discusses the two major types of prioritarian SWFs: Atkinson SWFs and Kolm-Pollak SWFs.

Section 2.10 explains the relation between prioritarian SWFs and inequality metrics.

Section 2.11 discusses variable population. The chapter generally simplifies the exposition of the SWF framework by assuming a fixed population of ethical concern: the very same individuals exist in each outcome. Section 2.11 relaxes this assumption.

The chapter includes an Appendix, which provides a more formal treatment of certain points in the main text.

Because the SWF framework ranks outcomes in light of their corresponding well-being vectors, it is insensitive to facts about outcomes except insofar as these "show up" in individuals' well-being. Assume that some individuals are better off in outcome y than outcome x, while others are better off in x than y. Now assume that the pattern of well-being in x^* is the same as in x, and the pattern of well-being in y^* is the same as in y. Then the prioritarian SWF, the utilitarian SWF, and indeed any (anonymous) SWF[6] will rank the first pair of outcomes the same way as the second. But there might be good non-welfare reasons to rank x better than y but y^* better than x^*. In particular,

[6] An "anonymous" SWF is one that satisfies the Anonymity axiom. All the major SWFs (utilitarian, prioritarian, leximin, rank-weighted and sufficientist) do so. If two outcomes have the same well-being pattern (in the sense that the allocation of well-being to the N individuals in the population in the second outcome is just a permutation of the allocation in the first), then Anonymity requires the two outcomes to be ranked equally good. See Section 2.3.

non-welfare facts regarding individual responsibility might argue for a differentiated ranking. (For example, some of the individuals who are at low well-being levels in x are responsible for their plight; they have knowingly made imprudent choices. In x^*, the counterpart individuals at these low well-being levels lack responsibility; they are the victims of "brute luck.")[7]

As already mentioned, it is the burden of Chapter 11 to discuss how to generalize prioritarianism to take account of responsibility. That topic is not addressed here.

2.2 The SWF Framework

The SWF framework is a welfare-consequentialist decision procedure. It is a rigorously structured methodology for implementing welfare-consequentialist constructs such as utilitarianism or prioritarianism.[8]

The framework's components are as follows: A set of outcomes $\mathbf{O} = \{x, y, \ldots\}$; a population of individuals of ethical concern, understood for now as a fixed and finite set of individuals $\mathbf{I} = \{1, \ldots, N\}$,[9] each of whom exists in all of the outcomes; a set of policies (possible governmental actions) $\mathbf{P} = \{P, P^*, P^{**}, \ldots\}$; a well-being measure $w(\cdot)$; an SWF, abbreviated as $\succcurlyeq$, which is a rule for ranking well-being vectors; and an uncertainty module for the SWF. I'll discuss each of these in turn.

2.2.1 *Outcomes, Individuals, Policies*

What is an "outcome"? As a first cut, we might say that each outcome is a "possible world." The consequentialist perspective on ethics says: the ethical ranking of the various choices available to a decisionmaker depends on what might happen as a result of each choice, and on how good those consequences are. A possible world is a complete

[7] The importance of individual responsibility as a component of ethical assessment is the core insight in the philosophical literature on "luck egalitarianism" (Knight, 2009; Lippert-Rasmussen, 2016), which in turn is the inspiration for the economic literature on equality of opportunity (Ferreira and Peragine, 2016).

[8] The SWF framework, as summarized in this section, is set forth in detail in Adler (2019).

[9] $N \geq 3$. $N = 1$ does not pose a problem of social choice; and with $N = 2$ the axiom of Separability is not fully distinct from the Pareto axiom but is rather implied by it (see Section 2.3 for statements of axioms).

description of a possible history of the universe. It tells us "what might happen" in full detail. The description is complete in the sense that every possible fact is either included within the description or precluded by it. (So, for example, a possible world will specify either that Matt Adler sneezes at 11 a.m. on December 17, 2019, or that he does not sneeze then.) Thinking about which possible worlds might result from each choice available to us brings into play literally everything we might care about, ethically.

However, *human* decisionmakers are cognitively bounded. A human being doesn't have the mental capacity to think about a possible world, described in full detail, let alone a set of possible worlds. In order for "outcomes" to play a role within a decision procedure that a human decisionmaker can actually use, outcomes can't be possible worlds. Rather, outcomes are cognitively tractable *models* of possible worlds. Each outcome in the set O is a description of a possible combination of *certain* facts, in particular certain facts of ethical relevance.

For welfare-consequentialists, the facts of ethical relevance are facts about individual well-being. An individual's well-being depends upon her characteristics or "attributes." Economists standardly model an individual's well-being as depending on some or all of the following attributes: income or consumption, leisure, health, longevity, and her level of public goods (e.g., environmental amenities). To be sure, many other types of attributes may be well-being-relevant; which ones *are* depends upon the theory of well-being (an issue I'll turn to momentarily). Further, for reasons of cognitive tractability, an outcome can't describe all of an individual's welfare-relevant attributes, but only a subset thereof.

Pulling this together: a given outcome x is a possible series of attribute bundles, one for each member of the population of concern. Let a denote an attribute bundle, and a_i the attribute bundle of individual i.[10] Then $x = (a_1, a_2, \ldots, a_N)$, namely the combination of a possible attribute bundle for individual 1, a possible attribute bundle for individual 2, …, a possible bundle for individual N. A given bundle specifies an individual's holdings of *some* of the attributes of well-being relevance: for example, her income and leisure; or her income, leisure, and health; or her income and longevity. Which attributes to include in

[10] Because we are interested in lifetime well-being, each attribute bundle is a lifetime sequence of attributes. See Section 2.2.2.

the bundle description is a modeling question. To repeat: cognitive tractability means that a bundle can't include *all* of the individual's welfare-relevant characteristics, but only some of them.[11]

Actually, this characterization of outcomes isn't quite adequate for a *preference-based* view of well-being. Those holding such a view give a special role to an individual's preferences in determining her well-being. They'll want to differentiate between two types of individual characteristics that are well-being relevant: non-preference characteristics, and preferences themselves. So as to accommodate this view, I'll use the term "attribute" to indicate some type of non-preference characteristic. An attribute bundle will be abbreviated as a, and a preference as R. Let a "history" denote a combination of an attribute bundle and a preference. History $h = (a, R)$. On a preference view, a given outcome is a possible series of *histories* (each history a combination of an attribute bundle and a preference), one history for each member of the population of concern.[12]

What is the population of ethical concern? The ethical perspective is *impartial.* Welfare-consequentialists, to be fully impartial, should

[11] It should be stated that the notion of an attribute bundle is meant to allow for relational attributes (expressing how an individual is situated relative to others, e.g., whether the individual has a below-average income) as well as the non-relational attributes more typically used by economic modelers (e.g., the individual's income). If a well-being theory counts certain relational attributes as a determinant of an individual's welfare, those can be included in the bundles. To be sure, if bundles include relational attributes, then the combination of bundles in a given outcome will need to be internally consistent. (For example, it's not possible for everyone to have below-average income.)

[12] That is: a given outcome $x = ((a_1, R_1), \ldots, (a_N, R_N))$, with (a_i, R_i) the history of individual i. Adler and Decancq, Chapter 3, this volume, explore how well-being is assigned to histories on the assumption that each R is a single preference; but the "history" concept can be generalized to allow for preference change by letting R be an intertemporal sequence of preferences.

It might be argued that conceptualizing each outcome as *merely* a series of attribute bundles or a series of histories is too restrictive. These welfare-relevant facts about outcomes are sufficient to translate each outcome into a well-being vector, but not for purposes of the SWF's uncertainty module, whereby a given policy maps states of nature onto outcomes. See Section 2.2.4. In order to ascertain that mapping, we will need to know the causally-relevant features of outcomes that determine which outcome would result from a given policy P in a given state of nature s.

This objection is easily handled. We can simply say that each outcome *includes* a list of attribute bundles/histories, one for each individual, and also may include further facts – as needed for the uncertainty module.

accord equal weight to the well-being of all human beings, at least. Actually, fully impartial welfare-consequentialists should give equal weight to the well-being of all humans and also of all non-human animals that (like humans) are "welfare subjects." However, so as to avoid a variety of difficult normative and implementation questions that arise in extending the SWF framework to animals, this chapter (and indeed the entire book) focuses on the simpler case of a population of ethical concern that includes only humans. "Person" and "individual" will be used as a synonym for "human being."[13]

[13] To be precise, I assume that each individual in the population is a human being and a person – that is, a human being with an array of psychological attributes sufficient to make him/her a person. These are attributes such as sentience, having preferences and beliefs, self-consciousness, the capacity for autonomous choice, etc. What these psychological attributes are is contested in the philosophical literature on personhood; for the purposes of this chapter, it's sufficient to say that the individuals in the population are persons, whatever exactly that means.

Various types of beings are *welfare subjects* – they have a well-being – but are not human persons. See generally Singer (2011). These include: (a) non-human animals that are sentient but are not persons; (b) non-human animals (if there are any) that are persons or close to persons in their psychological attributes; (c) human beings with psychological impairments so serious that they are not persons, but are still sentient and possess a well-being; and (d) non-living beings, such as highly intelligent computers, that are nonetheless persons or at least possess a well-being. Welfare-consequentialists ascribe ethical status to all such non-human-person welfare subjects ("NHP" welfare subjects). But extending the SWF framework and, specifically, prioritarianism to include them raises many complications. (1) Can we make well-being comparisons between human persons and NHP welfare subjects? (2) There is a strong case that the inputs to the SWF framework should be lifetime well-being numbers, in virtue of the psychological continuity of human persons over time. See Section 2.2.2. Some NHP welfare subjects lack such continuity. How should the SWF framework be specified to take account of the lifetime well-being of human persons as compared to the sublifetime (momentary?) well-being of such NHP welfare subjects? (3) Assuming we *can* make well-being comparisons between human persons and NHP welfare subjects, it seems intuitively plausible that many are worse off than human persons. For example, most species of sentient non-human animals would seem to be, on average, worse off than human persons. Applying a prioritarian SWF to all these beings would mean giving priority to the interests of the former over the latter – which seems quite counterintuitive (although this intuition may just reflect a pro-human bias on the part of the author!).

It is beyond the scope of this chapter to address these difficult questions. I simply assume that each individual in the population is a human person. Thus, throughout the text of the chapter, "human," "individual," and "person" are used interchangeably as shorthand for "human person." Further, although in the future the Prioritarianism-in-Practice project should certainly broaden its

Policymakers are rarely fully impartial, or even aspire to be. A governmental decisionmaker might well take as her aim the well-being of citizens; non-citizen interests might be ignored or down-weighted. The SWF framework is applicable to any population, whether that population is all humans or a subset – as long as everyone within the population is accorded equal weight.[14] Although powerful ethical arguments support the position that the population of ethical concern *is* all humans, not a subset, the SWF methodology can be used in a more restricted way. Further, all of the *other* issues regarding the specification of the methodology – the well-being measure, functional forms for the SWF, and application under uncertainty – are orthogonal to how the population is defined. Thus, for the remainder of the chapter, "population of ethical concern" or, for short, "population" will be either all humans or a subset (e.g., the citizenry of some country).

The most straightforward application of the SWF framework involves a *fixed* and *finite* population. "Fixed" means that the very same individuals exist in every outcome. **I**, the population of ethical concern, is such that each member of **I** exists in every outcome in **O**. "Finite" means that the number of individuals in **I** is some finite number N. As shorthand, I'll use a distinct number (rather than a distinct proper name) to refer to each member of **I**.

agenda to consider NHP welfare subjects, none of the chapters in the current volume do so. For an initial attempt to include non-human animals within the SWF framework, see Johansson-Stenman (2018).

A final note. No adult human being had the characteristics of a person at birth. Rather, any such adult acquired those characteristics at some point during her infancy or childhood. (What time that was depends on the precise list of characteristics sufficient for personhood.) Imagine that Lana, a human being, dies in outcome x at the age of three months, before becoming a person. How do we compare Lana's (lifetime?) well-being in x to that of human persons? Assuming we can make such comparison, it would seem that Lana in x is worse off than ordinary human persons, because her life is shorter. Should she, therefore, take priority over them? How the SWF framework should take account of human beings who die before becoming persons is, again, a quite important question but beyond what I can address in this chapter. I'll circumvent it by assuming that, in each outcome, each human being is old enough to be a full person. (Gamlund and Solberg [2019] grapple with the problem of determining the ethical value of saving newborns as compared with children and adults.)

14 Actually, the SWF framework itself doesn't require equal weighting. What does so is the Anonymity axiom, to be discussed below, Section 2.3, which I'll take as a foundational axiom.

So $\mathbf{I} = \{1, 2, \ldots, N\}$, with individual 1 a particular person, individual 2 another particular person, and so forth. The assumption of a fixed and finite population is adopted throughout the chapter until Section 2.11. See note 15 for an explanation of how this assumption is consistent with the analysis of policies that affect longevity, as in Cookson, Norheim and Skarda (Chapter 6, this volume) and Hammitt and Treich (Chapter 7).[15]

The set $\mathbf{P} = \{P, P^*, \ldots\}$ is a formal representation of some decisionmaker's choice situation. At a given point in time, the decisionmaker is selecting among possible choices – possible actions she might perform. **P**, the choice set, includes all the actions/choices that the decisionmaker is considering. The SWF framework will help her evaluate these choices. It will do so by ranking them, from best to worst.

I assume, specifically, that the decisionmaker is a governmental official of some type (or a governmental institution), and thus each choice in **P** is a *policy*: some course of action by government, such as enacting a particular statute, promulgating a particular regulation, building some particular infrastructure, distributing funds in some particular way, and so forth. (Thus the use of "**P**" to denote the set and "*P*" a member, as mnemonics for "policy.") Actually, the SWF framework is equally usable by private individuals and organizations. Consequentialism famously stipulates (notoriously so, for those ethicists who oppose consequentialism) that *everyone* is under an ethical injunction to promote ethically good outcomes. This is just as true for an ordinary person as for a governmental actor. Consequentialists draw no demarcation between the ethics of private and governmental choice. However, since in practice the SWF methodology has been, and will be, employed to provide guidance to governmental actors, the possible actions/choices in the choice set **P** are referred to as "policies," with P a particular policy, P^* a distinct policy, and so forth.

The end product of the SWF framework is a ranking of the choice set **P**: choice guidance, in the form of this best-to-worst ordering. The methodology arrives at this guidance (for any choice set) by means of

[15] If an individual lives a certain number of years in one outcome, and a longer or shorter number of years in a second, she exists in both. She "exists" if she is born (comes into being). Her longevity is a determinant of her lifetime well-being (see below, Section 2.2.2, for more on lifetime well-being), but doesn't change the fact of her existence. Thus the fixed-population assumption is fully consistent with using the SWF framework to assess policies that change longevity.

three crucial tools: the well-being measure, SWF, and uncertainty module. The well-being measure $w(\cdot)$ and SWF, together, function to order the outcome set. The uncertainty module, in turn, produces a choice ranking that is appropriately aligned (in consequentialist fashion) with the outcome ranking.

2.2.2 *The Well-Being Measure*

The well-being measure $w(\cdot)$ converts each outcome into a "vector" (ordered list) of well-being numbers. This vector has N entries – one for each member of the population. "$w_i(x)$" indicates the well-being number of individual i in outcome x, as assigned by the well-being measure. A given outcome x thus corresponds to the vector $(w_1(x), w_2(x), \ldots, w_N(x))$. This vector is a numerical representation of the pattern of well-being in outcome x (Adler, 2019, chapters 1–2).

For less mathematical readers, a more concrete illustration may help. Assume that N, the size of the population, is four. So there are four individuals, denoted as 1, 2, 3, and 4. The outcome set $\mathbf{O} = \{x, y, z, \ldots\}$. $w(\cdot)$ will map each outcome in $\mathbf{O}$ onto a vector with four entries – one for individual 1, one for individual 2, one for individual 3, and one for individual 4. For example, assume that $w_1(x) = 20$. The well-being number of individual 1 in outcome x – as a function of her attribute bundle in x or her history in x – is 20. Assume, further, that $w_2(x) = 60$. The well-being number of individual 2 in outcome x – as a function of *his* attribute bundle in x or history in x – is 60. Moreover, $w_3(x) = 37$ and $w_4(x) = 100$. Then the vector for outcome x is the four-entry list: (20, 60, 37, 100). There will be a similar four-entry list for each outcome in $\mathbf{O}$.

There is a rich philosophical literature concerning well-being. A range of competing accounts have been proposed and elaborated in this literature. Accounts often fall into one of three categories: hedonic accounts (an individual's well-being depends on her pains, pleasures, and/or similar mental states that feel good or feel bad); preference accounts (an individual's well-being depends on the extent to which her preferences are satisfied); and objective-good accounts (well-being depends on the realization of various "objective" goods, "objective" in the sense that whether an individual attains a given good is not merely a matter of what she wants or what she feels) (Adler, 2012, chapter 3; Bykvist, 2016; Fletcher, 2016; Griffin, 1986;

Haybron, 2016; Hurka, 2016; Scanlon, 1998, chapter 3; Sumner, 1996).

The $w(\cdot)$ numbers contain information about well-being comparisons – as per the account of well-being which has been adopted (be it a hedonic, preference-based, or objective-good account). In particular, I'll assume, those numbers represent intra- and interpersonal comparisons of both well-being levels and differences. $w_i(x) \geq w_j(y)$ indicates that individual i in x is at least as well off as individual j in y. (If $i = j$, we have here an *intrapersonal* comparison of well-being levels. If $i \neq j$, we have here an *interpersonal* comparison of well-being levels.) $w_i(x) - w_j(y) \geq w_k(z) - w_l(zz)$ indicates that the well-being difference between individual i in x and individual j in y is at least as large as the well-being difference between individual k in z and individual l in zz. (If $i = j = k = l$, we have here an *intrapersonal* comparison of well-being differences. If it is not the case that $i = j = k = l$, we have an *interpersonal* comparison of well-being differences.)

The SWF framework is consistent with *any* account of well-being (hedonic, preference-based, objective) – as long as the account doesn't eschew interpersonal comparisons, and as long as its comparisons can be represented via a well-being measure. Whatever the account, an individual's well-being will depend on her attributes (or, in the case of a preference account, her history). Thus we can say, generically, that $w_i(x)$ is a function of individual i's attributes/history in x.

See Section 2.5 for further discussion of the different types of well-being comparisons, and for an explanation of why the SWF framework requires some degree of interpersonal comparability; and see Adler and Decancq, Chapter 3, this volume, regarding the construction of an interpersonally comparable well-being measure.

While the SWF framework as presented here is inclusive in the sense of allowing for a wide range of accounts of well-being, it is restrictive in a different way. It assumes that the basis for the ethical assessment of outcomes and policies is individuals' *lifetime well-being*. This is implicit in the representation of an outcome as a series of well-being numbers, one number for each person in the population. x corresponds to $(w_1(x), w_2(x), \ldots, w_N(x))$, with $w_1(x)$ a number measuring the lifetime well-being of individual 1 in x, and so forth. Outcomes are ranked in light of the distributions of lifetime well-being that they embody. If, instead, the basis for ethical assessment were "sublifetime" well-being – well-being during a portion of an individual life, such as a year, a decade, a day, or a moment – then each outcome would correspond to a longer list of sublifetime numbers: for each individual, one number for her sublifetime well-being during each period in that outcome. Although the SWF framework *could* be specified in this "sublifetime" manner, such an approach is unusual.[16]

I have elsewhere presented a lengthy philosophical argument in favor of making lifetime well-being, not sublifetime well-being, the inputs to the SWF – and specifically in favor of lifetime rather than sublifetime prioritarianism (Adler 2012, chapter 6). In brief: (1) Human persons retain personal identity over their entire lifetimes, by virtue of psychological continuity between sublifetime stages.[17] (2) By virtue of such continuity, there is no non-arbitrary way to divide whole lifetimes into sublifetime stages longer than moments. Ordinarily, there is no sharp break in a person's psychological states at the end of a day, a week, a year, a decade.... Conversely, momentary welfarism is quite problematic because (on most accounts of well-being) there are many aspects of well-being that are only realized over longer stretches of time than a moment. (For example, individuals often have preferences for events or experiences that take longer than one moment.) (3) By virtue of intertemporal personal identity, distributional equity should take account of individuals' lifetime well-being. Imagine that, in outcome x, two individuals Avery and Blake have the same sublifetime well-being during period t of their lives. Outcome y is identical to outcome x, except that Avery's well-being in period t has improved by an increment Δw. Outcome y^* is identical to outcome x, except that now it is Blake who is better off by well-being increment Δw in period t. The

[16] The sublifetime specification would work as follows. Assume that each individual's life is divided into sublifetime periods (moments, days, ...), and that T is the maximum number of such periods that anyone lives in any outcome. Let $w_i{}^t(x)$ be the well-being of individual i during period t of her life, meaning a well-being number if she is alive during that period and a non-numerical symbol if she is not alive. Then x corresponds to a vector with $T \times N$ entries: $(w_1^1(x), ..., w_1^T(x), ..., w_i^1(x), ..., w_i^T(x), ..., w_N^1(x), ..., w_N^T(x))$. Possible rules for ranking $T \times N$ -entry vectors are specified, and are axiomatized in light of axioms stated in terms of sublifetime numbers (sublifetime Pareto, sublifetime Anonymity, sublifetime Pigou-Dalton, and so forth). At least in the theoretical literature on SWFs, such an approach is rarely (if ever) adopted.

[17] The case in which a human being has psychological attributes sufficient to be a person, but experiences a psychological break at some point sufficient to break intertemporal personal identity, presents an interesting but exceptional case that can be left aside for purposes of this chapter.

sublifetime specification of the SWF framework will be indifferent between y and y^*,[18] but it seems quite implausible that the two outcomes are necessarily equally good. For example, imagine that in x Avery is better off than Blake during each period except for t. Then it is only fair that Blake receive the benefit; y^* is a better outcome than y. The case for y^* being better than y presupposes that Avery remains the same person before, during, and after t. (If he and Blake were to experience psychological breaks at the beginning of t and at the end, then y and y^* would be equally good.)

Given space constraints, these arguments will not be recapitulated at greater length here. I take them as persuasive and, throughout the chapter, adopt the whole-lifetime approach—again, that is implicit in mapping an outcome onto *one* well-being number (a lifetime number) for each person.[19]

The whole-lifetime approach means that each attribute bundle is a lifetime bundle. It describes a possible combination of characteristics that an individual might have over an entire lifetime. Like the choice of attributes themselves, how fully to describe the intertemporal arc of a life is a matter of modelling tractability.[20]

2.2.3 *The SWF*

As already stated, an SWF ($\succcurlyeq$) is some rule for ranking well-being vectors. More precisely, it is an "ordering": a complete, transitive ranking.[21]

In presenting the various SWFs, it will be useful to have a compact notation for a well-being vector. A lower-case bold letter such as $\mathbf{w}$ or $\mathbf{v}$ will be used to indicate an N-entry vector, with $\mathbf{w}_i$ the well-being

[18] This assumes that the sublifetime SWF is such as to satisfy the sublifetime version of the Anonymity axiom. Sublifetime Anonymity requires indifference to a rearrangement of sublifetime numbers – which is what has occurred here, since Blake and Avery have simply swapped well-being numbers during period t.

[19] The reader who prefers the sublifetime approach can translate the formal apparatus of the chapter into sublifetime terms – by substituting $T \times N$-entry vectors for N-entry vectors. See note 16 above.

[20] See Adler and Decancq, Chapter 3, this volume.

[21] A quasiordering is a transitive, reflexive, binary relation. The SWF $\succcurlyeq$ is assumed to be a complete quasiordering, i.e., an ordering. $\mathbf{W}$, the set of well-being vectors ranked by $\succcurlyeq$, is either all N-dimensional vectors or some orthant of N-dimensional space. See Appendix.

number of individual i. (By contrast, the more cumbersome notation $(w_1(x), w_2(x), \ldots w_N(x))$ is used to indicate the vector associated with a given outcome, in this case x.)

$\mathbf{w} \succcurlyeq \mathbf{v}$ indicates that the SWF ranks vector **w** at least as good as vector **v**. $\mathbf{w} \succ \mathbf{v}$ indicates that the SWF ranks **w** strictly better than **v**. And $\mathbf{w} \sim \mathbf{v}$ indicates that the SWF ranks the two vectors as equally good. The $\succ$ and $\sim$ relations are linked to $\succcurlyeq$ as follows: $\mathbf{w} \succcurlyeq \mathbf{v}$ iff either (a) $\mathbf{w} \succ \mathbf{v}$, or (b) $\mathbf{w} \sim \mathbf{v}$. To say that one vector is "at least as good" as a second means that it is *either* better than the first *or* equally good as the first.

The major SWFs or families thereof are: the utilitarian SWF, prioritarian SWFs, the leximin SWF, rank-weighted SWFs, and sufficientist SWFs.[22] The first four are widely used in economic scholarship. The fifth is not, but is included here because it corresponds to an important position in philosophical work on welfare-consequentialism, namely sufficientism. On the different types of SWFs, see Adler (2019, chapter 3); Blackorby, Bossert, and Donaldson (2002; 2005, chapters 2–4); Boadway and Bruce (1984, chapter 5); Bossert and Weymark (2004); d'Aspremont and Gevers (2002); Mongin and d'Aspremont (1998); Weymark (2016).

Rules for all of these SWFs are provided in Table 2.1. The following concrete illustrations may help. Consider the two well-being vectors $\mathbf{v} = (115, 40, 100, 25)$ and $\mathbf{w} = (25, 112, 64, 70)$. The utilitarian SWF assigns each vector a number ("score") equaling the simple sum of well-being, and compares the vectors according to these scores. **v** is assigned the score $115 + 40 + 100 + 25 = 280$, while **w** is assigned the score $25 + 112 + 64 + 70 = 271$. **v** receives the larger sum-of-well-being score $(280 > 271)$, and hence is ranked better than **w** by the utilitarian SWF.

A prioritarian SWF employs some strictly increasing and strictly concave function $g(\cdot)$ (for short, the prioritarian "transformation" function); assigns each vector a score equaling the sum of transformed well-being numbers; and compares the vectors according to these

[22] The leximin SWF is an ordering of well-being vectors, but is not represented by a real-valued function. (In the terminology that will be used below, it is not "score-based.") This is also true of the sufficientist SWF. The description of these orderings as "social welfare functions" or "SWFs" is thus, strictly speaking, incorrect – but so as to avoid complicating the terminology, I will refer to any $\succcurlyeq$, whether or not score-based, as an "SWF."

Table 2.1. *The major SWFs*

Utilitarian SWF	Each vector **w** is assigned a utilitarian score $S^{Util}(\mathbf{w}) = \mathbf{w}_1 + \ldots + \mathbf{w}_N$. Vectors are ranked in the order of these scores: $\mathbf{w} \succcurlyeq \mathbf{v}$ iff $S^{Util}(\mathbf{w}) \geq S^{Util}(\mathbf{v})$.
Prioritarian SWFs	Each SWF within this family is defined by a strictly increasing and strictly concave function $g(\cdot)$. Each vector **w** is assigned a prioritarian score $S^{Prior}(\mathbf{w}) = g(\mathbf{w}_1) + \ldots + g(\mathbf{w}_N)$. Vectors are ranked in the order of these scores: $\mathbf{w} \succcurlyeq \mathbf{v}$ iff $S^{Prior}(\mathbf{w}) \geq S^{Prior}(\mathbf{v})$.
Leximin SWF	Let $\hat{\mathbf{w}}$ be a vector listing the elements of **w** from smallest to largest. For any two vectors **w**, **v**: (1) $\mathbf{w} \sim \mathbf{v}$ iff **w** is a permutation of **v**; and (2) $\mathbf{w} \succ \mathbf{v}$ iff there is $j \leq N$ such that $\hat{\mathbf{w}}_i = \hat{\mathbf{v}}_i$ for all $i < j$ and $\hat{\mathbf{w}}_j > \hat{\mathbf{v}}_j$.
Rank-weighted SWFs	Each SWF within this family is defined by a list of N positive and strictly decreasing weights: $k_1, k_2, \ldots, k_N$ such that $k_1 > k_2 > \ldots > k_N > 0$. Let $\hat{\mathbf{w}}$ be a vector listing the elements of **w** from smallest to largest. Each vector **w** is assigned a rank-weighted score $S^{RW}(\mathbf{w}) = k_1\, \hat{\mathbf{w}}_1 + \ldots + k_N\, \hat{\mathbf{w}}_N$. Vectors are ranked in the order of these scores: $\mathbf{w} \succcurlyeq \mathbf{v}$ iff $S^{RW}(\mathbf{w}) \geq S^{RW}(\mathbf{v})$.
Sufficientist SWFs	Each SWF within this family is defined by some threshold level of well-being w^{thresh}, and some strictly increasing and strictly concave function $g(\cdot)$. A given well-being vector **w** has two associated vectors: $\bar{\mathbf{w}}$, the elements of **w** truncated above at w^{thresh}; and $\underline{\mathbf{w}}$, the elements of **w** truncated below at w^{thresh}. For any two vectors **w**, **v**: (1) $\mathbf{w} \succ \mathbf{v}$ iff either (a) $g(\bar{\mathbf{w}}_1) + \ldots + g(\bar{\mathbf{w}}_N) > g(\bar{\mathbf{v}}_1) + \ldots + g(\bar{\mathbf{v}}_N)$ or (b) $g(\bar{\mathbf{w}}_1) + \ldots + g(\bar{\mathbf{w}}_N) = g(\bar{\mathbf{v}}_1) + \ldots + g(\bar{\mathbf{v}}_N)$ and $\underline{\mathbf{w}}_1 + \ldots + \underline{\mathbf{w}}_N > \underline{\mathbf{v}}_1 + \ldots + \underline{\mathbf{v}}_N$; and (2) $\mathbf{w} \sim \mathbf{v}$ iff $g(\bar{\mathbf{w}}_1) + \ldots + g(\bar{\mathbf{w}}_N) = g(\bar{\mathbf{v}}_1) + \ldots + g(\bar{\mathbf{v}}_N)$ and $\underline{\mathbf{w}}_1 + \ldots + \underline{\mathbf{w}}_N = \underline{\mathbf{v}}_1 + \ldots + \underline{\mathbf{v}}_N$.

Note: The rules for the utilitarian SWF, prioritarian SWFs, and rank-weighted SWFs are stated in a compact form giving necessary and sufficient conditions ("iff" conditions) for it to be the case that $\mathbf{w} \succcurlyeq \mathbf{v}$. The rules for the leximin and sufficientist SWFs could be stated in this compact form. However, so as to facilitate comprehension, I instead state them here as separate necessary and sufficient conditions for $\mathbf{w} \succ \mathbf{v}$ and for $\mathbf{w} \sim \mathbf{v}$.

scores. **v** is assigned the score $g(115) + g(40) + g(100) + g(25)$, while **w** is assigned the score $g(25) + g(112) + g(64) + g(70)$. Whether **v** or **w** gets the higher score, in this instance, depends upon which particular $g(\cdot)$ is chosen as the transformation function. For example, if $g(\cdot)$ is the

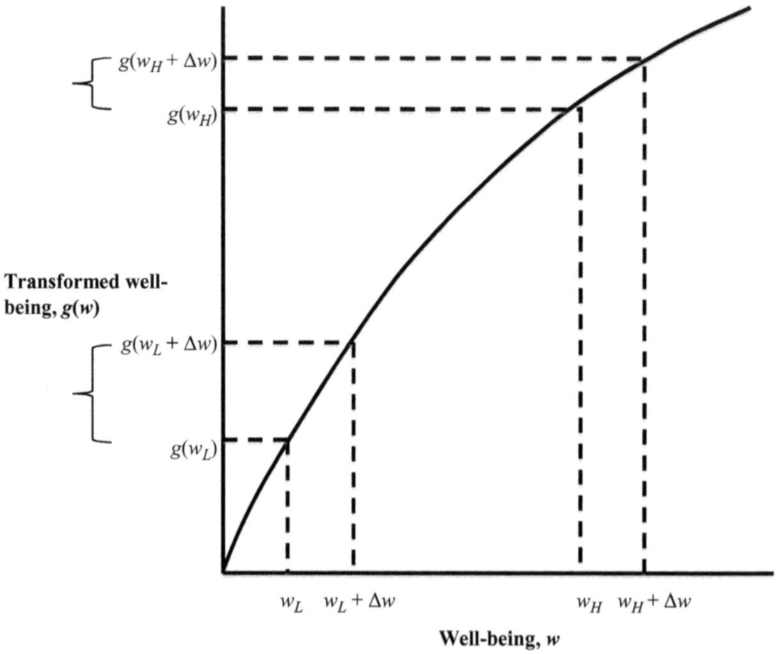

Figure 2.1 A prioritarian transformation function
(*Source*: Figure 1.1 in Matthew D. Adler, Measuring Social Welfare (2019), reproduced with permission of Oxford University Press)

square root, then **v** gets the higher score. If $g(\cdot)$ is the logarithm, **w** does.[23]

A terminological note: in some prior work (Adler 2012, 2019) I have referred to this SWF as a "continuous-prioritarian" SWF. In this chapter and volume, the terminology is simplified. "Prioritarian," here, means an SWF that sums a strictly increasing and strictly concave function of well-being.

"Prioritarian" SWFs are so-called because they accord greater weight (priority) to well-being changes affecting those at lower well-being levels. Figure 2.1 illustrates why the use of a strictly increasing

[23] The straight prioritarian formula assigns each well-being vector **w** the score $\sum_{i=1}^{N} g(\mathbf{w}_i)$. Sometimes a different prioritarian formula is used, the "equally distributed equivalent" (EDE) formula: $g^{-1}\left(\sum_{i=1}^{N} g(\mathbf{w}_i)/N\right)$. The two formulas are ordinally equivalent: they rank well-being vectors the same way. The choice between the straight and EDE formulas becomes significant in other contexts: for purposes of the uncertainty module, and for purposes of measuring social welfare on a ratio or translation scale. See Appendix, 2.A.2; Decancq and Schokkaert, Chapter 5, this volume.

and strictly concave transformation function means that a prioritarian SWF will indeed do this. Let w_L be the well-being level of a worse-off person, and w_H the well-being level of a better-off person: $w_L < w_H$. Imagine changing the worse-off person's well-being by adding a given amount of well-being, Δw, or instead changing the better-off person's well-being by adding the same amount. Because $g(\cdot)$ is strictly increasing, each change increases the prioritarian score. Because $g(\cdot)$ is strictly concave, the first change produces a larger increase in the prioritarian score than the second.

The leximin SWF ranks vectors according to the lowest well-being levels in each; if these are equal, the second-lowest; and so forth. The lowest well-being level in **v** (25, the well-being number of the fourth person) is the same as the lowest well-being level in **w** (25, the well-being number of the first person). However, the second-lowest well-being level in **v** (40, the well-being of the second person) is below the second-lowest well-being level in **w** (64, the well-being of the third person), and so the leximin SWF prefers **w**. Leximin is related to the notion of "maximin" introduced by John Rawls in *A Theory of Justice*[24] (Rawls 1999, first published in 1971).

[24] Rawls was not a welfare-consequentialist. Maximin as articulated in *A Theory of Justice* in the form of the "Difference Principle" applies to the distribution of "primary goods," not well-being; it says to maximize the bundle of primary goods held by the worst off. Maximin, transposed to the SWF format, takes the following form: **w** is better than **v** iff the lowest well-being level in **w** is greater than the lowest well-being level in **v**.

As a matter of theory, maximin is not a plausible SWF because it violates the Strong Pareto axiom (see Section 2.3). If the lowest well-being level in **w** is equal to the lowest well-being level in **v**, but some individuals are better off in **w** than **v** and none are worse off, then Strong Pareto requires **w** to be ranked above **v** – but maximin will be indifferent. Like maximin, leximin is such that an improvement in the well-being of the worst off is sufficient for an ethical improvement; unlike maximin, leximin satisfies Strong Pareto. For example, both maximin and leximin prefer $\mathbf{w}^* = (4, 25, 80, 60)$ to $\mathbf{v}^* = (3, 100, 100, 100)$, since the worst off improves from 3 to 4. However, maximin is indifferent between $\mathbf{v} = (15, 3, 9, 11)$ and $\mathbf{w} = (15, 3, 10, 14)$, since the worst off remains at 3; Strong Pareto applies and requires a preference for **w**; and leximin indeed prefers **w**.

Despite the axiomatic difficulties of the maximin SWF, it is sometimes used in applications. This can be justified by seeing maximin as a tractable approximation to leximin. Leximin is not score-based (see below, this subsection), while maximin is score-based – the score assigned to a vector is just the well-being number of the worst-off individual – which makes it more tractable.

A rank-weighted SWF uses a list of N fixed and positive weights, $k_1, k_2, \ldots, k_N$, which are strictly decreasing: $k_1 > k_2 > \ldots > k_N > 0$. Each vector is assigned a score by multiplying the lowest well-being number in that vector times k_1 plus the second-lowest number times k_2 plus . . . plus the highest number times k_N. For example, vector **v** would be assigned the score $k_1 \times 25 + k_2 \times 40 + k_3 \times 100 + k_4 \times 115$, while **w** would be assigned the score $k_1 \times 25 + k_2 \times 64 + k_3 \times 70 + k_4 \times 112$. In this instance, which vector is ranked higher depends upon the weights k_1, k_2, k_3 and k_4.

In a number of tables below, I illustrate the properties of rank-weighted SWFs using the rank-weighted SWF with "integer weights," by which I mean that: $k_1 = N$, $k_2 = N - 1$, . . ., $k_N = 1$.

A sufficientist SWF is defined by specifying some well-being threshold w^{thresh} and a strictly increasing and strictly concave transformation function $g(\cdot)$. The SWF is prioritarian below the threshold; gives absolutely priority to those below the threshold, over those above; and is utilitarian above the threshold. This is accomplished via a two-step rule: compare vectors by applying the prioritarian rule to well-being entries truncated above at w^{thresh}; if the vectors are ranked equal at the first step, compare them by applying the utilitarian rule to well-being entries truncated below at w^{thresh}. For example, let $w^{thresh} = 110$ and let $g(\cdot)$ be some strictly increasing and strictly concave function. The vectors **v** and **w** above are compared as follows. Let $\bar{\mathbf{v}}$ and $\bar{\mathbf{w}}$ denote the entries in those vectors truncated above at w^{thresh}, and $\underline{\mathbf{v}}$ and $\underline{\mathbf{w}}$ their entries truncated below at w^{thresh}. So $\bar{\mathbf{v}} = (110, 40, 100, 25)$, $\bar{\mathbf{w}} = (25, 110, 64, 70)$, $\underline{\mathbf{v}} = (115, 110, 110, 110)$, $\underline{\mathbf{w}} = (110, 112, 110, 110)$. Then we start by comparing $g(110) + g(40) + g(100) + g(25)$ to $g(25) + g(110) + g(64) + g(70)$. Depending on the $g(\cdot)$ function, the first sum might be greater (if so, the sufficientist SWF ranks **v** over **w**), the second might be greater (if so, it ranks **w** over **v**), or they might be equal. In this last case we move on to the second step, comparing $115 + 110 + 110 + 110$ to $110 + 112 + 110 + 110$ – so that the SWF ranks **v** over **w**.

Note that some *but not all* SWFs are "score-based." These SWFs employ some mathematical formula for assigning each vector a numerical score, and rank the vectors according to these scores. The utilitarian SWF, prioritarian SWFs, and rank-weighed SWFs are score-based. By contrast, the leximin SWF and sufficientist SWFs are not score-based. This difference, and the underlying axiomatics, will be further pursued below.

The SWF framework orders the outcome set via the combination of $w(\cdot)$ and $\succcurlyeq$. Let's call this the "Master Recipe."

The Master Recipe: x at least as good as y iff $(w_1(x), \ldots, w_N(x)) \succcurlyeq (w_1(y), \ldots, w_N(y))$.

Outcomes are ordered according to the SWF's ranking of their corresponding well-being vectors. Note how this implements *welfare*-consequentialism: the ethical comparison of any two outcomes hinges on a comparison of the patterns of well-being in the two (as represented numerically via well-being vectors). Note also that the Master Recipe is fully generic. How in fact a given outcome set will be ordered hinges on *which* well-being measure is used, and on *which* SWF is used.

2.2.4 *The Uncertainty Module*

Let's discuss, finally, the SWF's "uncertainty module." This tells us how to move *from* the ranking of outcomes according to the SWF (in conjunction with a given well-being measure) *to* the ranking of the choice set. On SWFs under uncertainty, see Adler (2012, chapter 7; 2019, chapters 3–4); Fleurbaey (2010); Mongin and Pivato (2016).

A standard device in decision theory is to represent choice under uncertainty via the state-of-nature set up (Gilboa, 2009, chapters 10–12; Joyce and Gibbard, 1998). There's a group of possible "states of nature." One or another of these is the actual state; the decisionmaker doesn't know which. The states should be such as to be causally independent of the choice at hand.[25] Moreover, they should be sufficient, in combination with the decisionmaker's choice, to yield one or another outcome. That is, each choice in the choice set, in conjunction with a given state, produces some outcome. This is the outcome that would occur, were that choice to be selected and that state to be the

[25] That is: the decisionmaker's selection from the choice set doesn't change which state is actual. Specifically, then, a possible state of nature should be thought of as a combination of (a) possible facts about the world at or prior to the time of choice and (b) possible causal laws. The "actual" state is, thus, a combination of possible facts about the world at or prior to the time of choice, and possible causal laws, which are such as to be true facts about the decisionmaker's world (facts about the world in which she actually finds herself) and true causal laws (the causal laws in her actual world).

Table 2.2. *The state-of-nature format for representing uncertainty*

States of nature	s	s^+	s^{++}	s^{+++}
Probabilities	$\pi(s)$	$\pi(s^+)$	$\pi(s^{++})$	$\pi(s^{+++})$
Policy P	x	y	z	zz
Policy P^*	x	z	zz	z
Policy P^{**}	z	y	y	x

Note: In this example, there are four states of nature: s, s^+, s^{++}, s^{+++}. The probability of a given state is denoted with "$\pi(\cdot)$"; for example, the probability of state s^+ is $\pi(s^+)$. The cumulative probability of the states is 1. Thus, here, $\pi(s) + \pi(s^+) + \pi(s^{++}) + \pi(s^{+++}) = 1$. In this example, there are four possible outcomes (x, y, z, and zz). A given policy associates each state with one of the outcomes; this is the outcome that would occur, were the policy to be chosen and that state to be the actual state of nature. For example, policy P^{**} produces outcome z in state s, outcome y in state s^+, outcome y in state s^{++}, and outcome x in state s^{+++}.

actual state. The decisionmaker's uncertainty regarding which state is actual is expressed probabilistically: the states are assigned probabilities, summing to 1.[26]

Let's now integrate this state-of-nature setup into the SWF framework. As illustrated in Table 2.2, a given policy in the choice set **P** yields some outcome in each state. Thus, for example, policy P produces outcome x in state s; outcome y in state s^+; z in state s^{++}; and zz in state s^{+++}. We might say that each policy is a state-by-state array of outcomes. Moreover, with the well-being measure $w(\cdot)$ in hand, each policy becomes a state-by-state array of well-being vectors. P in state s produces some outcome x; x is converted by the well-being measure into a well-being vector; and hence P is assigned that well-being vector in state s.

The uncertainty module for a given SWF is a procedure for ranking policies (each seen as a state-by-state array of well-being vectors). Interestingly, each SWF has *multiple* uncertainty modules. Of course, and trivially, every module for a given SWF should converge in its ranking of "degenerate" policies – a "degenerate" policy being one that yields the

[26] Sometimes, the term "uncertainty" is used to indicate the absence of precise probabilities, by contrast with "risk." In this chapter, however, "uncertainty" simply means the decisionmaker's absence of certainty regarding which outcome would result from a given policy; and I assume indeed – in line with classical decision theory – that the decisionmaker can always express her absence of certainty by an assignment of precise probabilities to states. How to apply an SWF absent such probabilities is beyond the scope of the chapter.

same vector in each state. (If all policies in the choice set are degenerate, there is no genuine, i.e., ethically relevant, uncertainty: no uncertainty regarding what the well-being pattern will be, were a particular policy to be selected.) But this basic requirement doesn't resolve how the SWF should be used to rank policies when there is genuine uncertainty.

The fact that a particular SWF has *multiple* uncertainty modules will be illustrated below in Section 2.7, where I describe three distinct modules for the prioritarian SWF.[27]

2.2.5 A Note on the Integral Representation

The theoretical literature on SWFs generally employs the formalism set forth here. There are a finite number of individuals in each outcome; an outcome corresponds to a well-being vector with a finite number of entries, one for each person. For short, call this the "vector" version of the SWF framework.

A different version of the framework employs an *integral* representation of the pattern of well-being. There are an uncountable infinity of individuals. An outcome corresponds to a well-being distribution across the uncountable population. Each such distribution is specified by a density function $f(\cdot)$. For a distribution with density $f(\cdot)$, the proportion of the population with well-being levels between w^* and w^{**} is $\int_{w^*}^{w^{**}} f(w)dw$. An SWF is a rule for ranking distributions. The utilitarian SWF ranks distributions according to the formula $\int_{-\infty}^{\infty} wf(w)dw$. The prioritarian SWF uses the formula $\int_{-\infty}^{\infty} g(w)f(w)dw$.

The integral formulation is the cornerstone of the SWF-based literature on optimal income taxation (Salanié, 2011; Tuomala, 2016). Indeed, the optimal taxation chapter in this volume (Tuomala and

[27] It's worth noting that the decisionmaker implementing the SWF framework doesn't literally need to specify states and a mapping from states to outcomes for each policy. Instead, she might circumvent the explicit representation of states and, for each policy, simply assign a probability to each outcome given the choice of that policy. However, such assignment should be consistent with the state framework. These should be causal probabilities. The probability of x given P should be the probability of P *causing* x to occur. That is, this probability should be the cumulative probability of the various possible states, each state causally independent of P, which are such that – were one of these states to obtain – the choice of P would cause x to occur.

Weinzierl, Chapter 4) uses this formulation. It also figures elsewhere in the volume (Decancq and Schokkaert, Chapter 5; Ooghe, Chapter 9).

The vector version has the theoretical virtue of mapping directly onto the structure of individuals and well-being. Individuals are discrete beings, each with a well-being level. Each possible world contains a finite number (or if not a finite number, then at most a countable infinity[28]) of these discrete beings, not an uncountable infinity. Further, it is more flexible theoretically than the integral approach, in that certain axiomatic possibilities are ruled out by the latter.[29] On the other hand, in some policy contexts, it may be easier to work with integrals than with finite sums; this seems to have been the experience, for example, of optimal tax scholars.

Although this chapter uses the vector formulation, readers should not be surprised when they see the integral formulation elsewhere in this volume and in the literature; and much of the analysis here could be transposed to that formulation.

2.2.6 A Note on Generalized-Lorenz Dominance

One way to employ the SWF framework for policy analysis is to choose a particular well-being measure $w(\cdot)$, a particular SWF, and a particular uncertainty module for that SWF, and then apply this specific measure-SWF-module combination in the policy domain of interest. This approach has the advantage of yielding a complete ranking of outcomes and policies. However, it requires a series of difficult ethical

[28] This chapter assumes throughout a finite population of individuals in each outcome. This is true both for the main case of a fixed and finite population (N individuals) in all outcomes; and for the extension, in Section 2.11, to allow for variable population (whereby it is allowed that the number of individuals each of whom exists in at least one outcome may be countably infinite, but the number in each outcome is finite). There is, in addition, an SWF-based literature on "infinite population" that allows for a countable infinity of individuals in an outcome – for example, a countable infinity of future generations. See Adler (2009, pp. 1511–1519), reviewing this literature.

[29] For example, Anonymity flows automatically from the integral approach. Well-being distributions are fully characterized by the density function, and so two distributions with the same density are ranked equally good regardless of which individuals are at the different percentiles of the distributions; while the vector approach allows for a violation of Anonymity. See Cowell (2000, pp. 91–92), discussing the two approaches.

judgments – namely those involved in ruling out all other well-being measures, SWFs, and modules.

A different, less demanding tactic is to leave the choice of well-being measure, SWF, and/or module partly unspecified. We could follow this route in an ad hoc manner. For example, pick a well-being measure, a family of SWFs, and a particular type of module for each SWF. See which policy comparisons are robust to the choice of any SWF within the family, and which policy comparisons are sensitive to that choice.

It would be useful, however, to have theoretical (not merely ad hoc) results regarding the application of the SWF framework without a fully specified well-being measure, SWF, and module – and indeed there *is* a theory literature on this topic. The literature goes under the heading of "dominance." It shows that if well-being vector **w** "dominates" vector **v** in some specified sense, then **w** is preferred to **v** by every SWF within some class, and vice versa[30] (Lambert, 2001, chapters 3–4; Cowell, 2016; Chakravarty, 2009, chapter 1; Shorrocks, 1983).

A headline finding of the "dominance" literature concerns "generalized-Lorenz" (GL) dominance. Consider any well-being vector **w** of length *N*. The generalized-Lorenz curve maps 1 onto the lowest well-being number in **w**, 2 onto the sum of the two lowest entries in **w**, 3 onto the sum of the three lowest entries, . . ., *N* onto the sum of the *N* lowest entries (total well-being).[31] Vector **w** GL-dominates vector **v** if the generalized-Lorenz curve for **w** is sometimes above the curve for **v**, and never below. A theorem of Shorrocks (1983) shows that **w** GL-dominates **v** iff every prioritarian SWF ranks **w** above **v**.

Ranking well-being vectors by the relation of GL-dominance has the advantage of avoiding contestable questions regarding the choice of prioritarian transformation function $g(\cdot)$. If one vector GL-dominates a second, then we know that every prioritarian – regardless of the functional form of her preferred transformation function and its degree of concavity – will count the first vector as better. A disadvantage of this approach is that it can be quite "gappy." Note that the relation of GL-dominance is a partial, rather than a complete ordering. It can be the case that the generalized-Lorenz curves of vectors **w** and **v** cross, so that

[30] The dominance literature is often formulated in terms of income vectors and social evaluation functions applied to income vectors; but dominance results of this sort can easily be transposed to vectors of well-being numbers and SWFs.

[31] We are assuming, as throughout this chapter until Section 2.11, that all vectors being compared have the same length *N*.

neither GL-dominates the other. (Indeed, by the Shorrocks theorem, this will occur whenever one prioritarian SWF prefers **w** and a second **v**.)

GL-dominance is further discussed in Brunori, Ferreira, and Peragine, Chapter 11, this volume, and is the basis for the empirical component of that chapter.

2.3 Axiomatic Characterization of SWFs

There are many different SWFs (indeed, an infinity!). We can structure ethical debate about the appropriate SWF by means of axioms. An axiom constrains the ranking of well-being vectors. By endorsing an axiom, we rule out SWFs inconsistent with it. On the axiomatic characterization of SWFs, see Adler (2019, chapter 3); Blackorby, Bossert, and Donaldson (2002; 2005, chapters 2–4); Boadway and Bruce (1984, chapter 5); Bossert and Weymark (2004); d'Aspremont and Gevers (2002); Mongin and d'Aspremont (1998); Weymark (2016).

Two fundamental axioms, widely accepted by scholars who work with SWFs and satisfied by all of the SWFs mentioned earlier (utilitarian, prioritarian, leximin, rank-weighted, and sufficientist) are: the Pareto axiom (which in turn has two parts, Pareto Indifference and Strong Pareto) and the Anonymity axiom.

I generally provide informal statements of the axioms; formal statements are provided in the Appendix. I also illustrate each axiom with an example.

Pareto. (1) *Pareto Indifference.* If each person is equally well off in vector **w** as in vector **v**, then $\mathbf{w} \sim \mathbf{v}$. *Example*: $(12, 25, 80, 3) \sim (12, 25, 80, 3)$.

(2) *Strong Pareto.* If each person is at least as well off in **w** as in **v**, and at least one person is strictly better off, then $\mathbf{w} \succ \mathbf{v}$. *Example*: $(3, 4, 10, 13) \succ (3, 4, 10, 12)$.

Anonymity. If the well-being numbers in **w** are a permutation (rearrangement) of the well-being numbers in **v**, then $\mathbf{w} \sim \mathbf{v}$. *Example*: $(7, 12, 4, 60) \sim (12, 60, 4, 7)$.

Pareto Indifference, as mentioned earlier, is the defining feature of welfare consequentialism. All SWFs satisfy it automatically. The other part of the Pareto axiom, Strong Pareto, is not automatically satisfied. But it should seem very plausible to a welfare consequentialist. The fact that some individuals have a higher well-being level in outcome x than

y is, prima facie, a reason to count the first outcome better. If none have a lower well-being level, what countervailing consideration would justify the conclusion that the first outcome is not better? Perhaps there is some non-welfare fact about the two outcomes such that, on balance, y is better than x or equally good. Non-welfarist-consequentialists might accept this line of argument, but welfare-consequentialists can't – since they deny that *anything* other than the pattern of welfare drives the outcome ranking.

Anonymity captures the ethical attitude of impartiality as between all members of the population. To say that **w** is a permutation (rearrangement) of the well-being numbers in **v** is just to say they contain the very same pattern of well-being – in the sense that, for any well-being level, the number of individuals in **w** at that level equals the number in **v**. The two vectors differ only as regards which particular individual is at a given well-being level. But, from an impartial point of view, that difference shouldn't matter.

Three further axioms are more controversial: the axioms of Pigou-Dalton (an equity axiom), Separability, and Continuity. These clarify what prioritarianism has in common with other SWFs, and what makes it distinctive. A prioritarian SWF satisfies all three of these axioms. None of the other SWFs that have been mentioned do. This is no coincidence: it can be shown that if an SWF satisfies Pigou-Dalton, Separability, and Continuity, along with the uncontroversial axioms of Pareto and Anonymity, then it must be prioritarian.[32]

Pigou-Dalton.[33] Assume that i is better off than j in vector **v**; that in **w** i's well-being has decreased by Δw, while j's well-being has increased

[32] See note 36 below.

[33] The Pigou-Dalton principle here is stated in terms of a transfer of *well-being* from someone with more well-being to someone with less. This is the appropriate form of the principle for a constraint on the ranking of well-being vectors. This version of the principle should be distinguished from a Pigou-Dalton principle framed in terms of some non-well-being attribute (an input to well-being) – for example, the Pigou-Dalton principle stated in terms of a transfer of income from someone with more income to someone with less, which is a mainstay of the literature on income inequality (Cowell, 2016).

The Pigou-Dalton principle with respect to well-being might be stated, as here, in terms of gap-diminishing transfers; or rather as a principle limited to non-rank-switching transfers (Adler, 2012 chapter 5). The version here implies the latter version; and, assuming Anonymity, the latter implies the version here. Thus, assuming Anonymity, the two are equivalent.

by the very same amount, and the gap between the two individuals has decreased; and that every other person is equally well off in **w** as she is in **v**. Then $\mathbf{w} \succ \mathbf{v}$. *Example*: $(3, 6, 8, 12) \succ (3, 4, 10, 12)$.

Separability. Assume that some individuals are "affected" with respect to the **w**/**v** comparison (each such individual is either better off in **w** or better off in **v**), while others are "unaffected" (each such individual is equally well off in **w** as she is in **v**). Let two other vectors, $\mathbf{w}^*$ and $\mathbf{v}^*$, be such that: (1) each individual who is affected in the **w**/**v** comparison is at the same well-being level in $\mathbf{w}^*$ as in **w**, and the same well-being level in $\mathbf{v}^*$ as in **v**; and (2) each individual who is unaffected in the **w**/**v** comparison is also unaffected in the $\mathbf{w}^*/\mathbf{v}^*$ comparison. Then the **w**/**v** ranking is the same as the $\mathbf{w}^*/\mathbf{v}^*$ ranking, i.e., $\mathbf{w} \succcurlyeq \mathbf{v}$ iff $\mathbf{w}^* \succcurlyeq \mathbf{v}^*$. *Example*: $(7, 100, 23, 7) \succcurlyeq (4, 100, 23, 12)$ iff $(7, 7, 7, 7) \succcurlyeq (4, 7, 7, 12)$.

Continuity. If $\mathbf{w} \succ \mathbf{v}$, then there is some region around **w** (perhaps small) such that for every $\mathbf{w}^+$ in this region, $\mathbf{w}^+ \succ \mathbf{v}$. Similarly, if $\mathbf{v} \succ \mathbf{w}$, then there is some region around **w** (perhaps small) such that for every $\mathbf{w}^*$ in this region, $\mathbf{v} \succ \mathbf{w}^*$. *Example*: If $(1, 3, 100, 100) \succ (1, 3, 6, 8)$, then $(1, 3 \pm \varepsilon, 100, 100) \succ (1, 3, 6, 8)$ for ε sufficiently small.

Utilitarianism fails Pigou-Dalton, but satisfies Separability and Continuity. Leximin, like prioritarianism, satisfies Pigou-Dalton and Separability, but it fails Continuity. Rank-weighted SWFs satisfy Pigou-Dalton and Continuity, but fail Separability. Sufficientist SWFs don't fully satisfy Pigou-Dalton,[34] satisfy Separability, but fail Continuity.[35]

Tables 2.3, 2.4, and 2.5 illustrate the properties of the various SWFs with respect to these three axioms.

Note now that the utilitarian SWF and prioritarian SWFs are axiomatically similar up to Pigou-Dalton, the equity axiom. They both satisfy Pareto, Anonymity, Separability, and Continuity; the axiomatic

[34] They satisfy it only if the worse-off individual is below the threshold. By contrast, if **w** is reached from **v** via a gap-diminishing pure transfer from a better-off individual above the threshold to a worse-off individual at or above the threshold, leaving everyone else unaffected, a sufficientist SWF will count **w** and **v** as equally good.

[35] This chapter uses the Pigou-Dalton axiom as the equity axiom for SWFs. Two other equity concepts also widely used by welfare economists are quasi-concavity and S-concavity (Chakravarty, 2009, chapter 1; Sen, 1973; Simon and Blume, 1994, pp. 522–527). A discussion of these concepts and how they relate to the Pigou-Dalton axiom will not be undertaken here. I will simply note that prioritarian SWFs are also equity-regarding in these senses: any prioritarian SWF is both strictly quasi-concave and strictly S-concave.

Table 2.3. *The Pigou–Dalton Axiom*

	Vector **w**	Vector **v**
Ariel	4	9
Ben	25	20
Camilla	36	36
Diego	16	16
Emile	100	100
Utilitarian score	181	181
Prioritarian score ($\sqrt{}$)	27	27.47
Rank-weighted score (integer weights)	331	341
Leximin	$\mathbf{v} \succ \mathbf{w}$	
Sufficientist:		
$w^{thresh} = 50$ and $\sqrt{}$	$\mathbf{v} \succ \mathbf{w}$	
$w^{thresh} = 15$ and $\sqrt{}$	$\mathbf{v} \succ \mathbf{w}$	
$w^{thresh} = 2$ and $\sqrt{}$	$\mathbf{v} \sim \mathbf{w}$	

Note: The Pigou-Dalton axiom requires that **v** be ranked above **w**. The table illustrates the ranking of these vectors by the utilitarian SWF; a prioritarian SWF with a square root transformation function; a rank-weighted SWF with integer weights; leximin; and a sufficientist SWF with a square root transformation function and various thresholds.

For the score-based SWFs (utilitarian, prioritarian, rank-weighted), the table displays the scores assigned to **v** and **w**; the ranking of the vectors is in the order of these scores. For the leximin and sufficientist SWFs, which are not score-based, the table directly displays the ranking of the two vectors. A similar approach is followed in Tables 2.4 and 2.5.

difference (an important one, to be sure) is that prioritarian SWFs *also* satisfy Pigou–Dalton.

In fact, by combining Pareto, Anonymity, Separability, and Continuity, we characterize a class of SWFs: generalized-utilitarian SWFs. Generalized-utilitarian SWFs are score-based, and assign each vector **w** a score equaling $f(\mathbf{w}_1) + f(\mathbf{w}_2) + \ldots + f(\mathbf{w}_N)$, with $f(\cdot)$ a strictly increasing and continuous function. Generalized-utilitarian SWFs clearly satisfy Pareto, Anonymity, Separability, and Continuity, and the converse can also be demonstrated: if an SWF satisfies these four axioms, then it must take the generalized-utilitarian form (Adler, 2018, appendix; Blackorby, Bossert and Donaldson, 2005, p. 116; Bossert and Weymark, 2004, p. 1159). The utilitarian SWF and prioritarian SWFs are members of the generalized-utilitarian class (there are others as well). In the case of utilitarianism, the $f(\cdot)$ function is the identity function: $f(\mathbf{w}_i) = \mathbf{w}_i$. In the case of prioritarianism, the $f(\cdot)$

Table 2.4. *The Separability Axiom*

	Vector **w**	Vector **v**	Vector **w***	Vector **v***
Ariel	30	32	30	32
Ben	60	57	60	57
Camilla	100	100	41	41
Diego	101	101	42	42
Emile	102	102	43	43
Utilitarian score	393	392	216	215
Prioritarian score (√)	43.37	43.36	32.66	32.65
Rank-weighted score (Integer weights)	994	992	586	593
Leximin	$\mathbf{v} \succ \mathbf{w}$		$\mathbf{v}^* \succ \mathbf{w}^*$	
Sufficientist: $w^{thresh} = 50$ and √	$\mathbf{v} \succ \mathbf{w}$		$\mathbf{v}^* \succ \mathbf{w}^*$	

Note: The Separability axiom requires that $\mathbf{w} \succcurlyeq \mathbf{v}$ iff $\mathbf{w}^* \succcurlyeq \mathbf{v}^*$. The table illustrates that the rank-weighted SWF fails Separability, while the other SWFs satisfy it. In this table, as in Table 2.3, the square root function is used as the transformation function for the prioritarian and sufficient SWFs; and the weights for the rank-weighted SWF are integer weights.

function is the prioritarian transformation function, i.e., $f(\cdot) = g(\cdot)$, with $g(\cdot)$ strictly increasing *and* strictly concave.[36]

2.4 Defending Generalized-Utilitarian SWFs

Generalized-utilitarian SWFs are considerably more tractable than other types of SWFs. Let's contrast them, first, with SWFs that fail Separability (such as rank-weighted SWFs); and, second, with SWFs that satisfy Separability but fail Continuity (such as the leximin SWF and sufficientist SWFs).

Separability is a precondition for an axiom regarding the uncertainty module, which I'll term "Policy Separability" (Adler, 2019, pp. 285–288).

[36] The prioritarian transformation function $g(\cdot)$ is also continuous. If the domain of $g(\cdot)$ is an open interval, this is automatic, since concave functions are continuous on open intervals.

Because $g(\cdot)$ is strictly increasing, continuous, *and* strictly concave, it is straightforward that the prioritarian SWF satisfies Pareto, Anonymity, Separability, Continuity, *and* Pigou-Dalton. The converse is also true. The first four axioms ensure that the SWF takes the generalized-utilitarian form – summing well-being transformed by a strictly increasing and continuous function $f(\cdot)$. Adding Pigou-Dalton entails that $f(\cdot)$ is strictly concave (Adler, 2019, p. 273).

Table 2.5. ***The Continuity axiom***

	Vector **w**	Vector **v**	Vector **w***	Vector **v**
Ariel	4	4	4.1	4
Ben	9	16	9	16
Camilla	81	25	81	25
Diego	121	100	121	100
Emile	144	225	144	225
Utilitarian score	359	370	359.1	370
Prioritarian score ($\sqrt{}$)	37	36	37.02	36
Rank-weighted score (Integer weights)	685	584	685.5	584
Leximin	$\mathbf{v} \succ \mathbf{w}$		$\mathbf{w}^* \succ \mathbf{v}$	
Sufficientist: $w^{thresh} = 7$ and $\sqrt{}$	$\mathbf{v} \succ \mathbf{w}$		$\mathbf{w}^* \succ \mathbf{v}$	

Note: Continuity requires that if $\mathbf{w} \succ \mathbf{v}$ then this is also true for every vector sufficiently close to **w**, and that if $\mathbf{v} \succ \mathbf{w}$ then this is also true for every vector sufficiently close to **w**. The table illustrates that Continuity is satisfied by the utilitarian SWF, prioritarian SWFs, and rank-weighted SWFs, but not the leximin SWF or sufficientist SWFs. In this table, as in Table 2.3 and 2.4, the square root function is used as the transformation function for the prioritarian and sufficient SWFs; and the weights for the rank-weighted SWF are integer weights.

Only SWFs that satisfy Separability can have an uncertainty module that satisfies Policy Separability. If an SWF fails Separability, then its uncertainty module necessarily fails Policy Separability.[37]

Policy Separability. To say that one or more individuals are "sure to be unaffected" as between two policies P and P^* means: each such individual with P has the same well-being level in any given state that she does with P^*. An uncertainty module satisfies the axiom of Policy Separability if its ranking of any two policies, P and P^*, is invariant to the state-by-state well-being levels of individuals who are sure to be unaffected as between P and P^*.

For an illustration of Policy Separability, see Table 2.6.

[37] This is straightforward. A given well-being vector **w** is equivalent to a "degenerate" policy: one that yields vector **w** in every state. If an SWF fails Separability, then any uncertainty module for that SWF necessarily fails Policy Separability (at least) in ranking the set of all degenerate policies, or any set that includes all degenerate policies.

Table 2.6. *Policy Separability*

	Policy P			Policy P^*		
	State s	State s'		State s	State s'	
	$\pi(s) = .5$	$\pi(s') = .5$		$\pi(s) = .5$	$\pi(s') = .5$	
Charles	1	2		4	4	
Deb	10	12		5	8	
Ernie	12	100		12	100	
			Expected			Expected
Utilitarian score	23	114	68.5	21	112	66.5
Prioritarian score (√)	7.63	14.88	11.25	7.70	14.83	11.26
EDE (√)	6.46	24.60	15.53	6.59	24.43	15.51
Rank-weighted score (Integer weights)	35	130	82.5	34	128	81

	Policy P^{+}			Policy P^{++}		
	State s	State s'		State s	State s'	
	$\pi(s) = .5$	$\pi(s') = .5$		$\pi(s) = .5$	$\pi(s') = .5$	
Charles	1	2		4	4	
Deb	10	12		5	8	
Ernie	5	6		5	6	
			Expected			Expected
Utilitarian score	16	20	18	14	18	16
Prioritarian score (√)	6.40	7.33	6.86	6.47	7.28	6.88
EDE (√)	4.55	5.97	5.26	4.65	5.89	5.27
Rank-weighed score (Integer weights)	23	30	26.5	27	32	29.5

Note: Ernie is sure to be unaffected as between P and P^*; he has the same well-being level in state s with each policy, and the same well-being level in state s' with each policy. Policy Separability requires that the P/P^* ranking be invariant to these state-by-state levels. For example, it requires that the P/P^* ranking be the same as the P^{+}/P^{++} ranking.

The table is meant to illustrate Section 2.7 of this chapter as well as the current section. It does so by showing how various uncertainty modules, described in Section 2.7 of this chapter, fare with respect to Policy Separability. The axiom is satisfied by UUU, the standard module for the utilitarian SWF (the expected sum of individual well-being) and by EPP, a module for the prioritarian SWF (the expected sum of transformed well-being, here with a square root transformation function). It is not satisfied by EEDEP, a different module for the prioritarian SWF ("EDE" is the equally-distributed-equivalent, here again with the square root transformation function; and EEDEP ranks policies according to the expected EDE).

Because the rank-weighted SWF violates Separability, no module for this SWF can satisfy Policy Separability. The table illustrates that one such module (the expected sum of rank-weighted well-being, with integer weights) violates Policy Separability.

Let's now say that an individual is "sure to be unaffected" relative to the policy set **P** if, for any pair of policies in the set, P and P^*, that individual is sure to be unaffected between the two. In other words, an individual is "sure to be unaffected" relative to the policy set **P** if his well-being is causally insulated from those policies. Whatever the state of nature may be, the decisionmaker's selection of one rather than another policy in **P** will have no causal impact on the individual's welfare. Conversely, an individual is "possibly affected" relative to the policy set **P** if he is not sure to be unaffected.

If an SWF's uncertainty module satisfies Policy Separability, then the population of ethical concern can be separated into two groups: those who are possibly affected by the policy choices at hand; and those who are sure to be unaffected. The decisionmaker can then "bracket" the well-being of the latter group. By this I mean that the decisionmaker need not incorporate their well-being into her calculations. To be clear, the sure-to-be-unaffected group remains part of the population of ethical concern. Their well-being is given the same weight as that of the possibly affected. But because the decisionmaker's module satisfies Policy Separability, the ranking of policies is independent of the state-by-state well-being levels of those in the sure-to-be-unaffected group. Their well-being can be bracketed.[38] More concretely, the decisionmaker does *not* need to assign probabilities to different possible well-being levels for each member of the sure-to-be-unaffected group, since her ranking of policies is the same for all such probability assignments.

By contrast, if the SWF's uncertainty module fails Policy Separability, then the decisionmaker *does* need to assign probabilities to different possible well-being levels for each member of the sure-to-be-unaffected group. She also may need to consider how the different possible well-being levels of sure-to-be-unaffected individuals correlate with the well-being levels of the rest of the population (the possibly affected).[39]

[38] I use the term "bracket" rather than "ignore" because the latter might suggest that the well-being of sure-to-be-unaffected individuals is given no weight. That is not the case: they remain fully part of the population of ethical concern.

[39] Some uncertainty modules that fail Policy Separability require the decisionmaker not only to assign probabilities to different possible well-being levels of sure-to-be-unaffected individuals, but also to consider how those levels correlate with those of the possibly affected. This is true, for example, of the EEDEP module for prioritarianism (described below in Section 2.7 and illustrated in Table 2.6), or the module for a rank-weighted SWF that ranks policies according to the

Being able to bracket the well-being of individuals who are sure-to-be-unaffected can be a great pragmatic advantage with respect to policy assessment. For example, imagine that the population of concern consists of the current population of a country, divided into twenty-six regions, A through Z. The policymaker is making a "local" policy choice, which (she is confident) will only causally impact those living within Region A. Although unsure about the well-being levels of those living in Regions B through Z, she is reasonably certain that these levels (whatever they are) will not be altered by her policy choice. Those levels are *fixed*, i.e., causally independent of her policy choice: whatever the state of nature, the well-being levels of those living in Regions B through Z remain the same regardless of which policy the decisionmaker selects.

If the SWF's uncertainty module fails Policy Separability, the policymaker needs to assign probabilities to different possible well-being levels for the various types of individuals living in Regions B through Z (the sure-to-be-unaffected), and perhaps also to consider how these levels would correlate with the well-being levels of those living in Region A (the possibly affected) as a result of each policy under consideration. By contrast, if the module satisfies Policy Separability, the policymaker can focus her modeling and information gathering on the individuals in Region A.

Policy Separability also facilitates the *delegation* of governmental choices to decisionmakers whose choices affect only a subset of the population. The regional example serves to illustrate this point. Imagine that a certain type of decision, type D*, directly impacts individuals living within a given region but has little effect on nonresidents; nonresidents are generally sure-to-be-unaffected with respect to decisions of type D*. (This might be the case, for example, regarding the level of public goods or governmental services that are provided only to residents, and that are funded by taxes borne by residents.) If so, and if a national policymaker endorses an SWF that satisfies Separability together with an uncertainty module that satisfies Policy

expected sum of rank-weighted well-being (illustrated in Table 2.6). Other uncertainty modules that fail Policy Separability are not sensitive to the correlation between the well-being levels of sure-to-be-unaffected and possibly affected individuals. This is true, for example, of a different module for a rank-weighted SWF: rank policies according to the sum of rank-weighted expected well-being.

Separability, the national policymaker can *delegate* decisions of type D* to a regional decisionmaker within each of the Regions A through Z. The national policymaker can instruct each regional decisionmaker to make decisions of that type by using the chosen SWF and uncertainty module, and to "bracket" the well-being of individuals living outside the region. If the national policymaker's preferred uncertainty module fails Policy Separability, delegation of this sort is not possible; rather, decisions of type D* within each region as well as other decisions must be made with reference to the well-being of the entire national population, affected or not.

A different type of example illustrating the advantages of Policy Separability involves prior generations. If the decisionmaker's uncertainty module satisfies Policy Separability, she can bracket the well-being of individuals within the population of concern who are no longer alive at the time of her choice ("prior generations"). Dead individuals are quintessentially sure-to-be-unaffected; current choices don't causally impact the well-being of the dead.

By contrast, how to handle prior generations creates a real dilemma for a decisionmaker with an uncertainty module that fails Policy Separability.[40] (a) One option is to drop prior generations from the population of ethical concern. However, doing so can lead to problems of time-inconsistency. As individuals die, the population of concern changes. (b) The decisionmaker can avoid time-inconsistency by including prior generations within the population of concern. But this makes decisionmaking less tractable, since the well-being levels of these dead individuals must now be considered.

The intention of the preceding paragraphs is to showcase the enhanced tractability of an uncertainty module that satisfies Policy Separability, and thereby to argue in favor of the Separability axiom. Again, satisfying the Separability axiom is a precondition (a necessary condition) for an SWF to have a uncertainty module that conforms to Policy Separability. Rank-weighted SWFs *violate* Separability, and thus are necessarily saddled with uncertainty modules attended by the difficulties that result from violating Policy Separability.

Leximin and sufficientist SWFs do satisfy Separability, but are not score-based, and hence are still not as tractable as generalized-

[40] For a discussion of this topic, see Fleurbaey (2010, pp. 663–669); Ferranna and Fleurbaey, Chapter 8, this volume.

utilitarian SWFs. It is quite economical to rank a set of outcomes by using a formula to assign each a score, and then ordering the outcomes as per the scores; leximin and sufficientist SWFs can't do this. Further, a score-based SWF has a natural, and highly tractable, uncertainty module: namely, taking the expected value of the score (or of some function of the score). Uncertainty modules for the leximin and sufficientist SWFs are more cumbersome. Finally, calculus techniques can be applied to the utilitarian and prioritarian scores (if differentiable) so as to identify optimal outcomes and policies (Adler, 2019, p. 262 and n.6, pp. 108–109, 279–280, 287–288). The fact that leximin and sufficientist SWFs are not score-based is closely connected to their failure to satisfy Continuity – since any SWF that satisfies this axiom is score-based (Adler, 2019, pp. 102–103).

To be sure, tractability is only one normative dimension by which to evaluate SWFs. By virtue of satisfying both Separability and Continuity, generalized-utilitarian SWFs are especially well situated on *this* dimension. It's certainly possible that other (more substantive) considerations might weigh in favor of SWFs outside the generalized-utilitarian class.

But are there, indeed, strong (substantive) considerations that argue in favor of SWFs outside the generalized-utilitarian class? Generalized utilitarians can plausibly deny that there are. To begin, note that a concern for *equity* – for the fair distribution of well-being – can be fully accomplished within the generalized-utilitarian class, by means of prioritarianism. Every prioritarian SWF fully satisfies the Pigou-Dalton axiom.

Further, the prioritarian family of SWFs offers flexibility with respect to the *degree* of concern for equity. Assume that one person ("Higher") is better off than a second ("Lower") in vector **v**. If **w** is reached from **v** via a *pure* gap-diminishing transfer of well-being from Higher to Lower, then every prioritarian SWF prefers **w**; this is what Pigou-Dalton requires. But what if **w** is reached from **v** via a *leaky* (impure) gap-diminishing transfer of well-being between the two? Higher's well-being goes down by Δw and Lower's well-being increases by a fraction thereof, $\rho\Delta w$, with $0 < \rho < 1$. Pigou-Dalton doesn't require a preference one way or the other, and indeed some prioritarian SWFs will prefer **w**, while others will prefer **v**.

More precisely, for any two well-being levels that Higher and Lower might have, and any degree of leakage in a gap-diminishing transfer between them, there are some prioritarian SWFs (with a transformation function sufficiently close to linear) that will disprefer the transfer, and other prioritarian SWFs (with a more concave transformation function) that will prefer the transfer.[41] As the prioritarian transformation function becomes less concave, it exhibits a lesser degree of concern for equity, approaching utilitarianism at the limit. Conversely, as the prioritarian transformation function becomes more concave, it exhibits a greater degree of concern for equity, approaching leximin at the limit (Bosmans, 2007).

In short, *equity* considerations don't seem to furnish a strong reason for departing from generalized-utilitarian SWFs. Such SWFs (via prioritarianism) permit both a concern for equity, and flexibility regarding the degree of such concern. Nor do there appear to be other major considerations cutting against the generalized-utilitarian form. As we'll see in detail in Section 2.7, prioritarianism under uncertainty has difficulty complying with the ex ante Pareto axiom. But this is *also* true of the leximin SWF, rank-weighted SWFs, and sufficientist SWFs (Adler, 2019, pp. 140–144).

Consider, now, the selection of an SWF *within* the generalized-utilitarian class. This chapter and book focus on the utilitarian SWF and prioritarian SWFs, ignoring generalized-utilitarian SWFs that are neither utilitarian nor prioritarian. Such SWFs have not been used much in economics, nor can they draw support from the philosophical literature. While the utilitarian SWF and prioritarian SWFs are the formal implementation of well-developed philosophical views (utilitarianism and prioritarianism, respectively), there appears to be virtually no philosophical argumentation in favor of a generalized-utilitarian approach that is neither utilitarian nor prioritarian.

Indeed, this absence of attention seems well justified. Generalized-utilitarian SWFs in this group, unlike prioritarian SWFs, can at most partly satisfy Pigou-Dalton (the equity axiom).[42] Like prioritarian

41 In particular, the degree of concavity of the Atkinson SWF, discussed in Section 2.9.1, is given by the parameter $\gamma > 0$. As γ increases, the Atkinson SWF becomes increasingly concave. For any gap-diminishing leaky transfer between a person at a given well-being level and a person at a lower well-being level, an Atkinson SWF with γ sufficiently small will disprefer the transfer, and an Atkinson SWF with γ sufficiently large will prefer it.

42 Recall that if an SWF is generalized-utilitarian (satisfying Pareto, Anonymity, Separability, and Continuity) *and* also satisfies Pigou-Dalton, then it is prioritarian. See note 36. A non-prioritarian, generalized-utilitarian SWF,

SWFs, but unlike the utilitarian SWF, these SWFs under uncertainty come into conflict with the ex ante Pareto axiom (Adler, 2019, pp. 140–144). So application under uncertainty is not grounds for choosing an SWF of this type, as opposed to a prioritarian SWF or the utilitarian SWF. Finally, they are no more tractable than prioritarian SWFs or the utilitarian SWF. Thus it is hard to see what would warrant their adoption.

The normative question that remains to be engaged is the debate between utilitarianism and prioritarianism. That will be undertaken in Section 2.8.

2.5 Utilitarianism, Prioritarianism and Interpersonal Comparisons

Some economists are skeptical about interpersonal well-being comparisons. However, the SWF methodology (including, in particular, the utilitarian SWF and prioritarian SWFs) requires some degree of interpersonal comparability. On SWFs and interpersonal comparability, see Adler (2019, chapter 2 and appendix); Bossert and Weymark (2004).

Assume that *only* intrapersonal well-being comparisons are meaningful. Let's refer to this position as No Interpersonal Comparisons. One, especially stark, version of No Interpersonal Comparisons says: only intrapersonal well-being *level* comparisons are meaningful. A different, less severe version, allows for both level and difference comparisons – but only intrapersonally, not interpersonally.

In order to explain the implications of No Interpersonal Comparisons for the SWF framework, I'll need to introduce the concept of an "individual-specific cardinal rescaling" of a well-being measure. Take a well-being measure $w(\cdot)$. Now define a new well-being measure $w^*(\cdot)$ as follows. For a given individual i, choose individual-specific constants $k_i > 0$ and l_i. Then our new well-being measure is the old measure rescaled by these constants. That is, for every outcome $x, w_i^*(x) = k_i \times w_i(x) + l_i$.

If No Interpersonal Comparisons is true, then the two well-being measures are *informationally equivalent*. They contain the very same

$\sum_{i=1}^{N} f(\mathbf{w}_i)$, if it is such that $f(\cdot)$ is strictly concave for some range of inputs, would partly satisfy Pigou-Dalton – for transfers between individuals with well-being levels in that range.

meaningful well-being information – meaningful according to the view at hand. Assume, first, that only intrapersonal level comparisons are meaningful. Note that $w^*(\cdot)$ contains the very same information as $w(\cdot)$ regarding these comparisons: whenever $w_i(x) \geq w_i(y)$, then $w_i^*(x) \geq w_i^*(y)$, and vice versa. Assume, next, that only intrapersonal level and difference comparisons are meaningful. Again, $w^*(\cdot)$ contains the very same information as $w(\cdot)$ regarding *these* comparisons. (1) Whenever $w_i(x) \geq w_i(y)$, then $w_i^*(x) \geq w_i^*(y)$, and vice versa. (2) Whenever $w_i(x) - w_i(y) \geq w_i(z) - w_i(zz)$, $w_i^*(x) - w_i^*(y) \geq w_i^*(z) - w_i^*(zz)$ and vice versa.

Observe, next, that our chosen SWF (whatever it might be) should be invariant to swapping a well-being measure for an informationally equivalent alternative. Assume that $w(\cdot)$ and $w^*(\cdot)$ are informationally equivalent. Imagine, now, that our chosen SWF ranks outcomes one way using $w(\cdot)$ and a different way using $w^*(\cdot)$. This would be quite problematic. If $w(\cdot)$ and $w^*(\cdot)$ are indeed informationally equivalent, they differ *only* numerically – only in terms of which numbers are being used to represent the very same well-being facts. Our chosen SWF, whatever it might be, shouldn't be sensitive to this *merely* numerical difference. Welfarists want outcomes to be ranked in light of their well-being patterns – and, if $w(\cdot)$ and $w^*(\cdot)$ are indeed informationally equivalent, the patterns of well-being in all the outcomes as signaled by $w(\cdot)$ are the same as those patterns as signaled by $w^*(\cdot)$.

Putting the last two paragraphs together, we arrive at the following conclusion. If No Interpersonal Comparisons is true, our chosen SWF (whatever it might be) should be invariant to swapping any given well-being measure $w(\cdot)$ for an individual-specific cardinal rescaling of $w(\cdot)$. But now a deep problem arises. A basic theorem of the SWF literature shows that *no* non-dictatorial Paretian SWF is invariant to individual-specific cardinal rescalings of the well-being measure (Adler, 2019, pp. 45–46; Bossert and Weymark, 2004, p. 1146; Weymark, 2016, p. 152).[43] Yet any *plausible* SWF, by welfare-consequentialist lights,

[43] The Cobb-Douglas SWF (the product of well-being numbers, assumed to be positive) is invariant to individual-specific *ratio* rescalings of well-being numbers. This SWF ranks well-being vectors the same way as the sum of the logarithm of well-being; in short, this is a type of prioritarian SWF. No other SWF that satisfies Strong Pareto and Anonymity is invariant to individual-specific ratio rescalings (Bossert and Weymark, 2004, p. 1148). However, an individual-specific ratio rescaling does preserve certain interpersonal

will be both non-dictatorial (this is an even weaker impartiality requirement than Anonymity) and Paretian. In short, no plausible SWF is invariant to individual-specific cardinal rescalings of the well-being measure. Every such SWF presupposes that well-being numbers contain *more* information than merely information about intrapersonal level and difference comparisons.

Table 2.7 illustrates specifically that neither the utilitarian SWF, nor a prioritarian SWF, nor the other major types of SWFs discussed in this chapter (leximin, rank-weighted, and sufficientist) will be invariant to individual-specific cardinal rescalings of the well-being measure.[44]

I've mentioned that a particular version of No Interpersonal Comparisons is especially stark – allowing only intrapersonal level comparisons. Some economists are suspicious of *difference* comparisons, and that is reflected in this severe view. It says, no difference comparisons of any type are meaningful, neither intra- nor interpersonal; intrapersonal level comparisons are meaningful; interpersonal level comparisons are not.

There is a view regarding well-being comparability that relaxes skepticism regarding interpersonal comparisons, but retains skepticism about difference comparisons. According to such a view, both intrapersonal and interpersonal level comparisons are meaningful, but neither intrapersonal nor interpersonal difference comparisons are.

Call such a view No Difference Comparisons. As illustrated by Table 2.8, the proponent of the leximin SWF can accept No Difference

information, namely whether individuals are above or below the zero point. Thus it is not correct to say that the Cobb-Douglas SWF is consistent with No Interpersonal Comparisons.

44 The example in Table 2.7, and the theorem mentioned in the previous paragraph, assume a profile-independent SWF. An SWF is profile-independent if its functional form does not depend upon $w(\cdot)$. The very same rule is used to rank well-being vectors, and thereby to rank outcomes via the Master Recipe, regardless of which well-being measure $w(\cdot)$ is used to map outcomes onto vectors. See Section 2.9.1. The utilitarian SWF is necessarily profile-independent; there is just one SWF here, namely the sum of well-being numbers. Profile-dependence becomes a possibility within the family of prioritarian SWFs; the transformation function $g(\cdot)$ might vary as $w(\cdot)$ does. This in turn raises the question whether No Interpersonal Comparisons might be consistent with a profile-dependent prioritarian SWF.

The question will not be pursued. Profile-independence is theoretically preferred; see Section 2.9.1. Thus, the fact that both the utilitarian SWF and any profile-independent prioritarian SWF are inconsistent with No Interpersonal Comparisons makes a strong case for interpersonal comparability.

Table 2.7. ***An individual-specific cardinal rescaling of the well-being measure***

Original well-being numbers				*Individual-specific cardinal rescaling*				Scaling factors	
	Outcome x	y	z		Outcome x	y	z	Times	Plus
Abel	9	4	21	Abel	9	4	21	1	0
Bob	25	25	21	Bob	230	230	190	10	–20
Chloe	49	16	21	Chloe	7.9	4.6	5.1	0.1	3
Diana	1	36	21	Diana	400	14400	8400	400	0
Util. score	84	81	84		646.9	14638.6	8616.1		
Prior. score(√)	16	17	18.3		41	139.3	112.3		
Rank-weighted score (Integer)	130	150	210		918.6	14889.8	8863.4		
Leximin		$z \succ y \succ x$				$x \succ z \succ y$			
Sufficientist (√) and $w^{thresh} = 100$		$z \succ y \succ x$				$z \succ x \succ y$			

Note: The left of the table displays well-being vectors assigned to outcomes x, y, and z by a well-being measure $w(\cdot)$, while the right displays vectors per an individual-specific cardinal rescaling of $w(\cdot)$. The table illustrates that neither the utilitarian SWF, nor a prioritarian SWF, nor a rank-weighted SWF, nor the leximin SWF, nor a sufficientist SWF is invariant to an individual-specific cardinal rescaling of well-being numbers. The square root transformation function is used for the prioritarian and sufficientist SWFs; and the rank-weighted SWF uses integer weights.

Table 2.8. *A common ordinal rescaling of the well-being measure*

Original well-being numbers				*Common ordinal rescaling*			
	Outcome x	y	z		Outcome x	y	z
Abel	1	4	9	Abel	100	101	102
Bob	36	25	16	Bob	110	104	103
Chloe	36	9	16	Chloe	110	102	103
Diana	1	25	16	Diana	100	104	103
Util. score	74	63	57		420	411	411
Prior. score(√)	14	15	15		40.976	40.545	40.546
Leximin	$z \succ y \succ x$				$z \succ y \succ x$		

Note: The left of the table displays well-being vectors assigned to outcomes x, y, and z by a well-being measure $w(\cdot)$, while the right displays vectors assigned by a common ordinal rescaling of $w(\cdot)$. The well-being numbers 1, 4, 9, 16, 25, and 36 are rescaled as 100, 101, 102, 103, 104 and 110 respectively. Common ordinal rescalings (see note 47 for a definition) preserve intra- and interpersonal well-being level information but not well-being difference information. As illustrated here, the leximin SWF is invariant to a common ordinal rescaling of the well-being measure, but the utilitarian SWF and prioritarian SWFs are not.

Comparisons without difficulty. But both the utilitarian SWF and prioritarian SWFs are inconsistent with No Difference Comparisons.

In short, anyone who endorses the utilitarian SWF or prioritarian SWFs must reject No Interpersonal Comparisons, and she must reject No Difference Comparisons. Our theory of well-being (whether hedonic, preference-based, or objective-good) should be such as to allow for both intra- and interpersonal comparisons, of both levels and differences. It should count all such comparisons as meaningful. And all four types of comparisons should be reflected in the well-being measure $w(\cdot)$.[45]

[45] Three possible views regarding intra- and interpersonal comparisons of well-being levels and differences have been considered and rejected here: that only intrapersonal level comparisons are meaningful; that only intrapersonal level and difference comparisons are meaningful; and that only intra- and interpersonal level comparisons are meaningful. Logically, rejecting these three views doesn't entail accepting that all four types of comparisons are meaningful. There are additional possibilities: for example, that only interpersonal comparisons are meaningful; that only intra- and interpersonal difference comparisons are meaningful; etc. However, these further possibilities can be rejected out of hand; none are even superficially plausible.

Indeed, making all four types of comparisons is common sense. No Interpersonal Comparisons and No Difference Comparisons fly in the face of common sense.

Imagine that John, in one possible world, is impoverished, has no friends, no job, is in poor health, and experiences chronic pain. In a second possible world, John has a good income, many friends, an engaging job, excellent health, and rarely feels pain. Then (*ceteris paribus*) John in the second world is better off than John in the first. This is an intrapersonal level comparison; no one disputes that such a comparison is meaningful.

But imagine now that John, in actuality, has a good income, many friends, an engaging job, excellent health, and rarely feels pain; while a different person, Jane, is impoverished, friendless, unemployed, in poor health, and experiences chronic pain. Surely John is better off than Jane (an *interpersonal* level comparison), just as John in the second world is better off than John in the first.

Difference comparisons are also common sense. Two days ago, Audra woke up with a slightly itchy elbow, but relieved the itch with a cortisone cream. Yesterday, she woke up with a terrible migraine headache, but it stopped after she took a pill. Intuitively, the headache pill made a bigger difference for Audra's well-being than the cortisone cream (an intrapersonal difference comparison). To insist that the two changes in Audra's well-being are incomparable (as does No Difference Comparisons) is counterintuitive.

Nor is it plausible to allow for intrapersonal difference comparisons, but reject interpersonal difference comparisons. Tweak the Audra case so that Audra, two days ago, wakes up with an itchy elbow while a different person, Brian, wakes up yesterday with the migraine. Intuitively, the headache pill made a bigger difference for Brian's well-being than the cream did for Audra's (an interpersonal difference comparison).

To reiterate: our theory of well-being (whether hedonic, preference-based, or objective-good) should be such as to allow for both intra- and interpersonal comparisons, of both levels and differences. And all four types of comparisons should be reflected in our well-being measure $w(\cdot)$.

Throughout this chapter, I will assume that $w(\cdot)$ does indeed represent both intra- and interpersonal well-being comparisons, of both levels and differences. How to construct such a $w(\cdot)$ is the topic of Chapter 3.

2.6 Is Prioritarianism Genuinely Different from Utilitarianism?

The prioritarian rule for ranking well-being vectors is different from the utilitarian rule. Prioritarianism assigns each vector **w** a score equaling $g(\mathbf{w}_1) + g(\mathbf{w}_2) + \ldots + g(\mathbf{w}_N)$ and ranks the vectors in the order of these scores; while utilitarianism assigns each vector **w** a score equaling $\mathbf{w}_1 + \mathbf{w}_2 + \ldots + \mathbf{w}_N$ and ranks the vectors in the order of *these* scores.

These rules are also axiomatically distinct. As explained above, the prioritarian vector-ranking rule satisfies the Pigou-Dalton axiom, while the utilitarian rule does not.

Finally, the prioritarian recipe for ranking outcomes is different from the utilitarian recipe. The prioritarian recipe is: outcome x at least as good as y iff $g(w_1(x)) + \ldots + g(w_N(x)) \geq g(w_1(y)) + \ldots + g(w_N(y))$. The utilitarian recipe is: outcome x at least as good as y iff $w_1(x) + \ldots + w_N(x) \geq w_1(y) + \ldots + w_N(y)$.

Still, the skeptic might argue that utilitarianism and prioritarianism are not genuinely distinct.[46] Why not? The prioritarian ranking of outcomes that results from combining well-being measure $w(\cdot)$ and transformation function $g(\cdot)$ is identical to the utilitarian outcome ranking using a different well-being measure, $w^*(\cdot)$. Simply define $w^*(\cdot)$ as follows: $w_i^*(x) = g(w_i(x))$ for every outcome x. In other words, our supposedly "prioritarian" outcome ranking can be expressed as a utilitarian outcome ranking by taking the transformed well-being numbers that result from our transformation function and initial well-being measure $w(\cdot)$, and relabeling them as straight well-being numbers according to a new well-being measure $w^*(\cdot)$.

The following example illustrates the skeptic's argument. Imagine that individuals are modeled as having two attributes, income and health quality, the latter quantified on a 0–1 scale (1 indicating perfect health, 0 a health state no better than death). Our well-being measure $w(\cdot)$ is defined as the product of health quality and the logarithm of income. Suppose now that we pick the square root function as the prioritarian transformation function. The "prioritarian" score assigned to each outcome is therefore calculated as follows: for each individual, multiply her health quality by the logarithm of her income to determine her well-being; take the square root of this well-being number to arrive at her transformed well-being; sum up these

[46] Broome (2015, pp. 225–227) suggests this line of argument.

transformed-well-being numbers. But this "prioritarian" score is nothing other than a utilitarian score calculated with a new well-being measure $w^*(\cdot)$ defined as follows: well-being is the square root of the product of health quality and the logarithm of income.

It is no doubt true that prioritarianism with a given well-being measure and transformation function is identical – in its outcome ranking – to utilitarianism with a different well-being measure. But the skeptic is wrong to conclude that prioritarianism is "the same" as utilitarianism. (1) Prioritarianism and utilitarianism are, obviously, distinct relative to a given well-being measure. If $w(\cdot)$ is our well-being measure, then the outcome ranking achieved using the prioritarian recipe is different from the ranking achieved using the utilitarian recipe. (2) It is true that, by combining $w(\cdot)$ and $g(\cdot)$, we can arrive at a new well-being measure $w^*(\cdot)$, such that the utilitarian outcome ranking with well-being measured by $w^*(\cdot)$ is the same as the prioritarian ranking with well-being measured by $w(\cdot)$ and transformed by $g(\cdot)$. But $w(\cdot)$ and $w^*(\cdot)$ are *different well-being measures*. In particular, intra- and interpersonal difference comparisons, as per $w^*(\cdot)$, are *different* from intra- and interpersonal difference comparisons, as per $w(\cdot)$. Our theory of well-being, we have supposed, allows for difference comparisons as well as level comparisons. If $w(\cdot)$ is an eligible measure – eligible according to our theory, in the sense of accurately representing the theory's level and difference comparisons – then $w^*(\cdot)$ is not an eligible measure.[47]

The discussion here illustrates a more general point about the SWF framework – namely, that this decision procedure is comprised of distinct components, meant to capture separable and distinctive aspects of ethical reasoning. One is the well-being component. We deliberate about what makes an individual life go well or badly, and thereby arrive

[47] $w^+(\cdot)$ is a common ordinal rescaling of $w(\cdot)$ if there exists a strictly increasing function $f(\cdot)$ such that $w_i^+(x) = f(w_i(x))$ for all i, x. $w^+(\cdot)$ is a common cardinal rescaling of $w(\cdot)$ if there exists $k > 0, l$, such that $w_i^+(x) = k \times w_i(x) + l$ for all i, x. Note that if $w^+(\cdot)$ is a common cardinal rescaling of $w(\cdot)$, then it is a common ordinal rescaling; but the converse is not true. Note also that if $w^+(\cdot)$ is a common ordinal rescaling of $w(\cdot)$ but not a common cardinal rescaling, $w^+(\cdot)$ *will* preserve the intra- and interpersonal level comparisons of $w(\cdot)$ but need not preserve the intra- and interpersonal difference comparisons of $w(\cdot)$.

$w^*(\cdot)$ defined as $w_i^*(x) = g(w_i(x))$, $g(\cdot)$ strictly increasing and strictly concave, is a common ordinal but not common cardinal rescaling of $w(\cdot)$ – hence need not preserve the difference information in $w(\cdot)$.

at a theory of well-being, mathematically represented via a well-being measure $w(\cdot)$. A second, separate component involves the specification of an SWF. Here, we deliberate about how the ethical goodness of outcomes depends upon the pattern of individual well-being. The question at *this* stage of ethical deliberation is not the nature of well-being, but its ethical role. Why would well-being vector **w** be better than, worse than, or equally good as well-being vector **v**? Should we endorse axioms such as Pareto, Anonymity, Pigou-Dalton, Separability, and Continuity? What is the specific form of the vector-ranking rule, $\succcurlyeq$? If we conflate the two components, it may look like prioritarianism and utilitarianism are the same. But if we are sensitive to the difference between debates about well-being and debates about the ethical role of well-being, the two SWFs are – clearly – different. Having settled upon a well-being measure $w(\cdot)$, it is a meaningful –and important! – question whether the ethical comparison of outcomes depends upon the simple sum of well-being, or instead the sum of transformed well-being.

2.7 Prioritarianism and Utilitarianism under Uncertainty

Recall that we are using the "state of nature" setup (Section 2.2.4) to conceptualize choice under uncertainty. Any particular policy that government might select can be represented as a state-by-state array of outcomes. With a well-being measure in hand, each policy corresponds to a state-by-state array of well-being vectors. Any given SWF $\succcurlyeq$ has various possible uncertainty "modules." An uncertainty module is some rule for ranking policies, understood as state-by-state arrays of well-being vectors. Each such module satisfies the basic constraint that it ranks degenerate policies consistently with the SWF.

Let's begin with prioritarianism. There is a substantial body of scholarship on prioritarianism under uncertainty.[48] The most widely discussed prioritarian uncertainty modules are the following three: (1) "ex post prioritarianism" (EPP), namely ranking policies according to the expected sum of transformed well-being; (2) "ex ante prioritarianism" (EAP), namely ranking policies according to the sum of transformed expected well-being; and (3) expected equally-distributed-equivalent prioritarianism (EEDEP), namely ranking policies

[48] That scholarship is reviewed in Adler (2012, chapter 7; 2019, chapters 3–4); Adler and Holtug (2019). See also Fleurbaey (2010); Mongin and Pivato (2016).

according to the expected value of the equally-distributed-equivalent of the well-being pattern in each state. See Appendix for formulas.

One might wonder why the literature hasn't settled on a single, canonical version of prioritarianism under uncertainty. Why the debate? The answer is axiomatic. Just as we posited axioms for the ranking of well-being vectors (Pareto, Anonymity, Pigou-Dalton, etc.), so we might posit axioms for the ranking of policies – for short, "uncertainty axioms." There are a variety of plausible uncertainty axioms, but I'll focus here on three: ex ante Pareto, Dominance, and Policy Separability (the last already mentioned). Each of the three seems *quite* plausible, and yet it is impossible for a prioritarian uncertainty module to satisfy all three. The debate between EPP, EAP, and EEDEP is fueled by disagreement about which of the three uncertainty axioms to drop given that all three can't be satisfied.

The uncertainty axioms are as follows. (See Appendix for precise statement.)

Ex Ante Pareto. (1) *Ex Ante Pareto Indifference.* If each person's expected well-being with policy P^* is the same as her expected well-being with policy P, then the two policies are equally good. (2) *Ex Ante Strong Pareto.* If each person's expected well-being with policy P^* is greater than or equal to her expected well-being with policy P, and at least one person's expected well-being with P^* is strictly greater than her expected well-being with P, then P^* is better than P.

Dominance. Assume that in each state of nature, the well-being vector produced by policy P^* is better than the well-being vector produced by policy P – better according to some given SWF. Then the uncertainty module for that SWF should be such as to rank P^* better than P.

Policy Separability. Assume that some individuals are "sure to be unaffected" as between two policies P and P^* (meaning that each such individual with P has the same well-being level in any given state that she does with P^*). If so, the ranking of the two policies should be invariant to the state-by-state well-being levels of these "sure-to-be-unaffected" individuals.

Table 2.9 illustrates the fundamental conflict between ex ante Pareto and Dominance, for a prioritarian SWF. As the table shows, it is impossible for an uncertainty module for a prioritarian SWF to satisfy both ex ante Pareto and Dominance.

Table 2.9. ***The conflict between ex ante Pareto and Dominance***

	Policy P			Policy P^+		
	State s	State s^*		State s	State s^*	
	$\pi(s) = .5$	$\pi(s^*) = .5$	expected well-being	$\pi(s) = .5$	$\pi(s^*) = .5$	expected well-being
Jasper	90	10	50	$50 - \varepsilon$	$50 - \varepsilon$	$50 - \varepsilon$
Karl	10	90	50	$50 - \varepsilon$	$50 - \varepsilon$	$50 - \varepsilon$

Note: Dominance requires the uncertainty module for a prioritarian SWF to rank P^+ over P for some $\varepsilon > 0$. However, ex ante Strong Pareto requires that P be preferred to P^+. Setting $\varepsilon = 0$ illustrates the conflict between Dominance and ex ante Pareto Indifference.

The EAP uncertainty module satisfies ex ante Pareto, but at the cost of violating Dominance. Conversely, the EPP and EEDEP uncertainty modules satisfy Dominance, but at the cost of violating ex ante Pareto.

As illustrated by Table 2.9, the prioritarian is forced to make an axiomatic choice. Ex ante Pareto and Dominance are each intuitively plausible, and yet can't be jointly satisfied (given a prioritarian $\succcurlyeq$). Thus the prioritarian needs to consider *relative* plausibility. Which of these competing uncertainty axioms – ex ante Pareto or Dominance – is *more* compelling?

This question of relative plausibility is, of course, debatable, but I believe a strong case can be made in favor of Dominance rather than ex ante Pareto. Dominance seems to flow directly from consequentialism. Any welfare-consequentialist agrees that the outcome ranking drives policy choice under conditions of certainty. In particular, and most fundamentally: If (1) we know for sure that policy P will lead to outcome x, with well-being pattern $\mathbf{w}$, and that policy P^* will lead to outcome x^*, with well-being pattern $\mathbf{w}^*$; and (2) our ranking of well-being patterns is such that $\mathbf{w}^*$ is better than $\mathbf{w}$, so that x^* is a better outcome than x; then (3) we should conclude that P^* is a better policy than P. (To accept *this* axiom seems definitional of welfare-consequentialism.) But it is very hard to justify accepting this axiom, yet rejecting Dominance. If P^* and P are as described by the Dominance axiom, we may not know for sure what outcomes and attendant well-being patterns (vectors) will result from the two policies; but what we *do* know is that, in each and every state, the P^* pattern (vector) is better than the P pattern.

Dominance can also be supported by appeal to an ideal, fully informed adviser. If P^* and P are as described by the Dominance axiom, then the decisionmaker can be sure that a fully informed adviser would recommend P^* (Fleurbaey, 2010, p. 655; Fleurbaey and Voorhoeve, 2013).

Let's now compare EPP and EEDEP. Again, both of these uncertainty modules for the prioritarian SWF satisfy Dominance. How do they differ axiomatically?

While both approaches violate the ex ante Pareto axiom, EEDEP satisfies this axiom in a restricted sense. In a nutshell, EEDEP satisfies the ex ante Pareto axiom when individuals are identically situated. (More precisely, if the well-being vector produced by policy P in each state is such that all individuals have the same well-being level, and the well-being vector produced by policy P^* in each state is such that all individuals have the same well-being level, then: the P/P^* ranking by EEDEP satisfies the ex ante Pareto axiom.) Conversely, EPP violates the ex ante Pareto axiom even when individuals are identically situated. However, EPP satisfies Policy Separability while EEDEP violates Policy Separability (see Table 2.6).

In my own view, EPP is on balance better justified than EEDEP. Consider, first, the axiom of Policy Separability. The pragmatic advantages of Policy Separability are large, as discussed earlier (Section 2.4). EEDEP can be criticized for failing to realize the *potential* pragmatic benefits of Separability – the pragmatic benefits that occur *if* the separable SWF is conjoined with a module that satisfies Policy Separability (as in the case of EPP). Further, as explained in the notes, it can be argued that the combination of a separable SWF with an uncertainty module that violates Policy Separability violates a maxim of rational choice – namely, don't rank choices in a manner that you know a fully informed adviser would disapprove.[49]

[49] Assume that Policy Separability applies and requires the P/P^* ranking to be the same as the P^+/P^{++} ranking. That is, there are some sure-to-be-unaffected individuals, each of whom has the same well-being in any given state s with P as she does with P^*. These individuals are also sure-to-be unaffected as between P^+ and P^{++}. And the state-by-state pattern of well-being for every other individual is the same in the P/P^* pair as in the P^+/P^{++} pair.

For any given state s, let $\mathbf{w}(P, s)$ denote the well-being vector that results in state s with a given policy P. Because the SWF is separable, it must be the case that, for every state s, $\mathbf{w}(P,s) \succcurlyeq \mathbf{w}(P^*,s)$ iff $\mathbf{w}(P^+,s) \succcurlyeq \mathbf{w}(P^{++},s)$. (This is illustrated in Table 2.6.) A fully informed adviser will know what the state of

On the other hand, EEDEP satisfies ex ante Pareto when individuals are identically situated. This is an axiomatic benefit, to be sure, but – arguably – not sufficient to justify dropping Policy Separability. The supposition that individuals are identically situated is quite restrictive. "Identically situated" means everyone in the entire population of ethical concern – not merely those in a subpopulation. Consider again the example of Regions A through Z (Section 2.4), with policies that affect only those in the first region. Tweak the example so that everyone in Region A is identically situated. (Prior policies and practices, let's imagine, have operated to produce an equal distribution of well-being within this region.) Now imagine a local policy choice that affects only those living in Region A. Assume that the expected well-being of those in Region A is greater with policy P^* than with policy P. If so, the ex ante Pareto axiom requires that P^* be ranked above P. EPP can violate ex ante Pareto in this case. *But EEDEP can also violate ex ante Pareto in this case.*

More generally, EEDEP (like EPP) can violate ex ante Pareto whenever some individuals in the population of ethical concern are differently situated from other individuals in that entire population. Even if the population can be partitioned into two subgroups, individuals identically situated (within the subgroup) and individuals sure to be unaffected – as in the example immediately above – EEDEP (like EPP) may violate ex ante Pareto.[50]

I've discussed prioritarianism under uncertainty at some length. The specification of an uncertainty module for the prioritarian SWF is not straightforward. EAP violates Dominance, but satisfies ex ante Pareto (and, as it happens, Policy Separability). EPP violates ex ante Pareto, but satisfies Dominance and Policy Separability. EEDEP satisfies Dominance; satisfies ex ante Pareto in the special case when individuals (in the entire population of ethical concern) are identically situated; but

nature is, and will rank P at least as good as P^* iff the adviser ranks P^+ at least as good as P^{++}. The imperfectly informed decision maker doesn't herself know what the state of nature is; but, by the structure of the problem, she knows that the adviser will never advise her to rank the P/P^* pair differently than the P^+/P^{++} pair.

[50] Adler (2019, pp. 130–138, 277–282) describes ex ante Pareto limited to cases in which individuals are either identically situated or sure-to-be-unaffected as "heartland ex ante Pareto," and discusses the fact that any prioritarian uncertainty module which satisfies Dominance violates heartland ex ante Pareto.

violates Policy Separability. I believe EPP to be on balance best justified, but this is certainly a matter for debate.

By contrast, the specification of an uncertainty module for the utilitarian SWF *is* straightforward. The module generally adopted in the literature (for short, UUU – utilitarianism under uncertainty) ranks policies according to the expected sum of individual well-being. This module satisfies Dominance *and* ex ante Pareto *and* Policy Separability. If the SWF is utilitarian, there exists an uncertainty module – UUU – that satisfies all three of these plausible uncertainty axioms.

2.8 Utilitarianism versus Prioritarianism

We now turn to the debate between utilitarianism and prioritarianism. To facilitate this debate, Table 2.10 displays how both the utilitarian SWF and prioritarian SWFs fare with respect to the SWF axioms discussed earlier.

The table adds a further axiom, Minimal Pigou-Dalton, which states the following.

Minimal Pigou-Dalton. There exists at least one pair of well-being vectors **w** and **v** such that $\mathbf{w} \succ \mathbf{v}$ and such that the two vectors are as follows: *i* is better off than *j* in vector **v**; in **w** *i*'s well-being has decreased by Δw, while *j*'s well-being has increased by the very same amount, and the gap between the two individuals has decreased; and every other person is equally well off in **w** as she is in **v**.

In other words, while the Pigou-Dalton axiom articulates a *universal* constraint, Minimal Pigou-Dalton articulates the corresponding *existential* constraint. Pigou-Dalton says: *whenever* vector **w** is reached from vector **v** via a pure, gap-diminishing transfer of well-being from someone better off to someone worse off, affecting no one else, **w** is better than **v**. Minimal Pigou-Dalton says: there exists at least one case in which vector **w** is reached from vector **v** via a pure, gap-diminishing transfer of well-being from someone better off, to someone worse off, affecting no one else, and **w** is better than **v**. Note that Pigou-Dalton implies Minimal Pigou-Dalton, but not vice versa.[51]

[51] That is, if an SWF satisfies Pigou-Dalton, it satisfies Minimal Pigou-Dalton. However, it is possible for an SWF to satisfy Minimal Pigou-Dalton but not Pigou-Dalton. (Indeed, this is true of sufficientist SWFs.)

Table 2.10. *The axiomatic properties of utilitarian and prioritarian SWFs*

	Utilitarian SWF	*Prioritarian SWFs*
Separability	Yes	Yes
Continuity	Yes	Yes
Pigou-Dalton	**No**	**Yes**
Minimal Pigou-Dalton	**No**	**Yes**
	with UUU uncertainty module	*with EPP uncertainty module*
Policy Separability	Yes	Yes
Dominance	Yes	Yes
Ex ante Pareto	**Yes**	**No**

In assessing the relative merits of the utilitarian SWF as compared to prioritarian SWFs, it's also important to consider the properties of the possible uncertainty modules associated with each. Here, I'll focus on the utilitarian SWF as implemented under uncertainty via the UUU module, as compared to the prioritarian SWF as implemented under uncertainty via the EPP module. (The reader who prefers EEDEP or EAP to EPP as a prioritarian procedure for handling uncertainty can undertake a similar exercise.) For the remainder of this Section, I'll use the terms "utilitarianism" or "the utilitarian SWF" to mean, specifically, the utilitarian SWF together with the UUU module; and I'll use the terms "prioritarianism" or "a prioritarian SWF" to mean, specifically, a prioritarian SWF together with the EPP module.

Table 2.10 also displays how the utilitarian SWF and prioritarian SWFs fare with respect to the uncertainty axioms discussed earlier.

As the table illustrates, utilitarianism and prioritarianism are alike in many respects. The features that distinguish them are twofold: ex ante Pareto and equity (Pigou-Dalton and Minimal Pigou-Dalton).

That prioritarianism violates ex ante Pareto is, no doubt, an intuitively problematic feature of the approach. (Again, we are focusing here on prioritarianism applied under uncertainty with EPP.)[52] It seems perverse for it to be the case that everyone has the same expected

[52] Recall that prioritarianism applied under uncertainty with EEDEP also violates ex ante Pareto, except when individuals are identically situated; prioritarianism applied with EAP satisfies ex ante Pareto, but at the cost of violating Dominance.

well-being with policy P^* as with policy P, and yet the policies are not ranked equal. It seems yet more perverse that (a) some or even all individuals have greater expected well-being with policy P^{++} than with policy P^+, and (b) no one has lower expected well-being with policy P^{++}, and yet P^{++} is *not* ranked better than P^+.

But we should remind ourselves that the prioritarian SWF *does* conform to the Pareto axiom, which is a constraint on the outcome ranking. Relatedly, the prioritarian SWF *does* satisfy ex ante Pareto with respect to degenerate policies. If the decisionmaker knows for sure that policy P yields vector $\mathbf{w}$, and that policy P^* yields vector $\mathbf{w}^*$, then she will rank P^* better than/equal to P if ex ante Pareto requires her to do so.[53]

Conversely, the failure of the prioritarian SWF to satisfy ex ante Pareto arises only by virtue of the decisionmaker's imperfect information. In the non-degenerate (imperfect information) case, the decisionmaker needs to compare P to P^* and yet does not know, for each person, what his well-being level would be were P to be chosen and what it would be were P^* to be chosen instead. Ex ante Pareto "extends" the Paretian idea to this imperfect-information context by calculating well-being expectations for each person. That extension seems intuitive, but also can have troubling results. The ex ante Pareto axiom can require that P^* be ranked above P even though, in fact – given the actual state of nature – some will be worse off with P^*. Indeed, the ex ante Pareto axiom can require that P^* be ranked above P even though, in fact, *everyone* will be worse off with P^*.

Let's now turn to the major weakness of utilitarianism, namely its failure to satisfy equity axioms.

In other work, I have offered a systematic defense of the Pigou-Dalton axiom, via the notion of "claims" (Adler, 2012, chapter 5). Imagine that we justify the ranking of any two well-being vectors (patterns of well-being) by considering that comparison from the perspective of each individual. Specifically, as between $\mathbf{w}$ and $\mathbf{v}$, a given person has a claim in favor of $\mathbf{w}$ over $\mathbf{v}$ if she is better off in $\mathbf{w}$ than $\mathbf{v}$; a claim in favor of $\mathbf{v}$ over $\mathbf{w}$ if she is better off in $\mathbf{v}$ than $\mathbf{w}$; and no claim if she is equally well off in the two vectors. This claim-based justificatory

[53] Moreover, if the well-being vector produced by P^* in each state is required by the Pareto axiom to be ranked better than/equally good as the well-being vector produced by P in that state, then prioritarianism will rank P^* better than/equally good as P.

framework tries to give specific content to the somewhat amorphous notion (introduced by John Rawls[54]) that ethics should take seriously the "separateness of persons." We do so, according to this framework, by proceeding person by person and, for each one, considering the direction and strength of her claim between the two possible well-being vectors.

This claims framework, I argue, reveals a deep unity between the Pareto and Pigou-Dalton axioms. It immediately supports Pareto. (If everyone is equally well off in two vectors, then none have claims between them, and so it follows that the two are equally good. If some are better off in **w** than **v**, then each of these persons has a claim in favor of **w**; if, further, none are worse off in **w**, then none have a claim in favor of **v**; since some claims point to **w**, and none to **v**, it follows that **w** is better.) But I have also argued, in a line of reasoning summarized in the footnotes, that the claims justificatory framework supports Pigou-Dalton.[55]

Quite apart from this specific line of justification, Pigou-Dalton has intuitive force. Suppose that we can transfer well-being from better-off Jamal to worse-off Kieran, without affecting anyone else; without losing any of the transferred well-being (a "pure" transfer); and with the well-being gap between them shrinking. Pigou-Dalton addresses this limiting case in which there is an equity "benefit" (the gap between a better-off and worse-off person shrinks) but no cost to overall well-being (the transfer is pure; overall well-being remains the same). Surely,

[54] See Rawls (1999, first published in 1971).

[55] Consider a non-rank-switching Pigou-Dalton transfer. In vector **v**, one individual ("Higher") is at well-being level w_H, a second ("Lower") at well-being level w_L, with $w_H > w_L$. In vector **w**, Higher's well-being decreases by $\Delta w > 0$, and Lower's well-being increases by Δw, without switching their ranks ($w_H - \Delta w \geq w_L + \Delta w$), and without affecting anyone else. In this case, everyone except for Lower and Higher has a zero claim between **v** and **w**. Further, it seems compelling that Lower's claim in favor of **w** over **v** is stronger than Higher's claim in favor of **v** over **w**. (The well-being differences are the same; and Lower is worse off than Higher, meaning specifically here that Lower's well-being level in **v** is strictly below that of Higher and that Lower's well-being level in **w** is weakly below that of Higher.) Thus **w** is better than **v** in light of the pattern of claims.

This is a claims-based argument for a Pigou-Dalton axiom limited to non-rank-switching transfers. That axiom, plus Anonymity, implies the broader Pigou-Dalton axiom (for gap-diminishing transfers) that we have been using in this chapter. See note 33.

at least in this case, equity considerations should come into play and recommend the transfer.

Minimal Pigou-Dalton is yet more intuitive. Surely there is *some* case in which a pure transfer from a better-off Jamal to a worse-off Kieran is a moral improvement. Yet utilitarianism denies that there is *ever* such a case – regardless of how much better off Jamal is than Kieran, regardless of the size of the transfer, and despite the fact that it is a pure one.

The utilitarian might defend her absence of concern for an equitable distribution of well-being (as axiomatized by Pigou-Dalton or, more weakly, Minimal Pigou-Dalton) by adducing the veil-of-ignorance (VOI) argument for utilitarianism, associated with John Harsanyi (1953, 1955, 1977). If we construct the outcome ranking by conceptualizing each outcome as an equiprobability lottery over the lives of the individuals therein, the upshot is a utilitarian SWF – which in turn implies rejecting Pigou-Dalton and even Minimal Pigou-Dalton. In short, accepting the VOI as the basis for justifying the outcome ranking explains why Pigou-Dalton and even Minimal Pigou-Dalton should be rejected, counterintuitive as that may be. But the status of the VOI as a justificatory framework is itself controversial. Is it really the case that outcome x is ethically better than outcome y iff everyone would choose x under a veil of ignorance? The dialectical situation is such that the proponent of prioritarianism can reject the VOI and instead endorse a different framework (for example, my claims-based approach), one that supports Pigou-Dalton (Adler, 2012, pp. 321–337; Moreno-Ternero and Roemer, 2008).

A second response is that the utilitarian SWF may support equity axioms in *attribute* space. In particular, it is often supposed that income has diminishing marginal utility, reflected in a well-being measure that is strictly increasing and strictly concave in income. If $w(\cdot)$ is indeed strictly increasing and strictly concave in income, the utilitarian SWF will satisfy a counterpart to the Pigou-Dalton axiom as stated here, namely one framed in terms of income. But it is less clear whether non-income attributes also have diminishing marginal utility. Note further that making the ethical case for attribute transfers depend upon diminishing marginal utility – as utilitarianism does – is itself counterintuitive. Assume that I am richer than you, but am a greedy materialist who loves money so much that I gain greater well-being from a unit of income than you do. Utilitarianism has no basis for an income transfer from me to you, while prioritarianism does.

2.9 Atkinson and Kolm-Pollak SWFs

A prioritarian SWF ranks well-being vectors by means of a "transformation" function: a strictly increasing, strictly concave function, abbreviated as "$g(\cdot)$" in this chapter. Each vector **w** is assigned a score equaling $g(\mathbf{w}_1) + \ldots + g(\mathbf{w}_N)$, and the vectors are ranked in the order of these scores.

But there are a multitude (an infinity!) of strictly increasing and strictly concave $g(\cdot)$ functions. Thus there are a multitude (an infinity!) of prioritarian SWFs, each defined by one such transformation function.

Two types of prioritarian SWFs are most widely discussed in the extant economic literature on prioritarianism. These are, first, Atkinson SWFs; and, second, Kolm-Pollak SWFs.[56] Each employs a quite tractable functional form for the $g(\cdot)$ function. Further, a plausible axiomatic case can be offered in defense of Atkinson SWFs. These two subfamilies of prioritarian SWFs will now be discussed in turn.

2.9.1 *Atkinson SWFs*

Atkinson SWFs define the $g(\cdot)$ function as follows: $g(w_i) = \frac{1}{1-\gamma} {w_i}^{1-\gamma}$, with $\gamma > 0$ (and $\gamma \neq 1$), and $g(w_i) = \log w_i$ in the special case of $\gamma = 1$. The γ parameter specifies the degree of priority for the worse off. The larger γ, the greater such priority. Adler (2012, pp. 378–399; 2019, pp. 154–158), discusses and defends Atkinson SWFs.

Atkinson SWFs are a subfamily of SWFs, within the broader family of prioritarian SWFs. The axiomatic argument in favor of this subfamily runs as follows. (1) To begin, let's assume that the prioritarian SWF is *profile-independent*. A "profile-independent" SWF is such that the functional form of the SWF is independent of our well-being measure.

[56] Atkinson SWFs are so-called because of their role in Atkinson's work on the measurement of inequality (Atkinson, 1970). They are also referred to as constant-elasticity-of-substitution SWFs, and sometimes as Kolm-Atkinson-Sen SWFs because they figure in Kolm (1969) and Sen (1973). Kolm-Pollak SWFs are credited to Kolm (1969) and Pollak (1971); they are discussed in Blackorby, Bossert and Donaldson (2005, chapter 4).

Whichever well-being measure is adopted to translate outcomes into well-being vectors – this depends on our theory of well-being – we use the very same rule to rank well-being vectors and thereby to rank outcomes via the Master Recipe. The prioritarian SWF, in particular, is profile-independent if we identify some single $g(\cdot)$ function as our transformation function, rather than a $g(\cdot)$ function that varies depending on which $w(\cdot)$ is being used.

The premise of a profile-independent SWF is often adopted in the theory literature on SWFs.[57] Further, this premise seems to capture the spirit of welfare-consequentialism. In comparing $\mathbf{w}$ to $\mathbf{v}$, we should care only about the pattern of well-being in each vector, not about the various individuals' bundles of attributes (income, health, longevity, leisure, etc.) or histories (combinations of attributes and preferences)[58] that happen to give rise to the two patterns. The mapping *from* attribute bundles/histories *to* well-being – that is, the specific $w(\cdot)$ that is being used to convert outcomes into vectors – should be irrelevant to how we compare the patterns themselves.

(2) Second, our profile-independent prioritarian SWF should satisfy an appropriate invariance axiom, namely that if $w(\cdot)$ is swapped for an informationally equivalent well-being measure $w^*(\cdot)$, the ranking of outcomes shouldn't change.

It is tempting to formulate this invariance requirement as follows:

Cardinal Invariance. Let $w^*(\cdot)$ be a common cardinal rescaling of $w(\cdot)$. Then the SWF should rank outcomes the very same way using $w^*(\cdot)$ and using $w(\cdot)$.

Note that if $w^*(\cdot)$ is a common cardinal rescaling of $w(\cdot)$, then $w^*(\cdot)$ and $w(\cdot)$ make the very same intra- and interpersonal comparisons of both well-being levels and well-being differences.

However, it can be shown that *no* profile-independent prioritarian SWF satisfies Cardinal Invariance (Bossert and Weymark, 2004, p. 1160; Weymark, 2016, p. 154). This impossibility can be avoided by weakening Cardinal Invariance to Ratio Invariance.

[57] For a discussion of profile-independence, see Weymark (2016). The so-called welfarism theorem (Weymark, 2016; Bossert and Weymark, 2004), a key theorem in the theoretical literature on SWFs, shows that profile-independence can be derived from Pareto Indifference plus an independence-of-irrelevant-alternatives axiom.

[58] See Section 2.2.1.

Ratio Invariance. Let $w^*(\cdot)$ be a common *ratio* rescaling of $w(\cdot)$. Then the SWF should rank outcomes the very same way using $w^*(\cdot)$ and $w(\cdot)$.

Ratio Invariance supposes that it is meaningful to make intra- and interpersonal comparisons of well-being levels, differences, *and* ratios, and that no other types of well-being comparisons are meaningful. A common ratio rescaling preserves all of the information regarding these six types of comparisons, and since there is no *further* well-being information to be had, the SWF's outcome ranking should be invariant to such a rescaling.[59]

To see how a common ratio rescaling preserves information regarding all six types of comparisons, suppose that there are three individuals, Amy, Barry, and Cindy. Outcome x is mapped by measure $w(\cdot)$ onto vector (10, 1, 5); y is mapped onto vector (8, 3, 4); and z is mapped onto vector (2, 2, 2). If we assume that intra- and interpersonal comparisons of levels, differences, and ratios are meaningful, we can "read off" various comparisons from these numbers: for example, that Amy in x is better off than Amy in y ($10 > 8$), an intrapersonal level comparison; that Amy in x is better off than Barry in z ($10 > 2$), an interpersonal level comparison; that the difference in well-being between Cindy in y and Cindy in z is greater than the difference in well-being between Cindy in x and Cindy in y ($4 - 2 > 5 - 4$), an intrapersonal difference comparison; that the difference in well-being between Amy in x and Amy in y is greater than the difference in well-being between Barry in y and Barry in z ($10 - 8 > 3 - 2$), an interpersonal difference comparison; that the well-being ratio between Amy in y and Amy in z is greater than the well-being ratio between Amy in x and Amy in y ($8/2 > 10/8$), an intrapersonal ratio comparison; or that the well-being ratio between Amy in x and Barry in x is greater than the well-being ratio between Barry in x and Cindy in y ($10/1 > 1/4$), an interpersonal ratio comparison.

Consider now a well-being measure $w^*(\cdot)$, which is a common ratio rescaling of the original well-being measure. Specifically, the values according to this new well-being measure are 10 times the values assigned by the original one. So outcome x is now mapped onto the

[59] As mentioned above in note 47, $w^*(\cdot)$ is a common cardinal rescaling of $w(\cdot)$ if there exists $k > 0, l$ such that $w_i^*(x) = kw_i(x) + l$ for all i, x. $w^*(\cdot)$ is a common ratio rescaling of $w(\cdot)$ if there exists $k > 0$ such that $w_i^*(x) = kw_i(x)$ for all i, x.

vector (100, 10, 50); outcome y is mapped onto the vector (80, 30, 40); and z is mapped onto the vector (20, 20, 20). It is straightforward to see that all of the information about intra- and interpersonal comparisons of levels, differences, and ratios contained in the original well-being measure is preserved by this new one.[60]

Putting together the stipulation that the prioritarian SWF be profile-independent and the axiom of Ratio Invariance, we end up with the Atkinson subfamily of SWFs. No other prioritarian SWF can satisfy both requirements (Boadway and Bruce, 1984, p. 160; Bossert and Weymark, 2004, pp. 1161–1162; Weymark, 2016, p. 154).

In order to implement the SWF methodology using a profile-independent SWF of the Atkinson form, two steps must be taken. First, we must construct a well-being measure that contains information not only about intra- and interpersonal comparisons of levels and differences (as discussed in Section 2.5), but *also* intra- and interpersonal comparisons of ratios. This can be done as follows. Assume that $w(\cdot)$ accurately reflects intra- and interpersonal level and difference information, as per our theory of well-being. Now identify a zero point, namely a particular attribute bundle or a particular history. This choice of zero point defines well-being ratios; for any two individual-outcome pairings (individual i in x and individual j in y), the ratio of their well-being levels is the ratio of their well-being differences from the zero point. Rescale $w(\cdot)$ so that the zero bundle/history is assigned the number 0 – that is, define a new well-being measure $w^+(\cdot)$ such that, for every individual i and outcome $x, w_i{}^+(x) = w_i(x) - Z$, with Z the number assigned by $w(\cdot)$ to the zero point. This new measure will contain the very same level and difference information as $w(\cdot)$ *and* will reflect intra- and interpersonal ratio information. (See Appendix for details.) Use this new measure $w^+(\cdot)$, in conjunction with the chosen Atkinson SWF and its uncertainty module, to rank outcomes and policies.

Second, we must specify the priority parameter γ. γ, as mentioned, determines the degree of priority for the worse off. The role of γ can be understood by imagining leaky transfers from a better-off to a worse-

60 Let $w_i^*(x) = kw_i(x), k > 0$, for all i, x. Then, for all individuals i, j, k, l (identical or wholly or partly distinct) and outcomes x, y, z, zz (identical or wholly or partly distinct): $w_i(x) \geq w_j(y)$ iff $w_i^*(x) \geq w_j^*(y)$; $w_i(x) - w_j(y) \geq w_k(z) - w_l(zz)$ iff $w_i^*(x) - w_j^*(y) \geq w_k^*(z) - w_l^*(zz)$; $w_i(x)/w_j(y) \geq w_k(z)/w_l(zz)$ iff $w_i^*(x)/w_j^*(y) \geq w_k^*(z)/w_l^*(zz)$.

off person. Imagine a better-off person at well-being level w_H and a worse-off person at well-being level w_L. Let K be the ratio between the two levels, larger divided by smaller: $K = w_H/w_L$. Consider a transfer in which the better-off individual loses some small amount of well-being Δw, while the worse-off one gains by some fraction of that loss, $\rho\Delta w$. If $\rho = 1$, every Atkinson SWF will approve it; this is required by the Pigou-Dalton principle. If $\rho = 0$, every Atkinson SWF will *disapprove* the transfer; disapproval is required by the Pareto axiom. Neither basic axiom constrains what happens in the case of *leaky* transfers – with ρ between 0 and 1 – and this is where the priority parameter γ comes into play. The minimum acceptable fraction ρ^{min} equals $(1/K)^{\gamma}$: it depends upon the well-being ratio and γ. This fraction decreases as the well-being ratio between the two individuals increases, and also decreases as γ does.

Reciprocally, picking the minimum acceptable fraction for a given well-being ratio suffices to fix γ. From the equation $\rho^{min} = (1/K)^{\gamma}$, it follows that $\gamma = -\left(\log \rho^{min}/\log K\right)$. (See Appendix for more detail.)

2.9.2 Kolm-Pollak SWFs

Atkinson SWFs, notwithstanding their axiomatic virtues, have a significant flaw; they require well-being numbers to be non-negative or, in the case of $\gamma \geq 1$, strictly positive. The Atkinson $g(\cdot)$ function is either undefined or, if defined, not both strictly increasing and strictly concave with negative well-being numbers as inputs (or with 0 as an input for $\gamma \geq 1$).

In other words, Atkinson SWFs provide a well-defined and prioritarian ranking of well-being vectors if, but only if, all the numbers in all the vectors are non-negative (indeed, positive if $\gamma \geq 1$).

Further, an Atkinson SWF exhibits extreme behavior near the zero point, even with low values of γ. As an individual's well-being level approaches the zero point, the relative weight given to increments in her well-being, as compared to changes in the well-being of someone better off, approaches infinity.

The Kolm-Pollak family of prioritarian SWFs avoids these limitations. Well-being numbers can be positive, negative, or zero. And there is no zero point around which Kolm-Pollak SWFs exhibit extreme behavior. Further, these SWFs – like Atkinson SWFs – have a simple functional form. The transformation function is defined as follows.

$g(w_i) = -\exp(-\beta w_i)$, with $\beta > 0$ now the parameter that defines the degree of priority for the worse off (the counterpart to the γ parameter for the Atkinson SWF).

However, there is a substantial theoretical downside to Kolm-Pollak SWFs. A profile-independent Kolm-Pollak SWF will fail to satisfy the axiom of Ratio Invariance. (Again, Atkinson SWFs are the only prioritarian SWFs that do.) In other words, a profile-independent Kolm-Pollak SWF might rank x better than y if the outcomes are represented, respectively, by the vectors $\mathbf{w} = (\mathbf{w}_1, \ldots, \mathbf{w}_N)$ and $\mathbf{v} = (\mathbf{v}_1, \ldots, \mathbf{v}_N)$; yet rank x equal to or worse than y if the outcomes are represented, respectively, by the vectors $k\mathbf{w} = (k\mathbf{w}_1, \ldots, k\mathbf{w}_N)$ and $k\mathbf{v} = (k\mathbf{v}_1, \ldots, k\mathbf{v}_N)$, $k > 0$ – even though representing the first outcome by $k\mathbf{w}$ and the second by $k\mathbf{v}$, rather than the first by $\mathbf{w}$ and the second by $\mathbf{v}$, is simply using a different numbering scheme to signify the very same two well-being patterns.

A closely related point is that it is not clear how to specify a profile-independent Kolm-Pollak SWF. Recall that we used the thought experiment of a leaky transfer between a better-off person, at w_H, and a worse-off person, at w_L, to fix the priority parameter (γ) for the Atkinson SWF. If we try to fix the priority parameter (β) for the Kolm-Pollak SWF using a parallel thought experiment, we end up with the following equation for the minimum acceptable fraction, ρ^{min} : $\rho^{min} = e^{-\beta[w_H - w_L]}$. This minimum fraction now depends upon the priority parameter (β) and the magnitude of the well-being difference between the two persons ($w_H - w_L$). But it doesn't seem meaningful to assign a magnitude to a well-being difference. What does it mean to say that the difference between Jada's well-being and Keith's well-being is a specific number (7, say, rather than 10)?[61]

A workable alternative is to specify a profile-dependent Kolm-Pollak SWF. Although this approach is theoretically somewhat dubious – it goes against the spirit of welfarism – it yields a workable prioritarian alternative to the Atkinson SWF. Specifically, rather than identifying a single β parameter for the Kolm-Pollak SWF, we use thought

[61] By contrast, the leaky-transfer thought experiment for specifying a profile-independent Atkinson SWF depends on the magnitude of the well-being ratio between the two individuals. Intuitively, it does seem meaningful to assign a magnitude to a well-being ratio. Further, there is a clear procedure for arriving at such magnitudes. If we have $w(\cdot)$ unique up to a common cardinal rescaling, and then fix a zero bundle/history, we end up with well-defined ratio magnitudes.

experiments regarding leaky transfers in *attributes* from better-off to worse-off persons to identify a β parameter that depends upon $w(\cdot)$. See Appendix for more details.

2.10 Prioritarian SWFs and Inequality Metrics

Inequality metrics (IMs) – such as the Gini coefficient, coefficient of variation, Atkinson inequality metric, or generalized-entropy family of metrics – are widely used in economics (Blackorby, Bossert and Donaldson, 2005, chapter 4; Chakravarty, 2009; Cowell, 2016; Lambert, 2001.) IMs quantify the distribution of some "currency." Much empirical work examines income inequality: in this body of work, the currency being plugged into an inequality metric is income. However, any item held by individuals can serve as the currency for inequality measurement. For example, the inequality of health, happiness, and longevity have each been studied.[62] And, as we'll see momentarily, well-being itself might be the currency for an IM.

Formally, an IM is a formula for assigning scores to currency vectors, quantifying the degree of inequality in each vector – a currency vector being a list of the holdings of the currency by each member of the population of interest. Standard IMs satisfy three axioms: an anonymity axiom (namely that a rearrangement of the currency among the population doesn't change the degree of inequality); a Pigou-Dalton axiom (a pure, gap-diminishing transfer of the currency from someone with more to someone with less, leaving everyone else's holdings unchanged, decreases the degree of inequality); and equality-as-a-lower bound (a perfectly equal distribution has the lowest inequality score) (Adler, 2012, p. 115). In what follows, I use "IM" to mean a metric that satisfies these axioms.

An important theorem from the SWF literature demonstrates a linkage between SWFs and IMs. Any SWF that satisfies the Pareto, Anonymity, Pigou-Dalton and Continuity axioms has a corresponding IM. The SWF's ranking of well-being vectors can be represented in a specific numerical form: as overall well-being discounted by the degree of inequality of well-being. Call this the Decomposition Theorem.

[62] See, e.g., Adler (2015), citing studies of income, longevity, and happiness inequality in examining the time trend of inequality in the US.

Decomposition Theorem. Let $\succcurlyeq$ be an SWF that satisfies Pareto, Anonymity, Pigou-Dalton and Continuity. Then there exists a corresponding IM $I^{\succcurlyeq}(\cdot)$ which is such that: for any well-being vectors **w** and **v**, $\mathbf{w} \succcurlyeq \mathbf{v}$ iff $(\sum_{i=1}^{N} \mathbf{w}_i)(1 - I^{\succcurlyeq}(\mathbf{w})) \geq (\sum_{i=1}^{N} \mathbf{v}_i)(1 - I^{\succcurlyeq}(\mathbf{v}))$.[63]

The formalism here bears close attention. There are many different IMs. $I^{\succcurlyeq}(\cdot)$ is that specific IM with a special representational property. We use well-being itself as the currency for $I^{\succcurlyeq}(\cdot)$. For each well-being vector **w**, we calculate an inequality score, $I^{\succcurlyeq}(\mathbf{w})$. This score will be 0 if well-being is distributed perfectly equally in **w** – everyone has the same well-being number – and is bounded above by 1. So $\left(1 - I^{\succcurlyeq}(\mathbf{w})\right)$ is an inequality discount factor. If well-being is perfectly equal in **w**, $\left(1 - I^{\succcurlyeq}(\mathbf{w})\right) = 1$. As the distribution becomes increasingly unequal, $\left(1 - I^{\succcurlyeq}(\mathbf{w})\right)$ decreases and is bounded below by 0.

We now calculate a composite score for each vector: overall well-being multiplied by the inequality discount factor $\left(1 - I^{\succcurlyeq}(\mathbf{w})\right)$. Then the ranking of vectors according to this composite score is exactly the same as the ranking according to the SWF $\succcurlyeq$. This is what the Decomposition Theorem shows.

The Decomposition Theorem applies to prioritarian SWFs. (Note that all such SWFs satisfy the axiomatic conditions of the theorem.) It shows that *prioritarianism* can be expressed as the hybrid of two ethical values: overall well-being and the equality of well-being.

Further, it may well be of interest to identify the inequality metric $I^{\succcurlyeq}(\cdot)$ corresponding to a prioritarian SWF and to use $I^{\succcurlyeq}(\cdot)$ alone to rank vectors and policies. This shows how vectors and policies

[63] The Decomposition Theorem with the multiplicative formula as stated here is true if all well-being numbers are positive. A proof of the theorem is given in Adler (2012, pp. 119–120); it derives originally from Atkinson (1970), Kolm (1969), and Sen (1973). For a generalization of that formula that allows for negative well-being numbers, see Blackorby, Bossert, and Donaldson (2005, pp. 101–102).

A different type of decomposition shows that an SWF that satisfies Pareto, Anonymity, Pigou-Dalton, and Continuity can be expressed, via an *additive* formula, as the combination of an inequality metric and overall well-being. There exists an IM $I^{\succcurlyeq *}(\cdot)$ corresponding to the SWF $\succcurlyeq$ such that: for any well-being vectors **w** and **v**, $\mathbf{w} \succcurlyeq \mathbf{v}$ iff $(\sum_{i=1}^{N} \mathbf{w}_i) - I^{\succcurlyeq *}(\mathbf{w}) \geq (\sum_{i=1}^{N} \mathbf{v}_i) - I^{\succcurlyeq *}(\mathbf{v})$. (Blackorby, Bossert, and Donaldson, 2005, pp. 102–103; Decancq and Schokkaert, Chapter 5, this volume). The discussion immediately below of the separability properties of $I^{\succcurlyeq}(\cdot)$ also applies to $I^{\succcurlyeq *}(\cdot)$.

Table 2.11. ***Inequality metrics (IMs) violate Separability***

	w	**v**	**w***	**v***
Iris	10	20	10	20
Joel	10	20	10	20
Karl	10	10	20	20
Laura	10	10	20	20

Note: Note that well-being is perfectly equally distributed in **w** but not **v** and in **v*** but not **w***. Thus any IM should assign a lower degree of inequality to **w** than **v** and to **v*** than **w***. However, this violates Separability. The **w/v** pair is the same as the **w*/v*** pair except for the fixed well-being levels of Karl and Laura – each fixed at 10 in the first case and 20 in the second.

compare with respect to the ethical value of equalizing well-being, with the degree of attainment of that value quantified by the inequality metric implicit in the SWF. But there's a difficulty: doing this sacrifices the pragmatic advantages of Separability.

Recall that prioritarian SWFs satisfy the Separability axiom with respect to the vector ranking. Moreover, every prioritarian SWF has an uncertainty module (specifically EPP[64]) that satisfies Policy Separability. The decisionmaker who adopts a prioritarian SWF and ranks policies with the EPP uncertainty module can "bracket" the well-being of individuals in the population of ethical concern who are sure to be unaffected (e.g., prior generations). The decisionmaker can focus her modeling and information-gathering efforts on the well-being *only* of potentially affected individuals (individuals who are not sure to be unaffected, e.g., the present and future generations). Because her uncertainty module is policy-separable, she need not assign probabilities to the well-being of those sure to be unaffected.[65]

However, no IM satisfies the Separability axiom. Even if the SWF $\succcurlyeq$ is prioritarian and hence satisfies Separability, its corresponding IM $I^{\succcurlyeq}(\cdot)$ will not. Table 2.11 illustrates why no IM can satisfy Separability.

Indeed, it is quite intuitive that the $I^{\succcurlyeq}(\cdot)$ ranking is not separable. $I^{\succcurlyeq}(\mathbf{w}) < I^{\succcurlyeq}(\mathbf{v})$ indicates that well-being is more equally distributed in

[64] EAP also satisfies Policy Separability, but is problematic because it fails Dominance. See Section 2.7.

[65] The advantages of Policy Separability were discussed in Section 2.4.

vector **w** than vector **v**. But in order to compare **w** and **v** with respect to inequality, we can't focus our attention just on the subset of affected individuals, those who are better off in **w** than **v** or vice versa. The degree of well-being inequality in **w** depends on the well-being levels of everyone in the population – including those who are equally well off in **w** and **v**. Similarly, the degree of well-being inequality in **v** depends on the well-being levels of everyone in the population – including those who are equally well off in **w** and **v**.

In order to use an IM to evaluate policies, we need an uncertainty module for the IM. We need a procedure for ranking policies understood as state-by-state arrays of well-being vectors, just as we do for an SWF. But because no IM satisfies Separability, no IM has an uncertainty module that satisfies Policy Separability. In considering how policies fare with respect to the inequality of well-being, the decision-maker cannot "bracket" the well-being of those sure to be unaffected (e.g., prior generations). The deliberational advantages that flow from Separability are not available when it comes to inequality assessment, even using the inequality metric that corresponds to a prioritarian and hence separable SWF.

2.11 Variable Population

The fixed-and-finite population setup, adopted until now, assumes a set of outcomes $\mathbf{O} = \{x, y, \ldots\}$ and a finite set of individuals $\mathbf{I} = \{1, \ldots, N\}$, each of whom exists in every outcome in **O**. But it's surely the case, for any individual, that this person might not have come into being. No person exists in every possible world. Of course, outcomes are cognitively tractable *models* of possible worlds, and **O** is a *model* of the set of all possible worlds. In many contexts, it may be adequate to employ the SWF framework with a fixed population. But in some contexts, this is not adequate. In particular, certain policies (for example, those concerning climate change) can be expected to significantly alter the number and identities of future individuals. If the SWF framework is to provide ethical guidance regarding such alterations, the fixed-population assumption needs to be relaxed.

In what follows, I continue to assume that a finite number of individuals exist in a given outcome, but relax the assumption that the population is fixed. As shorthand, I'll refer to this as the "variable-population" setup and to the case of a fixed-and-finite population as the "fixed-population" setup.[66]

In the variable-population setup, each outcome in $\mathbf{O} = \{x, y, \ldots\}$ has a finite number of existing individuals, but the number and identities of individuals may vary between outcomes. $\mathbf{I} = \{1, 2, \ldots\}$ is now everyone who exists in at least one outcome in **O**. **I** may be finite or infinite in size.[67]

A well-being vector has a slot for each person in **I**. If **I** is finite, then these are finite-length vectors; otherwise they are infinite vectors. Let's use "Ω" as a symbol to indicate an individual's nonexistence. Each slot in a well-being vector has as its entry either a well-being number or Ω. For example, if there are five individuals in **I**, then each well-being vector has five slots, and one such vector is as follows: (27, Ω, 15, 6, Ω). This indicates that individual 1 is at well-being level 27; individual 2 does not exist; individual 3 is at level 15; individual 4 is at level 6; individual 5 does not exist. Or, if there are an infinite number of individuals in **I**, then each well-being vector has an infinite number of slots and might be as follows: (Ω, 67, 8, Ω, , ...), indicating that individual 1 does not exist; individual 2 is at well-being level 67; individual 3 is at well-being level 8; individual 4 does not exist; and so on.

An SWF is a rule for ranking well-being vectors. As in the fixed-population context, each outcome is mapped by the well-being measure onto a well-being vector, and the ranking of outcomes is according to the ranking by the SWF of their corresponding vectors.

We can simplify a bit. It's very plausible to adopt a generalized anonymity axiom which implies that any vector with M existing individuals at various well-being levels is equally good as a vector in which the first M individuals are at those well-being levels and no one else exists. For example, the vector (27, Ω, 15, 6, Ω) is equally good as (27, 15, 6, Ω, Ω). Thus the ranking of (27, Ω, 15, 6, Ω) versus (Ω, 9, Ω, 12, Ω) should be the same as the ranking of (27, 15, 6, Ω, Ω) versus (9, 12, Ω, Ω, Ω).

We can therefore express the SWF's ranking of vectors that may have "Ω" entries in terms of a ranking of "reduced" vectors that lack

[66] See note 28, noting the possibility of a countably infinite number of individuals who exist in a given outcome. That possibility is not addressed here.

[67] The definitive text on the SWF framework in the variable-population case is Blackorby, Bossert, and Donaldson (2005). Adler (2019, pp. 237–248) provides a compact discussion.

such entries: vectors such as (27, 15, 6), (9, 12), (30, 30, 30, 30). The ranking of two such "reduced" vectors means that any pair of vectors of the same length with those numerical entries and any number of "Ω" entries is ranked accordingly. That is to say: the SWF's ranking of the vector (27, 15, 6) above (9, 12) means: it prefers (27, 15, 6) to (9, 12, Ω); it prefers (27, 15, 6, Ω) to (9, 12, Ω, Ω); it prefers (27, 15, 6, Ω, Ω) to (9, 12, Ω, Ω, Ω). The SWF's ranking of the vector (3, 3) above (2, 5) means: it prefers (3, 3) to (2, 5); (3, 3, Ω) to (2, 5, Ω); and so forth. In what follows, I express variable-population SWFs in these terms.

In the fixed-population case, of course, the vectors being compared all have the same number of numerical entries. Each SWF for the fixed-population case has a family of variable-number extensions. All such extensions converge in their ranking of same-number vectors, but differ in how they compare vectors with different numbers of numerical entries.

For example, the utilitarian SWF compares $\mathbf{w} = (27, 15, 6)$ to $\mathbf{v} = (14, 16, 15)$ by assigning each a score equaling the sum of its entries. **w** is assigned a score equaling $27+15+6 = 48$, **v** a score equaling $14+16+15 = 45$, and so **w** is ranked better than **v**. Each different-number *extension* of the utilitarian SWF will (a) rank **w** better than **v**, and (b) tell us how to make different-number comparisons, e.g., how to compare (27, 15, 6) to (9, 12).

Similarly, a given prioritarian SWF is identified by some strictly increasing and strictly concave transformation function $g(\cdot)$. **w** is assigned a score equaling $g(27) + g(15) + g(6)$, **v** a score equaling $g(14) + g(16) + g(15)$, and the two are ranked according to these scores. Each different-number *extension* of this prioritarian SWF will (a) preserve this ranking of **w** versus **v** and (b) tell us how to make different-number comparisons, e.g., how to compare (27, 15, 6) to (9, 12).

A variety of different-number extensions of the utilitarian SWF have been described in the literature. The three possibilities that have prompted the most discussion are "total" utilitarianism, "average" utilitarianism, and "critical-level" utilitarianism. The scoring system used by each is as follows. $w^{neutral}$ is the well-being level of the "neutral" life: a life equally good for well-being as non-existence. $w^{critical}$ is the well-being level of the "critical-level" life. $N(\mathbf{w})$ is the number of numerical entries. *Total utilitarianism*: $\sum(\mathbf{w}_i - w^{neutral})$. *Average utilitarianism*: $\sum \mathbf{w}_i / N(\mathbf{w})$. *Critical-level utilitarianism*: $\sum(\mathbf{w}_i - w^{critical})$.

For simplicity, in the illustrations that follow, I'll assume that $w^{neutral} = 0$.[68]

There is a vast philosophical literature regarding the pros and cons of total, average, and critical-level utilitarianism and other variable-population extensions of utilitarianism.[69] Suffice it to say that utilitarians are far from being in consensus about how the ethical goal of maximizing overall well-being should be generalized to outcomes with different numbers of individuals. The reason, in a nutshell, is that no variable-population SWF satisfies all the axioms that seem initially quite plausible.[70] Total utilitarianism runs afoul of the so-called "Repugnant Conclusion." For (a) any level of well-being w^h however high, (b) any vector **w** with every individual at level w^h, and (c) any level of well-being w^l arbitrarily close to neutral, $w^l > w^{neutral}$, there is a vector **v** with a sufficiently large number of individuals all at w^l which is better than **w**. For example, let $w^h = 1000$ and $w^l = 1$. Then a well-being vector with M individuals at level 1000 is worse than any well-being vector with a *much* larger population (a population with $1000M + k$ individuals, $k \geq 1$) at level 1.

Average utilitarianism avoids the Repugnant Conclusion, but has other difficulties. It is not separable in making different-number comparisons: (4, 6, 11) is preferred to (4, 6), but (20, 6, 11) is dispreferred to (20, 6).[71] Average utilitarianism also violates the "Negative Expansion" principle: adding an individual who is worse off than $w^{neutral}$ should

68 $w^{neutral}$ is often set to zero in the literature on population ethics, but this is not necessary. Indeed, setting $w^{neutral} = 0$ is problematic if the SWF is an Atkinson prioritarian SWF rather than a utilitarian SWF. As explained in Section 2.9.2, the Atkinson $g(\cdot)$ function cannot take negative well-being numbers as inputs. Setting $w^{neutral} = 0$ with an Atkinson SWF precludes well-being vectors with lives worse than neutral. Instead, with an Atkinson SWF, we should set $w^{neutral} > 0$, which allows for lives worse than neutral but with well-being values above 0 (Adler and Treich, 2015).

However, the examples in the text are illustrating the features of variable-population utilitarianism, and so I simplify by setting $w^{neutral} = 0$.

69 See Broome (2016), Greaves (2017) for overviews and Arrhenius, Bykvist, Campbell and Finneron-Burns (forthcoming) for an authoritative handbook.

70 See Adler (2019, pp. 244–248), discussing the axiomatic features of total, average, and critical-level utilitarianism described in the next several paragraphs.

71 Different-Number Separability requires that the ranking of two well-being vectors with different numbers of entries be independent of the well-being levels of individuals with the same well-being levels in both entries. This is what Blackorby, Bossert, and Donaldson (2005, p. 159) term "Utility Independence."

not be an improvement. According to average utilitarianism, (−10, −8, −3) is better than (−10, −8). Finally, and reciprocally, it violates the "Mere Addition" axiom: adding an individual with a life better than $w^{neutral}$ should not be a worsening. (15, 25, 10) is worse than (15, 25).

If $w^{critical} > w^{neutral}$, critical-level utilitarianism avoids the Repugnant Conclusion, satisfies the Negative Expansion principle, and is separable in making different-number comparisons. However it violates Mere Addition and also violates "Priority for Lives Worth Living": It shouldn't be the case that a vector with everyone above the neutral level is worse than one with everyone below the neutral level. For example, assume that $w^{critical} = 5$. Then (2, 4, 3, 1, 2) is assigned a critical-level utilitarian score of −13, which is less than the score of (−1, −1).

Prioritarian SWFs have different-number extensions analogous to those of utilitarianism. In particular, "total prioritarianism," "average prioritarianism" and "critical-level prioritarianism" can all be described, as follows. *Total prioritarianism*: $\sum(g(\mathbf{w}_i) - g(w^{neutral}))$. *Average prioritarianism*: $\sum g(\mathbf{w}_i)/N(\mathbf{w})$. *Critical-level prioritarianism*: $\sum(g(\mathbf{w}_i) - g(w^{critical}))$. The axiomatic features of these approaches with respect to the Repugnant Conclusion, Different-Number Separability, the Negative Expansion principle, Mere Addition and Priority for Lives Worth Living are the same as those of their utilitarian analogues. See Table 2.12, summarizing the axiomatic properties of total, average, and critical-level utilitarianism and prioritarianism.

I've said nothing thus far about *policies* in the variable-population case. The treatment, here, is the same as for the fixed-population case. There is a set **P** of policies $\{P, P^*, \ldots\}$. We continue to use the state-of-nature setup: a policy is a state-by-state array of outcomes and thus a state-by-state array of well-being vectors (replacing each outcome with its vector). Any given SWF for the fixed-population case has a whole family of different-number extensions, and each of *these* in turn has multiple uncertainty modules. For example, the total-utilitarian SWF has multiple modules, as do average and critical-level utilitarianism, and the same is true for total, average, and critical-level prioritarianism.

2.12 Conclusion

This chapter has explicated the theory of prioritarian SWFs. The SWF framework – the most rigorous methodology for implementing

Table 2.12. ***Total, average, and critical-level utilitarianism and prioritarianism***

	Total utilitarianism and prioritarianism	Average utilitarianism and prioritarianism	Critical-level utilitarianism and prioritarianism (with $w^{critical} > w^{neutral}$)
Avoids Repugnant Conclusion	No	Yes	Yes
Different-Number Separability	Yes	No	Yes
Negative Expansion	Yes	No	Yes
Mere Addition	Yes	No	No
Priority for Lives Worth Living	Yes	Yes	No

welfare-consequentialism – converts outcomes (models of possible worlds) into well-being vectors, and ranks the vectors using some rule (the SWF). Government policies are conceptualized as probability distributions over outcomes; and a given SWF is paired with an uncertainty module, for ranking policies thus conceptualized.

Prioritarianism is a family of SWFs. Each such SWF is defined by a strictly increasing and strictly concave transformation function, and ranks vectors according to the sum of well-being numbers plugged into this transformation function. All such SWFs satisfy the axioms of Pareto, Anonymity, Separability, Continuity, and Pigou-Dalton; and the converse is also true, namely that only prioritarian SWFs satisfy these axioms. The main uncertainty modules for a prioritarian SWF are ex post prioritarianism (EPP); ex ante prioritarianism (EAP); and expected equally-distributed-equivalent prioritarianism (EEDEP). These were compared with respect to uncertainty axioms, namely: ex ante Pareto, Dominance, and Policy Separability.

The chapter also reviewed two important subfamilies of prioritarian SWFs: Atkinson SWFs and Kolm-Pollak SWFs. These both employ specific and quite tractable formulas for the prioritarian transformation function. Atkinson and/or Kolm-Pollak SWFs are the versions of prioritarianism generally employed in the *Prioritarianism in Practice* volume and in previous applied work.

It is sometimes argued that prioritarianism is no different from utilitarianism. What animates the argument is a simple mathematical observation. Prioritarianism assigns a given outcome x the score $g(w_1(x)) + \ldots + g(w_N(x))$, with $w(\cdot)$ the well-being measure and $g(\cdot)$ the prioritarian transformation function. If we now define a new well-being measure $w^*(\cdot)$ as follows – $w_i^*(x) = g(w_i(x))$ – the utilitarian outcome ranking using $w^*(\cdot)$ is identical to the prioritarian outcome ranking using $g(\cdot)$ and $w(\cdot)$.

The mathematical observation is correct, but to leap from that observation to the conclusion that prioritarianism is just utilitarianism under a different name is problematic. Relative to any given well-being measure, the prioritarian and utilitarian outcome and policy rankings will generally be different. Moreover, the two measures immediately above, $w(\cdot)$ and $w^*(\cdot)$, are not the same. They imply distinct intra- and interpersonal comparisons of well-being differences; and a theory of well-being, insofar as it allows for such comparisons, will see the two well-being measures as distinct.[72]

The chapter not only explicated the theory of prioritarian SWFs, but also set forth a normative defense of prioritarianism. The key normative failing of utilitarianism is its insensitivity to the distribution of well-being. The utilitarian SWF fails to satisfy the Pigou-Dalton axiom, which stipulates that a gap-diminishing pure transfer of well-being from a better-off to a worse-off person is an ethical improvement. Indeed, the utilitarian SWF is such that a transfer of well-being from a better-off to a worse-off person that leaves unchanged the sum total of well-being is *always* a matter of ethical indifference – regardless of how much better off the better-off one is.

By contrast, prioritarianism satisfies Pigou-Dalton. To be sure, that is also true of other SWFs – most prominently the leximin SWF, rank-weighted SWFs, and sufficientist SWFs (which partly satisfy Pigou-Dalton[73]). But unlike these other equity-regarding, non-utilitarian

[72] Section 2.5 argued that well-being difference comparisons, not merely level comparisons, should be seen as admissible.

[73] On sufficientist SWFs and the Pigou-Dalton axiom, see note 34.

SWFs, prioritarian SWFs are especially tractable – an important consideration for a policy-analysis tool – in virtue of also satisfying the Separability and Continuity axioms. Pareto, Anonymity, Separability, and Continuity, taken together, characterize the *generalized-utilitarian* class of SWFs: all SWFs that sum a strictly increasing and continuous function of well-being. In the case of utilitarianism, this function is the identity function (utilitarianism simply adds up untransformed well-being). If we require, however, that a generalized-utilitarian SWF also be fully equity-regarding – that it satisfy Pigou-Dalton – we end up with prioritarianism.

2.A Appendix

The SWF framework has the following components. $\mathbf{O} = \{x, y, \ldots\}$ is a set of outcomes. $\mathbf{I} = \{1, 2, \ldots, N\}$ is a finite population of individuals, each of whom exists in all of the outcomes. $N \geq 3$. $w(\cdot)$ is a well-being measure, with $w_i(x)$ the well-being number of individual i in outcome x. x corresponds to the N-entry well-being vector $(w_1(x), w_2(x), \ldots, w_N(x))$. Well-being vectors are also denoted with bold-faced lower case letters such as **w** or **v**. **W** is the set of all N-entry well-being vectors.[74]

An SWF, $\succcurlyeq$, is an ordering of **W**. A quasiordering is a transitive, reflexive, binary relation and an ordering is a complete quasiordering. Transitive: For all **w**, **v**, **u**, if $\mathbf{w} \succcurlyeq \mathbf{v}$ and $\mathbf{v} \succcurlyeq \mathbf{u}$ then $\mathbf{w} \succcurlyeq \mathbf{u}$. Reflexive: For all **w**, $\mathbf{w} \succcurlyeq \mathbf{w}$. Complete: For all **w**, **v**, either $\mathbf{w} \succcurlyeq \mathbf{v}$ or $\mathbf{v} \succcurlyeq \mathbf{w}$ or both. $\mathbf{w} \succcurlyeq \mathbf{v}$ should be read as "**w** is at least as good as **v**." From this at-least-as-good relation, we generate an equally-good-as-relation ($\sim$) and better-than relation ($\succ$) as follows: $\mathbf{w} \sim \mathbf{v}$ iff $\mathbf{w} \succcurlyeq \mathbf{v}$ and $\mathbf{v} \succcurlyeq \mathbf{w}$. $\mathbf{w} \succ \mathbf{v}$ iff $\mathbf{w} \succcurlyeq \mathbf{v}$ and not $\mathbf{v} \succcurlyeq \mathbf{w}$. It follows that: $\mathbf{w} \succcurlyeq \mathbf{v}$ iff $\mathbf{w} \succ \mathbf{v}$ or $\mathbf{w} \sim \mathbf{v}$. (One item is at least as good as a second iff it is either equally good as or better than the second.)

An SWF ranks outcomes using the Master Recipe: x at least as good as y iff $(w_1(x), w_2(x), \ldots, w_N(x)) \succcurlyeq (w_1(y), w_2(y), \ldots, w_N(y))$.

$\mathbf{P} = \{P, P^*, \ldots\}$ is the set of policies, each understood as a state-by-state array of outcomes. A given SWF has different possible uncertainty modules. An uncertainty module specifies an ordering of **P**, denoted here as $\succcurlyeq^{\mathbf{P}}$.

In what follows, I first present formulas for the major SWFs and the axioms that characterize them; then discuss the policy ranking and uncertainty modules; and finally review the Atkinson and Kolm-Pollak functional forms for prioritarianism. Sources discussing the SWFs, axioms,

[74] Or all in some orthant of N-dimensional space. The possible need to restrict well-being vectors to an orthant is illustrated by Atkinson SWFs, which require well-being numbers to be non-negative (or positive if $\gamma \geq 1$).

and uncertainty are provided in Sections 2.2 and 2.3 of the main text; and discussing the Atkinson and Kolm-Pollak functional forms in Section 2.9.

2.A.1 SWFs: Formulas and Axioms

Major types of SWFs are as follows. (These formulas are given in Table 2.1 and, for convenience, are repeated here.)

The Utilitarian SWF: $\mathbf{w} \succcurlyeq \mathbf{v}$ iff $\sum_{i=1}^{N} \mathbf{w}_i \geq \sum_{i=1}^{N} \mathbf{v}_i$.

The Prioritarian Family of SWFs: $\mathbf{w} \succcurlyeq \mathbf{v}$ iff $\sum_{i=1}^{N} g(\mathbf{w}_i) \geq \sum_{i=1}^{N} g(\mathbf{v}_i)$, with $g(\cdot)$ a strictly increasing and strictly concave function.[75]

In presenting the next two types of SWF, I'll need some additional symbolism. For a given well-being vector $\mathbf{w}$, let $\hat{\mathbf{w}}$ be a vector listing the elements of $\mathbf{w}$ from smallest to largest.

The Leximin SWF: For any two vectors $\mathbf{w}$, $\mathbf{v}$: (1) $\mathbf{w} \sim \mathbf{v}$ iff $\mathbf{w}$ is a permutation of $\mathbf{v}$; and (2) $\mathbf{w} \succ \mathbf{v}$ iff there is $j \leq N$ such that $\hat{\mathbf{w}}_i = \hat{\mathbf{v}}_i$ for all $i < j$ and $\hat{\mathbf{w}}_j > \hat{\mathbf{v}}_j$.

The Rank-weighted Family of SWFs: Each SWF within this family is defined by a list of N positive and strictly decreasing weights: $k_1, k_2, \ldots, k_N$ such that $k_1 > k_2 > \ldots > k_N > 0$. $\mathbf{w} \succcurlyeq \mathbf{v}$ iff $\sum_{i=1}^{N} k_i \hat{\mathbf{w}}_i \geq \sum_{i=1}^{N} k_i \hat{\mathbf{v}}_i$.

The Sufficientist Family of SWFs: Each SWF within this family is defined by some threshold level of well-being w^{thresh}, and some strictly increasing and strictly concave function $g(\cdot)$. A given well-being vector $\mathbf{w}$ has two associated vectors: $\bar{\mathbf{w}}$, the elements of $\mathbf{w}$ truncated above at w^{thresh}; and $\underline{\mathbf{w}}$, the elements of $\mathbf{w}$ truncated below at w^{thresh}. (That is, $\bar{\mathbf{w}}_i = \min\{\mathbf{w}_i, w^{thresh}\}$; and $\underline{\mathbf{w}}_i = \max\{\mathbf{w}_i, w^{thresh}\}$.) For any two vectors $\mathbf{w}$, $\mathbf{v}$: (1) $\mathbf{w} \succ \mathbf{v}$ iff either (a) $g(\bar{\mathbf{w}}_1) + \ldots + g(\bar{\mathbf{w}}_N) > g(\bar{\mathbf{v}}_1) + \ldots + g(\bar{\mathbf{v}}_N)$ or (b) $g(\bar{\mathbf{w}}_1) + \ldots + g(\bar{\mathbf{w}}_N) = g(\bar{\mathbf{v}}_1) + \ldots + g(\bar{\mathbf{v}}_N)$ and $\underline{\mathbf{w}}_1 + \ldots + \underline{\mathbf{w}}_N > \underline{\mathbf{v}}_1 + \ldots + \underline{\mathbf{v}}_N$; and (2) $\mathbf{w} \sim \mathbf{v}$ iff $g(\bar{\mathbf{w}}_1) + \ldots + g(\bar{\mathbf{w}}_N) = g(\bar{\mathbf{v}}_1) + \ldots + g(\bar{\mathbf{v}}_N)$ and $\underline{\mathbf{w}}_1 + \ldots + \underline{\mathbf{w}}_N = \underline{\mathbf{v}}_1 + \ldots + \underline{\mathbf{v}}_N$.

The utilitarian SWF and prioritarian SWFs fall within a broader class of SWFs, namely *generalized-utilitarian* SWFs:

[75] $g(\cdot)$ is also continuous. If the domain of $g(\cdot)$ is an open interval, this is automatic, since concave functions are continuous on open intervals.

The generalized-utilitarian class of SWFs: $\mathbf{w} \succcurlyeq \mathbf{v}$ iff $\sum_{i=1}^{N} f(\mathbf{w}_i) \geq \sum_{i=1}^{N} f(\mathbf{v}_i)$, with $f(\cdot)$ strictly increasing and continuous.

At this juncture, it's worth introducing the "equally-distributed equivalent" (EDE) representation of a prioritarian SWF. Rank-weighted SWFs and generalized-utilitarian SWFs are "score-based": they rank vectors according to the values assigned to vectors by a real-valued function. For any such SWF, the ranking of vectors according to a given real-valued function, and according to any strictly increasing transformation of that function, are the same. In particular, consider a prioritarian SWF as defined immediately above. Let $H(\cdot)$ be any strictly increasing function. Then the ranking of vectors using the formula $\sum_{i=1}^{N} g(\mathbf{w}_i)$ is the same as that using the formula $H\left(\sum_{i=1}^{N} g(\mathbf{w}_i)\right)$: $\sum_{i=1}^{N} g(\mathbf{w}_i) \geq \sum_{i=1}^{N} g(\mathbf{v}_i)$ iff $H\left(\sum_{i=1}^{N} g(\mathbf{w}_i)\right) \geq H\left(\sum_{i=1}^{N} g(\mathbf{v}_i)\right)$.

For a given prioritarian transformation function (a strictly increasing and strictly concave function $g(\cdot)$), the equally distributed equivalent for a given well-being vector $\mathbf{w}$, $w^{EDE}(\mathbf{w})$, is the well-being level such that a vector with all N individuals at that level is equally good as $\mathbf{w}$. $w^{EDE}(\mathbf{w}) = g^{-1}\left(\sum_{i=1}^{N} g(\mathbf{w}_i)/N\right)$. Note now that $w^{\text{EDE}}(\mathbf{w}) = H\left(\sum_{i=1}^{N} g(\mathbf{w}_i)\right)$, with $H(m) = g^{-1}(m/N)$, and $H(\cdot)$ strictly increasing.

In short, the straight prioritarian formula $\sum_{i=1}^{N} g(\mathbf{w}_i)$ and the equally-distributed-equivalent formula $g^{-1}\left(\sum_{i=1}^{N} g(\mathbf{w}_i)/N\right)$ yield exactly the same rankings of well-being vectors. The choice between the two becomes significant in constructing an uncertainty module: the ranking of *policies* according to the expected value of the first formula (the EPP module) is not generally the same as the ranking of policies according to the expected value of the second formula (the EEDEP module). See Section 2.7; 2.A.2. The choice is also significant if one wishes not merely to rank well-being vectors, but to measure their social-welfare value on a supra-ordinal scale (e.g., a ratio or translation scale) (Decancq and Schokkaert, Chapter 5, this volume).

The most important axioms for characterizing SWFs, as discussed in the text, are as follows:

Pareto Indifference: If $\mathbf{w}_i = \mathbf{v}_i$ for all i, then $\mathbf{w} \sim \mathbf{v}$.[76]

[76] This is automatic, since $\succcurlyeq$ is just a ranking of well-being vectors, and can't differentiate between vectors with the same numbers in each of the N slots.

Strong Pareto: If $\mathbf{v}_i \geq \mathbf{w}_i$ for all i, and $\mathbf{v}_j > \mathbf{w}_j$ for at least one j, then $\mathbf{v} \succ \mathbf{w}$.

Anonymity: Let $\pi(\cdot)$ be a permutation mapping (a one-to-one, onto mapping) from the set of individuals **I** to **I**. $\pi(\cdot)$ associates each individual i with one and only one individual $\pi(i)$. If $\mathbf{w}_i = \mathbf{v}_{\pi(i)}$ for all i, $\mathbf{w} \sim \mathbf{v}$.

Pigou-Dalton: Let $\mathbf{w}$ and $\mathbf{v}$ be such that: $\mathbf{w}_i > \mathbf{w}_j$ for some i and j; $\mathbf{v}_i = \mathbf{w}_i - \Delta w, \mathbf{v}_j = \mathbf{w}_j + \Delta w$, with $\Delta w > 0$; $|\mathbf{w}_i - \mathbf{w}_j| > |\mathbf{v}_i - \mathbf{v}_j|$; and for all $k \neq i, j, \mathbf{w}_k = \mathbf{v}_k$. Then $\mathbf{v} \succ \mathbf{w}$.

Separability: Let **M** be any subset of **I**, and let $\mathbf{M}^+ = \mathbf{I} \setminus \mathbf{M}$ (all individuals not in **M**). Assume $\mathbf{w}, \mathbf{v}, \mathbf{w}^*, \mathbf{v}^*$ are as follows. For all $i \in \mathbf{M}$, $\mathbf{w}_i = \mathbf{v}_i$ and $\mathbf{w}_i^* = \mathbf{v}_i^*$. For all $j \in \mathbf{M}^+$, $\mathbf{w}_j = \mathbf{w}_j^*$ and $\mathbf{v}_j = \mathbf{v}_j^*$. Then $\mathbf{w} \succcurlyeq \mathbf{v}$ iff $\mathbf{w}^* \succcurlyeq \mathbf{v}^*$.

Continuity: Recall that **W** is the set of all well-being vectors. For any **w**, the sets $\{\mathbf{v} \in \mathbf{W}: \mathbf{v} \succ \mathbf{w}\}$ and $\{\mathbf{v} \in \mathbf{W}: \mathbf{w} \succ \mathbf{v}\}$ are open sets. Equivalently, the sets $\{\mathbf{v} \in \mathbf{W}: \mathbf{v} \succcurlyeq \mathbf{w}\}$ and $\{\mathbf{v} \in \mathbf{W}: \mathbf{w} \succcurlyeq \mathbf{v}\}$ are closed sets.

In comparing utilitarianism and prioritarianism (Section 2.8), the chapter introduces another axiom, Minimal Pigou-Dalton.

Minimal Pigou-Dalton: (1) There exist **w** and **v** such that $\mathbf{v} \succ \mathbf{w}$ and: $\mathbf{w}_i > \mathbf{w}_j$ for some i and j; $\mathbf{v}_i = \mathbf{w}_i - \Delta w, \mathbf{v}_j = \mathbf{w}_j + \Delta w$, with $\Delta w > 0$; $|\mathbf{w}_i - \mathbf{w}_j| > |\mathbf{v}_i - \mathbf{v}_j|$; and for all $k \neq i, j, \mathbf{w}_k = \mathbf{v}_k$. (2) Let **w** and **v** be such that: $\mathbf{w}_i \geq \mathbf{w}_j$ for some i and j; $\mathbf{v}_i = \mathbf{w}_i + \Delta w, \mathbf{v}_j = \mathbf{w}_j - \Delta w$, with $\Delta w > 0$; and for all $k \neq i, j, \mathbf{w}_k = \mathbf{v}_k$. Then $\mathbf{w} \succcurlyeq \mathbf{v}$.

2.A.2 Uncertainty and the Policy Ranking

Uncertainty is captured by a set $\mathbf{S} = \{s, s^*, \ldots\}$ of states of nature. **S** is finite. $\pi(s)$ is the probability of state s. $\sum_{s \in \mathbf{S}} \pi(s) = 1$. Zero-probability states can be ignored, and so I assume that $\pi(s) > 0$ for all s. There is a set **P** of policies, $\mathbf{P} = \{P, P^*, \ldots\}$. A policy associates each state with some outcome; this is the outcome that would occur, were that policy to be chosen and that state to be the actual state. Let $x_{P,s}$ denote the outcome in state s of policy P.

An uncertainty module for a given SWF $\succcurlyeq$ specifies an ordering $\succcurlyeq^{\mathbf{P}}$ of the set of policies **P**. The module is a formula for arriving at $\succcurlyeq^{\mathbf{P}}$, for any set of outcomes **O**, set of states **S** and state probabilities, set of policies

P, and well-being measure $w(\cdot)$. I assume that this formula takes account of the state probabilities and of the well-being vectors in each state (as per $w(\cdot)$), but is independent of the description of the states and of which specific outcome gives rise to the well-being vector in a given state.

All the modules for a given SWF converge in their ranking of "degenerate" policies – a degenerate policy being one that yields the same well-being vector in each state. This can be captured in a requirement of "Basic Consistency" which every module must satisfy.

Basic Consistency: Assume that (1) there exists some **w**, such that $(w_1(x_{P,s}), \ldots, w_N(x_{P,s})) = \mathbf{w}$ for every state s, and (2) there exists some $\mathbf{w}^*$ such that $(w_1(x_{P^*,s}), \ldots, w_N(x_{P^*,s})) = \mathbf{w}^*$ for every state s. Then $P \succcurlyeq^{\mathbf{P}} P^*$ iff $\mathbf{w} \succcurlyeq \mathbf{w}^*$.

The leading modules for the prioritarian SWF, as discussed in the text, are "ex post prioritarianism" (EPP); "ex ante prioritarianism" (EAP); and expected equally-distributed-equivalent prioritarianism (EEDEP). Their formulas are as follows. Throughout, $g(\cdot)$ is a strictly increasing and strictly concave function. As shorthand, I'll use $w_i(P)$ to denote i's expected well-being with policy P. $w_i(P) = \sum_{s \in S} \pi(s)\, w_i(x_{P,s})$.

EPP: $P \succcurlyeq^{\mathbf{P}} P^*$ iff $\sum_{s \in S} \pi(s) \sum_{i=1}^{N} g(w_i(x_{P,s})) \geq \sum_{s \in S} \pi(s) \sum_{i=1}^{N} g(w_i(x_{P^*,s}))$. Note that this formula is equivalent to summing individuals' expected transformed well-being. $\sum_{s \in S} \pi(s) \sum_{i=1}^{N} g(w_i(x_{P,s})) = \sum_{i=1}^{N} \sum_{s \in S} \pi(s) g(w_i(x_{P,s}))$

EAP: $P \succcurlyeq^{\mathbf{P}} P^*$ iff $\sum_{i=1}^{N} g(w_i(P)) \geq \sum_{i=1}^{N} g(w_i(P^*))$.

EEDEP: $P \succcurlyeq^{\mathbf{P}} P^*$ iff $\sum_{s \in S} \pi(s) g^{-1}\left(\sum_{i=1}^{N} g(w_i(x_{P,s}))/N\right) \geq \sum_{s \in S} \pi(s) g^{-1}\left(\sum_{i=1}^{N} g(w_i(x_{P^*,s}))/N\right)$.

The module for the utilitarian SWF, discussed in the text, is UUU.

UUU: $P \succcurlyeq^{\mathbf{P}} P^*$ iff $\sum_{s \in S} \pi(s) \sum_{i=1}^{N} w_i(x_{P,s}) \geq \sum_{s \in S} \pi(s) \sum_{i=1}^{N} w_i(x_{P^*,s})$. Note that this formula is equivalent to summing individuals' expected well-being. $\sum_{s \in S} \pi(s) \sum_{i=1}^{N} w_i(x_{P,s}) = \sum_{i=1}^{N} \sum_{s \in S} \pi(s) w_i(x_{P,s}) = \sum_{i=1}^{N} w_i(P)$

The uncertainty axioms that orient discussion in the text are the ex ante Pareto axiom (in two parts, Indifference and Strong); Dominance; and Policy Separability.

Ex ante Pareto Indifference: If $w_i(P) = w_i(P^*)$ for all i, then $P \sim^{\mathrm{P}} P^*$.

Ex ante Strong Pareto: If $w_i(P) \geq w_i(P^*)$ for all i, and $w_j(P) > w_j(P^*)$ for at least one j, then $P \succ^{\mathrm{P}} P^*$.

Dominance: Assume that, for all $s \in \mathbf{S}$, $(w_1(x_{P,s}), \ldots, w_N(x_{P,s})) \succ (w_1(x_{P^*,s}), \ldots, w_N(x_{P^*,s}))$. Then $P \succ^{\mathrm{P}} P^*$.

Policy Separability: Let $\mathbf{M}$ be any subset of $\mathbf{I}$ (the set of individuals), and let $\mathbf{M}^+ = \mathbf{I}\backslash\mathbf{M}$ (all individuals not in $\mathbf{M}$). Assume policies P, P^*, P^+, P^{++} are as follows. For each $i \in \mathbf{M}$, $w_i(x_{P,s}) = w_i(x_{P^*,s})$ and $w_i(x_{P^+,s}) = w_i(x_{P^{++},s})$ for every state s. For each $j \in \mathbf{M}^+$, $w_j(x_{P,s}) = w_j(x_{P^+,s})$ and $w_j(x_{P^*,s}) = w_j(x_{P^{++},s})$ for every state s. Then $P \succcurlyeq^{\mathrm{P}} P^*$ iff $P^+ \succcurlyeq^{\mathrm{P}} P^{++}$.

2.A.3 Functional Forms for Prioritarianism: Atkinson and Kolm-Pollak

The analysis that follows is formulated in terms of a preference-based view of well-being. An individual's well-being depends upon her history h, with a history a combination of a bundle of non-preference attributes a, and a preference structure R. $h = (a, R)$. (As explained in Adler and Decancq, Chapter 3, this volume, R might be an ordinal preference $\overline{R}$ or a lottery preference $\overline{\overline{R}}$. The analysis that follows applies equally to both cases.)

This section will be switching back and forth between a well-being measure that assigns well-being numbers to individuals in outcomes, and a well-being measure that assigns well-being numbers to *histories*. In order to avoid confusion, I'll continue to use $w(\cdot)$ to denote the former, and will use $\theta(\cdot)$ to denote the latter. $w_i(x) = \theta(h_i(x)) = \theta(a_i(x), R_i(x))$.

I assume, throughout, that $\theta(\cdot)$ is unique up to a positive affine transformation. If $\theta(\cdot)$ is unique up to a positive affine transformation, then $w(\cdot)$ is unique up to a common cardinal rescaling and represents both intra- and interpersonal comparisons of both well-being levels and differences.[77]

The analysis here translates in a straightforward way to non-preference-based views of well-being. This case is simpler, since the R can be dropped. $w_i(x) = \theta(a_i(x))$.

2.A.3.1 *Atkinson SWF (Profile-Independent)*

As discussed in the text, the theoretical literature on SWFs generally assumes that the SWF is *profile-independent*. $\succcurlyeq$ is a *single* ranking of well-being vectors, which is independent of $w(\cdot)$. Assume that $\succcurlyeq$ ranks well-being vectors **w**, **v**, **ww**, and **vv** a certain way. Imagine that we are using $w(\cdot)$ to assign well-being numbers to individuals in outcomes, and that outcomes x and y are such that $(w_1(x), \ldots, w_N(x)) = \mathbf{w}$ and $(w_1(y), \ldots, w_N(y)) = \mathbf{v}$. Then x at least as good as y iff $\mathbf{w} \succcurlyeq \mathbf{v}$. Imagine, now, that we switch to $w^+(\cdot)$ to assign well-being numbers to individuals in outcomes. The vector ranking remains the same. For example, $w^+(\cdot)$ is such that $({w_1}^+(x), \ldots, {w_N}^+(x)) = \mathbf{ww}$ and $({w_1}^+(y), \ldots, {w_N}^+(y)) = \mathbf{vv}$. Then x at least as good as y iff $\mathbf{ww} \succcurlyeq \mathbf{vv}$.

In the analytic setup here, with an individual's well-being determined by her history – $w_i(x) = \theta(a_i(x), R_i(x))$ – profile-independence means, more specifically, that $\succcurlyeq$ is independent of $\theta(\cdot)$. The ranking of well-being vectors remains the same, regardless of which $\theta(\cdot)$ is used to assign well-being numbers to histories.

To say that a *prioritarian* SWF is profile-independent means that the choice of $g(\cdot)$ is independent of $w(\cdot)$ – specifically, independent of $\theta(\cdot)$. Putting together the requirement of profile-independence with *invariance* considerations, we arrive at the Atkinson family of prioritarian SWFs. Atkinson SWFs define the $g(\cdot)$ function as follows: $g(w_i) = \frac{1}{1-\gamma} w_i^{1-\gamma}$, with $\gamma > 0$ (and $\gamma \neq 1$), and $g(w_i) = \log w_i$ in the special case of $\gamma = 1$.

No profile-independent prioritarian SWF is invariant to a common cardinal rescaling of $w(\cdot)$. If we relax the invariance requirement

[77] $w^*(\cdot)$ is a "common cardinal rescaling" of $w(\cdot)$ if there exists $k > 0, l$, s.t. $w_i^*(x) = kw_i(x) + l$ for all i, x. $\theta^*(\cdot)$ is a "positive affine transformation" of $\theta(\cdot)$ if there exists $r > 0, s$ s.t. $\theta^*(h) = r\theta(h) + s$ for every h. Consider any $\theta^*(\cdot)$ which is a positive affine transformation of $\theta(\cdot)$, and the corresponding $w^*(\cdot) : w_i^*(x) = \theta^*(h_i(x)).\theta^*(h_i(x)) = r\theta(h_i(x)) + s = rw_i(x) + s$. So $w^*(\cdot)$ is indeed a common cardinal rescaling of $w(\cdot)$, with $k = r$ and $l = s$.

somewhat – requiring invariance to a common ratio rescaling of $w(\cdot)$ – this impossibility is avoided. If the SWF is profile-independent, prioritarian, and invariant to a common ratio rescaling of $w(\cdot)$, then it must be an Atkinson SWF.

In the setup here, requiring that the SWF be invariant to a common ratio rescaling of $w(\cdot)$ is equivalent to requiring that $\theta(\cdot)$ be unique up to a positive *ratio* transformation.[78] That is to say, $\theta(\cdot)$ should contain information not only about the well-being levels of histories and well-being differences, but also about well-being ratios. In effect, we need to take $\theta(\cdot)$, which already represents levels and differences, and now "add in" information about well-being ratios.

We do so by picking a zero history $h^{zero} = (a^{zero}, R^{zero})$. Conceptually, well-being ratios are just ratios of differences from a zero point. The well-being ratio between history h and history h^+ is just the ratio of the well-being difference between h and a zero point h^{zero}, and the well-being difference between h^+ and that zero point. With h^{zero} in hand, we can now specify a new well-being measure $\theta^*(\cdot)$, with $\theta^*(a, R) = \theta(a, R) - \theta(a^{zero}, R^{zero})$. Note that $\theta^*(\cdot)$ preserves all of the well-being level and difference information in $\theta(\cdot)$, but also now represents well-being ratios, and is unique up to a positive ratio transformation.

How should h^{zero} be chosen? Relevant considerations are the following. (1) We might have intuitions about the well-being ratios between histories. Such intuitions can guide the choice of h^{zero}. For example, assume that $\theta(a, R) > \theta(a^+, R^+)$, and that we intuit that someone with history (a, R) is twice as well off as someone with history (a^+, R^+). Then we can choose $h^{zero} = (a^{zero}, R^{zero})$ so that $[\theta(a, R) - \theta(a^{zero}, R^{zero})]/[\theta(a^+, R^+) - \theta(a^{zero}, R^{zero})] = 2$. (2) A strong pragmatic consideration is that the well-being numbers inputted into the Atkinson SWF must be non-negative (or positive with $\gamma \geq 1$).[79] Thus, h^{zero} should be chosen so that every well-being vector that might

[78] $w^*(\cdot)$ is a "common ratio rescaling" of $w(\cdot)$ if there exists $k > 0$ s.t. $w_i^*(x) = kw_i(x)$ for all i, x. $\theta^*(\cdot)$ is a "positive ratio transformation" of $\theta(\cdot)$ if there exists $r > 0$ s.t. $\theta^*(h) = r\theta(h)$. Following an analysis parallel to that in note 77, it's clear that if $\theta^*(h) = r\theta(h)$, then the corresponding $w^*(\cdot)$ is such that $w_i^*(x) = kw_i(x)$, with $k = r$.

[79] As explained in the main text, the Atkinson $g(\cdot)$ function is either undefined or, if defined, not both strictly increasing and strictly concave with negative well-being numbers as inputs (or with 0 as an input for $\gamma \geq 1$).

arise with non-zero probability contains only non-negative (or positive, with $\gamma \geq 1$) entries. That is: h^{zero} should be a sufficiently "bad" history that, for every outcome y such that $x_{P,s} = y$ for some policy P in **P** and some state s, and for every i, $\theta(a_i(y), R_i(y)) \geq \theta(a^{zero}, R^{zero})$ – or $\theta(a_i(y), R_i(y)) > \theta(a^{zero}, R^{zero})$ for $\gamma \geq 1$. (3) h^{zero} is the point of absolute moral priority, in the following sense. As an individual's well-being level approaches h^{zero}, the relative weight given to changes in her well-being by an Atkinson SWF, as compared to that of better-off individuals, approaches infinity. For any prioritarian SWF, if individual i is at well-being level w_i, the marginal moral impact of a change to her well-being is $g'(w_i)$. For an Atkinson SWF, $g'(w_i) = w_i^{-\gamma}$. Consider two individuals i and j, $0 < w_i < w_j$. According to the Atkinson SWF, the marginal moral impact of a change to i's well-being, as a multiple of the marginal moral impact of a change to j's, is $\frac{g'(w_i)}{g'(w_j)} = \left(\frac{w_j}{w_i}\right)^{\gamma}$. For any value of $\gamma > 0$, this ratio approaches infinity as w_i approaches 0.

Atkinson SWFs, again, are a family of SWFs. Picking a value of γ identifies a particular SWF. How should γ be chosen? γ is a *priority* parameter.[80] As the equation immediately above shows, γ specifies the marginal moral impact of a change to a worse-off individual's well-being, as a multiple of the marginal moral impact of a change to a better-off person's well-being, depending on the ratio of their well-being levels (better off to worse off). If $w_j > w_i > 0$ and $(w_j/w_i) = K$, then this ratio of marginal moral impacts is $(w_j/w_i)^{\gamma} = K^{\gamma}$.

With $\gamma = 0$, the Atkinson SWF is no longer prioritarian but becomes utilitarian. (This can be seen immediately by plugging $\gamma = 0$ into the formula above.) As γ increases, the Atkinson SWF gives increasing priority to the worse off: the ratio of marginal moral impacts $(w_j/w_i)^{\gamma} = K^{\gamma}$ increases with γ for a given well-being ratio K between the better-off and worse-off individuals.

The ratio of marginal moral impacts can also be thought of in terms of leaky transfers. Imagine reducing the better-off individual's well-being by some small amount Δw and increasing the worse-off individual's well-being by a fraction of the loss to the better-off one, i.e., by

80 A standard mathematical indicator of the degree of concavity of a concave function $g(m)$ at a value m is the coefficient of relative risk aversion: $-g''(m)m/g'(m)$ (Lambert 2001, pp. 94–97). In the case of the Atkinson $g(\cdot)$ this coefficient is constant and equal to γ.

$\rho\Delta w, 0 < \rho < 1$. The moral impact of the loss to the better-off one is approximately $-(\Delta w)w_j^{-\gamma}$, while the moral impact of the gain to the worse-off one is approximately $(\rho\Delta w)w_i^{-\gamma}$. Let $\rho^{min} = (1/K)^{\gamma}$. Note that $(\rho\Delta w)w_i^{-\gamma} >< (\Delta w)w_j^{-\gamma}$ iff $\rho >< \rho^{min}$. So we can test whether the leaky transfer is a net moral gain or loss by seeing whether the fractional gain ρ to the worse-off one is greater than or less than ρ^{min}. This is an approximate test that becomes increasingly accurate as Δw approaches 0.

ρ^{min} is (approximately) the minimum acceptable fraction for a leaky transfer. Intuitions about ρ^{min} for a given K can be used to deliberate about the appropriate level of γ. Note that $\gamma = -(\log \rho^{min}/\log K)$.

Having chosen a value of γ, we now use the resultant Atkinson SWF together with a well-being measure $w^*(\cdot)$ that is unique up to a common ratio rescaling – with $w^*(\cdot)$ specified, as discussed above, by taking an $\theta(\cdot)$ that represents well-being levels and differences; identifying an $h^{zero} = (a^{zero}, R^{zero})$; defining $\theta^*(a, R) = \theta(a, R) - \theta(a^{zero}, R^{zero})$; and setting $w_i^*(x) = \theta^*(a_i(x), R_i(x))$. That is, we rank outcomes as follows – x at least as good as y iff $(1/(1-\gamma))\sum_{i=1}^{N} w_i^*(x)^{1-\gamma} \geq (1/(1-\gamma))\sum_{i=1}^{N} w_i^*(y)^{1-\gamma}$ – and we rank policies by using our chosen uncertainty module with $w^*(\cdot)$ as the well-being measure. For example, the EPP score assigned to a policy P would be: $\sum_{s\in S}\pi(s)(1/(1-\gamma))\sum_{i=1}^{N} w_i^*(x_{P,s})^{1-\gamma}$.

This approach is profile-independent because γ is independent of $w^*(\cdot)$, i.e., independent of $\theta^*(\cdot)$. Note that γ is not a function of $\theta(\cdot)$ and h^{zero}. Note also that, in the leaky-transfer thought experiment suggested above for specifying γ, the choice of γ is meant to depend upon intuitions about ρ^{min} for a given well-being ratio $K = w_j/w_i$. It is not meant to depend upon *which* well-being measure $\theta^*(\cdot)$ is used to map the two individuals' histories onto well-being numbers and thereby to determine the well-being ratio between them.

2.A.3.2 *Kolm-Pollak SWF (Profile-Dependent)*

Kolm-Pollak SWFs are a family of prioritarian SWFs that define the $g(\cdot)$ function as follows: $g(w_i) = -\exp(-\beta w_i), \beta > 0$. As compared to Atkinson SWFs, Kolm-Pollak SWFs have the advantage of allowing well-being numbers to take any value: positive, zero, or negative. Moreover, unlike Atkinson SWFs, which accord priority to a worse-off individual approaching infinity as her well-being level approaches 0,

Kolm-Pollak SWFs do not have this sort of property (a property that is intuitively troubling). With individual i at well-being level w_i, the marginal moral impact of a change to i's well-being is $\beta\exp(-\beta w_i)$. With $w_i < w_j$, the ratio of marginal moral impacts between the worse-off and better-off individuals is $\exp(\beta(w_j - w_i))$, which is finite for any number w_i (whether w_i is positive, negative, or zero) and approaches infinity only as $(w_j - w_i)$ does.

With $\beta = 0$, the Kolm-Pollak SWF is no longer prioritarian but becomes utilitarian.[81] As β increases, the Kolm-Pollak SWF gives increasing priority to the worse off: the ratio of marginal moral impacts $\exp(\beta(w_j - w_i))$ increases with β for a given well-being difference $(w_j - w_i)$ between the better-off and worse-off one.

Kolm-Pollak SWFs are not invariant to a common cardinal rescaling of $w(\cdot)$ (no prioritarian SWFs are), nor are they invariant to a common ratio rescaling of $w(\cdot)$ (only Atkinson SWFs are) – but Kolm-Pollak SWFs *do* have the property of being the only prioritarian SWFs that are invariant to a common *translation* rescaling of $w(\cdot)$(Bossert and Weymark, 2004, pp. 1160–1161). To say that $w^*(\cdot)$ is a common translation rescaling of $w(\cdot)$ means: $w_i^*(x) = w_i(x) + l$ for all i, x. With $w(\cdot)$ derived from $\theta(\cdot)$, requiring that $w(\cdot)$ be unique up to a common translation rescaling is equivalent to requiring that $\theta(\cdot)$ be unique up to a translation. $\theta^*(\cdot)$ is a translation of $\theta(\cdot)$ if $\theta^*(h) = \theta(h) + s$ for every history h.

Note that $\theta(\cdot)$ and all positive affine transformations thereof do *not* agree about the magnitude of the well-being difference between histories.[82] However, $\theta(\cdot)$ and all translations therefore *do* agree about that magnitude. If $\theta(h') - \theta(h) = D$, and $\theta^*(\cdot)$ is a translation of $\theta(\cdot)$, then $\theta^*(h') - \theta^*(h) = D$.

In principle, we could combine a profile-independent Kolm-Pollak SWF with a well-being measure $\theta^+(\cdot)$ unique up to a translation, as follows. (1) Starting with $\theta(\cdot)$, which represents our comparisons of

[81] Note that the ratio of marginal moral impacts, $\exp(\beta(w_j - w_i))$, is 1 with $\beta = 0$. Note also that the Kolm-Pollak SWF is ordinally equivalent to summing $g^*(w_i) = (-\exp(-\beta w_i) + 1)/\beta$. By l'Hôpital's rule, the limit of $g^*(\cdot)$ as β approaches 0 is w_i.

[82] Consider $\theta^*(\cdot) = r\theta(\cdot) + s$, with $r \neq 1$. If $\theta(h') - \theta(h) = D, \theta^*(h') - \theta^*(h) = rD \neq D$ if $D \neq 0$.

well-being levels and differences, we "add in" information about the magnitude of well-being differences. Assume that we judge that the well-being difference between h' and h is D, while in fact $\theta(h') - \theta(h) = d$. Then let $r = D/d$, and let $\theta^+(\cdot) = r\theta(\cdot)$. Then $\theta^+(\cdot)$ reflects this well-being information, as do all translations of $\theta^+(\cdot)$. (2) The priority parameter for the Kolm-Pollak SWF is β. We specify a profile-independent value for β – a value that is independent of how we choose $\theta(\cdot)$ and r – by deliberating about how the relative marginal moral impact of changes to the well-being of two individuals, w_i and w_j, $w_i < w_j$, depends upon the magnitude of the well-being difference between them. As already stated, this ratio of marginal moral impacts is just $\exp\left(\beta(w_j - w_i)\right)$. The minimum acceptable fraction for a leaky transfer is approximately $\rho^{min} = \exp\left(\beta(w_i - w_j)\right)$.

The difficulty with the approach sketched in the previous paragraph is that it's unclear what the magnitude of a well-being difference means. We can coherently judge that Philippe is better off than Suzanne, or that the well-being difference between Philippe and Suzanne is greater than the well-being difference between Ariela and Juan. But it doesn't seem meaningful to say that the well-being difference between Philippe and Suzanne is 7 rather than 5 or 110.

A more feasible approach, which doesn't require judgments about the magnitude of well-being differences, is to specify a profile-dependent Kolm-Pollak SWF so as to fit judgments regarding the moral weight of changes to individuals' attributes. Let a^m denote the attribute of type m. Assume that individual i has history (a^*, R^*), and individual j has history (a^+, R^+), with i worse off than j, i.e., $\theta(a^*, R^*) < \theta(a^+, R^+)$. The well-being impact of a marginal change Δa^m to i's holdings of a^m is approximately $\frac{\partial\theta}{\partial a^m}(a^*, R^*)\Delta a^m$, while the well-being impact of a marginal change Δa^m to j's holdings of a^m is approximately $\frac{\partial\theta}{\partial a^m}(a^+, R^+)\Delta a^m$. Using the Kolm-Pollak SWF, the moral impact of the first change is $\beta\exp\left(-\beta\theta(a^*, R^*)\right)\frac{\partial\theta}{\partial a^m}(a^*, R^*)\Delta a^m$, and that of the second is $\beta\exp\left(-\beta\theta(a^+, R^+)\right)\frac{\partial\theta}{\partial a^m}(a^+, R^+)\Delta a^m$, so that the ratio of marginal moral impacts, worse-off to better-off, is: $\exp\left(\beta[\theta(a^+, R^+) - \theta(a^*, R^*)]\right)\frac{\frac{\partial\theta}{\partial a^m}(a^*, R^*)}{\frac{\partial\theta}{\partial a^m}(a^+, R^+)} = Z$. We can use our intuitions about the magnitude of this ratio (Z) to solve for β. $\beta = [\log Z + \log\frac{\partial\theta}{\partial a^m}(a^+, R^+) - \log\frac{\partial\theta}{\partial a^m}(a^*, R^*)]/[\theta(a^+, R^+) - \theta(a^*, R^*)]$. Note that this approach is profile-dependent because β depends upon $\theta(\cdot)$.

The preceding is quite abstract, and a more concrete example may help. Some of the literature on SWFs contemplates using thought experiments about leaky transfers of *income* to specify an SWF. Assume that all histories have the same preference, so that $\theta(a, R)$ becomes $\theta(a)$. Let c denote income and b other attributes, so that $\theta(a) = \theta(c, b)$. Assume that income has a positive well-being impact: $\frac{\partial\theta}{\partial c} > 0$. Assume that individual i has income c^*, and individual j has income $c^+ > c^*$, with both individuals' non-income attributes at level b. Then the ratio between the marginal moral impact of a change Δc to i's income and a change Δc to j's income is $\exp\left(\beta[\theta(c^+, b) - \theta(c^*, b)]\right)\frac{\frac{\partial\theta}{\partial c}(c^*, b)}{\frac{\partial\theta}{\partial c}(c^+, b)} = Z$. Intuitions about this ratio are just intuitions about the minimum acceptable fraction $f^{\min}$ for a leaky transfer in *income* from individual j to individual i. $f^{\min} = 1/Z$.

2.A.3.3 *Atkinson SWF (Profile-Dependent)*

A third possibility is to have a profile-dependent Atkinson SWF. Since the Atkinson and Kolm-Pollak functional forms are the two most widely used types of $g(\cdot)$ functions, and since we have just discussed how to specify a profile-dependent Kolm-Pollak SWF, this possibility should also be mentioned.

In specifying a profile-dependent Atkinson SWF, there is no need to construct a $w^*(\cdot)$ unique up to a common ratio rescaling by starting with $\theta(\cdot)$, identifying a zero history h^{zero}, and thereby arriving at $\theta^*(\cdot)$ unique up to a positive ratio transformation and at $w^*(\cdot)$ defined from $\theta^*(\cdot)$.[83] Rather, we simply pick γ given $\theta(\cdot)$ so as to fit intuitions about the relative moral impact of changes to individuals' attributes.[84]

As with the Kolm-Pollak analysis above, let a^m denote the attribute of type m. Assume that individual i has history (a^*, R^*), and individual

[83] This is only needed for the profile-independent Atkinson SWF. That SWF is not invariant to a common cardinal rescaling, but is invariant to a common ratio rescaling.

[84] The profile-dependent Atkinson SWF does still require well-being numbers to be non-negative (or positive with $\gamma \geq 1$). If $\theta(\cdot)$ is such that well-being vectors with negative entries can arise, define $\theta^*(\cdot)$ as $\theta(\cdot) + t$, with t a sufficiently large positive number that all well-being numbers are positive: For every i, and for every y such that $x_{P,s} = y$ for some state s and some policy P in $\mathbf{P}, \theta^*(a_i(y), R_i(y)) > 0$. Then undertake the exercise that follows in terms of $\theta^*(\cdot)$, i.e., choose γ given $\theta^*(\cdot)$ to fit intuitions about the relative moral impact of attribute changes.

j has history (a^*, R^*). With $\theta(\cdot)$ in hand, the well-being impact of a marginal change Δa^m to i's holdings of a^m is approximately $\frac{\partial\theta}{\partial a^m}(a^*, R^*)\Delta a^m$, while the well-being impact of a marginal change Δa^m to j's holdings of a^m is approximately $\frac{\partial\theta}{\partial a^m}(a^+, R^+)\Delta a^m$. Now using the Atkinson SWF, the moral impact of the first change is $\theta(a^*,R^*)^{-\gamma}\frac{\partial\theta}{\partial a^m}(a^*, R^*)\Delta a^m$, and that of the second is $\theta(a^+,R^+)^{-\gamma}\frac{\partial\theta}{\partial a^m}(a^+, R^+)\Delta a^m$, so that the ratio of marginal moral impacts is: $\left(\frac{\theta(a^+,R^+)}{\theta(a^*,R^*)}\right)^{\gamma}\frac{\frac{\partial\theta}{\partial a^m}(a^*,R^*)}{\frac{\partial\theta}{\partial a^m}(a^+,R^+)} = Z$. We can use our intuitions about the magnitude of this ratio (Z) to solve for γ. $\gamma = [\log Z + \log\frac{\partial\theta}{\partial a^m}(a^+, R^+) - \log\frac{\partial\theta}{\partial a^m}(a^*, R^*)]/[\log\theta(a^+, R^+) - \log\theta(a^*, R^*)]$.

References

Adler, M.D. (2009). "Future generations: A prioritarian view." *George Washington Law Review*, 77: 1478–1520.

(2012). *Well-Being and Fair Distribution: Beyond Cost-Benefit Analysis*. New York: Oxford University Press.

(2015). "Equity by the numbers: Measuring poverty, inequality, and injustice." *Alabama Law Review*, 66: 551–607.

(2018). "Prioritarianism: Room for desert?" *Utilitas*, 30: 172–197.

(2019). *Measuring Social Welfare: An Introduction*. New York: Oxford University Press.

Adler, M.D., and Holtug, N. (2019). "Prioritarianism: A response to critics." *Politics, Philosophy & Economics*, 18: 101–144.

Adler, M.D., and Treich, N. (2015). "Prioritarianism and climate change." *Environmental and Resource Economics*, 62: 279–308.

Arrhenius, G., Bykvist, K., Campbell, T., and Finneron-Burns, E., eds. (forthcoming). *The Oxford Handbook of Population Ethics*. Oxford: Oxford University Press.

Atkinson, A.B. (1970). "On the measurement of inequality." *Journal of Economic Theory*, 2: 244–263.

Blackorby, C., Bossert, W., and Donaldson, D. (2002). "Utilitarianism and the theory of justice." In K.J. Arrow, A.K. Sen and K. Suzumura, eds., *Handbook of Social Choice and Welfare*, vol. 1. Amsterdam: Elsevier, pp. 543–596.

(2005). *Population Issues in Social Choice Theory, Welfare Economics, and Ethics*. Cambridge: Cambridge University Press.

Boadway, R., and Bruce, N. (1984). *Welfare Economics*. Oxford: Basil Blackwell.

Bosmans, K. (2007). "Extreme inequality aversion without separability." *Economic Theory*, 32: 589–594.

Bossert, W., and Weymark, J.A. (2004). "Utility in social choice." In S. Barberà, P.J. Hammond and C. Seidl, eds., *Handbook of Utility Theory*, vol. 2 (*Extensions*). Boston: Kluwer Academic, pp. 1099–1177.

Brandt, R.B. (1979). *A Theory of the Right and the Good*. Oxford: Oxford University Press.

Broome, J. (1991). *Weighing Goods: Equality, Uncertainty, and Time*. Oxford: Basil Blackwell.

(2015). "Equality versus priority: A useful distinction." *Economics and Philosophy*, 31: 219–228.

(2016). "The well-being of future generations." In M.D. Adler and M. Fleurbaey, eds., *The Oxford Handbook of Well-Being and Public Policy*. New York: Oxford University Press, pp. 901–927.

Bykvist, K. (2016). "Preference-based views of well-being." In M.D. Adler and M. Fleurbaey, eds., *The Oxford Handbook of Well-Being and Public Policy*. New York: Oxford University Press, pp. 321–346.

Chakravarty, S.R. (2009). *Inequality, Polarization and Poverty: Advances in Distributional Analysis*. New York: Springer.

Cowell, F.A. (2000). "Measurement of inequality." In A.B. Atkinson and F. Bourguignon, eds., *Handbook of Income Distribution*, vol. 1. Amsterdam: Elsevier, pp. 87–166.

(2016). "Inequality and poverty measures." In M.D. Adler and M. Fleurbaey, eds., *The Oxford Handbook of Well-Being and Public Policy*. New York: Oxford University Press, pp. 82–125.

d'Aspremont, C., and Gevers, L. (2002). "Social welfare functionals and interpersonal comparability." In K.J. Arrow, A.K. Sen and K. Suzumura, eds., *Handbook of Social Choice and Welfare*, vol. 1. Amsterdam: Elsevier, pp. 459–541.

Eggleston, B., and Miller, D.E., eds. (2014). *The Cambridge Companion to Utilitarianism*. Cambridge: Cambridge University Press.

Ferreira, F.H.G., and Peragine, V. (2016). "Individual responsibility and equality of opportunity." In M.D. Adler and M. Fleurbaey, eds., *The Oxford Handbook of Well-Being and Public Policy*. New York: Oxford University Press, pp. 746–784.

Fletcher, G., ed. (2016). *The Routledge Handbook of Philosophy of Well-Being*. Milton Park: Routledge.

Fleurbaey, M. (2010). "Assessing risky social situations." *Journal of Political Economy*, 118: 649–680.

Fleurbaey, M., and Voorhoeve, A. (2013). "Decide as you would with full information! An argument against *ex ante* Pareto." In N. Eyal et al., eds., *Inequalities in Health: Concepts, Measures, and Ethics*. Oxford: Oxford University Press, pp. 113–128.

Gamlund, E., and Solberg, C.T., eds. (2019). *Saving People from the Harm of Death*. New York: Oxford University Press.

Gilboa, I. (2009). *Theory of Decision under Uncertainty*. Cambridge: Cambridge University Press.

Greaves, H. (2017). "Population axiology." *Philosophy Compass*, 12: e12442.

Griffin, J. (1986). *Well-Being: Its Meaning, Measurement, and Moral Importance*. Oxford: Clarendon Press.

Hare, R.M. (1981). *Moral Thinking: Its Levels, Methods, and Point*. Oxford: Clarendon Press.

Harsanyi, J.C. (1953). "Cardinal utility in welfare economics and in the theory of risk-taking." *Journal of Political Economy*, 61: 434–435.

(1955). "Cardinal welfare, individualistic ethics, and interpersonal comparisons of utility." *Journal of Political Economy*, 63: 309–321.

(1977). *Rational Behavior and Bargaining Equilibrium in Games and Social Situations*. Cambridge: Cambridge University Press.

Haybron, D.M. (2016). "Mental state approaches to well-being." In M.D. Adler and M. Fleurbaey, eds., *The Oxford Handbook of Well-Being and Public Policy*. New York: Oxford University Press, pp. 347–378.

Holtug, N. (2010). *Persons, Interests, and Justice*. Oxford: Oxford University Press.

(2017). "Prioritarianism." *Oxford Research Encyclopedia of Politics*, http://dx.doi.org/10.1093/acrefore/9780190228637.013.232.

Hurka, T. (2016). "Objective goods." In M.D. Adler and M. Fleurbaey, eds., *The Oxford Handbook of Well-Being and Public Policy*. New York: Oxford University Press, pp. 379–402.

Johansson-Stenman, O. (2018). "Animal welfare and social decisions: Is it time to take Bentham seriously?" *Ecological Economics*, 145: 90–103.

Joyce, J.M., and Gibbard, A. (1998). "Causal decision theory." In S. Barberà, P.J. Hammond and C. Seidl, eds., *Handbook of Utility Theory*, vol. 1 (*Principles*). Dordrecht: Kluwer Academic, pp. 627–666.

Knight, C. (2009). *Luck Egalitarianism: Equality, Responsibility, and Justice*. Edinburgh: Edinburgh University Press.

Kolm, S. (1969). "The optimal production of social justice." In J. Margolis and H. Guitton, eds., *Public Economics*. London: Macmillan, pp. 145–200.

Lambert, P.J. (2001). *The Distribution and Redistribution of Income*, 3rd ed. Manchester: Manchester University Press.

Lippert-Rasmussen, K. (2016). *Luck Egalitarianism*. London: Bloomsbury Academic.

McKerlie, D. (1984). "Egalitarianism." *Dialogue*, 23: 223–237.

Mongin, P., and d'Aspremont, C. (1998). "Utility theory and ethics." In S. Barberà, P.J. Hammond, and C. Seidl, eds., *Handbook of Utility Theory*, vol. 1 (*Principles*). Dordrecht: Kluwer Academic, pp. 371–481.

Mongin, P., and Pivato, M. (2016). "Social evaluation under risk and uncertainty." In M.D. Adler and M. Fleurbaey, eds., *The Oxford Handbook of Well-Being and Public Policy*. New York: Oxford University Press, pp. 711–745.

Moreno-Ternero, J.D., and Roemer, J.E. (2008). "The veil of ignorance violates priority." *Economics and Philosophy*, 24: 233–257.

Otsuka, M., and Voorhoeve, A. (2018). "Equality versus priority." In S. Olsaretti, ed., *The Oxford Handbook of Distributive Justice*. Oxford: Oxford University Press, pp. 65–85.

Parfit. D. (2000). "Equality or priority?" In M. Clayton and A. Williams, eds., *The Ideal of Equality*. Houndmills: Palgrave, pp. 81–125. Delivered as the Lindley Lecture at the University of Kansas in 1991.

Pollak, R. (1971). "Additive utility functions and linear Engel curves." *Review of Economic Studies*, 38: 401–414.

Rawls, J. (1999). *A Theory of Justice*, rev. ed. Cambridge, MA: Belknap Press of Harvard University Press. First published in 1971.

Salanié, B. (2011). *The Economics of Taxation*, 2nd ed. Cambridge, MA: MIT Press.

Scanlon, T.M. (1998). *What We Owe to Each Other*. Cambridge, MA: Belknap Press of Harvard University Press.

Sen, A. (1973). *On Economic Inequality*. Oxford: Oxford University Press.

Sen, A., and Williams, B., eds. (1982). *Utilitarianism and Beyond*. Cambridge: Cambridge University Press.

Shorrocks, A.F. (1983). "Ranking income distributions." *Economica*, 50: 3–17.

Simon, C.P., and Blume, L. (1994). *Mathematics for Economists*. New York: W.W. Norton & Co.

Singer, P. (2011). *Practical Ethics*. New York: Cambridge University Press, 3rd ed.

Smart, J.J.C., and Williams, B. (1973). *Utilitarianism: For and Against*. Cambridge: Cambridge University Press.

Sumner, L.W. (1996). *Welfare, Happiness, and Ethics*. Oxford: Clarendon Press.

Temkin, L. (1983). *Inequality*. Ph.D. Thesis, Princeton University.

Tuomala, M. (2016). *Optimal Redistributive Taxation*. Oxford: Oxford University Press.

Weirich, P. (1983). "Utility tempered with equality." *Nous*, 17: 423–439.

Weymark, J.A. (2016). "Social welfare functions." In M.D. Adler and M. Fleurbaey, eds., *The Oxford Handbook of Well-Being and Public Policy*. New York: Oxford University Press, pp. 126–159.

3 Well-Being Measurement*

MATTHEW D. ADLER AND KOEN DECANCQ

3.1 Introduction

This chapter discusses the construction of a well-being measure for purposes of the social welfare function (SWF) framework. Together with Chapter 2, it provides a theoretical foundation for the *Prioritarianism in Practice* volume.

As discussed in Chapter 2, the SWF framework includes three major components: a well-being measure $w(\cdot)$, for converting outcomes into vectors (lists) of well-being numbers; the SWF itself, which is a rule for ranking well-being vectors; and an uncertainty module, for ranking policies understood as probability distributions over outcomes. A given outcome x corresponds to the well-being vector $(w_1(x), \ldots, w_N(x))$, with $w_i(x)$ denoting the well-being of individual i in outcome x.

Chapter 2 also discussed the question of well-being comparability. It explored four different types of well-being comparisons: intra- and interpersonal comparisons of well-being levels and differences. The chapter defended all four types of comparisons, both for reasons having to do with the informational requirements of utilitarian and prioritarian SWFs, and as a matter of common sense. The well-being measure should be such as to embody information about all four types of comparisons.[1]

* We thank Erwin Ooghe, Paolo Piacquadio and participants in conferences at the University of Bergen and Duke University for comments and discussion. Decancq gratefully acknowledges support of the Research Foundation – Flanders.

[1] A well-being measure $w(\cdot)$ embodies information about these comparisons as follows. *Intra- and interpersonal comparisons of well-being levels.* $w_i(x) \geq w_j(y)$ iff (if and only if) individual i in outcome x is at least as well off as individual j in outcome y, with x and y identical or distinct. If $i = j$, this is an intrapersonal level comparison. If $i \neq j$, this is an interpersonal level comparison. *Intra- and interpersonal comparisons of well-being differences.* $w_i(x) - w_j(y) \geq w_k(z) - w_l(zz)$ iff the well-being difference between individual i in outcome x and individual j in outcome y is at least as large as the well-being difference between individual k in outcome z and individual l in outcome zz, with x, y, z, zz the same

But how indeed are we to construct a well-being measure that embodies these various kinds of well-being information? That is the topic of this chapter.

We start, in Section 3.2, by introducing the notion of a preference-based well-being measure. Generically, an individual's well-being in an outcome depends upon her "attributes" (income, health, longevity, happiness, etc.) and may also depend upon her preferences. A preference-based well-being measure builds in such dependence on preferences, in a systematic way. The succeeding two sections focus on the two principal approaches to constructing an interpersonally comparable preference-based well-being measure: the equivalence approach (Section 3.3) and the vNM approach (Section 3.4).[2] Section 3.5 addresses two non-preference-based approaches: objective goods and "capabilities", on the one hand, and subjective well-being (SWB), on the other. Although the authors of this chapter favor a preference account of well-being, the SWF framework is not committed to such an account.

A terminological note: The reader will observe that the term "iff" is used with some frequency in the text and notes. This is shorthand for "if and only if."

3.2 Attributes, Preferences, and Well-Being Measures

The SWF framework is meant to be a tractable decision procedure for evaluating governmental policies. In order for this procedure to be tractable, a given outcome x cannot be a complete "possible world"; thinking in detail about whole possible worlds is beyond the cognitive capacity of human decisionmakers. Rather, an outcome is a *model* of a possible world. (See Adler, Chapter 2, Section 2.2, this volume).

outcome or partly or wholly distinct. If $i = j = k = l$, this is an intrapersonal difference comparison. If not $i = j = k = l$, this is an interpersonal difference comparison. See Adler, Chapter 2, Sections 2.2, 2.5, this volume.

2 A vast amount of work in economics is devoted to the theory and estimation of individual utility functions – a utility function being a representation of individual preferences. However, most writing about utility functions is either skeptical about interpersonal comparability or simply does not address the issue. What is distinctive about the scholarship that we label the "equivalence approach" and "vNM approach" is its ambition both to make interpersonal comparisons and to respect preferences. The literatures covered in Sections 3.3 and 3.4 are – as far as we're aware – the most systematic attempts to do both.

In particular, the *welfarist* decisionmaker—who believes that ethical evaluation depends upon individual well-being—conceptualizes an outcome as a series of attribute bundles for each member of the population of ethical concern. A given outcome x assigns to each individual i an attribute bundle. Let $a_i(x)$ be the attribute bundle of a particular individual i in outcome x. To avoid notational clutter we drop the explicit reference to the outcome or the individual when that is convenient and use a as our generic symbol for an attribute bundle. The set of all attribute bundles under consideration is denoted **A**.[3]

The types of individual attributes described by an attribute bundle are *some* (not necessarily all) of the characteristics of an individual that determine her well-being, such as her income or consumption; her leisure; her health; and/or the level of various public goods that she and others experience (e.g., environmental quality). This list is not exhaustive and other characteristics can be added to the list. Nor is it mandatory to include all these characteristics. Indeed, in most applied work only some of these standard attributes are included. For example, the optimal tax tradition in SWF scholarship often assumes that an individual's attribute bundle consists of her consumption and her leisure and does not describe her health, the quality of her environment, or other characteristics (see Tuomala and Weinzierl, Chapter 4, this volume). How fully to describe attribute bundles is a matter of balancing the accuracy gains of more complicated bundles against the tractability costs. The literature, to date, lacks a rigorous account of how to undertake this balancing, and we will not attempt to tackle the problem here. Rather, we direct our attention to an orthogonal problem, namely how to construct a well-being measure for any characterization of individual attributes.

In principle, the well-being numbers inputted into an SWF are *lifetime numbers*. (See Adler, Chapter 2, Section 2.2, this volume.) Outcome x corresponds to the vector $(w_1(x), \ldots, w_N(x))$, with $w_i(x)$ indicating the lifetime well-being of individual i in outcome x. Note that if well-being numbers were meant instead to measure an individual's "sublifetime well-being" – her well-being during a portion of her life, e.g., a year – then the vector corresponding to each outcome would consist of a series of numbers for each individual i, rather than a single number $w_i(x)$.

[3] **A** should include, at least, every bundle which is possessed by some individual i in some outcome x in the set **O** of outcomes that is being used in the analysis (Adler, Chapter 2, Section 2.2, this volume.) It may include additional bundles. Our analysis in this chapter doesn't depend on which bundles are included in **A**.

Some policy-analysis scholarship employs multi-period models; an individual is described as living for one or more periods, and as having characteristics that can vary from period to period. An explicitly multi-period representation of individual lives is often adopted, for example, in public health scholarship. (See Cookson, Norheim and Skarda, Chapter 6, this volume. See also Hammitt and Treich, Chapter 7, this volume.) Individuals are seen as endowed with a lifespan and with a health state for each year alive. Much of the economics literature, however, employs simple, one-period models. Each individual has some single cluster of characteristics during the one period. In effect, the one-period framework ignores both interpersonal heterogeneity in lifespan and variation over time in a given person's attributes. This one-period setup is quite unrealistic, to be sure – individuals in reality *do* die at different ages and *do* experience intertemporal change in their characteristics – but may be substantially more tractable than the multi-period approach.

What follows is agnostic as between single-period and multi-period models. If the one-period representation is used, then each bundle a describes a combination of attributes during the single period. If the modeler instead follows the multi-period route, then each bundle a is a series of period bundles; it describes the individual's lifespan (the number of periods she exists) and, for each period, her attributes at that time.

On a preference view of well-being, an individual's well-being in outcome x depends on her attribute bundle, plus her preferences. We denote the preference of individual i in outcome x as $R_i(x)$.[4] Again, we drop the explicit reference to the outcome or individual when that is convenient. Moreover, it will be useful for the rest of this chapter to introduce a clear symbolism that allows us to make a distinction between *ordinal* preferences and *lottery* preferences. Ordinal preferences play a central role in the "equivalence approach" (Section 3.3), while lottery preferences are central to the "vNM approach" (Section 3.4).

We use R with a single bar on top to denote an ordinal preference: $\bar{R}$. A given ordinal preference $\bar{R}$ is a ranking of the set **A** of attribute bundles. When we write $a \; \bar{R} \; a^*$, this should be read as: attribute bundle

[4] Note that we are assuming that an individual's preferences remain the same over her lifetime. In a multi-period model, this assumption is genuinely restrictive. See Fleurbaey and Tadenuma (2014) and Adler (2020) discussing how, respectively, the equivalence approach and vNM approach might be generalized to allow for variation in preferences over time. Space limitations prevent our discussing this here.

a is weakly preferred to a^* according to the ordinal preference $\bar{R}$. The set of all ordinal preferences under consideration is denoted $\bar{\mathbf{R}}$.[5] We use R with a double bar on top to denote a lottery preference: $\bar{\bar{R}}$. A given lottery preference $\bar{\bar{R}}$ is a ranking of the lottery set $\mathbf{L}^{\mathbf{A}}$, i.e., the set of all (finite) lotteries over $\mathbf{A}$. The set of all lottery preferences under consideration is denoted $\bar{\bar{\mathbf{R}}}$. $a\,\bar{\bar{R}}\,a^*$ means that the lottery preference $\bar{\bar{R}}$ weakly prefers bundle a to bundle a^*.[6]

The generic symbol R (without bar) will be used as an umbrella term to refer both to an ordinal preference $\bar{R}$ and to a lottery preference $\bar{\bar{R}}$. Having the generic symbol R at hand will make it easier to express what the equivalence and vNM approaches have in common.

The history $h_i(x)$ of individual i in outcome x is a combination of her attribute bundle $a_i(x)$ and her preference $R_i(x)$, so that $h_i(x) = (a_i(x), R_i(x))$. Also here we drop the explicit reference to the outcome or individual in the symbol when that is convenient. We write $h = (a, R)$ to indicate that a history consists of an attribute bundle and a preference. The project of well-being measurement can be seen as assigning well-being numbers to histories: $w(\cdot) = w(a, R)$, with R either an ordinal preference $\bar{R}$ (in the equivalence approach) or a lottery preference $\bar{\bar{R}}$ (in the vNM approach).[7]

5 "Under consideration," here, has an analogous meaning as for the set $\mathbf{A}$ of attributes bundles (see note 3). $\bar{\mathbf{R}}$ should include every preference $\bar{R}$ possessed by some individual i in some outcome x in the set $\mathbf{O}$ of outcomes, and may include additional preferences. "Under consideration" with respect to the set $\bar{\bar{\mathbf{R}}}$ of lottery preferences, as stated in the text immediately below, is defined similarly.

6 More precisely: $\bar{R}$ is a transitive, reflexive, and complete binary relation (an ordering) on $\mathbf{A}$. From the weak preference $\bar{R}$ we can derive strict preference $\bar{P}$ and indifference $\bar{I}$ in the standard manner. $a\bar{P}a^*$ iff $a\bar{R}a^*$ and not $a^*\bar{R}a$. $a\bar{I}a^*$ iff $a\bar{R}a^*$ and $a^*\bar{R}a$.

A finite lottery l in $\mathbf{L}^{\mathbf{A}}$ assigns a probability number $\pi_l(a)$ to each attribute bundle in $\mathbf{A}$ such that: $0 \leq \pi_l(a) \leq 1, \pi_l(a) > 0$ for only a finite number of a, and $\sum_{a \in \mathbf{A}} \pi_l(a) = 1$. A lottery preference $\bar{\bar{R}}$ is an ordering of $\mathbf{L}^{\mathbf{A}}$.

Note that each attribute bundle a corresponds to a "degenerate" lottery: the lottery that assigns probability 1 to that bundle, and 0 to every other bundle. Thus, a lottery preference $\bar{\bar{R}}$, in its ranking of the lottery set $\mathbf{L}^{\mathbf{A}}$, includes a ranking of the attribute set $\mathbf{A}$ itself. We require a lottery preference only to rank finite rather than infinite lotteries because the apparatus of vNM utility theory, and thus the vNM approach to well-being measurement, can be formulated without the additional complexity of infinite lotteries. See Adler (2016, p. 482, n. 11).

7 Let $(a_i(x), \bar{R}_i(x))$ denote the history (according to the equivalence approach) of individual i in outcome x. The equivalence approach then sets $w_i(x)$ equal to the well-being number of $(a_i(x), \bar{R}_i(x))$. Abusing symbolism slightly:

At this juncture, it's important to concede that not all preference relations are equally appealing for a preference-based well-being analysis. Consider, for instance, Ann, who has whimsical preferences that are internally inconsistent, or Bob, whose preferences are formed based on fake news and other forms of misinformation. Preferences can therefore be "laundered" first, so that the resulting laundered preference relations tell us how individuals would rank attribute bundles were they sufficiently well-informed and satisfied stipulated rationality criteria. The laundering may even go further and correct some preferences that are considered ethically unappealing, such as sadistic preferences. To be sure, the precise nature of this laundering is itself a topic for normative discussion (see, e.g., Goodin, 1986). Laundered preferences may differ from the preferences which are revealed by actual behavior (see Gul and Pesendorfer, 2008 for a discussion).

In any event, the preferences that we will be discussing in this chapter have been laundered according to whichever criteria of rationality, good information, and ethical acceptability are endorsed as singling out *well-being relevant* preferences.[8] We don't take a position here about the specifics of laundering, beyond assuming that preferences satisfy certain basic formal rationality criteria.[9]

We can now bring to the fore two major similarities between the equivalence and vNM approaches. First, as already stated in the introduction to this chapter, both accept interpersonal comparability.

$w_i(x) = w(a_i(x), \bar{R}_i(x))$. Strictly speaking $w(\cdot)$, which assigns well-being numbers to individuals in outcomes, is a different function from one that assigns well-being numbers to histories. We should use a different symbol for the latter function, e.g., $\theta(\cdot)$, and say that: $w_i(x) = \theta(a_i(x), \bar{R}_i(x))$. See Adler, Chapter 2, Section 2.A.3, this volume. However, so as to avoid multiplying symbols, we'll use $w(\cdot)$ to mean both types of function. For most of this chapter, $w(\cdot)$ is used in the sense $w(a, R)$, so there isn't much risk of confusion.

Let $(a_i(x), \bar{\bar{R}}_i(x))$ denote the history (according to the vNM approach) of individual i in outcome x. The vNM approach then sets $w_i(x)$ equal to the well-being number of $(a_i(x), \bar{\bar{R}}_i(x))$. Again abusing symbolism slightly: $w_i(x) = w(a_i(x), \bar{\bar{R}}_i(x))$.

8 $\bar{R}$ is a *laundered* ordinal preference, and $\bar{\mathbf{R}}$ the set of all laundered ordinal preferences under consideration. $\bar{\bar{R}}$ is a *laundered* lottery preference, and $\bar{\bar{\mathbf{R}}}$ the set of all laundered lottery preferences under consideration.

9 See note 6. See, however, Fleurbaey and Schokkaert (2013) and Decancq and Nys (2021) on the equivalence approach when individuals have incomplete preferences.

Specifically, both endorse some version of the Same History Principle.[10]

Same History Principle: For any two individuals i and j, and any two outcomes x and y, if the history of i in x is (a, R) and the history of j in y is (a, R), then i in x is equally well off as j in y.

If two individuals have the same history – the same attributes and the same preferences – then they are equally well off. The Same History Principle seems compelling and makes rigorous the common-sense case for interpersonal comparability (see Adler, Chapter 2, Section 2.5, this volume). If two individuals, Isaac and Jules, are identical with respect to everything that determines well-being – they have the same attribute bundle *and* the same preferences – then surely their well-being levels are identical.

The direct upshot of the Same History Principle is to allow for interpersonal comparisons of well-being *levels*. But it also implies that differentiating between intra- and interpersonal comparisons of well-being *differences* is arbitrary. *If* intrapersonal comparisons of differences are meaningful then so, too, must be interpersonal difference comparisons.[11]

Second, both the equivalence and vNM approaches yield *preference-based* well-being measures, in a precise sense. A well-being measure $w(\cdot)$ is *preference-based* if it conforms to the following Deference Principle (namely, deference to preferences):

Deference Principle: For all attribute bundles a and a^* and all preferences R, $w(a, R) \geq w(a^*, R)$ iff $a \; R \; a^*$.

[10] The equivalence approach endorses the ordinal-preference version of the Same History Principle, namely: if two individuals have the same attributes and the same ordinal preferences, then they are equally well off. The vNM approach rejects this version of the Same History Principle, for reasons to be explored in Section 3.4.2, but endorses the lottery-preference version: if two individuals have the same attributes and the same lottery preferences, then they are equally well off.

[11] Assume that we endorse *intrapersonal* difference comparisons. We are willing to say, concerning one individual (Stacey), that the difference in Stacey's well-being between outcomes x and y is greater than the difference in Stacey's well-being between outcomes z and zz. Now imagine that a second individual, Thom, has the same history in outcome z^* as Stacey does in z, and the same history in zz^* as Stacey does in zz. Then, by the Same History Principle, we should accept that the difference in Stacey's well-being between x and y is greater than the difference in Thom's well-being between z^* and zz^* – an *interpersonal* difference comparison.

The Deference Principle states that well-being is higher in a preferred attribute bundle. The equivalence and vNM approaches both satisfy the Deference Principle. Whether to adopt the Deference Principle is a normative question. While the underlying idea of sovereignty is a central tenet of economics, the linkage between preferences and well-being is a contested topic in the philosophical literature on well-being (see Section 3.5). In our view, the case for the principle rests upon individual autonomy.

Consider, first, the *intrapersonal* case in which we are determining what the well-being of a given individual (Philippe) would be with two histories. That is to say: we are comparing Philippe having attribute bundle a to Philippe having attribute bundle a^*, on the supposition that Philippe's preferences are R. The attribute bundle a^* may be obtained from a as the result of a policy intervention, for instance. If Philippe weakly prefers the initial attribute bundle, $a \, R \, a^*$, but the social planner assigns a higher well-being score to the post-intervention history, $w(a, R) < w(a^*, R)$, the social planner is substituting her own judgment for Philippe's about what makes his life go well.

Turn now to the *interpersonal* case where (a, R) is being considered as a possible history for one person, and (a^*, R) as a possible history for a second, distinct, person. We are comparing, for example, the well-being of Philippe with (a, R) to the well-being of Stacey with (a^*, R). Note that, while the attribute bundles of Philippe and Stacey differ, they have the same preferences.[12] If $a \, R \, a^*$, but $w(a, R) < w(a^*, R)$, the social planner goes against the shared view of Philippe and Stacey that Philippe with attribute bundle a is at least as well off as Stacey with attribute bundle a^*. We believe that in both examples the social planner would violate the autonomy of the concerned individuals.

3.3 The Equivalence Approach

In this section, we discuss the equivalence approach to constructing a well-being measure in line with the Deference Principle.[13] Recall that,

[12] Decancq et al. (2015a) refer to the Deference Principle in interpersonal comparisons as the Same Preference Principle.

[13] An excellent introduction to the equivalence approach can be found in Fleurbaey and Blanchet (2013, chapter 4). A more technical discussion can be found in

for the equivalence approach, an individual's well-being depends upon her attributes and her ordinal preference. A history $h = (a, \bar{R})$ is a combination of an attribute bundle and an ordinal preference $\bar{R}$. A well-being measure $w(\cdot)$ is a function that assigns a numerical value to each history, which can be used as input to an SWF.

An ordinal preference relation is an *indifference map*. The equivalence approach is built on the idea that this indifference map can be used to identify histories that are equally good from a well-being perspective. More precisely, attribute bundles situated on indifference curves that coincide (even if the curves belong to distinct preference orderings) are considered as equally good according to the equivalence approach. The history $(a, \bar{R})$ is equally good as $(a^*, \bar{R}^*)$ if $\bar{R}$ and $\bar{R}^*$ share an identical indifference curve and a and a^* are on it. Consequently, one can say that well-being measures of the equivalence approach assign a numerical value to indifference curves.[14] The various well-being measures that belong to the equivalence approach disagree, however, on how to assign a numerical value to histories which are situated on non-coinciding indifference curves.

Two important families of well-being measures can be discerned within the equivalence approach, each with their roots in the theory of fair allocation (see Fleurbaey and Maniquet, 2011). In the first family, a collection of *reference sets* is used to assign a numerical value to each indifference curve. A prominent member of this family is the money metric well-being measure. In the second family, each indifference curve is labelled by its intersection with a *monotone path*. A prominent member of the second family is the ray utility well-being measure.[15] First, we discuss these families and then turn to the use of the so-called *equivalent-income* measure of well-being. Interestingly, the equivalent-income measure can be interpreted as a member of both families. We conclude with a clarification regarding difference

Fleurbaey and Maniquet (2011); and older, but still very relevant, sources are by Deaton (1980) and Deaton and Muellbauer (1980).

14 Hence, all preference information that is not contained in the shape of the indifference curves is ignored, such as risk aversion (see Adler, 2016; Section 3.4, this chapter) or other information about the intensity of preferences (see Sen 1979, p. 11).

15 In a series of recent papers, Fleurbaey and Maniquet (2017, 2018, 2019) have compared the axiomatic properties of the money metric and ray utility well-being measures.

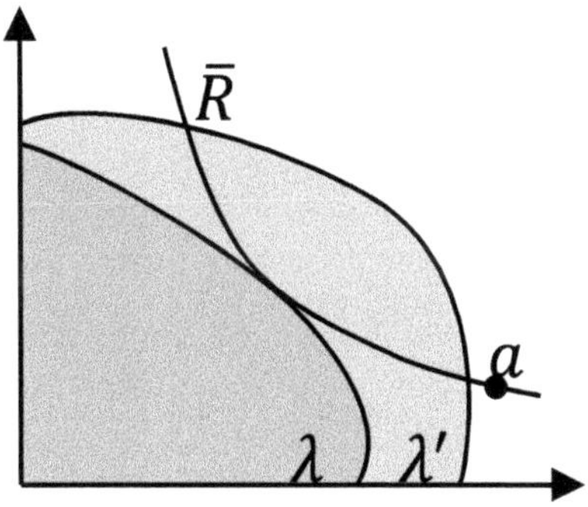

Figure 3.1 Two nested reference sets and a history

comparisons. Except where explicitly stated, we simplify our presentation of the equivalence approach by assuming that preferences are monotonic.[16]

3.3.1 Measuring Well-being with a Collection of Reference Sets

In the first family of well-being measures, a collection of nested reference sets $B = (B_\lambda)_{\lambda \in \mathbb{R}^+}$ is used to assign a numerical value to each indifference curve that can be used as input in an SWF. Each member of the collection of reference sets is indexed by a real number λ in such a way that larger reference sets get larger numbers, so that $\lambda \leq \lambda'$ iff $B_\lambda \subseteq B_{\lambda'}$. Figure 3.1 provides an example where two reference sets are depicted in a two-attribute space. The reference sets are nested and indexed so that $\lambda < \lambda'$.

Well-being measures of this family assign the index of the reference set to the history to which it is *equivalent*. A reference set B_λ is said to be equivalent to a history $(a, \bar{R})$ when the individual at hand is indifferent (with her preferences $\bar{R}$) between her bundle of attributes a and being able to choose freely from the reference set B_λ. In the example of Figure 3.1, the individual is indifferent between her attribute bundle a and being able to choose freely from the reference set indexed by λ. Once each history is assigned a reference set from the collection of reference sets, they can be compared using the indices of the equivalent

[16] That is: each ordinal preference $\bar{R}$ in $\bar{\mathbf{R}}$ is such that, if attribute bundle a has a higher level than a^* of at least one type of attribute, and no lower level of any, then $a \, \bar{P} \, a^*$.

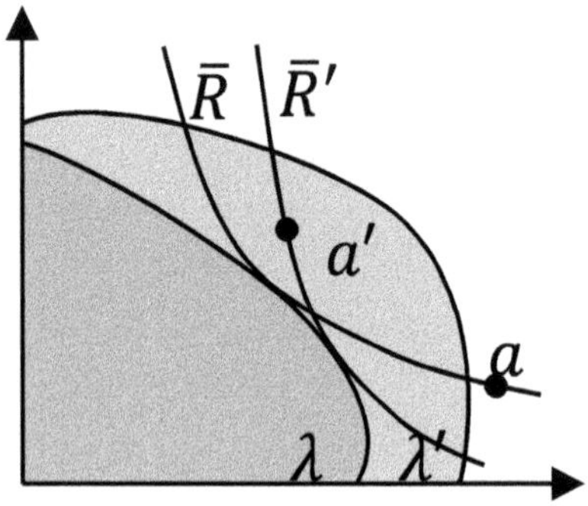

Figure 3.2 Two histories that are equivalent to the same reference set

reference sets.[17] This captures the intuition that choosing freely from a larger reference set cannot be worse than being able to choose from a smaller reference set. Note furthermore that larger well-being numbers are attached to histories which are situated on higher indifference curves. Hence, we have that $w(a', \bar{R}) \geq w(a, \bar{R})$ iff $a' \bar{R} a$. This observation illustrates that the Deference Principle is indeed satisfied.[18]

The same well-being level is given to all histories that are equivalent to the same reference set, as illustrated in Figure 3.2. Both individuals are indifferent between their own attribute bundle and choosing freely from the same set B_λ. Even though they have very different attribute bundles and different preferences, the well-being level of both histories is said to be the same because both histories are considered equally good as being able to choose freely from the same reference set. The question which histories are equally good from a well-being perspective is particularly relevant when the well-being measures are used as arguments of a prioritarian SWF. As discussed in Chapter 2, prioritarian SWFs are averse to well-being inequality, and the choice of the well-being measure determines what the ideal of equality precisely

[17] We assume that the collection of reference sets is such that: for each indifference curve there is one and only one equivalent reference set.

[18] The analytic argument for why the Deference Principle is satisfied runs as follows. We assume (see note 17) that for any two attribute bundles a and a^*, there is a single reference set B_λ to which a is equivalent according to $\bar{R}$, and a single reference set B_{λ^*} to which a^* is equivalent according to $\bar{R}$. If $a \bar{I} a^*$, then it must be the case that $B_\lambda = B_{\lambda^*}$, hence $\lambda = \lambda^*$. If $a \bar{P} a^*$, then it can't be the case that $B_\lambda = B_{\lambda^*}$; nor can it be the case that B_λ is a proper subset of B_{λ^*}; hence B_{λ^*} is a proper subset of B_λ and thus $\lambda > \lambda^*$.

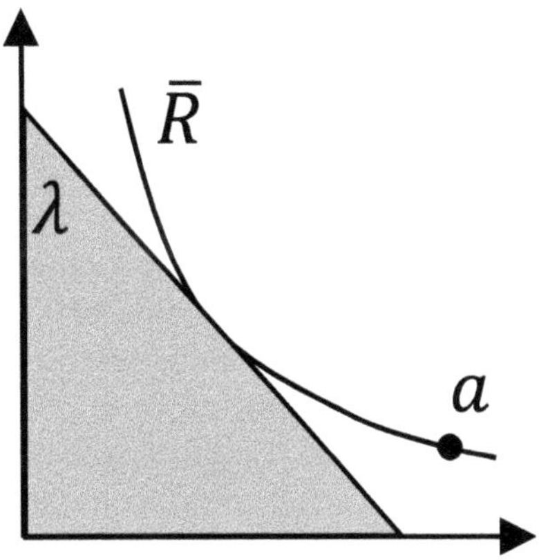

Figure 3.3 The money metric well-being measure

entails. When using a well-being measure based on a reference set, the goal is to offer all individuals the same equivalent reference set to choose from. In this sense, the equivalence approach connects the measurement of well-being to an evaluation of opportunity sets. This idea was evoked by Deaton and Muellbauer (1980, chapter 1) and received renewed attention in the capability approach (Sen, 1985).

The choice of the collection of reference sets, and the way in which they are indexed, matters for the precise well-being levels that are attached to the histories. This choice is a normative one, which should ideally be guided by an ethical theory.[19] In the general case, however, it may seem hard to come up with a natural and intuitive way of indexing the reference sets. Specific cases are arguably easier.

One specific case is the so-called *money metric* well-being measure.[20] Consider a collection of reference sets that are defined as follows: $B_\lambda = \left\{a | \sum a_j \times p_j^* \leq \lambda\right\}$, where $p^* = \left(p_1^*, \ldots, p_j^*, \ldots, p_k^*\right)$ is a positive reference price vector. These reference sets are reminiscent of standard budget constraints, which contain all (attribute) bundles that can be afforded with an income λ, at prices p^*. In a two-dimensional setting, the reference sets are right-angled triangles with their right angle in the origin, see Figure 3.3. For a given reference price vector,

19 See Fleurbaey and Blanchet (2013, p. 141) for some suggestions regarding how such an ethical theory may be developed.

20 Money metrics were introduced by McKenzie (1957) and Samuelson (1974) as a tool to number indifference curves.

the reference sets are indeed nested, as more attribute bundles can be afforded with a higher income level.

When a money metric measure of well-being is used, well-being is evaluated by looking at the minimal income that is necessary to afford an attribute bundle that is at least as good (according to preferences $\bar{R}$) as the attribute bundle a, given reference prices p^*. Multiplying all reference prices with a constant does not change the shape of the reference sets, but multiplies the well-being measure with the constant. Using a scale invariant SWF to aggregate the well-being measure (e.g., an Atkinson SWF; see Adler, Chapter 2, Section 2.9, this volume) introduces a convenient independence of the social evaluation with respect to the constant.

The use of money metrics has been criticized for its dependence on the choice of the reference prices p^* (see, for instance, Roberts 1980). But the choice of reference prices need not be arbitrary and should ideally be part of a full-fledged ethical theory of social welfare. When the attributes are all market goods and the reference prices are chosen equal to the market prices, the money metric well-being measure coincides with ordinary income and, hence, social states will be evaluated with an SWF defined over ordinary incomes. When a lower price is chosen than the market price for a specific attribute, the well-being level of individuals who have a lot of this attribute in their bundle is lowered. However, when using money metrics in a context where the attributes are not available on the market (such as health, political freedom, or social interactions), market prices do not exist to provide a benchmark.

A second critique against the use of money metric well-being measures has been formulated by Blackorby and Donaldson (1988). They observe that a standard *quasi-concave* SWF (e.g., a prioritarian SWF) combined with money metric well-being measures may fail to approve transfers from richer to poorer individuals. Only an SWF that gives absolute priority to the worst-off approves all richer-to-poorer transfers.

It should be stressed that the prioritarian SWF conforms to the Pigou-Dalton axiom in terms of well-being (see Adler, Chapter 2, Section 2.3, this volume). A pure, gap-diminishing transfer of well-being from someone better off, to someone worse off, will be approved by the prioritarian SWF. If $w(\cdot)$ is constructed using the money metric approach, then the prioritarian SWF will approve pure, gap-diminishing transfers of money metric well-being from those at higher levels of money metric well-being, to those at lower levels. The

Blackorby and Donaldson critique concerns the Pigou-Dalton axiom *in the space of attributes*. A quasi-concave (e.g., prioritarian) SWF defined over money metric well-being will fail to approve some *attribute* transfers from richer to poorer individuals.

This observation has led to several different responses in the literature. First, Blackorby and Donaldson (1988, p. 129) themselves conclude that a social welfare analysis based on money metric well-being measures is flawed. Their conclusion struck a heavy blow against the use of money metric well-being measures in (applied) social welfare analysis. Fleurbaey and Maniquet (2011, p. 21), by contrast, conclude that this observation justifies the leximin (or maximin) SWF, rather than undermining the use of money metric measures as arguments in a social welfare analysis. Recently, Bosmans et al. (2018) have revisited the observation by Blackorby and Donaldson (1988) and question the premise that the approval of richer-to-poorer transfers is an essential requirement for an SWF in a multi-attribute setting. While such transfers clearly lead to a more equitable situation, their price in terms of efficiency may be large. Indeed, a richer-to-poorer transfer in a multi-attribute setting may transfer attributes from a rich person who values the attributes greatly to a poor person who does not value these attributes. Only SWFs that give an absolute priority to equity considerations over efficiency concerns (such as leximin or maximin) consider all such transfers desirable.

3.3.2 Measuring Well-being with a Monotone Path

We turn now to the second family of well-being measures that belong to the equivalence approach.[21] In this family, a so-called *monotone path* is used to assign a numerical value to each indifference curve. A monotone path is a set of attribute bundles such that, for any two bundles on the path, one of the two "vector-dominates" the other – meaning that one of the two bundles has at least as much of each type of attribute as the other bundle, and strictly more of at least one type of attribute.[22] Let the

[21] Formally, this second family can be seen as a special case of the first. (Consider a collection of reference sets which each consist of the bundle on the monotone path plus all the attribute bundles which are vector-dominated by that bundle.) Yet, we believe that it is pedagogical to treat it as a separate family.

[22] We assume that each indifference curve intersects once and only once with the monotone path.

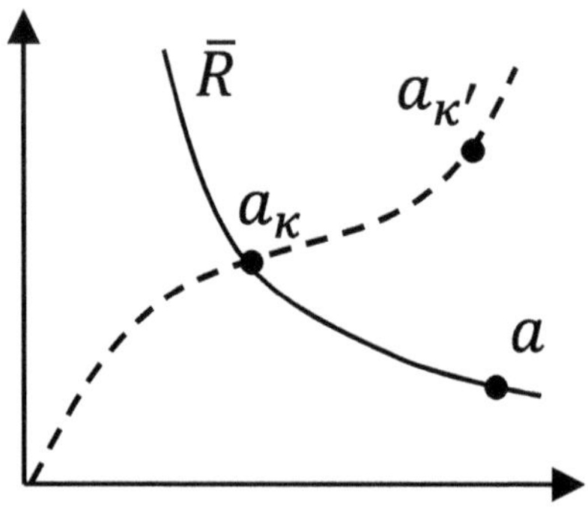

Figure 3.4 A monotone path and a history

attribute bundles on the monotone path be indexed by a real number κ in such a way that vector-dominating attribute bundles get a larger number; that is, $\kappa' > \kappa$ iff $a_{\kappa'}$ vector dominates a_κ in the sense just stated; see Figure 3.4 for an illustration. Attribute bundles on the monotone path can be ranked by the index κ, irrespective of the preferences of the concerned individuals. That means that attribute bundles on the monotone path that have more in some attributes and no less in any are better from the perspective of well-being.[23]

Each history $(a, \bar{R})$ can be assigned an equivalent attribute bundle on the monotone path, which is situated where the indifference curve of preference $\bar{R}$ through a and the monotone path cross. The index of the equivalent attribute bundle can then be used to quantify the well-being of all histories that are situated on the indifference curve. Once each history is assigned an index, comparing them in terms of well-being is straightforward. The indices can also be used as arguments of an SWF. Furthermore, we see that larger indices are attached to histories which are situated on higher indifference curves, so that the Deference Principle is satisfied.[24]

[23] Fleurbaey and Trannoy (2003) prove that ranking attribute bundles with vector dominance is in general incompatible with the idea of respecting preferences. Restricting vector dominance to a monotone path, on the other hand, is compatible with respect for preferences, as shown by Decancq et al. (2015b).

[24] The Deference Principle follows immediately from the definition of monotone path plus the assumption of monotonic preferences. If $\bar{R}$ is monotonic, then – as between any two bundles on the monotone path – it must strictly prefer the one that vector-dominates the other and is assigned a larger index number.

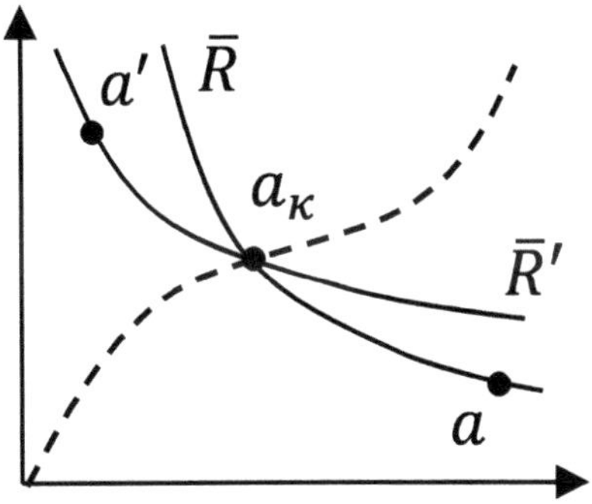

Figure 3.5 Two histories that are equivalent to the same attribute bundle on the monotone path

Well-being measures of this family assign the same well-being level to all histories that are equivalent to the same attribute bundle on the monotone path, as illustrated in Figure 3.5. Both individuals in the figure are indifferent between their own attribute bundle and the attribute bundle a_κ that is situated on the monotone path. By comparing Figure 3.2 and 3.5, it is clear that the underlying logic to identifying the histories which are equally good from a well-being perspective differs between the two families of the equivalence approach. Hence, also the ideal of well-being equality differs. While for the first family the ideal of equality is to offer all individuals the same equivalent reference set to choose from, the ideal for the second family is that the actual attribute bundles are equivalent to the same bundle on the monotone path.

Analogous to the first family, the choice of the monotone path and the way in which the attribute bundles on the monotone path are indexed is a normative one, with important consequences for the precise well-being numbers that are attached to the histories.

The so-called *ray utilities* (or quantity metrics according to Deaton and Muellbauer, 1980, pp. 179–182) are prominent examples of well-being measures that use a monotone path to assign a numerical value to indifference curves.[25] In this case, the monotone path is a straight line or ray that connects the origin with a reference bundle r, and the

[25] Ray utilities were introduced by Samuelson (1977), Pazner, and Schmeidler (1978), and Deaton (1979). See Fleurbaey and Tadenuma (2014) for a recent discussion.

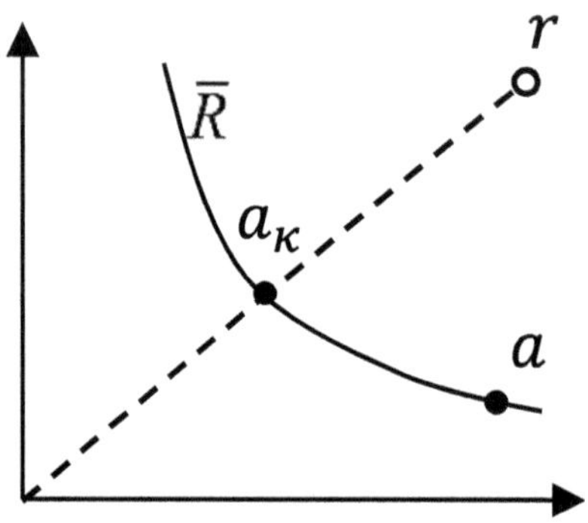

Figure 3.6 The ray utility well-being measure

index κ is the ratio of the distance from the origin to a_κ to the distance to r. In other words, the well-being of history $(a, \bar{R})$ is measured by the proportional share of the reference bundle r that is considered equally good (according to preferences $\bar{R}$) as the attribute bundle a. In the illustration of Figure 3.6, the history $(a, \bar{R})$ obtains a ray utility well-being number of 0.5 since the equivalent attribute bundle a_κ is situated halfway on the ray through the reference bundle r.

How to choose the reference bundle is a normative question. Ray utilities can be criticized along the same lines as the money metrics and a similar challenge arises to develop a full-fledged ethical theory of the choice of the reference bundle. The specific context may determine the appeal of the choice of a specific reference bundle. The reference bundle can consist of the total amount of resources available in the society for each attribute, for instance (Pazner and Schmeidler, 1978). In the context of multidimensional poverty measurement, Decancq et al. (2019) propose to select the bundle that contains the poverty threshold in each attribute as the reference bundle.

Once each history is assigned an equivalent attribute bundle on the ray, evaluating the social welfare of the social outcome becomes a one-dimensional problem (along the ray). Note that shifting the reference bundle r itself along the ray leads to a rescaling of all well-being numbers by a multiplicative constant. When a scale invariant SWF is used to aggregate the well-being numbers in a second stage (e.g., an Atkinson SWF; see Adler, Chapter 2, Section 2.9, this volume), the precise position of the reference bundle along the ray becomes irrelevant, so that only the direction of the ray matters.

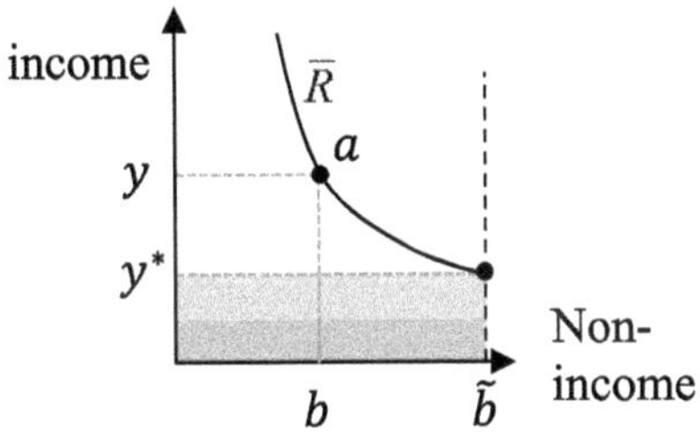

Figure 3.7 The equivalent-income well-being measure

3.3.3 Measuring Well-being with Equivalent Incomes

In this subsection we discuss the equivalent-income well-being measure, which has received some recent attention in theoretical and empirical work.[26] To introduce the equivalent-income well-being measure, let us write the attribute bundle $a = (y, b)$ in which y denotes income and b a vector of non-income dimensions. For the non-income attributes we select a reference value (denoted $\tilde{b}$), for instance the situation in which the individual suffers no health problems, obtains the desired level of social interactions, etc. The equivalent income y^* is the income level that, combined with the reference value on the non-income attributes, would place the individual in a situation that she finds equally good as her actual situation. More precisely, the equivalent income y^* is defined by

$$(y, b)\, \bar{I}\, (y^*, \tilde{b})$$

where $\bar{I}$ denotes indifference (according to ordinal preferences $\bar{R}$).

Figure 3.7 illustrates the case in which there is one non-income dimension, specifically health. The individual is indifferent between the current attribute bundle $a = (y, b)$ and a hypothetical bundle $(y^*, \tilde{b})$. She considers having the equivalent-income level and being in the reference health situation equally good as her current situation with more income and a worse health. We call the difference between the current income level y and the equivalent-income level y^*, the *willingness-to-pay* to be in the reference situation.

[26] See Fleurbaey and Schokkaert (2013), Decancq et al. (2015a, b), Decancq and Schokkaert (2016), or Fleurbaey (2016) for recent discussions of the equivalent-income well-being measure.

The equivalent-income well-being measure can be interpreted as a member of both families that belong to the equivalence approach. Equivalent incomes result from a specific choice of reference sets as well as a specific choice of the monotone path. Figure 3.7 illustrates two rectangular reference sets $B_\lambda = \{(y,b)|y \leq \lambda, b \leq \tilde{b}\}$, for which the index λ coincides with the equivalent income measure y^*. Alternatively, the dashed line formed by all attribute bundles with non-income dimension equal to $\tilde{b}$ is a monotone path. By indexing the attribute bundles on this monotone path with their income level, the resulting well-being measure coincides with the equivalent-income measure.

How to choose the reference value $\tilde{b}$? Similar to other examples of the equivalence approach, selecting the reference value is a normative choice. Observe that two histories on the monotone path can be ranked based on their income level, *irrespective of the preferences*. In the case when the attributes are income and health, Fleurbaey and Schokkaert (2013) argue that "perfect health" (i.e., a situation without health problems) constitutes an appealing reference value. The argument is that in the hypothetical situation where nobody suffers from health problems, well-being comparisons can be made based on income, without taking preferences or the willingness-to-pay for health improvements into account. Yet, as soon as some people suffer from health problems, their willingness-to-pay for health improvements matters to evaluate the severity of their health problems. Preferences about the importance of health matter when comparing situations with poor health, but not when health is perfect.

Reference values need not be the same for all individuals. Fleurbaey and Blanchet (2013, p. 149) and Decancq et al. (2015a) propose to use individualized reference values. These reference values can be chosen as the best value of the non-income attribute for each individual, for instance. They may prefer a certain amount of leisure time, for instance. Deviations from this best value are considered as worse by the individual; see Figure 3.8 for an illustration.[27]

Conveniently, equivalent income is measured in monetary units (in the same units as the income dimension). This has the advantage that the values can be easily interpreted. Yet, the monetary measurement

[27] In Figure 3.8, the preferences are not monotonic. We assume merely that each indifference curve intersects once with the monotone path (the vertical line at $\tilde{b}$) and that more income is always preferred to less. If so, the Deference Principle is satisfied.

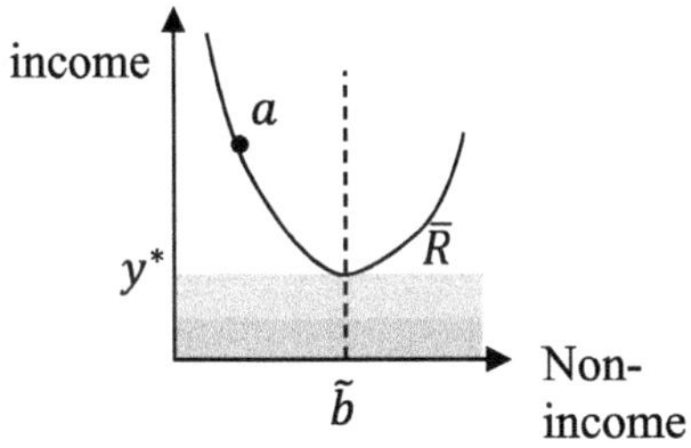

Figure 3.8 Equivalent incomes when preferences are not monotonic

unit of equivalent income should not be interpreted as a reductionist attempt to neglect the importance of the non-income attributes. On the contrary, when using equivalent incomes, each individual values the difference between her actual achievements in the non-income attributes and the reference situation according to her own preferences, by means of her willingness-to-pay.

3.3.4 The Equivalence Approach and Difference Comparisons

Finally, we turn to the question of how the equivalence approach can provide information about well-being differences. Comparisons of well-being levels are insufficient for a prioritarian SWF or the utilitarian SWF (see Adler, Chapter 2, Section 2.5, this volume).[28] Both require *more* than well-being level information. At a minimum, these SWFs require well-being *difference* information.[29] How can the equivalence approach provide such information?

[28] Imagine a well-being measure $w(\cdot)$ that assigns well-being numbers to histories, but is understood only to contain information about the well-being levels of the histories. If so, we can define a new measure $w^+(\cdot)$, by picking any strictly increasing function $f(\cdot)$, and defining $w^+(\cdot)$ as follows: $w^+(a, \bar{R}) = f(w(a, \bar{R}))$ for every history $(a, \bar{R})$. Note that $w^+(\cdot)$ and $w(\cdot)$ agree in their intra- and interpersonal comparisons of well-being levels. Moreover, the leximin SWF will be invariant to the substitution of $w^+(\cdot)$ for $w(\cdot)$. But this is not true of either the utilitarian SWF or a prioritarian SWF. See Adler, Chapter 2, Section 2.5, this volume.

[29] As discussed in Chapter 2, Section 2.9.1, prioritarian SWFs indeed require *more* than level and difference information. While utilitarian SWFs are invariant to a common cardinal rescaling of well-being numbers, prioritarian SWFs are not. Atkinson prioritarian SWFs *are* invariant to a common ratio rescaling of well-being numbers. How to go from a well-being measure that contains well-being level and difference information, to one that contains well-being level, difference, and ratio information, is addressed in Chapter 2, Section 2.9.1, 2.A.3.1. Our

The answer, in a nutshell, is that the equivalence approach assigns a unique number to each history $(a, \bar{R})$. In the reference-set version of the approach, this is accomplished by assigning an index number to each reference set; the unique number $w(a, \bar{R})$ is, then, the index number of the reference set such that $\bar{R}$ is indifferent between a and that set. In the monotone-path version, this is accomplished by picking an index number for each location along the path. The unique number $w(a, \bar{R})$ is then the index number of the location along the path such that $\bar{R}$ is indifferent between a and that location.

We need to be cautious in how we use the unique well-being number assigned to each history $(a, \bar{R})$. The numbers may contain spurious information. They may "indicate" a well-being fact regarding histories that we don't believe to be meaningful.[30]

However, if we *do* believe that well-being difference comparisons are meaningful, then we *can* read off such information from $w(\cdot)$ as constructed with the equivalence approach. We can say that the well-being difference between $(a, \bar{R})$ and $(a^*, \bar{R}^*)$ is at least as large as the well-being difference between $(a^+, \bar{R}^+)$ and $(a^{++}, \bar{R}^{++})$ iff $w(a, \bar{R}) - w(a^*, \bar{R}^*) \geq w(a^+, \bar{R}^+) - w(a^{++}, \bar{R}^{++})$.

Conversely, in choosing an indexing scheme for reference sets or monotone paths, we should be sensitive to what these numbers imply as regards both well-being level and well-being difference comparisons. This is critical if we will be using the numbers as inputs into a utilitarian or prioritarian SWF. Indeed, we have stressed throughout this section that the choice of reference sets or a monotone path involves normative judgment. *If* we will be interpreting $w(\cdot)$ numbers to indicate not only well-being levels but also well-being differences, then the normative judgment in indexing reference sets or a monotone path

focus in this chapter is simply how to construct a $w(\cdot)$ that is preference-based and contains both well-being level and well-being difference information.

30 For example, we may not believe that it is meaningful to assign a single magnitude to the well-being difference between histories. See Chapter 2, Section 2.9.2, 2.A.3.2. If so, we should not interpret a well-being measure $w(\cdot)$ as constructed with the equivalence approach as containing such information. For example, $w(\cdot)$ may be such that $w(a, \bar{R})$ is 10, while $w(a^*, \bar{R}^*)$ is 7. The numbers "indicate" that the magnitude of the well-being difference between the two histories is 3. But if we believe that such a magnitude is spurious information, we shouldn't read $w(\cdot)$ as indicating this.

is – precisely – a normative judgment regarding both level and difference comparisons between histories.[31]

3.4 The vNM Approach

The vNM approach conceptualizes a history as a combination of an attribute bundle and a lottery preference: $h = (a, \overline{\overline{R}})$. It assumes, further, that the lottery preference satisfies the axioms of vNM utility theory, and that the ranking of history lotteries satisfies a principle of Lottery Deference. Using these assumptions plus several others, the vNM approach derives its "Fundamental Formula," which states that the well-being number of a given history is the *utility* number of the attribute bundle in that history – as per an appropriately scaled vNM utility function representing the lottery preference.

The vNM approach originates with the pioneering scholarship of John Harsanyi. Adler, building upon Harsanyi's foundational work, has further developed the methodology; and the version of the vNM approach set forth here will be as presented in Adler (2016; 2019 chapter 2, appendix). vNM utilities (shorthand for "von Neumann-Morgenstern") are, of course, a pervasive tool in modern economics. What is distinctive about the line of thought originating with Harsanyi is the use of vNM utility functions as the linchpin of a theory of interpersonal comparisons. We use the term "vNM approach" to mean, specifically, this theoretical apparatus – as opposed to vNM utility theory more generally.

To date, little empirical work has been undertaken that explicitly references the vNM approach. (By contrast, the equivalence approach has been implemented in a sizeable empirical literature.) See Decancq and Neumann (2016); Decancq and Schokkaert, Chapter 5, this volume, for empirical applications of the vNM approach. However, some scholarship on SWFs does employ vNM utility functions as the input to an SWF.[32] The vNM approach (or something like it) is implicit in such scholarship.

[31] While the Deference Principle itself determines our well-being level comparisons of two histories with the same preference, it *doesn't* determine our well-being level comparisons of histories containing different preferences, nor does it determine our difference comparisons between histories.

[32] For example, the SWF-based literature on climate change often uses a utilitarian SWF with individual utility, as a function of consumption, calculated with a

In what follows, we first present the approach; then contrast it with the equivalence approach; and finally discuss the special case of homogeneous preferences.

3.4.1 The vNM Approach: Elements

vNM utility functions are ubiquitous in modern economics, as mentioned. vNM utility theory shows the following (Gilboa 2009; Kreps 2013): If we require that a lottery preference $\overline{\overline{R}}$ (an ordering of the set of lotteries)[33] conform to a few basic rationality axioms, then $\overline{\overline{R}}$ can be *expectationally represented* by a vNM utility function, $u^{\overline{\overline{R}}}(\cdot)$. For any two lotteries, the first is preferred to the second by $\overline{\overline{R}}$ iff the expected utility of the first lottery is greater than the expected utility of the second, and $\overline{\overline{R}}$ is indifferent between the two lotteries iff the two lotteries have the same expected utilities – these expected utilities calculated using $u^{\overline{\overline{R}}}(\cdot)$.[34] The symbolism $u^{\overline{\overline{R}}}(\cdot)$ indicates that this is a utility function corresponding to $\overline{\overline{R}}$: the numbers it assigns to lotteries, by taking expected values, are such as to mirror the ranking of lotteries by $\overline{\overline{R}}$.

vNM utility theory also shows that a utility function representing a lottery preference is *unique up to a positive affine transformation.* A utility function $u^{\overline{\overline{R}}}(\cdot)$ that expectationally represents lottery preference $\overline{\overline{R}}$ is not unique. Rather, there is an entire family of utility functions that do so. If we pick one member of this family ($u^{\overline{\overline{R}}}(\cdot)$), then every other member can be derived from $u^{\overline{\overline{R}}}(\cdot)$ by multiplying by a positive constant and adding a constant.

The vNM approach constructs a well-being measure $w(\cdot)$ for histories as follows. The ethical deliberator is posited to have a ranking of histories and of differences between histories. If this ranking is well-behaved, there exists a $w(\cdot)$ that represents it. $w(h) \geq w(h^*)$ iff history h is judged by the deliberator to be at least as good for well-being as history h^*. $w(h) - w(h^*) \geq w(h^+) - w(h^{++})$ iff the well-being difference between h and h^* is judged by the deliberator to be at least as large as the well-being difference between h^+ and h^{++}.

vNM utility function of the constant-relative-risk-aversion form. See Botzen and van den Bergh (2014, p. 3).

33 See note 6.

34 That is: $l\,\overline{\overline{R}}\,l^*$ iff $\sum_{a\in \mathbf{A}}\pi_l(a)u^{\overline{\overline{R}}}(a) \geq \sum_{a\in \mathbf{A}}\pi_{l^*}(a)u^{\overline{\overline{R}}}(a)$.

The ethical deliberator is also posited to have a ranking of *history lotteries*. From the set **A** of attribute bundles and set $\overline{\overline{\mathbf{R}}}$ of lottery preferences, we arrive at a set **H** of histories (all pairings of an attribute bundle and a lottery preference). $\mathbf{L}^{\mathbf{H}}$ is the set of all lotteries over **H**. Each lottery L in this set is such as to assign probability numbers, summing to unity, to various histories. The deliberator is posited to have a ranking of $\mathbf{L}^{\mathbf{H}}$. Further, this ranking is formally well-behaved so that there exists a function $\zeta(\cdot)$ that expectationally represents it. One history lottery L is judged by the deliberator to be at least as good as a second history lottery L^* iff the expected $\zeta(\cdot)$ value of L is at least as large as the expected $\zeta(\cdot)$ value of L^*.[35]

So we have three different mathematical indicators: a vNM utility function $u^{\overline{\overline{R}}}(\cdot)$ for each preference $\overline{\overline{R}}$ regarding lotteries over attribute bundles; $w(\cdot)$ representing the deliberator's judgments regarding the well-being levels of histories and well-being differences between them; and $\zeta(\cdot)$ expectationally representing the deliberator's ranking of history lotteries. The vNM approach now posits two axioms that create a tight linkage between these indicators.

First, it posits a "Lottery Deference" principle. The vNM approach accepts the Deference Principle (above) but goes further. It says not only that the ranking of histories with a common preference defers to that preference, but that the ranking of *lotteries* over histories with a common preference defers to that preference.

Lottery Deference Principle: If history lotteries L and L^* are such as to assign non-zero probabilities to histories all of which contain the very same preference $\overline{\overline{R}}$, then the deliberator defers to $\overline{\overline{R}}$ in ranking the history lotteries.[36]

Adler defends the Lottery Deference Principle by appealing to the very same considerations of individual autonomy that justify the

[35] Let $\pi_L(h)$ be the probability assigned to history h by L. Then $\zeta(\cdot)$ is such that the deliberator judges L to be at least as good for well-being as L^* iff $\sum_{h\in \mathbf{H}}\pi_L(h)\zeta(h) \geq \sum_{h\in \mathbf{H}}\pi_{L^*}(h)\zeta(h)$.

[36] Here is a precise statement of Lottery Deference. Let L, L^*, and $\overline{\overline{R}}^{+}$ be such that: For all a, $\overline{\overline{R}}$ if $\pi_L(a, \overline{\overline{R}}) > 0$ then $\overline{\overline{R}} = \overline{\overline{R}}^{+}$ and if $\pi_{L^*}(a, \overline{\overline{R}}) > 0$ then $\overline{\overline{R}} = \overline{\overline{R}}^{+}$. Let l and l^* be the two attribute-bundle lotteries corresponding to L and L^*, respectively, namely: $\pi_l(a) = \pi_L(a, \overline{\overline{R}}^{+})$ and $\pi_{l^*}(a) = \pi_{L^*}(a, \overline{\overline{R}}^{+})$ for all a. Then the deliberator judges L to be at least as good for well-being as L^* iff $l\,\overline{\overline{R}}^{+}\,l^*$.

Deference Principle. Consider, for simplicity, the intrapersonal case. Consider the subset of histories constructed by combining attribute bundles with the very same lottery preference $\overline{\overline{R}}^{+}$. L and L^* are lotteries over this subset. Let's imagine that $\overline{\overline{R}}^{+}$ is indeed the actual lottery preference of Philippe. In comparing L to L^*, then, we are comparing lotteries over different possible lives for Philippe – that is, lives consisting of one or another attribute bundle paired with Philippe's lottery preference $\overline{\overline{R}}^{+}$.

The Deference Principle says we should respect Philippe's preference in determining which would be a better life for him to lead for certain. If $\overline{\overline{R}}^{+}$ prefers a to a^* – that is, Philippe, holding preference $\overline{\overline{R}}^{+}$, favors a over a^* – then the Deference Principle tells us to prefer the life in which Philippe has a, to the one in which he has a^*. Surely then (or so Adler argues) we should also respect Philippe's preference in comparing one lottery over lives he might lead to a second.

It turns out that Lottery Deference implies a tight linkage between $\zeta(\cdot)$ and each $u^{\overline{\overline{R}}}(\cdot)$. The $\zeta(\cdot)$ value assigned to any given history $(a, \overline{\overline{R}})$ must be either equal to the utility value assigned to bundle a by $u^{\overline{\overline{R}}}(\cdot)$ or a positive affine transformation of that utility value.

Second, the vNM approach posits a "Bernoulli" principle, which won't be discussed at length here, but says – in a nutshell – that the deliberator is risk neutral with respect to well-being in ranking history lotteries. As between a history that yields a well-being value w, and a lottery with a 50 percent chance of increasing well-being to $w + \Delta w$, and a 50 percent chance of decreasing well-being to $w - \Delta w$, the deliberator judges the two to be equally good. She does not give more weight to a chance of a well-being gain over an equal chance of a well-being loss, or vice versa. Bernoulli (which is intuitively quite plausible) has powerful implications. Simplifying slightly, it implies that $w(h) = \zeta(h)$ for every h.[37] Understand that these indicators are conceptually distinct: $w(\cdot)$ tracks the deliberator's judgments of levels and differences, $\zeta(\cdot)$ her judgments regarding lotteries. Bernoulli means that the $w(\cdot)$ numbers assigned to histories are equal to the $\zeta(\cdot)$ numbers.

[37] Strictly, it implies that $w(\cdot)$ is a positive affine transformation of $\zeta(\cdot)$; but since all positive affine transformations of $w(\cdot)$ equally well represent comparisons of history levels and differences, and all positive affine transformations of $\zeta(\cdot)$ equally well expectationally represent comparisons of history lotteries, we can without loss of generality set $w(\cdot) = \zeta(\cdot)$.

Putting together Lottery Deference and Bernoulli, we end up with the Fundamental Formula of the vNM approach:

Fundamental Formula: $w(a, \overline{\overline{R}}) = s(u^{\overline{\overline{R}}})u^{\overline{\overline{R}}}(a) + t(u^{\overline{\overline{R}}}), s(u^{\overline{\overline{R}}}) > 0$

The Fundamental Formula says that the well-being number assigned to a history $(a, \overline{\overline{R}})$ is equal to, or a positive affine transformation of, the utility number of the attribute bundle in that history (a) as per a vNM utility function $u^{\overline{\overline{R}}}(\cdot)$ expectationally representing the preference in that history $(\overline{\overline{R}})$.

The Fundamental Formula means that the ethical deliberator's judgments regarding well-being levels and differences are tightly constrained by the vNM utility functions representing the various preferences. Each lottery preference in $\overline{\overline{\mathbf{R}}}$ is represented by a vNM utility function $u^{\overline{\overline{R}}}(\cdot)$. For each such function, the deliberator chooses two scaling factors, $s(u^{\overline{\overline{R}}}) > 0$ and $t(u^{\overline{\overline{R}}})$. (The scaling factors used for the vNM utility function representing one lottery preference need not be the same as the factors used for the vNM utility function representing a different lottery preference; hence the scaling factors are written as $s(u^{\overline{\overline{R}}})$ and $t(u^{\overline{\overline{R}}})$ rather than simply s and t.) Having chosen these utility-function scaling factors, the deliberator has fully specified $w(\cdot)$. See Table 3.1 for an illustration of the role of the utility-function scaling factors. The axioms of Lottery Deference and Bernoulli mean that the deliberator's *only* flexibility in constructing $w(\cdot)$ is in choosing the scaling factors.

Although the intellectual path to the Fundamental Formula is complicated, the formula itself is reasonably intuitive. It says, simply, that the well-being number of a history is a rescaling of the vNM utility number of the attribute bundle in the history. Because vNM utility functions are only unique up to a positive affine transformation, the deliberator has flexibility to rescale the utility numbers – and that's where the choice of scaling factors comes into play.

The final component of the vNM approach is some theory as to how the scaling factors should be selected. The strong principle of deference to preferences (Deference and indeed Lottery Deference) and risk neutrality in well-being (Bernoulli) do not themselves provide guidance on this topic. Adler (2019, chapter 2) suggests a "high–low" approach: choose two attribute bundles, a "high" bundle a^{high} and a "low" bundle a^{low}, such that individuals are judged to be equally well off with a^{high} independent of their preferences, and equally well off with

Table 3.1. *The role of scaling factors in the vNM approach*

Attribute bundle (a)	$u^{\overline{\overline{R}}}(a)$	$u^{\overline{\overline{R}}^{+}}(a)$
a^*	1	1
a^{**}	3	5
a^{***}	5	4
Attribute bundle (a)	$s(u^{\overline{\overline{R}}}) = 50$ $t(u^{\overline{\overline{R}}}) = 0$ $w(a, \overline{\overline{R}})$	$s(u^{\overline{\overline{R}}^{+}}) = 1$ $t(u^{\overline{\overline{R}}^{+}}) = 0$ $w(a, \overline{\overline{R}}^{+})$
a^*	50	1
a^{**}	150	5
a^{***}	250	4
Attribute bundle (a)	$s(u^{\overline{\overline{R}}}) = 1$ $t(u^{\overline{\overline{R}}}) = 0$ $w(a, \overline{\overline{R}})$	$s(u^{\overline{\overline{R}}^{+}}) = 1$ $t(u^{\overline{\overline{R}}^{+}}) = 10$ $w(a, \overline{\overline{R}}^{+})$
a^*	1	11
a^{**}	3	15
a^{***}	5	14
Attribute bundle (a)	$s(u^{\overline{\overline{R}}}) = 1$ $t(u^{\overline{\overline{R}}}) = 3$ $w(a, \overline{\overline{R}})$	$s(u^{\overline{\overline{R}}^{+}}) = 100$ $t(u^{\overline{\overline{R}}^{+}}) = -99$ $w(a, \overline{\overline{R}}^{+})$
a^*	4	1
a^{**}	6	401
a^{***}	8	301

Note: The top part of the table displays two vNM utility functions: $u^{\overline{\overline{R}}}(\cdot)$, a vNM utility function representing preference $\overline{\overline{R}}$; and $u^{\overline{\overline{R}}^{+}}(\cdot)$, a vNM utility function representing preference $\overline{\overline{R}}^{+}$. This part of the table shows the values that each of these utility functions assigns to three attribute bundles: a^*, a^{**}, a^{***}. The three lower parts of the table show the well-being numbers assigned to six histories (the six possible combinations of the three bundles and the two preferences), using the Fundamental Formula – given the choice of scaling factors for utility function $u^{\overline{\overline{R}}}(\cdot)$, namely $s(u^{\overline{\overline{R}}})$ and $t(u^{\overline{\overline{R}}})$, and scaling factors for utility function $u^{\overline{\overline{R}}^{+}}(\cdot)$, namely $s(u^{\overline{\overline{R}}^{+}})$ and $t(u^{\overline{\overline{R}}^{+}})$.

Note that the well-being level and difference comparisons between histories with the same lottery preference are independent of the choice of scaling factors. For example, regardless of the scaling factors selected in the lower parts of the table, $w(a^{**}, \overline{\overline{R}}^{+}) > w(a^{***}, \overline{\overline{R}}^{+}) > w(a^{*}, \overline{\overline{R}}^{+})$ and $w(a^{***}, \overline{\overline{R}}^{+}) - w(a^{*}, \overline{\overline{R}}^{+}) > w(a^{**}, \overline{\overline{R}}^{+}) - w(a^{***}, \overline{\overline{R}}^{+})$. However, well-being level and difference comparisons between histories with different lottery preferences are sensitive to the choice of scaling factors. For example, using the scaling factors in the first lower part of the table $\left(s(u^{\overline{\overline{R}}}) = 50, t(u^{\overline{\overline{R}}}) = 0, s(u^{\overline{\overline{R}}^{+}}) = 1, t(u^{\overline{\overline{R}}^{+}}) = 0\right)$, we have that $w(a^{*}, \overline{\overline{R}}) > w(a^{*}, \overline{\overline{R}}^{+})$ and that $w(a^{**}, \overline{\overline{R}}) - w(a^{*}, \overline{\overline{R}}) > w(a^{**}, \overline{\overline{R}}^{+}) - w(a^{*}, \overline{\overline{R}}^{+})$. But using the scaling factors in the second lower part of the table $\left(s(u^{\overline{\overline{R}}}) = 1, t(u^{\overline{\overline{R}}}) = 0,\ s(u^{\overline{\overline{R}}^{+}}) = 1,\ t(u^{\overline{\overline{R}}^{+}}) = 10\right)$, these inequalities are reversed.

a^{low} independent of their preferences. This suffices to fix the scaling factors. For a different theory of the choice of scaling factors, see Fleurbaey and Zuber (2021).

3.4.2 *The vNM Approach versus the Equivalence Approach*

The two preference-based methodologies for measuring well-being that have been reviewed in this chapter are similar in many ways. But there is one key structural difference, which we have highlighted: the vNM approach insists on making well-being a function of an individual's lottery preferences, while the equivalence approach relies on ordinal preferences alone.

To see how the use of lottery rather than ordinal preferences drives a wedge between the two approaches, consider the following example. Assume that there are two lottery preferences, $\overline{\overline{R}}^{*}$ and $\overline{\overline{R}}^{+}$, that rank attribute bundles the very same way. That is, the two lottery preferences share the very same ordinal preference (let's denote it as $\bar{R}'$). They have the very same indifference curves in the space of attribute bundles, but disagree in how they rank lotteries over attribute bundles. For each given attribute bundle a, there is the history $(a, \overline{\overline{R}}^{*})$ and its counterpart history $(a, \overline{\overline{R}}^{+})$. The vNM approach distinguishes between the two histories. Further, and critically, the vNM approach *cannot* assign the very same well-being number to $(a, \overline{\overline{R}}^{*})$ and $(a, \overline{\overline{R}}^{+})$ for every attribute bundle.[38] By contrast, the equivalence approach does not differentiate between $(a, \overline{\overline{R}}^{*})$ and $(a, \overline{\overline{R}}^{+})$. As both lottery preferences share the same ordinal preference $\bar{R}'$, the two counterparts are represented as one and the same history, $(a, \bar{R}')$, and assigned the very same well-being number.

The vNM approach's conceptualization of histories is, at first blush, quite puzzling. An outcome (as explained earlier and in Chapter 2, Section 2.2, this volume) is a simplified model of a possible world.

38 If we take vNM utility functions representing each preference, $u^{\overline{\overline{R}}^{*}}(\cdot)$ and $u^{\overline{\overline{R}}^{+}}(\cdot)$, there is no way to rescale the two so that they assign the very same rescaled utilities to each and every attribute bundle. If there were scaling factors $s(u^{\overline{\overline{R}}^{*}})$, $t(u^{\overline{\overline{R}}^{*}})$, $s(u^{\overline{\overline{R}}^{+}})$, $t(u^{\overline{\overline{R}}^{+}})$ such that $s(u^{\overline{\overline{R}}^{*}})u^{\overline{\overline{R}}^{*}}(a) + t(u^{\overline{\overline{R}}^{*}}) = s(u^{\overline{\overline{R}}^{+}})u^{\overline{\overline{R}}^{+}}(a)+ t(u^{\overline{\overline{R}}^{+}})$ for every a, the two utility functions would be positive affine transformations of each other – which is impossible if, as supposed, the two lottery preferences are different.

A possible world includes a complete description of each person's characteristics. For short, call this a "complete possible life." There is no uncertainty in a complete possible life. For any given person, and any possible characteristic that this person might have, a complete possible life will specify either that the person has or that he lacks that characteristic. In one possible life, Lia gets a Ph.D. in economics; in another possible life, she does not earn a Ph.D. In no possible life for Lia is it uncertain whether she earns a Ph.D. or, if so, what the subject is (or, if so, how many pages the dissertation is, etc., etc.).

A history is a *model* of a possible life. And just as possible lives "squeeze out" all uncertainty, so do histories. Certain types of individual attributes are selected for description; each type of attribute is modeled as having different "attainments" (e.g., different amounts of income for the income attribute, different quality levels for the health attribute). An attribute bundle specifies the individual's attainment of each of the characterized types of attributes. There is no uncertainty regarding the attainments of the attribute bundles.

Advocates of the equivalence approach argue that, in such a risk-free setting, only ordinal preferences should matter. They think of a history as a combination of an attribute bundle and an *ordinal* preference.[39] Advocates of the vNM approach disagree and argue that a history is best seen as a combination of an attribute bundle and a *lottery* preference. Why is that?

We refer the reader to Adler (2016) for an elaborated defense and to Fleurbaey (2016) for a critique. In brief, the argument of Adler runs as follows. Although histories themselves contain no uncertainty about attribute bundles, a full theory of *well-being* cannot ignore uncertainty entirely. Individuals constantly make choices under uncertainty and wonder, what is the better choice in light of my interests? What is the

[39] Although the equivalent-income measure as discussed in Section 3.3.3 does not take account of individuals' lottery preferences – it is discussed there as one version of the equivalence approach, in turn understood as taking account only of individuals' ordinal preferences – it is possible to extend the equivalent income idea so as to take account of lottery preferences. Let l denote a lottery over attribute bundles. Fleurbaey (2016, pp. 462–463) discusses the possibility of computing a certainty-equivalent income, i.e., the sure income that, combined with the reference value on the non-income attributes, would place the individual in a situation that she finds equally good as l. A more risk-averse individual would request a larger risk premium and, hence, obtains a lower certainty-equivalent income. While computing such certainty-equivalent incomes is a possibility that Fleurbaey describes, he does not in fact advocate their use in social assessment. (See *id.*)

more *prudent* choice? It would be problematic for a theory of well-being to fail to address such questions.

Thus a full theory of well-being will include a ranking not merely of histories, but also of history lotteries, argues Adler. A very plausible axiom for the ranking of history lotteries is what Adler terms "Welfare Stochastic Indifference." If two lotteries assign the same probabilities to each of a series of well-being levels, then the lotteries are equally good for well-being. The core of Adler's argument for why histories should specify lottery preferences is this: if a history merely specifies each individual's ordinal preference, then it's impossible for the well-being ranking of histories to satisfy both Welfare Stochastic Indifference and the axiom of Lottery Deference (see Adler, 2016, pp. 507–508).

Pragmatically, the vNM approach is more demanding than the equivalence approach, since we need to estimate lottery preferences. It remains to be seen whether using lottery rather than ordinal preferences makes a significant difference in policy assessment. In a head-to-head comparison of a vNM measure of well-being and an equivalent-income measure, as implemented in a sample of about 20,000 German subjects (the German Socio-Economic Panel of 2010), Decancq and Neumann (2016) find the two measures to be more similar to each other – in terms of the characteristics of individuals in the bottom well-being decile and individuals' well-being ranks in the whole population –than to well-being as measured via income, an objective index, or subjective well-being. In Chapter 5 of this volume, Schokkaert and Decancq study how the question of whether there was social progress in Russia between 1995 and 2005 depends on which well-being measure is used. They introduce equivalent-income measures of well-being, vNM measures, and (standard) expenditures as arguments in SWFs of the Atkinson and Kolm-Pollak family. In this analysis, Schokkaert and Decancq do find some substantial differences between the equivalent-income and vNM measures.

3.4.3 Homogeneous Preferences

Both the vNM approach and the equivalence approach are methodologies for interpersonal well-being comparisons that allow for heterogeneous preferences. The set **R** of preferences (ordinal preferences in the case of the equivalence approach, lottery preferences in the case of the vNM approach) may have multiple members. A central ambition of both frameworks is to allow for heterogeneous preferences and to do so in a manner that satisfies the Deference Principle.

However, SWF scholarship often simplifies matters by positing homogeneous preferences. For example, the classic optimal tax model, deriving from Mirrlees, posits that everyone has the same preferences regarding consumption-leisure bundles (Tuomala, 2016, chapter 4).

The equivalence approach does not operate any differently with homogeneous preferences than it does with heterogeneous preferences. **R** is, specifically, the set $\bar{\mathbf{R}}$ of ordinal preferences – which in the case of homogeneous preferences is a singleton set, containing a single ordinal preference $\bar{R}$. All histories are combinations of attribute bundles with this one preference $\bar{R}$. Well-being numbers are assigned to those histories by numbering the indifference curves of $\bar{R}$, using either reference sets or a monotone path.

With homogeneous preferences, the vNM approach simplifies significantly (and in an intuitive way). Now, **R** is, specifically, the set $\bar{\bar{\mathbf{R}}}$ of lottery preferences – which in the case of homogeneous preferences contains a single lottery preference $\bar{\bar{R}}$. There is no need to choose scaling factors – their function is to commensurate heterogeneous lottery preferences – and $w(\cdot)$ can be set equal to any vNM utility function $u^{\bar{\bar{R}}}(\cdot)$ representing the single preference. That is, $w(a, \bar{\bar{R}}) = u^{\bar{\bar{R}}}(a)$.[40]

The intellectual divide between the two approaches also becomes smaller with homogeneous preferences. Recall that, with multiple lottery preferences, the vNM approach may assign different numbers to the very same indifference curve depending upon which lottery preference that curve is associated with (see Section 3.4.2). However, if there is but a single lottery preference $\bar{\bar{R}}$, with a single corresponding ordinal preference $\bar{R}'$, then all attribute bundles on the same indifference curve of $\bar{R}'$ are now assigned the same well-being number – namely, the vNM utility level of all bundles on that curve according to $u^{\bar{\bar{R}}}(\cdot)$.[41] In effect,

[40] In this case, because vNM utility functions are unique up to a positive affine transformation, assigning well-being numbers to histories via the formula $w(a, \bar{\bar{R}}) = u^{\bar{\bar{R}}}(a)$ produces the same well-being level and difference comparisons between histories regardless of which vNM utility function representing $\bar{\bar{R}}$ is chosen.

[41] Recall that each attribute bundle a is equivalent to a "degenerate" lottery: a lottery that assigns this bundle probability 1. To say that a and a^* lie on the same indifference curve of $\bar{R}'$, the ordinal preference corresponding to $\bar{\bar{R}}$, is equivalent to saying: lottery preference $\bar{\bar{R}}$ is indifferent between a degenerate

in the case of homogeneous preferences, the only difference between the equivalence and vNM approaches is *how* indifference curves are numbered. If the population is modeled as having a single lottery preference $\overline{\overline{R}}$ and a single corresponding ordinal preference $\bar{R}'$, the equivalence approach ignores $\overline{\overline{R}}$ and assigns numbers to the indifference curves of $\bar{R}'$ via reference sets or a monotone path. The vNM approach, instead, numbers indifference curves by applying $u^{\overline{\overline{R}}}(\cdot)$. In both cases, the well-being number assigned to a given attribute bundle a is just the number of the indifference curve of ordinal preference $\bar{R}'$ on which a lies.

3.5 Non-Preference-Based Well-Being Measures

3.5.1 *Objective Goods and Capabilities*

We have defined a well-being measure as *preference-based* if it operates on histories, of the form (a, R) – with R either an ordinal or lottery preference – and satisfies the Deference Principle. The view that well-being depends upon preferences is very widespread in economics, of course, and is also well represented in the philosophical literature on well-being. Our definition is an attempt to make precise (within our framework of measurement) this preferentialist tradition in the conceptualization of well-being.

But the dependency of well-being on preferences has been disputed. There is also a long tradition in philosophy, going back to Aristotle, of so-called *objective-good* accounts of well-being. Such accounts deny that well-being consists in preference satisfaction. Contemporary objective-good theorists posit lists of goods as the components of individual well-being. The goods (or at least some of them[42]) are preference-independent, in the sense that an individual can have more of the good without preferring it. For example, John Finnis argues that

lottery with probability 1 to a and a degenerate lottery with probability 1 to a^*. If that is true, then – if $u^{\overline{\overline{R}}}(\cdot)$ is indeed a vNM utility function representing $\overline{\overline{R}}$ – it must be the case that $u^{\overline{\overline{R}}}(a) = u^{\overline{\overline{R}}}(a^*)$.

42 If an account includes some goods that are preference-dependent while others are not, it's still possible for an individual to be better off (according to the account) with a bundle of goods that she disprefers. (Consider two bundles that differ only with respect to the preference-independent goods.) This is the hallmark of an objective-good account.

well-being consists in the attainment of the following goods: life, knowledge, play, aesthetic experience, sociability, practical reasonableness, religion (Finnis, 1988, chapter 4). James Griffin sets forth a different list: accomplishment, "the components of human existence" (roughly, autonomy and physical integrity), understanding, enjoyment, deep personal relations (Griffin, 1996, pp. 29–30). Guy Fletcher suggests: achievement, friendship, happiness, pleasure, self-respect, virtue (Fletcher, 2016). George Sher endorses this list of goods: moral goodness, rational activity, development of abilities, having children and being a good parent, knowledge, awareness of true beauty (Sher, 1997, p. 201). (See Alkire, 2002, for a survey with more examples.)

There are evident linkages between this corpus of philosophical scholarship and the contemporary literature on the *capability approach*, originating with work by Amartya Sen and Martha Nussbaum. In the capability approach, well-being is assessed in terms of individual "functionings" and "capabilities" (opportunities to function) that are not reducible either to preference satisfaction or to hedonic states (Sen, 1985).[43] Capability scholars often suggest leaving the identification of functionings and capabilities to democratic discussion (Sen, 2004). Martha Nussbaum, however, has famously defended a specific list of capabilities: life; bodily health; bodily integrity; the senses, imagination and thought; emotions; practical reason; affiliation; other species; play; and control over one's environment (Nussbaum, 2000, 2006). This list of capabilities looks very much like a philosophical list of objective goods.

Under the impetus of the capability approach (and objective-good accounts of well-being) several international institutions have developed and implemented so-called *composite indicators of well-being*, which aggregate different aspects of well-being by means of a mathematical procedure that often takes the form of a (weighted) average. The Human Development Index (HDI) of the United Nations Development Programme or the Better Life Index (BLI) of the Organisation for Economic Cooperation and Development (OECD) are popular examples.[44] While these composite indicators

[43] See, however, Decancq et al. (2021) for a preferentialist interpretation of the capability approach and an application with Colombian data.

[44] The Human Development Index is published yearly in the Human Development Report by the United Nations Development Programme; see www.undp.org. The Better Life Index can be computed by the user on www.oecdbetterlifeindex.org. Decancq (2017) compares these indices.

are mostly measured at the country (or regional) level based on average attainments, they can also be computed at the individual level, leaving room to introduce distributional or prioritarian concerns in the social evaluation. Building on a multidimensional version of the Atkinson SWF, Alkire and Foster (2011) and Decancq (2017) provide distribution-sensitive versions of the HDI and BLI, respectively. See also Decancq and Schokkaert, Chapter 5, this volume.[45]

Multidimensional composite well-being indicators have a clear advantage over so-called "dashboards" of several (one-dimensional) policy indicators, such as the Millennium or Sustainable Development Goals.[46] These dashboards are popular in empirical applications of the capability approach, for instance. They display a policy's impact on well-being with respect to a series of indicators and, hence, leave it to the decisionmaker to balance the plural impacts so that an overall assessment can be made. The difficulty is that dashboards are insensitive to the correlation between the attainments. A pragmatic advantage, however, is that dashboards can be constructed using different dimension-specific datasets, which is obviously not possible for well-being measures that consider different attainments of the same individual.

Leaving aside data issues, one important challenge to constructing a composite indicator of well-being is to select an operational procedure to aggregate the different attainments and to determine the relative weights of these attainments (see Decancq and Lugo, 2013, for a critical review). This challenge brings us back to the – fundamental – question of what information can be used when making such decisions and, in particular, what role preferences can or should play therein.

Consider the simplest case of an objective-good theory that posits a list of goods, each one of which is preference-independent. Such a theory can be captured in our formalism by supposing that the well-being level of histories is wholly independent of their component preferences: $w(a, R) = w(a^{\star}, R^{\star})$ if $a = a^{\star}$. Two histories with the same

[45] These, and other, proposals are built on the literature on the measurement of multidimensional inequality. Measures of multidimensional inequality summarize the joint distribution of multiple attainments in a single number. However, most multidimensional inequality measures do not explicitly measure each individual's well-being as a product of her multidimensional attainments. See Aaberge and Brandolini (2015), Chakravarty and Lugo (2016) or Weymark (2006) for surveys.

[46] For the Millennium Development Goals, see www.un.org/millenniumgoals and for the Sustainable Development Goals, see https://sdgs.un.org.

attribute bundle lead to the same well-being level, irrespective of the preferences. Clearly, this position does not satisfy the Deference Principle. Interestingly, however, objective well-being measures that do not take account of preferences are the only ones that can satisfy the so-called dominance principle – which states that an attribute bundle with higher attainments for all attributes leads to higher well-being, irrespective of the preferences (see Fleurbaey and Trannoy, 2003).[47]

If individuals' preferences are not used to aggregate the different attainments and to construct a measure of well-being that allows for intra- and interpersonal comparisons of levels and differences, one may wonder which information can be used to determine the well-being function $w(\cdot)$. Unfortunately, there is no off-the-shelf theory that we can borrow from the objective-good literature or the capability approach to determine the shape of this function (at least not that we are aware of). In most applied work on composite indicators of well-being, one often works with simple well-being functions that are essentially (weighted) averages of the attainments (the HDI is an example of this approach) or, alternatively, one relies on complex statistical algorithms, such as principal component analysis (Ram, 1982) or Data Envelopment Analysis (Cherchye et al., 2007) to make intra- and interpersonal comparisons of well-being.

A different approach to handling the case under consideration flows most naturally from the earlier sections of this chapter.[48] A deliberator can have her own preference with respect to attribute bundles – her own sense of how different bundles compare with respect to well-being. That is, she has her own ordinal ranking of the set **A** of attribute bundles (let's denote this as $\bar{R}^d$) which she uses to evaluate well-being using some version of the equivalence approach – either via reference sets, or via a monotone path. The well-being number of a given attribute bundle a is just $w(a, \bar{R}^d)$. In other words, we locate each attribute bundle on the deliberator's indifference curves and then apply the equivalence approach. While the Deference Principle with respect to the individual's own preferences is not satisfied, the Deference Principle with respect to the deliberator's preferences is. The deliberator's preferences may or may not depend on the individual preferences

[47] Decancq et al. (2015a) show how equivalent incomes can be obtained by combining respect for preferences with a weaker version of the dominance principle, restricted to a monotone path.

[48] We thank Paolo Piacquadio for raising this point.

of the individuals in the society, through a process of democratic decision. The BLI of the OECD may be interpreted as an – arguably crude – operational version of an approach based on the deliberator's preferences. On an interactive website,[49] users can choose some parameters of the deliberator's preferences over the eleven attributes considered. These preferences are then used to compare the average well-being of the OECD member states in a graphical way.[50]

A more complicated case arises if the objective-good account of well-being includes *some* preference-dependent goods. Although the account overall is still objective because it denies that a given person's well-being levels with different possible attribute bundles always hinges on the person's preferences over those bundles, the theory does not ignore preferences entirely. Note, for example, that James Griffin above includes the good of "accomplishment" on his list of goods, while Guy Fletcher includes the good of "achievement." A state of affairs is an accomplishment/achievement for some individual only if she prefers that state of affairs.

In our framework, an objective-good theory with some preference-dependent goods could be represented as follows. On the one hand, the Deference Principle is rejected: this is what makes the theory objective. It is not the case that $w(a, R) \geq w(a^*, R)$ iff $a\ R\ a^*$. On the other hand, preferences are *not* ignored entirely in assigning well-being numbers. It is *not* the case that $w(a, R) = w(a^*, R^*)$ if $a = a^*$. How to construct the well-being measure for *this* type of objective-good account is beyond the scope of what we can address here.

3.5.2 Subjective Well-Being

A large body of work in economics and psychology now examines individuals' subjective well-being (SWB) – the term that is used by this

49 www.oecdbetterlifeindex.org.

50 Alternatively, the deliberator might have her own lottery preference with respect to the set of attribute bundles, $\overline{\overline{R}}^d$, and assign a given attribute bundle a the well-being number $w(a, \overline{\overline{R}}^d)$ as per the vNM approach. Because the vNM approach in this application is ignoring all lottery preferences except $\overline{\overline{R}}^d$, the set of lottery preferences is a singleton and we have that $w(a, \overline{\overline{R}}^d) = u^{\overline{\overline{R}}^d}(a)$, with $u^{\overline{\overline{R}}^d}(\cdot)$ any vNM utility function representing $\overline{\overline{R}}^d$. See above, Section 3.4.3.

literature to refer to happiness, pain and pleasure, satisfaction with life, and related affective or cognitive mental states. SWB is typically assessed with surveys, which ask respondents to quantify some aspect of their SWB. For example, the respondent might be asked: "All things considered, how satisfied would you say you are with your life these days? Please tell me on a scale of 1 to 10, where 1 means very dissatisfied and 10 means very satisfied." Or: "Taken all together, would you say that you are very happy, pretty happy, or not too happy?" (Graham, 2016; Lucas, 2016).

An emerging policy-analytic strand within this scholarship uses SWB data for policy evaluation or the assessment of social condition (see, e.g., Layard, 2005; Adler, 2013). For example, SWB-based cost-benefit analysis has been theorized and implemented (Fujiwara and Dolan, 2016). Inequality metrics have been used to study the inequality of SWB (see, e.g., Dutta and Foster, 2013). Gross-national-happiness indicators (analogous to GDP) have been calculated. Indeed, many countries now collect SWB statistics regularly.

It is therefore worth considering how SWB data might be used to inform the well-being measure in our social welfare framework. We lack space to consider the issue in detail here, so will simply sketch the main possibilities.

First, an objective-good account of well-being might include certain SWB states on its list of objective goods. For example, we included above the lists of goods endorsed by the philosophers Guy Fletcher and James Griffin. Note that Fletcher's list includes the goods of happiness and pleasure, while Griffin's includes enjoyment.

At the limit, an objective-good theory might include *only* SWB states as goods. This is true, indeed, of the classic hedonic account of well-being adopted by Jeremy Bentham. Such a view construes pleasure and pain as positive and negative *sensations*; posits pleasure and pain as preference-independent goods (namely, that an individual's well-being is increased if she feels pleasure and decreased if she feels pain, independent of her preferring pleasure and dispreferring pain); and posits these hedonic goods as the only intrinsic components of well-being (Sumner, 1996, chapter 4).

Second, a preference-based view of well-being will take the position that pain or pleasure, happiness, or some other SWB state – like every other aspect of some individual's life – is better for that person's well-being if and any only if she has a (laundered) preference for that SWB state. Leaving aside considerations of tractability, then, attribute bundles should describe individuals' SWB states along with non-SWB attributes such as income, health, and longevity. The preference-based well-being measures we described in detail above (the equivalence approach and the vNM approach), which take the form $w(\cdot) = w(a, R)$, can be extended without difficulty to the case in which a includes both SWB and non-SWB dimensions. To be sure, tractability considerations mean that a can only include some, not all, welfare-relevant characteristics. However, if individuals tend to have strong preferences regarding some SWB state, policy modeling with the SWF framework will be significantly more accurate if it includes that SWB state in the attribute bundle.

Third, there is a plausible linkage between a particular SWB state – life satisfaction – and preferences. Life satisfaction has a cognitive component, namely judging that one's life is going well. Let us denote the life satisfaction reported by an individual i with attribute bundle a as $SWB_i(a)$. Note that the life satisfaction function is individual-specific because life satisfaction scores are not only determined by the attribute bundle at hand, but also by other (idiosyncratic) scaling factors such as personality traits, cultural norms, expectations and aspirations. An optimistic person with a particular attribute bundle a will report a higher life satisfaction than a pessimistic person.

Decancq et al. (2015a) study the link between life satisfaction and ordinal preferences and define the so-called *consistency assumption*, which states that $SWB_i(a) \geq SWB_i(a^\star)$ iff $a\,\bar{R}_i\,a^\star$.[51] Under this assumption, life satisfaction scores provide a well-being measure which satisfies the Deference Principle in *intrapersonal* comparisons. Yet, due to the presence of the individual-specific scaling factors, interpersonal comparisons of life satisfaction are not necessarily consistent with unanimously held preferences. Indeed, the optimistic individual Anne may report a higher life satisfaction than the pessimistic Bob, even when both Anne and Bob have the same ordinal preferences which agree that Bob's attribute bundle is preferred over Anne's. This example shows that raw life satisfaction scores should not be used as preferentialist well-being measures in our social welfare framework.

[51] Testing whether the consistency assumption holds in real-life situations is an open avenue for further research. Benjamin et al. (2012) provide some cautionary evidence.

Building on the consistency assumption, however, a significant body of empirical work uses life satisfaction surveys to estimate ordinal preferences or indifference curves (see Decancq et al. (2015a) and Decancq and Neumann (2016), for instance). In these estimations, one aims to control econometrically for the effect of the individual-specific scaling factors on life satisfaction scores. When this method is used to estimate preferences so as to implement the equivalence approach, there is a substantial difference between the raw life satisfaction scores and the equivalence measure of well-being. Decancq et al. (2015a), for instance, find a significant divergence between life satisfaction scores and equivalent incomes in identifying the worst-off individuals (in a nutshell, "the subjectively least satisfied individuals have larger expenditures, better health and nicer houses than those with the lowest value of equivalent incomes" [p. 1099]); while Decancq and Neumann (2016) find a significant divergence between life satisfaction and both equivalent-income and vNM well-being measures.

In sum: there are a number of connections between SWB and well-being. But an SWB measure of well-being (even a life satisfaction measure) is not a preference-based measure, and those who endorse a preference account of well-being should resist using it this way.

3.6 Conclusion

Economists traditionally define well-being in terms of preference-satisfaction. It might seem that a preference account of well-being undercuts interpersonal well-being comparisons. In particular, consider well-being comparisons between individuals with different preferences. Imagine that Muriel prefers attribute bundle a to bundle a^*, while Nate has the opposite preference. We can't say unequivocally that either bundle is better than the other. Muriel is better off with a than a^*, while Nate is better off with a^* than a. An interpersonal comparison between the two based merely on their bundles would ignore their preferences; and so perhaps the lesson of this sort of case is that, if we want to respect preferences, we should give up on across-person comparability of well-being. Indeed, one line of thought within economics rejects interpersonal comparisons (Adler, 2019, pp. 76–79).

However, rejecting interpersonal comparisons is not an option for those who propose to use a social welfare function (SWF) to evaluate governmental policy – in particular a prioritarian SWF, the focus of this volume. Such rejection also flies in the face of common sense. (See Adler, Chapter 2, this volume.) For those who understand well-being in terms of preferences *and* accept interpersonal well-being comparisons – as we do – the lesson of the sort of case just described is that *both* preferences *and* attributes (not attributes alone) are the inputs into well-being. A well-being measure $w(\cdot)$ should be understood as operating on "histories," each history being a combination of an attribute bundle a and a preference structure R: $w(\cdot)$ takes the form $w(a, R)$. The Same History Principle then stipulates that if two individuals have the same history – the same attributes and the same preferences – they are equally well off.

The formalism of making an individual's well-being a function of her history (a, R) does not itself imply that the account of well-being is preference-based. This formalism *allows* for preferences to be followed in determining well-being, but doesn't *require* that they be. We could use the history formalism together with a well-being measure $w(\cdot)$ that ignores preferences.[52] What is distinctive about a *preference-based* well-being measure is that it satisfies the Deference Principle. The Deference Principle says: $w(a, R) \geq w(a^*, R)$ iff $a\ R\ a^*$ (preference R weakly prefers a to a^*). In other words, the well-being ranking of histories that incorporate different bundles but the same preference *tracks* that preference.

This chapter, although also covering well-being measures that violate the Deference Principle, has mainly focused on two approaches that satisfy it: the equivalence approach and the vNM approach. These approaches differ in significant respects; the first focuses on ordinal preferences, the second on lottery preferences. But the two approaches are alike in more fundamental regards: each respects the Same History Principle, each respects the Deference Principle, and each constructs a well-being measure that assigns a well-being number to every history – so that the well-being of two histories is commensurable even if the two contain different preferences.[53] Both approaches, in somewhat different ways, show how to develop an interpersonally comparable well-being measure suitable for the SWF framework while also respecting preferences.

[52] That is, $w(a, R) = w(a, R^*)$ for all a, R, R^*.

[53] For every (a, R) and (a^*, R^*), either $w(a, R) > w(a^*, R^*)$; $w(a, R) = w(a^*, R^*)$; or $w(a, R) < w(a^*, R^*)$.

References

Aaberge, R., and Brandolini, A. (2015). "Multidimensional poverty and inequality." In A.B. Atkinson and F. Bourguignon, eds., *Handbook of Income Distribution*, vol. 2A. Amsterdam: Elsevier, pp. 141–216.

Adler, M.D. (2013). "Happiness surveys and public policy. What's the use?" *Duke Law Journal*, 62: 1509–1601.

(2016). "Extended preferences." In M.D. Adler and M. Fleurbaey, eds., *The Oxford Handbook of Well-Being and Public Policy*. New York: Oxford University Press, pp. 476–517.

(2019). *Measuring Social Welfare: An Introduction*. New York: Oxford University Press.

(2020). "Extended preferences and the valuation of health." In N. Eyal et al. eds., *Measuring the Global Burden of Disease: Philosophical Dimensions*. New York: Oxford University Press, pp. 86–106.

Alkire, S. (2002). "Dimensions of human development." *World Development*, 30: 181–205.

Alkire, S., and Foster, J. (2011). "Counting and multidimensional poverty measurement." *Journal of Public Economics*, 95: 476–487.

Benjamin, D. J., Heffetz, O., Kimball, M.S., and Rees-Jones, A. (2012). "What do you think would make you happier? What do you think you would choose?" *American Economic Review*, 102: 2083–2110.

Blackorby, C., and Donaldson, D. (1988). "Money metric utility: A harmless normalization?" *Journal of Economic Theory*, 46: 120–129.

Bosmans, K., Decancq, K., and Ooghe, E. (2018). "Who's afraid of aggregating money metrics?" *Theoretical Economics*, 13: 467–484.

Botzen, W.J. Wouter, and van den Bergh, J.C.J.M. (2014). "Specifications of social welfare in economic studies of climate policy: Overview of criteria and related policy insights." *Environmental and Resource Economics*, 58: 1–33.

Chakravarty, S.R., and Lugo, M.A. (2016). "Multidimensional indicators of inequality and poverty." In M.D. Adler and M. Fleurbaey, eds., *The Oxford Handbook of Well-Being and Public Policy*. New York: Oxford University Press, pp. 246–285.

Cherchye, L., Moesen, W., Rogge, N., and Van Puyenbroeck, T. (2007). "An introduction to 'benefit of the doubt' composite indicators." *Social Indicators Research*, 82: 111–145.

Deaton, A. (1979). "The distance function in consumer behaviour with applications to index numbers and optimal taxation." *The Review of Economic Studies*, 46: 391–405.

(1980). "The measurement of welfare: theory and practical guidelines." Living Standards Measurement Study (LSMS) Working Paper No. 7, World Bank.

Deaton, A., and Muellbauer, J. (1980). *Economics and Consumer Behavior.* Cambridge: Cambridge University Press.

Decancq, K. (2017). "Measuring multidimensional inequality in the OECD member countries with a distribution-sensitive better life index." *Social Indicators Research*, 131: 1057–1086.

Decancq, K., Fleurbaey, M., and Maniquet, F. (2019). "Multidimensional poverty measurement with individual preferences." *Journal of Economic Inequality*, 17: 29–49.

Decancq, K., Fleurbaey, M., and Schokkaert, E. (2015a). "Happiness, equivalent incomes, and respect for individual preferences." *Economica*, 82: 1082–1106.

(2015b). "Inequality, income, and well-being." In A.B. Atkinson and F. Bourguignon, eds., *Handbook of Income Distribution*, vol. 2A. Amsterdam: Elsevier, pp. 67–140.

Decancq, K., and Lugo, M. A. (2013). "Weights in multidimensional indices of well-being: An overview." *Econometric Reviews*, 32: 7–34.

Decancq, K., and Neumann, D. (2016). "Does the choice of well-being measure matter empirically?" In M.D. Adler and M. Fleurbaey, eds., *The Oxford Handbook of Well-Being and Public Policy*. New York: Oxford University Press, pp. 553–587.

Decancq, K., and Nys, A. (2021). "Nonparametric well-being comparisons." *European Economic Review*, 133: 103666.

Decancq, K., and Schokkaert, E. (2016). "Beyond GDP: Using equivalent incomes to measure well-being in Europe." *Social Indicators Research*, 126: 21–55.

Decancq, K., Schokkaert, E., and Zuluaga, B. (2021). "Implementing the capability approach with respect for individual valuations." In E. Chiappero-Martinetti et al. eds., *The Cambridge Handbook of the Capability Approach*. Cambridge: Cambridge University Press, pp. 307–332.

Dutta, I., and Foster, J. (2013). "Inequality of happiness in the United States: 1972–2010." *Review of Income and Wealth*, 59: 393–415.

Finnis, J. (1988). *Natural Law and Natural Rights*. Oxford: Clarendon Press.

Fletcher, G. (2016). "Objective list theories." In G. Fletcher, ed., *The Routledge Handbook of Philosophy of Well-Being*. Milton Park, UK: Routledge, pp. 148–160.

Fleurbaey, M. (2016). "Equivalent income." In M.D. Adler and M. Fleurbaey, eds., *The Oxford Handbook of Well-Being and Public Policy*. New York: Oxford University Press, pp. 453–475.

Fleurbaey, M., and Blanchet, D. (2013). *Beyond GDP: Measuring Welfare and Assessing Sustainability*. New York: Oxford University Press.

Fleurbaey, M., and Maniquet, F. (2011). *A Theory of Fairness and Social Welfare*. Cambridge: Cambridge University Press.

(2017). "Fairness and well-being measurement." *Mathematical Social Sciences*, 90: 119–126.

(2018). "Inequality-averse well-being measurement." *International Journal of Economic Theory*, 14: 35–50.

(2019) "Well-being measurement with non-classical goods." *Economic Theory*, 68: 765–786.

Fleurbaey, M., and Schokkaert, E. (2013). "Behavioral welfare economics and redistribution." *American Economic Journal: Microeconomics*, 5: 180–205.

Fleurbaey, M., and Tadenuma, K. (2014). "Universal social orderings: An integrated theory of policy evaluation, inter-society comparisons, and interpersonal comparisons." *The Review of Economic Studies*, 81: 1071–1101.

Fleurbaey, M., and Trannoy, A. (2003). "The impossibility of a Paretian egalitarian." *Social Choice and Welfare*, 21: 243–263.

Fleurbaey, M., and Zuber, S. (2021). "Fair utilitarianism." *American Economic Journal: Microeconomics*, 13: 370–401.

Fujiwara, D., and Dolan, P. (2016). "Happiness-based policy analysis." In M.D. Adler and M. Fleurbaey, eds., *The Oxford Handbook of Well-Being and Public Policy*. New York: Oxford University Press, pp. 286–317.

Gilboa, I. (2009). *Theory of Decision under Uncertainty*. Cambridge: Cambridge University Press.

Goodin, R. E. (1986). "Laundering preferences." In J. Elster and A. Hylland, eds., *Foundations of Social Choice Theory*. Cambridge: Cambridge University Press, pp. 75–101.

Graham, C. (2016). "Subjective Well-Being in Economics." In M.D. Adler and M. Fleurbaey, eds., *The Oxford Handbook of Well-Being and Public Policy*. New York: Oxford University Press, pp. 424–450.

Griffin, J. (1996). *Value Judgement: Improving our Ethical Beliefs*. Oxford: Clarendon Press.

Gul, F., and Pesendorfer, W. (2008). "The case for mindless economics." In A. Caplin and A. Schotter, eds., *The Foundations of Positive and Normative Economics: A Handbook*. New York: Oxford University Press, pp. 3–42.

Kreps, D.M. (2013). *Microeconomic Foundations I: Choice and Competitive Markets*. Princeton, NJ: Princeton University Press.

Layard, R. (2005). *Happiness: Lessons from a New Science*. New York: Penguin Press.

Lucas, R.E. (2016). "Subjective Well-Being in Psychology." In M.D. Adler and M. Fleurbaey, eds., *The Oxford Handbook of Well-Being and Public Policy*. New York: Oxford University Press, pp. 403–423.

McKenzie, L. (1957). "Demand theory without a utility index." *The Review of Economic Studies*, 24: 185–189.

Nussbaum, M.C. (2000). *Women and Human Development: The Capabilities Approach*. Cambridge: Cambridge University Press.

(2006). *Frontiers of Justice: Disability, Nationality, Species Membership*. Cambridge, MA: Harvard University Press.

Pazner, E. A., and Schmeidler, D. (1978). "Egalitarian equivalent allocations: A new concept of economic equity." *The Quarterly Journal of Economics*, 92: 671–687.

Ram, R. (1982). "Composite indices of physical quality of life, basic needs fulfillment and income: A 'principal component' representation." *Journal of Development Economics*, 11: 227–247.

Roberts, K. (1980). "Price-independent welfare prescriptions." *Journal of Public Economics*, 13: 277–297.

Samuelson, P.A. (1974). "Complementarity: an essay on the 40th anniversary of the Hicks-Allen revolution in demand theory." *Journal of Economic Literature*, 12: 1255–1289.

(1977). "Reaffirming the existence of 'reasonable' Bergson-Samuelson social welfare functions." *Economica*, 44: 81–88.

Sen, A. (1979). "The welfare basis of real income comparisons: A survey." *Journal of Economic Literature*, 17: 1–45.

(1985). *Commodities and Capabilities*. North-Holland: Amsterdam.

(2004). "Capabilities, lists, and public reason: Continuing the conversation." *Feminist Economics*, 10: 77–80.

Sher, G. (1997). *Beyond Neutrality: Perfectionism and Politics*. Cambridge: Cambridge University Press.

Sumner, L.W. (1996). *Welfare, Happiness, and Ethics*. Oxford: Clarendon Press.

Tuomala, M. (2016). *Optimal Redistributive Taxation*. Oxford: Oxford University Press.

Weymark, J. A. (2006). "The normative approach to the measurement of multidimensional inequality." In F. Farina and E. Savaglio, eds., *Inequality and Economic Integration*. London: Routledge, pp. 303–328.

4 Prioritarianism and Optimal Taxation

MATTI TUOMALA AND
MATTHEW WEINZIERL*

In this chapter, we trace out the implications of adopting prioritarianism as the normative standard for the design of labor income taxation, and we examine the extent to which prevailing tax policies fit with those implications. Labor income taxation embodies, perhaps more directly and with broader reach than any other policy decision, social judgments on the proper role of government and distribution of economic resources.[1] The design of "optimal" taxation therefore depends critically on what we assume optimality entails. In other words, normative choices are at the heart of the study of optimal taxation.

First, we discuss and build on over nearly five decades of research in optimal tax theory to provide both analytical and numerical results on prioritarian-optimal tax policy. Though little appreciated even by most tax theorists, James Mirrlees (1971) specified an objective for tax policy in the founding paper of that literature which directly translated the core idea of prioritarianism into his model's formal mathematical language. Emmanuel Saez (2001), in his important and influential restatement of Mirrlees's analysis, followed his lead, as have most others. Optimal tax theorists' use of prioritarianism is typically motivated by technical convenience, however, rather than explicit normative reasoning. In fact, most optimal tax theorists prefer to avoid normative judgments altogether and evaluate only the (Pareto) efficiency of policies, focusing their efforts on managing an array of positive (not normative) complexities. The objective used by Mirrlees, Saez, and most other theorists admits a prioritarian specification, but it also

* Matti Tuomala, University of Tampere, Matti.Tuomala@tuni.fi; Matthew Weinzierl, Harvard Business School and NBER, mweinzierl@hbs.edu. Thanks to Robert Scherf for excellent research assistance and this volume's editors for helpful comments.

[1] While we focus on labor income taxation, adopting prioritarianism would have implications for the design of related policies such as social insurance and capital taxation, as well.

admits a utilitarian or maximin specification, and when forced to choose among efficient allocations, the convention in modern optimal tax theory has been to default to these extreme cases. Thus, much more can be done to develop the normative case for prioritarianism in modern optimal tax theory.[2]

Second, we examine the extent to which prevailing tax policies and attitudes toward taxation appear to embrace prioritarian goals. We provide an overview of the results of both recent so-called inverse optimum analyses, in which a society's apparent normative preferences are inferred from its chosen tax policies, and recent positive optimal taxation analyses, in which carefully designed surveys are used to elicit popular views on taxation. Although we do not find widespread evidence of the influence of prioritarianism in either case, much more work remains to be done along these lines. Our hope is that this chapter will help inspire that work.

This chapter proceeds as follows. Section 4.1 examines what prioritarianism can teach us about optimal taxation through theoretical analysis and numerical simulations. In Section 4.2, we turn from theory to practice, as we look for evidence on the influence of prioritarianism in prevailing tax policies and attitudes toward taxes. Section 4.3 raises and discusses prominent reservations about prioritarianism and looks to the future, considering arguments for prioritarianism that economists may find appealing and suggesting approaches that future research might take.

4.1 Prioritarianism and the Theory of Optimal Taxation

Modern optimal tax theory is written in the formal language of constrained optimization. Society is assumed to have an objective for its tax policy and to face economic constraints on what its policies can achieve. The task of the optimal tax theorist – and the hypothetical

[2] At several points in this chapter, we discuss the maximin criterion as a limit case of the standard social welfare function used in optimal tax. An alternative criterion is the leximin criterion, discussed in Chapter 2, which can diverge from the maximin when the worst-off individuals are unaffected by policy and which is arguably the limiting case of prioritarianism. The near absence of discussion of leximin in the optimal tax literature, perhaps because it is analytically less convenient than maximin, leads us to focus on maximin in this chapter. But the differences between maximin and leximin imply that some critiques of the former do not apply directly to prioritarianism.

"social planner" assumed to have authority over tax policy – is to derive the tax policy that will best achieve this objective given these constraints.

In a typical optimal tax analysis, the objective for policy is to maximize social welfare, an object that is calculated through a social welfare function that depends upon only the welfare (i.e., well-being) levels of the individuals in society. The founding modern optimal tax analysis of Mirrlees (1971) has the social planner maximize the following expression:

$$W = G\left(U\left(c, \frac{y}{n}; n\right)\right) f(n) dn \tag{4.1}$$

In expression (4.1), W denotes social welfare, $U(\cdot)$ individual utility[3], c consumption, y income, n an individual's exogenous and unobserved productivity (with $f(n)$ as the associated density), and $\frac{y}{n}$ labor effort. $G(\cdot)$ is the social welfare function that takes individual utilities as its arguments.

Prioritarianism fits seamlessly into this formal structure, requiring only that the social welfare function be strictly concave (and increasing) in individual welfare levels; that is, for $U_j > U_i, G'(U_j) < G'(U_i)$. In words, strict concavity of the social welfare function means that an additional unit of utility for an individual with a high level of utility increases social welfare by less than an additional unit of utility for an individual with low utility.

In fact, Mirrlees (1971) assumes the following specific form for $G(U)$ when conducting numerical analysis:

$$G(U) = \frac{-1}{\beta} e^{-\beta U} \tag{4.2}$$

Marginal social welfare from an increase in utility is thus given by:

$$G'(U) = e^{-\beta U} \tag{4.3}$$

[3] Note that we assume a one-period model of utility with homogenous preferences over consumption and leisure. Both are commonplace in optimal tax research. The former reflects that the model is best understood as a lifetime model. The latter relates to a fairly extensive literature on heterogeneous preferences both in the context of labor and capital income taxation (see Tuomala (2016), chapter 10 for a discussion). Two-dimensional problems tend to lead to difficult technical and normative problems.

Consistent with a prioritarian objective, this marginal social welfare is decreasing in the level of U for $\beta > 0$. Mirrlees assumes $\beta \geq 0$, thus putting a prioritarian objective at the heart of his analysis.[4]

In his baseline quantitative analyses, however, Mirrlees uses $\beta = 0$, the utilitarian specification in which $G'(U) = 1$, "for simplicity," leaving the prioritarian objective for robustness checks. These choices set the stage for the next nearly five decades of research in optimal tax, where prioritarianism plays an active but mostly implicit role in both analytical and quantitative results, and the default parameterization of the social welfare function that admits prioritarianism has been, instead, utilitarian.

4.1.1 Prioritarianism's Effects on Analytical Optimal Tax Results

Mirrlees (1971) derived an analytical expression for marginal tax rates that shows the central place of prioritarianism – or at least optimal tax theorists' formalization of it – in the literature. Marginal tax rates are the key determinant of the income tax structure in the Mirrlees model, and they are obtained by maximizing the objective specified in expression (4.1) subject to two sets of constraints: (1) the government needs to raise enough tax revenue to fund its spending, and (2) taxpayers will respond to tax policy to maximize their own well-being. The details of the analysis are not important to this chapter, so we skip directly to the result.[5]

Saez (2001) provided the most widely used version of this expression for optimal marginal tax rates. It is:

$$\frac{T'(y)}{1 - T'(y)} = \frac{1 - F(y)}{\varepsilon y f(y)} \int_{y}^{\infty} \frac{1 - h(z)}{1 - F(y)} dF(z) \tag{4.4}$$

In this expression, T'(y) is the marginal tax rate at income level y. The income distribution is *F(y)*, with density *f(y)*, and ε denotes the elasticity (responsiveness) of income to taxation.[6]

4 Mirrlees (1982) wrote, in the context of this welfare function: "At [the] time I used it, I had no intention of avoiding the addition of utilities, but rather of looking at the effect on optimal policies of having a more inequality averse utility function" (p. 77).

5 For derivations, see Diamond (1998) and Saez (2001) or Tuomala (2016).

6 This form was also found in Atkinson (1990) and Atkinson (1995).

Briefly, the intuition behind this formula is as follows. The optimal marginal tax rate at income y is greater when it transfers income from a larger population that earns more than y (i.e., when $1\text{-}F(y)$ is greater), when it directly distorts a smaller tax base (i.e., when $yf(y)$ is smaller), when the responsiveness of taxable income is less (i.e., when ε is smaller), and when the welfare gains of transferring resources from those with incomes greater than y are larger (i.e., when the final integrand is larger).

For the purposes of this chapter, the key term in expression (4.4) is $h(y)$, which is typically called the marginal social welfare weight (MSWW) of an individual earning income y and is defined as the social welfare generated by a marginal increase in consumption for this individual relative to a marginal increase in consumption spread equally across the entire population. Mathematically, this MSWW is made up of two components: the increase in the individual's well-being due to an increase in consumption, and the increase in social welfare that arises from an increase in that individual's well-being.

The distinction between the two components of a MSWW is important to understanding how prioritarianism differs from alternative normative principles for optimal tax theorists. In a prioritarian objective, as shown above in the case of Mirrlees' specification in expression (4.3), the second component of the MSWW has a specific feature: the increase in social welfare due to an increase in an individual's well-being is decreasing in that individual's level of well-being. Specifically, $h(y)$ decreases with y in a prioritarian objective even if the (assumed non-increasing) marginal utility of consumption is constant, because marginal social welfare is decreasing in utility and thus income. In other words, the marginal value to society of an extra unit of consumption is greater if it goes to the worse-off even if individuals' utility from income is nondecreasing because a gain in utility for the worse-off is worth more to society than a gain in utility for the better-off.

The implication of moving to a prioritarian objective from a utilitarian objective, and thus moving to an $h(y)$ in expression (4.4) that declines more rapidly with y, is that marginal tax rates are greater along the income distribution, enabling greater redistribution to individuals earning less. This result is, of course, consistent with the intention to give priority to those with less well-being. To see more specific results on its optimal policy effects, however, we need to turn to numerical simulations.

4.1.2 Prioritarianism's Effects on Quantitative Optimal Tax Results

A voluminous literature has explored how a range of specifications of the social welfare function, including those that capture a prioritarian objective, translate into quantitative optimal tax results. To solve the optimal nonlinear income tax model numerically requires four key elements.[7] We consider each in turn.

The first factor is the social welfare function (SWF). As in Mirrlees (1971), we will suppose the $G(U)$ function in the SWF takes the form in expression (4.2), where β measures the degree of inequality aversion in the SWF of the government. In the case of $\beta = 0$, we define $G(U) = U$ and have the utilitarian SWF; in the limit as $\beta \rightarrow \infty$, we have the maximin criterion in which $W = \min(U)$. Recall that the curvature in the individual's utility from consumption modifies $G'(U)\, U_c$ and makes social preferences (implicitly) more redistributive.

The second factor is the distribution of income-earning abilities. Following Mirrlees (1971), much work on optimal non-linear and linear income taxation used a lognormal distribution of productivities (e.g., Atkinson (1972), Stern (1976), Tuomala (1984), Kanbur and Tuomala (1994), Mankiw et al. (2009)). As is commonly known, the lognormal distribution fits data on incomes reasonably well over a large part of the income distribution but diverges from it markedly at both tails. The Pareto distribution in turn fits well at the upper tail. Here we will use the two-parameter version of the Champernowne distribution, with parameters m (scale parameter) and θ (shape parameter).[8] This distribution approaches asymptotically a form of the Pareto distribution for large values of wages but it also has an interior

[7] For details on these simulations, Appendix 5.2 in Tuomala (2016) describes the computational procedure and the FORTRAN program used. Standard optimal tax models simplify reality in many ways to focus on specific questions. Unfortunately, in many cases these simplifications may affect the results. For example, the interplay between marginal rates and public provision is missing in the standard optimal income tax model. Blomquist, Christiansen and Micheletto (2010) examine implications of public provision for tax distortions. They suppose public provision is strictly tied to working hours (e.g., daycare) and paid by the income tax. Then part of the tax is a direct payment, like a service fee or market price. Hence, not all of the marginal tax rate is distortionary, and one must also look at how tax revenue is spent as well as raised to get the full picture.

[8] It is also known as the Fisk distribution.

maximum. A small value for the shape parameter, say $\theta = 2$, reflects high inequality, while a larger value such as $\theta = 3$ reflects low inequality. Among two parameter distributions, it is the best fitting for pre-tax income distribution in Finland (1990–2010), where the θ parameter varies from 2.78 to 2.40 over the period and was approximately constant at 2.50 from the latter part of the 1990s to 2010.

The third factor is the shape of individual preferences. Of course, many representations of preferences are possible, and, as we will see below, which representation we choose will matter for our results. Here, we consider a utility function of the following CES form, which has been frequently used in numerical simulations:

$$U = \frac{-1}{c} - \frac{1}{1-l}, \tag{4.5}$$

where the elasticity of substitution between consumption (c) and leisure ($1 - l$) equals one-half. In the absence of taxation, the labor supply function is backward-bending given these preferences.

The fourth factor is the government's revenue requirement R, specified as the fraction of total income not used for consumption by individuals

$$R = 1 - \int \frac{c(n)f(n)dn}{y(n)f(n)dn}$$

This revenue can be interpreted as what is required to fund public goods, and its size affects the cost of raising revenue to fund transfers to poor individuals, a key distributive tool in these models.[9]

To see the effect of prioritarianism on quantitative results in optimal tax theory, we now examine what happens when we change the values for the four inputs described above.

First, the most direct effects of prioritarianism are apparent when we vary inequality aversion (i.e., through the parameter β, where prioritarianism requires $\beta > 0$). In Table 4.1 and Figures 4.1 through 4.3, we show tax schedules for different levels of β (note that these taxes should be compared with the schedules for the overall taxation of income and expenditures in real economies). All the calculated tax schedules take the form of a lump sum credit (or basic income)

[9] Weinzierl (2018) raises the concern that how tax revenue is spent may matter for the distribution of income, a dependence largely assumed away in the literature.

Table 4.1. ***Tax schedules for different social objective parameterizations***

Table 4.1. f = Champernowne distribution holding mean constant $m = e^{-1}$, $\theta = 2.5$, R = 0.1, $u = -\frac{1}{c} - \frac{1}{(1-l)}$

	F(n) = Percentiles of wage distribution									
	$\beta = 0$	$\beta = 0$	$\beta = 0.5$	$\beta = 0.5$	$\beta = 1$	$\beta = 1$	$\beta = 2$	$\beta = 2$	$\beta = \infty$	$\beta = \infty$
F(n)	ATR	MTR	ATR	MTR	ATR	MTR	ATR	MTR	ATR	MTR
	%	%	%	%	%	%	%	%	%	%
0.10	−133	62	−198	70	−200	74	−400	77		
0.50	3	61	−8	69	−7	73	−12	75	−6	79
0.90	35	63	39	69	42	69	43	72	47	72
0.97	45	64	51	69	52	64	55	70	57	70
0.99	52	64	57	67	54	47	59	67	60	63

Note: Table 4.1 shows the average tax rate (ATR) and marginal tax rate (MTR) schedules – along points in the income distribution F(n) – for different values of the parameter β in the social welfare function, given the parameter values shown atop the table.

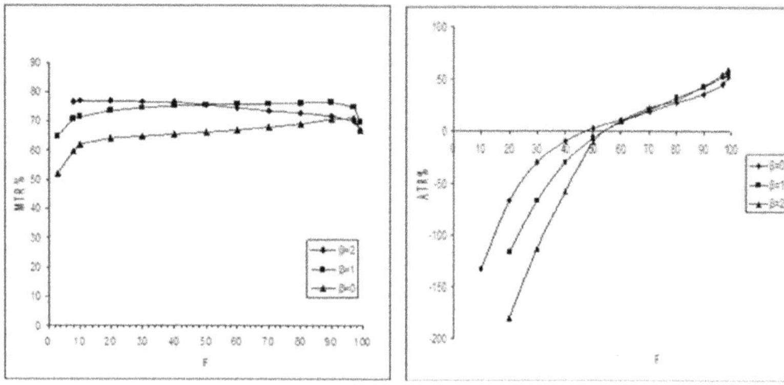

Figure 4.1 Tax schedules for prioritarian and utilitarian social objectives
Note: Figure 4.1a plots the marginal tax rate (MTR) and Figure 4.1b the average tax rate (ATR) schedules – over the income distribution F(n) – for values of the parameter β in the social welfare function, given the parameter values shown atop the table.

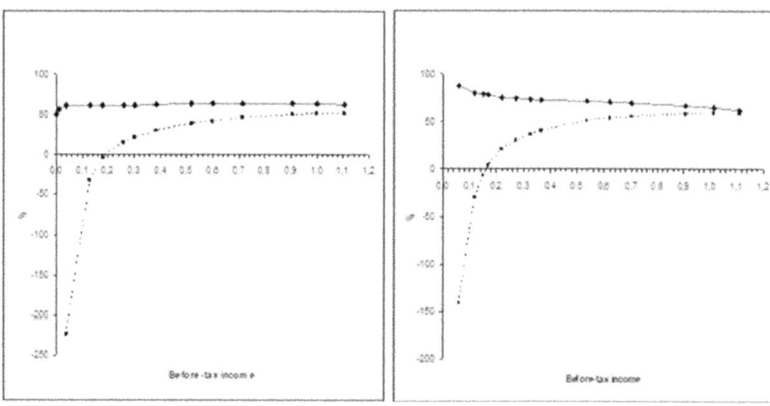

Figure 4.2 Tax schedules for utilitarian and maximin social objectives
Note: Figure 4.2a plots the MTR and ATR schedules – against before-tax labor income – for the utilitarian social welfare function ($\beta = 0$), given the parameter values shown atop the table. Figure 4.2b does the same for the maximin social welfare function ($\beta \rightarrow \infty$).

followed by marginal tax rates, and we plot these schedules against incomes.

Our numerical results suggest that marginal tax rates tend to increase for all taxpayers with increasing inequality aversion. One

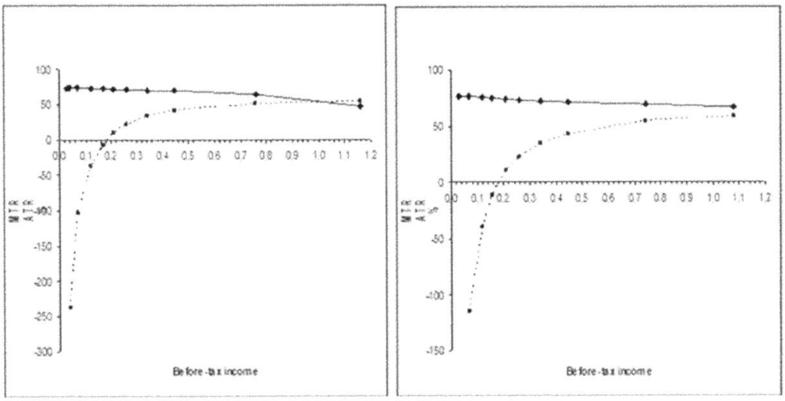

Figures 4.3a and 4.3b Tax schedules for prioritarian social objectives
Note: Figure 4.3a plots the MTR and ATR schedules – against before-tax income – for the social welfare function with $\beta = 1$, given the parameter values shown atop the table. Figure 4.3b does the same for $\beta = 2$.

might have expected that increasing β above 1.0 would have a particularly large effect, but our calculations show that this is not true. In fact, it can be seen that the difference in the marginal rates between the case $\beta = 1$ (or $\beta = 2$) and the maximin solution (the limit as $\beta \rightarrow\infty$) is not very large, whereas it is much more marked between the case $\beta = 1$ and the utilitarian case $\beta = 0$. Our results also seem to suggest that a sufficiently high level of inequality aversion (a large enough β) leads to a pattern of optimally declining marginal tax rates, and indeed in the maximin case we find that marginal tax rates decline monotonically with income. It may be surprising that the maximin (Rawlsian, as in Rawls (1971)) objective does not lead to increasing marginal tax rates, but this pattern follows from the fact that this objective is not concerned with inequality among those not in the "least fortunate group". Average tax rates rise with income much more steeply in the maximin case than in the utilitarian case considered in our simulations. On the other hand, it can be seen that the maximin case and the case $\beta = 2$ do not differ much in terms of average tax rates. That is, they do not differ much in the extent of redistribution. We will return to the extent of the redistribution later in this chapter.

In addition to exploring different parameter values within the SWF of the form in expression (4.2), called the Kolm–Pollak form or

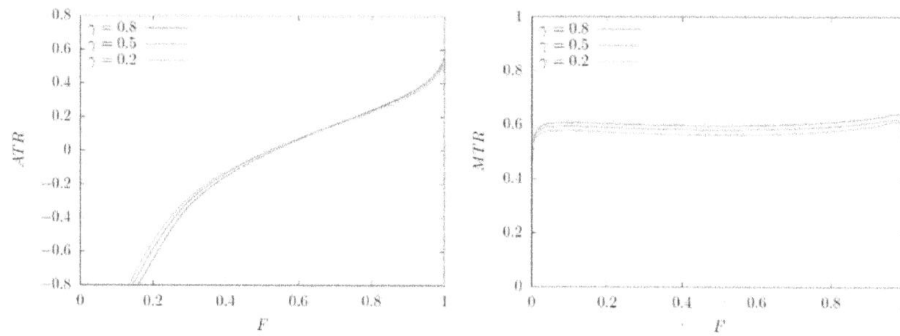

Figures 4.3c and 4.3d Tax schedules for Atkinson form of the social objective
Note: These figures plot the MTR and ATR schedules – over the income distribution F(n) – for the Atkinson form of the social welfare function with several values for γ, given CES utility and a Champernowne ability distribution.

(especially in this chapter's context) the Kolm–Mirrlees–Pollak form, we also consider a constant relative utility-inequality aversion form: the so-called Atkinson form of

$$V(U) = \frac{U^{1-\gamma}}{1-\gamma}$$

The numerical simulations with the Atkinson form prove cumbersome when γ is greater than 1. We settled for numerical solutions where γ is less than 1. The results of the simulations are summarized in Figures 4.3c and 4.3d, using the CES case (expression 4.5) with a Champernowne distribution. The revenue requirement $R = 0.1$ in all cases. As expected, an increase in γ leads to higher marginal tax rates in both specifications. The pattern and the levels of MTR's and ATR's are similar to those we have in the Kolm–Mirrlees–Pollak case for β between 0 and 0.5.

The discussion of tax structures in the optimal income tax literature has been almost entirely about marginal tax rates. Notably, almost all analytical results focus on the structure of marginal tax rates to the neglect of average tax rates, the latter of which are arguably more important indicators of income tax progressivity. After all, high marginal tax rates as such perform no direct distributional function; their purpose is to increase average tax rates higher up the income scale. In fact, in all cases shown in our tables and figures, average tax rates are increasing in income. Analytically it is difficult to establish this, but computational techniques can demonstrate these patterns.

Second, we gauge the sensitivity of the shape of the tax schedule to the joint choice of the parameter θ in the Champernowne distribution and the parameter β, the degree of inequality aversion. In Table 4.2, we computed solutions when θ varies from 2.0 to 3.3 with the CES utility function in (expression 4.5) and different β parameters. When $\theta = 3.3$, marginal tax rates are declining. When $\theta = 2.0$ and $\beta = 0$, marginal tax rates are increasing with income to around the 98th percentile; when $\beta = 1$ they are increasing to the 96th percentile.

As an alternative SWF, we calculate solutions for rank order SWFs. Aaberge (2007) provides a parametric variant for rank order social preferences as follows

$$G_k = \begin{cases} -lnF \;\; for\; k = 1 \\ \frac{k}{k-1}\left(1 - F^{k-1}\right) \; for\; k = 2, 3, 4 \ldots \end{cases},$$

where F denotes the percentile of the income distribution for an individual. When k approaches ∞, this weighting function approaches the utilitarian case and there is no concern for inequality. When $k = 2$, then $G_2 = 2(1\text{-}F)$, which is in effect the weighting underlying the Gini coefficient, as shown by Sen (1974) who provided an axiomatic justification for such a social welfare function. In this case, the social marginal valuation declines linearly with F from twice the average for the lowest paid taxpayer to zero for the highest paid taxpayer. The optimal tax schedules with utilitarian and Gini weights differ considerably, with marginal rates being higher in the latter (see Figure 4.4).

Third, we consider different expressions for individual preferences. Most previous simulations (see Mirrlees (1971), Atkinson (1972), Tuomala (1984), Kanbur and Tuomala (1994)) have used either logarithmic (Cobb-Douglas) utility of consumption or what is shown in expression (4.5), both of which are instances of the utility functional form in which the coefficient of relative risk aversion (the CRRA, which controls the curvature of utility over consumption) is constant (in these cases, it is 1.0 and 2.0, respectively). In light of Table 1 in Chetty (2006), those values may be too high. In addition, other preferences yield more complex – and arguably more realistic – relationships between net wage and labour supply. In empirical labor supply studies, e.g. Keane and Moffitt (2001), preferences over working time and net income are given by a utility function that is quadratic in hours and net

Table 4.2. ***Tax schedules for different social objective and ability distribution parameterizations***

Table 4.2. f = Champernowne distribution holding mean constant $m = e^{-1}$, $\theta = 3.3, 2.0$, $R = 0.1$, $u = -\frac{1}{c} - \frac{1}{(1-l)}$

F(n) = Percentiles of wage distribution								
	$\beta = 0$	$\beta = 0$	$\beta = 1$	$\beta = 1$	$\beta = 0$	$\beta = 0$	$\beta = 1$	$\beta = 1$
	$\theta = 3.3$	$\theta = 3.3$	$\theta = 3.3$	$\theta = 3.3$	$\theta = 2.0$	$\theta = 2.0$	$\theta = 2.0$	$\theta = 2.0$
F(n)	ATR%	MTR%	ATR%	MTR%	ATR%	MTR%	ATR%	MTR%
0.10	−50	58	−100	73	−100	62	−100	71
0.50	6	52	3	67	−18	66	−29	75
0.90	27	52	55	64	41	71	47	76
0.97	33	53	44	61	55	71	61	75
0.99	39	51	47	58	60	68	65	70

Note: Table 4.2 shows the average tax rate (ATR) and marginal tax rate (MTR) schedules – along points in the income distribution F(n) – for different values of the distributional parameter θ and the parameter β in the social welfare function, given the other parameter values shown atop the table.

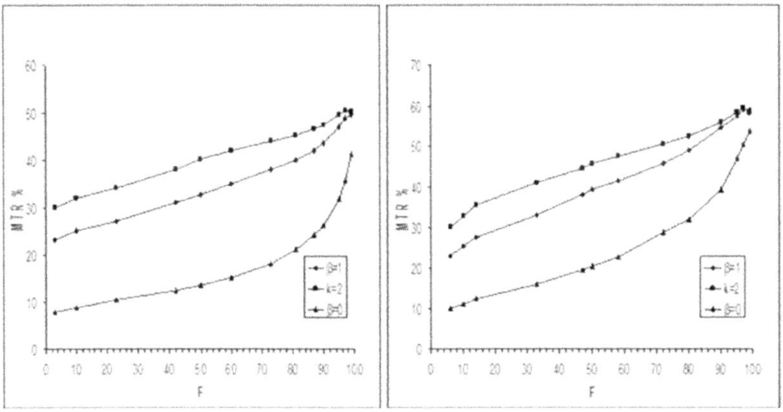

Figure 4.4 Tax schedules for different social objectives, quadratic utility specification

Note: Figures 4.4a and 4.4b plot the marginal tax rate (MTR) schedules – over the income distribution F(n) – for different social welfare functions, assuming the quadratic form for utility in expression (4.6) and the parameter values shown atop the figures.

income. To illustrate the effects of using this alternative specification, we solve numerically cases in which the utility function is quadratic in consumption:

$$u = (c-1) - a(c-1)^2 - (1-l) \tag{4.6}$$

The curvature in the utility from consumption in (4.6) is smaller than that used in the previous simulations, and the coefficient of relative risk aversion varies at different values of c. With the parameterization used in our computations (including $a = 5$), the values of the coefficient of relative risk aversion are smaller and more in line with the empirical labor supply literature. Moreover, the elasticity-based marginal tax formulas turn out to be useful because we can calculate traditional labor supply elasticities at each point of the distribution.

The striking thing in the numerical results shown in Figures 4.4 (plotted against income percentiles) and 4.5 (plotted against income levels) is that once we assume that preferences are given by the utility function that is quadratic in consumption, the shape of optimum tax schedules may be altered drastically. The marginal tax

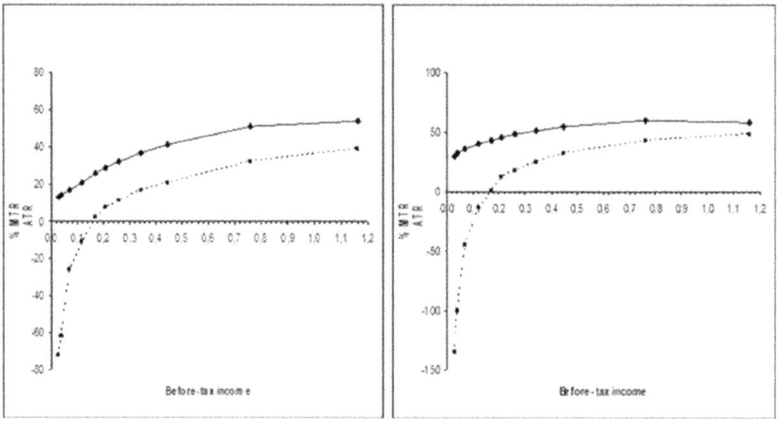

Figure 4.5 Tax schedules for utilitarian and prioritarian social objectives, quadratic utility specification

Note: Figures 4.5a and 4.5b plot the MTR and ATR schedules – against before-tax incomes – for utilitarian and prioritarian social welfare functions, assuming the quadratic form for utility in expression (4.6) and the parameter values shown atop the figures.

rates rise with income, practically speaking, over the whole range (up to the 99.7 percentile point), except that in cases $\beta = 1$ and $\beta = 2$ marginal rates decline slightly at the very top of the earnings distribution. The reason for this is that this utility function with an upper bound on consumption implies a concave budget constraint in the Mirrlees model.

Next, we explore how sensitive is the level of the lump sum transfer (or basic income) component of the tax system to the specification of the model. Tables 4.3 and 4.4 display the ratios of the basic income to the average net income with different welfare weights and values for θ when utility is either (expression 4.5) or (expression 4.6) and the revenue requirement is 10 percent of total income.

This ratio is clearly higher in the case of $\beta = 1$ and Gini weights 2 $(1 - F)$(when $k = 2$) than in the case of the pure utilitarian $\beta = 0$. The ratio is increasing with pre-tax inequality (i.e., decreasing in θ).

Since marginal tax rates may be a poor indication of the redistribution powers of an optimal tax structure, we measure the extent of redistribution, denoted by *RD*, as the proportional reduction between the percentile ratio P90/P50 for market income y and disposable

Tables 4.3. and 4.4. ***Level of basic income under different utility and social objective specifications***

Table 4.3. The ratio of x_o (basic income) to the average net income

	$u = -\frac{1}{c} - \frac{1}{(1-l)}$ and R = 0.1		
θ	$\beta = 0$	$\beta = 1$	k = 2, Gini weights
3.0	0.53	0.66	0.62
2.5	0.61	0.69	0.67
2.0	0.62	0.70	0.65

Table 4.4. The ratio of x_o (basic income) to the average net income

	$u = (c-1) - a(c-1)^2 - (1-l)^{-1}$, a = 5 and R = 0.1		
θ	$\beta = 0$	$\beta = 1$	k = 2, Gini weights
3.3	0.06	0.25	0.33
2.5	0.15	0.35	0.42
2.0	0.25	0.44	0.51

Note: Tables 4.3 and 4.4 show the basic income level as a share of the average income level for different specifications of utility, the ability distribution, and the social welfare function (as shown atop each table).

income c.[10] In other words, *RD* captures the extent to which pre-tax inequality between these points in the income distribution is reduced through taxation. Tables 4.5 and 4.6 show the extent of redistribution (in terms of our measure) for the two forms of the utility function we consider and different distributional objectives.

We can ask: Is pre-tax inequality (which is decreasing in θ) more important than redistributional preferences in determining the extent of redistribution? In response, perhaps the most interesting finding in our simulations can be seen in Table 4.7.

It turns out that increasing β above 1 has a very modest effect to the effect of redistribution. This is true for all three values of θ. Hence, the extent of redistribution is about the same in the $\beta = 1$ case as in the

[10] Unlike the scalar inequality measures, the use of fractile measures such as the percentile ratio allows us to consider changes in inequality at various different points in the distribution.

Tables 4.5. and 4.6. *Extent of redistribution under different utility and social objective specifications*

Table 4.5. The extent of redistribution (RD)

	$u = -\frac{1}{c} - \frac{1}{(1-l)}$, R = 0.1		
θ	$\beta = 0$	$\beta = 1$	k = 2, Gini weights
3.0	60.0	67.0	61.6
2.5	71.8	86.1	80.3
2.0	84.3	93	92.9

Table 4.6. The extent of redistribution (RD):

	$u = (c-1) - a(c-1)^2 - (1-l)^{-1}$, a = 5 R = 0.1		
θ	$\beta = 0$	$\beta = 1$	k = 2, Gini weights
3.3	31.1	49.5	28.1
2.5	52.3	55.0	44.4
2.0		61.6	57.3

Note: Tables 4.5 and 4.6 show a measure of redistribution – defined in the text – for different specifications of utility, the ability distribution, and the social welfare function (as shown atop each table).

Table 4.7. *Extent of redistribution under different utility and social objective specifications*

Table 4.7. The extent of redistribution (RD); utility function $u = -\frac{1}{c} - \frac{1}{(1-l)}$, P90/P50, R = 0.1

θ	β = 0	β = 1	Maximin	Gini weights
3.3	22.6	34.0	36.8	33.0
2.5	37.3	47.5	50.7	44.3
2.0	47.0	60.0	61.7	60.5

Note: Table 4.7 shows a measure of redistribution – defined in the text – for different specifications of utility, the ability distribution, and the social welfare function (as shown atop the table).

maximin case. It is important to note that the extent of redistribution and rising marginal tax rates may be quite different things. The extent of redistribution is larger with higher β, but the marginal tax schedule may be rising in the case of $\beta = 0$.

Tables 4.8. and 4.9. ***Extent of redistribution under different revenue requirements***

Table 4.8. The extent of redistribution (RD), utility function, $u = -\frac{1}{c} - \frac{1}{(1-l)}$, P90/P50, θ = 3

R	$\beta = 0$	$\beta = 1$
0.1	22.9	33.0
0.2	9.1	32.0

Table 4.9. The extent of redistribution (RD), utility function $u = -\frac{1}{c} - \frac{1}{(1-l)}$, P90/P10, θ = 3

R	$\beta = 0$	$\beta = 1$
0.1	51.6	69.1
0.2	14.0	67.4

Note: Tables 4.8 and 4.9 show a measure of redistribution – defined in the text – for different values of β and the revenue requirement R, given the parameters shown atop each table.

Finally, if larger tax revenues are to be raised, would it mean significant changes in the shape of the tax schedule? Our earlier numerical results seem to suggest that marginal tax rates tend to increase for most taxpayers with increasing net government expenditure. The shape of the tax schedule remains quite similar, however, in spite of changes in government expenditure. As expected, in the following tables we see the extent of redistribution is much smaller in the utilitarian case than in the prioritarian case (with $\beta = 1$). Perhaps slightly surprising, in the utilitarian case the extent of redistribution declines dramatically with an increased revenue requirement, whereas in the prioritarian case it changes little (see Tables 4.8 and 4.9).

In sum, the optimal income tax schedule is very sensitive to many key modeling choices and parameter assumptions. Moreover, these choices interact in complicated ways. For example, consider the choice of the form of utility from consumption. Unlike in most of cases with the CES utility function (expression 4.5), marginal tax rates rise with income when we assume that utility is quadratic in consumption. Hence, the interaction between two components of an MSWW plays a central role in determining the shape of the tax schedule.

4.2 Prioritarianism and the Practice of Taxation

We now turn from the task of designing prioritarian-optimal taxation to that of examining prioritarianism's place in prevailing tax policies and attitudes toward them. After all, the scholarly study of taxation must be in dialogue with the reality of taxation if it is to be seen as relevant to those who vote on and are affected by it.

4.2.1 Are Existing Taxes Prioritarian? An Overview of Inverse Optimum Research

A recent literature tries to extract the implicit judgments of society – e.g., society's MSWWs in the Mirrlees model discussed above – from existing tax policy. Called the "inverse optimum" approach, the idea of this research is that the optimal tax model can be run "in reverse" to back out society's objective function, once we assume a set of constraints and have data on outcomes. That is, an implied schedule of marginal social welfare weights can be inferred from optimal tax formulas by populating them with existing tax schedules and values for all non-normative parameters, leaving the welfare weights as the only unknowns.

Inverse optimum researchers have generally found that MSWWs are non-negative and greater on low earners than high earners, but consensus on more specific normative implications – such as the policies' fit with prioritarianism – remains elusive. An inventory of results would include, among others, the following. A very early contribution was Christiansen and Jansen (1978), who study Norway and find that its implicit inequality aversion parameter is quite far from the utilitarian value, giving more social weight to low-income people. A similar study was carried out in India by Ahmad and Stern (1984); they also infer substantial inequality aversion. Stern (1977) finds, however, that the UK system implicitly fits with an equal sacrifice principle quite far from prioritarianism (and discussed below). More recent studies have used micro data, such as the pioneering work of Bourguignon and Spadaro (2012), who consider the revealed social preferences of the French tax-benefit system. Spadaro et al. (2012) study the tax and transfer systems of 26 European countries, finding evidence of Rawlsian policies in some countries but less redistributive policies in others. Bargain et al. (2014) consider the tax and transfer systems of 17 EU countries and the United States and find that social welfare weights are always positive, though they are not monotonically declining for low-income groups, and that there are significant differences in social welfare weights between, but not within, groups of countries (e.g., the US vs Continental Europe, Scandinavia, and Southern Europe). Lockwood and Weinzierl (2016) examine the US tax system over time, highlighting the relative stability of implicit weights over the last several decades. Jacobs, Jongen, and Zoutman (2017) use this method to find the redistributive preferences implicit in the reform proposals of Dutch political parties and find that all parties give a higher social weight to the poor than the rich.

Such an inventory of results is difficult to synthesize, however, and (as far as we are aware) no meta-analysis of the inverse optimum literature exists. Complicating a synthesis is that existing results span a range of countries, time periods, and estimation approaches, and they are communicated in many different ways. While most authors discuss whether their estimated weights are consistent with Pareto efficiency (i.e., whether they are non-negative) and their overall shape (e.g., whether they are declining in income), only some authors discuss whether their estimates are consistent with utilitarian, Rawlsian, libertarian, prioritarian, or other more specific normative principles. We hope to begin filling this gap, and in the process provide some evidence on the role of prioritarianism in the practice of taxation.

Given the diversity within the inverse optimum literature, performing a meta-analysis requires us to impose some structure if we hope to say something informative about prevailing policy and prioritarianism. We will rely on the functional forms discussed above: in particular, we will use the form

$$G(U) = \frac{-1}{\beta} e^{-\beta U}$$

for social welfare as a function of individual utility and

$$U(c) = \frac{(c - \bar{c})^{1-\lambda} - 1}{1 - \lambda}$$

for utility, which is a generalization of the CES form (i.e., where $\lambda = 2$). The only unfamiliar term in these expressions is $\bar{c}$, which we include to represent a "minimum acceptable" level of consumption. While this term is somewhat unconventional, it plays an important role in making our numerical analysis suitable to existing policies because, fortunately, no households in the advanced economies for which inverse optimum analyses have been completed face the prospect of zero consumption. Rather, these societies appear to have established a minimum level of consumption below which individuals are not allowed to fall. By including the $\bar{c}$ term, we assign the high marginal utilities of consumption implied by $\lambda > 0$ to the individuals whose after-tax incomes place them nearest to this minimum acceptable level.[11]

Our procedure is as follows. We survey the inverse optimum literature by country. For each analysis, we record the estimated marginal social welfare weights at a set of income percentiles (0, 10, 25, 50, 75, and 90 where available). Each of these points corresponds to a level of disposable (after-tax and -transfer) income. We then numerically find the value of β for a range of values of λ that, assuming our functional forms above, imply marginal social welfare weights that minimize the unweighted sum of squared errors from these recorded estimates.

For reference, recall that $\beta = 0$ is a utilitarian SWF, and prioritarianism corresponds to $\beta > 0$. Similarly, $\lambda = 0$ implies utility that is linear in consumption, while concave utility corresponds to $\lambda > 0$ (with $\lambda = 1$, log utility, a standard benchmark).

To illustrate our results, consider the following figures for Finland:

The top figure plots the pairs of β and λ that provide the best fit to two separate, well-known, inverse optimum estimates: those by Bargain et al. (2014) and Spadaro et al. (2015). The bottom figure shows the estimated MSWWs from these papers at the discrete points in the income distribution (the dots) along with an example of the fitted MSWW curves for each (in fact, it shows the best- fitting curves among the possible parameter pairs for each paper). Note that consumption of zero in the bottom figure is the point at which $c = \bar{c}$ not c = 0.

These results for Finland reveal two lessons that appear, from our early steps in this analysis, to apply across a wide range of countries.

First, the estimated MSWWs are "too flat for too long" to be well-described by a SWF with substantial concavity over consumption. The dots for both papers lie above the fitted curves at higher-income percentiles, as the SWF has a difficult time assigning sizeable positive

[11] Note that this modification to the utility function is not a positive affine transformation – so that the transformed utility function is not CRRA – and it is not the kind of rescaling proposed in Chapter 2 and undertaken in Chapter 8.

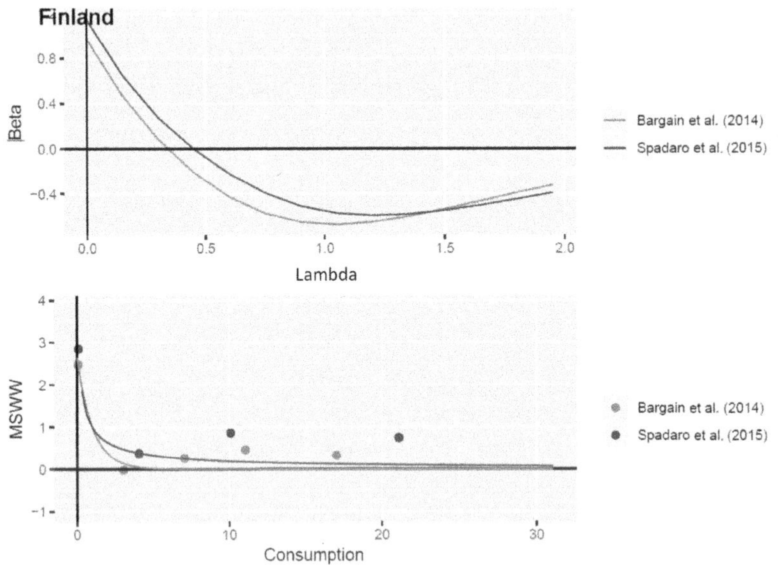

Figure 4.6 Inverse optimum results for tax policy in Finland
Note: Figure 4.6 shows the pairs (λ, β) that best explain existing tax policy (top graph) and the marginal social welfare weights implied by the best-fitting (λ, β) pair (bottom graph).

weights to the relatively well-off, explaining why this "too flat for too long result" appears to apply to the inferred values, not the fitted curve.

Second, a prioritarian objective for policy can be inferred from the data only if the concavity of individual utility is well below levels typically assumed. That is, the trade-off between concavity in the social welfare function ($\beta > 0$) and in the individual utility function ($\lambda > 0$) is severe, and $\beta > 0$ obtains only at values for λ far below the standard benchmark of $\lambda = 1$. The utilitarian case ($\beta = 0$) is consistent with a value of $\lambda = 0.5$, larger than for prioritarianism but still substantially lower than typically estimated.

Other countries yield similar lessons. Take, for example, the United States.

Here, the two lessons are even more stark. The estimated welfare weights are far too flat at too high incomes for $\beta > 0$ and $\lambda > 0$ to hold. Strikingly, the estimates for Lockwood (2017) and Lockwood and Weinzierl (2016) lie below their best-fit lines only because these lines are upward-sloping, using a $\beta < 0$ to generate increasing MSWWs.

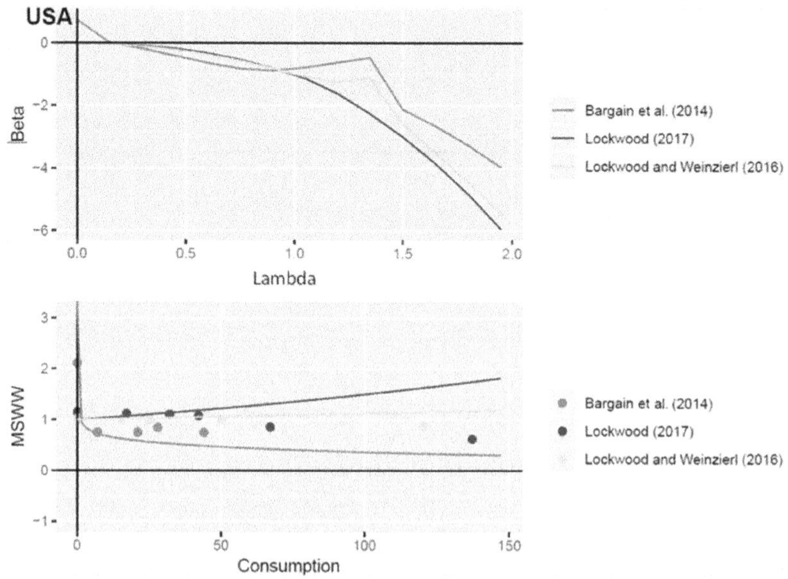

Figure 4.7 Inverse optimum results for tax policy in the United States
Note: Figure 4.7 shows the pairs (λ, β) that best explain existing tax policy (top graph) and the marginal social welfare weights implied by the best-fitting (λ, β) pair (bottom graph).

Moreover, the scope for $\beta > 0$ is extremely limited in the case of the United States (as shown in the top panel). For virtually all values of λ, the SWF must give greater weight to those with greater utility levels – a sort of anti-prioritarianism – to be consistent with prevailing policies.

Similar figures can be generated for a range of economies. These two lessons apply in nearly all cases.

Of course, our analysis could be improved in many ways in future research. Most important would be to have additional inverse optimum results to fit. Experimenting with the MSWWs implied by different underlying functional forms, as our simulations from earlier in the chapter suggested, can affect optimal rates substantially. And an important step will be to clarify the role of different policy components (e.g., taxes versus medical insurance) in driving the MSWW estimates. Perhaps these and other improvements in the elicitation or analysis of inverse optimum estimates will revise the implication that is hard to avoid from the current results: we lack strong evidence that prioritarianism is a prominent guiding principle of existing tax policy.

4.2.2 Are Tax Policy Preferences Prioritarian? Positive Optimal Taxation

A recent literature, referred to as positive optimal tax theory, studies prevailing views on distributive justice and thus taxation among the general public. Using both theory and empirics, this new literature attempts to complement philosophical introspection with the use of empirically verifiable evidence for social preferences. In this way, the positive optimal tax theory project can be seen as a way to accommodate both discomfort with imposing normative judgments and a desire to go beyond Pareto efficiency.

Early papers in positive optimal tax theory are Weinzierl (2014, 2017) and Saez and Statcheva (2015), each of which finds evidence suggesting that prevailing normative priorities in the United States are not well-captured by prioritarianism. Weinzierl (2014) asks US survey respondents to choose between two tax policy alternatives: one based on the standard utilitarian criterion and the other based on the principle of Equal Sacrifice, a less redistributive alternative supported by John Stuart Mill (1871) in which each individual's tax burden imposes the same sacrifice in absolute utility terms. He finds that a majority of the respondents choose the latter, suggesting that support for the more redistributive prioritarian objective (as the sole guide to policy) would be quite limited. In subsequent work, Weinzierl (2017) finds similar enthusiasm for the principle of taxation preferred by Adam Smith (1776), referred to by Richard Musgrave (1959) as Classical Benefit-Based Taxation. As with Equal Sacrifice, popular support for this principle is sharply at odds with any claim that prioritarianism captures the public's priorities for tax policy. Saez and Stantcheva (2016) introduce the formal tool of Generalized Social Marginal Welfare Weights to the modern optimal tax model, where prioritarianism could be easily captured formally (i.e., by weights that decline even if individual marginal utility from consumption is constant). They gather survey evidence on preferred values for those weights in the United States, and they find substantial support for values reflecting a mix of principles: "...social preferences are in between the polar utilitarian and libertarian cases," they write. In sum, recent evidence points away from prioritarianism (or utilitarianism) as a good guide to how the public thinks about tax policy, at least in the US context. (Also see Chapter 10 for related evidence)

What can this evidence tell us about which normative principles are consistent with existing policy? One possibility is that policies reflect a mix of priorities that, together, generate a strong interest in helping the worse-off but a weak interest in redistribution across the rest of the income distribution. Perhaps the preferences of Richard Musgrave (in Buchanan and Musgrave, 1999) are as good a guide as any: "Moreover, observers such as myself who tend to be egalitarian should not rule out the norm of Lockean entitlement to earnings (Locke 1690, Nozick 1974) as an alternative criterion that also deserves consideration. Most people, I suggest, would wish to assign some weight to both norms. . . . I would give it, say, one-quarter weight with three-quarters to the Rawlsian concept."

4.3 The Future of Prioritarianism in Optimal Tax Theory and Practice

Consider this striking fact: none of five of the most important, authoritative book-length treatments of modern optimal tax theory includes "prioritarianism" in its index (nor, aside from minor exceptions that we have found, in their texts). In order of publication, these are Louis Kaplow (2008), The Mirrlees Review (2010, 2011), Bernard Salanie (2011), Robin Boadway (2012), and Matti Tuomala (2016). Of course, all of these books prominently feature the implicitly prioritarian social welfare function discussed earlier, but none considers the case for a prioritarian specification of it by that name.

The lack of explicit engagement with prioritarianism may reflect the youth of prioritarianism as a named concept (it was first introduced into published philosophical works around 2000) or economists' naivete regarding normative considerations, but it may also reflect an underlying discomfort with the principle. After all, the bar for embracing a particular normative standard is extremely high among most economists, including optimal tax theorists, who are hesitant to wade into philosophical debate and have long been tempted to limit their analysis to determining only the (Pareto) efficiency of tax policy.

As discussed above, utilitarianism serves as something like a default normative principle for many economists. To prioritarianism's supporters, its delineation from utilitarianism is a selling point, but to most optimal tax theorists it is an obstacle. Skepticism toward prioritarianism can be traced to the tremendously influential – among economists, at least – arguments of William Vickrey and John Harsanyi, as well as Kenneth Arrow's defense of them, in which utilitarianism was derived as a social analogue to individual expected utility maximization. Many economists view debates over the normative objective of policy as having been essentially resolved by their contributions – resolved, that is, in favor of utilitarianism.[12] As Louis Kaplow (2008) notes, when choosing among possible allocations from behind a veil of ignorance, a prioritarian social welfare function will recommend policies that deliver lower expected utilities to everyone in society, violating an ex ante version of the Pareto criterion that economists tend to hold in high esteem. A utilitarian social welfare function avoids this concern. Of course, respecting ex ante Pareto comes at a cost: utilitarianism cannot

[12] Economists have tended to see the prioritarian view as a less extreme version of John Rawls's difference principle under which priority is given to the worst-off in society. (The use of maximin in much optimal tax research is driven – at least in part – by its tractability and its position opposite utilitarianism on a redistributive spectrum). Skepticism toward Rawls's claims, therefore, has contaminated economists' views of prioritarianism. Kenneth Arrow (1973) famously compared Rawls's principle to the analysis of William Vickrey and John Harsanyi, who employed similar thought experiments to Rawls's veil of ignorance but obtained strikingly different results. Vickrey and Harsanyi approached the problem of choosing an SWF as formally equivalent to the problem of individual choice under uncertainty. They argued that rational individuals choosing economic policy with an equal probability of becoming any realized person – e.g., from behind what Rawls called the veil of ignorance – would choose a utilitarian social welfare function so as to maximize their expected level of well-being. Rawls (1972) thought this logic for utilitarianism failed to adequately account for the degree of risk aversion that agents behind the veil of ignorance would surely feel when faced with such high-stakes consequences. But Arrow disputed that argument by noting that Rawls, in turn, failed to account for Vickrey and Harsanyi's representation of utility, which already embedded risk aversion. Arrow then demonstrated that, far from being opposed to utilitarianism, the difference principle could be viewed as "a limiting case of it." That is, if individual preferences were represented by von Neumann-Morgenstern utility and the degree of risk aversion approached infinity, a properly scaled utilitarian social welfare function would approach the maximin criterion. Rawls (1972) objected to Arrow's interpretation of his difference principle as a limiting case of utilitarianism. He thought it was wrong to suggest that we can "shift smoothly from the moral conception to another simply by varying the parameter" (p. 664). In fact, Rawls thought that an important feature of a distributive criterion is that it should serve as a public principle. He wrote that "citizens generally should be able to understand it and have some confidence that it is realized" (Rawls, 1972 p. 143). He claimed that the maximin, unlike utilitarianism, satisfies this criterion of sharpness or transparency.

respect the Pigou-Dalton principle at the heart of prioritarianism. (See Chapter 2 of this volume for a more detailed discussion of this trade-off.)

A closely related critique of prioritarianism (also discussed in Chapter 2) is that it may invite confusion over the root of concavity in distributional judgments. In the first several decades following Mirrlees (1971), most optimal tax theorists explicitly stated a separate utility function and social welfare function. More recently, however, and often in numerical applications, it has become common to adopt a "reduced form" implicit composition of these two functions and, thus, conceptually combine their concavities (over utility levels and income, respectively). Louis Kaplow (2010) strongly objects to this approach, arguing that these two layers of concavity are conceptually distinct and showing that they are not mathematically additive in the way some theorists assume. Prioritarians agree with Kaplow, separating clearly these two layers of concavity. But anti-prioritarians prefer avoiding the confusion altogether by simply omitting concavity in the social welfare function, in part because the concavity of the individual utility function reflects declining marginal utility of income that is (arguably) empirically verifiable while the concavity of the social welfare function involves a value judgment that is not.

Perhaps the most direct path for prioritarianism to gain acceptance is for it to be seen as a plausible – even preferable – alternative to utilitarianism. After all, it shares the tractability that economists so value in utilitarianism, so if philosophers were to give economists good reasons to prefer it on normative grounds, the latter would likely be receptive. For example, prioritarianism might be put forward as a viable candidate for a sufficiently flexible and general single objective that can capture the normative pluralism behind existing tax policies and prevailing tax policy preferences identified in this chapter. As another example, the work of Fleurbaey and Maniquet (2006, 2018) provides an axiomatic derivation of "fair taxation" designed to incorporate a careful response to preference heterogeneity – a long-standing concern in the optimal tax literature[13] – and derives the following

[13] While earlier theorists such as Mill (1871) and Edgeworth (1897) were comfortable using cardinal measures of utility across individuals, the rise of the New New Welfare Economics of the 1930s caused many economists to view utility as an ordinal rather than a cardinal object. If utility levels and changes have no cardinal meaning for individuals, then redistributive preferences – e.g., prioritarian preferences – that compare levels and changes in utilities across

result: "the optimal tax should give the greatest subsidies to the working poor (the agents having the lowest skill and choosing the largest labour)."[14] This conclusion is resonant with the ideals of prioritarianism, which is perhaps not surprising given that one of Fleurbaey and Maniquet's axioms is the Pigou-Dalton principle.

individuals are similarly meaningless. Instead, all one can say is whether individuals gain or lose from a policy change.

To economists, the attractiveness of analyses limited to ordinal comparisons survives to the present day. For example, Ivan Werning, a leading modern optimal tax theorist, provides conditions for Pareto efficient bounds on tax rates in Werning (2007) and notes, at the outset of the paper, "It is worth remarking that, given the focus on Pareto efficiency, no interpersonal comparisons of utility will be needed. Thus, the cardinality of preferences is completely irrelevant and only the ordinal features of preferences matter."

Compelling as it remains, resistance to interpersonal comparisons of utility was weakened in the 1970s with the rise of what Stiglitz (1987) called the New New Welfare Economics. While economists of this era retained a respect for the Pareto criterion, they sought a way around the limits it imposed. As Stiglitz noted, "it still remains the case that many of the critical choices necessitate interpersonal trade-offs, choices among alternative Pareto-efficient allocations." In response, these economists – led by Mirrlees – advocated the use of the social welfare function to evaluate and even compare different Pareto efficient allocations. This shift made room for the use of normative principles such as prioritarianism in the leading models of optimal taxation.

While modern theorists have thus embraced interpersonal utility comparisons of the sort required by prioritarianism, following through on this choice raises a number of difficulties. To cite just one example, most modern optimal tax analyses assume all individuals have the same utility function in order to aggregate utilities. If preferences across goods are heterogeneous, however, the way these preferences are represented in the utility function will matter for optimal policy and requires a normative judgment.

14 There are well-known technical difficulties related to incentive constraints to study multidimensional optimal tax problems including both of the elements. Another problem is how to incorporate heterogeneous preferences into a social welfare function (SWF) in analyzing optimal tax policy. There is a growing body of literature which studies multidimensional optimal tax problems by avoiding the technical complications by assuming that multidimensionalities can be represented with a one-dimensional aggregation of the multidimensional characters. Lockwood and Weinzierl (2015) take this approach.

In the spirit of Roemer (1998) and Van de Gaer (1993) another approach is to apply a compromise between the principle of compensation and the principle of responsibility. For individuals with the same preferences but different wage rates, the maximin criterion is applied (of course we can apply less extreme prioritarianism). In other words a zero aversion of inequality can be applied along the dimension of responsibility preference, whereas a high aversion to inequality is acceptable along the dimension of circumstances (in skill). Ravaska, Tenhunen, and Tuomala applied this approach.

At this point in the optimal tax literature's development, perhaps the best summary of the relationship between optimal tax theory and prioritarianism is the following: optimal tax theorists can, and sometimes do, use prioritarian objectives to define optimal policy, but they don't give reasons – theoretical or empirical – why they should. One implication of this state of affairs is that those committed to prioritarianism ought to guide optimal tax theorists toward a more satisfying way to use it in their work and toward analyses that would demonstrate its appeal through some combination of its normative force, its desirable implications for taxation, and its real-world relevance.

References

Aaberge, Rolf (2007). "Gini's nuclear family," *The Journal of Economic Inequality*, Springer; Society for the Study of Economic Inequality, 5: 305–322.

Ahmad, Ehtisham, and Nicholas Stern (1984). "The theory of reform and Indian indirect taxes." *Journal of Public Economics*, 25: 259–298.

Arrow, Kenneth J. (1973). "Some ordinalist-utilitarian notes on Rawls's theory of justice by John Rawls." *The Journal of Philosophy*, 70: 245–263.

Atkinson, A.B. (1972), La Maxi-Min' et l'imposition optimale des revenus, *Cahiers du Séminaire d'Econométrie,* 1975, No 16 : 73–86 (French version of University of Essex discussion paper No 47, 1972, Maximin' and optimal income taxation, accepted for publication by the Review of Economic Studies, but never resubmitted).

(1995), *Public Economics in Action*. Oxford: Oxford University Press.

Atkinson, Anthony B. (1990) "Public economics and the economic public." *European Economic Review*, 34: 225–248.

Bargain, Olivier, et al. (2014). "Tax-benefit revealed social preferences in Europe and the US." *Annals of Economics and Statistics/Annales d'Economie et de Statistique*, 113: 257–289.

Blomquist, Soren, Vidar Christiansen, and Luca Micheletto (2010). "Public provision of private goods and nondistortionary marginal tax rates." *American Economic Journal: Economic Policy*, 2: 1–27.

Boadway, Robin (2012). *From Optimal Tax Theory to Tax Policy.* Cambridge: MIT Press.

Bourguignon, Francois, and Amedeo Spadaro (2012). "Tax-benefit revealed social preferences." *The Journal of Economic Inequality*, 10: 75–108.

Chetty, Raj (2006). "A new method of estimating risk aversion." *American Economic Review*, 96: 1821–1834.

Christiansen, Vidar, and Eilev S. Jansen (1978). "Implicit social preferences in the Norwegian system of indirect taxation." *Journal of Public Economics*, 10: 217–245.

Diamond, Peter A. (1998). "Optimal income taxation: an example with a U-shaped pattern of optimal marginal tax rates." *American Economic Review*, 88: 83–95.

Edgeworth, Francis Y. (1897). "The pure theory of taxation." *The Economic Journal*, 7: 46–70.

Fleurbaey, Marc, and Francois Maniquet (2006). "Fair income tax," *Review of Economic Studies*, 73: 55–83.

(2018). "Optimal income taxation theory and principles of fairness." *Journal of Economic Literature*, 56: 1029–1079.

Jacobs, Bas, Egbert L. Jongen, and Floris T. Zoutman (2017). "Revealed social preferences of Dutch political parties." *Journal of Public Economics*, 156: 81–100.

Kanbur, Ravi, and Matti Tuomala (1994). "Inherent inequality and the optimal graduation of marginal tax rates." *The Scandinavian Journal of Economics*, 96: 275–282.

Kaplow, Louis (2008). *The Theory of Taxation and Public Economics*, Princeton: Princeton University Press.

(2010). "Concavity of utility, concavity of welfare, and redistribution of income." *International Tax and Public Finance*, 17: 25–42.

Keane, Michael, and Robert Moffitt (1998). "A structural model of multiple welfare program participation and labor supply." *International Economic Review*, Aug: 553–589.

Locke, John (1690). *Second treatise of government: An essay concerning the true original, extent and end of civil government.* John Wiley & Sons, 2014.

Lockwood, B., and M. Weinzierl (2015). "De Gustibus non est Taxandum." *Journal of Public Economics*, 124: 74–80.

(2016). "Positive and normative judgments implicit in U.S. tax policy, and the costs of unequal growth and recessions." *Journal of Monetary Economics*, 77: 30–47.

Lockwood, Benjamin B. (2017). "Optimal income taxation with present bias," Working Paper, University of Pennsylvania.

Mankiw, N. Gregory, Matthew Weinzierl, and Danny Yagan (2009). "Optimal taxation in theory and practice." *Journal of Economic Perspectives*, 23: 147–174.

Mill, John Stuart (1871). *Principles of Political Economy*. Oxford University Press, 1994.

Mirrlees Review (1971). "An exploration in the theory of optimal income taxation." *Review of Economic Studies*, 38: 175–208.

Mirrlees Review (1982). “The economic uses of utilitarianism.” In *Utilitarianism and Beyond,* Sen, A., Williams, B. and Williams, B.A.O. eds., Cambridge University Press.

Mirrlees, James A., and Stuart Adam (2010). *Dimensions of Tax Design: The Mirrlees Review.* Oxford University Press.

Mirrlees, James A., et al. (2011). “The Mirrlees Review: conclusions and recommendations for reform.” *Fiscal Studies*, 32: 331–359.

Musgrave, Richard A. (1959). *The Theory of Public Finance*. McGraw-Hill.

Musgrave, Richard A. and James Buchanan (1999). *Public Finance and Public Choice: Two Contrasting Visions of the State*, Cambridge: MIT Press.

Nozick, Robert (1974). *Anarchy, State, and Utopia*. New York: Basic Books.

Ravaska, Terhi, Sanna Tenhunen, and Matti Tuomala (2018). “On the optimal lifetime redistribution and social objectives: a multidimensional approach.” *International Tax and Public Finance*, 25: 631–653.

Rawls, John (1971). *A Theory of Justice*. Cambridge: Harvard University Press.

Rawls John (1972). “Some reasons for the Maxi-Min Criterion.” *American Economic Review, Papers and Proceedings*, 64: 141–146.

Roemer, John (1998). *Equality of Opportunity*, Cambridge: Harvard University Press.

Saez, Emmanuel (2001). “Using elasticities to derive optimal income tax rates.” *The Review of Economic Studies*, 68: 205–229.

Saez, Emmanuel, and Stefanie Stantcheva (2016). “Generalized Social Welfare Weights for Optimal Tax Theory.” *American Economic Review*, 106: 24–45.

Salanie, Bernard (2011). *The economics of taxation*. Cambridge: MIT press.

Sen, Amartya (1974). “Informational bases of alternative welfare approaches: aggregation and income distribution.” *Journal of Public Economics*, 3: 387–403.

Smith, Adam (1776). *An Inquiry into the Nature and Causes of the Wealth of Nations*. Homewood, IL: Irwin.

Spadaro, Amedeo, Luca Piccoli, and Lucia Mangiavacchi (2015). “Optimal taxation, social preferences and the four worlds of welfare capitalism in Europe.” *Economica*, 82: 448–485.

Stern, Nicholas (1976). “On the specification of models of optimum income taxation.” *Journal of Public Economics*, 6: 123–162.

Stern, Nicholas (1977). “Welfare weights and the elasticity of the marginal valuation of income.” In Artis, M., and Nobay, R., (eds.) *Proceedings of the Aute Edinburgh Meeting of April 1976*. Oxford: Basil Blackwell.

Stiglitz, Joseph (1987). “Pareto Efficient and Optimal Taxation and the New Welfare Economics.” In A. Auerbach and M. Feldstein (eds.) *Handbook of Public Economics*. Amsterdam: North Holland.

Tuomala, Matti (1984). "On the optimal income taxation: Some further numerical results." *Journal of Public Economics*, 23: 351–366.

(2016). *Optimal Redistributive Taxation*. Oxford: Oxford University Press.

Van De Gaer, D. (1993). "Equality of opportunity and investment in human capital." Katholieke Uni- versiteit Leuven.

Weinzierl, Matthew (2014). "The promise of positive optimal taxation: normative diversity and a role for equal sacrifice." *Journal of Public Economics*, 118: 128–142.

(2017). "Popular acceptance of inequality due to innate brute luck and support for classical benefit-based taxation." *Journal of Public Economics*, 155: 54–63.

(2018). "Revisiting the classical view of benefit-based taxation." *Economic Journal*, 128: F37–F64.

Werning, Ivan, (2007). "Pareto Efficient Income Taxation," Working Paper, MIT.

5 Prioritarianism and Measuring Social Progress

KOEN DECANCQ AND ERIK SCHOKKAERT*

5.1 Introduction

Are the individuals in society x better off than the individuals in society y? How much social progress is society x making over time? The standard (and still most popular) approach to address these questions is to look at GDP per capita. The society with the highest GDP per capita is considered as better off and social progress is measured by the growth of GDP per capita. Yet, while GDP per capita is arguably a useful measure of the size of economic activity, it is by now generally accepted that it is not a good measure of overall social welfare. We see at least two reasons. First, GDP per capita remains blind for non-monetary aspects of well-being and, second, the distribution of well-being across the individuals is left out of the picture. Various proposals have therefore been made to go *"Beyond GDP"*(see Stiglitz et al. (2009) for a survey).

In this chapter, we critically survey the academic literature that deals with the question of how social conditions can be assessed and compared through a multidimensional and prioritarian (or, better, generalized utilitarian) lens. To avoid a sprawling discussion of this vast and rapidly expanding field,[1] we focus here primarily on the topic of the measurement of social progress, i.e., the question of how much the well-being of the individuals in a particular society has improved over time. Yet, most of the surveyed results and tools can be applied to the broader topic of the general assessment and comparison of social conditions.

* We thank the Editors, Marc Fleurbaey, Erwin Ooghe and participants to presentations at Duke University and the University of Bergen for helpful comments. We are grateful to Vladimir Gimpelson for providing additional data from an ad-hoc module to the RLMS-HSE. Support of the Research Foundation - Flanders is gratefully acknowledged.

1 See, for instance, Sen (1979), Deaton (1980), Slesnick (1998), Fleurbaey (2009), Ferreira (2012), Fleurbaey and Blanchet (2013), Decancq et al. (2015a) and Jorgenson (2018).

Broadly speaking, measuring and comparing social progress entails two challenges which echo the critiques raised against GDP per capita. First, including non-monetary information in a measure of social progress requires an operational measure of individual well-being. We group the different approaches in this survey according to the underlying definition of individual well-being. We make a distinction between approaches based on objective, subjective (or hedonic) and preferentialist well-being measures (see Chapter 3 of this book). Second, information needs to be included about where progress takes place in the distribution of well-being. Has the well-being of the worst-off improved or is well-being growth rather benefiting individuals in more favourable positions? A central role in our chapter is occupied by the growth incidence curve that was proposed by Ravallion and Chen (2003). This curve is a useful device to chart and visualize well-being growth across the entire distribution. We relate the growth incidence curve to the literature on prioritarian social welfare functions developed in the wake of the work by Atkinson (1970) and Kolm-Pollak (Pollak (1971); Kolm (1976)).

The chapter is organized as follows. In Section 5.2, we sketch a general theoretical framework to measure social progress in a prioritarian setting. We present two decompositions that provide additional insights into the structure of the prioritarian considerations in any given context and we discuss how to introduce lifetime well-being and population issues into the analysis. In the third section, we take a critical look at the existing (applied) literature on social progress. Section 5.4 illustrates the different theoretical concepts introduced in the previous sections with an empirical application based on Russian data from the RMLS-HSE between 1995 and 2005. During this turbulent decade, the Russian economy underwent sharp changes, including the financial crisis of August 1998. We conclude in Section 5.5.

5.2 Social Welfare and Social Progress

5.2.1 Social Welfare Functions

Let there be N individuals in society. We start by assuming that N is constant over time. We discuss and relax that assumption in Section 5.2.4.2. The well-being situation of individual i in period t is described by the bundle of attributes a_{it}. Examples of attributes are income (or consumption), health, job satisfaction, quality of social relations, etc. Since income plays a crucial role in many approaches, we introduce it explicitly in our notation, when that is useful, by splitting the attribute vector a_{it} in two parts (y_{it}, x_{it}), in which y_{it} represents the income attribute and the vector x_{it} the non-income attributes.

Define $\boldsymbol{a}_t = (a_{1t}, \ldots, a_{Nt})$ as the attribute matrix in period t, which contains for each individual i her attribute vector a_{it}. We assume that social welfare is given by an instantaneous social welfare function $S(\cdot)$ that only takes the attribute matrix $\boldsymbol{a}_t$ of period t as argument (we return to that assumption in Section 5.2.4.1). Furthermore, we restrict our attention to the *generalized utilitarian* social welfare functions:

$$S(\boldsymbol{a}_t) = \frac{1}{N} \sum\nolimits_{i=1}^{N} g(w_i(a_{it})), \tag{5.1}$$

where $g(\cdot)$ is an increasing transformation function. Eq. (5.1) captures an explicit two-step approach where in a first step a well-being measure $w_{it} = w_i(a_{it})$ is computed for each individual i. These N well-being measures form a vector $\boldsymbol{w}_t = (w_{1t}, \ldots, w_{Nt})$. In a second step, the well-being measures are transformed by the function $g(\cdot)$ and averaged. When $g(\cdot)$ is the identity function, we call $S(\cdot)$ a *utilitarian* social welfare function. When $g(\cdot)$ is a strictly increasing and strictly concave function, we call $S(\cdot)$ a *prioritarian* social welfare function. In this section, we follow this two-step approach without specifying the precise content of individual well-being. In the next section we briefly discuss three different interpretations of the well-being measures (i.e., objective, subjective and preferentialist); see also Chapter 3 of this book.

As soon as we have specified a social welfare function, it is natural to assess society's condition on the basis of that function. A society with attribute matrix $\boldsymbol{a}_t$ is "better off", i.e., reaches a higher level of social welfare, than a society with attribute matrix $\boldsymbol{a}'_t$, if $S(\boldsymbol{a}_t) > S(\boldsymbol{a}'_t)$. In the same vein, we say that there is social progress if the level of social welfare increases over time:

$$\Delta S = S(\boldsymbol{a}_{t+1}) - S(\boldsymbol{a}_t) > 0. \tag{5.2}$$

In the generalized utilitarian case[2] of Eq. (5.1), we say that there is social progress if:

[2] Bossert and Dutta (2019) discuss the measurement of welfare change using generalized Gini social welfare functions.

$$\Delta S = \frac{1}{N}\sum_{i=1}^{N}\left[\left(g\left(w_i\left(a_{i(t+1)}\right)\right) - g\left(w_i\left(a_{it}\right)\right)\right] > 0. \tag{5.3}$$

Note that the social welfare function (5.1) and the measures of social progress according to Eqs (5.2) and (5.3) satisfy an anonymity principle with respect to well-being in each period. Reshuffling the names of the individuals in the attribute matrix of one period does not affect the measurement of social progress. This has the advantage that only cross-sectional data are needed. In Section 5.2.4.1 we discuss how life-cycle considerations can be introduced in a cross-sectional setting.

If we want to compare the social welfare levels of two societies, or check whether there is social progress or regress, i.e., whether the Eqs (5.2)–(5.3) are positive or negative, it is sufficient that social welfare is measured at an ordinal level. To interpret the numerical value of ΔS as the increase in social welfare, however, social welfare must be measured on a translation-scale that is defined up to a constant term. Yet, it is common to measure social progress in terms of growth rates. In the current setting, this means calculating the growth rate of social welfare $\Delta S/S(a_t)$. This growth rate can only be meaningfully interpreted if it can be assumed that social welfare is measured on a ratio-scale that is defined up to a constant factor. Note that we are not talking here about the measurability level of the individual well-being functions $w(.)$, but about the measurability level of the function $S(.)$. Both aspects are closely linked if we choose for the social welfare function a representation in terms of its equally-distributed equivalent.

The equally-distributed equivalent is the well-being level which, if it were equally enjoyed by all individuals, would yield the same level of social welfare as the current distribution of well-being. In the generalized utilitarian case, it is given by:

$$\widetilde{S}(a_t) = g^{-1}\left[\frac{1}{N}\sum_{i=1}^{N} g\left(w_i\left(a_{it}\right)\right)\right]. \tag{5.4}$$

In the following, we use the notation $\widetilde{S}$ to refer to the equally-distributed equivalent representation of the social welfare function. One of the advantages of working with the equally-distributed equivalent representation is that it is expressed in the same units as individual well-being and, hence, more easily interpreted. When all individuals have the same well-being level $\bar{w}$, the equally-distributed equivalent is also equal to $\bar{w}$ (see Eq. (5.4)). When there is some inequality in the well-being distribution, the equally-distributed equivalent will be strictly lower than the average well-being level in the prioritarian case when the transformation function $g(\cdot)$ is strictly increasing and strictly concave.[3]

If we are willing to assume that individual well-being is perfectly measurable (i.e., both ratio-scale and translation-scale measurable), the equally-distributed equivalent representation of the social welfare function is also perfectly measurable and, hence, absolute changes and growth rates of social welfare can be computed. Perfect measurability is an extremely demanding condition, however. We illustrate less demanding approaches for the two most important subfamilies of prioritarian social welfare functions, the Atkinson and Kolm-Pollak social welfare functions (see Chapter 2 of this book for a more detailed discussion). In the recent literature, the Atkinson specification has been more popular than the Kolm-Pollak specification. In our own empirical application in Section 5.4, we show the results for both subfamilies.

The Atkinson Social Welfare Function

To obtain the Atkinson social welfare function, the transformation function g is chosen as follows:

$$g^{ATK}(w_{it}) = \frac{w_{it}^{1-\gamma}}{1-\gamma}, \tag{5.5}$$

with $\gamma > 0$ being a parameter of inequality aversion. The larger γ, the larger the degree of priority given to the worse off. In the case when $\gamma = 1$, $g^{ATK}(\cdot)$ is the logarithmic transformation function. The equally-distributed equivalent of the Atkinson social welfare function is given by:

$$\widetilde{S}_{\gamma}^{ATK}(a_t) = \left[\frac{1}{N}\sum\nolimits_{i=1}^{N}(w_i(a_{it}))^{1-\gamma}\right]^{1/1-\gamma}. \tag{5.6}$$

[3] The so-called normative inequality measures are derived from the discrepancy between the level of the equally-distributed equivalent and the average of a distribution. They measure the welfare loss due to inequality. Some examples are given in the next section.

If the individual well-being measure is ratio-scale measureable – a necessary condition for the Atkinson social welfare function to make sense – then the growth rate in $\widetilde{S}_{\gamma}^{ATK}(a_t)$ is also meaningfully defined.

The Kolm-Pollak Social Welfare Function
We obtain the Kolm-Pollak social welfare function by selecting the following transformation function g:

$$g^{KP}(w_{it}) = \frac{-\,exp\,(-\beta w_{it})}{\beta}, \tag{5.7}$$

with $\beta > 0$ a parameter of inequality aversion. The equally-distributed equivalent of the Kolm-Pollak social welfare function can be written as follows:

$$\widetilde{S}_{\beta}^{KP}(a_t) = -\frac{1}{\beta}\,log\left[\frac{1}{N}\sum\nolimits_{i=1}^{N} exp\,(-\beta w_i(a_{it}))\right]. \tag{5.8}$$

If the well-being measure is translation-scale measurable, we can meaningfully measure the value of $\Delta\widetilde{S}_{\beta}^{KP}(a_t)$, i.e., the absolute change in social welfare.

5.2.2 *Decomposing Social Progress*

The crucial difference between the utilitarian and the prioritarian approach to the measurement of social welfare is that in the latter approach a redistribution from the better-off to the worse-off is seen as a social improvement due to the strict concavity of the transformation function $g(.)$ in Eq. (5.1). The degree of concavity determines the relative weight given to the worse-off. The importance of prioritarian considerations can be made more salient by two decompositions. First, we discuss a decomposition of the level of social welfare and, second, we present a decomposition of the change in social welfare.

5.2.2.1 Mean and Inequality

A first decomposition is to write the equally-distributed equivalent representation of social welfare as a function of the average and the inequality of individual well-being. As discussed in Chapter 2 of this book, it is convenient to use a different decomposition for the Atkinson and the Kolm-Pollak social welfare functions, so that a relative inequality index is obtained in the former case and an absolute inequality index in the latter.[4]

For the Atkinson specification, we can write:

$$\widetilde{S}_{\gamma}^{ATK}(\boldsymbol{a_t}) = \mu(\boldsymbol{a_t})\left[1 - A_{\gamma}(\boldsymbol{a_t})\right], \tag{5.9}$$

with $\mu(\boldsymbol{a_t}) = \sum_i (w_i(a_{it}))/N$ being the average well-being in period t and $A_{\gamma}(\boldsymbol{a_t})$ the Atkinson index of inequality in well-being for the inequality aversion parameter γ. In Eq. (5.9), the inequality index "corrects" the average well-being to take the loss in social welfare due to well-being inequality into account. The larger the well-being inequality, the larger this correction becomes. In the utilitarian case ($\gamma = 0$) we have that $A_{\gamma}(\boldsymbol{a_t}) = 0$ for any attribute matrix $\boldsymbol{a_t}$, and social welfare equals average well-being. In this case, social progress equals the change in average well-being.

A similar decomposition is possible for the Kolm-Pollak specification, for which:

$$\widetilde{S}_{\beta}^{KP}(\boldsymbol{a_t}) = \boldsymbol{\mu}(\boldsymbol{a_t}) - KP_{\beta}(\boldsymbol{a_t}), \tag{5.10}$$

with $KP_{\beta}(\boldsymbol{a_t})$ the Kolm-Pollak measure of inequality for the inequality aversion parameter β. Again, for the utilitarian social welfare function ($\beta = 0$), the inequality measure equals 0 and in this case social welfare equals average well-being, so that social progress is measured by the change in average well-being.

5.2.2.2 Visualizing Well-Being Changes: Growth Incidence Curves

The second decomposition deals with the change in social welfare over time and is based on the concept of a growth incidence curve. For this decomposition it is useful to distinguish between the relative approach in terms of percentage-wise growth rates (using the Atkinson social welfare function) and an absolute approach in terms of social welfare differences (using the Kolm-Pollak social welfare function). We discuss both approaches here and illustrate them with Russian data in Section 5.4. In this section, we switch to continuous notation because this is more convenient to introduce the decompositions.

[4] A relative inequality index is invariant to a rescaling of all values with a common factor and an absolute inequality index is invariant to a translation of all values with a common constant.

Let Q_t be the quantile function of the well-being distribution w_t, i.e., the function that returns the well-being level at time t for each percentile p.[5] In this continuous framework, we can restate Eq. (5.4) as:

$$\widetilde{S}_t = \widetilde{S}(a_t) = g^{-1}\left[\int_0^1 g(Q_t(p))dp\right]. \tag{5.11}$$

The relative growth incidence curve and the Atkinson social welfare function

Ravallion and Chen (2003) have introduced the relative growth incidence curve, which we denote $rGIC_t(p)$. This curve shows the (relative) well-being growth rate at percentile p:

$$rGIC_t(p) = \frac{dQ_t(p)/Q_t(p)}{dt}. \tag{5.12}$$

Interestingly, there is a direct link between this relative growth incidence curve and the relative growth rate of (the equally-distributed equivalent of) the Atkinson social welfare function.[6] As shown in Appendix 5.A.1 we can decompose the relative growth rate of the Atkinson social welfare function as follows:

$$\frac{d\widetilde{S}_t^{ATK}/\widetilde{S}_t^{ATK}}{dt} = \int_0^1 \left[\frac{g^{ATK}(Q(p))}{\int_0^1 g^{ATK}(Q(q))dq}\right] \times rGIC_t(p) \times dp. \tag{5.13}$$

This means that the growth rate of the Atkinson social welfare function can be written as a weighted sum of the growth rates of well-being at the different percentiles as given by the relative growth incidence curve. The weights, which are indicated between square brackets in Eq. (5.13), are given by the ratio of the transformed well-being at each percentile and the average transformed well-being across all percentiles.

In the utilitarian case ($\gamma = 0$), the weights are equal to the ratio of well-being at each perentile and average well-being. Perhaps counter-intuitively, higher percentiles then get a larger weight. In the

5 If F_t is the cumulative distribution function of the individual well-being measures in period t, we have that for each percentile $p, Q_t(p) = w_i(a_{it})$ if and only if $p = F_t(w_i(a_{it}))$.

6 See also Kraay (2006) and Ferreira (2012) for similar discussions.

prioritarian case ($\gamma > 0$), however, the higher the parameter γ, the larger the weight that is given to the growth rates of the worse-off percentiles.

The absolute growth incidence curve and the Kolm-Pollak social welfare function

The absolute growth incidence curve, denoted $aGIC_t(p)$, shows the (absolute) growth of well-being at percentile p of the well-being distribution:

$$aGIC_t(p) = \frac{dQ_t(p)}{dt}. \tag{5.14}$$

Comparing Eqs (5.12) and (5.14), we see that $rGIC_t(p) = aGIC_t(p)/Q_t(p)$.

In the case of the Kolm-Pollak social welfare function, there is an analogous link between the absolute growth incidence curve and the absolute change in social welfare. As shown in Appendix 5.A.1, we obtain:

$$\frac{d\widetilde{S}_t^{KP}}{dt} = \int_0^1 \left[\frac{g^{KP}(Q(p))}{\int_0^1 g^{KP}(Q(q))dq} \right] \times aGIC_t(p) \times dp. \tag{5.15}$$

The absolute growth of the Kolm-Pollak social welfare function can be written as a weighted sum of the growth of well-being at the different percentiles, as given by the absolute growth incidence curve. Similarly to the Atkinson social welfare function, the weights assigned to the absolute growth incidence curve at each percentile are given by the ratio of the transformed well-being at each percentile and the average transformed well-being across all percentiles.

In the utilitarian case ($\beta = 0$), all weights become equal to 1 and the growth of social welfare is equal to the average change in individual well-being. In the prioritarian case ($\beta > 0$), the larger the parameter β is, the larger the weight that is given to the well-being growth of the worse off. Contrary to the decomposition of the percentage-wise change in social welfare in the Atkinson case, the weights in the decomposition of the change in the Kolm-Pollak social welfare function are decreasing with p.

5.2.3 Inequality Aversion and the Well-Being Measure

Eq. (5.1) allows us to focus on two central choices when measuring social progress, i.e., the choice of the social welfare function (see Chapter 2, this volume) and the choice of the individual well-being (or utility) function (see Chapter 3, this volume). These two choices can be made independently of each other. However, in much of the applied work, the two choices are intertwined so that it is impossible to identify (the curvature of) both functions separately.

Let us illustrate the issue for the simple case in which social welfare is measured based on information about the income distribution $y_t = (y_{1t}, \ldots, y_{Nt})$. It is common to work with the functional form:

$$S(y_t) = \frac{1}{N}\sum_{i=1}^{N} h(y_{it}). \tag{5.16}$$

From the perspective of Eq. (5.1), it is tempting to interpret Eq. (5.16) as utilitarian. However, this is not the common interpretation in the literature, which interprets $h(.)$ as the concatenation of $g(.)$ and $w(.)$, i.e., $h = g \circ w$. This means that "inequality aversion" (of the social welfare function) and "risk aversion" (of the utility function) can no longer be distinguished, if one wishes to do so. This can be easily illustrated. Suppose one takes a utility function:

$$w(y_{it}) = \frac{y_{it}^{1-\lambda}}{1-\lambda}, \tag{5.17}$$

with λ representing relative risk aversion, and the Atkinson social welfare function

$$S(y_t) = \frac{1}{1-\gamma}\frac{1}{N}\sum_{i=1}^{N} w(y_{it})^{1-\gamma}, \tag{5.18}$$

with γ the parameter of inequality aversion. Combining Eqs (5.17) and (5.18) yields

$$S(y_t) = \frac{1}{(1-\gamma)(1-\lambda)}\frac{1}{N}\sum_{i=1}^{N} y_{it}^{(1-\gamma)(1-\lambda)}, \tag{5.19}$$

and this can also be interpreted as a specification with a linear utility function and inequality aversion equal to $1-(1-\gamma)(1-\lambda)$. The interpretation goes both ways: it would be wrong to say that all applied studies that implement Eq. (5.19) are assuming a linear (risk-neutral) utility function. The specification (5.16) has become popular, precisely because it avoids the difficult issue of separating risk aversion and inequality aversion and allows us to focus directly on the ethical issues raised by the unequal distribution of incomes.

5.2.4 Issues of Life and Death: Lifetime Well-Being and Variable Population

The prioritarian approach to social welfare naturally starts from a lifetime perspective on individual well-being. If we want to determine which individuals are better-off, it is indeed necessary to consider their entire life course. Most applied work, however, focuses on social welfare in one period (usually a year). Introducing life-cycle considerations into an empirical analysis raises a host of tricky issues, both from a conceptual (see, e.g., Adler (2012), Ponthière (2016)) and a practical viewpoint. In Section 5.2.4.1, we focus on the latter. In Section 5.2.4.2, we briefly discuss the related issue of how to handle variable populations.

5.2.4.1 Lifetime Well-Being

At each moment in time we have a situation with overlapping generations, i.e., with persons of different generations living together. To illustrate the implications of that, we have to extend the framework of the previous section by including more periods. Let us consider a simple example with three individuals i, j and k and three periods $(t-1)$, t and $(t+1)$. Assume that the world begins in period $(t-1)$ and ends immediately after period $(t+1)$. Suppose that we can measure the well-being of individual i in period t as ω_{it}, with $\omega_{it}=0$ if individual i is not alive in period t. The well-being of the three individuals follows the trajectories that are summarized in Table 5.1.

The overall lifetime social welfare can be written as a double aggregation, one across individuals and one across periods (the rows and columns of Table 5.1, respectively):

$$SW = \mathcal{S}\big(\omega_{i(t-1)}, \omega_{it}, 0, 0, \omega_{jt}, 0, \omega_{k(t-1)}, \omega_{kt}, \omega_{k(t+1)}\big). \qquad (5.20)$$

The lifetime prioritarian approach takes into account the well-being of individuals over their whole lifetime and assumes separability between

Table 5.1. *Three life courses*

	$t-1$	t	$t+1$
ind. i	$\omega_{i(t-1)}$	ω_{it}	0
ind. j	0	ω_{jt}	0
ind. k	$\omega_{k(t-1)}$	ω_{kt}	$\omega_{k(t+1)}$

individuals. Hence, the social welfare function has the following separable structure[7]

$$SW^1 = \mathcal{S}\big(w_i(\omega_{i(t-1)}, \omega_{it}, 0), w_j\big(0, \omega_{jt}, 0\big), w_k(\omega_{k(t-1)}, \omega_{kt}, \omega_{k(t+1)})\big). \tag{5.21}$$

One first calculates the lifetime well-being for each individual, and then aggregates these lifetime well-being levels through a social welfare function of the prioritarian type. Applied to Eq. (5.1), this means that we would interpret $w_{it}(.)$ as the lifetime well-being of the individual i at time t.

Yet this is not the common practice in empirical work, which is mostly restricted to cross-sectional data for a given period. This means that one changes the sequence of the aggregations, by first aggregating across individuals and then across periods. This period-by-period approach assumes another separable structure for $\mathcal{S}(.)$:

$$SW^2 = \mathcal{S}\big(S(\omega_{i(t-1)}, 0, \omega_{k(t-1)}), S\big(\omega_{it}, \omega_{jt}, \omega_{kt}\big), S(0, 0, \omega_{k(t+1)})\big), \tag{5.22}$$

so that it becomes possible to focus on each period separately. The individual well-being levels in the analysis then become period-specific values, not the lifetime well-being levels. This has important consequences in a prioritarian setting. Indeed, it implies that the relative weights given to the well-being of the different individuals in period t are independent of their well-being in the other periods. An individual who reaches a high well-being level in period t, but a very low one in

[7] The subscripts attached to $w(.)$ indicate that individuals may have different preferences about the relative weight given to different periods of their life in the evaluation of overall lifetime well-being.

the rest of his life, would get the same weight in t as an individual who maintains the same high well-being level during his entire life. Differences in longevity are a striking example. In the simple example of Table 5.1, it is possible that individual j has a very high well-being in period t, although his life is shorter than that of the other two individuals. This result may go against the fairness intuition of many prioritarians.[8]

In principle, we should therefore work with the aggregation sequence underlying Eq. (5.21): first aggregate across periods for each individual and then across individuals. Yet, this approach faces at least three difficulties in an empirical application. First, how to introduce differences in longevity in the analysis? In fact, this is a typical example of cumulative deprivation, as the economically weakest groups on average also have a shorter life. Second, there is a practical data problem. The available data rarely contain complete information on the past situation of the individuals. Third, there is a conceptual issue. When we calculate social welfare in period t, we often do not know the future life course of all individuals. Hence, our estimates of individual well-being are truncated. What is worse, the moment of truncation depends on the age of the individuals at the time of the analysis. Summarizing, we need an exceptionally rich dataset to implement Eq. (5.21).

How can we proceed in practice? One possibility is suggested by the so-called non-anonymous approach to measuring economic growth. In fact, the term "non-anonymous" is a misnomer, since the basic idea of this approach is to take the starting positions of the individuals into account when evaluating social progress. Loosely speaking, this can be seen as a correction on the weights that introduces information on the past life course of individuals and, hence, a lifetime perspective in the analysis. In this approach, the growth in social welfare GR_t is defined as a weighted average of the growth rates in the well-being of the individuals gr_{it}, with weights that are decreasing with their initial well-being level. A typical example is the measure proposed by Genicot and Ray (2013):

[8] In fact, combining Eqs (5.21) and (5.22) implies that the function $S(.)$ is additive in the temporal well-being levels, clearly illustrating that it becomes difficult to introduce lifetime considerations.

$$GR_t = \sum_{i=1}^{N} \left[\frac{(w_{it})^{-\varepsilon}}{\sum_{j=1}^{N} (w_{jt})^{-\varepsilon}} \right] \times gr_{it}. \tag{5.23}$$

This measure gives a larger weight to the growth of well-being of those that start at a lower initial level of well-being. The weights become more sensitive to the initial distribution as the parameter ε grows. When $\varepsilon = 0$, social progress reduces to the unweighted average of the individual growth rates and the past does not matter. Note that the weights in Eq. (5.23) are similar to the weights in the Atkinson approach to the relative growth incidence curve (see Eq. (5.13)). Of course, the growth rates to which these weights are applied are defined differently: Eq. (5.13) includes the growth rates at each percentile, in Eq. (5.23) we have the growth rates for each individual i. By incorporating the past into the analysis, this non-anonymous approach gives us some idea about how a lifetime approach could be different from a temporal approach.

A second (pragmatic) approach is to focus on representative individuals within a cohort and introduce life expectancy in the measure of individual well-being. A simple approach to this issue has been proposed (among others) in the paper by Becker et al. (2005). Dropping the subscript i for notational convenience, they write the indirect utility function $V(Y, \sigma)$ of an individual with lifetime income Y and survival function σ as:

$$V(Y, \sigma) = \max \int_0^{\infty} \exp(-\rho t)\sigma_t u(c_t) dt \tag{5.24}$$

subject to

$$Y = \int_0^{\infty} \exp(-rt)\sigma_t y_t dt = \int_0^{\infty} \exp(-rt)\sigma_t c_t dt, \tag{5.25}$$

where c_t is consumption in period t, $u(.)$ a utility function and $r = \rho$ the interest rate and time preference. This indirect utility function can be seen as a simple example of the lifetime well-being function that was introduced in Eq. (5.21), in which only two attributes are considered: consumption and life expectancy.

Let us now consider the special case in which the individual receives the same income y in all years of his life. With the budget constraint (5.25), this implies that consumption also remains constant, i.e., that $c_t = c = y$. The indirect utility function (5.24) can then be written as

$$V(y,\sigma) = u(y)L(\sigma), \tag{5.26}$$

with $L(\sigma) = \int_0^\infty \exp(-rt)\sigma_t dt$. Eq. (5.26) nicely separates instantaneous utility $u(y)$ and the utility related to longevity $L(\sigma)$. Of course, this simple decomposition no longer holds if we consider the allocation of more attributes over the whole life-cycle or specify a more realistic income-generating process. Moreover, life expectancy is an *ex ante* concept and the actual length of life may be very different for different individuals within a group with the same life expectancy.

5.2.4.2 Variable Population

In the previous sections we have assumed that the population size, N, remains constant. In most applications, however, N may vary. When comparing the social condition of different countries, we have to take differences in their population size into account. When looking at changes over time of the social condition of a given country, again the size of the population of that country may change. Moreover, in both comparisons the people making up the society are not the same. This is obvious for international comparisons. In comparisons over time, some individuals in the initial situation will have died, and the final situation will also include newborns. This "non-identity" problem has been discussed at great length in the philosophical literature in the wake of Parfit (1984) but we leave it aside in this chapter. Instead, we focus on the issue of how to handle different population sizes in the measurement of social welfare (this issue is also discussed in Chapter 2, this volume).

Implicitly, we have already addressed the issue by taking in Eq. (5.1) the average and not the sum of the (transformed) well-being levels. This approach could be called "average prioritarianism". If we had taken the sum (what could be called "total prioritarianism"), it would be easier for larger countries to be better-off than smaller countries. In fact, total prioritarianism (like total utilitarianism, which has been the main focus of the literature) implies what Parfit (1984) has called the "repugnant conclusion": for any society in which individuals are at a high level of well-being, there is a second society that is ranked higher in terms of social welfare and in which everyone is at a very low level of well-being. Average prioritarianism avoids that implication, but it has other debatable consequences. Adding a person to a rich society (with a high average individual well-being) decreases social welfare if the well-being of that individual (weighted by the function $g(.)$) is smaller than the overall average.[9] As a specific example, low-skilled immigration in a rich country is evaluated as negative for the social condition of that country, even if these migrants reach a decent level of well-being, as long as that level of well-being is below the average in the receiving country. On the other hand, in a very poor country, with an average below the subsistence level, adding another person below that subsistence level (but above the average), could be welfare improving.[10] Neither of these two implications is very attractive from a welfare point of view. The latter problem is avoided by an alternative approach, which could be called "critical-level prioritarianism" (Blackorby et al. 2005) in which Eq. (5.1) is replaced by

$$S^{CRIT}(a_t) = \sum_{i=1}^{N} \left(g(w_i(a_{it})) - g\left(w^{CRIT}\right)\right). \tag{5.27}$$

Critical-level prioritarianism also avoids the repugnant conclusion. However, it still implies that adding a person with a well-being level below w^{CRIT} would lead to a decrease in social welfare, which is not very attractive if w^{CRIT} is large.

The literature on population ethics is rapidly growing and at this stage it has not yet reached a consensus. The issue is largely neglected in the applied work, however, where "per capita" (average) approaches, such as Eq. (5.1) take almost a monopoly position.

5.3 Applications: Social Welfare with Different Measures of Individual Well-Being

The prioritarian approach to social progress, as described in the previous section, can be implemented with different concepts of well-being. The use of different concepts may lead to different results. Inevitably, hard normative and modelling choices are needed to do applied work. In this section, we give a brief overview of the three main approaches to the measurement of well-being: objective, subjective and preferentialist. For further details we refer to Chapter 3 in this volume by Adler and Decancq. The focus of this book and of the empirical illustration in

[9] This is a variant of what is called in the literature for a utilitarian framework the "mere addition principle".

[10] This has been called in the literature the "negative expansion principle".

Section 5.4 is on the preferentialist approach, but we also discuss the other two approaches, since they are prominently present in the applied literature. For each of the three approaches, we discuss some illustrative applications. While the applied literature is large, only very few studies explicitly implement a prioritarian social welfare function. The aim of this section is not to be complete, but to illustrate some normative and modelling choices with examples. While we refer sporadically to inter-country comparisons, our main focus is on the evaluation of changes of social conditions over time, i.e., on measuring social progress.

We only discuss approaches that implement an explicit and inclusive measure of individual well-being. Other methods are found in the applied literature. One is the calculation of multidimensional inequality measures (see Weymark (2006) for a survey). Combining a multi-dimensional transfer principle with other axioms (e.g. scale invariance) yields inequality measures that implicitly suggest a functional specification for $S(\boldsymbol{a}_t)$ and $w(\boldsymbol{a}_{it})$, with the latter assumed to be the same for all individuals. Unfortunately this justification is not rooted in an explicit theory of individual well-being. Another method is to introduce richer information in the social evaluation by constructing a "*dashboard*" that collects information on various one-dimensional outcomes and their evolution over time (see Atkinson et al. (2002) for a dashboard of social indicators to monitor the performance of the EU with respect to social inclusion, for instance). Although useful to monitor dimension-specific policy outcomes, we consider the dashboard approach a non-starter for the measurement of social condition and social progress. The reason is that it remains blind to the phenomenon of "cumulative deprivation" or, more generally, the correlation between the different dimensions of well-being (see Decancq and Schokkaert (2016) for a more extensive argument and Ravallion (2011) for a critique of this position).

5.3.1 *Objective Measures of Well-Being*

5.3.1.1 Income

The most popular approach in applied work remains to look at income y_{it} as a measure of well-being.[11] In the utilitarian interpretation of

[11] Prioritarian social welfare functions are defined over *individual* well-being levels. Much of the empirical work, however, relies on *household-level* data (e.g.,

Eq. (5.3), the social welfare function then becomes (some variant of) per capita GDP and social progress becomes GDP growth. In a prioritarian interpretation, inequality can be introduced as in Eqs (5.9) or (5.10). Interestingly, Atkinson himself presented an empirical comparison of 12 countries in his seminal paper (Atkinson (1970), pp. 258–261). He compared seven advanced and five developing countries based on the equally-distributed equivalent of their income distribution for several values of the inequality aversion parameter. Countries with a high average income perform better when the inequality aversion parameter is low and countries with a more equal income distribution perform better when the parameter is high. The application illustrates that the equally-distributed equivalent is a flexible tool to make international comparisons. In its wake, many studies have implemented the simple decomposition (5.9), but, to the best of our knowledge, only few of them have interpreted their results explicitly within a prioritarian framework. Empirical work using Kolm's prioritarian social welfare function is even more scarce.

The (relative) growth incidence curve (see Section 5.2.2.2) has also been mainly applied in an income setting, for which it was introduced from the very start. A recent famous example of its use is the "Elephant curve" proposed by Lakner and Milanovic (2016), showing the income growth at different percentiles of the global income distribution (see Figure 5.1). The curve illustrates the relative decline in the income of the middle class in the richer countries.[12]

household income, household consumption), mainly because of data limitations. Traditionally, equivalence scales are used to "equivalize" household income (or consumption) into individual income (or consumption). Underlying the use of equivalence scales is the assumption that household income (and hence, in this narrow framework, well-being) is distributed equally within the household. This is definitely not a realistic assumption. Recently, the theory of household behaviour has moved from the unitary approach (the household as one unit) to the collective approach (the household as a collective of individuals), allowing for the separate evaluation of the well-being of the different household members (Chiappori and Meghir, 2015). To the best of our knowledge, this approach has not yet led to applications from a prioritarian perspective.

[12] Figure 1.1 from *Global Inequality: A New Approach for the Age of Globalization* by Branko Milanovic, Cambridge, Mass.: Harvard University Press, Copyright © 2016 by the President and Fellows of Harvard College. Reprinted with permission from Harvard University Press.

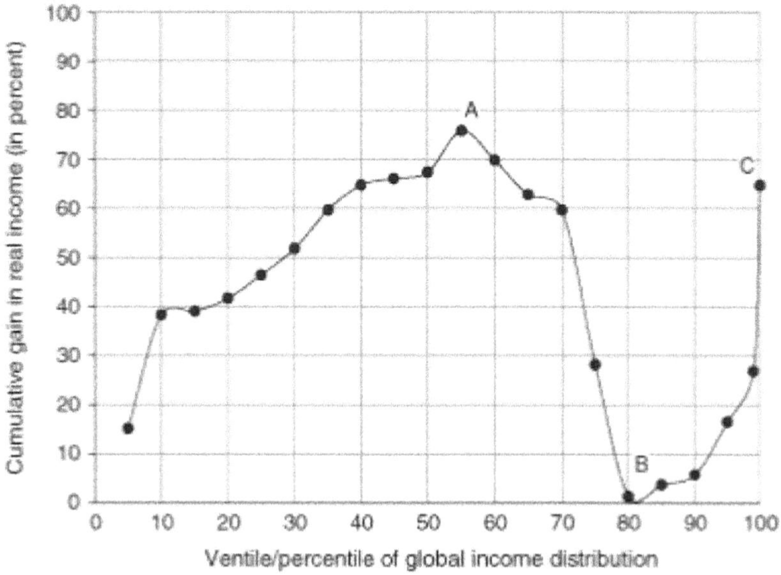

Figure 5.1 Growth incidence curve of the global income distribution
(Source: Milanovic (2016))

Income is relatively easy to measure. Moreover, focusing only on income means that one does not have to tackle the thorny issue of how to aggregate the different attributes in one measure of individual well-being. Yet, this is precisely its main weakness. Most people would agree that income is not the *only* relevant attribute of individual well-being and that non-monetary attributes (such as health, job characteristics and social relations) are essential components of a good life too.

5.3.1.2 Multidimensional Composite Indices of Well-Being

Some scholars have claimed that individual well-being or individual flourishing is an objective notion that does not depend on individual preferences (see Chapter 3, this volume for an overview and discussion). They argue that preferences can be misguided, biased, or even ill-defined. In an objective approach, the weighting of the different attributes is decided by the analyst, not by the individuals themselves – and is usually assumed to be uniform for all individuals. Without necessarily referring to a sophisticated theory, much of the applied work has – for practical reasons – also resorted to an objectively given weighting scheme. (See Decancq and Lugo (2013) for an overview of different methods to select a weighting scheme.)[13]

Two international institutions are particularly active in the production of such objective indices of well-being: the UNDP and the OECD. The UNDP has computed the "Human Development Index" (HDI) annually since the early 1990s and, more recently, the OECD has launched its "Better Life Index" (BLI).[14] Whereas the HDI covers all countries of the world for a limited number of dimensions, the BLI covers only the OECD member countries for a broader set of dimensions of well-being. To be more precise, the HDI consists of three dimensions: standard of living, education and life expectancy. The BLI consists of 11 dimensions grouped in two categories: quality of life and material conditions. Quality of life is measured by eight dimensions: health status, work–life balance, education and skills, social connections, civic engagement and governance, environmental quality, personal security and subjective well-being. Material conditions are measured by three dimensions: income and wealth, jobs and earnings and housing.

Neither the HDI nor the BLI uses data at the individual level, and they do not include any distributional concerns. Hence, it may be best to interpret them as (objective) specifications of the well-being function of a representative individual i in the various countries:

$$w_{it}^{obj} = w(a_{it}) = \left(\sum_{j=1}^{m} \omega_j \times a_{ijt}^{1-\mu} \right)^{1/1-\mu}. \tag{5.28}$$

In this mathematical structure two sets of parameters need to be selected; a weight ω_j for each dimension j and a parameter μ that captures the degree of complementarity between the dimensions of well-being. For the HDI all weights are fixed at 1/3, and after its revision in 2010 the complementarity parameter μ equals 1 (in which case Eq. (5.28) becomes multiplicative). For the BLI, the weights can be selected by the user in an online web application and the parameter $\mu = 0$.

One can of course also see Eq. (5.28) as the specification of well-being for each individual separately, and then aggregate all individual well-being levels through a prioritarian social welfare function. As an

13 Such an objective, "perfectionist" approach is often followed in the literature on educational policies; see Chapter 9, this volume.

14 For the Better Life Index, see www.oecdbetterlifeindex.org.

example, Bosmans et al. (2015) present the following specification, which introduces Eq. (5.28) in (the equally-distributed equivalent of) an Atkinson social welfare function:

$$\widetilde{S}(a_t) = \left(\frac{1}{N}\sum_{i=1}^{N}\left(\sum_{j=1}^{m}\omega_j \times a_{ijt}^{1-\mu}\right)^{1-\gamma/1-\mu}\right)^{1/1-\gamma}. \tag{5.29}$$

This specification contains an additional parameter γ to capture the degree of inequality aversion. The special case in which $\gamma = \mu$ has been proposed by Foster et al. (2005) and Alkire and Foster (2010) to derive the inequality-adjusted Human Development Index, which has been published every year in the Human Development Report since 2010. Decancq (2017) argues in favour of keeping both parameters to have the flexibility to capture the degree of complementarity (μ) and the aversion to inequality (γ) independently. He proposed a distribution-sensitive Better Life Index, based on an Atkinson social welfare function, and applies it to a synthetic micro dataset for all OECD member countries. His work illustrates how the welfare ranking of countries crucially depends on the inequality aversion parameter: as an example, while the United States obtains a higher social welfare for low values of the parameter γ, Austria scores better for a more inequality averse social welfare function.

Decancq and Ooghe (2010) use the framework of Eq. (5.29) to study the question whether the world has moved forward. Since their analysis is at the country level, they do not take up within-country inequality, but they do integrate in their analysis between-country inequality in well-being. Analogously to what we have discussed in Section 5.2.2.1, they decompose Eq. (5.29) to obtain a measure of multidimensional inequality $I(a_t)$

$$\widetilde{S}(a_t) = \widetilde{S}(\bar{a}_t) \times \left[1 - \underbrace{\left(1 - \frac{\widetilde{S}(a_t)}{\widetilde{S}(\bar{a}_t)}\right)}_{I(a_t)}\right], \tag{5.30}$$

where $\bar{a}_t$ is the matrix that contains the average outcomes in each dimension. They consider the three dimensions of the HDI and fix the parameter $\mu = 1$.[15] They perform a sensitivity analysis for the role

[15] This restriction follows from imposing a strong invariance principle, see also Tsui (1995).

of the aversion to inequality (γ) and the different possible weighting schemes. They find that between-country social welfare has increased between 1980 and 2008. When focusing on between-country multidimensional inequality, they find that if life expectancy or standard of living get a large weight, the inequality trend depends on the level of inequality aversion.

5.3.2 Happiness and Life Satisfaction

Completely neglecting the differences in the relative importance that people attach to the various life dimensions goes against the economic tradition of "consumer sovereignty". In recent years, this criticism of the objective approach has been vigorously restated by researchers active in the field of measuring happiness. Layard (2005, p. 121) puts it bluntly: "Ethical theory should surely focus on what people feel, rather than what people think is good for them. If we accept the Marxist idea of false consciousness, we play God and decide what is good for others, even if they will never feel it to be so." Layard himself is advocating a subjective well-being approach, in which well-being is reduced to a mental state such as happiness. This emphasis on feelings brings us back to a version of Benthamite utilitarianism. With one important difference, though: "individual happiness" can be measured in large-scale surveys and is therefore readily available as a measure of individual well-being.

These large-scale surveys typically also enquire how satisfied people are with their lives, all things considered. Although the results on this question are highly correlated with reported feelings of happiness, conceptually they are different since life satisfaction refers to a more cognitive (albeit still subjective) evaluation of life. It seems natural to interpret "happiness feelings" as one possible dimension of life (one element in the vector a_{it}) and "life satisfaction" as an overall evaluation of the attributes contained in a_{it}. This interpretation brings us close to the preferentialist approach.

Recently, the literature on happiness and life satisfaction is booming. The bulk of the applied work looks at average happiness or life satisfaction, and can therefore be interpreted as an application of average utilitarianism. A calculation of averages is only meaningful if one assumes that happiness or life satisfaction can be measured at a cardinal level and that the response scale is used in the same way by all respondents, so that the resulting values are interpersonally comparable. Yet, the data on happiness or life satisfaction are typically measured on an ordinal scale (see Ferrer-i-Carbonell and Frijters (2004) for a discussion). Moreover, there is evidence of heterogeneous use of the response scale by different respondents (see Beegle et al. (2012), Angelini et al. (2014), Ravallion et al. (2016) and Fleurbaey and Blanchet (2013) for a more general theoretical analysis).[16] If these interpersonal differences reflect differences in expectations and aspirations, it is debatable whether they should be respected in interpersonal well-being comparisons: if two individuals are in the same objective situation and have identical preferences, but one is less happy (or less satisfied) because she has more demanding aspirations, should she get a larger weight in a prioritarian evaluation of social states? One could perhaps argue that differences in scaling reflect individual idiosyncrasies that are likely to be wiped out in the averaging process. This does not solve the problem that the cardinalization is an arbitrary one, however. Moreover, even if we can see the response scale differences as noise, they cannot be neglected for interpersonal comparisons at the individual level. As an example, it has been shown that they have a strong influence on the identification of who are the poor in a given society (see, e.g., Decancq et al. (2015b)).[17]

Most of the applied empirical literature neglects these measurement issues and analyses the happiness and life satisfaction data as if they were cardinally measurable and interpersonally comparable. An example is offered by the yearly published "World Happiness Reports" (Helliwell et al., 2019). In the period 2016–2018, average happiness was highest in Finland, Denmark and Norway and lowest in South Sudan, the Central African Republic and Afghanistan. In the period from 2005–2008 to 2016–2018, the largest increase in average happiness was realized in Benin, Nicaragua, Bulgaria and Latvia, the largest decrease in average happiness was found in (not surprisingly) Syria and Venezuela – both with a large decrease of almost two points on a 10-point-scale. The authors also report results on the inequality of

[16] King et al. (2004) have proposed the use of vignettes to model and correct for differential use of the response scale, see also Angelini et al. (2014).

[17] We focus here only on the measurement issues. Even if the measurement were perfect, the use of happiness or life satisfaction as measures of individual well-being would still raise serious ethical issues. See the seminal analysis in Sen (1985), Dworkin (1981) and Chapter 3, this volume.

happiness, measured by the standard deviation of the distribution of the individual evaluations of life satisfaction (also on a 10-point-scale). Comparing the results for different regions in the world yields interesting insights. As an example, they find that in the period 2006–2018, average life satisfaction has remained almost constant in Sub-Saharan Africa, but has declined considerably in the Middle East. In the same period inequality in life satisfaction has increased in the two regions and very strongly so in Sub-Saharan Africa.

Some authors have calculated the inequality in life satisfaction while taking due account of the ordinal nature of the data (see, e.g., Dutta and Foster (2013)), but to the best of our knowledge, there are no applications in which hedonic measures have been used in a prioritarian social welfare function as given by Eq. (5.1).

5.3.3 Preferentialist Approaches

In a preference-based approach, the well-being measure is a representation of the individual preferences. If we denote the preference relation of individual i by R_i, preferentialist measures of well-being satisfy the condition[18]

$$w_i(a_{it}) \geq w_i(a'_{it}) \Leftrightarrow a_{it} R_i a'_{it}. \tag{5.31}$$

All functions $w(\cdot)$ that satisfy Eq. (5.31) are representations of a preference relation and, hence, utility functions. The ethical issue is how to choose between different possible cardinalizations. In fact, if one accepts that the answers to a life satisfaction question reflect individual preferences, life satisfaction is one of these possible cardinalizations. As is discussed in Section 5.3.2, it raises some ethical questions, however.

The literature has suggested many other possibilities with a specific ethical rationale for the chosen cardinalization (see Chapter 3, this volume, for a more extensive discussion).[19] In Section 5.3.3.1, we

[18] This condition is called the "Deference Principle" in Chapter 3 of this volume.

[19] The equivalent income is one possible choice within the "equivalence approach" (Fleurbaey and Maniquet (2011)). Another popular family of well-being measures within the same approach is that of ray utilities (Deaton, 1979; Fleurbaey and Tadenuma, 2014). Note that Eq. (5.32) implicitly defines an "instantaneous" equivalent income for period t. The extension to a life-cycle equivalent income is straightforward.

discuss money metric utilities, which have been particularly influential in consumption theory. Going beyond market outcomes, we discuss in Section 5.3.3.2 the so-called equivalent income.

The equivalent income y_{it}^* is defined implicitly by the equation:

$$\left(y_{it}^*, \tilde{x}_{it}\right) I_i (y_{it}, x_{it}), \tag{5.32}$$

where $\tilde{x}_{it}$ is a vector with reference values for the non-income attributes. We formulate these reference values here in a flexible way as dependent both on the individual and on the time period concerned. In empirical applications it is common to assume that these reference values are constant across individuals and time, so that $\tilde{x}_{it} = \tilde{x}$. It is easily seen that

$$y_{it}^* = y_{it} - WTP_i\left(x_{it} \rightarrow \tilde{x}_{it}\right), \tag{5.33}$$

where $WTP_i\left(x_{it} \rightarrow \tilde{x}_{it}\right)$ denotes the willingness-to-pay of individual i for a move from x_{it} to $\tilde{x}_{it}$.

Equivalent incomes respect individual preferences in a risk-free setting, but they do not take up individual differences in risk aversion. An alternative cardinalization, going back to the seminal work of Harsanyi (1977) and recently advocated by Adler (2016), makes use of von Neumann–Morgenstern (vNM) utility functions (see Chapter 3, this volume).

Preference-based approaches raise a challenging implementation issue: how to estimate preferences over attributes? If we only consider market commodities (or, more precisely, attributes that can be chosen by the individuals), revealed preference techniques can be used. As soon as we introduce non-market commodities (such as health) where freedom of choice is limited, one has to resort to stated preferences (see, e.g., Fleurbaey et al. (2013)) or to deriving ordinal information from life satisfaction data (see, e.g., Decancq et al. (2015b)). The latter method is used in the empirical illustration in Section 5.4. It retrieves (ordinal) information about the marginal rates of substitution from an estimated life satisfaction equation. This ordinal information allows us to estimate equivalent incomes. Indeed, if we write the life satisfaction equation as $SWB_{it} = f_i(y_{it}, x_{it}, u_{it})$ with x_{it} capturing the non-income attributes of well-being and u_{it} an error term with zero mean, the equivalent income can be derived from solving the following implicit equation:

$$f_i(y_{it}, x_{it}, u_{it}) = f_i(y_{it}^*, \tilde{x}_{it}, 0), \tag{5.34}$$

with $\tilde{x}_{it}$ the reference values for the non-income attributes.[20] In the case of vNM utilities, one needs additional information about risk aversion. We return to the implementation of the vNM approach in our empirical application of Section 5.4.

Many cross-sectional studies attempt to take into account preference heterogeneity. However, when analysing changes over time, it is usually assumed that preferences do not change. This is obviously not realistic, but introducing changing preferences into the analysis raises challenging normative and empirical questions (see Fleurbaey and Tadenuma (2014) for a discussion).

5.3.3.1 Market Commodities

The preference-based approach has taken a prominent place in theories of social welfare based on consumption theory (see, e.g., Deaton and Muellbauer (1980)). A typical example is the work of Jorgenson and co-authors. Denote by q_{it} the quantities of market commodities consumed by household i in period t, and write $U(q_{it}, A_i)$ as the utility representation of the preferences over market commodities of household i with characteristics A_i. To estimate the preference parameters, Jorgenson (1990) assumes that household preferences can be represented by a translog indirect utility function. Since he focuses on market commodities only, all the parameters in that function can be estimated from household consumption data. To move to social welfare, Jorgenson and Slesnick (2014) propose the following social welfare function:

$$SW(V_1, \cdots, V_N) = \ln\bar{V} - \gamma(\mathbf{q}) \left[\frac{\sum_i m_0(p, A_i) |\ln V_i - \ln\bar{V}|^{-\rho}}{\sum_k m_0(p, A_k)} \right]^{-1/\rho}, \tag{5.35}$$

with V_i the translog indirect utility function and $m_0(p, A_i)$ the general household equivalence scale. Eq. (5.35) can be interpreted as follows. The first term $\ln\bar{V} = \sum_i \frac{m_0(p, A_i)}{\sum_k m_0(p, A_k)} \ln V_i$ captures average social welfare,

[20] Eq. (5.34) makes the life satisfaction equation individual-specific. Of course, in empirical work with the available panel data, the degree of inter-individual variation has to be restricted.

while the second term is a measure of inequality. It is a homogeneous function of the deviations of the individual welfare levels from the average. The parameter ρ measures the degree of inequality aversion: if $\rho = -\infty$, the dispersion term vanishes and social welfare reduces to the simple average of the logarithm of individual well-being. Jorgenson and Slesnick (2014) call this the "utilitarian" case, while they denote the case of $\rho = -1$ as "egalitarian".

From the perspective of the rest of the literature, the social welfare specification (5.35) is rather idiosyncratic.[21] However, it is not difficult to use the individual welfare levels, as estimated from consumption behaviour, in another social welfare function. One possibility, mentioned in Jorgenson and Schreyer (2017), is the Atkinson-specification (as in Eq. (5.9)).

The strengths and limitations of this approach are both linked to the fact that the authors only consider market commodities. This makes it possible to estimate and implement the revealed preference approach. When working with individual household data, it becomes possible to introduce (and estimate) a considerable amount of preference variation: in addition to household size, the vector A_i includes age and gender of the household head, and urban versus rural residence. Moreover, the focus on consumption allows for the integration of equity considerations in the regular National Accounts framework. This is one of the main aims of the recent work by Jorgenson and Schreyer (2017). The application of their methodology to the US data for the period 1948–2010 shows a positive contribution of the change in equity for the period 1948–1973. However, since the mid-seventies the equity component has turned negative and the growing inequity has led to a decrease in the growth rate of social welfare.

Despite these practical advantages, it remains difficult to accept that individual well-being and social progress would only depend on the consumption of market commodities. We now turn to approaches that have tried to incorporate other, non-material, considerations.

5.3.3.2 Including Non-Market Commodities

As soon as non-market commodities are included in the vector a_{it}, the estimation of preferences becomes a real challenge. We first present

[21] For Eq. (5.35) to satisfy the Pareto principle, the function $\gamma(q)$ has to be restricted. Jorgenson and Slesnick (2014) assume that it takes the maximum value consistent with the Pareto principle.

some studies that have tried to circumvent the estimation of the preferences by calibrating them. We then discuss an application in which preferences are estimated on the basis of a life satisfaction equation. This approach is also used in the empirical illustration in Section 5.4.

Calibrated Preferences

A central non-market commodity is health. As described in Section 5.2.4.1, Becker et al. (2005) have proposed to introduce longevity into the analysis by specifying a country-level indirect utility function $V(y_t, \sigma_t) = u(y_t)L(\sigma_t)$, where y_t is GDP per capita, σ_t the survival function of the country in period t and $L(\sigma_t) = \int_0^\infty \exp(-rt)\sigma_t dt$ (see Eq. (5.26)). In their empirical analysis, the authors assume a constant relative risk aversion specification for $u(.)$ to arrive at:[22]

$$V(y_t, \sigma_t) = \left(\frac{y_t^{1-1/\gamma}}{1-1/\gamma} + \alpha\right) \times L(\sigma_t). \tag{5.36}$$

The authors calibrate the parameter values of this Eq. based on findings from the literature about relative risk aversion and the value of life (they set $\alpha = -16.2$, $\gamma = 1.250$ and $r = 0.03$). Based on Eq. 5.36, they compute for each country a full income y^* so that:

$$V(y^*, \sigma_t) = V(y_{t+1}, \sigma_{t+1}). \tag{5.37}$$

The growth rate rate $(y^* - y_t)/y_t$ captures both the increase of GDP and the improvement in longevity and is their measure of social progress between the periods t and $t+1$. Becker et al. (2005) implement this approach at the country level, so that their results are insensitive to the within-country distribution of full income. They focus on the inequality in social progress between countries. Their results show that improvements in longevity have contributed considerably to growth in full income, especially for the poorest countries.

Jones and Klenow (2016) extend the framework of Becker et al. (2005) substantially. They include the disutility of labour and use consumption rather than income. Their specification of flow utility is

$$u(C, l) = \bar{u} + log(C) - \frac{\theta\varepsilon}{1+\varepsilon}(1-l)^{\frac{1+\varepsilon}{\varepsilon}}, \tag{5.38}$$

[22] The constant α is used to obtain a realistic calibration of the value of longevity.

where C is consumption, l is leisure, θ is the weight given to leisure and ε is the Frisch-elasticity of labour supply. Longevity is entered as in Eq. (5.26). Importantly, in their empirical work they make use of individual survey data, so that inequality can also be taken into account. Like Becker et al. (2005), they implement a consumption equivalent measure to answer questions such as: what proportion of consumption in the United States, given the US values of leisure, mortality and inequality, would deliver the same utility level as the values in France? Since they calculate expected utility for each country, their social welfare function is utilitarian.

After calibrating all the parameter values in the model, Jones and Klenow (2016) find that the level of social welfare in Western Europe is much closer to that in the United States than it would appear from looking at GDP per capita alone. Longer lives with more leisure time and more equal consumption in Western Europe largely offset their lower average consumption. In addition to these country-level comparisons, they also calculate social progress as the growth rates of the consumption equivalents over time. Some detailed results are shown in Table 5.2. Life expectancy is again the main driver of the differences between welfare growth and income growth.

Both Becker et al. (2005) and Jones and Klenow (2016) have assumed preference homogeneity and calibrated a single indirect utility function for a representative agent for each country. Fleurbaey and Gaulier (2009) calculate equivalent incomes with reference values as they are defined in Eq. (5.32). They extend the parametric specification given in Eq. (5.36) by including the disutility of labour, the risk of unemployment and household composition. They allow for inter-country differences in preferences for leisure by taking the observed net wage rate as an estimate of the marginal rate of substitution between consumption and leisure. The resulting equivalent incomes are then introduced in an Atkinson prioritarian social welfare function which penalizes average full income for the inequality in its distribution. The penalty for inequality in the distribution of full incomes is approximated by the inequality in the distribution of ordinary incomes. Their empirical work focuses on instantaneous comparisons of different countries, rather than the measurement of social progress. The authors implement their approach for 24 OECD member countries and find that the obtained ranking of countries differs when the social welfare function becomes inequality averse ($\gamma = 1, 5$) compared

Table 5.2. ***Income and welfare growth***

	Welfare growth (in %)	Income growth (in %)	Diff. (in %)	Decomposition of difference				
				Life exp.	Consumption/ income	Leis.	Cons. ineq.	Leis. ineq.
UK (1998–2007)	4.42	3.12	1.30	1.16	0.12	−0.01	0.02	0.05
India (1983–2005)	4.08	4.05	0.03	1.14	−1.04	0.04	−0.13	0.02
France (1984–2005)	3.15	2.15	1.00	1.04	0.10	−0.05	−0.16	0.07
US (1984–2006)	3.09	2.11	0.98	0.89	0.51	−0.10	−0.24	0.08
Italy (1987–2006)	2.73	2.02	0.72	1.33	0.03	−0.17	−0.24	−0.22
Indonesia (1993–2006)	2.65	0.39	2.25	1.43	0.81	0.18	−0.16	−0.00
Mexico (1984–2006)	1.87	1.05	0.82	1.09	0.26	−0.23	−0.16	−0.14
Average	3.14	2.13	1.02	1.15	0.11	−0.05	−0.16	−0.04

Note: Adapted from Jones and Klenow (2016).

to the utilitarian (inequality-neutral) case. Especially Japan and the northern European countries improve their position, while Ireland, the UK, the US, Australia, Portugal and Italy worsen their position.

Estimated Preferences

As mentioned before, preferences for non-market commodities can also be estimated on the basis of a life satisfaction equation, rather than calibrated. This approach is illustrated by Decancq and Schokkaert (2016), who have estimated a life satisfaction equation with pooled information from the European Social Survey for 2008 and 2010 and for 15 EU-members, Switzerland, Norway and the Russian Federation. The attributes included in the analysis are income, health, employment, social relations and safety. Interaction effects between demographic variables and attributes are introduced to incorporate intergroup preference heterogeneity. Decancq and Schokkaert find, for example, that higher educated respondents give a higher weight to income and a lower weight to health. The estimated parameters of the life satisfaction equation are then used to estimate equivalent incomes for all individuals in the sample on the basis of Eq. (5.34).

Decancq and Schokkaert (2016) use a rank-dependent generalized Gini social welfare function and decompose its equally-distributed equivalent for a country in period t as follows:

$$\widetilde{S}_{\rho}^{DS}(\boldsymbol{a}_t) = \mu(\boldsymbol{a}_t)\left[1 - GI_{\rho}(\boldsymbol{a}_t)\right], \tag{5.39}$$

where $\mu(\boldsymbol{a}_t) = \sum_i (w_i(a_{it}))/N$ is the average equivalent income in period t and GI_{ρ} is a generalized Gini inequality measure with ρ a parameter of inequality aversion (with $\rho = 1$, $GI_{\rho} = 0$ and social welfare reduces to mean individual well-being, with $\rho = 2$, GI_{ρ} becomes the well-known Gini coefficient). While the decomposition of Eq. (5.39) resembles (5.9), the social welfare function does not have the separable structure of Eq. (5.1) and, hence, their approach is not generalized utilitarian (see Chapter 2, this volume, for a discussion).

They find that the introduction of health as a dimension of well-being has a strong effect on country rankings based on social welfare. The growth rate of social welfare is summarized in Table 5.3. It shows that the inter-country ranking of the growth rates of social welfare ("social progress") is crucially affected both by the move from income to equivalent income and by the introduction of a sensitivity to the

Table 5.3. ***Growth rates of income and equivalent income in period 2008–2010***

	Income (%)			Equivalent income (%)		
Country	$\rho = 1$	$\rho = 2$	$\rho = 5$	$\rho = 1$	$\rho = 2$	$\rho = 5$
BE	−0.55	−0.55	1.69	0.05	−1.11	−3.52
	4	*5*	*4*	*8*	*6*	*4*
CH	7.35	10.18	9.73	3.95	4.89	1.14
	1	*1*	*1*	*2*	*2*	*2*
CZ	−4.26	−5.42	−5.26	−7.74	−12.59	−17.21
	14	*16*	*14*	*17*	*17*	*17*
DE	0.09	0.85	1.26	2.94	−3.35	−10.12
	3	*3*	*5*	*4*	*7*	*10*
DK	−1.73	−2.53	−3.62	−4.01	−6.67	−10.85
	8	*9*	*12*	*12*	*13*	*11*
EE	−8.60	−8.67	−8.51	−6.89	−11.33	−12.40
	18	*18*	*17*	*16*	*16*	*13*
ES	−2.24	−3.87	−6.59	0.58	−6.43	−16.29
	11	*13*	*16*	*7*	*12*	*16*
FI	−3.37	−3.04	−3.18	−4.60	−6.39	−13.89
	13	*12*	*10*	*13*	*11*	*14*
FR	−1.53	−1.02	−2.96	−6.42	−8.89	−10.90
	6	*7*	*9*	*15*	*15*	*12*
GB	−2.16	0.36	1.81	−0.85	−3.90	−8.66
	10	*4*	*2*	*9*	*9*	*8*
GR	−5.81	−6.96	−9.76	−9.04	−17.47	−25.45
	17	*17*	*18*	*18*	*18*	*18*
HU	−2.32	−2.65	−2.62	−1.55	−3.52	1.00
	12	*10*	*8*	*10*	*8*	*3*
NL	−2.03	−0.91	0.36	−4.73	−8.35	−15.50
	9	*6*	*6*	*14*	*14*	*15*
NO	−1.54	−2.92	−4.13	−3.10	−5.19	−9.56
	7	*11*	*13*	*11*	*10*	*9*
PL	2.72	2.72	1.80	2.16	−0.68	−3.97
	2	*2*	*3*	*5*	*5*	*5*
RU	−4.69	−4.35	−6.41	3.79	5.98	4.79
	16	*15*	*15*	*3*	*1*	*1*
SE	−1.25	−1.46	−2.12	5.11	−0.37	−7.69
	5	*8*	*7*	*1*	*4*	*7*
SI	−4.5	−4.3	−3.5	1.2	0.6	−5.1
	15	*14*	*11*	*6*	*3*	*6*

Note: Adapted from Decancq and Schokkaert (2016).

distribution of well-being, i.e., by selecting the parameter of inequality aversion at a value larger than 1.[23]

5.4 An Empirical Illustration: Social Progress in Russia

Between 1995 and 2005, the Russian economy underwent sharp changes, including a deep financial crisis in August 1998. One may wonder how much social progress there was over the considered decade, and for whom? We use three waves of the Russia Longitudinal Monitoring Survey (RLMS-HSE) in 1995, 2000 and 2005 to investigate this question and illustrate some issues that were discussed in this chapter. We measure social progress using the Atkinson and Kolm-Pollak social welfare function for several values of the inequality aversion parameters, relying on three different well-being measures: expenditures, equivalent incomes and vNM-utilities.

Because the shape of the distribution of these well-being measures differs considerably, it is a challenge to choose the inequality aversion parameters γ and β in a "comparable" way. We therefore consider a thought experiment with a leaky bucket transfer between a person at the 90th percentile of the well-being distribution and a person at the 10th percentile.[24] We consider four cases in which κ, the leak of the leaky bucket transfer, amounts to 0 per cent, 50 per cent, 90 per cent and 99 per cent, respectively. If the leak κ equals 99 per cent, for instance, and the person at the 90th percentile sends a transfer of 100 rubles, only 1 ruble is received by the person at the 10th percentile. The remaining 99 rubles are lost. The leaky bucket transfer generates two opposing forces on social welfare: the leak reduces total well-being, but the transfer also makes the well-being distribution more equal. We select the inequality aversion parameters of the social welfare function so that both forces precisely compensate each other and social welfare remains the same before and after the leaky bucket transfer. When the social welfare-neutral leak is 0 per cent, the social planner is not willing to accept any leak in compensation for the

[23] Table 12 from K. Decancq and E. Schokkaert, "Beyond GDP: Using Equivalent Incomes to Measure Well-Being in Europe." Social Indicators Research 126: 21–55 (2016), Copyright © 2016. Reprinted with permission from Springer Nature.

[24] See also Chapter 2, this volume for a similar thought experiment with a leaky bucket transfer.

Table 5.4. ***Inequality aversion parameters γ and β for different values of the social welfare-neutral leak κ***

	Expenditures		Equivalent income		vNM utility	
κ	γ	β	γ	β	γ	β
0%	0	0	0	0	0	0
50%	0.36	0.00008	0.15	0.00022	1.25	1.892
90%	1.21	0.00028	0.50	0.00074	4.15	6.287
99%	2.41	0.00056	0.99	0.00147	8.31	12.57

reduction in well-being inequality. Hence, the social welfare function that the planner is using is inequality-neutral. The larger the welfare-neutral leak κ is, the more weight the social planner gives to the reduction in well-being inequality, and, hence, the more inequality averse the social welfare function becomes. The implied inequality aversion parameters γ and β for the distribution of the considered well-being measures in 1995 are given in Table 5.4.[25] The implied parameter values are quite different across the different well-being measures. These differences reflect the differences in the shape of the well-being distribution in 1995. The absolute difference between the 10th and 90th percentile of the distribution of expenditures is smaller than for equivalent incomes, for instance, whereas the ratio is larger (leading to larger γ values and smaller β values for the same κ value, respectively).

Tables 5.5 and 5.6 present the equally-distributed equivalent of social welfare for the three considered well-being measures using the Atkinson social welfare function (Table 5.5) and the Kolm-Pollak social welfare function (Table 5.6) in 1995, 2000 and 2005. In the following subsections we discuss for each well-being measure how it is

[25] The γ and β parameter values for the considered well-being measures are obtained by using Eq. (5.11) and equalizing $(1-\kappa) \times d\tilde{S}/dQ(p)$ at the 10th percentile and $d\tilde{S}/dQ(p)$ at the 90th percentile for the Atkinson and Kolm-Pollak transformation functions. After some reworking, this yields that $\gamma = -\ln(1-\kappa)/\ln[Q(0,9)/Q(0,1)]$ and $\beta = -\ln(1-\kappa)/[Q(0,9) - Q(0,1)]$ in which the appropriate percentile values of the well-being distribution and value for the welfare-neutral leak κ can be substituted.

Table 5.5. *Equally-distributed equivalent ($\widetilde{S}$), average (μ) and inequality (A) for the Atkinson social welfare function, using expenditures, equivalent incomes and vNM utilities as well-being measure*

		Expenditures			Equiv. income			vNM utility		
t	κ	$\widetilde{S}$	μ	A	$\widetilde{S}$	μ	A	$\widetilde{S}$	μ	A
1995	0%	4863	4863	0	1164	1164	0	0.688	0.688	0
	50%	4411	4863	0.093	1034	1164	0.112	0.668	0.688	0.028
	90%	3505	4863	0.279	746	1164	0.359	0.611	0.688	0.112
	99%	2486	4863	0.489	388	1164	0.667	0.512	0.688	0.256
2000	0%	4126	4126	0	1172	1172	0	0.680	0.680	0
	50%	3699	4126	0.103	1040	1172	0.113	0.654	0.680	0.039
	90%	2894	4126	0.299	743	1172	0.366	0.564	0.680	0.172
	99%	2047	4126	0.504	358	1172	0.694	0.417	0.680	0.386
2005	0%	5732	5732	0	1606	1606	0	0.704	0.704	0
	50%	5203	5732	0.092	1440	1606	0.104	0.681	0.704	0.033
	90%	4156	5732	0.275	1056	1606	0.343	0.610	0.704	0.133
	99%	2999	5732	0.477	531	1606	0.669	0.497	0.704	0.294

Table 5.6. *Equally-distributed equivalent ($\widetilde{S}$), average (μ) and inequality (KP) for the Kolm-Pollak social welfare function, using expenditures, equivalent incomes and vNM utilities as well-being measure*

		Expenditures			Equiv. income			vNM utility		
t	κ	$\widetilde{S}$	μ	KP	$\widetilde{S}$	μ	KP	$\widetilde{S}$	μ	KP
1995	0%	4863	4863	0	1164	1164	0	0.688	0.688	0
	50%	4321	4863	541	923	1164	241	0.669	0.688	0.018
	90%	3623	4863	1240	667	1164	497	0.623	0.688	0.064
	99%	3072	4863	1791	502	1164	662	0.559	0.688	0.128
2000	0%	4126	4126	0	1172	1172	0	0.680	0.680	0
	50%	3661	4126	465	928	1172	244	0.656	0.680	0.024
	90%	3096	4126	1030	670	1172	502	0.595	0.680	0.085
	99%	2654	4126	1472	502	1172	670	0.511	0.680	0.169
2005	0%	5732	5732	0	1606	1606	0	0.704	0.704	0
	50%	5008	5732	724	1230	1606	376	0.683	0.704	0.022
	90%	4141	5732	1591	848	1606	758	0.627	0.704	0.078
	99%	3476	5732	2256	617	1606	989	0.552	0.704	0.153

operationalized and we compare the results of the two decompositions introduced in Section 5.2.2. First, we look at the decomposition of the level of social welfare in the mean and inequality and, second, we turn to the decomposition of the change in social welfare using the growth incidence curves.

5.4.1 Expenditures

The real household expenditures are measured by adding the expenditures of all household members and applying the square root equivalence scale to capture differences in household composition. The first column of Table 5.5 presents the level of the equally-distributed equivalent of the Atkinson social welfare function and the first column of Table 5.6 shows the level of the equally-distributed equivalent of the Kolm-Pollak social welfare function. We use the inequality aversion parameters γ and β that are implied by the four values of the welfare-neutral leak κ (see Table 5.4). We see that for all parameter values of the two social welfare functions, the lowest level of social welfare is reached in 2000, in the aftermath of the Russian financial crisis. After 2000, social welfare increases again and reaches a higher level in 2005 compared to 1995.

The decomposition of social welfare in the mean and inequality (shown in the second and third columns of Tables 5.5 and 5.6) reveals some additional interesting findings. First, the more inequality averse the social welfare function is, the bigger the welfare loss due to inequality measured by the inequality measure A in Table 5.5 and KP in Table 5.6. Remarkably, the welfare loss due to inequality shows a different trend for the Atkinson and Kolm-Pollak social welfare functions over time. While it is inversely U-shaped for the Atkinson social welfare function, it is U-shaped in the case of Kolm-Pollak.

The second decomposition, relating social progress to the relative and absolute growth incidence curves, allows us to investigate this finding further. Figures 5.2 and 5.3 show the relative and absolute growth incidence curves in the top and bottom panel, respectively. Figure 5.2 focuses on the period between 1995 and 2000, whereas Figure 5.3 covers the entire period between 1995 and 2005.

Let us start from Figure 5.2. The difference between the top and bottom panel of this figure is striking. It illustrates why the social welfare loss due to inequality shows a different trend for the

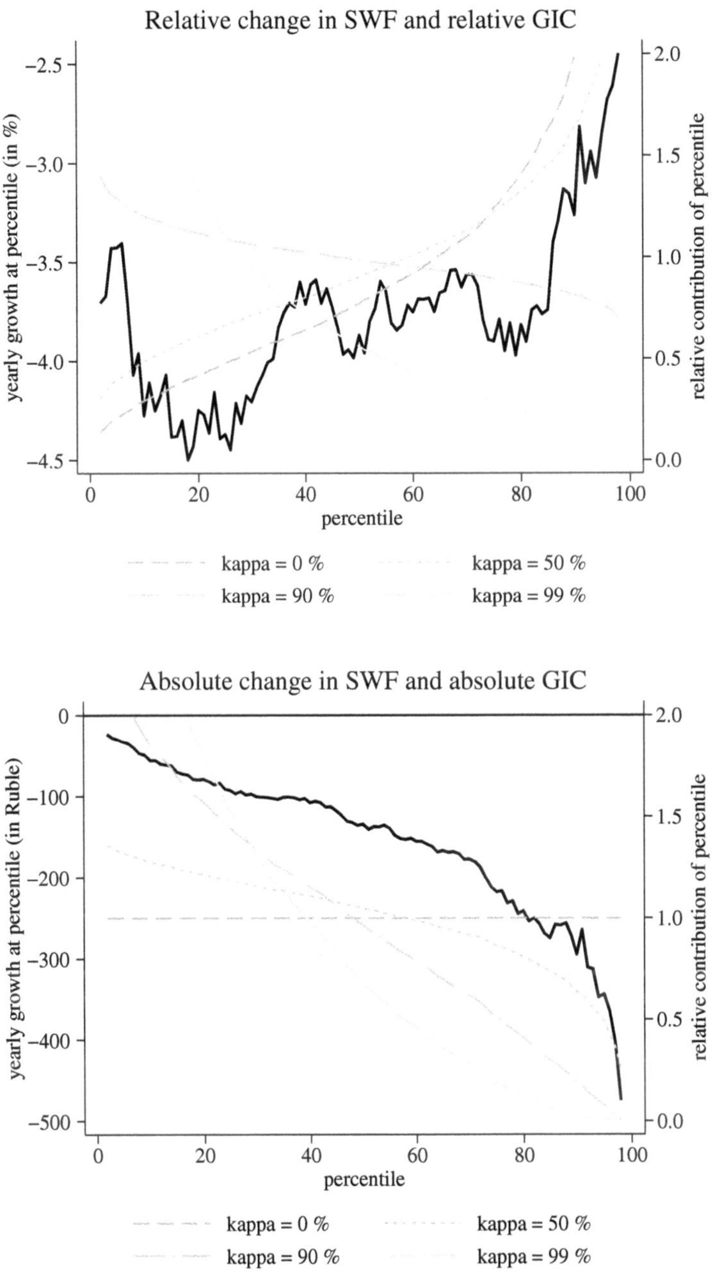

Figure 5.2 Growth incidence and change in social welfare between 1995 and 2000 for Atkinson (top) and Kolm-Pollak (bottom) social welfare functions, using expenditures as well-being measure

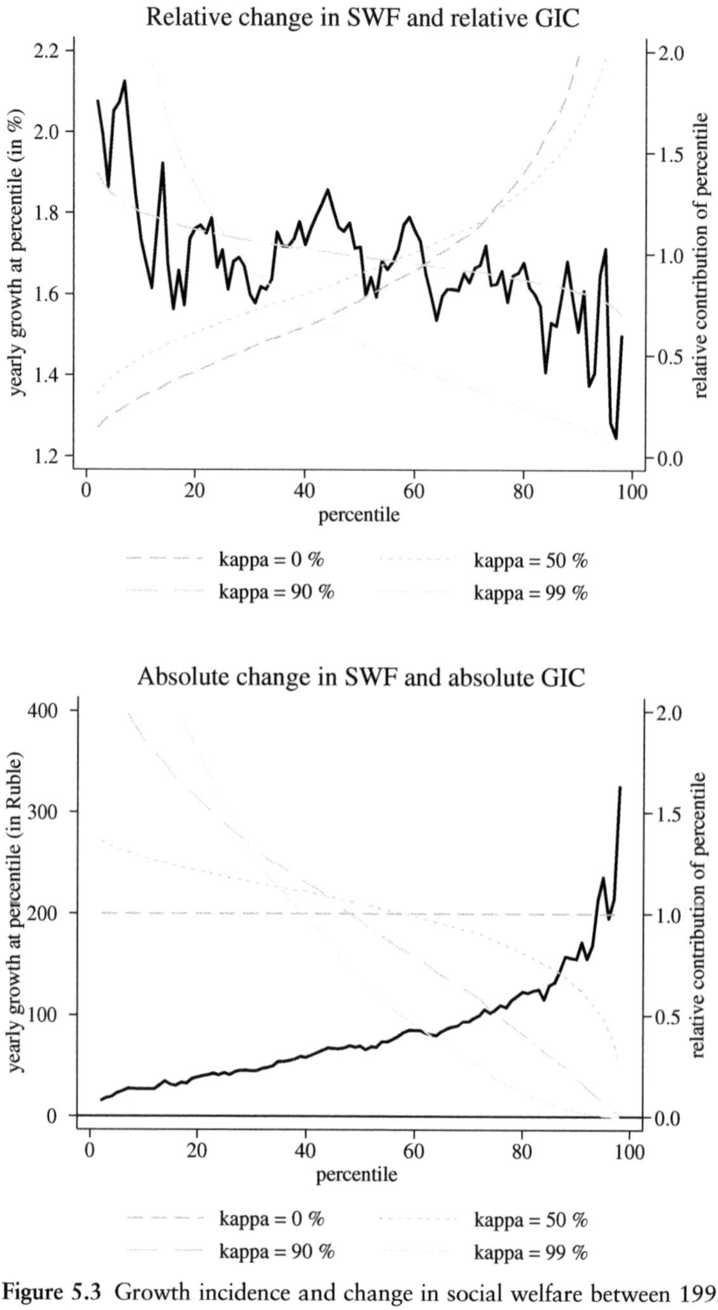

Figure 5.3 Growth incidence and change in social welfare between 1995 and 2005 for Atkinson (top) and Kolm-Pollak (bottom) social welfare functions, using expenditures as well-being measure

Atkinson and Kolm-Pollak inequality measures. In the period between 1995 and 2000, the top panel shows that the growth rate of expenditures was negative throughout the entire distribution, being more negative for the poorest individuals. The annual growth rate of expenditures reached −4.5 per cent at the 20th percentile, while it was "only" −2.5 per cent at the top of the distribution. The bottom panel shows the same period, but tells a quite different story by looking at the absolute changes in expenditures (expressed in rubles), rather than their relative growth rate. The absolute reduction of expenditures during the crisis is larger for persons higher in the distribution. Both findings are not inconsistent in the presence of large initial expenditure inequalities: the loss of 2.5 per cent of a large expenditure level at the top of the distribution turns out to be larger than 4.5 per cent of a smaller expenditure level at the bottom. Both growth incidence curves tell a different (and complementary) story. As we have seen in Section 5.2.2.2, the relative growth incidence curve in the top panel of Figure 5.2 is closely related to the relative change in the Atkinson social welfare function.[26] The growth rate of the Atkinson social welfare can be written as a weighted sum of the growth rates of well-being at the different percentiles with the weights being equal to the ratio of the transformed well-being at each percentile and the average transformed well-being across all percentiles. The weights at each percentile for four different κ values are indicated in Figures 5.2 and 5.3 in greyscale. The higher this weight, the higher the impact on the change in social welfare. The size of the weight depends on the shape of the distribution and also on the selected welfare-neutral leak κ and the inequality aversion parameter γ it implies (see Table 5.4). Remember that for the Atkinson social welfare function, the weight increases with well-being if the selected welfare-neutral leak κ and the implied inequality aversion γ are sufficiently low. This is exactly what we observe in the figure. For more inequality averse social welfare functions, however, the weights are larger at the bottom of the distribution, reflecting that the relative growth of social welfare is more sensitive to the well-being growth of the worse-off.

Figure 5.3 shows the relative and absolute growth incidence curves for the entire period between 1995 and 2005. The relative growth rates in the top panel turn out to be positive throughout the distribution, and

[26] The relative (yearly) growth rates can be computed from the first column of Table 5.5 and the absolute yearly growth can be computed from the first column of Table 5.6.

are overall modestly pro-poor. While the 10th percentile obtains an annual growth rate of 2 per cent, the top of the distribution reaches only 1.5 per cent. The bottom panel shows, however, that the absolute growth of the rich expressed in rubles remained much larger than the growth of the poor. Even with a larger annual growth rate at the bottom of the distribution, the absolute expenditure differences have increased during the considered period. The later phenomenon is picked up by the increased inequality measure *KP* in Table 5.6.

5.4.2 Equivalent Incomes

We now turn to the preference-based measures of well-being. A *conditio sine qua non* to implement a preference-based well-being measure, is to know the preferences of the respondents. We follow Decancq et al. (2017), who have used a life satisfaction approach to estimate the ordinal preferences over expenditures, health, housing quality, employment status and the presence of wage arrears for the respondents in the nine waves of the RLMS-HSE between 1995 and 2005.[27] The estimation allows for preference heterogeneity at the level of socio-demographic groups that are determined by a series of binary indicators that capture whether the respondent is living in a rural area, is young (below the age of 33), is male, and reports to have obtained higher education.

With these estimates of the ordinal preferences, the equivalent income well-being measure y_{it}^* as defined by Eq. (5.32) in Section 5.3.3 can be computed for all respondents in the dataset. These equivalent incomes are used as arguments of a social welfare function, similarly to the expenditures in the previous subsection. The fourth columns of Tables 5.5 and 5.6 show the evolution of the (equally-distributed equivalent of the) Atkinson social welfare function and the Kolm-Pollak social welfare function, respectively. Columns five and six present the decomposition of social welfare in the mean and inequality. The parameters are set based on the leak in a welfare-neutral leaky bucket transfer between a person on the 90th percentile of the distribution of equivalent incomes and the 10th percentile. As we have discussed in Section 5.3.3, the equivalent incomes are obtained by

[27] For more information on the definition of the variables, the econometric model and the estimated coefficients, see Decancq et al. (2017). Decancq et al. (2015b) and Decancq et al. (2019) use a similar approach to estimate ordinal preferences for the RLMS-HSE.

subtracting the willingness-to-pay to be in the reference situation for all non-income attributes, from the expenditures. Since the estimated willingness-to-pay is non-negative for all respondents, the level of social welfare using equivalent incomes as a measure of individual well-being is lower than the level of social welfare with expenditures as a well-being measure. Note that the evolution of equivalent income over time, as shown in Tables 5.5 and 5.6, does not show the sharp drop in 2000 that is observed for expenditures.

The change in social welfare can be decomposed using the relative and absolute growth incidence curves. The top panel of Figure 5.4 shows that the equivalent incomes of the worse-off decrease in the initial period between 1995 and 2000 at a stunning annual rate of about 15 per cent, but that the equivalent incomes of the 60 per cent best-off people remain relatively stable during the financial crisis of the late nineties. The bottom panel shows, interestingly, that also for the worst-off the decrease in well-being remains modest when it is expressed in monetary values. Yet, the initial well-being levels are so low at the bottom of the distribution, that a modest decrease in monetary value leads to a large decrease when it is expressed as a percentage. Similar to Figures 5.2 and 5.3, the weights at each percentile for four different κ values are indicated in Figures 5.4 and 5.5 in greyscale. Given the low well-being values at the bottom of the distribution, the share of well-being going to the top of the distribution is large, leading to a sharp increase of the weight across the percentiles in the top panels, except for a large κ value.

The relative and absolute growth incidence curves for the period between 1995 and 2005, shown in Figure 5.5, indicate social progress for almost the entire distribution. Only those in the bottom decile have experienced a negative relative growth rate and are worse-off in 2005 compared to 1995.

5.4.3 *Von Neumann–Morgenstern Utilities*

To compute the second preference-based well-being measure based on von Neumann–Morgenstern (vNM) utilities, we use the "high-low" method proposed in Adler (2016) and discussed in Chapter 3, this volume. We start from the ordinal preferences estimated by the life satisfaction approach for the computation of the equivalent incomes. Based on the (estimated) risk attitudes of the respondents, we select a vNM utility function that is consistent with these preferences. The cardinal well-being

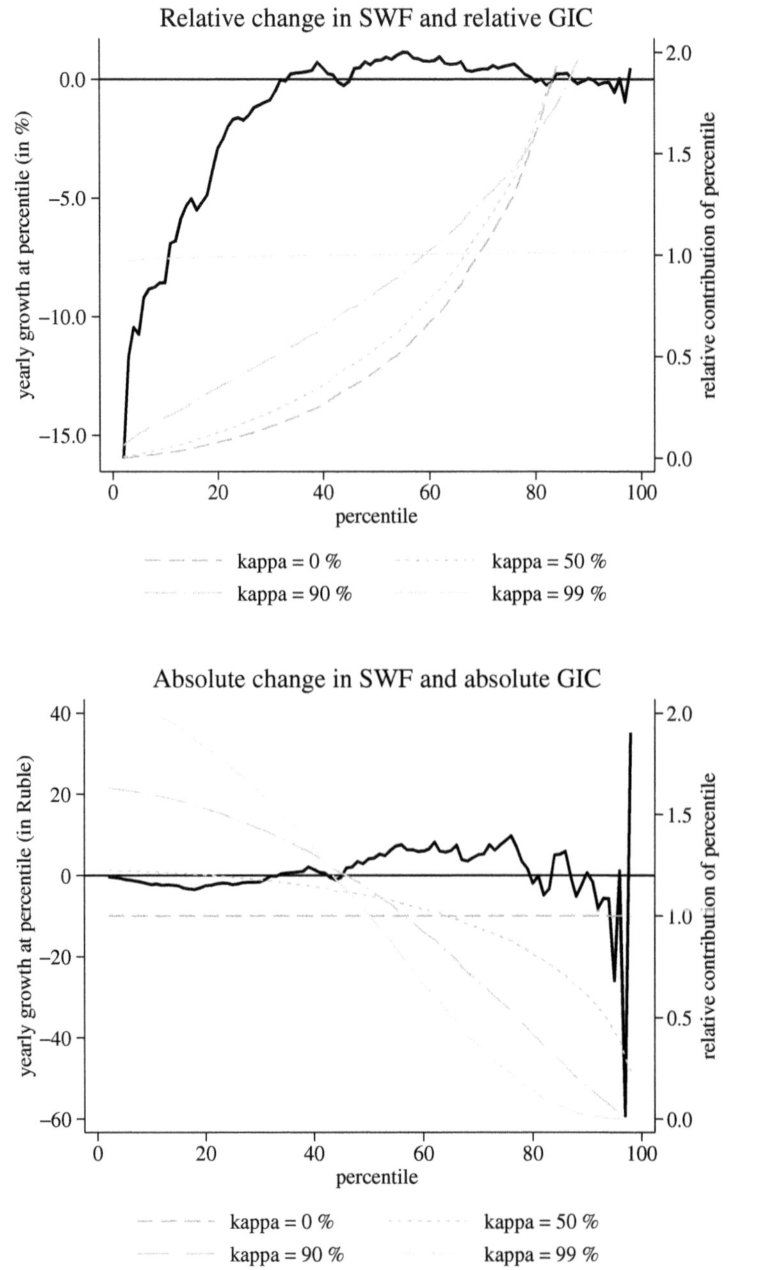

Figure 5.4 Growth incidence and change in social welfare between 1995 and 2000 for Atkinson (top) and Kolm-Pollak (bottom) social welfare functions, using equivalent incomes as well-being measure

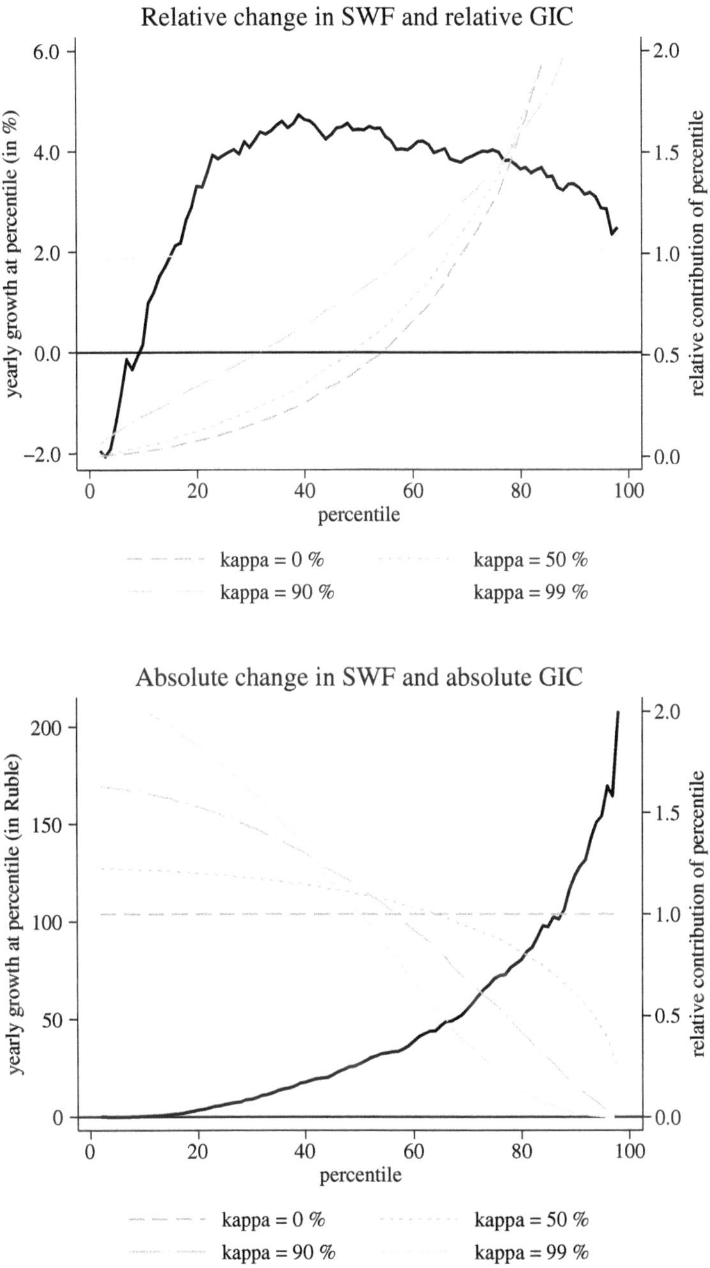

Figure 5.5 Growth incidence and change in social welfare between 1995 and 2005 for Atkinson (top) and Kolm-Pollak (bottom) social welfare functions, using equivalent incomes as well-being measure

levels are then determined by selecting two attribute bundles where the well-being level is calibrated at the level of 0 and 1, respectively. That is, we measure well-being by the following equation.

$$WB = \frac{V_i(\ell_i) - V_i(\ell_i^+)}{V_i(\ell_i^{++}) - V_i(\ell_i^+)}, \tag{5.40}$$

where V_i is the vNM utility function of person i, and ℓ_i^+ and ℓ_i^{++} are calibration points that are chosen such that $WB = 0$ and $WB = 1$ respectively. The main difference between the vNM approach and equivalent incomes is the transformation of Eq. (5.40) and the treatment of the cardinal information about the risk aversion of the respondents (Chapter 3, this volume provides a more detailed comparison between equivalent incomes and the vNM approach). Whereas cardinal information plays no role in the computation of equivalent incomes, the risk aversion determines the curvature of the vNM utility function V_i and, hence, also the well-being level of the person.[28] To compute the well-being measures with Eq. (5.40), we set the attribute bundle ℓ_i^+ equal to the attribute bundle that consists of the lowest value in all dimensions of well-being and ℓ_i^{++} equal to the attribute bundle that consists of the 99th percentile of expenditures and the reference value for all non-income dimensions. The obtained well-being measures can then be used as arguments in the Atkinson and Kolm-Pollak social welfare functions. The seventh columns of Tables 5.5 and 5.6 show the evolution of the social welfare measure with the (equally-distributed equivalent of the) Atkinson social welfare function and the Kolm-Pollak social welfare function, respectively. The parameters are set by means of the leaky bucket thought experiment and are given in Table 5.4.[29] Columns eight and nine present the decomposition of social welfare in the mean and inequality. We see that the lowest level of social welfare is reached in 2000 for all inequality aversion parameter values.

The specific cardinalization of the vNM well-being measure leads to a smaller difference between the relative and absolute growth incidence curve, as shown in Figures 5.6 and 5.7. The worse-off experience

[28] Appendix 5.A.2 describes how the risk aversion of the respondents is estimated and imputed with the RLMS-HSE.

[29] By construction, the vNM well-being measures take values between 0 and 1. This is different from the monetary scale of expenditures and equivalent incomes. The absolute difference between the 10th and 90th percentile is smaller, as is the ratio. The corresponding γ and β are, hence, much larger.

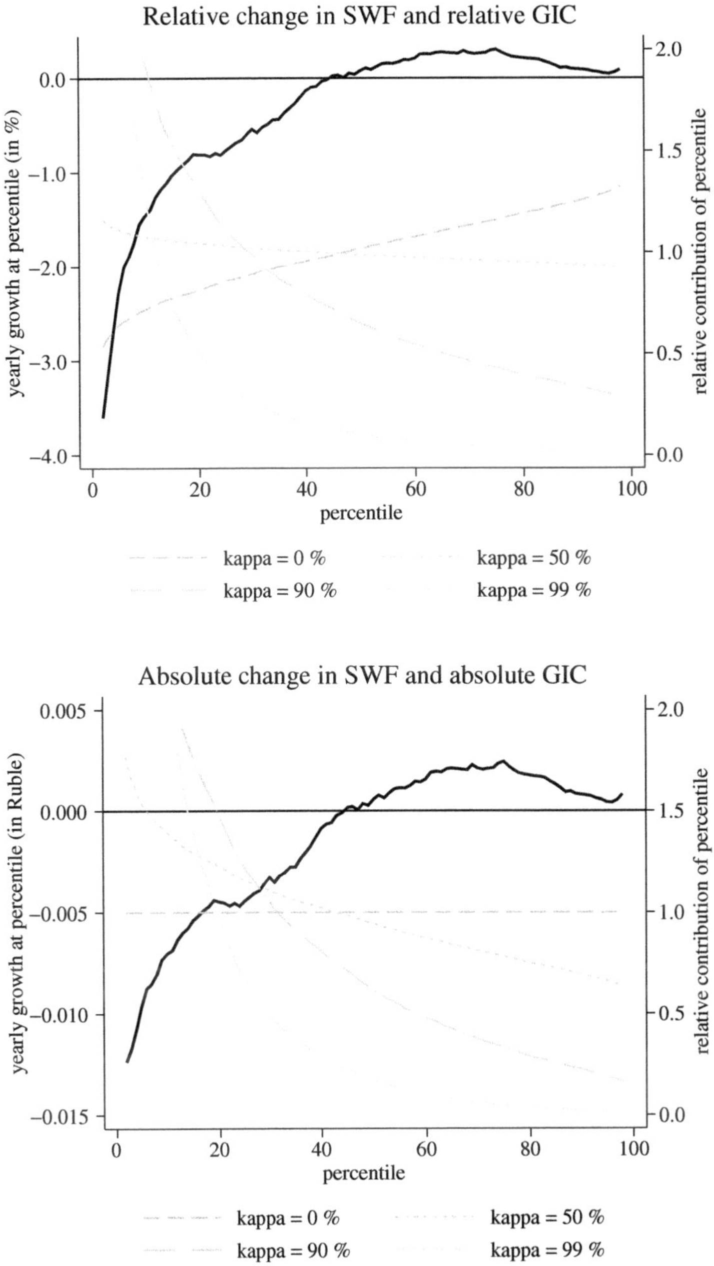

Figure 5.6 Growth incidence and change in social welfare between 1995 and 2000 for Atkinson (top) and Kolm-Pollak (bottom) social welfare functions, using vNM utility as well-being measure

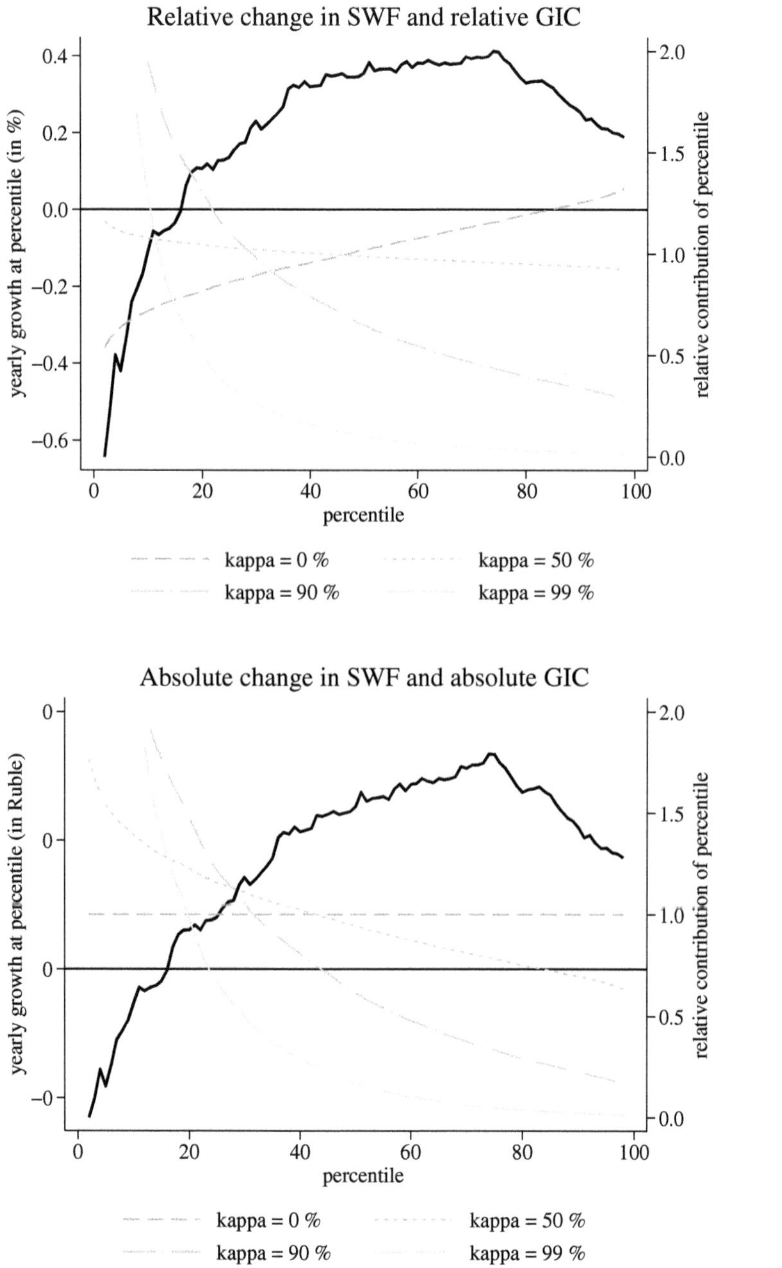

Figure 5.7 Growth incidence and change in social welfare between 1995 and 2005 for Atkinson (top) and Kolm-Pollak (bottom) social welfare functions, using vNM utility as well-being measure

regress when the vNM approach is used to measure well-being, whereas the better-off make progress, irrespective of whether an Atkinson or Kolm-Pollak social welfare function is used.

Although the broad-brush picture about the evolution of social welfare in Russia between 1995 and 2005 that the different well-being measures and social welfare functions reveal is rather similar, a more nuanced and subtle story emerges from the complementary use of the different measures and social welfare functions.

5.5 Conclusion

Assessing social conditions is an essential step in the evaluation of economic policies or the overall performance of economic and political systems. This is crucial for comparisons between countries as well as for analysing social progress over time. If one accepts that such assessments should take into account that the quality of individual lives depends on more than only income and that the evaluation of a social condition involves distributional issues, the prioritarian social welfare framework is a natural candidate. In this chapter, we have discussed briefly the main theoretical issues and surveyed some empirical applications. The applied literature is large and we have focused on the measurement of social progress over time rather than on international comparisons. Assessing social conditions is essentially a normative exercise and the results crucially depend on the choice of the measure of individual well-being and of the degree of inequality aversion.

Throughout the chapter, we used the equally-distributed equivalent representation of social welfare and we distinguished the Atkinson and the Kolm-Pollak social welfare functions. We proposed a decomposition of social welfare into the average and the inequality of individual well-being. To analyse changes in social welfare over time, we related the growth incidence curve to the prioritarian social welfare framework. All these concepts were illustrated with an empirical application on Russian data for the turbulent period between 1995 and 2005. Our application shows that the prioritarian framework is indeed a powerful tool to assess social conditions.

Appendix 5.A.1 Decomposing the Change of Social Welfare

Using the continuous notation of Section 5.2.2, we define the social welfare function and its equally-distributed equivalent as follows:

$$S_t = \int_0^1 g(Q_t(p))dp. \tag{5.41}$$

$$\widetilde{S}_t = g^{-1}\left[\int_0^1 g(Q_t(p))dp\right] = g^{-1}(S_t). \tag{5.42}$$

The absolute change in the equally-distributed equivalent $\widetilde{S}_t$ over time can be written as follows:

$$\frac{d\widetilde{S}_t}{dt} = \underbrace{\frac{dg^{-1}(S_t)}{dS_t}}_{(1)} \times \int_0^1 \left[\underbrace{\frac{dg(Q_t(p))}{dQ_t(p)}}_{(2)} \times \underbrace{\frac{dQ_t(p)}{dt}}_{(3)}\right] dp, \tag{5.43}$$

where the third component equals the absolute growth incidence curve *aGIC* (Eq. (5.14)).

Likewise, the relative change in the equally-distributed equivalent $\widetilde{S}_t$ over time can be obtained:

$$\frac{d\widetilde{S}_t/\widetilde{S}_t}{dt} = \underbrace{\frac{dg^{-1}(S_t)}{dS_t}}_{(1)} \times \int_0^1 \left[\underbrace{\frac{dg(Q_t(p))}{dQ_t(p)} \frac{Q_t(p)}{\widetilde{S}_t}}_{(2)} \times \underbrace{\frac{dQ_t(p)}{dt} \frac{1}{Q_t(p)}}_{(3)}\right] dp, \tag{5.44}$$

where the third component equals the relative growth incidence curve *rGIC* (Eq. (5.12)).

First, using the Atkinson transformation function

$$g_A(Q_t(p)) = \frac{Q_t(p)^{1-\gamma}}{1-\gamma}, \tag{5.45}$$

we obtain that the first component of Eq. (5.44) equals:

$$\frac{dg_A^{-1}(S_t^{ATK})}{dS_t^{ATK}} = \left[(1-\gamma)S_t^{ATK}\right]^{\frac{\gamma}{1-\gamma}}. \tag{5.46}$$

The second component of the same expression equals:

$$\frac{dg_A(Q_t(p))}{dQ_t(p)}\frac{Q_t(p)}{\widetilde{S}_t^{ATK}} = \frac{Q_t(p)^{1-\gamma}}{\left[(1-\gamma)S_t^{ATK}\right]^{\frac{1}{1-\gamma}}}. \tag{5.47}$$

Multiplying Eqs (5.46) and (5.47) yields Eq. (5.13).

Second, using the Kolm-Pollak transformation function

$$g_K(Q_t(p)) = -\frac{exp\,(-\beta Q_t(p))}{\beta}, \tag{5.48}$$

we obtain that the first component of Eq. (5.43) equals:

$$\frac{dg_K^{-1}(S_t^{KP})}{dS_t^{KP}} = \frac{1}{\int_0^1 exp(-\beta Q_t(p))dp}. \tag{5.49}$$

The second component of the same expression equals:

$$\frac{dg_K(Q_t(p))}{dQ_t(p)} = exp\,(-\beta Q_t(p)). \tag{5.50}$$

Multiplying Eqs (5.49) and (5.50) yields Eq. (5.15).

Appendix 5.A.2 Imputation of the Risk Attitudes Based on the RLMS-HSE Data

To determine a level of risk aversion for each respondent in our dataset, we use additional information from an ad hoc risk module to the RLMS-HSE in 2009.[30] This module is inspired by the work of Dohmen et al. (2011) and contains a specific question about risk attitudes: "*Are you generally a person who is willing to take risks or do you try to avoid risks?*" Respondents use an 11-point response scale between 0 (not at all willing to take risks) and 10 (very willing to take risks). Based on the responses to this question, the risk attitude can be predicted for each respondent in the data between 1995 and 2005 using some socio-economic variables (the coefficients are given in Table 5.7). These predicted risk attitudes are obviously an imperfect approximation of the risk aversion of the respondents, but the dataset does not permit us to make more detailed estimates. Based on the predicted risk attitudes, the respondents are classified in four equal-sized groups (called risk neutral, low risk aversion, medium risk aversion, high risk aversion, respectively). The higher the predicted risk attitude, the more curvature is assumed on the vNM utility function V_i, see also Decancq and Neumann (2016).

Table 5.7. ***Estimation of the individual risk attitudes***

	Risk attitude	
female	−1.016***	(0.0740)
logarithm of expenditures	0.215***	(0.0471)
unemployed	0.989***	(0.262)
retired	0.386	(0.352)
education	−0.00566	(0.0158)
high status	1.244***	(0.193)

[30] We are grateful to Professor Vladimir Gimpelson for making this additional information available.

Table 5.7. (*cont.*)

	Risk attitude	
middle status	0.289 **	(0.101)
married	−0.265 **	(0.102)
living as married	−0.0532	(0.159)
divorced	0.273 *	(0.131)
widowed	−0.0330	(0.188)
wage arrears	0.442 **	(0.167)
self-assessed health	0.0873	(0.0616)
age between 20 and 29	−0.0256	(0.279)
age between 30 and 39	−0.440	(0.285)
age between 40 and 49	−1.029 ***	(0.291)
age between 50 and 59	−1.525 ***	(0.294)
age between 60 and 69	−1.787 ***	(0.328)
age between 70 and 79	−1.949 ***	(0.427)
age 80 and above	−4.957 +	(2.819)
constant	2.882 ***	(0.567)
N	6403	
R^2	0.099	

Standard errors in parentheses
Note: $^{+}$ $p < 0.10$, * $p < 0.05$, ** $p < 0.01$, *** $p < 0.001$.

References

Adler, M. D. (2012). *Well-Being and Fair Distribution: Beyond Cost-Benefit Analysis*. Oxford University Press.

(2016). "Extended Preferences." In Adler, M. and Fleurbaey, M., eds., *Oxford Handbook on Well-being and Public Policy*, Oxford University Press, pp. 476–517.

Alkire, S. and Foster, J. (2010). "Designing the inequality-adjusted Human Development Index (HDI)" Oxford Poverty and Human Development Initiative Working Paper 37.

Angelini, V., Cavapozzi, D., Corazzini, L. and Paccagnella, O. (2014). "Do Danes and Italians rate life satisfaction in the same way? Using vignettes to correct for individual-specific scale biases." *Oxford Bulletin of Economics and Statistics*, 76: 643–666.

Atkinson, A.B. (1970). "On the measurement of inequality." *Journal of Economic Theory*, 2: 244–263.

Atkinson, A.B., Cantillon, B., Marlier, E. and Nolan, B. (2002). *Social Indicators: The EU and Social Exclusion*. Oxford University Press.

Becker, G.S., Philipson, T.J. and Soares, R.R. (2005). "The quantity and quality of life and the evolution of world inequality." *The American Economic Review*, 95: 277–291.

Beegle, K., Himelein, K. and Ravallion, M. (2012). "Frame-of-reference bias in subjective welfare." *Journal of Economic Behavior and Organization*, 81: 556–570.

Blackorby, C., Bossert, W. and Donaldson, D. J. (2005). *Population Issues in Social Choice Theory, Welfare Economics, and Ethics*. Cambridge University Press.

Bosmans, K., Decancq, K. and Ooghe, E. (2015). "What do normative indices of multidimensional inequality really measure?" *Journal of Public Economics*, 130: 94–104.

Bossert, W. and Dutta, B. (2019). "The measurement of welfare change." *Social Choice and Welfare*, 53: 603–619.

Chiappori, P.A. and Meghir, C. (2015). "Intra-household Inequality." In Atkinson, A. B. and Bourguignon, F., eds., *Handbook of Income Distribution*, Elsevier, pp. 1369–1418.

Deaton, A. (1979). "The distance function in consumer behaviour with applications to index numbers and optimal taxation." *The Review of Economic Studies*, 46: 391–405.

(1980). "The measurement of welfare: theory and practical guidelines" , Living Standards Measurement Study Working Paper No. 7, World Bank.

Deaton, A. and Muellbauer, J. (1980). *Economics and Consumer Behavior*. Cambridge University Press.

Decancq, K. (2017). "Measuring multidimensional inequality in the OECD Member Countries with a distribution-sensitive Better Life Index." *Social Indicators Research*, 131: 1057–1086.

Decancq, K., Fleurbaey, M. and Maniquet, F. (2019) "Multidimensional poverty measurement with individual preferences." *The Journal of Economic Inequality*, 17: 29–49.

Decancq, K., Fleurbaey, M. and Schokkaert, E. (2015a). "Inequality, Income, and Well-Being." In Atkinson, A.B. and Bourguignon, F., eds., *Handbook of Income Distribution*, Elsevier, pp. 67–140.

(2015b). "Happiness, equivalent incomes, and respect for individual preferences." *Economica*, 82: 1082–1106.

(2017). "Well-being inequality and preference heterogeneity." *Economica*, 84: 210–238.

Decancq, K. and Lugo, M.A. (2013). "Weights in multidimensional indices of well-being: An overview." *Econometric Reviews*, 32: 7–34.

Decancq, K. and Neumann, D. (2016). "Does the choice of well-being measure matter empirically?" In Adler, M.D. and Fleurbaey, M., eds., *Oxford Handbook on Well-being and Public Policy*, Oxford University Press, pp. 553–587.

Decancq, K. and Ooghe, E. (2010). "Has the world moved forward? A robust multidimensional evaluation." *Economics Letters*, 107: 266–269.

Decancq, K. and Schokkaert, E. (2016). "Beyond GDP: Using equivalent incomes to measure well-being in Europe." *Social Indicators Research*, 126: 21–55.

Dohmen, T., Falk, A., Huffman, D., Sunde, U., Schupp, J. and Wagner, G. G. (2011). "Individual risk attitudes: Measurement, determinants, and behavioral consequences." *Journal of the European Economic Association*, 9: 522–550.

Dutta, I. and Foster, J. (2013). "Inequality of Happiness in the US: 1972–2010." *The Review of Income and Wealth*, 59: 393–415.

Dworkin, R. (1981). "What is equality? Part 1: Equality of welfare." *Philosophy and Public Affairs,* 10: 185–246.

Ferreira, F.H.G. (2012). "Distributions in motion: Economic growth, inequality, and poverty dynamics". In Jefferson, P., ed., *Oxford Handbook of the Economics of Poverty*, Oxford University Press, pp. 427–462.

Ferrer-i-Carbonell, A. and Frijters, P. (2004). "How important is methodology for the estimates of the determinants of happiness?" *Economic Journal*, 114: 641–659.

Fleurbaey, M. (2009). "Beyond GDP: the quest for a measure of social welfare." *Journal of Economic Literature*, 47: 1029–1075.

Fleurbaey, M. and Blanchet, D. (2013). *Beyond GDP: Measuring Welfare and Assessing Sustainability*. Oxford University Press.

Fleurbaey, M. and Gaulier, G. (2009). "International comparisons of living standards by equivalent incomes." *Scandinavian Journal of Economics*, 111: 597–624.

Fleurbaey, M., Luchini, S., Muller, C. and Schokkaert, E. (2013). "Equivalent income and fair evaluation of health care." *Health Economics*, 22: 711–729.

Fleurbaey, M. and Maniquet, F. (2011). *A Theory of Fairness and Social Welfare*. Cambridge University Press.

Fleurbaey, M. and Tadenuma, K. (2014). "Universal social orderings: An integrated theory of policy evaluation, inter-society comparisons, and interpersonal comparisons." *The Review of Economic Studies*, 81: 1071–1101.

Foster, J., Lopez-Calva, L.F. and Szekely, M. (2005). "Measuring the distribution of human development: Methodology and an application to Mexico." *Journal of Human Development*, 6: 5–25.

Genicot, G. and Ray, D. (2013). "Measuring upward mobility." Unpublished paper, Georgetown University and New York University.

Harsanyi, J. C. (1977). "Morality and the theory of rational behavior." *Social Research*, 44: 623–656.

Helliwell, J., Layard, R., Sachs, J. and Neve, J.-E.D. (2019). *World Happiness Report 2019*. New York: Sustainable Development Solutions Network.

Jones, C. I. and Klenow, P. J. (2016). "Beyond GDP? Welfare across countries and time." *The American Economic Review*, 106: 2426–2457.

Jorgenson, D.W. (1990). "Aggregate Consumer Behavior and the measurement of social welfare." *Econometrica*, 58: 1007–1040.

(2018). "Production and welfare: Progress in economic measurement." *Journal of Economic Literature*, 56: 867–919.

Jorgenson, D.W. and Schreyer, P. (2017). "Measuring individual economic well-being and social welfare within the framework of the system of national accounts." *The Review of Income and Wealth*, 63: S460–S477.

Jorgenson, D.W. and Slesnick, D.T. (2014). "Measuring Social Welfare in the U.S. National Accounts." In Jorgenson, D.W., Landefeld, J.S. and Schreyer, P., eds., *Measuring Economic Sustainability and Progress*, University of Chicago Press.

King, G., Murray, C.J.L., Salomon, J.A. and Tandon, A. (2004). "Enhancing the validity and cross-cultural comparability of measurement in survey research." *The American Political Science Review*, 98: 191–207.

Kolm, S.-C. (1976). "Unequal inequalities. I." *Journal of Economic Theory*, 12: 416–442.

Kraay, A. (2006). "When is growth pro-poor? Evidence from a panel of countries." *Journal of Development Economics*, 80: 198–227.

Lakner, C. and Milanovic, B. (2016). "Global income distribution: From the fall of the Berlin Wall to the Great Recession." *World Bank Economic Review*, 30: 203–232.

Layard, R. (2005). *Happiness: Lessons for a new Science*. Penguin.

Milanovic, B. (2016). *Global Inequality: A New Approach for the Age of Globalization*. Harvard University Press.

Parfit, D. (1984). *Reasons and Persons*. Oxford University Press.

Pollak, R. A. (1971). "Additive utility functions and linear Engel curves." *The Review of Economic Studies*, 38: 401–414.

Ponthière, G. (2016). "Lifetime Well-Being." In Adler, M. and Fleurbaey, M., eds., *Oxford handbook on Well-being and Public Policy*, Oxford University Press, pp. 871–900.

Ravallion, M. (2011). "Mashup indices of development." *The World Bank Research Observer*, 27: 1–32.

Ravallion, M. and Chen, S. (2003). "Measuring pro-poor growth." *Economics Letters*, 78: 93–99.

Ravallion, M., Himelein, K. and Beegle, K. (2016). "Can Subjective Questions on Economic Welfare Be Trusted?" *Economic Development and Cultural Change*, 64: 697–726.

Sen, A.K. (1979). "The welfare basis of real income comparisons: A survey." *Journal of Economic Literature*, 17: 1–45.

(1985). *Commodities and Capabilities*. North-Holland.

Slesnick, D.T. (1998). "Empirical approaches to the measurement of welfare." *Journal of Economic Literature*, 36: 2108–2165.

Stiglitz, J.E., Sen, A. and Fitoussi, J.-P. (2009). "Report by the Commission on the Measurement of Economic Performance and Social Progress." Commission on the Measurement of Economic Performance and Social Progress, Paris.

Tsui, K.Y. (1995). "Multidimensional generalizations of the relative and absolute inequality indices: the Atkinson-Kolm-Sen approach." *Journal of Economic Theory*, 67: 251–265.

Weymark, J.A. (2006). "The normative approach to the measurement of multidimensional inequality." In Farina, F. and Savaglio, E., eds., *Inequality and Economic Integration*, Routledge, London, pp. 3101–3335.

6 *Prioritarianism and Health Policy*

RICHARD COOKSON, OLE F. NORHEIM AND IEVA SKARDA*

6.1 Introduction

This chapter aims to present a practical prioritarian approach to economic evaluation of health programmes with impacts on both health and income, with an illustrative application that compares the results of prioritarianism (both *ex ante* and *ex post* variants), utilitarianism, and cost-benefit analysis. More specifically, it presents a lifetime prioritarian approach that gives priority to the worse off in terms of lifetime well-being defined as the sum of current period well-being over the lifetime.

This chapter is a contribution to the "Prioritarianism in Practice" programme, which aims to advance our understanding of generalized utilitarian approaches to assessing governmental policy and social

* We have followed the convention in the economics discipline of listing authors in alphabetical order. The author contributions were as follows. The main text was lead-authored by Ole F. Norheim, who also led the design and construction of the illustrative decision model. Ieva Skarda lead authored the section on lifetime well-being metrics within the context of the equivalence approach and the technical appendix, co-designed and validated the illustrative decision model, and used the model outputs to create the figures and tables. Richard Cookson advised on study design and drafted the background section. All authors made substantial contributions to re-drafting the manuscript.

For helpful comments, we would like to thank Matt Adler, Jim Hammitt, Lisa Robinson, Marc Fleurbaey, Grégory Ponthière and participants at various PiP and BCEPS workshops. Ieva Skarda was supported by the Wellcome Trust (Grant No. 205427/Z/16/Z). Richard Cookson and Ole F. Norheim were supported by the Bergen Centre for Ethics and Priority Setting (BCEPS), University of Bergen, via grants from the Trond Mohn Foundation (Grant No. BFS2019TMT02) and the Norwegian Agency for Development Cooperation (Grant No. RAF 18/009, "Decision Support for Universal Health Coverage"). Norheim's work was also supported by the Research Council of Norway through the project Inclusive Evaluation of Public Health Interventions (Grant No. 260588). The errors and opinions expressed in this chapter are the responsibility of the authors alone.

progress, including both prioritarian and utilitarian approaches, and including comparisons with standard approaches such as benefit-cost analysis (BCA) and cost-effectiveness analysis (CEA). We define "prioritarian" approaches as those that rank social outcomes according to the sum of a strictly increasing and strictly concave transformation of individual levels of well-being (Adler, 2012, 2019; Adler and Holtug, 2019; see also Adler, Chapter 2, this volume), and reserve the term "utilitarian" for those that rank social outcomes according to the sum of untransformed individual levels of well-being. We use the term "generalized utilitarian" approaches to cover both prioritarian and utilitarian approaches, though not egalitarian approaches involving non-separable functions of individual welfare, such as rank-dependent social welfare functions which respect to the strong Pareto principle and strictly egalitarian ones which do not (O'Donnel and Van Ourti, 2020; O'Donnell & Van Ourti, 2020).

In principle, the lifetime prioritarian approach described in this chapter can be applied to decisions about:

(a) specific health care technologies (e.g., reimbursement decisions for new, expensive drugs);
(b) designing health care benefit packages (e.g., whether to cover type 2 diabetes in a public health insurance plan and, if so, which treatments and with what co-payments);
(c) public health policies and regulations (e.g., bans on smoking in public places, "sin" taxes, health promotion campaigns, subsidies for sport and physical activity); and
d) cross-sectoral social policies with important impacts on health as well as non-health outcomes (e.g., policies on education, transport and social protection).

Our illustrative example relates to a decision of the first kind – the funding of an expensive cancer drug in a low-income country – but the methods we describe are in principle applicable to all these kinds of decisions.

Hitherto, most empirical applications of prioritarianism in the health sector have focused on health as the measure of individual value.[1] This is fine for informing health care and public health

[1] One reason for restricting information to health only has been pragmatic and institutional. The policy questions relevant for priority setting, e.g., the relative

decisions that are primarily intended to improve health and that are not also expected to have non-health consequences of direct concern to decision makers and stakeholders. However, it is less satisfactory for informing decisions which are expected to have important non-health consequences – for example, impacts on financial protection from the out-of-pocket costs of health care and the wider costs of illness.

In this chapter, therefore, we will focus on the broad and challenging question of how to apply prioritarianism to multi-dimensional measures of well-being that combine information about health and non-health dimensions of well-being. Applications of prioritarianism to health outcomes only, which have already been extensively documented elsewhere (Cookson et al., 2020), can then be seen as special cases of this more general problem. We examine two different well-being concepts: equivalent life and equivalent income. To keep things simple and tractable, however, we focus on operationalizing these concepts using information about health and just one other dimension of individual well-being: the consumption of privately funded goods and services. We call this "income" and measure it using household income after taxes and cash benefits, adjusted for household size and composition. Both equivalent life and equivalent income can be extended to cover other non-health outcomes – for example, the consumption of publicly funded goods and services, the quality of personal relationships and adverse experiences such as maltreatment, unemployment and incarceration – but we do not examine such extensions here.

In the health sector, methods for measuring health outcomes are well developed and health programmes are often assessed though economic evaluations before they are introduced through public finance. The dominant method for economic evaluation is cost-effectiveness

rank of new expensive drugs, are typically formulated in terms of health-, not well-being-impact. The health sector (with its limited budget) is responsible for improving health, not well-being. The standard methods used to inform these decisions are cost per health-adjusted life years analysis, where HALY is a measure of health, not well-being. Health policy makers see their job as primarily to improve health rather than income, and it has been argued that direct redistribution of income by fiscal instruments is more appropriate and efficient than indirect redistribution through the health service (For some limitations of this argument, see Robinson, Hammitt and Zeckhauser, 2016.)

analysis using a general summary measure of health outcome that allows comparison between different diseases and conditions, for example in terms of cost per quality-adjusted life year (QALY) gained or a cost per disability-adjusted life year (DALY) averted (Drummond et al., 2015; Neumann et al., 2017; Sanders et al., 2016). This is a quasi-utilitarian approach: it ranks distributions of health according to the sum of untransformed individual levels of health. In other words, cost-effectiveness analysis aims to maximize sum total net health benefit in terms of health gains minus health opportunity costs.

In the health sector, special concern for the worse off in terms of health has been identified as important in addition to the standard objective of health maximization (Dolan et al., 2005; Fleurbaey and Schokkaert, 2009; Johri and Norheim, 2012; Sassi et al., 2001). Early contributions to this idea were typically made in the context of equity-efficiency trade-offs (Anand, 2002; Anand et al., 2001; Anand & Nanthikesan, 2001; Nord, 1993; Nord, 1999; Wagstaff, 1991). The worse off are sometimes defined using a lifetime perspective – for example, expected healthy years from birth to death – and sometimes using a current period perspective – e.g., expected remaining future healthy years from the time of decision to death (Johansson et al. 2020). In a health context, the use of lifetime versus current period concepts of well-being can make an extremely important difference to who is considered badly-off. For example, a 100 year-old with skin cancer may be extremely well-off in terms of lifetime health but extremely badly-off in terms of current and remaining healthy years of life. In the health policy literature, current period health is typically what people have in mind when they talk about "severity of illness", whereas lifetime health is typically what they have in mind when talking about "health inequality" – though policy rhetoric is often ambiguous about this and the concepts of "severity of illness" and "health inequality" can be measured from both lifetime and current period perspectives. There are strong theoretical arguments favouring a lifetime health perspective, and considerable evidence of public concern for the worse off in lifetime health in many different countries (Bleichrodt et al., 2004; Bleichrodt et al., 2005; Dolan and Tsuchiya, 2012; Ottersen, 2013).

There may also be special concern for the worse off more broadly in terms of well-being, including non-health dimensions of well-being such as income.[2] The same issue of temporal perspective arises in this broader context, as to whether prioritarian concern focuses on current well-being or lifetime well-being. In this chapter we adopt a lifetime well-being perspective to prioritarian concern – that is, we explore the implications of giving priority to individuals with lower lifetime well-being.[3] As we shall see later, however, when measuring current period well-being as a function of consumption we also assume that current period consumption is subject to diminishing marginal value. This could be seen as a kind of prioritarian concern in the space of current period income – i.e., concern to give priority to those who are worse off in terms of current period income. Under this interpretation, our approach could be thought of as a kind of "double prioritarianism" – priority to the worse off in terms of current period income, and then also priority to the worse off in terms of lifetime well-being. However, we prefer to interpret the assumption of diminishing marginal value of current period consumption as being motivated by concern to measure current period well-being accurately – a concern shared by utilitarians and prioritarians alike. So we interpret our approach as prioritarianism in the space of lifetime well-being, properly measured, without any additional concern for those who are worse off in terms of current period well-being.

In the health literature, applications of prioritarianism have departed from the more general approach described in earlier chapters of this book in three ways (see, e.g., Anand et al., 2001; Asaria et al., 2016; Asaria et al., 2015; Cookson et al., 2020; Cookson et al., 2021a; Cookson et al., 2017; Hernæs et al., 2017; Johansson and Norheim, 2011; Norheim, 2013; Norheim et al., 2020; Norheim et al., 2019; Ottersen, 2013; Ottersen et al., 2014). First, as already discussed, they have focused on health as the measure of individual advantage to define who is worse off, rather than well-being more broadly including health and non-health dimensions. Second, they have focused on group-level distributions (e.g., based on social groups defined by

[2] In this chapter we will use income interchangeably with consumption. From a theoretical perspective consumption is a better indicator of well-being than income, but convention in the "equivalent income" literature makes it easier to use the term "income" which is also more user-friendly for non-economists.

[3] Adler (2012), chapter 6, provides a philosophical defence of prioritarianism applied to lifetime well-being rather than shorter time-slices.

socioeconomic status, ethnicity, geographical location or disease groups defined by disease classification) rather than individual-level distributions. Third, they have focused exclusively on *ex ante* prioritarianism based on expected health outcomes rather also on *ex post* prioritarianism based on realized health outcomes.

Prioritarianism in this narrower health-oriented sense has informed the development of various methods of "distributional" cost-effectiveness analysis (DCEA) in the health sector which provides information about the distribution of costs and effects as well as value-for-money in terms of total costs and effects (Cookson et al., 2020). In this literature, normative concerns about differences in health and well-being between people are often labelled as "equity" considerations and normative concerns about sum total health and well-being are often labelled as "efficiency" considerations. Empirical studies rarely distinguish explicitly between prioritarian and egalitarian frameworks, though they are typically based implicitly on a prioritarian approach.

The chapter is organized as follows. The next section provides background on standard approaches to economic evaluation in the health sector: cost-effectiveness analysis (CEA), benefit-cost analysis (BCA). Section 6.3 then examines two ways of constructing an index of lifetime well-being, suitable for prioritarian evaluation, based on information on length of life, health-related quality of life and income. Section 6.4 then illustrates the application of generalized utilitarian social welfare functions to these two measures of lifetime well-being compared with standard CEA and BCA, including both *ex post* as well as *ex ante* prioritarian approaches, using a common example involving a hypothetical cancer treatment programme in a low-income country. The final section concludes.

6.2 Background on Standard Economic Evaluation in the Health Sector

This section provides some background on how standard methods of cost-effectiveness analysis (CEA) (Drummond et al., 2015) and benefit-cost analysis (BCA) (McIntosh et al., 2010; Robinson et al., 2019a) are usually applied in practice in the health sector. Background on the theory and practice of BCA more generally is provided elsewhere (Adler, 2019; Boardman et al., 2018; McIntosh et al., 2010).

In practice, CEA and BCA studies used to inform health sector decision making usually measure health effects in terms of a summary measure of health such as QALYs or DALYs. That is because summary measures of health allow comparisons between mortality and morbidity effects of different kinds across different health conditions.

We therefore start this section by introducing summary measures of health before describing how they are used in practice in CEA and BCA studies. We also briefly discuss the use of distributional weights in CEA and BCA. As well as presenting aggregate headline findings, both CEA and BCA studies can also present a range of disaggregated information about costs and effects in a "dashboard" or "impact inventory", along with qualitative information about potentially important costs and effects that were not quantified in the analysis.

6.2.1 Summary Measures Of Health: Health-Adjusted Life Years (HALYs)

Conceptually, the only important difference between a QALY and a DALY is the sign; a QALY is a healthy year gained and a DALY is a healthy year lost (Gold et al., 2002; Robberstad, 2005). So we will use the term "health-adjusted life year" (HALY) to mean either a QALY gained or an averted DALY or other similar summary measure of health in terms of healthy years. There are differences in the technical details of construction, just as there are differences in the technical details of construction of different kinds of QALYs and different kinds of DALYs. Not all QALYs and DALYs are comparable, but they share the same basic conceptual motivation and underpinnings, which we describe below.

When making priority-setting decisions, health sector decision makers implicitly or explicitly have to compare the value of different kinds of health effect for different people with different diseases and conditions – for example, a five-point gain in a mental health symptom score for one group of patients versus a 10 per cent reduction in the risk of dying from cardiovascular disease for another group. HALYs provide a systematic method for comparing condition-specific health effects in terms of gains in healthy years of life, based on evidence and explicit value judgements. They also allow value for money to be assessed in a standardized way, by establishing a common cost-effectiveness benchmark (e.g. in terms of a cost per HALY gained) that can be used for deciding which services are best included in health care coverage (Culyer, 2016). There are many different ways of constructing HALYs and different HALY metrics are not fully comparable with one another.

An index of health-related quality of life in the current time period combines information on multiple dimensions of health-related quality of life to produce a single number on a ratio scale anchored at 0 (as bad as death) and bounded above at 1 (full health in the current period). The corresponding index of health-related disability is the same thing but with the scale inverted – i.e., a number anchored at 1 (as bad as death) and 0 (full health in the current period). This is then multiplied by the duration of the time period (in years) and summed across all relevant time periods to yield a HALY score that combines information on both length of life and health-related quality of life. The HALY is measured on a ratio scale and then normalized so that 1 represents a year of health gained or lost. Any set of numbers will serve for a ratio scale, so long as they are related by a constant multiplicative term; for example, one can measure distance in miles or kilometres, and one mile is always the same distance as 0.62 kilometres. However, normalizing the HALY to mean a healthy year means choosing one specific version of the HALY ratio scale. This is analogous to normalizing the measure of distance – for example, measuring distance in terms of light-years. Other normalizations could be chosen, but this specific unit is convenient for certain purposes.

In principle you can even go below 0 for states of health considered to be worse than death; though thankfully such states are rarely encountered in practice.

The resemblance that a HALY has to some usages of "utility" in welfare economics has led some authors to describe HALYs as utilities, which can be misleading on a number of grounds (Bleichrodt and Gafni, 1996; Garber and Phelps, 1997; Hammitt, 2002, 2013, 2017). The term "utility" in welfare economics generally refers to an index of individual preference ("decision utility") or well-being ("experienced utility"). The typical use of a HALY, however, is not necessarily as an indication of what any individual wants, or thinks, or feels, or chooses, or how well their life is going overall, but rather as a general measure of health (of which, doubtless, more will indeed usually be preferred). The HALY is not a value-free scientific measure of health, however, as the process of selecting, scoring and weighing the different dimensions of health requires a series of value judgements.

The HALY might be seen as a component of well-being, or as a partial indicator of health-related well-being, but it is by no means a complete measure of well-being. For most practical applications in the health sector, the objective is cast entirely in terms of health, with other outcomes considered only for their impact on health or the effectiveness of health interventions. To avoid confusion with the standard usage of the word "utility" in economics to mean preference or well-being, we avoid the use of terms like "cost-utility analysis" and do not refer to HALYs, QALYs or DALYs as "utilities".

6.2.2 *Cost-Effectiveness Analysis (CEA)*

We now review the nuts and bolts of CEA using HALYs, including the cost-effectiveness plane and the basic concepts of the cost-effectiveness threshold value, health opportunity cost and net health benefit.

Cost-effectiveness analysis of a single decision option compared with an alternative entails estimating the incremental costs and health effects of that option compared to the current or reference situation. An option that reduces costs and increases health is a "dominant" or "win–win" option (i.e. clearly cost-effective). An option that increases costs and reduces health is a "dominated" or "lose–lose" option (i.e. clearly not cost-effective). If the consequences are estimated to be either increased costs accompanied by increased health, or reduced costs accompanied by reduced health, then an additional piece of information is required to determine whether the decision is cost-effective, i.e. the "threshold value" at which investments are considered cost-effective. This threshold value may be implicit and it may be an imprecise range rather than a precise point estimate, but it is needed if wants to claim that an option is cost-effective rather than not cost-effective.

This can be shown diagrammatically using a cost-effectiveness plane (see Figure 6.1). The origin represents a baseline comparator of no change from the reference situation. Other points in the plane represent the total expected incremental costs and effects of alternative decisions

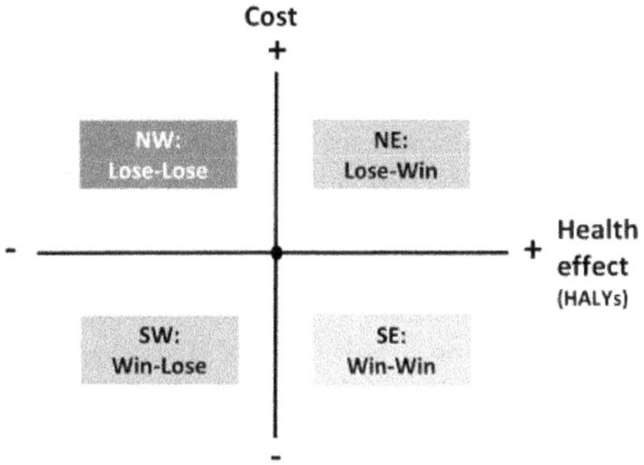

Figure 6.1 Cost-effectiveness plane

compared with this baseline decision. The cost-effectiveness plane thus has four quadrants representing four logically possible cases: (1) North-East for cost-increasing and health-improving; (2) North-West for cost-increasing and health-harming (i.e., "dominated" in the cost-effectiveness sense); (3) South-East for cost-saving and health-improving (i.e., "dominant" in the cost-effectiveness sense), and (4) South-West for cost-saving and health-harming ("win–lose").

The threshold value at which an option is considered cost-effective compared with an alternative can be given various interpretations (Faria and Lomas, 2020). For example, it can be given a "demand-side" interpretation in terms of the average willingness to pay for a HALY among the relevant population of individuals. Or a "supply-side" interpretation as the marginal production cost of a HALY from foregone activity that can no longer be undertaken. Or a "social norm" interpretation based on precedent from past decisions or benchmarks set by decision making bodies or other authoritative organizations. On the "supply-side" interpretation, cost-effectiveness can be interpreted as a test of whether the decision increases net health benefit, i.e., sum total health gains minus sum total health opportunity costs. If so, cost-effectiveness analysis can be seen as a quasi-utilitarian approach to evaluation that seeks to maximize health (Cookson, 2015).

Whatever interpretation is used, the basic idea is that a cost-increasing policy option can be considered "cost-effective" if its health gain per unit of cost compares favourably with (i.e., is higher than) the most attractive alternative way of using resources. The recognition of opportunity costs – i.e., that resources used in the provision of a programme would have generated value if used in their most highly valued use elsewhere – is fundamental to cost-effectiveness analysis. Every benefit attributed to a programme must be assessed relative to the benefits displaced when resources are diverted from alternative activities.

In a public health system with an exogenously fixed budget, the displaced activities will usually be alternative health programmes that would otherwise have been producing health benefits. This is as true when the budget is due to expand or contract over time as it is when it is due to remain constant. If the budget is set to grow, then the question is: "where to spend the next dollar?" The displaced activity is then the alternative health programme the next dollar could otherwise have been spent on. In this context, "exogenously fixed" does not necessarily mean "constant over time". Rather, it means "beyond the control of the health sector decision maker who is making the priority setting decision".

Things are different if the health budget is endogenous, however, in the sense that the decision maker can choose to increase the health budget rather than displace other health programmes. In such settings, the displaced activities may include alternative health services, but they may also include other activities having both health and non-health benefits – such as other forms of public expenditure (e.g., education, transport, poverty reduction) or reduced taxes or insurance premiums allowing people to enjoy improved material living conditions. Whatever activity is displaced, there may be both health and non-health opportunity costs.

The estimation of health opportunity costs is more problematic if opportunity costs do in fact primarily fall on household consumption (via increased taxes or insurance premiums) or on reductions in public expenditure on programmes not primarily designed to improve health. In that case, it may be more helpful to conduct benefit-cost analysis rather than cost-effectiveness analysis, or to use a multi-dimensional index of well-being as we propose later in this chapter.

When assessing cost-effectiveness in this way, the process of adding up HALY gains and opportunity costs across individuals and groups embodies the value judgement that all healthy years count the same, no matter who gains or loses them – i.e., "a HALY is a HALY is a HALY". The one caveat to this statement relates to the discounting of future costs and effects; a HALY in ten years' time may be considered less valuable than a HALY this year. There are various reasons for discounting future costs and effects on efficiency grounds related to producing a more accurate estimate of sum total health and well-being – for example, "pure" time preference, allowing for the risk of a future "apocalyptic event" causing mass extinction, and allowing for economic growth and technological innovation (Claxton et al., 2011). There are also further equity considerations related to intergenerational equity in the distribution of costs and effects between age groups and birth cohort groups, which we do not address in this chapter.

6.2.3 *Benefit-Cost Analysis (BCA)*

Benefit-cost analysis is less commonly encountered in the health sector but may be applied to evaluations of cross-sectoral policies with important health and non-health impacts (Chang et al., 2018; McIntosh et al., 2010; Robinson et al., 2019a; Robinson and Hammitt, 2016; U.S. Department of Health and Human Services, 2016). The basic idea is to measure the most important health and non-health effects, value them in monetary terms and then compare them with the costs. In practice,[4] BCA in the health sector is often applied using the following simple additively separable equation, where health effects are measured in HALYs and all costs and benefits are discounted to their net present values:

$$\begin{aligned}&\text{Total cost}: \quad \Delta c\\&\text{Total benefit}: \Delta y + \Delta s + \Delta h^{*} v^{h} + \Delta x^{*} v^{x}\end{aligned}$$

where

Δc is the sum total cost in terms of both public expenditure and private consumption

Δs is the sum total benefit in terms of long-term savings in public expenditure

Δy is the sum total benefit in terms of increase in private consumption

Δh is the sum total benefit in terms of increase in HALYs

[4] BCA can also be applied in more complicated ways, allowing for differences in willingness to pay (WTP) for health for different kinds of individuals, and for non-separable functional forms.

v^h is the consumption value of a HALY (usually estimated based on willingness to pay data)

Δx is the sum total benefit in terms of any other relevant non-health outcome

v^x is the consumption value of any other non-health outcome (= average willingness to pay for one unit of that outcome)

The benefit-cost ratio is the ratio of total benefit to total cost; and the net monetary benefit is the total benefit minus the total cost. Notice that this simple applied approach uses the same monetary consumption value of health for all individuals, and does not use differential values based on differential willingness to pay by income and age group. This goes against the standard welfare economic theory of the Hicks–Kaldor compensation test but can be justified not only on grounds of simplicity but also on grounds of procedural egalitarian concern to value the same gains in lifespan and health-related quality of life equally for all individuals, irrespective of income, age, gender, disability or other characteristics.

The key advantage of BCA is that in principle it can account for a full range of benefits of any kind, rather than being restricted to health benefits only.[5] It can therefore be used to evaluate health programmes with effects on financial protection as well as health, and cross-sectoral programmes involving expenditure across different policy sectors (e.g. education, transport, environment and social protection as well as health). If applied in this simple additively separable form, it also retains the other great advantage of CEA, which is that it only needs information on total or average effects: we do not need to know how effects are distributed between different kinds of individual.

6.2.3.1 Distributional Weights

A common criticism of BCA is that it fails to allow for differences in the marginal value of income to different people (Adler, 2016; Robinson et al., 2016). To take an extreme example, a billionaire might be willing to pay a billion dollars for three months of poor-quality life extension (0.2 of a HALY) whereas a million poor families might be unable, and therefore unwilling, to pay 1,000 dollars each for their sick child to access life-saving treatment bringing 50 years of good quality

[5] In principle, CEA can count non-health effects as "costs" (so non-health benefits are reduced costs), but standard CEAs rarely do so.

life extension each (50m HALYs). So, in theory, BCA could recommend treating the billionaire rather than the million sick children, despite the latter programme yielding 250 million times more healthy years (50m/0.2). As already described, this problem is partly addressed in practice by using a common consumption value of health across all population groups.

However, this problem persists in relation to private consumption benefits; for example, increased employment, reduced commuting times and reduced work-days lost to illness will all generate larger private consumption benefits in prosperous geographical areas where individual incomes are higher. And the problem re-emerges in relation to health if one starts applying BCA in more sophisticated ways than the simple additive equations above, which start to reflect large differences between individuals in their ability to pay for health gains.

To address distributional issues of this kind, "distributional weights" can be applied in BCA whereby monetary benefits to poorer individuals are valued more highly than monetary benefits to well-off individuals (Adler, 2016; Boadway, 2016). This is sometimes done in the UK, though in the US most textbooks and guidance take a negative view of distributional weights (Boardman et al., 2018; Robinson et al., 2018; Robinson et al., 2016).

Distributional weights are a numerical way of valuing benefits and opportunity costs more highly for some specific subgroups of the population than others. In practice, distributional weights are rarely applied in BCA, but there are simple approaches that are sometimes used outside the health sector. For example, one simple approach to distributional weighting by income quintile groups is recommended by the UK Treasury in its "Green Book" of guidance for economic evaluation (HM Treasury, 2018). This approach is based on a simple individual well-being function whereby well-being is the log of median consumption or household income within each income quintile group. Under this approach, the distributional weight for income quintile group *g* is given by:

$$\frac{y_j^{-1}}{\bar{y}^{-1}} \tag{6.1}$$

where y_g is the median income of group j and $\bar{y}$ is the median income in the general population. A similar approach is recommend by the UK Department for Work and Pensions (DWP), based on an individual well-being function whereby well-being is an isoelastic function of income with an elasticity of the marginal value of income of 1.3 – reflecting an estimate by Layard and colleagues based on subjective well-being data from various countries (Fujiwara, 2010; Layard et al., 2008). According to this approach, the distributional weight for income group *j* is:

$$\frac{y_j^{-1.3}}{\bar{y}^{-1.3}} \tag{6.2}$$

At levels of income in the UK in the late 2010s, this yields a weight to the poorest income quintile group compared with the middle group of between 2 (Treasury approach) and 2.5 (DWP approach).

Arguably, these distributional weights for monetary benefits are not "prioritarian" but "utilitarian" in nature, insofar as they adjust income benefits to allow for diminishing marginal individual value of income. They can thus be seen as utilitarian adjustments to income that measure well-being more accurately rather than prioritarian transformations of well-being that give priority to the worse off.

In CEA, by contrast, distributional weights are sometimes used that are prioritarian in nature – they aim to give priority to the worse off in terms of health (Bobinac et al., 2012; Lal et al., 2018; Nord et al., 1999; Wailoo et al., 2009). The standard approach is to use direct distributional weights that are applied in whatever *ad hoc* pattern is preferred by the decision maker; for example, health benefits to severely ill individuals might be assigned a weight that is two or three times higher than health benefits to the average individual. Typically, direct distributional weights are applied in relation to some measure of disadvantage – for example, greater weight to benefits and burdens for persons with low income, poor health, an orphan condition, or some other equity-relevant characteristic. To that extent, direct distributional weighting in CEA is an informal prioritarian approach giving priority to the worse off. However, as we shall see later (Section 6.4), it is also possible to adopt more formal prioritarian approaches by using indirect distributional weights which are derived from a prioritarian social welfare function.

6.3 Lifetime Well-Being Metrics for Prioritarian Evaluation

In what follows, we explore two ways of constructing a lifetime well-being metric suitable for generalized utilitarian evaluation of health policies, based on individual-level data on period-specific mortality risk, health-related quality of life and consumption. We discuss two candidate measures, both of which are based on the "equivalence approach": equivalent life and equivalent income.

Equivalent life values the components of well-being in terms of lifespan. This approach is a generalization of the "quality-adjusted life year" concept in health economics, the idea being to measure well-being in terms of years of life adjusted for other dimensions of well-being, such as income, health-related quality of life and so on – and so is sometimes known as the "well-being QALY" approach. By contrast, equivalent income values the components of well-being in terms of income; i.e., the idea is to measure well-being in terms of income adjusted for various dimensions of well-being such as lifespan, health-related quality of life and other dimensions. More specifically, the equivalent life metric can be thought of as years of "good" life with a "good" reference level of income, health-related quality of life and other dimensions of well-being. The equivalent income metric can be thought of as dollars of "good" consumption with a "good" reference level of lifespan, health-related quality of life and other dimensions of well-being.

For simplicity we will focus just on income and health, but both approaches can readily be extended to include further dimensions of well-being as appropriate. Both approaches have more demanding information requirements than standard CEA and BCA, which only require separate modelling of health and income outcomes. Equivalent life and equivalent income approaches require joint modelling of both outcomes to provide information on health, income and potentially other dimensions of well-being at each time period for each individual or subgroup.

In theory, if all individuals have the same preferences then equivalent life and equivalent income metrics should yield the same rankings of individual and social well-being. Differences emerge, however, if individual preferences differ (Onder et al., 2019). Take two people with equal income and health, both below the reference levels for "good" income and health. If their preferences are the same, then their well-being is the same using either metric. However, imagine that person A cares more about health than person B. They would therefore be willing to pay a larger amount of their income to achieve "good" health, and would be willing to accept a smaller deterioration in their health to achieve a "good" income. Who is worse off? According to the equivalent income approach, person A is worse off than person B – because their equivalent income is their current income minus their (larger) willingness to pay for "good" health. By contrast, according to the equivalent life approach, person A is better off than person B – because their equivalent life is their current health minus their (smaller) willingness to sacrifice health to achieve a "good" income.

In practice, however, it is hard to measure differences in preferences between individuals and economic evaluation studies usually rely on estimates of population average preferences, sometimes broken down into subgroups using one or two readily measurable variables such as age or income. However, differences between the two metrics can still emerge in practice due to differences in the ways that they are estimated. We illustrate by constructing the two metrics in different ways. We construct equivalent life using a simple parametric approach, based on an explicit current period well-being function, and we construct equivalent income using a simple non-parametric approach, based on evidence about average current period willingness to pay for health-related quality of life broken down by five different income groups. Neither of these simple practical approaches allows for individual-level preference heterogeneity, but they can give different rankings of programmes. It is possible to adopt the same simple non-parametric approach to equivalent life (i.e., using data on willingness to sacrifice health-related quality of life to achieve "good" income by the five socioeconomic groups) and the same simple parametric approach to equivalent income (as we show in Appendix 5.A.1). It is also possible to adopt different parametric and non-parametric approaches to estimating both metrics. We merely use these specific approaches as illustrations of our general point that the specific empirical approach to estimating these metrics matters and needs to be given careful consideration, as well as the theory lying behind the metrics.

Below we spell out in more detail how our measures of equivalent life and income relate to the general "equivalence approach" in the welfare economics literature (Deaton and Muellbauer, 1980; Fleurbaey and Blanchet, 2013; Fleurbaey and Maniquet, 2011, also discussed in Adler and Decancq, Chapter 3, this volume), and the specific measure of life-metric utility derived by Canning (Canning, 2013). Then we show how we operationalize equivalent life in a simple parametric way by making specific assumptions about the period-specific well-being function. Finally, we show how we operationalize equivalent income in a simple non-parametric way using estimates of willingness to pay for full health by income group.

6.3.1 *Using the "Equivalence Approach" to Derive "Equivalent Life" and "Equivalent Income"*

Both equivalent life and equivalent income follow the "equivalence approach" to constructing well-being measures (Deaton and Muellbauer, 1980; Fleurbaey and Blanchet, 2013; Fleurbaey and Maniquet, 2011). This is based on the idea that bundles of income, health and other attributes that individuals derive utility (well-being) from can be considered equally good as long as they are on the same indifference curve.

Similar to Canning (2013), we focus on three types of goods – period-specific consumption of traded goods, period-specific health quality and lifespan. Our aim is exclusively normative: we aim to value bundles of consumption, health quality and lifespan by constructing an index of well-being, but not to predict individual behaviour using the same well-being index.[6] In particular, we do not need to assume that individuals always make "optimal" long-term plans as if they were fully informed rational self-interested maximizers of total well-being over the lifetime with rational expectations and infallible computational abilities. We are therefore not constrained by the potential behavioural paradoxes that might emerge if one were to make that behavioural assumption.

An individual's lifetime profile of different traded goods consumed in different time periods is represented by the vector $\mathbf{x}$ (with a corresponding vector of prices $\mathbf{p}$), their profile of different health-quality attributes over time is represented by the vector $\mathbf{h}$ (with an upper bound representing full health $\mathbf{h} \leq \mathbf{1}$)[7], and their lifespan in years is represented by the scalar l.[8]

Individuals are also endowed with an exogenous flow of period-specific income over their lifetime, represented by the vector $\mathbf{y}$. Hence,

[6] We leave open the question of whether well-being is supposed to represent "true" individual preferences – i.e., behavioural preferences that have been suitably "laundered" to ensure they meet appropriate theoretical conditions such as being well-informed and consistent – or some other philosophical construct.

[7] In Canning's original framework, health quality is a multi-dimensional concept with multiple health attributes. We simplify this to a uni-dimensional concept of health quality, i.e. we summarize the multi-dimensional health attributes $\mathbf{m_t}$ in time period t in the standard way by $h_t(\mathbf{m_t})$, where h_t is scalar measured on the standard ratio scale of health-related quality of life used in health economics, anchored at 0 (to mean a health state not worth living through) and bounded above at 1 (to mean full health). We use year-specific scalar values, h_t to represent the individual's health-related quality of life in year t.

[8] We denote individual lifetime vectors in bold.

an individual can be described by their allocation of the bundle $(\mathbf{x}, \mathbf{h}, l)$ and their endowment of income $\mathbf{y}$. The expression $\mathbf{xp} \leq \mathbf{y}$ defines the set of individual budget constraints in each period, i.e. it says that the individual cannot afford to consume more traded goods in a given period than their income in that period allows. We assume that the period-specific flows of income and health quality are exogenously given, and our only concern is to value different lifetime bundles of these goods from a normative perspective rather than to predict long-term savings, consumption and health behaviours.

Our general lifetime well-being function depends on income and health over the lifetime, as well as lifespan, and thus can be represented by $w(\mathbf{y}, \mathbf{h}, l)$. The function is consistent with more income being better for the individual, more current period health quality being better, and more lifespan being better as long as one's life is "worth living", but in our general theoretical framework we make no further normative or behavioural assumptions.

Canning (2013), on the other hand, does make a set of standard assumptions about individual preferences. He assumes preferences are represented on the bounded set of all the possible bundles F by a continuous utility function *u(.)* increasing in each argument, and strictly increasing in life-span l; this latter assumption, however, rules out the possibility of some health states being valued as worse than being dead; and also similarly rules out states with consumption so low that it would make "life not worth living".

When operationalizing the framework later in this chapter, we do assume a specific functional form for the well-being function $w(\mathbf{y}, \mathbf{h}, l)$, which also respects most of the assumptions for the utility function by Canning (2013). One key difference, however, is that like the standard HALY approach, we allow the existence of states worse than being dead. States worse than being dead raise possible behavioural puzzles for rational choice theorists – for example, the question of why people in states worse than dead do not always kill themselves. However, as our aim is to value well-being rather than to predict behaviour, this issue does not constrain us.

In Canning's framework, when the individual consumes a bundle of traded goods $\mathbf{x}$, her indirect utility from income, health and lifespan can be represented by $v(\mathbf{y}, \mathbf{h}, l) = max_x \{u(\mathbf{x}, \mathbf{h}, l) | (\mathbf{x}, \mathbf{h}, l) \in F, \mathbf{xp} \leq \mathbf{y}\}$, where F is the set of all possible bundles of traded goods, health attributes and lifespan. This means that, given prices, the individual indirect utility $v(.)$ can be defined as a function of income, health attributes and lifespan.[9]

Consistent with the equivalence approach, Canning (2013) defines equivalent life (or what he calls "life-metric utility") using a hypothetical trade-off between the individual's actual life with their actual lifespan, income and health profile and a hypothetical life with assumed reference levels of "good" income and full health.

We follow a similar approach. More specifically, we define "equivalent life", l^*, as the hypothetical number of life years that together with full health quality $\mathbf{h}_{max}$ and a reference "good" level of income $\mathbf{y}_{ref}$ would generate the same well-being for the individual as her actual situation:

$$w(\mathbf{y}_{ref}, \mathbf{h}_{max}, l^*) = w(\mathbf{y}, \mathbf{h}, l) \tag{6.3}$$

This condition states that the utility derived from consuming the reference bundle of income and health over a lifespan of l^* is the same as the utility derived from consuming the actual bundle of income and health over the actual lifespan l.

Canning (2013) proves the uniqueness and existence of the equivalent life for the general case that satisfies his assumptions. In our specific case with the specific utility function that we will define, it is straightforward to also derive a unique l^* from the equivalence condition in equation 6.3.

We will use a similar approach to derive equivalent income (y^*) – defined as 'the hypothetical income that together with perfect health (and lifespan) would put the individual in a situation that is for her as good as her actual situation' (Samson et al., 2018). To do this, we need to specify both a lifetime vector of reference "perfect" level of health quality, $\mathbf{h}_{max}$, and a reference "perfect" length of life, which we shall denote by l_{max}.[10]

We can then modify the "equivalence condition" in equation 6.3 to implicitly define a lifetime vector of equivalent income $\mathbf{y}^*$ (instead of equivalent life):

[9] For brevity, we have omitted the price vector **p** from the list of arguments of $v()$.

[10] Notice that to derive the equivalent income, we now need to set not only a reference value for health quality $\mathbf{h}_{max}$, but also a reference value for lifespan l_{max}.

$$w(\mathbf{y}^*, \mathbf{h}_{\mathbf{max}}, l_{max}) = w(\mathbf{y}, \mathbf{h}, l) \tag{6.4}$$

Empirically, one way to find the lifetime vector of the hypothetical equivalent income $\mathbf{y}^*$ is to use information on individual *i's* willingness to pay (WTP) for perfect health (Samson et al., 2018). For example, if we set the benchmark for perfect health at 1 in each time period, i.e. $\mathbf{h}_{\mathbf{max}}=\mathbf{1}$, then the aggregate lifetime equivalent income could be calculated using information on the WTP for a year in full health:

$$\sum_{t=0}^{l-1} y_t^* = \sum_{t=0}^{l-1} (y_t - WTP(h_t \rightarrow 1)) \tag{6.5}$$

where $WTP(h_t \rightarrow 1)$ is the individual WTP for a year in full health of 1 (one HALY), given their actual health.[11]

6.3.2 A Parametric Approach to Operationalizing Equivalent Life

One parametric way of operationalizing the equivalent life approach is to follow Cookson et.al.(2021b), and assume a simple additive period-specific well-being function, which requires three normative parameters to be set based on various sources of evidence and value judgement. Individual well-being at time t can be expressed as:[12]

$$w_t = h_t + u(y_t) - 1, \text{ where } u(y_{i,t}) = A - B \times (y_t)^{1-\eta} \tag{6.6}$$

In equation 6.6, h_t is individual health quality at time t measured in HALYs, y_t is individual consumption at time t measured in dollars, and the instantaneous utility from consumption *u(.)* is specifically defined as $u(y_{i,t}) = A - B \times (y_t)^{1-\eta}$, where $\eta > 1$ ("eta") is a parameter representing the elasticity of the marginal value of consumption, and "-1", A and B are normalization constants ensuring that the well-being measure scale is appropriately anchored, so that the value 1 is a "good

11 Alternatively, this could be expressed in terms of the aggregate individual WTP for a full lifespan in full health: $\sum_{t=0}^{l_{max}-1} y_t^* = \sum_{t=0}^{l-1} y_t - WTP\left(\sum_{t=0}^{l-1} h_t \rightarrow l_{max}\right)$, where $WTP\left(\sum_{t=0}^{l-1} h_t \rightarrow l_{max}\right)$ is the WTP for a life with full lifespan (to be defined) and in full health.

12 For simplicity, we ignore the individual-level subscript *i*, but the well-being is derived for each individual *i*.

year of life" and the value 0 is a "state in which life is barely worth living" (Cookson et al., 2021b).

More specifically, the constants A and B are defined as

$$A = y_{min}^{(1-\eta)} / \left(y_{min}^{(1-\eta)} - y_{std}^{(1-\eta)} \right) \quad \text{and } B = 1 / \left(y_{min}^{(1-\eta)} - y_{std}^{(1-\eta)} \right), \text{where :}$$

- y_{std} is standard consumption for a good standard of living, set at a level that the relevant social decision makers consider to represent a good living standard; one way of operationalizing this is to assume that the reference level of income is equal to the median income in the relevant population.
- y_{min} is minimal consumption for a life worth living, set at a level that the relevant social decision makers consider to represent a living standard so extremely bad that life is barely worth living.[13,14]

The higher the eta parameter, the more rapidly diminishing returns set in as consumption increases. The theoretical literature on "eta" supports the possibility that $\eta \leq 1$, in which case the well-being function is not bounded from above. However, the empirical literature supports values of "eta" of at least 1 (Layard et al., 2008).

We now assume the period-specific well-being function defined in equation 6.6, to operationalize the equivalent life measure using the trade-off represented by the equivalence condition in equation 6.3.

First, consistent with the approach for quantifying equivalent life described in the previous section, we set a reference "good" level of current period income, $\mathbf{y_{ref}} = \mathbf{y_{std}}$, and a reference "good" level of current period health quality, $\mathbf{h_{max}} = \mathbf{1}$, as common benchmarks which apply to all individuals. This is consistent with the equivalence condition (6.3) in the following form $w(\mathbf{y_{std}}, \mathbf{1}, l^*) = w(\mathbf{y}, \mathbf{h}, l)$. After substituting equation 6.6 in this, to represent well-being,

[13] This does not necessarily mean it would be better for the person to die, since death is irreversible (lasting for all future periods) whereas we are here defining well-being for a single period only. Rather than thinking of zero well-being as being as bad as death, therefore, it may be more helpful to think of it as a period of life that is no better than unconsciousness. This is a normative judgement which does not have to coincide with the subsistence level of consumption needed to sustain life.

[14] If we know the proportional estimate of minimal consumption as a share of standard consumption ($k = \frac{y_{min}}{y_{std}}$), it is possible to simplify the parameters by setting $A = \frac{k^{1-\eta}}{k^{1-\eta}-1}$ and $B = \frac{A}{y_{min}}$.

$w(\mathbf{y}, \mathbf{h}, l) = \sum_{t=0}^{l-1} \left\{ h_t + A - B \times (y_t)^{1-\eta} - 1 \right\}$, the equivalence condition becomes:

$$\sum_{t=0}^{l^*-1} \left\{ 1 + A - B \times y_{std}^{1-\eta} - 1 \right\} = \sum_{t=0}^{l-1} \left\{ h_t + A - B \times y^{1-\eta} - 1 \right\} \tag{6.7}$$

From 6.7 we express the equivalent life, adjusted for health and income, l^*:

$$l^* = \sum_{t=0}^{l-1} \left\{ h_t + A - B \times y^{1-\eta} - 1 \right\} \tag{6.8}$$

Consistent with the framework outlined above, the difference $l - l^*$ represents the number of life years that an individual would be willing to give up to exchange a life with their actual lifetime income and health $(\mathbf{y}, \mathbf{h})$ for a life with a "good" level of lifetime income and in full lifetime health $(\mathbf{y}_{\text{std}}, \mathbf{1})$.

Equation 6.8 shows that the equivalent life measure can be derived using the equivalence approach for constructing well-being measures, or the hypothetical trade-off between individual's actual levels of lifetime income and health and assumed reference levels of "good" of income and full health. Therefore, the lifetime well-being QALY can also be interpreted as a measure of equivalent life.

It is also possible to operationalize equivalent income using a parametric approach analogous to the one used to operationalize equivalent life (see Appendix 6.A.1). However, in this chapter we use a different non-parametric approach to operationalizing equivalent income.

6.3.3 A Simple Non-Parametric Approach to Operationalizing Equivalent Income

In this section we describe a non-parametric approach used to operationalize equivalent income based on estimates of willingness to pay (WTP) for full health quality by income group. We estimate WTP for a life year (value of a statistical life year (VSLY)), and by assumption WTP for a year in full health (a HALY), in a given country and for income subgroups, in three steps (Verguet and Norheim, 2021). First, following Robinson et al., for a given country *a*, the value of a statistical life (VSL_a) can be estimated from country *b*, adjusting for income differences (Robinson et al., 2019b).

$$VSL_a = VSL_b \left(\frac{GNI_a}{GNI_b} \right)^{\epsilon},$$

where GNI is per capita gross national income for countries a and b, and ϵ is income elasticity.

We convert VSL to the value of VSLY by starting from the fact that WTP studies typically have asked about preferences over risk reductions for persons with an average age of 35 years. We assume:

$$VSLY_a = \frac{VSL_a}{e_{35}},$$

where e_{35} is life expectancy at age 35 for country a.

Third, for different income groups within a country, we treat groups similarly and estimate $VSLY_i$ by income group, adjusting for variation in income with the income elasticity parameter:

$$VSLY_g = VSLY_a \left(\frac{I_j}{I_a} \right)^{\epsilon},$$

where I_j is income for a given income group and I_a is mean income in that country. In our example below, we use $\epsilon = 1.2$ and assume that all individuals in the same income group have the same WTP (see Table 6.3, shown later).

6.4 Illustrative Example – Cancer in Ethiopia

We now illustrate the application of generalized utilitarian social welfare functions to these two measures of lifetime well-being compared with standard CEA and BCA in a simple, stylized example: cancer treatment for patients in a low-income country such as Ethiopia.

6.4.1 Baseline Distributions

Consider a cohort of 100,000 people in a low-income country, all aged 50 years and observed for the next 30 years.[15] For simplicity, we

[15] All inputs are available data for Ethiopia, a country with a population of about 100 million people, a low-income country according to World Bank classification of country income groups. Incidence of cancer is stylized so as to illustrate distributions better.

assume the cohort has enjoyed 50 healthy years since birth and that the maximum lifespan is 80. Mean income is about US$ 790 per year per person, and we assume that all income is consumed each year.[16] We create an individual-level distribution of income within the cohort with a Gini index of 0.30 using a gamma distribution. This distribution is then split into five income quintile groups (with annual income ranging from US$ 311 to US$ 1371), and for simplicity we assume that individuals belong to their income group from birth and have no mobility over time across income groups. At age 50, 50 per cent of individuals are diagnosed with a cancer that gives them a substantially shorter health-adjusted life expectancy (HALE) – an unrealistically high incidence rate that we use for illustrative purposes. We assume that low-income groups have a higher cancer mortality risk than high-income groups, but for simplicity we assume there are no differences between income groups in cancer incidence. The remainder of the cohort is healthy with background mortality typical for their income group. At baseline, the group with cancer pays US$ 10 out-of-pocket per year they are alive for palliative care with low effectiveness. No other treatment is available.

Thus, we construct a highly stylized example where we can estimate lifetime health and lifetime income over the lifespan of the cohort. Lifetime income and expected healthy lifespan (measured in HALYs) by quintile for both groups at baseline are given in Figure 6.2.

Next, a new cancer treatment is proven effective in a randomized controlled trial and if introduced will improve survival and quality of life. The cost of the treatment is US$ 250 per year and treatment reduces the annual risk of death from 0.4 (on average across quintiles) to 0.1; quality of life improves from 0.8 to 0.9 per year alive.

With these inputs, we created a Markov model (Figure 6.3) following a cohort of 100,000 people, divided into subgroups, over 30 years and compared costs, survival and quality of life across subgroups.

As seen from the figure, the population is divided into ten subgroups, by quintile 1–5 and by health status. Each group is followed over 30 cycles, facing a given annual mortality risk that differs by income and health status. The healthy groups face annual background mortality as given in standard life tables for this population. Groups with cancer face higher mortality due to their disease. In the intervention arm,

[16] GNI per capita in US$, 2018 (World Bank database, Atlas method).

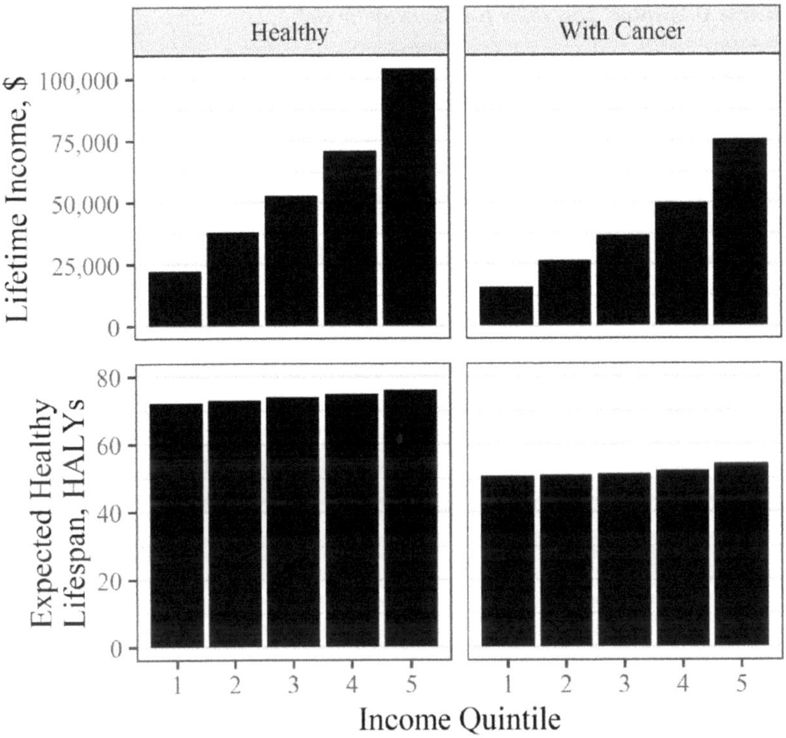

Figure 6.2 Baseline distributions of income and health

annual mortality risk and quality of life differ from the status quo. Key input parameters for the Markov model are provided in Table 6.1. We assumed a social gradient in annual mortality risk with cancer, and applied the same gradient to estimate background mortality for the healthy groups, by quintile.

When the model is run for 30 years, this gives us the proportion in each subgroup surviving by year, their quality of life by year, associated annual treatment costs, and their income by year. Expected survival and HALYs by subgroup over 30 years are also provided.

The first result of this modelling exercise is a simplified cost-effectiveness analysis where only direct treatment costs are included; other indirect costs are not taken into account. Treatment costs are considered regardless of whether they are covered through public finance or out of pocket. For simplicity, neither costs or health outcomes are discounted.

Table 6.1. ***Input variables for Markov model***

Parameter variables	Q1	Q2	Q3	Q4	Q5
Probability of survival without treatment	0.36	0.48	0.6	0.72	0.84
Probability of survival with treatment	0.9	0.9	0.9	0.9	0.9
Cost of ineffective treatment per year ($)	10	10	10	10	10
Cost of treatment per year alive ($)	250	250	250	250	250
Quality of life with untreated cancer	0.8	0.8	0.8	0.8	0.8
Quality of life with treated cancer	0.9	0.9	0.9	0.9	0.9

Note: We only show parameters related to cancer patients, all others for healthy groups are held constant. Q1–Q5 = quintile 1–5.

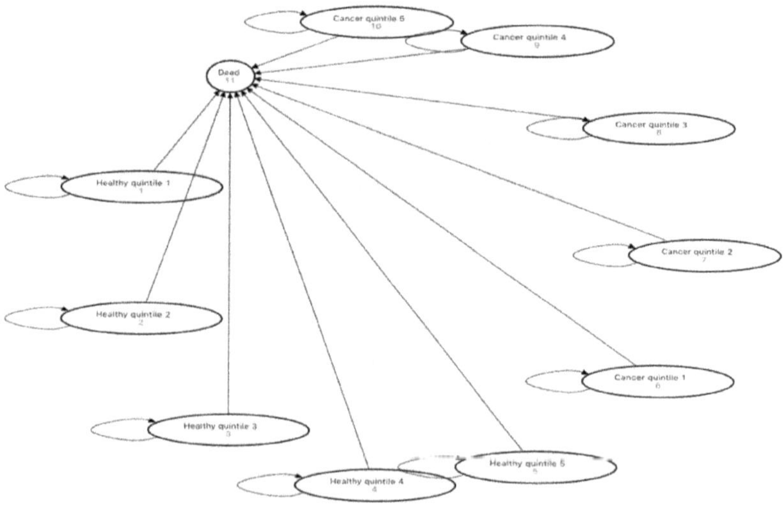

Figure 6.3 State transition diagram for the Markov model. The population is divided into ten subgroups, by quintile 1 (lowest income)–5 (highest income), and by health status (healthy or with cancer)

We see from Table 6.2 that incremental cost per HALY gained per person is about US$ 390. This ICER is about 50% of GDP per capita (US$ 790) and would probably be considered cost-effective by criteria suggested for low-income countries (Woods et al., 2016). Observe that all costs and all health gains are summarized across all subgroups and over the complete time horizon and divided by population size. Results are thus, by convention, expressed as averages per capita.

Table 6.2. *Results from cost-effectiveness analysis ICER = incremental cost-effectiveness ratio ($/HALYs)*

Strategy	Cost ($)	Incremental cost ($)	Health (HALYs)	Incremental health (HALYs)	ICER
Baseline	16		12.9		
UPF	1,197	1,181	15.9	3.0	392

Note: All costs and health gains are per capita. ICER = incremental cost-effectiveness ratio ($/HALYs).

The Markov model provides additional information about subgroups that we use for further analysis. For example, the model produces survival curves for each subgroup that we now extend and use to evaluate lifetime health and lifetime income, and their distribution.

With Markov modelling,[17] we can project new health (Figures 6.4 and 6.5) and income (Figure 6.6) distributions for two policy options: introduce the new cancer treatment with universal public finance (UPF) based on taxes or compulsory insurance premiums proportional to income, or let the cost be borne by the patients, out-of-pocket, at the point of consumption (OOP).

With the latter policy option (OOP), we assume that the poorest quintile cannot afford treatment, so they pay no treatment cost and gain no health benefit (see Figure 6.5), while all other patients do pay for treatment.[18] Under UPF, all cancer patients receive treatment, including those in the poorest quintile group, so total cost and health gains will be somewhat higher.

Under the out-of-pocket finance policy (OOP), individuals with cancer, except quintile 1 with no ability to pay out of pocket, receive an effective treatment which costs US$ 250 per year out-of-pocket. This yields a benefit for the treated individuals in the form of added life years and quality of life in each year. Better survival increases the

[17] Note that we simply add the first 50 years where everyone is healthy and belongs to their income group to get a lifetime perspective. This is obviously a simplifying assumption.

[18] In Appendix 6.A.5 (Table 6.A.5.1), we show results under the assumption that the poorest quintile pays out-of-pocket for treatment. This less realistic scenario has the advantage of equal costs under OOP and UPF, so is simpler to compare.

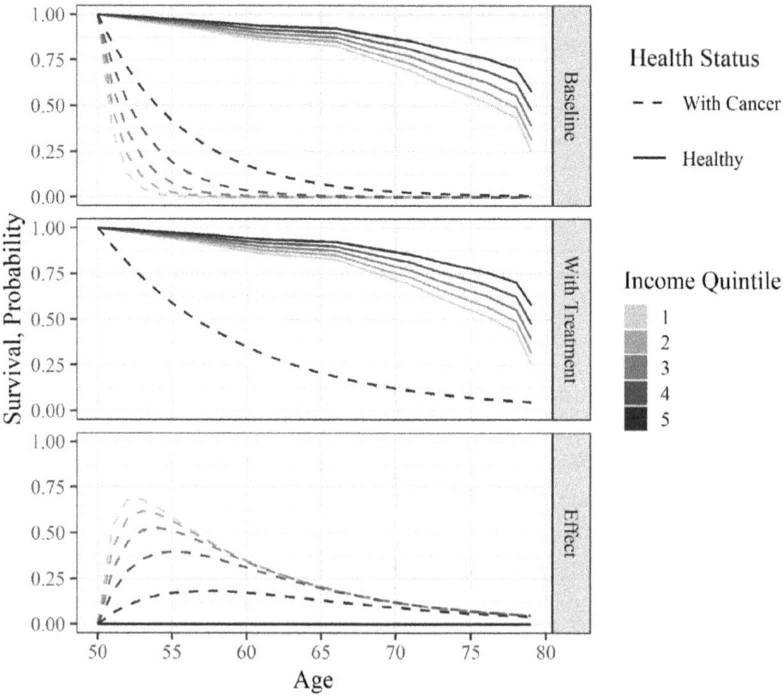

Figure 6.4 Survival by income quintile group with and without treatment, and the resulting effects, comparing the healthy (solid lines) and cancer (dotted lines) populations

lifespan and hence also lifetime income despite their out-of-pocket payment. Individuals without cancer pay nothing, so they have no loss of income under OOP.

Under the universal public finance policy (UPF), the cancer treatment is covered by a public tax, defined as a proportion of income. In this case, individuals without cancer pay taxes and get somewhat lower income. All cancer patients, including quintile 1, receive treatment. Survival is therefore improved for cancer patients in quintile 1. For all other groups, survival is the same as under the OOP policy.

We see from Figure 6.6 that the distribution of lifetime income is unequal at baseline, and the pattern changes when treatment is introduced. Cancer patients live longer and therefore have more net income (except the poorest quintile 1 that cannot pay out-of-pocket for treatment). The healthy groups pay taxes under UPF, and net income for them is lower than under OOP, and more so for the better off. Among

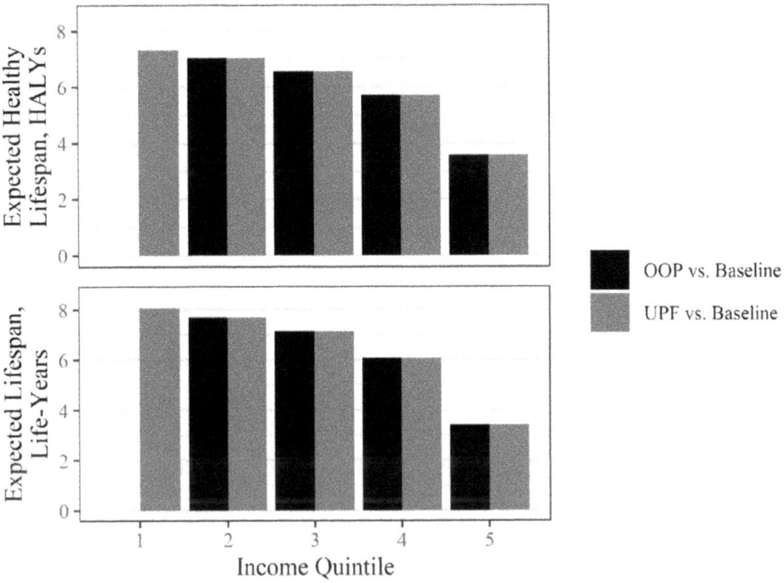

Figure 6.5 Treatment effect (net increase) on expected lifespan measured in years and health-adjusted life years for the cancer patients with OOP and UPF, by income quintile

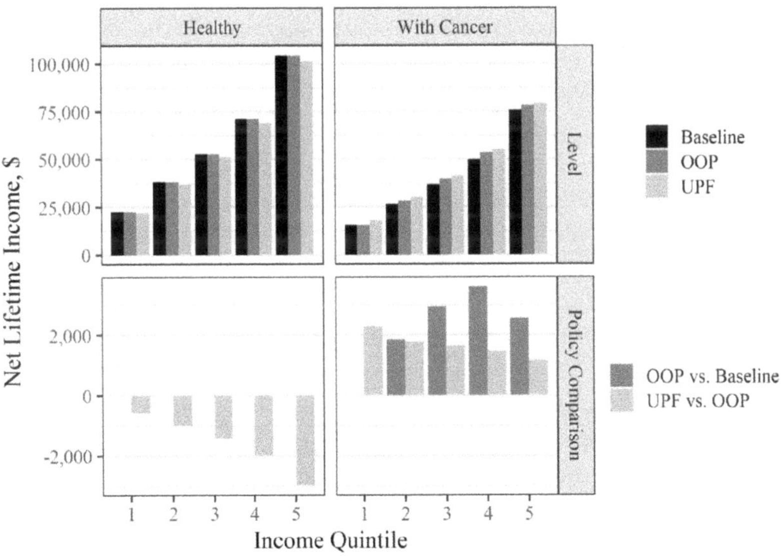

Figure 6.6 Net per capita lifetime income at baseline, with OOP and UPF for the healthy and cancer groups, by income quintile – levels and incremental comparisons

the cancer patients, net income is higher under UPF compared to OOP, and more so for the worse off quintiles.

We assume zero administrative and deadweight loss costs of UPF taxation. The task is to evaluate these distributions in a framework that includes both health and income.

6.4.2 *Calculation of Lifetime Well-Being*

Recall that in this example we follow a cohort of individuals from age 50 for a further 30 years, and assume a maximum lifespan of 80 years. Assume that the cohort P consists of N individuals, each denoted by i. We assume all individuals live their previous 50 years with full health quality, 1, at their existing level of income, y_i. Then each individual's remaining lifetime *income* (starting at $t = 50$) y_i can be calculated as $y_i = \sum_{t=50}^{l_i} y_{it}$ and remaining lifetime *health* as $h_i = \sum_{t=50}^{l_i} h_{it}$, where l_i is the individual's lifespan. All of these variables can also be aggregated over the entire lifetime, i.e. starting from $t = 0$.

We want to compare two alternative policies that both improve well-being compared to the baseline. We have already shown in Figure 6.2 the estimated distribution of health and lifetime income at baseline in each group. For the subset of individuals with cancer, with no policies implemented, they pay out-of-pocket US$ 10 per year they are alive for ineffective palliative care; the rest of the individuals pay nothing.

The next step involves transforming lifetime health and income in each quintile under each policy into a well-being number.

6.4.2.1 Equivalent Life in the Different Scenarios

Recall that equivalent life as a measure of well-being, $w(y_i, h_i)$, uses health and income as inputs and these are calculated using the well-being functions discussed above for equation 6.6. In this example, we set the elasticity of the marginal value of income $\eta = 1.26$, minimal income y_{min} to US$ 50 and standard income $y_{std} =$ US$713 (mean income), and obtain the values of equivalent life in each year.[19] The yearly values can then be aggregated over the lifetime to obtain the individual- and quintile group-level lifetime well-being. The net

[19] For a discussion of these assumptions, see (Cookson et al., 2021b).

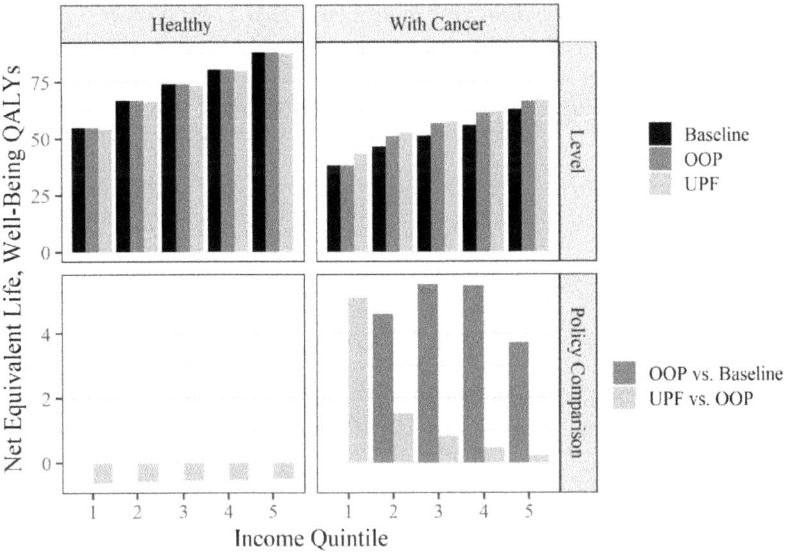

Figure 6.7 Net lifetime equivalent life at baseline, with OOP and UPF for the healthy and cancer groups, by income quintile – levels and incremental comparisons

difference in equivalent life in the two scenarios (OOP vs UPF) is illustrated in Figure 6.7.

We see from Figure 6.7 that among the healthy, the proportional tax with UPF imposes a slightly larger well-being loss on the poor compared to the rich (lower-left quadrant). Among the cancer patients, the well-being gains are largest in quintile 1 (the poorest) under UPF compared to OOP (lower-right quadrant). Observe, however, that OOP will also improve net well-being compared to baseline.

6.4.2.2 Equivalent Income

We make various simplifying assumptions empirically to estimate equivalent income, and we do not use the same well-being equation approach as for equivalent life, as discussed in Section 6.3.3, but rather use willingness to pay estimates from previous studies.

We denote by $WTP_i(h_i \to h^*)$ the individual's willingness to pay for a year in normal health compared to their health (quality of life) in the baseline scenario, and the individual's marginal willingness to pay for one HALY by wtp_i. We then make the further simplifying assumption that when this marginal value is constant with respect to income,

Table 6.3. *Estimated willingness to pay for a HALY, by income quintile group*

Income quintile group	Mean annual income (US$)	WTP for a HALY
1	311	285
2	520	528
3	713	772
4	948	1087
5	1371	1691

health and time period, the marginal value for a health improvement for individual i can be calculated as WTP for full health multiplied with full minus actual health $WTP_i(h_i \rightarrow h^*) = (wtp_i \times (h^* - h_i))$. Full health as a reference point is set to one HALY.

We further assume that individual WTP is constant at the margin but varies according to individual income quintile group, denoted by g. An individual's marginal WTP for a HALY thus does not vary as their own level of lifetime income and lifetime health change, but it does depend on their fixed income group – thus capturing the concept of increasing marginal value of health at group level but not at individual level (people with higher income have higher WTP for health improvements). Then we can express individual WTP as WTP at the margin for each quintile (wtp_g) times the actual health increase from a move from actual health to full health, i.e. $WTP_g(h \rightarrow h^*) = wtp_g \times (h_{max} - h)$.

In our example, the marginal willingness to pay for a HALY in our low-income country is estimated from US WTP data by quintile groups of income, as explained in Section 6.3.3. If available, it would be better to use more fine-grained empirical estimates. In our example, we assume that all individuals in the same income group have the same WTP (Table 6.3).

We see from Table 6.3 that people in lower income groups have lower WTP for a HALY, in line with an increasing marginal rate of substitution of income for health at group level.

6.4.3 *Equivalent Income in the Different Scenarios*

Net lifetime income and lifetime health can then be estimated as equivalent income as explained for equation 6.5 above. Figure 6.8 illustrates the distribution of equivalent income under baseline, OOP and UPF.

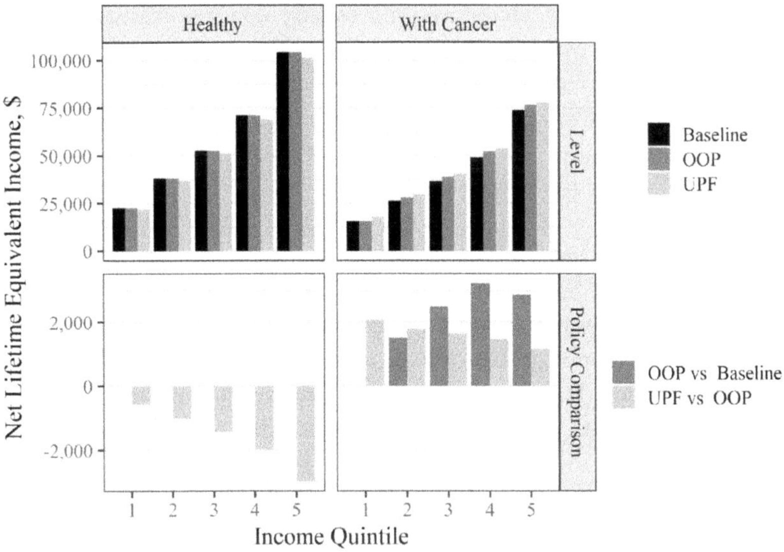

Figure 6.8 Net lifetime equivalent income at baseline, with OOP and UPF for the healthy and cancer groups, by income quintile – levels and incremental comparisons

We see from Figure 6.8 that among the healthy, the proportional tax with UPF imposes a loss of lifetime equivalent income. For cancer patients, the level of equivalent income is higher with UPF than with OOP. Among the cancer patients, with UPF, the gain in equivalent income is highest among the poorest (quintile 1). If we compare UPF and OOP, we see that UPF is redistributive, with the healthy getting somewhat lower equivalent income (and a larger well-being loss on the richer quintiles) while the cancer patients get higher equivalent income (they live longer and do not pay out-of-pocket).

Our task is, next, to compare and evaluate these distributions of well-being, measured as equivalent life or equivalent income, by the use of social welfare functions.

6.4.4 Prioritarian SWF for Equivalent Life and Equivalent Income: Comparing the Two Scenarios

Social welfare can be quantified by transforming individual-level lifetime well-being numbers (measured as equivalent life or equivalent income) by a strictly increasing and strictly concave transformation function (as discussed in Adler, Chapter 2, this volume) and then aggregating over individuals (for further details, see Appendix 6.A.3). We use these SWFs to compare *distributions* of equivalent life (as illustrated in Figure 6.7) and equivalent income (as illustrated in Figure 6.8) under the two polices.

6.4.4.1 Ex Ante and Ex Post Evaluations

To evaluate distributions of health and income under OOP and UPF from the *ex ante* and *ex post* perspective[20], we use information on survival by income group and year available as output from the Markov model. For *ex ante* evaluations, we simply use as input expected life years at t_0 for each quintile, with and without cancer (see Figure 6.5, lower panel). Expected healthy lifespan is used to generate health distributions, and expected life years multiplied with net income (with OOP or UPF) gives us distributions of expected lifetime income. These are then converted into well-being numbers and the transformed sum of expected well-being for each policy is calculated as described above.

For *ex post* evaluations, we use information on survival by year, the survival curve method, as described by Adler and others Adler (2019, chapter 5), see also Adler (2020); Jamison et al., (2020). We do not have information about identified individuals, but we have information on the expected proportion of each quintile in the cohort surviving each year, and we convert this information to a distribution profile of age at death by quintile (see Figure 6.9). For example, treatment for cancer patients, compared to the baseline, will shift a left-skewed distribution profile to the right (Figure 6.8, right panel).

A higher proportion in each quintile survives for more years. Improvements in quality of life and lifetime income follow the same pattern. *Ex post* distributions in each quintile are aggregated by taking into account the expected proportion of people alive each year, their quality of life, and their net income, then these are transformed to equivalent life or equivalent income by year, and finally transformed and summarized by a prioritarian social welfare function (for more

[20] We follow the distinction made by Adler, Chapter 2, this volume: (1) *ex ante* prioritarianism: the sum across individuals of transformed expected well-being; and (2) *ex post* prioritarianism: the sum across individuals of expected transformed well-being.

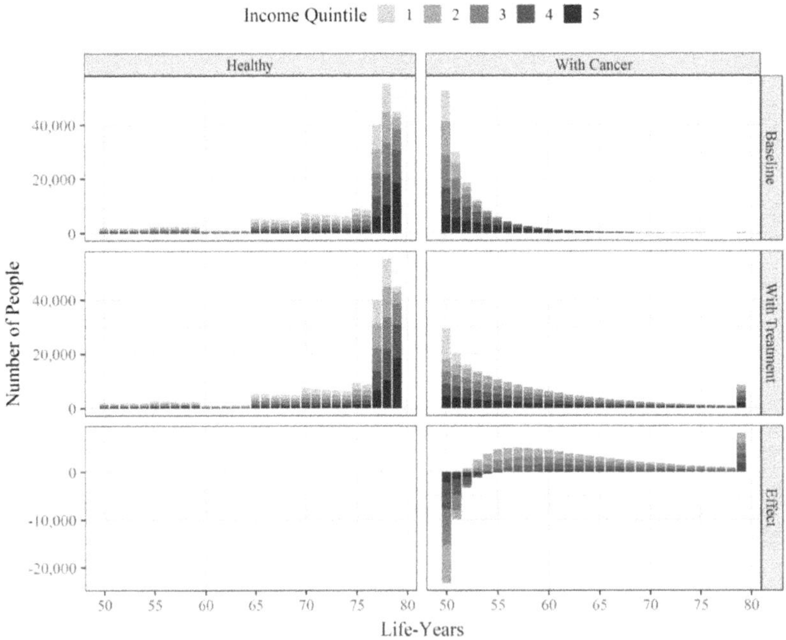

Figure 6.9 *Ex post* evaluation: Distribution of age at death (measured in life years after age 50) by quintile and health status in the cohort of 100,000

details, see Appendix: 6.A.3). This gives us the sum across individuals of expected transformed well-being.

6.4.4.2 Equally Distributed Equivalent Well-Being

For ease of comparison, we calculate equally distributed equivalent well-being (EDE_w) for each scenario and for *ex ante* and *ex post* evaluations. The EDE_w is the level of well-being that if equally distributed would generate the same level of social welfare as that generated by the actual distribution of well-being. EDE_w is ordinally equivalent to the index of social welfare; i.e., it ranks well-being distributions in the same order. EDE_w expresses the level of social welfare represented by a prioritarian SWF on the same scale as the measure of well-being. In Table 6.4, EDE is expressed as equivalent life (measured in good life years) or equivalent income (measured in dollars).[21]

21 Note that EDE_w is not the same as expected EDE discussed in chapter 2, this volume. Rather, we are simply giving an ordinal rescaling of the *ex ante* and *ex post* valuation on the same scale as the measure of well-being.

Table 6.4. *Summary per capita results for all evaluation approaches*

	Baseline		OOP		UPF	
Gamma	Equivalent income, US$	Equivalent life, well-being QALYs	Equivalent income, US$	Equivalent life, well-being QALYs	Equivalent income, US$	Equivalent life, well-being QALYs
Utilitarian						
0	49,023	61.8	50,032	63.8	50,046	64.3
Ex ante prioritarian, EDE$_w$						
0.5	45,641	60.9	46,644	63.0	46,929	63.7
1	42,297	60.0	43,251	62.2	43,826	63.1
1.5	39,109	59.1	39,972	61.3	40,845	62.4
2	36,184	58.3	36,926	60.5	38,084	61.8
Ex post, EDE$_w$						
0.5	45,560	60.8	46,540	62.8	46,799	63.5
1	42,152	59.8	43,062	61.8	43,575	62.7
1.5	38,916	58.9	39,720	60.9	40,483	61.8
2	35,958	57.9	36,635	59.9	37,624	61.0

6.4.5 *Summary Results*

Table 6.4 compares social welfare per capita (expressed as EDE_w) calculated using equivalent income and equivalent life (with eta = 1.26) across the two scenarios OOP and UPF, *ex ante* and *ex post*. We use the Atkinson SWF (as discussed in detail in Adler, Chapter 2, this volume) and we use five values for γ, the gamma parameter, 0, 0.5; 1.0; 1.5; and 2. In the case when $\gamma = 0$, γ represents a utilitarian social welfare function, i.e. the welfare of people is not assumed to have diminishing social value.

Our example is set up so that universal public finance increases utilization of the cancer treatment among patients in the lowest-income group, increases consumption for other cancer patients (who no longer have to pay out-of-pocket treatment costs) and reduces consumption for the rest of the population (who have to pay additional taxes).

We see from Table 6.4 that EDE_w is higher for UPF and OOP than at baseline, and favours UPF over OOP. This holds, in this case, for all values of gamma tested, including gamma = 0 (utilitarian SWF). In this case, the choice of well-being metric does not make a difference. Neither does the choice of *ex ante* versus *ex post* perspective.

The UPF scenario is favoured for two reasons: first, it generates additional health benefits in the worse-off groups (low-income cancer patients) and second, it delivers a progressive income redistribution favouring worse off groups, i.e., from rich to poor and healthy to sick.

Utilitarian evaluation based on equivalent life is also sensitive to the difference between OOP and UPF because equivalent life allows for diminishing marginal value of consumption in terms of health (or, equivalently, increasing willingness to pay for marginal health gains as consumption increases), although it is not sensitive to transfers of well-being.[22]

Although SWF analysis is always at population level, we first present social welfare in per capita terms in Table 6.4 because we believe it is easier to understand. Table 6.5 compares aggregate social welfare in a cohort of 100,000 individuals.

[22] Utilitarian evaluation based on equivalent income would not be sensitive to this difference, if costs and survival were the same in the two scenarios, e.g., if cancer patients in quintile 1 also receive and pay for treatment out-of-pocket (as shown in Appendix 6.A.4, Table 6.A.4.1). This is so because the method to translate health and income allows for no diminishing marginal value of consumption.

Table 6.5. *Summary results for all evaluation approaches (incremental over 30 years in the cohort of 100,000 people)*

	OOP vs baseline		UPF vs OOP	
Gamma	Equivalent income, US$	Equivalent life, well-being QALYs	Equivalent income, US$	Equivalent life, well-being QALYs
Utilitarian				
0	100,898,997	193,523	1,428,816	53,701
Ex ante prioritarian, EDE_w				
0.5	100,363,584	204,222	28,464,253	69,812
1	95,414,154	213,088	57,541,133	88,004
1.5	86,268,077	219,718	87,290,136	108,317
2	74,178,028	223,787	115,839,364	130,710
Ex post, EDE_w				
0.5	97,978,068	198,093	25,881,318	66,885
1	90,997,985	200,512	51,312,206	81,202
1.5	80,436,311	200,603	76,261,587	96,508
2	67,674,075	198,311	98,960,294	112,594

Table 6.5 shows the results from a population-level rather than individual-level perspective and also in incremental terms making two pairwise comparisons: OOP versus baseline and UPF versus OOP. From a decision-making perspective, the relevant comparison is between the two relevant policy options: UPF versus OOP. Under utilitarian evaluation, this comparison shows that UPF provides a gain of US$1.4m dollars of equivalent income (US$14 per capita) or 53.7 thousand years of equivalent life or "well-being QALYs" (0.53 per capita). Under prioritarian evaluation these gains are valued more highly, because they are concentrated among worse off individuals – and the higher the gamma parameter value representing concern for the worse off, the larger the gains.

Finally, we compare the two policy options using benefit-cost analysis, with results provided in Table 6.6. We show both benefits that include survivor consumption (benefits consist of income and health benefits) and benefits that exclude survivor consumption (benefits consist only of health benefits). Health benefits are converted to monetary terms using the population average willingness to pay for health.

Table 6.6. ***Benefit-cost analysis, total costs and benefits over 30 years in a cohort of 100,000 people***

	OOP vs baseline		UPF vs OOP	
	Health care benefit, US$	Health care cost, US$	Incremental health care benefit, US$	Incremental health care cost, US$
Including survivor consumption benefits				
	285,930,999	85,163,168	59,971,344	21,489,949
Benefit-cost ratio	3.36		2.79	
net benefit	200,767,832		38,481,395	
Excluding survivor consumption benefits				
	176,429,032	85,163,168	56,407,196	21,489,949
Benefit-cost ratio	2.07		2.62	
net benefit	91,265,865		34,917,247	

Costs are health care costs, whether paid for privately via OOP or publicly via UPF. We follow the standard convention in applied benefit-cost analysis of valuing health gains for rich and poor the same, rather than valuing them differentially at willingness to pay values that reflect differential ability to pay in rich and poor groups. This means that the health gains to poorer individuals under UPF compared with OOP are valued substantially more highly than their willingness to pay values. For this reason, the net benefit of UPF compared with OOP shown in Table 6.6 (US$38.4m with survivor consumption benefits and US$34.9m without) is much higher than the gain in equivalent income under utilitarian evaluation shown in Table 6.5 above (only US$1.4m).

If we slightly change our example so that cancer patients in the poorest quintile group receive and pay for treatment out-of-pocket, aggregate costs and survival are the same in the two scenarios – and so there is no health benefit of UPF, only an income redistribution effect. Benefit-cost analysis will then not distinguish between the OOP and UPF policy, while a prioritarian SWF will clearly do so (see Appendix 6.A.4, Table 6.A.4.1 and 6.A.4.2).

6.5 Conclusion

This chapter presents a practical prioritarian approach to economic evaluation of health programmes, taking into account impacts on income as well as health. Our approach proceeds in three steps.

First, we need information on the impact of health programmes, both on changes in health and changes in income after all costs are taken into account, and on baseline levels of income and health. Second, we combine individual-level information on income and health to generate an index of well-being. We describe two ways of constructing a well-being index: the equivalent life and the equivalent income approach. We measure equivalent life using a well-being function with three parameters (reference income, minimum income and the elasticity of the marginal value of income). We measure equivalent income using empirical data on willingness to pay for full health quality by income group. Third, we compare and rank health programmes by the sum of a strictly increasing and strictly concave transformation of individual levels of lifetime well-being.

We have illustrated how these two metrics can be used to conduct a lifetime prioritarian evaluation using a simple hypothetical comparison of two funding options for cancer treatment in a low-income country – out-of-pocket payment (OOP) and universal public funding (UPF) funded by taxes or compulsory insurance premiums proportional to income. In our simple example, OOP had treatment and health effects for all cancer sufferers, except the poorest part of the population without ability to pay. UPF had treatment and health effects for all cancer sufferers, and income effects for all population subgroups through taxation. Compared with OOP, UPF increases utilization of cancer treatment and reduces current period income in the lowest-income group of cancer sufferers: they now receive treatment, rather than remaining untreated, but have to pay insurance premiums. The overall effect is to increase lifetime income as well as lifetime health in this subgroup, since they live longer. UPF has no effect on utilization, health or total income in other groups, but effects a progressive income redistribution from healthy (people without cancer) to sick (people with cancer) – people without cancer now pay additional insurance premiums while people with cancer only pay insurance but not higher out-of-pocket costs – with further progressivity since premiums are proportional to income.

We find that standard cost-effectiveness analysis and benefit-cost analysis are not sensitive to income redistribution, and so in our example their recommendations depend only on the total effects on health and income in the poorest group of cancer sufferers. Lifetime prioritarian evaluation is sensitive not only to total effects on health and income but also to progressive redistribution of lifetime income, health and well-being favouring the worse off. It is more data intensive, however, since it requires effect estimates to be broken down by social group and it also requires baseline estimates of income and health for each social group from birth to death.

6.A Appendix

6.A.1 A Simple Parameterization of the Equivalent Income

In this appendix section we show how equivalent income could be operationalized in the same parametric way used to operationalize equivalent life, rather than in the non-parametric way used in the chapter based on estimates of willingness to pay for full health by income groups. We can impose the assumption of the well-being function in (6.6), and then use the equivalence condition in (6.4), to derive the expression for equivalent income under these assumptions.

More specifically, substitute equation 6.6 for the period-specific well-being function in the equivalence condition in 6.4, and get:

$$\sum_{t=0}^{l_{max}-1} \left\{ h_{max} + A - B \times \left(y_t^*\right)^{1-\eta} - 1 \right\} = \sum_{t=0}^{l-1} \left\{ h_t + A - B \times y_t^{1-\eta} - 1 \right\} \tag{6.A.1.1}$$

This is the equivalence condition expressed as a trade-off over lifetime. To express lifetime equivalent income from it, it is useful to re-write the condition as multiple short-term trade offs in each year up to the full lifespan l_{max}:[23],[24]

[23] When assuming the well-being function defined by (6.6) and the annual stream of income to be exogenously given, analysing the lifetime equivalence condition or trade-off in (6.A.1.1.) will yield the same expression for lifetime equivalent income as analysing the multiple short-term trade-offs in each year as in (6.A.1.2), and then aggregating the annual equivalent income.

[24] In the potential extra life years t of full lifespan which go beyond the individual's actual lifespan, i.e., for t values when $l<t\leq l_{max}$, we are comparing the well-being from full health and equivalent income, with the well-being from being dead, i.e., zero well-being.

$$\begin{cases} h_{max} + A - B \times \left(y_t^*\right)^{1-\eta} - 1 = h_t + A - B \times y_t^{1-\eta} - 1, & for\ 0 \le t < l \\ h_{max} + A - B \times \left(y_t^*\right)^{1-\eta} - 1 = 0, & for\ l \le t \le l_{max} \end{cases} \tag{6.A.1.2}$$

When we express y_t^* from equation 6.A.1.2 and substitute in the equations for constants *A, B* as defined for equation 6.6, we obtain the following expression for equivalent income annually for each year *t*:

$$y_t^* = \begin{cases} \left(y_t^{1-\eta} + \left(y_{min}^{1-\eta} - y_{std}^{1-\eta}\right)(1 - h_t)\right)^{\frac{1}{1-\eta}}, & for\ 0 \le t < l \\ y_{min}, & for\ l \le t \le l_{max} \end{cases} \tag{6.A.1.3}$$

We can aggregate the yearly equivalent income in 6.A.1.3 over the full lifespan to get the expression for full lifetime equivalent income as:

$$\sum_{t=0}^{l_{max}-1} y_t^* = \sum_{t=0}^{l-1} \left(y_t^{1-\eta} + \left(y_{min}^{1-\eta} - y_{std}^{1-\eta}\right)(1 - h_t)\right)^{\frac{1}{1-\eta}} + (l_{max} - l) y_{min} \tag{6.A.1.4}$$

From (6.A.1.4) we can also express WTP for each year of full health over one's life and up to the full lifespan, as the difference between one's actual income and the hypothetical equivalent income each year:

$$\begin{aligned} WTP(h_t \to 1) &= y_t - y_t^* \\ &= \begin{cases} y_t - \left(y_t^{1-\eta} + \left(y_{min}^{1-\eta} - y_{std}^{1-\eta}\right)(1 - h_t)\right)^{\frac{1}{1-\eta}}, & for\ 0 \le t < l \\ 0 - y_t^* = -y_{min}, & for\ l \le t \le l_{max} \end{cases} \end{aligned} \tag{6.A.1.5}$$

In the years up to one's actual lifespan, i.e., for *t*-values such that $0 \le t < l$, the WTP for full health is a function of one's income and health $WTP(h_t \to 1) = f(y_t, h_t)$, moreover this function is increasing in one's actual income and decreasing in one's actual health quality, i.e. $\frac{\partial f(y_t, h_t)}{\partial y_t} > 0$ and $\frac{\partial f(y_t, h_t)}{\partial h_t} < 0$. In the potential extra years that go beyond one's actual lifespan, i.e. for values of *t* such that $l \le t \le l_{max}$, the WTP is simply "minus y_{min}". It means that an individual would be willing to "trade off being dead with being alive" if they were given at least the income of y_{min}, which would "make the year of life barely worth living" (which is the anchor point of the well-being function characterized in (6.6), for a year in full health but with income of y_{min}).

6.A.2. When Are Equivalent Life and Equivalent Health Equivalent?

In this appendix section we show that equivalent life and equivalent health will yield the same recommendations if they are both operationalized using the well-being function represented by equation 6.6. This result only holds, however, if we use a function that is additively separable in health and income.

Let us re-write the equivalence condition in 6.3 so that it defines the lifetime vector of "equivalent health quality" $\mathbf{h}^*$:

$$w\left(\mathbf{y}_{\mathrm{std}}, \mathbf{h}^*, l_{max}\right) = w(\mathbf{y}, \mathbf{h}, l) \tag{6.A.2.1}$$

$\mathbf{h}^*$ here represents "equivalent health": it is the hypothetical lifetime vector of health quality that, together with full lifespan l_{max} and a reference "good" level of income $\mathbf{y}_{\mathrm{std}}$, would generate the same well-being for the individual as her actual situation.

To express lifetime equivalent health, it is useful to re-write the condition as multiple short-term trade-offs in each year up to the full lifespan l_{max}:[25]

$$\begin{cases} h_t^* + A - B \times y_{std}^{1-\eta} - 1 = h_t + A - B \times y_t^{1-\eta} - 1, & for\ 0 \leq t < l \\ h_t^* + A - B \times y_{std}^{1-\eta} - 1 = 0, & for\ l \leq t \leq l_{max} \end{cases} \tag{6.A.2.2}$$

In 6.A.2.2 the trade-offs in the years beyond one's death, i.e. for t such that $l < t \leq l_{max}$ involves making the comparison to "being dead" which would yield a well-being of zero.

When we express the annual equivalent health h_t^* from 6.A.2.2, we get:

$$h_t^* = \begin{cases} h_t + A - B \times y_t^{1-\eta} - 1, & for\ 0 \leq t < l \\ 0, & for\ l \leq t \leq l_{max} \end{cases} \tag{6.A.2.3}$$

When the annual expressions up to the full lifespan are aggregated, then one gets the expression for lifetime equivalent health

[25] When we assume the well-being function in 6.6 and the annual stream of income to be exogenously given, analysing the lifetime trade-off in equation 6.A.2.1 will yield the same answer for equivalent health as analyzing multiple short-term trade-offs in each year, up to the full lifespan l_{max}, as in 6.A.2.2.

$h^* = \sum_{t=0}^{l-1}\left\{h_t + A - B \times y_t^{1-\eta} - 1\right\}$, which is the same as the expression for equivalent life in equation 6.8.

This result would not necessarily hold, however, if health and income were not additively separable in the well-being function, e.g. in the case when there are important interactions between health and income.

6.A.3 Prioritarian SWFs for Equivalent Life and Equivalent Income

In this appendix we write down the formal equations for the prioritarian SWFs used in the illustrative example. If we assume a population of N individuals, indexed by *i=1..N*, and denote by w_i the lifetime well-being of individual i, then we can quantify social welfare S as:

$$S = \sum_{i=1}^{N} g(w_i), \text{ where}$$
$$g(w_i) = \begin{cases} \dfrac{1}{1-\gamma}\{w_i\}^{1-\gamma} \; for\, \gamma \geq 0 \; and\, \gamma \neq 1 \\ g(w_i) = ln\, w_i \; for\, \gamma = 1 \end{cases} \tag{6.A.3.1}$$

When $\gamma = 0$, equation 6.A.3.1 represents a utilitarian evaluation, and when $\gamma > 0$, then it represents a prioritarian evaluation.

In Section 6.4 (illustrative example – cancer in Ethiopia), we evaluate social welfare in three policy scenarios – the baseline scenario, out-of-pocket finance policy scenario and universal public finance policy scenario. We use both well-being measures:

- equivalent life, i.e., $w_i(h_i, y_i) = l_i^*$ where l_i^* is defined by equation (6.8); and
- equivalent income, i.e., $w_i(h_i, y_i) = y_i^*$ where y_i^* defined by equation (6.5).

Below, we show how to derive these well-being measures in the three scenarios.

6.A.3.1 Baseline Scenario

Assume that a subset of individuals $i \in C$ are ill with cancer, and they pay an out-of-pocket fixed cost $e > 0$ per year they are alive for ineffective palliative care; the rest of the individuals pay nothing.

The lifetime equivalent income of individual i can be expressed as:

$$\begin{aligned} y^*_i &= \sum_{t=0}^{49} y^*_{it} + \sum_{t=50}^{l_i-1} y^*_{it} \\ &= \sum_{t=0}^{49} (y_{it} - WTP_i \times (1 - h_{it})) + \sum_{t=50}^{l_i-1} (y_{it} - e_{|i\in C} - WTP_i \times (1 - h_{it})) \end{aligned} \tag{6.A.3.2}$$

where $e_{|i\in C}$ means that the cost e is faced only if an individual is in the group with cancer, $i \in C$, and is zero otherwise.

Similarly, we will use this notation for other variables, e.g. for any variable x:

$$x_{|i\in C} = \begin{cases} x, & if\ i \in C \\ 0, & if\ otherwise \end{cases}$$

The equivalent life of individual i can be quantified as:

$$\begin{aligned} l^*_i = \sum_{t=0}^{49} l^*_{it} + \sum_{t=50}^{l_i-1} l^*_{it} &= \sum_{t=0}^{49} \left\{ h_{it} + A - B \times (y_{it})^{1-\eta} - 1 \right\} \\ &+ \sum_{t=50}^{l_i-1} \left\{ h_{it} + A - B \times \left(y_{it} - e_{|i\in C}\right)^{1-\eta} - 1 \right\} \end{aligned} \tag{6.A.3.3}$$

where A and B, are the constants as defined for equation 6.6.

6.A.3.2 *Out-of-Pocket Finance Policy Scenario*

Assume that the subset of individuals with cancer $i \in C$ can now receive an effective treatment which costs z per year out-of-pocket to the cancer patient and yields a benefit for the treated individual i in the form of l_i' added life years and added health quality in each year equal to h_i'. Also, this treatment cannot be afforded by the poorest individuals in the lowest income quintile group (i.e., income quintile group 1), marked by $g = 1$.

In this scenario, the lifetime equivalent income of individual i can be expressed as:

$$y^*_i = \sum_{t=0}^{49} y^*_{it} + \sum_{t=50}^{l_i - 1 + l'_{i|i\in C\&g\neq 1}} y^*_{it} = \sum_{t=0}^{49} (y_{it} - WTP_i \times (1 - h_{it})) + \sum_{t=50}^{l_i - 1 + l'_{i|i\in C\&g\neq 1}} \Big(y_{it} - z_{|i\in C\&g\neq 1} - e_{|i\in C\&g=1} - WTP_i \times \Big(1 - h_{it} - h'_{i|i\in C\&g\neq 1}\Big)\Big) \quad (6.A.3.4)$$

Where for any variable $x_{|i\in C\&g\neq 1} = \begin{cases} x, & if\ i \in C\ and\ g \neq 1 \\ 0, & if\ otherwise \end{cases}$, which means that any variable x applies only to the cancer patients not in the first income quintile group, and is zero otherwise; and where $e_{|i\in C\&g=1} = \begin{cases} e, & if\ i \in C\ and\ g = 1 \\ 0, & if\ otherwise \end{cases}$ means that the palliative care cost e is faced by the cancer patients in the bottom income quintile group only.

Similarly, the equivalent life of individual i can be quantified as:

$$l^*_i = \sum_{t=0}^{49} l^*_{it} + \sum_{t=50}^{l_i - 1 + l'_{i|i\in C\&g\neq 1}} l^*_{it} = \sum_{t=0}^{49} \Big\{h_{it} + A - B \times (y_{it})^{1-\eta} - 1\Big\} + \sum_{t=50}^{l_i - 1 + l'_{i|i\in C\&g\neq 1}} \Big\{h_{it} + h'_{i|i\in C\&g\neq 1} + A - B \times \big(y_{it} - z_{|i\in C\&g\neq 1} - e_{|i\in C\&g=1}\big)^{1-\eta} - 1\Big\} \quad (6.A.3.5)$$

6.A.3.3 *Universal Public Finance Policy*

Assume the scenario above, but the cancer treatment is covered by a public tax, defined as a proportion τ of income. In this case, cancer patients in quintile 1, with low ability to pay out-of-pocket, will also receive treatment. Also, we assume $\sum_{i=1}^{N} \Big(l_i - 1 + l'_{i|i\in C} - 49\Big) \times z_{|i\in C} = \tau \times \sum_{i=1}^{N} \sum_{t=50}^{l_i - 1 + l'_{i|i\in C}} y_{it}$ (the tax rate is such that it exactly covers the cohort health care costs).

In this scenario, the lifetime equivalent income of individual i can be expressed as:

$$y^*_i = \sum_{t=0}^{49} y^*_{it} + \sum_{t=50}^{l_i-1+l'_{i|i\in C}} y^*_{it} = \sum_{t=0}^{49} (y_{it} - WTP_i \times (1 - h_{it})) + \sum_{t=50}^{l_i-1+l'_{i|i\in C}} \left((1-\tau) \times y_{it} - WTP_i \times \left(1 - h_{it} - h'_{i|i\in C}\right)\right) \quad (6.A.3.6)$$

Similarly, the equivalent life of individual i can be quantified as:

$$l^*_i = \sum_{t=0}^{49} l^*_{it} + \sum_{t=50}^{l_i-1+l'_{i|i\in C}} l^*_{it} = \sum_{t=0}^{49} \left\{ h_{it} + A - B \times (y_{it})^{1-\eta} - 1 \right\} + \sum_{t=50}^{l_i-1+l'_{i|i\in C}} \left\{ h_{it} + h'_{i|i\in C} + A - B \times ((1-\tau) \times y_{it})^{1-\eta} - 1 \right\} \quad (6.A.3.7)$$

6.A.3.4 *Ex Ante Evaluation*

To calculate the *ex ante* social welfare, we use $E(w_j)$ as input in the social welfare transform *g()*, where $E(w_j)$ denotes the expected lifetime well-being at *t=0* for an individual in quintile group *j*, calculated for all quintile groups *j=1,..,5*:

$$S^{EAP} = \frac{N}{5} \sum_{j=1}^{5} g(\, E(w_j) \,) = \frac{N}{5} \sum_{j=1}^{5} g\left(\sum_{t=0}^{l_{max}-1} w_{jt}\, p_{jt} \right)$$

The expected lifetime well-being for group *j*, is calculated as $E(w_j) = \sum_{t=0}^{l_{max}-1} w_{jt}\, p_{jt}$, where p_{jt} is the probability that an individual in group *j* survives up to age *t*. Finally, we multiply the term with $\frac{N}{5}$ which is the number of people in each quintile group.

For simplicity, we do not distinguish here between individuals with and without cancer, but we carry out this calculation separately for both groups – the group with cancer and the group without cancer.

6.A.3.5 *Ex Post Evaluation*

If individual-level data were available, we could calculate the *ex post* social welfare as follows:

$$S^{EPP} = \sum_{i=1}^{N} g\left(\sum_{t=0}^{l_i-1} w_{it}\right)$$

However, as we do not have individual-level data on well-being, we estimate the *ex post* well-being distribution using period-specific survival probabilities for each income quintile group (that we extract from our Markov model), and then use that as input in the social welfare transform *g()*:

$$S^{EPP} = \frac{N}{5}\sum_{j=1}^{5}\sum_{t=0}^{l_{max}-1}\left\{\left(p_{jt} - p_{j\,t+1}\right) g\left(\sum_{\tau=0}^{t} w_{j\tau}\right)\right\}$$

More specifically, as we do not have information on w_{it} but only on w_{jt}, we estimate the proportion of people in each quintile group *j* who have survived up to age t (or, alternatively, people dying at age *t+1*) as $p_{jt} - p_{jt+1}$ and multiply that with their lifetime well-being, which can be calculated as the cumulative sum of well-being up to age *t*, $\sum_{\tau=0}^{t} w_{j\tau}$.

6.A.4 Alternative Tables (Equal Costs in OOP and UPF: Cancer Patients in Quintile 1 Receive Treatment under OOP)

Table 6.A.4.1. *Summary results for all evaluation approaches*

	Baseline		OOP		UPF	
Gamma	Equivalent income, US$	Equivalent life, well-being QALYs	Equivalent income, US$	Equivalent life, well-being QALYs	Equivalent income, US$	Equivalent life, well-being QALYs
Utilitarian						
0	49,022	61.8	50,046	63.7	50,046	64.3
Ex ante prioritarian, EDE						
0.5	45,641	60.9	46,669	62.9	46,929	63.7
1	42,297	60.0	43,290	62.1	43,826	63.0
1.5	39,109	59.1	40,029	61.3	40,845	62.4
2	36,184	58.3	37,005	60.4	38,084	61.8
Ex post, EDE						
0.5	45,560	60.8	46,565	62.8	46,799	63.5
1	42,152	59.8	43,101	61.8	43,575	62.7
1.5	38,916	58.9	39,777	60.8	40,483	61.8
2	35,958	57.9	36,711	59.8	37,624	61.0

Table 6.A.4.2. *Benefit–cost analysis*

	OOP vs baseline		UPF vs OOP	
	Benefit, US$	Cost, US$	Benefit, US$	Cost, US$
Including survivor consumption benefits				
	3,459	1,067	0.00	0.00
Benefit-cost ratio	3.24		NA	
Excluding survivor consumption benefits				
	2,328	1,067	564.07	214.90
Benefit-cost ratio	2.18		2.68	

Note: The benefits including survivor consumption benefits consist of income and health benefits. The benefits excluding survivor consumption benefits consist only of health benefits. Health benefits are converted to monetary terms using the population average willingness to pay for health.

References

Adler, M. (2012). *Well-Being and Fair Distribution: Beyond Cost-Benefit Analysis*. New York: Oxford University Press.

(2016). Benefit–cost analysis and distributional weights: An overview. *Review of Environmental Economics and Policy*, 10, 264–285.

(2019). *Measuring Social Welfare: An Introduction*. New York: Oxford University Press.

(2020). Social Welfare Functions. In O.F. Norheim, E. Emanuel, and J. Millum (eds.), *Global Health Priority-Setting: Beyond Cost-Effectiveness*. New York: Oxford University Press.

Adler, M., and Holtug, N. (2019). Prioritarianism: A response to critics. *Politics, Philosophy & Economics*, 18 101–144.

Anand, S. (2002). The concern for equity in health. *Journal of Epidemiology and Community Health*, 56, 485–487.

Anand, S., Diderichsen, F., Evans, T., Shkolnikov, V.M., and Wirth, M. (2001). Measuring disparities in health: methods and indicators. In T. Evans, M. Whitehead, F. Diderichsen, A. Bhuiya, and M. Wirth (eds.), *Challenging Inequities in Health: From Ethics to Action*, pp. 49–67. Oxford: Oxford University Press.

Anand, S., and Nanthikesan, N. (2001). A compilation of length-of-life distribution measures for abridged life tables. Working paper. Harvard Center for Population and Development Studies.

Asaria, M., Griffin, S., and Cookson, R. (2016). Distributional cost-effectiveness analysis: A tutorial. *Medical Decision Making*, 36, 8–19.

Asaria, M., Griffin, S., Cookson, R., Whyte, S., and Tappenden, P. (2015). Distributional cost-effectiveness analysis of health care programmes – a methodological case study of the UK Bowel Cancer Screening Programme. *Health Economics*, 24, 742–754.

Bleichrodt, H., Diecidue, E., and Quiggin, J. (2004). Equity weights in the allocation of health care: the rank-dependent QALY model. *Journal of Health Economics*, 23, 157–171.

Bleichrodt, H., Doctor, J., and Stolk, E. (2005). A nonparametric elicitation of the equity-efficiency trade-off in cost-utility analysis. *Journal of Health Economics*, 24, 655–678.

Bleichrodt, H., and Gafni, A. (1996). Time preference, the discounted utility model and health. *Journal of Health Economics*, 15, 49–66.

Boadway, R.W. (2016). Cost-Benefit Analysis. In M.D. Adler, and M. Fleurbaey (eds.), *The Oxford Handbook of Well-Being and Public Policy*, pp. 47–81. New York: Oxford University Press.

Boardman, A.E., Greenberg, D.H., Vining, A., and Weimer, D.L. (2018). *Cost-Benefit Analysis: Concepts and Practice*, 5th ed. Boston: Cambridge University Press.

Bobinac, A., van Exel, N.J., Rutten, F.F., and Brouwer, W.B. (2012). Inquiry into the relationship between equity weights and the value of the QALY. *Value in Health*, 15, 1119–1126.

Canning, D. (2013). Axiomatic foundations for cost-effectiveness analysis. *Health Economics*, 22, 1405–1416.

Chang, A., Horton, S., and Jamison, D.T. (2018). Chapter 9. Benefit-Cost Analysis in Disease Control Priorities, 3rd ed. In D.T. Jamison, H. Gelband, S. Horton, P. Jha, R. Laxminarayan, C.N. Mock, et al. (eds.), *Disease Control Priorities: Improving Health and Reducing Poverty. Disease Control Priorities* (3rd ed.), Volume 9. Washington, DC.: World Bank.

Claxton, K., Paulden, M., Gravelle, H., Brouwer, W., and Culyer, A.J. (2011). Discounting and decision making in the economic evaluation of health-care technologies. *Health Economics*, 20, 2–15.

Cookson, R. (2015). Justice and the NICE approach. *Journal of Medical Ethics*, 41, 99–102.

Cookson, R., Griffin, S., Norheim, O.F., and Culyer, A.C. (eds.) (2020). *Distributional Cost-Effectiveness Analysis. Quantifying Health Equity Impacts and Trade-Offs*. Oxford: Oxford University Press.

Cookson, R., Griffin, S., Norheim, O.F., Culyer, A.J., and Chalkidou, K. (2021a). Distributional cost-effectiveness analysis comes of age. *Value in Health*, 24, 118–120.

Cookson, R., Mirelman, A.J., Griffin, S., et al. (2017). Using cost-effectiveness analysis to address health equity concerns. *Value in Health*, 20, 206–212.

Cookson, R., Skarda, I., Cotton-Barratt, O., Adler, M., Asaria, M., and Ord, T. (2021b). Quality adjusted life years based on health and consumption: A summary wellbeing measure for cross-sectoral economic evaluation. *Health Economics*, 30, 70–85.

Culyer, A.J. (2016). Cost-effectiveness thresholds in health care: A bookshelf guide to their meaning and use. *Health Economics, Policy and Law*, 11, 415–432.

Deaton, A. and Muellbauer, J. (1980). *Economics and Consumer Behavior.* Cambridge: Cambridge University Press.

Dolan, P., Shaw, R., Tsuchiya, A., and Williams, A. (2005). QALY maximisation and people's preferences: A methodological review of the literature. *Health Economics*, 14, 197–208.

Dolan, P., and Tsuchiya, A. (2012). It is the lifetime that matters: Public preferences over maximising health and reducing inequalities in health. *Journal of Medical Ethics*, 38, 571–573.

Drummond, M.F., Sculpher, M., Claxton, K., Stoddart, G.L., and Torrance, G.W. (2015). *Methods for the Economic Evaluation of Health Care Programmes*. Oxford: Oxford University Press.

Faria, R.O. J., and Lomas, J. (2020). Opportunity costs, marginal productivity, and cost-effectiveness thresholds: what are they and how are they related https://aheblog.com/2020/09/23/opportunity-costs-marginal-productivity-and-cost-effectiveness-thresholds-what-are-they-and-how-are-they-related/ (accessed January 4, 2020).

Fleurbaey, M. and Blanchet, D. (2013). *Beyond GDP: Measuring Welfare and Assessing Sustainability*. Oxford: Oxford University Press.

Fleurbaey, M. and Maniquet, F.A. (2011). *Theory of Fairness and Social Welfare*. Cambridge: Cambridge University Press.

Fleurbaey, M., and Schokkaert, E. (2009). Unfair inequalities in health and health care. *Journal of Health Economics*, 28, 73–90, 28, 73-90.

Fujiwara, D. (2010). The Department for Work and Pensions Social Cost-Benefit Analysis framework Methodologies for estimating and incorporating the wider social and economic impacts of work in Cost- Benefit Analysis of employment programmes. A report of research carried out by the Department for Work and Pensions. Working Paper No 86. London.

Garber, A.M., and Phelps, C.E. (1997). Economic foundations of cost-effectiveness analysis. *Journal of Health Economics*, 16, 1–31.

Gold, M.R., Stevenson, D., and Fryback, D.G. (2002). HALYS and QALYS and DALYS, Oh My: similarities and differences in summary measures of population Health. *Annual Review of Public Health*, 23, 115–134.

Hammitt, J.K. (2002). QALYs versus WTP. *Risk Analysis*, 22, 985–1001.

(2013). Admissible Utility Functions for Health, Longevity, and Wealth: Integrating Monetary and Life-Year Measures. *Journal of Risk and Uncertainty*, 47, 311–325.

(2017). Valuing Non-Fatal Health Risks: Monetary and Health-Utility Measures. *Revue Économique*, 68, 335–356.

Hernæs, U.J.V., Johansson, K.A., Ottersen, T., and Norheim, O.F. (2017). Distribution-weighted cost-effectiveness analysis using lifetime health loss. *Pharmacoeconomics*, 35, 965–974.

HM Treasury. (2018). *The Green Book. Central Government Guidance on Appraisal and Evaluation*. London: Crown copyright.

Jamison, D.T., Jamison, J., Norheim, O.F., and Verguet, S. (2020). Inequality in Survival. In O.F. Norheim, E. Emanuel, and J. Millum (eds.), *Global Health Priority-Setting: Beyond Cost-Effectiveness*. New York: Oxford University Press.

Johansson, Kjell Arne et al. (2020) Health by disease categories. In Richard Cookson, Susan Griffin, Ole F. Norheim, and Anthony Culyer, (eds.), *Distributional Cost-Effectiveness Analysis: Quantifying Health Equity Impacts and Trade-Offs*. Oxford: Oxford University Press.

Johansson, K.A., and Norheim, O.F. (2011). Problems with prioritization: exploring ethical solutions to inequalities in HIV care. *American Journal of Bioethics*, 11, 32–40.

Johri, M., and Norheim, O.F. (2012). Can cost-effectiveness analysis integrate concerns for equity? Systematic review. *International Journal of Technology Assessment in Health Care*, 28, 125–132.

Lal, A., Moodie, M., Peeters, A., and Carter, R. (2018). Inclusion of equity in economic analyses of public health policies: systematic review and future directions. *Australian and New Zealand Journal of Public Health*, 42, 207–213.

Layard, R., Mayraz, G., and Nickell, S. (2008). The marginal utility of income. *Journal of Public Economics*, 92, 1846–1857.

McIntosh, E., Clarke, P., Frew, E., and Louviere, J. (eds.) (2010). *Applied Methods of Cost-Benefit Analysis in Health Care*. London: Oxford University Press.

Neumann, P.J., Sanders, G.D., Russell, L.B., Siegel, J.E. and Ganiats, T.G. (eds.) (2017). *Cost-Effectiveness in Health and Medicine.* 2nd ed. New York: Oxford University Press.

Nord, E. (1993). [Health care politicians are not concerned about maximum health gain per crown]. [Norwegian]. *Tidsskrift for Den Norske Laegeforening*, 113, 1371–1373.

(1999). *Cost-Value Analysis in Health Care*. Cambridge: Cambridge University Press.

Nord, E., Pinto, J.L., Richardson, J., Menzel, P., and Ubel, P. (1999). Incorporating societal concerns for fairness in numerical valuations of health programmes. *Health Economics*, 8, 25–39.

Norheim, O.F. (2013). Atkinson's index applied to health: can measures of economic inequality help us understand trade-offs in health care priority setting? In N. Eyal, S. Hurst, O.F. Norheim, and D. Wikler (eds.), *Inequalities in Health: Ethics and Measurement*, pp. 214–230. New York: Oxford University Press.

Norheim, O.F., Asaria, M., Johansson, K.A., Ottersen, T., and Tsuchiya, A. (2020). Chapter 13: Level-dependent equity weights. In R. Cookson, A.J. Culyer, S. Griffin, and O.F. Norheim (eds.), *Distributional Cost-Effectiveness Analysis. Quantifying Health Equity Impacts and Trade-Offs*, pp. 253–274. Oxford: Oxford University Press.

Norheim, O.F., Ottersen, T., Tolla, M.T., Memirie, S.T., and Johansson, K.A. (2019). Incorporating distributional concerns into practical tools for priority setting. In O.F. Norheim, E. Emanuel, and J. Millum (eds.), *Global Health Priority-Setting: Beyond Cost-Effectiveness*. New York: Oxford University Press.

O'Donnel, O., and Van Ourti, T. (2020). Chapter 11: Dominance analysis. In R. Cookson, S. Griffin, O.F. Norheim, and A.C. Culyer (eds.), *Distributional Cost-Effectiveness Analysis. Quantifying Health Equity Impacts and Trade-Offs. Handbooks in Health Economic Evaluation*. Oxford: Oxford University Press.

O'Donnell, O., and Van Ourti, T. (2020). Chapter 12: Rank-dependent equity weights. In R. Cookson, S. Griffin, O.F. Norheim, and A.C. Culyer (eds.), *Distributional Cost-Effectiveness Analysis. Quantifying Health Equity Impacts and Trade-Offs. Handbooks in Health Economic Evaluation*. Oxford: Oxford University Press.

Onder, H., Pestieau, P., and Ponthière, G. (2019). Equivalent income versus equivalent lifetime: does the metric matter? Paris School of Economics, Working Paper No. 41. halshs-02187803

Ottersen, T. (2013). Lifetime QALY prioritarianism in priority setting. *Journal of Medical Ethics*, 39, 175–180.

Ottersen, T., Mæstad, O., and Norheim, O.F. (2014). Lifetime QALY prioritarianism in priority setting: quantification of the inherent trade-off. *Cost-Effectiveness and Resource Allocation*, 12, 2.

Robberstad, B. (2005). QALYs vs DALYs vs LYs gained: What are the differences, and what difference do they make for health care priority setting? *Norsk Epidemiologi*, 15, 183–191.

Robinson, L., Hammitt, J., Cecchini, M., et al. (2019a). *Reference Case Guidelines for Benefit-Cost Analysis in Global Health and Development* (accessed December 16, 2020).

Robinson, L., Hammitt, J., Jamison, D., and Walker, D. (2019b). Conducting benefit-cost analysis in low- and middle-income countries: introduction to the special issue. *Journal of Benefit-Cost Analysis*, 10, 1–14.

Robinson, L.A., and Hammitt, J.K. (2016). Valuing reductions in fatal illness risks: implications of recent research. *Health Economics*, 25, 1039–1052.

Robinson, L.A., Hammitt, J.K., and Hammitt, M.D. A. (2018). Assessing the Distribution of Impacts in Global Benefit-Cost Analysis, Guidelines for Benefit-Cost Analysis Project, Working Paper No. 3.

Robinson, L.A., Hammitt, J.K., and Zeckhauser, R.J. (2016). Attention to distribution in U.S. regulatory analyses. *Review of Environmental Economics and Policy*, 10, 308–328.

Samson, A.L., Schokkaert, E., Thébaut, C., et al. (2018). Fairness in cost-benefit analysis: A methodology for health technology assessment. *Health Economics*, 27, 102–114.

Sanders, G.D., Neumann, P.J., Basu, A., et al. (2016). Recommendations for conduct, methodological practices, and reporting of cost-effectiveness analyses: second panel on cost-effectiveness in health and medicine. *Journal of the American Medical Association*, 316, 1093–1103.

Sassi, F., Archard, L., and Le Grand, J. (2001). Equity and the economic evaluation of healthcare. *Health Technology Assessment*, 5.

US Department of Health and Human Services. (2016). Guidelines for Regulatory Impact Analysis.

Verguet, S., and Norheim, O.F. (2021). Estimating and comparing health and financial risk protection outcomes in economic evaluations: *Value in Health* (in press).

Wagstaff, A. (1991). QALYs and the equity-efficiency trade-off. *Journal of Health Economics*, 10, 21–41.

Wailoo, A., Tsuchiya, A., and McCabe, C. (2009). Weighting must wait: Incorporating equity concerns into cost-effectiveness analysis may take longer than expected. *Pharmacoeconomics*, 27, 983–989.

Woods, B., Revill, P., Sculpher, M., and Claxton, K. (2016). Country-level cost-effectiveness thresholds: Initial estimates and the need for further research. *Value in Health*, 19, 929–935.

7 Prioritarianism and Fatality Risk Regulation

JAMES K. HAMMITT AND
NICOLAS TREICH*

7.1 Introduction

Many forms of government regulation are designed to decrease risks of death from particular hazards, leading to increases in life expectancy. In some cases, reducing risks of death (and of nonfatal illness or injury) is the primary objective (as in food, transportation, and occupational safety); in other cases, reducing health risks is but one of several objectives (as in much of environmental regulation). Even when it is not the sole objective, reduction of fatality risks can dominate the quantified benefits. For example, estimates of the benefits of the U.S. 1990 Clean Air Act amendments find that 85 to 95 percent of the quantified annual benefit is due to the reduction in mortality risk (U.S. Environmental Protection Agency 2011, table 7.1). Lee and Taylor (2019) estimate that reductions in mortality risk account for up to 70 percent of the quantified benefits of recent major U.S. federal regulations. In part this dominance reflects the much greater value estimated for reducing fatal rather than nonfatal health risks. It also reflects the fact that many nonfatal health effects and environmental consequences are not included in the evaluation because monetary values have not been estimated for many of these numerous and diverse effects.

Regulations that affect fatality risks are frequently evaluated using benefit-cost analysis (BCA). In the United States, such evaluation has been required for federal regulations under a series of presidential executive orders beginning in 1981; regulatory impact analysis, including quantification of benefits, costs, and distributional effects, is

* The authors thank Matthew Adler, Ole Norheim, and Maddalena Ferranna for useful comments. This work was supported by the Chair AMEP-IDEX at the University of Toulouse Capitole. James Hammitt acknowledges support from the U.S. National Science Foundation (award number 1824492). Nicolas Treich acknowledges financial support from the ANR under grant ANR-17-EURE-0010 (the Investissements d'Avenir program) and the TSE-P SCOR chair.

required by nearly all OECD member states (OECD 2018). We describe the way fatality risks are evaluated using BCA and contrast it with evaluation under several prominent social-welfare functions (SWFs).

As described in the following section, the approach to valuing mortality risk used in BCA centers on the "value per statistical life" or VSL (called the "value of a prevented fatality" or VPF in the United Kingdom). Under standard theory, the VSL is expected to vary across individuals who differ in wealth, baseline mortality risk, and other dimensions such as age. Differences in VSL between individuals imply that the benefits of reducing fatality risk depend on whose risk is reduced. Government actors and others are often uncomfortable with explicitly valuing risk reductions differently across individuals; there has been sharp public criticism when values have been differentiated based on income or age (e.g., Cameron 2010, Robinson 2007, Viscusi 2009). Perhaps as a result, it is common practice to use the same VSL for all affected individuals in a country (although it is also common to assume that VSL will increase over time in response to assumed future increases in income). The reluctance to allow VSL to vary across individuals may also reflect the tension between efficiency and distributional concerns; conventional BCA measures allocative efficiency, setting concerns about the distribution of effects aside on the assumption they will be addressed through supplementary distributional analysis.

Although most distributional analysis of U.S. regulations is qualitative (Robinson et al. 2016), a growing literature explores the use of inequality measures to quantify distributional effects, especially in the context of environmental justice. This literature uses inequality indices to evaluate the distribution of risk from, or exposure to, environmental hazards and whether racial/ethnic or low-income groups are particularly burdened. It has been applied to multiple case studies. (See Levy 2021 and Sheriff and Maguire 2020 for citations.) Key issues include adapting measures of the distribution of goods (e.g., income) to the distribution of bads (e.g., mortality risk), evaluating absolute or proportional differences, the importance of parameterizing inequality aversion, and whether inequality is evaluated across groups that are ordered (e.g., by income) or unordered (e.g., by race or ethnicity) (Levy 2021). Levy et al. (2006) reviewed multiple indices and recommended use of the Atkinson index, which measures relative differences; Sheriff and Maguire (2020) recommended the use of Fleurbaey's equally distributed equivalent measure with the Kolm-Pollak inequality index. The Kolm-Pollak index is sensitive to absolute differences and hence yields the same result when measuring differences in mortality risk as differences in survival probability; in contrast, the Atkinson index is sensitive to proportional differences and yields different results.[1]

In contrast to conventional BCA, SWFs can integrate concerns about equitable distribution with those about efficiency. We present and describe the results of using SWFs to characterize the value of reducing mortality risk through regulation. For consistency with the literature that applies BCA to environmental, health, and safety risks, we measure individual wellbeing using von Neumann-Morgenstern utility functions; for simplicity, we assume that utility functions are homogenous (i.e., that individuals have the same utility function but may differ in wealth, baseline risk, or other characteristics). Adler and Decancq (Chapter 3, this volume) describe alternative measures of individual wellbeing.

We examine three benchmark SWFs: utilitarian, ex ante prioritarian, and ex post prioritarian. The utilitarian SWF is the dominant approach in the SWF literature; prioritarian SWFs add a concern for the distribution of wellbeing (Adler, Chapter 2, this volume). In the context of fatality risk, the difference between ex ante and ex post perspectives is important, and so we examine both ex ante and ex post prioritarian SWFs.[2]

This chapter is closely related to other chapters in this volume concerned with health risk, particularly Chapter 6 on health care (Cookson, Norheim, and Skarda) and Chapter 12 on COVID-19 (Bloom, Ferranna, and Sevilla).

In the following section, the standard one-period model for VSL is presented, together with an analysis of how VSL varies with individual characteristics, specifically wealth and baseline risk. Sections 7.3 and 7.4 apply the benchmark SWFs, both utilitarian and prioritarian, to

[1] Atkinson and Kolm-Pollak measures of inequality are described by Decancq and Schokkaert (Chapter 5, this volume).

[2] Adler (Chapter 2, this volume) uses the term SWF to mean a rule for ranking wellbeing vectors and the term "uncertainty module" to mean a method for incorporating uncertainty about the vector. We use the term SWF to mean the combination of an SWF and an uncertainty module and hence describe ex ante prioritarianism and ex post prioritarianism as different SWFs.

evaluate the social value of mortality-risk reduction and how it depends on individuals' wealth and baseline risk. Section 7.3 analyzes the one-period model introduced in Section 7.2 and Section 7.4 describes a multi-period model, which permits consideration of the effects of individuals' ages. Section 7.5 presents simulations calibrated to the U.S. population that illustrate how the value of mortality-risk reduction varies by age and income under BCA and the benchmark SWFs. Section 7.6 describes two extensions: alternative SWFs that can incorporate aversion to catastrophes that produce many deaths, and evaluating effects of health and nonfatal health risks using BCA and the benchmark SWFs. Section 7.7 concludes.

7.2 Valuing Mortality Risk Changes in BCA: The Value Per Statistical Life

Benefit-cost analysis is based on measuring changes in individuals' wellbeing as monetary values. These values are positive for individuals who are better off with a policy and negative for those who are worse off. The sum of these values across the population is described as the net social benefit; if it is positive, then hypothetical compensation payments (from those who gain to those who are harmed) could be arranged such that everyone would be better off with the policy change and payment or receipt of compensation than without the policy change and compensation.

There are two alternative definitions of the monetary value of the effect of a change in mortality risk (or other policy effect). The compensating surplus is the change in wealth that compensates for the change in risk in the sense that the individual's wellbeing is unaffected by the combination of the change in risk and wealth. The compensating surplus is the individual's willingness to pay (WTP) for a risk reduction and willingness to accept compensation (WTA) for a risk increase. The equivalent surplus is the change in wealth that is equivalent to the change in risk, in the sense that either change alone has the same effect on her wellbeing. Equivalent surplus is the individual's WTA to forgo a risk decrease and WTP to prevent a risk increase. For small changes in risk, the two values are approximately equal in theory, although stated-preference studies find that the equivalent surplus (WTA to forgo a risk reduction) is often substantially larger than the compensating surplus (WTP for a risk reduction), by a factor on the order of five (Tunçel and Hammitt 2014).

The value per statistical life (VSL) is conceptualized as an individual-specific quantity equal to the individual's marginal rate of substitution of wealth for a reduction of her mortality risk in a specified period. It is the ratio of her compensating surplus for a change in mortality risk to the magnitude of the change, for infinitesimally small changes in risk. The time period is generally short (e.g., a year). Risk is defined as the probability of dying in a specified period (as a hazard rate per unit time). The value of surviving a period may depend on its duration; the value of surviving the current decade generally exceeds the value of surviving the current hour.

The conventional one-period model (Drèze 1962, Jones-Lee 1974, Weinstein et al. 1980) assumes the individual wishes to maximize her expected utility, which depends on her probability of surviving the current period and her utility conditional on surviving and on not surviving (each of which may depend on wealth). Specifically, expected utility

$$\mathrm{U = p\,u(c) + (1 - p)\,v(c)} \tag{7.1}$$

where p is the probability of surviving the period, $u(c)$ and $v(c)$ are utility conditional on surviving and not surviving the period, and c is wealth. The utility of wealth conditional on surviving the period depends on the lottery over future conditions the individual will face if she survives, including her future longevity, health, and income. The utility of wealth conditional on dying during the period is often called a bequest function; it represents the utility gained by knowing one's wealth will be passed on to one's children or other heirs in the event of one's death. Any monetary effect of dying, such as medical bills or funeral expenses, can be incorporated in the definition of the bequest function.

It is conventional and usually reasonable to assume that survival is preferred to death $(u(c) > v(c))$, the marginal utility of wealth is strictly larger given survival than as a bequest $(u'(c) > v'(c))$ and the marginal utility of a bequest is greater than or equal to zero $(v'(c) \geq 0)$. In words, it is never harmful to die with more wealth but it is better to spend it while living. It is also assumed the individual is risk averse (or risk neutral) with respect to wealth, i.e., $u''(c) \leq 0$ and $v''(c) \leq 0$.[3]

[3] A single prime denotes first derivative and a double prime denotes second derivative.

The VSL or marginal rate of substitution of wealth for survival probability is the change in wealth accompanying an infinitesimal change in survival probability that leaves the individual no better and no worse off than before (i.e., holding expected utility U constant). VSL can be obtained by differentiating equation (7.1) to obtain

$$VSL = -\frac{dw}{dp} = \frac{u(c) - v(c)}{pu'(c) + (1-p)v'(c)} = \frac{\Delta u(c)}{Eu'(c)}. \tag{7.2}$$

Equation (7.2) shows that VSL is the ratio of the gain in utility from surviving the period rather than dying ($\Delta u(c)$) to the expected opportunity cost of wealth ($EU'(c)$), which is the rate at which utility could be obtained by spending on other goods and services rather than on reducing mortality risk.

As illustrated in Figure 7.1, VSL is (the absolute value of) the slope of the individual's indifference curve between wealth and survival probability at her current wealth and mortality risk, and the monetary value of a small risk change is approximately equal to the product of VSL and the magnitude of the risk change. Under the assumptions described above, indifference curves are downward sloping and convex, as illustrated. Because increases in wealth and survival probability are both desirable, indifference curves are downward sloping (the individual is willing to give up some of one attribute to obtain more of the other). The indifference curves are convex because holding survival probability fixed, an increase in wealth increases VSL[4] and holding wealth fixed, an increase in survival probability decreases VSL.[5]

A slope is quantified as rise over run; by convention, VSL is measured for a run (change in survival probability) from 0 to 1. As is clear from Figure 7.1, the amount an individual would accept as compensation for a decrease in survival probability from 1 to 0 is much larger

[4] An increase in wealth increases the numerator of equation (7.2) (because the marginal utility of wealth is larger conditional on survival than on death) and (weakly) decreases the denominator (because the utility conditional on survival and the bequest exhibit weakly decreasing marginal utility).

[5] An increase in survival probability has no effect on the numerator of equation (7.2) but increases the denominator as it puts more weight on the (larger) marginal utility of wealth conditional on survival and less weight on the (smaller) marginal utility of a bequest. Pratt and Zeckhauser (1996) call this the "dead-anyway effect" because if survival probability is low, spending is likely to come out of the bequest and the opportunity cost of spending is small.

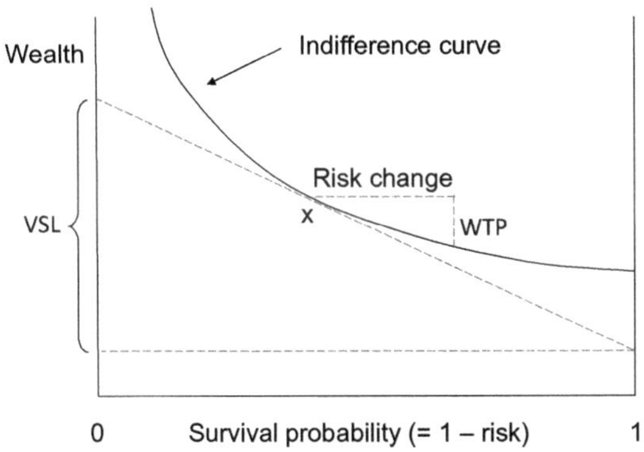

Figure 7.1 VSL is the slope of the indifference curve between the individual's wealth and survival probability at her current position

than her VSL (at survival probability 1) and may be infinite (if the indifference curve does not intersect the vertical axis); the amount she would pay to increase survival probability from 0 to 1 is much less than her VSL (at survival probability near zero). Indeed, conventional estimates of VSL greatly exceed individual wealth, and so an individual would be unable to pay as much as her VSL to avoid certain death.

Government agents and the public can be uncomfortable applying different values of risk reduction to different people. This concern is exacerbated by the term value per statistical life, which is easily misunderstood as measuring the total value of an individual's life (Cameron 2010, Simon et al. 2019). Benefit-cost analyses of policies that affect a domestic population almost invariably value risk reductions to different individuals using a common VSL, independent of income, age, health, and other factors. For policies that reduce current mortality risk by the same amount for each person, or for which individual risk reductions are uncorrelated with factors such as age and income that affect VSL, the use of a common value is unproblematic.[6] When comparing policies that disproportionately affect different subpopulations (e.g., young v. old, rich v. poor), use of a common VSL may be

[6] Under BCA, the social value of reducing mortality risk by a small amount for many people equals the sum of the affected individuals' monetary values, which are approximately equal to the product of each individual's risk reduction and VSL. If the individual risk reductions are equal to each other or are uncorrelated with individuals' VSLs, this sum is equal to the sum of the average risk reduction multiplied by the average VSL.

inconsistent with the principles on which BCA is based and can produce biased results. Use of a common VSL may produce results that better accord with preferences for equity that might be obtained using a weighted BCA. Baker et al. (2008) examined the question of when a common VSL might exist and suggest using weighted BCA.

Social-welfare functions provide a means for explicitly incorporating concerns for both efficiency and equity in a policy evaluation. In Section 7.3, we describe the application of SWFs to valuing fatality risk in the context of the standard one-period model described above. In Section 7.4, we extend the analysis to life-cycle models that allow comparison of the value of reducing risk to individuals of different ages. We present simulation results illustrating the magnitudes of the effects in Section 7.5.

7.3 SWFs Applied To a Single-Period Model

Using the single-period model described above (equation (7.1)), Adler et al. (2014) evaluated how changes to individuals' survival probabilities affect social welfare as measured by alternative social-welfare functions. They defined the "social value of risk reduction" (SVRR) as the rate of increase in social welfare resulting from a small increase to an individual's survival probability, i.e., as the partial derivative of social welfare with respect to an individual's survival probability. SVRR for an SWF is the analog of VSL for BCA, as VSL measures the rate of increase of net social benefits associated with a small increase to an individual's survival probability. Exploiting this analogy, we describe VSL as the SVRR under BCA. Adler et al. (2014) examined how SVRR depends on wealth and baseline risk under different SWFs; as noted above, VSL is increasing in these attributes. In this section, we describe the results for three benchmark SWFs: the utilitarian, ex ante prioritarian and ex post prioritarian SWFs.

To account for possible dependence of the realization of the mortality risk among individuals (examined in Section 7.6.1), the formalization is slightly more complex than that introduced in Section 7.2. Specifically, assume there are N individuals indexed by i. Let s denote the state of nature and π_s denote the probability of state s. An individual's outcome in each state includes her wealth c_i (which is assumed to be constant across states) and realization of the mortality risk, i.e., whether she survives or dies during the period. An individual's expected utility $U_i = \sum_s \pi_s[l_i^s u(c_i) + (1 - l_i^s)v(c_i)]$ where l_i^s is an indicator variable equal to 1 if she survives in state s and 0 otherwise. The utility functions conditional on survival and death, u and v, are assumed to be interpersonally comparable, to satisfy the standard conditions described in Section 7.2, and to be identical across individuals (to allow us to focus on the effects of other interpersonal differences). An individual's probability of surviving the period equals the sum of the probabilities of the states in which she survives, $p_i = \sum_s \pi_s l_i^s$.

An SWF ranks vectors that describe the wellbeing of all individuals. In the context of mortality risk, individuals' wellbeing is uncertain (they may live or die) and so the SWF requires a procedure for ranking risks over wellbeing vectors, an uncertainty module (Adler, Chapter 2, this volume). Two natural uncertainty modules for a given SWF are (a) to calculate the expected value of the SWF and (b) to apply the SWF to the vector of expected utilities associated with a policy. In the case of utilitarianism, these are mathematically equivalent. In the case of prioritarianism, they are not.

The utilitarian SWF is the sum of individual utilities. Let S^U denote social welfare under the utilitarian SWF. Because it is the sum of individual utilities, its ex ante and ex post forms are equal:

$$\begin{aligned} S^U &= \sum_s \pi_s \left[\sum_i l_i^s u(c_i) + (1 - l_i^s) v(c_i) \right] \\ &= \sum_i \left[\sum_s \pi_s \left[l_i^s u(c_i) + (1 - l_i^s) v(c_i) \right] \right] \\ &= \sum_i p_i u(c_i) + (1 - p_i) v(c_i). \end{aligned} \tag{7.3}$$

Note that the first expression (the ex post form) equals the expected value (across states) of the sum of individuals' realized (ex post) utilities. The second expression (the ex ante form) equals the sum across individuals of their expected utilities, before the mortality risks are resolved. The last expression is a simplification of the second expression, using the fact that an individual's survival probability is the sum of the probabilities of the states in which she survives.

In contrast to the utilitarian SWF, the ex post and ex ante prioritarian SWFs differ from each other. Let $g(\cdot)$ be the prioritarian transformation function, which is assumed to be continuously differentiable, strictly increasing, and strictly concave.

The ex post prioritarian SWF is

$$\begin{aligned} S^{EPP} &= \sum_s \pi_s \left[\sum_i g\left[l_i^s u(c_i) + (1 - l_i^s) v(c_i)\right] \right] \\ &= \sum_i p_i g[u(c_i)] + (1 - p_i) g[v(c_i)], \end{aligned} \tag{7.4}$$

which is the expected value (across states) of the sum of individuals' realized utilities as transformed by the function g.

The ex ante prioritarian SWF is

$$S^{EAP} = \sum_i g[p_i u(c_i) + (1 - p_i) v(c_i)], \tag{7.5}$$

which is the sum of the individuals' expected utilities as transformed by the function g.

All three of the benchmark SWFs are separable across individuals. Social welfare is the population sum of some individual-specific quantity: expected utility in the case of the utilitarian SWF, expected transformed utility in the case of the ex post prioritarian SWF, and transformed expected utility in the case of the ex ante prioritarian SWF. This implies that the effect on social welfare of a change to an individual's risk is independent of the risk and other characteristics of everyone else.

As noted above, the social value of risk reduction (SVRR) for an individual is defined as the rate of change in social welfare in response to a small change to the individual's survival probability, $\frac{\partial S}{\partial p_i}$, for each SWF. VSL is the analogous rate of change of net social benefits under BCA.

For the utilitarian SWF (equation (7.3)), the SVRR for individual i is $u(c_i) - v(c_i)$. Note this is the numerator of the VSL (equation (7.2)), which equals the difference in utility between survival and death.

For the ex post prioritarian SWF (equation (7.4)), the SVRR is $g[u(c_i)] - g[v(c_i)]$. This is similar to the SVRR for the utilitarian SWF, except the realized utilities are transformed by the function g.

For the ex ante prioritarian SWF (equation (7.5)), the SVRR is $g'[p_i u(c_i) + (1 - p_i) v(c_i)][u(c_i) - v(c_i)]$. In words, it equals the SVRR for the utilitarian SWF (the second term, in brackets) multiplied by a factor that depends on the individual's expected utility; this priority factor is larger for individuals with smaller expected utility (because g is concave).

Table 7.1. ***Effects of baseline risk, wealth, and health on SVRR in the single-period model***

	Mortality risk	Wealth	Health
BCA	+	+	+/−
Utilitarian SWF	0	+	+
Ex ante prioritarian SWF	+	+/−	+/−
Ex post prioritarian SWF	0	+/−	+

Note: Symbols describe the sign of the effect of an increase in the column parameter on the SVRR under each evaluation framework. Symbols denote increase (+), decrease (−), no effect (0), ambiguous effect (+/−). An effect is ambiguous if it depends on parameter values; the effect of wealth on SVRR for the two prioritarian SWFs is negative if the transformation function is strongly concave and positive if it is close to linear.

Recall that VSL is increasing in the individual's wealth and mortality risk. Consider the effects of mortality risk and wealth on the SVRR under the three benchmark SWFs, summarized in Table 7.1 (the effects of health, shown in the last column, are discussed in Section 7.6.2). Unlike VSL, the SVRR under the utilitarian and ex post prioritarian SWFs are independent of mortality risk, because these SWFs are expected values (of individual wellbeing or transformed wellbeing, respectively) and hence are linear functions of an individual's survival probability. In contrast, the SVRR under the ex ante prioritarian SWF is increasing in mortality risk (because that decreases the individual's expected utility and hence increases her social priority). The sensitivity to baseline risk of VSL and SVRR under the ex ante prioritarian SWF implies that BCA and the ex ante prioritarian SWF exhibit a preference for risk equity, defined as a more equal distribution of risk holding the expected number of fatalities constant. In contrast, the utilitarian and ex post prioritarian SWFs are neutral with respect to risk equity.[7]

Turning to wealth, SVRR under the utilitarian SWF is increasing in wealth, as is VSL. However, the utilitarian SVRR is less sensitive to wealth than is VSL. Recall that SVRR under the utilitarian SWF equals the numerator of VSL (equation (7.2)), which increases with wealth under the assumption that the marginal utility of wealth conditional on survival is greater than as a bequest. The denominator of VSL

[7] Risk equity is discussed in Section 7.6.1.

decreases with wealth, increasing the sensitivity of VSL to wealth compared with the sensitivity of the SVRR under the utilitarian SWF.[8] The effect of wealth on the SVRR under the two prioritarian SWFs depends on the curvature of the transformation function g. Although greater wealth increases an individual's utility, it decreases her social priority and the combined effect of wealth on SVRR can be positive, negative, or zero. If g is close to linear, the prioritarian SWFs are close to the utilitarian SWF and the effect of wealth on SVRR is positive; if g is sufficiently concave, the effect is negative.

To summarize, the effects of mortality risk and wealth on the social value of risk reduction differ between BCA and the three benchmark SWFs. Baseline risk increases the SVRR under BCA and the ex ante prioritarian SWF but it has no effect on the SVRR under the utilitarian and ex post prioritarian SWFs. In contrast, wealth increases the SVRR under BCA and the utilitarian SWF, but its effect under the two prioritarian SWFs can be positive, negative, or zero. The only SWF under which the SVRR can be equal across individuals differing in wealth and baseline risk is the ex post prioritarian SWF, and then only if the curvature of the transformation function exactly offsets the positive effect of wealth on individual utility.

7.4 SWFs Applied To a Lifetime Model

The effect of an individual's age on the social value of reducing her current-period mortality risk is of significant policy interest. Over most of the lifespan, mortality risk increases with age at an accelerating rate. Many important sources of mortality risk increase sharply with age, including cardiovascular disease and many cancers. One of the largest environmental-health risks, exposure to fine-particulate air pollution, is believed to increase mortality risk more for older than younger individuals; the effect of exposure on mortality risk is consistent with the assumption that exposure increases baseline risk by a constant factor, a so-called constant proportional hazard. In contrast, motor-vehicle safety programs often produce larger risk reductions for young

[8] If the utility of wealth conditional on survival and on death is risk neutral ($u'' = v'' = 0$), then the denominator is unaffected by wealth and SVRR under the utilitarian SWF and VSL are equally sensitive to wealth.

adults, who face larger fatality risk from this hazard than do older individuals.

Because (remaining) life expectancy conditional on surviving the current period tends to be negatively associated with age,[9] it seems intuitive that the social value of risk reduction is larger for younger than for older individuals. Consistent with this perspective, cost-effectiveness analysis (CEA) of health interventions often measures effectiveness by the expected increase in quality-adjusted life years. Under this metric, decreasing mortality risk to a younger individual (with greater life expectancy) generally produces greater benefits. Some commentators go further, endorsing a "fair innings" argument that "everyone be given an equal chance to have a fair innings, to reach the appropriate threshold but, having reached it, they have received their entitlement. The rest of their life is the sort of bonus which may be canceled when this is necessary to help others reach the threshold" (Harris 1985). The fair innings perspective recommends giving greater priority to the young than would be justified by their larger expected increase in quality-adjusted life years (Williams 1997).

As described below, neither VSL nor the SVRR under any of the benchmark SWFs we consider necessarily decrease with age; in each case, there are conditions under which the social value of risk reduction is larger for an older than an otherwise identical younger individual. However, both the ex ante and ex post prioritarian SWFs give more priority to a younger individual than does the utilitarian SWF, a property that Adler et al. (2021) denote "priority to the young".

The effects of age and life expectancy are implicit in the single-period model introduced in Section 7.2. Utility conditional on survival $u(c)$ implicitly depends on the individual's uncertain prospects if she survives the period, including her future longevity, health, income, and other factors. Hence $u(c)$ can be interpreted as her expected utility conditional on surviving the period. Normally, greater life expectancy will increase the utility of surviving the current period, the utility gain from survival (the numerator of equation (7.2), holding the bequest $v(c)$ constant), and hence the SVRR under the utilitarian and ex post prioritarian SWFs. However, it need not increase SVRR under the ex ante prioritarian SWF or VSL. Under the ex ante prioritarian SWF, the

[9] Life expectancy is decreasing in age if the hazard rate (the current mortality risk) does not decrease with age.

increase in the utility of survival can be more than offset by the decrease in the social priority of the individual. For VSL, the increase in the numerator can be offset by an increase in the expected opportunity cost of spending (the denominator of equation (7.2)). For example, if the individual will have no future income and must support herself from current wealth, the opportunity cost of spending conditional on survival $u'(c)$ will be larger when life expectancy is greater. Depending on the relative magnitudes of its effects on $u(c)$ and on $u'(c)$, the effect of life expectancy on VSL may be positive, zero, or negative.

Further progress in evaluating how the SVRR depends on age requires a more-explicit model of how wellbeing depends on age and life expectancy. The conventional multi-period model assumes wellbeing depends on the present value of future utility, where utility in each period depends on consumption (and implicitly on health and other factors). Although the utility of a bequest might depend on the age at death (or on the age of one's children, which is correlated with age at death), applications of this model set the utility of a bequest to zero (primarily for simplicity).

Under the conventional multi-period model, the individual seeks to maximize her expected lifetime wellbeing, subject to a budget constraint. The age-dependence of VSL depends on the conditions under which an individual can reallocate income[10] to consumption in different periods, e.g., whether she can borrow against future income or save past income to adjust her consumption over time. It also depends on how the rate at which she discounts future utility compares with the interest rate, which affects returns to saving and costs of borrowing. When income increases with age (as it usually does over younger ages), if the individual cannot borrow against future income her VSL first rises then falls with age, exhibiting an inverted-U pattern (Shepard and Zeckhauser 1984). When the individual can both save past income and borrow against future income and the interest rate and utility discount rate are equal, optimal consumption is constant over time and VSL decreases with age (Shepard and Zeckhauser 1984). In contrast, when the utility discount rate is smaller than the interest rate, it is optimal to defer consumption, at least at younger ages, and the opportunity cost

[10] It is conventional in these models to assume that income in each period is exogenous. A richer model could allow the individual to alter her income trajectory by investing in education or choosing how many hours to work each period.

of spending decreases with age. In this case, VSL again follows an inverted-U pattern (Ng 1992).

Adler et al. (2021) analyzed the social value of risk reduction for individuals of different ages using the standard multi-period model under the same benchmark SWFs described in Section 7.3: utilitarian, ex ante and ex post prioritarian. In the base case, individuals face identical time paths of mortality risk and income, but their current ages differ because of differences in birth date. The SWFs are functions of individuals' lifetime utility. In the model, an individual experiences the utility of consuming in a period only if she survives that period; if not, her lifetime utility includes only the periods before the current period. This assumption is not limiting (periods can be arbitrarily short) but it influences the interpretation of some of the results.

The SVRR depends on whether the individual can save or borrow and, if she can, on whether the policy that reduces mortality risk is anticipated (which affects her planned consumption path) or comes as a surprise. In the base case, an individual's consumption is assumed to be equal to her (exogenously determined) income in each year that she survives; she can neither save nor borrow. In an extension (Adler et al. 2019), the individual is assumed to be able to save or borrow at actuarially fair rates, so she can allocate her expected lifetime wealth to consumption across all periods, but the policy comes as a surprise and so does not affect her consumption plan.

7.4.1 Effects of Age and Priority To the Young

As noted above, the effect of age on VSL depends on whether the individual can finance current consumption by borrowing against future income and on how she discounts future utility compared with the interest rate. Under some conditions, VSL decreases with age; under others, it increases over younger ages then decreases over older ages. Similarly, SVRR under the benchmark SWFs can but does not necessarily decrease with age. However, compared with the utilitarian SWF, both the ex ante and ex post prioritarian SWFs give more priority to reducing risk to younger than to older individuals.

Consider a simple two-period example. At birth each individual has probability p_1 of surviving her first period ("youth") and, conditional on surviving the first period, probability p_2 of surviving her second period ("adulthood"). Her utility of surviving the first period is u_1 and utility of surviving the second period is u_2 (utility for a period she does not survive is zero). A young person, in her first period, has expected lifetime utility $p_1 u_1 + p_1 p_2 u_2$. An old person, in her second period, has already survived her first period and has expected lifetime utility $u_1 + p_2 u_2$. A reduction in current-period risk increases p_1 for the young person and increases p_2 for the old person.

Under the utilitarian SWF, the SVRR for the young person is $u_1 + p_2 u_2$ and the SVRR for the old person is u_2. The difference, SVRR(young) – SVRR(old) = $u_1 + (p_2 - 1)\, u_2$, can be interpreted as the sum of two effects, a "duration effect" u_1, which reflects the longer future life the young person may live (two periods rather than one) and a "risk effect" $(p_2 - 1)\, u_2$, which reflects the fact that the young person has a smaller chance of living during her second period, because she might not survive her first period, while the old person already has. The duration effect is positive and the risk effect is negative, hence the SVRR may be larger or smaller for the young than for the old person. Typically the difference in SVRR will be positive but it can be negative if u_1 is small compared with u_2 and p_2 is small compared with one.

Similarly, under the ex ante and ex post prioritarian SWFs, the SVRR for the young person is not necessarily larger than for the old person. However, the ratio of the SVRR for the young person to the SVRR for the old person is always larger under either of the prioritarian SWFs than it is under the utilitarian SWF. In this sense, the two prioritarian SWFs exhibit a property that Adler et al. (2021) call "ratio priority to the young."

Continuing with the two-period example, the ratio SVRR(young)/SVRR(old) for the utilitarian SWF equals $\frac{u_1 + p_2 u_2}{u_2} = \frac{u_1}{u_2} + p_2$. For the ex ante prioritarian SWF, the ratio SVRR(young)/SVRR(old) equals $\frac{g'(s_1 u_1 + p_1 p_2 u_2)(u_1 + p_2 u_2)}{g'(u_1 + p_2 u_2) u_2} = \frac{g'(p_1 u_1 + p_1 p_2 u_2)}{g'(u_1 + p_2 u_2)} \left(\frac{u_1}{u_2} + p_2 \right)$. The last term (in parentheses) is the ratio for the utilitarian SWF. It is multiplied by a term that depends on the slope of the transformation function g evaluated at the expected lifetime wellbeing of the young person (in the numerator) and at the expected lifetime wellbeing of the old person (in the denominator). Because the expected lifetime wellbeing of the young person is less than that of the old person, the numerator is larger than the denominator and so the ratio SVRR(young)/SVRR(old) is larger than under the utilitarian SWF. For the ex post prioritarian SWF, the ratio SVRR(young)/SVRR(old) equals $\frac{g(u_1)-g(0)+p_2[g(u_1+u_2)-g(u_1)]}{g(u_1+u_2)-g(u_1)} = \frac{g(u_1)-g(0)}{g(u_1+u_2)-g(u_1)} + p_2$. This ratio is larger than the ratio for the utilitarian SWF because the concavity of g implies that the first term on the right-hand side is larger than $\frac{u_1}{u_2}$.

These results can be extended to a model with more than two periods. For example, let each period be one year. Consider two individuals whose age-specific mortality risks and consumption levels are identical; the only difference between them is their year of birth. Let A_0 and A_1 denote the ages of the younger and older individuals, respectively. Consider the utilitarian SWF. Reducing current-period mortality risk increases each individual's chances of being alive in all future years and hence gain utility from consumption in those years. The duration effect is that, although both individuals increase their chances of living at ages greater than A_1, the younger individual also stands to gain the utility of living at ages between A_0 and A_1; the older individual has already lived these years. The risk effect is that the chance of experiencing the utility of living at each age greater than A_1 is smaller for the younger individual, who may die before reaching age A_1. If the utility of living each year is constant or decreasing with age (e.g., because income is constant, consumption is perfectly smoothed, or utility decreases as health declines with age) and the probability of surviving a period does not increase with age, then the duration effect exceeds the risk effect and the SVRR is larger for the younger individual. But if the utility of living per year or the probability of surviving a year can increase with age, then the risk effect can outweigh the duration effect and the utilitarian SWF can give priority to reducing risk to the older individual.

Under the ex ante prioritarian SWF, the difference in social welfare associated with reducing current risk to the younger rather than the older individual includes the same duration and risk terms as the utilitarian SWF. In addition, there is a third term which has the same sign as $g'(V_0) - g'(V_1)$, where V_0 and V_1 are the expected lifetime utilities of the younger and older individuals, respectively (Adler et al. 2021). The older individual's expected lifetime utility is larger than that of the younger individual's ($V_0 < V_1$) because the older individual has already survived the risk of dying between ages A_0 and A_1. Hence the difference $g'(V_0) - g'(V_1)$ is positive. This term is denoted the "priority to the young" term and it ensures that the ex ante prioritarian

SWF gives greater priority to the young than does the utilitarian SWF. Indeed, Adler et al. (2021) prove a stronger result: that the ratio of the SVRR for the younger individual to the SVRR for the older individual is strictly larger under the ex ante prioritarian SWF than under the utilitarian SWF.

The ex post prioritarian SWF also assigns greater priority (than the utilitarian SWF) to reducing current risk to the younger than to the older individual. Although the formula differs from that for the ex ante prioritarian SWF, the same three effects are present: duration, risk, and priority to the young. The stronger result also holds, i.e., that the ratio of the SVRR for the younger individual to the SVRR for the older individual is strictly larger under the ex post prioritarian SWF than under the utilitarian SWF.

While both ex ante and ex post prioritarian SWFs give priority to the young compared with the utilitarian SWF, it is not true that one of these always gives more priority to the young than the other. To demonstrate, return to the two-period example and let $u_1 = u_2 = 1$, $p_2 \approx 1$, and $g(u) = \sqrt{u}$. The ratio SVRR(young)/SVRR(old) equals approximately $2/\sqrt{p_1}$ under the ex ante prioritarian SWF and approximately $\sqrt{2}/(\sqrt{2}-1)$ under the ex post prioritarian SWF. Both ratios are of course larger than the corresponding ratio under the utilitarian SWF, which equals approximately 2. The ratio for the ex ante prioritarian SWF depends on the value of p_1 but the ratio for the ex post prioritarian SWF does not. For values of p_1 larger than $(2-\sqrt{2})^2 \approx 0.34$ the ratio for the ex ante prioritarian SWF is smaller than the ratio for the ex post prioritarian SWF; for values of p_1 smaller than this threshold the situation is reversed.

7.4.2 *Effects of Income and Baseline Risk*

When analyzing the effects on the SVRR of differences in income or in risk, one must distinguish between differences that last for only a single period, for multiple periods, or throughout the lifetime. Moreover, the effects of a change for a single period can depend on whether that period is in the past, the present, or the future.

The effects of single-period and all-period differences in income and survival probability on the SVRR are summarized in Table 7.2, for the case in which the individual can neither borrow nor save, so consumption equals income in each period. Note that the SVRR under BCA and

Table 7.2. ***Effects of income and baseline risk on SVRR in the multi-period model***

SVRR	Income: single-period difference	Income: permanent difference	Survival probability: single-period difference	Survival probability: permanent difference
BCA	Past period: *Independent* Current period: *Increasing* Future period: *Increasing*	*Increasing*	Current period: *Decreasing* Future period: *Increasing*	*Ambiguous*
Utilitarian	Past period: *Independent* Current period: *Increasing* Future period: *Increasing*	*Increasing*	Current period: *Independent* Future period: *Increasing*	*Increasing*
Ex ante prioritarian	Past period: *Decreasing* Current period: *Ambiguous* Future period: *Ambiguous*	*Ambiguous*	Current period: *Decreasing* Future period: *Ambiguous*	*Ambiguous*
Ex post prioritarian	Past period: *Decreasing* Current period: *Increasing* Future period: *Increasing*	*Ambiguous*	Current period: *Independent* Future period: *Increasing*	*Increasing*

Note: Adapted from Adler et al. (2021), table 2.

the utilitarian SWF are unaffected by differences in past-period income but SVRR under the prioritarian SWFs is affected. Prioritarian SWFs are history-dependent; they give priority to individuals with lower lifetime utility (expected utility in the case of the ex ante and possible realized utility in the case of the ex post prioritarian SWF). Greater income in a previous period increases lifetime utility and hence decreases the priority associated with improving an individual's well-being under both prioritarian SWFs. Because it has no effect on the gain from surviving the current period, greater income in a previous period decreases the SVRR.

Greater income in the current or a future period increases SVRR under BCA, the utilitarian, and the ex post prioritarian SWF. In all three cases, greater income increases wellbeing conditional on survival.[11] In contrast, the effect is ambiguous under the ex ante prioritarian SWF; higher income increases the utility gain from survival but decreases the priority given to the individual. If the transformation function g is not too concave, the ex ante prioritarian is similar to the utilitarian SWF and higher current or future income increases the SVRR; if the transformation function is sufficiently concave, the decrease in priority more than offsets the increase in wellbeing. Combining the effects of changes in past, present, or future income implies that the effect of an increase in income in all periods increases the SVRR under BCA and the utilitarian SWF but has an ambiguous effect under the two prioritarian SWFs. For the ex ante case, higher expected lifetime utility reduces social priority, and this effect can be large enough to offset the gain in expected lifetime utility if the transformation function is sufficiently concave. For the ex post case, the ambiguity arises because an increase in current or future income increases SVRR but an increase in past income decreases SVRR; the net effect depends on the relative magnitudes of these effects.

The effects of a change in survival probability in a past period have no effect on the SVRR under BCA or any of the benchmark SWFs. This is because the risk of dying in these periods has already been resolved, so the values of the probabilities are irrelevant to lifetime wellbeing.

An increase in current survival probability has no effect on SVRR under the utilitarian and ex post prioritarian SWFs because it has no

[11] Recall that an individual gains utility from the current period only if she survives it.

effect on lifetime wellbeing conditional on surviving the current period. In contrast, it decreases the SVRR under BCA and the ex ante prioritarian SWF. For BCA, an increase in current survival probability has no effect on the utility gain from survival (the numerator of equation (7.2)) but increases the expected opportunity cost of reduced consumption (the denominator of equation (7.2), the dead-anyway effect). Under the ex ante prioritarian SWF, the change in survival probability has no effect on the expected gain in utility from surviving the current period but increases expected lifetime utility and hence decreases social priority.

The effect of an increase in a future-period survival probability is to increase SVRR under BCA,[12] the utilitarian, and the ex post prioritarian SWF; in all three cases, the change increases expected lifetime wellbeing conditional on surviving the current period for BCA and the utilitarian SWF, and expected transformed lifetime wellbeing for the ex post prioritarian SWF. In contrast, the effect is ambiguous under the ex ante prioritarian SWF because the increase in expected lifetime wellbeing can be more than offset by the associated decrease in priority if the transformation function g is sufficiently concave.

Because the effect of an increase in current or future survival probabilities is to increase SVRR under the utilitarian and ex post prioritarian SWFs, so is the effect of a permanent increase in survival probabilities. In contrast, because the effects of an increase in current or future survival probabilities differ from each other under BCA and can differ under the ex ante prioritarian SWF, the effects of a permanent change are ambiguous and depend on which effect is larger.

In an extension to this model, Adler et al. (2019) analyze the case in which the individual can save and borrow against future income, which allows her to reallocate consumption over time. Specifically, they assume the individual can sign a contract at birth pledging her income in each year she survives to an insurer that will pay her a defined annuity (that she will spend on consumption) each year she survives. The expected present value of her planned consumption path is equal to the expected present value of her (exogenous) income path; these depend on her time path of mortality risk and the interest rate.

[12] As noted above, in the single-period model an increase in life expectancy conditional on survival can decrease VSL if it increases the opportunity cost of spending. In the model of Adler et al. (2021), the individual receives income each period she survives and sets consumption equal to income, so an increase in life expectancy has no effect on the opportunity cost of spending.

The individual's optimal consumption path increases, decreases, or does not change with age if she discounts future utility at a rate that is smaller than, larger than, or equal to the interest rate, respectively.

The effect of being able to reallocate consumption over time on the SVRR depends on whether the policy that decreases mortality risk is anticipated (perhaps with some probability) or not. An anticipated change in mortality risk could affect the terms on which the individual can exchange her income stream for an annuity stream. Adler et al. (2019) analyze the case in which the policy that reduces risk is unanticipated; it comes as a surprise and does not affect the terms on which the individual can purchase her annuity or her planned consumption path. Hence the findings that the ex ante and ex post prioritarian SWFs exhibit priority to the young (compared with the utilitarian SWF) remain true in this extension to the model. The effect of a change in income on the SVRR does not depend on whether the income change occurs for a period in the past, present, or future; in each case, a higher income in one period increases the expected present value of lifetime income. This implies that the effect of a change in income in any period is qualitatively the same as a permanent increase in income under the base-case model; it increases SVRR under BCA and the utilitarian SWF and has an ambiguous effect on SVRR under the two prioritarian SWFs (see Table 7.2). In contrast, the effect on the SVRR of a change in risk for a single period or for all periods differs from the base case; it is ambiguous under all of the evaluation frameworks. The intuition is that two individuals of the same age having identical lifetime income paths but different survival-probability paths will have different paths of planned consumption.

This section reveals a diversity of qualitative effects of differences in income and baseline risk on SVRR across the different SWFs but gives little indication of their magnitudes. In the following section we report simulation exercises to help evaluate how large the effects of different evaluation methods may be on the SVRR of reducing mortality risk to individuals of different age and income.

7.5 Simulations

Adler et al. (2021) calculated the SVRR under BCA and each of the benchmark SWFs for a simulated population calibrated to the U.S. population. At each age, the distribution of income is based on U.S.

Census data and the survival probability is based on the CDC lifetable, adjusted upward for higher and downward for lower incomes.[13] It is assumed there is no income mobility and an individual's income path over time corresponds to the median income of a fixed quintile of the income distribution at each age (i.e., the 10th, 30th, 50th, 70th, or 90th percentile).[14] The simulation is conducted for ages 20 through 100. Consumption is assumed to be equal to income in each year. Results for ages 20–24 and 75 and older are in part artifacts of setting income at these ages equal to their values at ages 25 and 74, respectively, due to limitations in how the income data are reported.

The within-period individual utility function is ln(c) – ln($1,000), where c is annual income or consumption in dollars and the threshold level of $1,000 is based on the World Bank's estimate of subsistence income; the utility discount rate is zero. For the prioritarian SWFs, the transformation function $g(\cdot)$ is the Atkinson (isoelastic) function $g(u) = \frac{u^{1-\gamma}}{1-\gamma}$ with two values of the inequality-aversion parameter, $\gamma = 1, 2$.[15]

Figure 7.2 presents the SVRR by age and income quintile for BCA and the benchmark SWFs. For BCA, the SVRR is VSL. For this simulation, it tends to decrease with age while also exhibiting an inverted-U pattern, which is more pronounced for the higher-income quintiles. Because consumption is set equal to income, the inverted-U reflects the pattern of income with age rather than any saving or borrowing. The variation with income (and associated mortality risk) is large; as shown by Figure 7.3, at age 40 the VSL for an individual in the highest-income quintile is about 30 times as large as for an individual in the lowest-income quintile.

The SVRR is monotonically decreasing as a function of age for all the SWFs. Under the utilitarian SWF, the SVRR is increasing in income but the effect is much smaller than for VSL; the ratio of the SVRR for

13 Annual mortality risk in each income quintile (lowest to highest) equals population risk multiplied by the following factors, derived from Chetty et al. (2016): 1.5, 1.2, 1, 0.9, 0.7.

14 Income data are from the U.S. Census Bureau, Current Population Survey, data on individual money income in 2016 (www.census.gov/data/tables/time-series/demo/income-poverty/cps-pinc/pinc-01.html). This table reports income distribution by five-year age increments from ages 25 to 74 but pools ages 15 to 24 years and 75 years and older. Survival data are from the United States Life Tables for 2014 (www.cdc.gov/nchs/products/life_tables.htm).

15 When $\gamma = 1$, $g(u) = \ln(u)$.

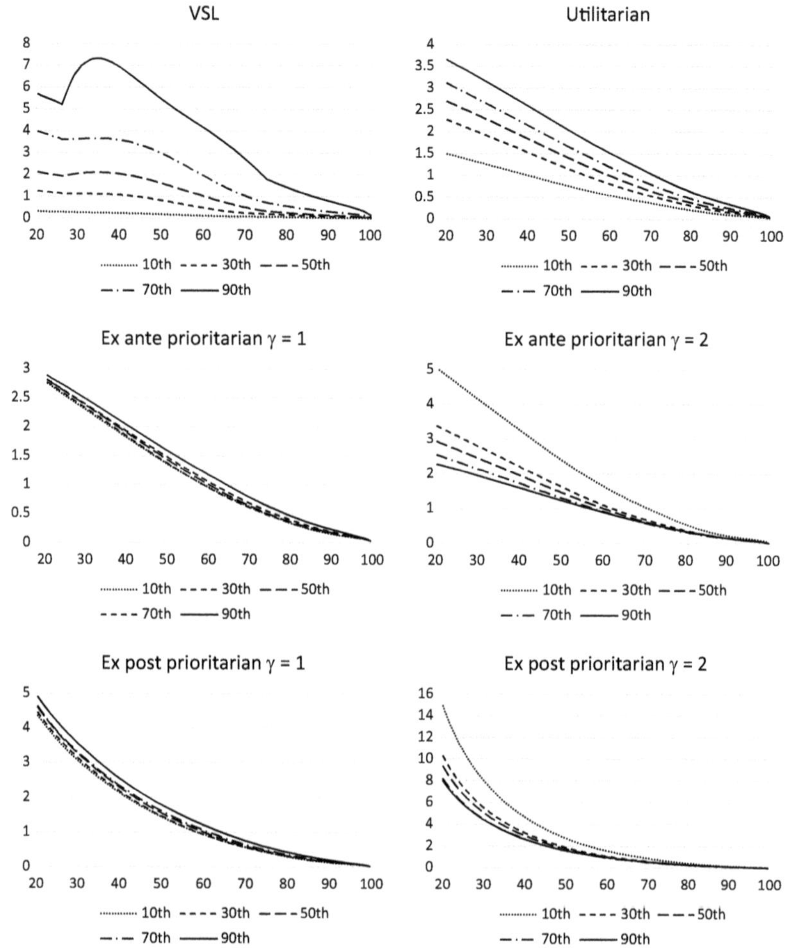

Figure 7.2. SVRR normalized for age and income (= 1 for age 60, median income) for BCA and alternative SWFs

the highest- to the lowest-income quintile is between 2.5 and 3 for ages between about 20 and 80 (see Figure 7.3). The increase with income reflects two factors: expected future utility is larger because it is increasing in consumption, and life expectancy conditional on surviving the period is larger because it is increasing in income. For the prioritarian SWFs with inequality-aversion coefficient $\gamma = 1$ (both ex ante and ex post), the effect of income is very small, though the SVRR is increasing with income. In contrast, with the larger coefficient of

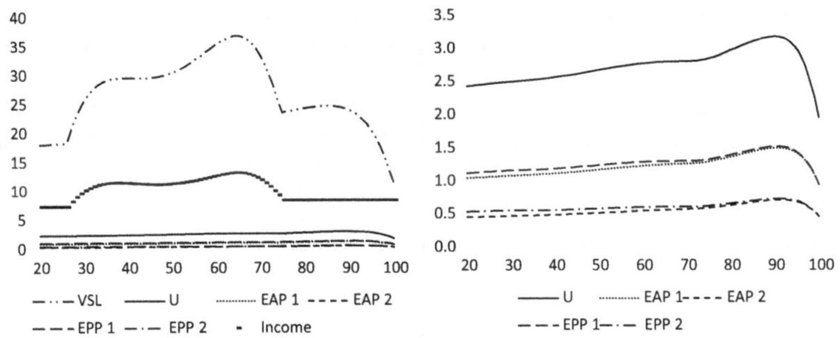

Figure 7.3. Ratio of SVRR at 90th percentile to 10th percentile of income under BCA and alternative SWFs. Left panel includes ratio of income at 90th to 10th percentile

inequality aversion $\gamma = 2$, the ordering by income is reversed with SVRR larger for lower- than for higher-income individuals. Individuals in lower-income quintiles receive greater priority because their consumption is lower and their expected lifetime is shorter.

The effects of income and the associated difference in mortality risk on the SVRR are illustrated more clearly in Figure 7.3, which shows the ratio of SVRR for the highest-income quintile to SVRR for the lowest-income quintile as a function of age. The left-hand panel includes the ratios for VSL and for income in addition to those for the SVRR under the benchmark SWFs; the right-hand panel excludes VSL and income so that the differences among the SWFs are more clearly seen.

For VSL, the ratio of SVRR for the highest to SVRR for the lowest-income quintile is greater than 20 at most ages. Its variation over time mirrors and exaggerates that of the ratio of income between the highest- and lowest-income quintiles, which increases from a value of about 8 to a peak of about 13 near age 65 then decreases. For the SWFs, the proportional effect of income rises very slightly with age (except for the sharp drop at ages greater than about 90 years); it is largest for the utilitarian SWF (a factor of about 3). The results under the prioritarian SWFs are more sensitive to the coefficient of inequality aversion than to the difference between the ex ante and ex post forms. With inequality aversion equal to 1, the ratio of SVRR for the highest- to the lowest-income quintile rises with age from about 1 to 1.5. With inequality aversion equal to 2, the SVRR is smaller for the highest- than for the

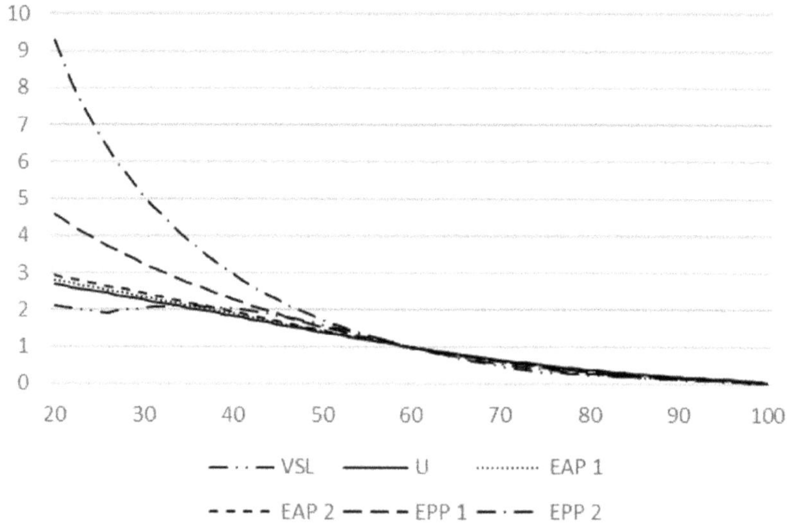

Figure 7.4. SVRR for median income normalized for age (= 1 for age 60) for BCA and alternative SWFs

lowest-income quintile; the ratio rises from about 0.5 to 0.7 (which implies the effect of income decreases with age, contrary to the patterns for the other SWFs). Recall that income is assumed to be constant for ages younger than 25 and older than 74, so patterns at these younger and older ages are influenced by this perhaps unrealistic assumption.

The effects of age for median-income individuals are illustrated by Figure 7.4. Compared with the SVRR at age 60, the ex post prioritarian SWF produces the largest SVRR at young ages; the highest curve is with the inequality-aversion coefficient γ equal to 2 and the second highest is with the coefficient equal to 1. The ex ante prioritarian SWF with inequality-aversion coefficients of 1 and 2 and the utilitarian SWF produce very similar patterns of SVRR as a function of age that are nearly indistinguishable on this plot. As noted earlier, the evaluation under BCA is the outlier, with the SVRR increasing with age for younger ages then decreasing at older ages.

Adler (2019, chapter 5) presents a similar simulation in which he evaluates policies that reduce current mortality risk but at a cost that decreases individuals' current consumption. The population is divided into quintiles by income, with survival curves similar to those in the simulation described above. Wellbeing is measured using the same logarithmic utility function. In contrast, income is assumed to be

Table 7.3. ***Breakeven average cost ($) for policy that reduces average annual mortality risk by 1/100,000***

Policy	BCA	Utilitarian	Ex post prioritarian
Uniform risk reduction			
Uniform cost	91	48	78
Cost proportional to income	91	77	159
Risk reduction for youngest quintile			
Uniform cost	132	71	178
Cost proportional to income	132	108	360
Risk reduction for poorest quintile			
Uniform cost	15	32	98
Cost proportional to income	15	51	201

Source: Adapted from Adler (2019), table 5.12.

constant over an individual's lifetime. Using this framework, Adler evaluates policies that reduce current mortality risk (for one year) by 1 per 100,000 on average. The risk reduction may be distributed uniformly across individuals aged 20, 30, 40, 50, and 60 years (present in equal numbers) or targeted to either the youngest quintile (20-year-olds) or the poorest quintile. A targeted policy reduces mortality risk by 5 per 100,000 for individuals in the targeted quintile and zero for all others. The one-year cost is distributed either uniformly or in proportion to income. Adler calculates the maximum cost of each policy (average reduction in individual consumption) such that the policy is preferred to the status quo, using BCA, the utilitarian, and ex post prioritarian SWFs (using the Atkinson transformation function with inequality-aversion coefficient $\gamma = 2$). A policy increases social welfare if its average cost is less than the breakeven cost, i.e., more desirable policies have larger breakeven costs.

Results are summarized in Table 7.3. Under BCA, the breakeven cost is unaffected by its allocation. It is smaller when the risk reduction is targeted to the poorest quintile (whose VSL is smaller). The breakeven cost is larger when the risk reduction is targeted to the youngest quintile, who have a larger VSL than do older cohorts. (In the simulation, VSL decreases with age because consumption is assumed to be constant over time.)

Under the utilitarian and ex post prioritarian SWFs, the breakeven cost is always larger when costs are allocated in proportion to income rather than uniformly, because the utility loss of a reduction in consumption is smaller at higher incomes. The proportional difference is larger for the ex post prioritarian than for the utilitarian SWF, because the former exhibits aversion to inequality in wellbeing. Under both SWFs, the policy that targets risk reduction to the youngest quintile has a higher breakeven cost than does the uniform risk reduction. In contrast, the policy that targets risk reduction to the poorest quintile has a smaller breakeven cost than the uniform risk reduction under the utilitarian SWF, but a higher breakeven cost under the ex post prioritarian SWF. The poorest quintile experiences a smaller than average gain in wellbeing from risk reduction, but the ex post prioritarian SWF assigns sufficient priority to this quintile to offset the difference in wellbeing compared with a uniform risk reduction.

These simulations show that the use of alternative evaluation methods, whether BCA or a specific SWF, can have a dramatic effect on the relative social value of reducing risk to individuals with different characteristics. The SVRR is increasing with income (and associated life expectancy) under BCA and the utilitarian SWF; the effect is much larger under BCA. In contrast, SVRR can increase or decrease with income under the ex ante and ex post prioritarian SWFs, depending on the degree of inequality aversion. All of the benchmark SWFs produce a larger SVRR for younger than older individuals in the simulations; this contrasts with BCA, which yields an SVRR that rises over younger ages then falls over older ages for some income quintiles. The ex post prioritarian SWF gives more priority to the young than does the ex ante prioritarian SWF in the simulations, though as described in Section 7.4 this is not always true theoretically.

7.6 Extensions

In this section we consider two extensions. The first is the use of SWFs that are not additively separable across individuals, which can exhibit catastrophe aversion. The second is a more general model that includes health and nonfatal health risks.

7.6.1 Catastrophe Aversion and Nonseparable SWFs

Hazards that lead to mass casualties, such as hurricanes, earthquakes, floods, volcanic eruptions and other natural disasters, airliner crashes, and terrorist attacks, are often perceived to be of greater social concern than hazards that produce an equal or even greater number of deaths that occur in separate incidents, such as traffic crashes and ambient air pollution. Arguably, resistance to nuclear power plants and acceptance of coal-fired alternatives is rationalized by the perceived chance of a catastrophic loss of life in a nuclear accident as opposed to the routine mortality toll from fine-particulate air pollution.

Catastrophe aversion is defined as the preference for a higher probability of a smaller number of deaths over a lower probability of a larger number of deaths, holding the expected number of deaths constant. Keeney (1980) showed that, when risks are independent, catastrophe aversion conflicts with a preference for risk equity, defined as greater equality among individuals' risks. To illustrate, consider a population of N people, each facing independent mortality probability p_i. If the individual risks are all equal to $1/N$, the expected number of deaths is one. Because the individuals' risks are equal, the risk distribution is perfectly equitable. Alternatively, if individuals 1 and 2 each face a risk of 1/2 and all the others face zero risk, the expected number of deaths is also 1. This distribution is less equitable, because two people face higher risk than everyone else. The actual number of deaths can be very different: in the first case, it can be any number between 0 and N; in the second case, any number between 0 and 2. Catastrophe aversion implies a preference for the second risk over the first, which conflicts with a preference for risk equity.

Adler et al. (2014) and Rheinberger and Treich (2017) generalized Keeney's definition of catastrophe aversion; they define it as a preference for any mean-preserving contraction[16] in the probability distribution of the number of fatalities. When risks are independent, a pure transfer of risk from one individual to another that decreases the difference between them increases risk equity and yields a mean-preserving spread in the distribution of fatalities, i.e., it makes the risk more catastrophic. Hence the conflict between catastrophe aversion and a preference for risk equity also exists under this more general definition of catastrophic risk. When risks are dependent (before or after the risk transfer) and there are more than two people in the

[16] A mean-preserving contraction shifts probability away from the tails of a distribution without changing the mean. A mean-preserving spread shifts probability toward the tails.

population, the relationship between risk equity and catastrophic risks is more complicated because a risk transfer can affect the correlation of risks within the population (Bernard et al. 2018).

Rheinberger and Treich (2017) reviewed the empirical literature and found that catastrophe aversion is supported less often than not, perhaps because of a greater concern for risk equity. Another rationale for preferring a more-catastrophic risk is common-fate preference. As Schelling (1968) observed, a family may prefer to travel together on a single airliner rather than traveling on separate flights; traveling separately reduces the chance of a catastrophe in which the entire family dies but increases the chance of losing at least one family member, leaving the survivors to grieve.

Of the evaluation frameworks evaluated to this point, BCA and the ex ante prioritarian SWF prefer policies in which risk is distributed more equally, and the utilitarian and ex post prioritarian SWFs are insensitive to how individual risks are distributed. This implies that, when risks are independent, BCA and the ex ante prioritarian SWF exhibit catastrophe acceptance and the utilitarian and ex post prioritarian SWFs exhibit catastrophe neutrality. In contrast, when risks are dependent the link between a preference for risk equity and catastrophe acceptance need not hold. For example, all four evaluation frameworks (BCA, the utilitarian, ex ante and ex post prioritarian SWFs) are indifferent between the case in which there is a $1/N$ chance that all N (identical) members of a population will die (with a complementary chance that all survive) and the case in which one of the N members to be selected at random will die for sure. In both cases, every individual faces a $1/N$ chance of death.

The utilitarian, ex ante and ex post prioritarian SWFs are each defined as sums over individuals; this implies the evaluation is unaffected by any correlation or dependence between individuals' outcomes. That is, the effect on social welfare of whether an individual survives or dies is the same regardless of whether other individuals survive or die. Other SWFs can account for such dependence. For example, the ex post transformed utilitarian and ex post transformed prioritarian SWFs are sensitive to dependence among individuals' outcomes.

These SWFs are obtained by introducing a strictly increasing function $h(\cdot)$ that transforms each possible social outcome and calculating the expected value of the transformed outcomes. For the single-period model defined in Section 7.3, the ex post transformed utilitarian SWF is given by

$$S^{EPTU} = \sum_s \pi_s h\left[\sum_i \{l_i^s u(c_i) + (1 - l_i^s)v(c_i)\}\right] \tag{7.6}$$

and the ex post transformed prioritarian SWF is given by

$$S^{EPTP} = \sum_s \pi_s h\left[\sum_i g\{l_i^s u(c_i) + (1 - l_i^s)v(c_i)\}\right]. \tag{7.7}$$

As shown by Adler et al. (2014), these SWFs exhibit catastrophe aversion if and only if the transformation function h is concave. The intuition is that introducing a concave h is like introducing risk aversion over the evaluation of the possible outcomes. This implies the ex post transformed utilitarian and prioritarian SWFs prefer policies that are associated with a mean-contracting spread of the evaluation of the outcomes, e.g., a less-catastrophic risk. The utilitarian SWF (equation (7.3)) calculates the expected value of the sum of individuals' utilities in each state. In contrast, the ex post transformed utilitarian SWF (equation (7.6)) calculates the expected value of this sum transformed by the function h. Analogously, the ex post prioritarian SWF (equation (7.4)) calculates the expected value of the sum of individuals' utilities transformed by the function g. The ex post transformed prioritarian SWF (equation (7.7)) calculates the expected value of this sum transformed by the function h.

An important special case of the transformation function h is Fleurbaey's (2010) equally distributed equivalent (EDE).[17] For any distribution of wellbeing in a population, the equally distributed equivalent is the level of individual wellbeing that, if held by everyone in a population, would yield the same social welfare. For the utilitarian SWF, the equally distributed equivalent is the average utility in the population and the transformation function h^{EDE} is the identity function. Hence the ex post transformed utilitarian SWF using h^{EDE} is catastrophe neutral. For the prioritarian SWF, the equally distributed equivalent is $g^{-1}\left[\frac{1}{N}\sum_1^N g(u_i)\right]$ where u_i is the wellbeing of individual i. Because g is concave, its inverse g^{-1} and hence h^{EDE} are convex.

[17] EDE is discussed by Adler (Chapter 2, this volume). Ferranna and Fleurbaey (Chapter 8, this volume) compare ex ante, ex post, and expected EDE prioritarianism in the context of climate policy.

This implies that ex post transformed prioritarianism using h^{EDE} is catastrophe accepting. The intuition is that a more catastrophic situation is also more equitable ex post in the sense that more people live or die together, which is socially valued under this SWF.

7.6.2 Health

In the single-period model defined in Section 7.2, the effect of health is implicit; the utility of surviving the current period $u(c)$ depends on the individual's uncertain future health, longevity, income, and other factors. This model can be adapted to incorporate the effects of health and the possibility of suffering nonfatal illness or injury. In this section, we first examine the effect of future health on the social value of reducing current-period mortality risk.[18] Second, we generalize the single-period model to include the possibility that an individual may suffer an illness or injury that diminishes her health and may prove fatal. In this richer model, the set of possible actions is broader than for fatal risks. In addition to reducing the probability of suffering the condition, one can potentially reduce its severity or its lethality. We examine the social value of each of these actions under BCA and the benchmark SWFs, and how they depend on the baseline risk of illness, its severity, and the probability that it is fatal.

In the single-period model introduced in Section 7.2, utility conditional on surviving the current period $u(c)$ can be interpreted as the certainty-equivalent utility conditional on survival, which depends on the individual's lottery over future health prospects. Define "better future health" as any change in this lottery that increases its certainty equivalent $u(c)$ and hence increases the utility of survival. Better health increases SVRR under the utilitarian and ex post prioritarian SWFs but it can increase or decrease SVRR under the ex ante prioritarian SWF and BCA, as summarized in the last column of Table 7.1. Moreover, comparing two individuals who are identical except that one has better future health than the other, the ex post and ex ante prioritarian SWFs give relatively greater priority to reducing mortality risk for the individual with worse future health than does the utilitarian SWF. This

[18] Here we depart from the assumption that the utility function $u(c)$ is identical across individuals.

result parallels the finding that the two prioritarian SWFs give priority to younger individuals, discussed in Section 7.4.1.

Recall the SVRR under the utilitarian SWF is $u(c_i) - v(c_i)$ and the SVRR under the ex post prioritarian SWF is $g[u(c_i)] - g[v(c_i)]$. In both cases, increasing utility conditional on survival $u(c_i)$ while holding constant the bequest $v(c_i)$ increases the SVRR. For the ex ante prioritarian SWF, the SVRR is $g'[p_i u(c_i) + (1 - p_i)v(c_i)][u(c_i) - v(c_i)]$. The second term (in brackets) is the SVRR under the utilitarian SWF (which is increasing in $u(c_i)$) but the first term is decreasing in $u(c_i)$. If the transformation function g is sufficiently concave, the decrease in the first term can more than offset the increase in the second term so that the SVRR decreases with future health. For BCA, if (as is plausible) better health increases the marginal utility of wealth conditional on survival, the corresponding increase in the denominator of equation (7.2) can more than offset the increase in utility (the numerator), decreasing VSL.

Under both the ex post and ex ante prioritarian SWFs, the ratio of the SVRR for someone with worse future health to the SVRR for an otherwise identical individual with better future health is larger than the corresponding ratio under the utilitarian SWF. That is, although the utilitarian and ex post prioritarian SWFs give priority to reducing risk to an individual with better future health (all else equal), the ex post prioritarian SWF gives less priority to such an individual. The ex ante prioritarian SWF also gives less weight to such an individual, and can even favor reducing mortality risk to the individual with worse future health.

As shown in Table 7.1, the effects of health on SVRR differ from the effects of both baseline risk and income. Neither VSL nor the SVRR under any of the benchmark SWFs can be equal across individuals differing in baseline risk, wealth, and health.

To capture the possibility of illness or injury that may prove fatal, consider the single-period model developed by Rheinberger et al. (2016). An individual faces a probability p of illness. Conditional on illness, mortality risk is q.[19] If ill, health deteriorates by a fraction h defined such that $h = 0$ corresponds to full health and $h = 1$ to a health state as bad as dead (h is limited to the interval between 0 and 1).

[19] Rheinerger et al. (2016) denote the probability of illness by q and the conditional mortality risk by p.

Utility depends on wealth c; the utility of a bequest is $v(c)$ and the utility of survival equals $(1-h)\,u(c)+v(c)$.[20] As in the standard model for mortality risk (equation (7.1)), we assume survival is preferred to death ($u(c)>0$), the marginal utility of wealth conditional on survival is greater than the marginal utility of a bequest ($u'(c)>0$), the marginal utility of a bequest is non-negative ($v'(c)\geq 0$), and the individual is averse to financial risk conditional on survival and on death ($u''(c)\leq 0$ and $v''(c)\leq 0$).

Individual expected utility

$$\begin{aligned} U &= (1-p)[u(c)+v(c)]+p(1-q)[(1-h)u(c)+v(c)]+pqv(c) \\ &= [1-p(q+h-qh)]u(c)+v(c) \end{aligned} \tag{7.8}$$

One implication of this specification is that the marginal utility of wealth decreases as the health deterioration increases; this is often but not always assumed. This model is most naturally interpreted as a model of chronic illness because the individual cannot recover. It provides a model for acute illness if the utility if ill is interpreted as expected future lifetime utility conditional on becoming ill in the current period and recovering. Nonfatal health conditions can be represented by setting lethality $q=0$. Note that the roles of lethality q and health deterioration h are symmetric; they appear in the last expression of equation (7.8) only in the term $(q+h-q\,h)$. This has implications that are addressed below.

Decreases in any of the three parameters (risk of illness p, severity h, and lethality q) increase expected utility. We describe the marginal value of decreases in each of these parameters (and of an increase in wealth c) under BCA and under the three benchmark SWFs. We then describe how these marginal values depend on the values of the other parameters (e.g., how the value of reducing the risk of an illness depends on its severity and lethality). Finally, we compare the relative social values of decreases in each parameter. Derivations are reported by Hammitt (2021).

[20] Note that $u(c)$ is the difference in utility between survival in full health and death. This differs from the model for mortality risk (equation (7.1)), in which $u(c)$ is the utility of wealth conditional on survival. This specification is convenient for representing ill health as a fractional deterioration toward a health state as bad as dead.

Table 7.4. *Social value of reducing alternative dimensions of health risk*

	Parameter decreased	Incidence (p)	Lethality (q)	Severity (h)	Wealth (c)
BCA	Prevention (p)	+	+	+	+
	Lethality (q)	+	+	−	+
	Severity (h)	+	−	+	+
Utilitarian SWF	Prevention (p)	0	+	+	+
	Lethality (q)	+	0	−	+
	Severity (h)	+	−	0	+
Ex ante prioritarian SWF	Prevention (p)	+	+	+	+/−
	Lethality (q)	+	+	+/−	+/−
	Severity (h)	+	+/−	+	+/−
Ex post prioritarian SWF	Prevention (p)	0	+	+	+/−
	Lethality (q)	+	0	−	+/−
	Severity (h)	+	−	+	+/−

Note: Symbols describe the sign of the effect of an increase in the column parameter on the social value of a marginal decrease of the row parameter under each evaluation framework. Symbols denote increase (+), decrease (−), no effect (0), ambiguous effect (+/−).

Under BCA, the social value of a marginal improvement in any dimension of the health risk equals the individual's WTP for that improvement. By analogy to VSL, this value can be normalized to a one-unit change and reported as a value per statistical case. Marginal WTP for prevention (reducing p), treatment (reducing q), and palliative care (reducing h) are positive and depend on wealth and the values of the risk parameters. These results are summarized in Table 7.4. WTP for an improvement in each dimension is increasing in wealth. Higher baseline risk (larger p) increases WTP for prevention (that reduces p), treatment (that reduces q), and care (that reduces h). Greater lethality (larger q) increases WTP for prevention (that reduces p) and treatment (that reduces q) but decreases WTP for care (that reduces h). Greater severity (larger h) increases WTP for prevention (that reduces p) and care (that reduces h) but decreases WTP for treatment (that reduces q) (Rheinberger et al. 2016, Hammitt 2021).

The social value of a decrease in baseline risk, lethality, or severity for an individual is defined as the rate of increase of social welfare resulting from a decrease in the corresponding parameter, i.e., the negative of the partial derivative of social welfare with respect to that parameter. Similarly, the social value of an increase in an individual's wealth is the partial derivative of social welfare with respect to the individual's wealth. These definitions are analogous to the definition of the social value of risk reduction in the case of mortality.

Under the utilitarian SWF, social welfare is the sum of each individual's expected utility (equation (7.8)). The contribution to social welfare of a single individual[21]

$$V^U = U = [1 - p(q + h - qh)]u(c) + v(c). \tag{7.9}$$

The social value of a reduction in parameter θ is $-\frac{\partial V^U}{d\theta} = -\frac{\partial U}{d\theta}$, where $\theta = p$, q, or h. A decrease in baseline risk, lethality, or severity increases individual expected utility, and so the social value of a decrease in each of these dimensions is positive. The sensitivity of the social values to the parameter values are summarized in Table 7.4.

The social value of an improvement (reduction) in baseline risk p, lethality q, and severity h is independent of the value of that parameter and is increasing in wealth. An increase in baseline risk p increases the social value of both treatment (reducing lethality q) and care (reducing severity h). The intuition is that, the more likely the individual is to become sick, the more likely it is that she will benefit from a reduction in lethality or severity. An increase in either lethality or severity decreases the social value of reducing the other, because it makes it less likely the individual will benefit from that reduction.

Under the ex ante prioritarian SWF, social welfare is the sum of each individual's expected utility U transformed by an increasing, concave function g. The contribution to social welfare of a single individual

$$V^{EAP} = g[U] = g\{[1 - p(q + h - qh)]u(c) + v(c)\}. \tag{7.10}$$

The social value of a reduction in parameter θ is given by $-\frac{\partial V^{EAP}}{d\theta} = -g'(U)\frac{\partial U}{d\theta}$, i.e., the social value of reducing that parameter under the utilitarian SWF multiplied by a priority factor that is equal to the slope of the transformation function g evaluated at the individual's expected utility. Under this SWF, many of the effects are ambiguous because a change in a parameter that increases the individual's expected utility (and hence the social value under the utilitarian SWF) decreases priority to the individual. The effects of an increase

[21] We omit individual subscripts for simplicity.

in wealth on the social values of prevention, treatment, and care are ambiguous for this reason. The sign of the effect depends on the concavity of the function g: if the function is nearly linear, the effects go in the same direction as those under the utilitarian SWF; if it is sharply concave, the directions of the effects can be reversed.

One effect that is unambiguous under the ex ante prioritarian SWF is that an increase in baseline risk p increases the social value of all three actions: prevention, treatment, and care. Although the social value of prevention under the utilitarian SWF is independent of baseline risk, an increase in risk decreases expected utility and hence increases the priority given to the individual under the ex ante prioritarian SWF. Because of the symmetry of lethality and health in the model, their effects are symmetric: an increase in either parameter increases the social value of reducing that parameter but has an ambiguous effect on the social value of reducing the other parameter. The difference from the results under the utilitarian SWF is that an increase in lethality or severity decreases expected utility and increases priority to the individual. If the function g is sufficiently concave, the increase in social priority can more than offset the decreased gain in expected utility.

Under the ex post prioritarian SWF, social welfare is the sum of each individual's expected transformed utility. The contribution to social welfare of a single individual

$$V^{EPP} = (1-p)g[u(c)+v(c)] + p(1-q)g[(1-h)u(c)+v(c)] + pqg[v(c)] \tag{7.11}$$

and the social value of a reduction in parameter θ is given by $-\frac{\partial V^{EPP}}{d\theta}$. Results are almost identical to those under the utilitarian SWF, with the major exception that the effect of an increase in wealth on the social value of prevention, treatment, and care is ambiguous rather than positive; the social values of these changes can decrease if the function g is sufficiently concave. The only other difference from the results under the utilitarian SWF is that an increase in severity h increases the social value of care (that reduces h) while it has no effect under the utilitarian SWF; in contrast, an increase in lethality has no effect on the social value of treatment (that reduces q) under both the ex post prioritarian and utilitarian SWFs. This result breaks the symmetry of the effects of severity h and lethality q seen under the utilitarian and ex ante prioritarian SWFs. The reason is that the two parameters do not enter the ex post prioritarian SWF (equation

(7.11)) in a symmetric fashion. Severity h is a parameter of utility conditional on illness, so it enters as part of the argument of the transformation function g, specifically as $g[(1 - h)\, u(c) + v(c)]$. In contrast, lethality q is a probability and so it never appears in the argument of g.

Comparison of the relative social values of reducing each of the three dimensions of health risk reveals that results are identical for BCA, the utilitarian and the ex ante prioritarian SWF. This follows because the social value of reducing each parameter under BCA equals the social value under the utilitarian SWF divided by the expected marginal utility of wealth, and the social value under the ex ante prioritarian SWF equals the social value under the utilitarian SWF multiplied by the slope of the transformation function g evaluated at the individual's expected utility. Hence if the social value of reducing one parameter is larger than the social value of reducing another under the utilitarian SWF, the same is true under BCA and the ex ante prioritarian SWF.

Because of the symmetry of the roles of lethality q and health deterioration h in the model (except under the ex post prioritarian SWF), the relative social values of treatment (to reduce q) and care (to reduce h) are determined by their relative magnitudes. Under BCA, the utilitarian SWF, and the ex ante prioritarian SWF, the marginal social value of decreasing one of these parameters is always greater for the larger of the two parameters. That is, treatment (to reduce q) has a higher social value than care (to reduce h) if and only if $q > h$.

The social value of prevention (to reduce p) is larger than the social value of treatment (to reduce q) if and only if $\frac{h}{1-h} > p - q$. This condition is satisfied for diseases that are uncommon and lethal (for which $p < q$). For diseases that are rarely fatal ($q \approx 0$), the condition is satisfied only if health deterioration is large compared with baseline risk; for common, mild, nonfatal illnesses, the social value of treatment can exceed that of prevention. The social value of prevention is larger than that of care (to reduce h) if and only if $\frac{q}{1-q} > p - h$. This condition is satisfied for diseases that are uncommon and severe (for which $p < h$), and for highly lethal diseases (with $q \approx 1$). For common, mild, nonfatal illnesses, the social value of care can exceed that of prevention.

Under the ex post prioritarian SWF, the social value of treatment (decreasing lethality q) exceeds the social value of palliative care (decreasing health deterioration h) if $q \geq h$. The social value of prevention (decreasing risk p) is greater than that of treatment (decreasing lethality q) if baseline risk p is near zero or health deterioration h is near one, i.e., for very rare or very severe disease. If lethality q and health deterioration h are both small, and risk p is not too small, then treatment has a larger social value than prevention. Prevention (to reduce risk) has a larger social value than care (to reduce severity) if h is small and q is larger than p or if h and q are large and p is small. Care has a larger social value than prevention if the disease is rarely fatal ($q \approx 0$) and if health deterioration is smaller than baseline risk.

In summary, in the case of fatal risk, better health conditional on survival increases SVRR under the utilitarian and ex post prioritarian SWFs but can increase or decrease SVRR under the ex ante prioritarian SWF and BCA. In the case of more general health risks, the social value of an improvement in any of the three dimensions of health risk (baseline risk, lethality, and severity of condition) is positive under BCA and the three benchmark SWFs. The sensitivities of the social values of risk reduction to changes in parameters differ substantially across the evaluation methods. One general result is that the social values are all increasing in wealth under BCA and the utilitarian SWF, but can increase, decrease, or be unaffected by wealth under the ex ante and ex post prioritarian SWFs. Another result is that the social value of prevention is larger when the health condition is more lethal or more severe; it is also larger when the baseline risk is higher under BCA and the ex ante prioritarian SWF, but is unaffected by baseline risk under the utilitarian and ex post prioritarian SWFs.

7.7 Conclusion

Concern about how to value reductions in mortality risk to people of different ages, incomes, and other characteristics has been a perennial issue in the evaluation of environmental, health, and safety policies. Typically, these policies have been evaluated using benefit-cost analysis and the value of reducing mortality risk is quantified as a value per statistical life (VSL). Analyses within a national population generally use a common VSL, independent of individual characteristics. In contrast, evaluation of medical and public health interventions such as vaccination often use a constant value per unit increase in life expectancy, i.e., a constant value per life year or per life year adjusted for health (such as quality-adjusted or disability-adjusted life years).[22]

[22] These analyses are often framed as cost-effectiveness analyses, where the health effect is valued in terms of the expected increase in quality-adjusted life years (or some other measure of health and longevity).

Obviously the two approaches are mutually inconsistent as the gain in life expectancy associated with a reduction in current-period mortality risk is proportional to life expectancy conditional on surviving the current period, which typically decreases with age.

The use of social-welfare functions may help to defuse this tension. An important reason for the use of a common value, either per expected life saved or per expected life year gained, is a desire to treat individuals equitably, perhaps equally. Conventional BCA attempts to separate evaluation of efficiency and equity, where efficiency is defined by the Kaldor-Hicks compensation test: a policy is efficient if the individuals who benefit from the policy could hypothetically compensate the individuals harmed by the policy with money, so that everyone would prefer the policy change plus compensation to the status quo. Recognizing that this compensation is hypothetical and is typically not made, it is conventional to supplement BCA (or at least to recommend it be supplemented) with an analysis of the distributional effects. The notion is that decision makers can choose policies recognizing both efficiency and distributional effects and make appropriate trade-offs between these dimensions.

Unlike conventional BCA, social-welfare functions can explicitly incorporate concerns for distribution together with concerns for efficiency. In principle, there is no need, and perhaps no advantage, to supplement an SWF analysis with a distributional analysis. Agreement on an appropriate SWF (including the functional form and parameter values), or at least agreement on a limited set of SWFs and parameter values, might reduce some of the tension about balancing effects on efficiency and equity. Use of an SWF requires choice of an interpersonally comparable measure of wellbeing, which is not required for BCA.

The simulations reported in Section 7.5 suggest that differences in the social value of reducing risk to individuals with different incomes (and associated baseline mortality risks) are much smaller under any of the benchmark social-welfare functions than they are under BCA. Plausible SWFs treat individuals with different incomes more similarly than does BCA and for this reason may be perceived as more equitable. In contrast, the effect of differences in age can be smaller or larger under the benchmark SWFs than under BCA. If differences in the social value of risk reduction are justified by a particular model of equity that is embedded in the chosen SWF, they may be more acceptable to decision makers and the public than the differences that arise under BCA.

To determine whether the use of SWFs in evaluation of fatality risk regulations will help to better inform policy choice, much work remains to be done. Incorporating distributional effects in policy analysis requires more information on how policy effects are distributed than is necessary for BCA. In particular, information about how costs (reductions in disposable income) are distributed in a population is not needed for BCA but can be critical when applying an SWF (or conducting a distributional analysis). Because costs often appear in the form of increases in taxes or product prices, or decreases in wages, their incidence depends on how people respond to these market changes and can be difficult to estimate. Moreover, under prioritarian SWFs, the evaluation depends on history; the priority given to different individuals depends on their lifetime wellbeing, which depends on their wellbeing in previous periods. Collecting and organizing the information needed to adequately represent the distribution of lifetime wellbeing and its relationship to the distribution of possible consequences is a challenging topic for future work.

References

Adler, M.D. (2019). *Measuring Social Welfare: An Introduction*, Oxford: Oxford University Press.

Adler, M.D., Ferranna, M., Hammitt, J.K. and Treich, N. (2019). "Fair innings? The utilitarian and prioritarian value of risk reduction over a whole lifetime," Duke Law School Public Law and Legal Theory Working Paper No. 2019-79. Available at https://ssrn.com/abstract=3493976.

(2021). "Fair innings? The utilitarian and prioritarian value of risk reduction over a whole lifetime," *Journal of Health Economics* 75: 102–412.

Adler, M.D., Hammitt, J.K. and Treich, N. (2014). "The social value of mortality risk reduction: VSL versus the social welfare function approach," *Journal of Health Economics* 35: 82–93.

Baker, R., Chilton, S., Jones-Lee, M. and Metcalf, H. (2008). "Valuing lives equally: defensible premise or unwarranted promise?" *Journal of Risk and Uncertainty* 36: 125–138.

Bernard, C., Rheinberger, C.M. and Treich, N. (2018). "Catastrophe aversion and risk equity in an interdependent world," *Management Science* 64: 4490–4504.

Cameron, T.A. (2010). "Euthanizing the value of a statistical life," *Review of Environmental Economics and Policy* 4: 161–178.

Chetty, R., Stepner, M., Abraham, S., Lin, S., Scuderi, B., Turner, N., Bergeron, A. and Cutler, D. (2016). "The association between income and life expectancy in the United States, 2001–2014," *JAMA* 315: 1750–1766.

Drèze J. (1962). "L'Utilité sociale d'une vie humaine," *Revue Française de Recherche Opérationelle*, 6: 93–118.

Fleurbaey, M. (2010). "Assessing risky social situations," *Journal of Political Economy* 118: 649–680.

Hammitt, J.K. (2021). "Prevention, treatment, and palliative care: the relative value of health improvements under alternative evaluation frameworks," mimeo, February.

Harris, J. (1985). *The Value of Life*, London: Routledge and Kegan Paul.

Jones-Lee, M.W. (1974). "The value of changes in the probability of death or injury," *Journal of Political Economy* 82: 835–849.

Keeney, R.L. (1980). "Equity and public risk," *Operations Research* 28: 527–534.

Lee, J.M. and Taylor, L.O. (2019). "Randomized safety inspections and risk exposure on the job: quasi-experimental estimates of the value of a statistical life," *American Economic Journal: Economic Policy* 11: 350–374.

Levy, J.I. (2021). "Accounting for health risk inequality in regulatory impact analysis: barriers and opportunities," *Risk Analysis* 41: 610–618.

Levy, J.I., Chemerynski, S.M. and Tuchmann, J.L. (2006). "Incorporating Concepts of Inequality and Inequity into Health Benefits Analysis," *International Journal for Equity in Health* 5: Article 2.

Ng, Y.-K. (1992). "The older the more valuable: divergence between utility and dollar values of life as one ages," *Journal of Economics* 55: 1–16.

OECD. (2018). *OECD Regulatory Policy Outlook 2018*, Paris: OECD Publishing.

Pratt, J.W. and Zeckhauser, R.J. (1996). "Willingness to pay and the distribution of risk and wealth," *Journal of Political Economy* 104: 747–763.

Rheinberger, C.M., Herrera-Araujo, D. and Hammitt, J.K. (2016). "The value of disease prevention vs. treatment," *Journal of Health Economics* 50: 247–255.

Rheinberger, C.M. and Treich, N. (2017). "Attitudes toward catastrophe," *Environmental and Resource Economics* 67: 609–636.

Robinson, L.A. (2007). "How US government agencies value mortality risk reductions," *Review of Environmental Economics and Policy* 1: 283–299.

Robinson, L.A., Hammitt, J.K. and Zeckhauser, R.J. (2016). "Attention to distribution in U.S. regulatory analyses," *Review of Environmental Economics and Policy* 10: 308–328.

Schelling T.C. (1968). The life you save may be your own. In S.B. Chase, Jr., ed., *Problems in Public Expenditure Analysis*. Washington, DC: Brookings Institution, pp. 127–162.

Shepard, D.S. and Zeckhauser, R.J. (1984). "Survival versus consumption," *Management Science* 30: 423–439.

Sheriff, G. and Maguire, K.B. (2020). "Health Risk, Inequality Indexes, and Environmental Justice," *Risk Analysis* 40: 2661–2674.

Simon, N.B., Dockins, C., Maguire, K.B., Newbold, S.C., Krupnick, A.J. and Taylor, L.O. (2019). "What's in a name? a search for alternatives to 'VSL'," *Review of Environmental Economics and Policy* 13: 155–161.

Tunçel, T. and Hammitt, J.K. (2014). "A New meta-analysis on the WTP/WTA disparity," *Journal of Environmental Economics and Management* 68: 175–187.

U.S. Environmental Protection Agency. (2011). *The Benefits and Costs of the Clean Air Act from 1990 to 2020*, Final Report, Rev. A, Washington, D.C.

Viscusi, W.K. (2009). "The devaluation of life," *Regulation and Governance* 3: 103–127.

Weinstein, M.C., Shepard, D.S. and Pliskin, J.S. (1980). "The economic value of changing mortality probabilities: a decision-theoretic approach," *Quarterly Journal of Economics* 94: 373–396.

Williams, A. (1997). "Intergenerational equity: an exploration of the 'fair innings' argument," *Health Economics* 6: 117–132.

8 *Prioritarianism and Climate Change*

MADDALENA FERRANNA AND
MARC FLEURBAEY*

8.1 Introduction

Judgments about what is fair and morally defensible play a central role in designing climate policies. Climate change is, first of all, an intergenerational equity issue. The carbon emissions produced today will generate damages only in the future; on the other hand, future generations are likely to be richer than the current one, and climate policy will impose costs on the relatively poor people and benefit the relatively richer ones. Climate change also exacerbates intra-generational inequality. Climate policies are likely to be regressive, imposing higher costs on the current poor; on the other hand, climate change will likely fall hard on the future poor. On top of that, climate change entails huge risks and uncertainties. It might have catastrophic consequences, to the point of reducing human beings to subsistence levels or even wiping out human life on earth. The key word here is "might," since we do not know whether that is even possible. We also do not know how future people will value climate damages and ecosystem services. In addition, climate change will likely determine the identity and existence of future people; thus, any climate policy will have an impact on who our descendants will be.

When studying the desirable characteristics of climate policy, ethical considerations are incorporated in a social welfare function, which aggregates the well-being of the individuals in the (present, future, and possibly past) population. The social welfare function adjudicates the conflicting interests of present and future people, of rich and poor, and of existing and possible individuals. Most of the climate change literature adopts a utilitarian welfare framework. Policy

* We thank participants at the Prioritarianism in Practice meetings on May 3–4, 2019 and May 21–22, 2020 for useful comments.

recommendations that are analyzed in the literature, and that fuel the debate in the policy arena, are mostly based on the utilitarian social welfare approach. This chapter discusses some of the implications for climate policy if we move from a utilitarian to a prioritarian welfare framework.

The chapter has two main objectives: first, to determine whether prioritarianism is a feasible approach in the climate change context, by highlighting the main advantages and drawbacks from a practical point of view; and second, to discuss the main features of a prioritarian climate policy. In particular, we are interested in understanding to which extent the prioritarian climate policy differs, in practice, from the utilitarian one. Our main conclusion is that, given the specific characteristics of the climate problem, and the way they are represented in the literature, in the simplest deterministic setting the utilitarian social welfare function can be re-interpreted as a prioritarian one.[1] Thus, prioritarianism and utilitarianism often lead to similar policy implications. The switch to a prioritarian approach matters in specific contexts, for example when we want to emphasize the role of climate risks. The utilitarian climate policy may not be sensitive enough to the presence of risk because the curvature of the utility function represents both attitudes to risk and attitudes to inequality, whereas the two attitudes should arguably have contrasting effects on the optimal climate policy. In contrast, the prioritarian approach allows us to disentangle attitudes to risk and attitudes to well-being inequality, thereby putting separate emphasis on risk and inequality.

The chapter is structured as follows. Section 8.2 reviews some of the main debates concerning climate policies, and shows how they relate to the social welfare function approach. In particular, this section discusses issues related to discounting, the treatment of intra-generational inequality, catastrophic risks, population ethics and non-human species. Section 8.3 discusses the discounted utilitarian welfare framework frequently used in climate policies, and describes the different prioritarian approaches that can be applied in the climate change context. Section 8.4 compares the policy recommendations of the discounted utilitarian approach to those derived from a prioritarian

[1] See also Adler, Chapter 2, this volume on how prioritarianism relative to one well-being measure is equivalent to utilitarianism relative to a different well-being measure.

welfare function. This section focuses on a deterministic environment, while Section 8.5 considers a risky environment. Section 8.6 discusses some extensions: heterogeneous preferences, equivalent income, uncertainty (as distinct from risk), and population ethics. Section 8.7 concludes.

8.2 Hot topics in climate policy: a brief introduction to the economics of climate change

When analyzing the type of interventions that are needed to fight climate change, the usual starting point is a so-called Integrated Assessment Model (IAM). An IAM is a model that describes the interactions between the economy and the climate system. Production and consumption processes generate CO2 emissions, which accumulate in the atmosphere, alter the climate dynamics and induce an increase in temperature. Higher temperatures negatively affect the production and consumption possibilities of individuals, and, as a consequence, their well-being. Climate damages affect multiple dimensions of well-being, and they can range from productivity losses to increases in health risks and biodiversity impacts. Because of the inertia in the climate system, climate damages occur years after the carbon emissions are released into the atmosphere. This creates an intergenerational tension, as damages are produced by the current generation but they are borne mainly by future generations. Conversely, the introduction of a climate policy aimed at reducing the amount of carbon emissions is costly for the current generation and beneficial to future generations.[2] The prescribed climate policy is derived by maximizing a social welfare function that aggregates the well-being of different

[2] In the chapter we will focus mainly on policies that prescribe a temporal path of emission reductions (mitigation policy). Alternative climate policies include investments in technologies that help individuals to adapt to the modified climate and reduce the amount of suffering (e.g., using more climate-resistant crops or improving building insulation), and geoengineering programs that artificially modify the climate. The normative issues with adaptation and geoengineering policies are slightly different than with mitigation policies. Adaptation policies often have short-term impacts, i.e., both the costs and the benefits of the policy occur in the same generation. Geoengineering the climate might impose new unpredictable risks, thereby raising issues of the morality of trading one risk with another.

generations and individuals, and trades off conflicting interests between those that have to pay for the policy (the present generation) and those that are expected to benefit from it (future generations).[3]

One of the main outputs of an IAM is the Social Cost of Carbon (SCC). The SCC represents the monetized value of all the damages caused by a single ton of carbon emitted into the atmosphere. It is a central figure in any climate change discussion. The higher the SCC, the larger the amount of emission reductions that should be implemented. The SCC can serve as the basis of a carbon tax, or be used to set the cap in a cap-and-trade emission system. More generally, the SCC can be used in any cost-benefit analysis exercise to assess the value of a climate-related project and predict its returns (e.g., improving the energy-efficiency of buildings). For instance, in the United States, the potential use in federal cost-benefit analysis induced the Obama administration to establish a standardized range of SCC figures.[4]

Computationally, the SCC is equivalent to the present value of the sum of future monetized damages. Two main ingredients contribute to its value: the size of damages produced by one ton of carbon, and a rule to discount them in present terms so as to be able to compare the SCC figure to the current costs of the policy. Ethical considerations, and, in particular, the choice of the social welfare function, affect both ingredients.[5] We will now briefly review four of the most debated topics related to the SCC (and to climate policy in general), and discuss how they interact with the choice of the social welfare function.

[3] Note that IAMs can be divided into two broad categories: i) relatively simple, aggregate models aimed at determining the desired temporal path of emission reductions; ii) very sophisticated models, with a lot of details about the spectrum of technologies, that look at the least costly way to implement the desired emission reductions. Throughout the chapter, we will refer exclusively to the first type of models.

[4] See www.epa.gov/sites/production/files/2016-12/documents/sc_co2_tsd_august_2016.pdf and the most recent review under the Trump administration www.epa.gov/sites/production/files/2017-10/documents/ria_proposed-cpp-repeal_2017-10.pdf. The Interagency Working Group on the Social Cost of Carbon made use of three frequently used IAMs: FUND (Framework for Uncertainty, Negotiation and Distribution, www.fund-model.org/), DICE (Dynamic Integrated Climate Economy model, https://sites.google.com/site/williamdnordhaus/dice-rice), and PAGE (Policy Analysis of the Greenhouse Effect, Hope 2006).

[5] See, for instance, Fleurbaey et al. (2019) for a discussion of the role of different ethical values in the determination of the SCC.

Discounting.[6] Discounting has probably been the hottest topic in climate change economics.[7] To understand the importance of discounting, let us consider the following example. Suppose one ton of carbon produces $100 damages in 100 years. If future dollars are discounted at 1 percent per year, $100 in 100 years are equivalent to about $37 today. If future dollars are discounted at 3 percent per year, $100 in 100 years are equivalent to just $5 today.[8] The larger the discount rate, the lower the monetized value of damages in present terms, and, as a consequence, the lower the SCC and the more lenient the climate policy. As a more concrete example, the Obama administration proposed a 3 percent discount rate to be used, as a central estimate, in climate change projects, resulting in an SCC of $42 for the year 2020 (in 2007 dollars per metric of CO2). Under the Trump administration, the US federal government's central figure fell to $1 due to the preferred choice of a 7 percent discount rate and the restriction of climate change impacts to national impacts only.

The choice of the discount rate is inherently linked to the characteristics of the social welfare function. The discount rate reflects how much less valuable it is to give $1 to a future generation rather than giving the same $1 to the current generation. And the role of a social welfare function is exactly to mediate conflicting interests and set priorities. However, the discount rate is not a purely ethical parameter. The value of consuming in the future vs consumption today depends also on empirical predictions about economic growth or the distribution of future climate damages and risks (Gollier 2012). For example, if the future is going to be richer than the present, that is a reason for discounting and giving priority to the consumption of the current generation. If the future generation faces the possibility of catastrophic climate damages, that is a reason for not discounting and for giving

[6] This paragraph discusses the concept of "consumption discounting", i.e., the value attached to future $ amounts as compared to current $ amounts. Consumption discounting (or simply discounting from now on) should not be confused with "utility" or "time" discounting (or rate of pure time preference), a concept that will be introduced in Section 8.3 and that refers to the relative value attached to the well-being of future generations (as distinct from future $). Note that we can have consumption discounting without imposing time discounting.

[7] See Gollier (2012) on how to compute the consumption discount rate in climate change projects.

[8] If r is the (constant) annual discount rate, then the present value of $100 in t years is equal to: $\frac{\$100}{(1+r)^t}$.

priority to a future generation (Weitzman 2009). If damages from climate change are borne mainly by future *poor* people, that is again a reason for not discounting (Schelling 1995, Dennig et al. 2015). The strength of these opposite reasons is related to the social welfare function.

The debate on discounting can be divided into two main streams. A few papers focus on the type of social welfare function that should be used in climate policy. Most of the analyses based on IAMs adopt a utilitarian approach. However, other contenders have been proposed: prioritarian approaches (Adler et al. 2017), sustainable discounted utilitarianism (Dietz and Asheim 2012), rank discounted social welfare functions (Zuber and Asheim 2012), Epstein-Zin preferences to better represent preferences for risk (Traeger 2009, Gollier 2002), and ambiguity-sensitive criteria (Millner et al. 2013). This chapter contributes to this stream of the literature, and we will see later how a utilitarian vs. a prioritarian social welfare function affects the discount rate, and, as a consequence, the SCC.

Most of the literature on discounting retains a utilitarian approach, and discusses how to choose its parameter values and calibrate the discounting rule. A broad distinction can be made between prescriptive and descriptive approaches to discounting (Kelleher 2017). Descriptivists posit that the utilitarian function used in IAMs describes the preferences of a hypothetical representative agent in the economy; its calibration, then, should be based on market data. In contrast, prescriptivists posit that the utilitarian social welfare function is a representation of ethical premises, and the choice of its form cannot be based on individuals' behavior but on normative considerations. The famous Stern–Nordhaus debate revolves exactly around this point. Stern (2007) takes an ethical stance in calibrating the welfare function, and proposes an annual discount rate of 1.4 percent, which results in a SCC of more than $200 per ton of CO2. Instead, Nordhaus (2007) suggests a discount rate of around 5 percent to match financial market data, which results in a much lower SCC.

Inequality. The representative agent idea behind the descriptive approach is widespread in the climate change economics literature, and not only when it comes to the selection of the parameters that enter into the welfare function. Many studies using IAMs only look at inequality among generations, thereby neglecting inequalities within generations, despite the fact that background inequality, and, in particular, who is expected to pay for the climate policy, plays a central role in any political discussion of climate interventions.[9]

Some IAMs do introduce intra-generational inequality, but they often rely on the so-called Negishi weights to separate efficiency and distributional considerations, i.e., to avoid that the climate policy (or its absence) is defined by the extent to which it is capable of redistributing resources and reducing inequality (Nordhaus 2008). Formally, Negishi weights are utility weights set proportionally to the inverse of the marginal utility of consumption such that, under the standard utilitarian social welfare function, the existing distribution of consumption across individuals is the optimal one, no matter how unequal it is. Equivalently, it is implicitly assumed that there exists another (and better) way to redistribute resources both in the present and future generations, and that climate policy should not be concerned with that. However, imperfections in existing risk sharing schemes within and among countries undermine the idea that better redistributive policies will be put in place.[10]

Catastrophes. A third hot topic in the climate change economics literature is the presence of catastrophic risks. If climate change entails catastrophic outcomes, such as the destruction of life on earth as we know it, and brings humanity back to subsistence consumption levels, and if the likelihood of those outcomes is sufficiently high, then climate policy might prescribe to do whatever would prevent it. Weitzman's "dismal theorem" drives attention to the fat tails of the probability distribution of climate sensitivity, which is suggested to be an inevitable consequence of the deep structural uncertainty surrounding the effects of carbon emissions on climate (Weitzman 2009). In particular, if the risk of catastrophic outcomes is relevant, the debate about inter- and intra-generational inequality becomes of second-order importance, and the focus of the analysis should be shifted to assessing the value of catastrophes and the probability of very negative consequences.[11]

[9] See, for instance, the "Yellow Vests" protest against the introduction of a carbon tax in France (www.nytimes.com/2018/12/06/world/europe/france-fuel-carbon-tax.html).

[10] If one is worried about the excessive redistributive impacts of climate policy, one can always study climate policy in conjunction with other redistributive policies. See, for instance, Kornek et al. (2021) on the relation between national redistributive policies and the SCC.

[11] For example, Pindyck (2019) suggests completely dismissing the IAM tool (and the related social welfare function), and just focusing on the likelihood of extreme losses in consumption when computing the SCC.

Population size and non-human species. Catastrophic outcomes refer not only to drastic reductions in consumption possibilities of future generations. A catastrophe may also mean that the entire human species is wiped out, or its population substantially reduced. And a catastrophe may also refer to the fact that non-human species go extinct. More generally, climate change and climate policy will likely influence both the identity of people that will live in the future and their number, by affecting patterns of fertility and mortality, and, possibly, the preferences of future individuals. Also, climate change and climate policy will likely affect biodiversity and ecosystem services, thereby raising issues related to the rights and welfare of non-human species. This set of topics is related to population ethics and they are still relatively unexplored, although frequently debated in political and philosophical circles.

Most IAMs neglect to consider the impact of climate change on future human population size. A few exceptions include Millner (2013) and Méjean et al. (2020), who both integrate population issues in a utilitarian approach. Moreover, existing IAMs poorly incorporate the impact of climate change on non-human species. The few existing estimates focus on the instrumental value of non-human species, and the environment in general, while they overlook their intrinsic value.[12] In addition, the instrumental value that is captured often refers only to services and amenities with a clear market value, while it neglects non-market attributes, such as cultural values or the value of enjoying a pristine environment.[13]

8.3 Utilitarianism vs Prioritarianism: Basic Concepts

Most IAMs adopt a discounted utilitarian social welfare function. This section discusses the characteristics of the discounted utilitarian approach as applied to climate policy. Given the complexity of the climate problem, IAMs make a number of simplifying assumptions: homogeneous individual preferences, consumption as the only attribute of individual well-being, no impact of climate change on the number and identity of future individuals. Under those restrictive assumptions, we will first formalize prioritarian social welfare

[12] For a pioneering attempt at taking account of the well-being of other species in an IAM, see Budolfson and Spears (2018).

[13] See, for instance, Tol (2009) for a discussion of the damage estimates related to ecosystem services and biodiversity.

functions applied to climate change, and then, in Sections 8.4 and 8.5 we will discuss the implications of prioritarianism for climate policy in a deterministic and in a risky context, respectively. Extensions of the framework will be considered in Section 8.6.

8.3.1 Expected Discounted Utilitarianism

The Expected Discounted Utilitarian (EDU) social welfare function adds up the expected well-being of present and future generations and attaches an exponentially decreasing weight to people living in the future. Let $t = \{0, .., T\}$ denote the time period, with T the maximum horizon of human species existence,[14] $i = \{1, .., I\}$ a social group or region of the world. Furthermore, let $s = \{1, .., S\}$ denote the state of the world, and π_s the probability that state s occurs, with $\sum_{s=1}^{S} \pi_s = 1$. The EDU social welfare function W^{EDU} widely used in the climate change literature is given by the following expression:[15]

$$W^{EDU} = \sum_{t=0}^{T} \frac{1}{(1+\rho)^t} \left(\sum_{s=1}^{S} \pi_s \left(\sum_{i=1}^{I} N_{it} u(c_{sit}) \right) \right) \tag{8.1}$$

where $\rho \geq 0$ represents the "time discount rate" (the rate ranges from 0.1 percent to 1.5 percent in the literature), c_{sit} the per capita consumption level, N_{it} the number of people in group i living in period t, and u a von Neumann-Morgenstern (vNM) utility function which measures individuals' well-being.

Several assumptions are embedded in the EDU formula. Because of utility discounting, people living in the present have more weight in social evaluation than people living in future generations.[16] For instance, if $\rho = 1\%$, the utility of individuals living in period $t = 1$ is weighted 1 percent less than the utility of individuals living in the current period $t = 0$, while the utility of individuals living in period $t = 10$ is weighted 9 percent less and the utility of individuals living in period $t = 100$ is weighted 63 percent less than the utility of

[14] $t = 0$ is considered the current period. Note that the maximum length T may be infinity.

[15] To avoid confusion with the symbol for states of nature s, we depart by the norm of this volume and use W to denote the social welfare function instead of S.

[16] Remember that the concept of utility discounting should not be confused with the concept of consumption discounting discussed in Section 8.2. Utility discounting is not a prerequisite of consumption discounting, although it may be an element of it.

individuals living in the current period.[17] Because of utility discounting, the well-being of individuals living in the far future is practically neglected when choosing the climate policy.

The difference between the descriptive and the prescriptive approach has been stark about the calibration of the parameter ρ. The authors endorsing an ethical approach support a close-to-zero value of ρ to represent an exogenous risk of human extinction (Dasgupta and Heal 1979; Cline 1992; Stern 2007). Since we are not sure that future generations will exist (independently from the climate change phenomenon), their well-being should be assigned a lower value in line with their probability of existing.[18] On the other side, the descriptivists call for larger values of ρ on the basis of preferences revealed in financial markets (Nordhaus 2007; Weitzman 2007). The main argument is that a zero time discount rate would imply too much sacrifice for the current generation for the sake of future generations, a propensity to sacrifice that is not supported by existing behavior. Financial markets, according to this view, reveal how much individuals really care for the future.

In applications, a period is often a decade. This makes it difficult to interpret each period as corresponding to a different generation. But if each individual's utility is a discounted sum of instantaneous utility, with the same discount rate ρ,[19] and if consumption in every period is distributed equally across people, then the EDU formula is actually the discounted sum of individuals' lifetime utilities, each lifetime utility being inserted into the formula at the period of birth of the individual.[20]

17 If the rate of time preference is 1 percent, the weight attached to individuals living in period $t = 1$ is $\frac{1}{1+0.01} = 0.99$, the weight attached to individuals living in period $t = 10$ is $\left(\frac{1}{1+0.01}\right)^{10} = 0.91$, and the weight attached to individuals living in period $t = 100$ is $\left(\frac{1}{1+0.01}\right)^{100} = 0.37$.

18 For instance, Stern (2007) assumes that the risk of extinction is 1/1,000 per year, which implies a 10 percent probability of human extinction in the coming 100 years.

19 Such a coincidence is unlikely. The rate of time preference for the purpose of intrapersonal discounting is a matter for each individual's self-interested preferences, whereas the choice of the rate of time preference for discounted utilitarianism is either (a) an ethical matter (an ethical judgment that we should discount the future, e.g., to avoid a utilitarianism that sacrifices the present for the future), or (b) a matter of society's revealed intergenerational preference.

20 For a rigorous overlapping generations modeling see, for instance, Schneider et al. (2012). Alternatively, the EDU formula can be read as assuming that each individual lives for more than one period but is regarded as a distinct self in each period.

The utility function is increasing in consumption as individuals prefer more consumption to less. Consumption is usually interpreted as incorporating additional amenities such as longevity, and this will be discussed in Section 8.6.2. The utility function is also concave due to a "diminishing marginal utility assumption," according to which the effect on u of an additional unit of consumption decreases with the level of consumption. The diminishing marginal utility assumption implies that reductions in consumption are less harmful the richer the individual is.

Most IAMs assume that the function u has an isoelastic form: $u(c_{sit}) = \frac{c_{sit}^{1-\eta}}{1-\eta}$, where $\eta \neq 1$ is the elasticity of the marginal utility of consumption.[21] The larger η is, the more weight is given to changes in consumption at low consumption levels. The parameter η has been interpreted in at least three different ways (Anthoff et al. 2009): individuals' coefficient of relative risk aversion; individuals' (inverse) elasticity of intertemporal substitution; the coefficient of relative inequality aversion of a social evaluator. Advocates of a descriptive approach posit that the curvature of the function u can (and should) be empirically estimated from individuals' behavior concerning time and risk. Then, the parameter η would represent either risk aversion or aversion to fluctuations of consumption over time (Nordhaus 2008). Some proponents of the prescriptive approach agree that we should defer to individual preferences when calibrating the parameter η since the function u is a preference-based measure of individual well-being, whereas the choice of the time discount rate ρ is based purely on ethical principles (e.g., Stern 2007). Other proponents of the prescriptive approach view η as the propensity to trade off consumption between the rich and the poor, thereby representing ethical aversion to consumption inequality (Dasgupta 2008). Note that, in this sense, the parameter η can be interpreted as an implicit prioritarian parameter as it requires to attach larger weight to the consumption changes of the poorest. The next section will discuss that in more detail.

Independently of the meaning of the parameter η, its role is to smooth consumption across individuals, either belonging to the same generation or to different generations. As a result, (undiscounted)

[21] If η=1, then $u(c_{it}) = \log(c_{it})$. Note a small departure from the norm of the volume: since the climate literature commonly uses η to denote the elasticity parameter of the utility function, we stick with this notation instead of using λ, as other chapters of this volume do.

utilitarianism will prefer policies that benefit the poor individuals more. The introduction of time discounting will switch the ranking of policies in favor of policies that benefit the poor individuals living in the initial periods more.

In the EDU expression, climate damages operate through a reduction in the consumption level c. In many applications, climate change has no impact on the number of people N_{it} living in the future and no impact on the identity of future individuals. That explains why in expression (8.1) the same number of people live in all future states of nature, i.e., N_{it} is independent of s. Climate change affects only how much those individuals can consume.

8.3.2 Prioritarian Social Welfare Functions

8.3.2.1 Deterministic Setting

A prioritarian welfare framework applied to climate change is considered in Adler and Treich (2015) and Adler et al. (2017). Both papers mainly focus on a deterministic setting, where the consumption of present and future individuals is known for sure (in other words, there is only one possible state of the world). While maintaining the same assumptions as before, the prioritarian social welfare function looks like the following:

$$W^P = \sum_{t=0}^{T} \sum_{i=1}^{I} N_{it} g(u(c_{it})) \tag{8.2}$$

where g is a strictly increasing and concave transformation of individual well-being, u is lifetime individual well-being (under the homogeneous preferences assumption), and c_{it} is the consumption of individual i living in period t. As before, we assume that u is a von Neumann-Morgenstern utility function, although alternative well-being measures (e.g., equivalent income) can be embodied in the formula.

There are two main differences with respect to the discounted utilitarian expression (8.1). First of all, there is no time discounting. Current people do not have more social importance just because they live in the present. In theory, prioritarianism could take a discounted form by adding the discount factor $\frac{1}{(1+\rho)^t}$. However, the existing work on climate prioritarianism has adopted a non-discounted version. Within a prescriptive approach to identify the social welfare function, discounted prioritarianism is normatively unattractive, since time discounting is normatively unattractive.

The second difference concerns the presence of the concave transformation function *g*, which gives substance to the prioritarian statement by giving greater weight to well-being improvements affecting individuals at lower well-being levels.

The prioritarian approach requires the specification of an ethically defensible transformation function *g*. Adler, Chapter 2 this volume, has presented arguments in favor of an Atkinson transformation function, with $W^P = \sum_{\text{it}} N_{it} \frac{(u(c_{it}) - u^{zero})^{1-\gamma}}{1-\gamma}$. If that is the case, the choice of *g* entails the choice of the priority parameter γ and consumption subsistence level c_{zero}, such that $u^{zero} \equiv u(c_{zero})$, to rescale the well-being so as to avoid negative numbers. Under the common assumption of isoelastic utility function, $u(c_{it}) = \frac{c_{it}^{1-\eta}}{1-\eta}$, the prioritarian social welfare function is fully characterized by three parameters: the priority parameter γ, the consumption subsistence level c_{zero}, and the coefficient η, which represents risk aversion if one measures well-being by (suitably normalized) von Neumann-Morgenstern utilities. When $\gamma = 0$, we fall back on (undiscounted) utilitarianism.

An alternative transformation function presented in Adler, Chapter 2 this volume, is the Kolm-Pollak prioritarian function, according to which $g(w_i) = -e^{-\beta w_i}$ for any well-being measure w_i. The parameter $\beta > 0$ captures the degree of priority for the worse off. The prioritarian objective would then be $-\sum_{it} N_{it} e^{-\beta u(c_{it})}$. Under the standard assumption of isoelastic utility function, the social welfare function is fully characterized by two parameters: the priority parameter β and the elasticity of marginal utility of consumption η.

If we consider either an Atkinson or a Kolm-Pollak transformation function, the coefficient η is an empirical parameter that represents individuals' self-interested attitudes toward risk in consumption. Instead, the choice of the priority parameters γ and β is an ethical issue, capturing the social evaluator's attitudes towards inequality in individuals' well-being.

The larger the concavity of the function *g* (i.e., the higher γ or β is), the higher the priority given to the worse-off individuals. Since the framework considered so far assumes that individual well-being depends only on consumption, and that individuals have homogenous preferences, the worse-off individuals coincide with the poorest ones. Therefore, prioritarianism will prefer policies whose benefits accrue more to the poor individuals. In the simplified framework often used in the climate change literature, the implications of prioritarianism look similar to those of undiscounted utilitarianism, as both approaches favor policies that redistribute resources towards the poorest individuals. However, notice that, for a given well-being measure $u(c_{it})$, the strength of concern for the poorest is larger under prioritarianism than under utilitarianism. Indeed, under utilitarianism the degree of priority to the poor is given by the concavity of the function u, while in the prioritarian case the degree of priority is given by the concavity of the function $g \circ u$, where $\circ$ denotes a composition of functions. The utilitarian prioritizes the poor because marginal utility is decreasing (an additional unit of consumption increases the well-being of the poor more than the well-being of the rich). The prioritarian prioritizes the poor both because marginal utility is decreasing, and because marginal welfare is decreasing (an additional unit of well-being to the poor is more socially valuable than an additional unit of well-being to the rich).

In the previous section, we mentioned that the discounted utilitarian formula (8.1) is flexible to the chosen welfare criterion, and that it can be re-interpreted as a prioritarian social welfare function with respect to consumption. Indeed, although (undiscounted) utilitarianism and prioritarianism are distinct when a given well-being measure u is fixed, they can be understood as different forms of prioritarianism relative to consumption, using different concave transformations of consumption, $u(c)$ in the case of utilitarianism, and $h(c) = g(u(c))$ in the case of prioritarianism. In a deterministic setting, a prioritarian social evaluator behaves in practice as a very risk averse utilitarian social evaluator, or, vice versa, a utilitarian social evaluator behaves as a less inequality averse prioritarian social evaluator.

8.3.2.2 Prioritarianism under Risk

Expected utilitarianism defines the social objective as the sum of individual expected well-being, or, equivalently, the expected value of the sum of individual well-being (Harsanyi 1955). As a consequence, as explained in Adler, Chapter 2, this volume, expected utilitarianism is the only welfare framework that respects both individual preferences (ex-ante Pareto) and social rationality (the Dominance criterion).[22]

[22] Dominance states that if an option is preferred in all states of the world, then that option should still be preferred when the state of the world is unknown.

If we want to introduce fairness concerns (the Pigou-Dalton principle), we need to drop either ex-ante Pareto or Dominance.

By retaining ex-ante Pareto, an ex-ante prioritarian (EAP) social welfare function can be derived. The ex-ante approach consists in summing a concave transformation of individual expected utilities. In our context, where preferences are homogenous and depend on a single consumption good, the ex-ante prioritarian social welfare function is given by:

$$W^{EAP} = \sum_{t=0}^{T} \sum_{i=1}^{I} N_{it} g\left(\sum_{s \in S} \pi_s u(c_{sit}) \right) \tag{8.3}$$

where the function g captures attitudes to inequality in *expected* individual well-being. If g is linear, we are back to the expected (undiscounted) utilitarian framework.[23]

As discussed in Adler, Chapter 2 this volume, EAP violates social rationality, and, in particular, the Dominance axiom. Applied to the climate change problem, assume that we know for sure that climate change is harmful; we just do not know who is going to bear the climate damages. Social rationality requires us to prevent climate change because ex-post, it decreases well-being. However, since individuals do not know if they will actually end up suffering from climate change, their expected utilities may not be diminished ex-ante. Individuals may unanimously agree not to invest in a climate policy because climate change is not harmful from an ex-ante point of view, even though everyone knows that ex-post, someone will certainly pay for the climate damages and will regret not having invested in the policy. Violation of social rationality leads to counter-intuitive results.

In addition, EAP leads to time inconsistent preferences. The ex-ante prioritarian social evaluator may decide at time $t = 0$ how much to mitigate in each future period, and then deviate from her plan when the future arrives, even if no new information has arrived. Time consistency is considered a desirable property of public policies, although we

[23] For simplicity, population is assumed to be the same in all states of the world here. If different states can have different populations, then individuals' expected utilities have to be computed conditional on existence of the individual. In the extreme case, if every state of the world has a totally different population, then individual expected utility becomes the actual utility of the individual in that state.

could always assume that the social evaluator is sophisticated, i.e., she anticipates the time inconsistency problem and incorporates it into policy making.

If we relax the ex-ante Pareto principle and retain the Dominance axiom, we obtain an ex-post prioritarian (EPP) social welfare function, where the social objective consists in the expected value of state-dependent social welfare:

$$W^{EPP} = \sum_{s \in S} \pi_s \left(\sum_{t=1}^{T} \sum_{i=1}^{I} N_{it} g(u(c_{sit})) \right) \tag{8.4}$$

where the function g captures the social evaluator's attitudes to inequality in the distribution of individuals' *realized* well-being, and the term in parentheses can be interpreted as a prioritarian welfare function if state s occurs for sure.

The main drawback of the EPP approach is that it partly relies on the social evaluator's concerns for inequality (represented by the concavity of g) to guide risky choices, imposing a greater risk aversion than the individuals' one. For instance, suppose that there is no inequality: all individuals and generations consume the same amount, which, however, depends on the state of the world that is realized. Then, the recommendation of the social evaluator about what to do in the presence of risk differs from what the individuals would unanimously choose to do.[24] Of course, this form of paternalism might be considered a welcome feature, as more risk aversion in policy making may be advisable (Rabinowicz 2002).

Fleurbaey (2010) proposes a different version of ex-post prioritarianism, which relaxes the ex-ante Pareto principle only when there is inequality, thereby respecting individual preferences when all individuals face exactly the same risk. As EPP, the social objective consists in the expected value of a social welfare function, but the welfare function takes an "equally distributed equivalent" (EDE) form: $g^{-1}\left(\frac{1}{N}\sum_{t,i} N_{it} g(u(c_{its}))\right)$, where $N = \sum_{t,i} N_{it}$ denotes the total population. The function g^{-1} denotes the inverse of the function g. The equally distributed equivalent prioritarianism (EDE-P) approach is given by:[25]

[24] Indeed, the social evaluator chooses according to $g(u(c_s))$, while individuals use the utility function $u(c_s)$, where c_s is the consumption level in state s.

[25] Alder, Chapter 2 this volume, abbreviates "expected equally distributed equivalent prioritarianism" as EEDEP. We shorten this to EDE-P.

$$W^{EDE-P} = N\sum_{s}\pi_s g^{-1}\left(\frac{1}{N}\sum_{t,i} N_{it} g(u(c_{sit}))\right) \tag{8.5}$$

where g represents the social evaluator's attitude to inequality in realized well-being, as in the EPP approach. If there is no inequality, i.e., $c_{sit} = c_s$ for all i and t, the EDE-P approach falls back to the (undiscounted) utilitarian one: $N\sum_s \pi_s g^{-1}(\frac{1}{N}\sum_{it} N_{it} g(u(c_s))) = \sum_s \pi_s u(c_s)$.

Concavity of the function g implies that individuals with low realized well-being have higher priority in policy making. Since g is concave, the equally distributed equivalent transformation g^{-1} is convex. Therefore, an additional unit of realized well-being increases social welfare more if it occurs in a state of the world with high total welfare $\sum_{it} N_{it} g(u(c_{it}))$. The EDE-P social evaluator gives priority to individuals with low realized well-being (through the concavity of g) who suffer a low well-being in states of the world where total welfare is high. Notice that total welfare is high if: (i) individuals are on a high well-being path (i.e., in state s well-being is relatively high for all individuals); (ii) in state s inequality in well-being is relatively low (i.e., not only all individuals are doing well compared to other states, but also the gaps in well-being across individuals are small).

The main problem with the EDE-P framework is the non-separability property. The derivation of social welfare, and, as a consequence, the evaluation of any policy, depends on the fate of all individuals and generations, including the non-affected ones. In particular, the social objective is non-separable with respect to the past. This appears problematic, both because past generations have no say on current policies, and because the destiny of current and future individuals would be indissolubly anchored to what happened in the past. For instance, the non-separability assumption would reject risks for the present and future generations that create inequalities only with respect to the unconcerned past generations.

To avoid the dependence on the past issue, we could restrict attention to present and future generations in the evaluation. However, the drawback is possible time inconsistency in the policy, since the evaluation depends on the time at which it is made.[26]

[26] We could of course assume that the social evaluator is sophisticated, in the sense that she anticipates the time inconsistency issue and factors it into her evaluations. Alternatively, we could impose more structure on the welfare

Actually, dependence on the past is not such a daunting assumption after all. In most situations, future generations are going to be better off than past generations in spite of the risks they take. Thus, including the past would have little impact on the choice made by the social evaluator. Inequalities with respect to the past matter mostly when future generations risk ending up worse off than past generations. In that case, including the past would force the social evaluator to be more cautious in her assessments (Fleurbaey 2010).

Moreover, the time inconsistency that would arise by excluding past generations is unlikely to be serious in practice. If the length of the policy is far shorter than the horizon of human survival (including past and future generations), the repercussions of the policy itself on the total well-being (past, present, and future) is likely to be small, making it possible to ignore the larger picture.[27]

8.4 Prioritarian Climate Policies in a Deterministic Setting

Most of the climate economics literature focuses on intergenerational inequalities in consumption, thereby assuming that consumption is equally shared among the individuals living in the same period t. The occurrence of climate change will reduce the consumption of future generations, while a climate policy imposes costs (mainly) on the current generations due to the inertia of the climate system and the long-term nature of the problem. As a consequence, climate change raises intergenerational distribution issues. Section 8.4.1 discusses the prioritarian solution to such an intergenerational problem as compared to the undiscounted and discounted utilitarian ones.

Although undiscounted utilitarianism would be the natural comparator of (undiscounted) prioritarianism, discounted utilitarianism

function, for instance by assuming that the function g has an exponential form. In that case, the past enters only through a multiplicative factor and has no impact on the policy maker's choice. See, for instance, Fleurbaey and Zuber (2013) for welfare criteria of the EDE-P family that satisfy some separability requirements.

27 For instance, using historical data from the Maddison Project, Ferranna (2020) shows the existence of a relatively small bias in the Social Cost of Carbon figure when using an EDE-prioritarian welfare function and neglecting the past. The Maddison Project collects historical data about GDP and population back until the year 1 AD (www.ggdc.net/maddison/maddison-project/home.htm).

is the standard framework in climate policy. Therefore, we will compare the prioritarian framework to both undiscounted and discounted utilitarianism, and we will make clear in the discussion which comparison we are making. As we will explain shortly, there is also an analytical reason for comparing prioritarianism and discounted utilitarianism, i.e., prioritarianism gives the blessing to utility discounting if future generations are better off than the current one.

After discussing the differences between (undiscounted) prioritarianism and (undiscounted and discounted) utilitarianism in the baseline model, Section 8.4.2 considers the policy implications of prioritarianism if intra-generational inequality is added to the picture. Section 8.5 extends the analysis to a risky scenario. When discussing prioritarianism, we will mainly focus on an Atkinson social welfare function.

8.4.1 The Green Prioritarian Dilemma

In the absence of intra-generational inequality, the typical utilitarian welfare framework used in IAMs is given by: $W^{EDU} = \sum_{t=0}^{T} \frac{1}{(1+\rho)^t} N_t \frac{c_t^{1-\eta}}{1-\eta}$, where N_t is the total number of people living in period t, and c_t the per capita normalized consumption level. The parameter η captures the propensity to smooth consumption across generations. When $\rho \neq 0$, we obtain the discounted utilitarian expression, while $\rho = 0$ implies undiscounted utilitarianism.

Given the usual assumption of economic and social progress, future generations are assumed to be on average better-off than the current generation. As a consequence, since the climate policy entails costs for the relatively poorer present generation and benefits for relatively richer future generations, the larger the parameter η (the higher the concavity of u), the lower the urgency to act against climate change. A positive rate of pure time preference ρ reinforces this argument, since the well-being of the present generation matters more than the well-being of later generations. High ρ and high η both prescribe to postpone emission reductions in the future. The famous Stern–Nordhaus debate reduces to the choice of those two parameters. Stern (2007) calls for immediate actions by picking a low time discount rate $\rho = 0.1\%$ and a low elasticity of utility $\eta = 1$. In contrast, Nordhaus (2007) favors a "policy ramp", with a lenient climate policy today that tightens over time, due to his preferred choice of the parameters $\rho = 1.5\%$ and $\eta = 2$.[28]

With an undiscounted prioritarian Atkinson social welfare function, the welfare objective can instead be written as $W^P = \sum_t N_t \frac{1}{1-\gamma}\left(\frac{c_t^{1-\eta} - c_{zero}^{1-\eta}}{1-\eta}\right)^{1-\gamma}$ (this formula appears in Adler et al. 2017). If we neglect intra-generational inequality, the worse-off generation is the current one under the usual assumption of economic and social progress. Therefore, for a given value of η and c_{zero}, the higher the priority given to the worse-off (i.e., the larger the priority parameter γ), the lower the incentives to invest in a policy that would benefit the better-off future generations at the expense of the worse-off current generation.

Let us first compare (undiscounted) prioritarianism with undiscounted utilitarianism. The prioritarian welfare objective W^P coincides with the undiscounted utilitarian one when $\gamma = 0$. Since the prioritarian climate policy gets less stringent as γ increases (the larger γ is, the lower the incentives to invest in a policy that benefits the better-off future generations), prioritarianism recommends less stringent climate policies compared to utilitarianism.

Thus, a green prioritarian dilemma arises. Compared to utilitarianism, the switch to a prioritarian framework usually favors more redistributive policies because of the larger weight attached to well-being changes accruing to the worse-off. However, with an intergenerational issue like climate change, prioritarianism calls for less redistribution

[28] The different choices for the rate of pure time preference ρ and the elasticity of utility η explain also why Stern and Nordhaus differ in their choice of the consumption discount rate to be applied when evaluating climate policies (with Stern suggesting 1.4 percent and Nordhaus values around 5 percent; see Section 8.2). A simple formula to compute the consumption discount rate implicitly used in policy evaluation is the so-called Ramsey rule (Gollier 2012), which states that, in a deterministic setting, the consumption discount rate r is approximately equal to:

$$r = \rho + \eta * g$$

with g the annual growth rate of the economy. Therefore, larger ρ and η lead to a larger consumption discount rate (note that Stern and Nordhaus also have different assumptions about the economic growth rate). The larger the consumption discount rate, the less stringent the climate policy. Since a large consumption discount rate is due to large values for ρ and η, we can simply discuss the implications of these parameters for the stringency of climate policy while skipping the intermediary passage of computing the consumption discount rate.

under the form of a more lenient climate policy. Prioritizing the worse-off means doing less for the future. In other words, prioritarianism gives a blessing to the practice of discounting future utility: improvements in future well-being should be discounted because of the higher well-being that future generations are expected to enjoy. This adds to the reasons offered in Section 8.3.1 as to why the well-being of future generations should be valued less than the well-being of current generations.

Let us now turn to the comparison between (undiscounted) prioritarianism and *discounted* utilitarianism. Both welfare frameworks discount the utility of future generations, although in different ways. Discounted utilitarianism discounts future utility levels through the rate of time preference ρ, while prioritarianism does so through the concavity of function g. Which type of discounting is stronger (thus recommending a less stringent climate policy) depends on the specific values chosen for ρ and γ, and on the assumptions about the stream of well-being across generations (i.e., how much worse off present people are with respect to future people). As shown in Adler et al. (2017) when studying the impact of prioritarianism on the Social Cost of Carbon, the comparison between discounted utilitarianism and prioritarianism is a priori ambiguous.

8.4.2 Intra-Generational Inequality

In a model with only intergenerational inequality the expectation of economic and social progress calls for a cautious approach to climate change, as any climate policy would impose costs on the relatively worse-off current generation for the sake of future relatively better-off generations. Both utilitarianism and prioritarianism support this conclusion. Undiscounted utilitarianism supports this conclusion because future generations are expected to be richer than current ones. The decreasing marginal value of money assumption implies that policies that increase the income of future generations (e.g., through a reduction in climate damages) at the expense of the income of the current poor generation are not so desirable. The utility discounting term in discounted utilitarianism reinforces this result. Prioritarianism supports a cautious approach to climate change because future generations are expected to be richer than current generations, and, as a consequence, they are expected to have a relatively higher well-being than current generations. The concern for the worse off reinforces the undiscounted utilitarian argument for having lenient climate policies.

However, this conclusion fails to consider distributional issues within a generation, and, in particular, who is expected to pay for the costs of the climate policy and who is expected to bear the brunt of climate damages. For instance, even though the average US citizen in 50 years is likely to be richer than the average US citizen today, we may doubt the assumption that, let's say, the average Nigerian citizen in 50 years will be richer than the average US citizen today. Therefore, if we were considering a policy that is paid mainly by developed countries today and that will benefit mainly the developing world in 50 years, the incentives to invest in such a policy would increase with the concavity of both u and g. The more we care about the poorest, the more we will reduce emissions, either because the social evaluator is concerned about their low consumption (under utilitarianism) or because she is concerned about their low consumption and well-being (under prioritarianism).

The matter is of course not so simple. Climate policy is believed to be regressive, at least in developed countries (Grainger and Kolstad 2010, Schwerhoff et al. 2017, Levinson 2019): the consumption of goods with high carbon content is decreasing with income. Moreover, carbon emissions are the fuel of economic growth in developing countries. Thus, the introduction of a climate policy is likely to trade off the interests of the current poor against the interests of the future poor. Ultimately, the impact of inequality on the policy choice depends on which type of inequality is expected to be larger (inter-generational or intra-generational), and on how the policy itself will affect those inequalities. For instance, Dennig et al. (2015) show that, under discounted utilitarianism, even when taking Nordhaus' calibration of the discounted utilitarian welfare function (i.e., with high values for ρ and η), the optimal carbon price trajectory resembles the one recommended by Stern if the climate damages fall especially hard on the poor.

Prioritarianism calls for giving more weight to the worse-off individuals independently of when and where they live. If the current poor pay for the climate policy, then prioritarianism tends to loosen the climate policy with respect to undiscounted utilitarianism. If the future poor benefit most from the policy, the opposite occurs. The comparison with undiscounted utilitarianism is thus ambiguous. Prioritarianism calls for a present bias approach through the "discounting" effect due to economic and social progress.[29] But prioritarianism also calls for giving priority to the poor today and tomorrow. The result of the comparison is affected by which type of inequality is expected to be larger (inter-generational, among people living in the present or among people living in the future).[30]

What is striking in the previous analysis is that the policy implications of the prioritarian social welfare function are similar to those of the discounted utilitarian approach, although there are different reasons underlying those policy implications (time discounting and decreasing marginal utility vs priority to the worst off). In particular, both frameworks ultimately favor policies that redistribute towards the poorest.

8.5 Prioritarian Climate Policies under Risk

This section describes the main implications of ex-ante and ex-post prioritarianism for the SCC as compared to expected utilitarianism. Explicit formulae for the SCC under the different welfare frameworks are included in Appendix 8.A.1. As in the deterministic setting, we focus primarily on an Atkinson social welfare function. Moreover, we retain the assumption that the only inequality-relevant dimension is the intergenerational one (consumption is uniformly distributed across people living in the same period).

Suppose that the consumption of the current generation $t = 0$ is known, while the consumption of future generations, and the extent of possible climate damages, are unknown. Future consumption and

[29] Note, however, that prioritarianism, unlike discounted utilitarianism, is not *biased* towards the present in the sense that the current generation is allocated a higher importance in policy evaluation just because they live in the present. The current generation has a higher weight in evaluation because they are worse-off compared to future generations. The utility discount factor is a direct violation of impartiality/anonymity, while non-discounted prioritarianism *satisfies* impartiality/anonymity.

[30] Comparison with discounted utilitarianism is even more difficult because of the presence of the time discount rate and its ambiguous relation with the discounting term in the prioritarian setting (see Adler et al. 2017 for some sensitivity exercises). In particular, Adler et al. (2017) find that an increase in the concavity of the g function (an increase in priority for the worse-off) tends to reduce the Social Cost of Carbon, but the effect is not directly comparable to an increase in the utility discount rate ρ (which also reduces the social cost of carbon).

future climate damages are risky, in the sense that they may be worse or better than expected. As usual, assume that future generations are, on average, better off than the current one. Compared to the deterministic setting, the utilitarian SCC tends to be larger. This occurs for two reasons. First of all, future generations may enjoy lower economic and social progress than expected, and with risk aversion the less favorable states of the world loom larger than the best states. The concern that climate policy might increase intergenerational inequality (by imposing costs on relatively poor current people and benefitting relatively rich future people) thus becomes less important. Second, climate change may have catastrophic consequences, that lead to a sharp reduction in future consumption and well-being. Even a small chance of such a climate catastrophe will prompt a utilitarian social evaluator to prescribe stringent climate policies so as to protect the living conditions of future individuals who potentially end up with a bad outcome, thereby calling for a high SCC (Weitzman 2009, Millner 2013).

Therefore, two opposite effects arise. On the one hand, future generations are expected to be, on average, better off than the current one. Intergenerational inequality calls for less stringent climate policies, and, as a consequence, a lower SCC. On the other hand, climate change may pose threats to the well-being of future generations. Catastrophic risk calls for more stringent climate policies, mirrored in a higher SCC. In the expected utilitarian framework, both incentives are governed by the shape of the function u. If we adopt the standard isoelastic utility function $u(c_{sit}) = \frac{c_{sit}^{1-\eta}}{1-\eta}$, the parameter η measures both attitudes towards intergenerational inequality, and attitudes towards risk. The larger η is, the larger the aversion to transfer resources to the (on average) better-off future, thereby leading to a lower SCC. However, the larger η is, the higher the propensity to transfer resources to the future so as to prevent very bad outcomes occurring, thereby inducing a higher SCC. As a result, the sensitivity of the SCC to η is a priori ambiguous, and depends on which type of inequality is expected to be larger (whether across generations or across states of the world). Most IAMs implicitly or explicitly assume that the prospects of economic growth create a larger inequality across generations than the inequality created within a generation by the likelihood of adverse climate outcomes (see Ackerman et al. 2013 for a discussion of this point). As a consequence, the SCC is typically found to decrease as the parameter η increases.

A prioritarian social welfare function, in contrast to the utilitarian approach, allows us to separate individuals' preferences over consumption lotteries (represented by the function u) and the social evaluator's preferences over unequal distributions of well-being (encapsulated in the function g).[31]

Let us first consider the ex-ante prioritarian social welfare function described in formula (8.3). An ex-ante prioritarian social evaluator cares about the distribution of expected individual utilities. Ex-ante prioritarianism attaches high priority to individuals with low expected utility. If expected economic growth is so high that, all things considered (i.e., despite the threat of a climate catastrophe), the future is very likely to be better-off than the present, then the ex-ante prioritarian social evaluator attaches higher priority to individuals living in the present than in the future. Therefore, the ex-ante prioritarian SCC will be lower than the undiscounted utilitarian one. The opposite occurs if the probability of a climate catastrophe is so high as to make the prospects of future generations very grim (i.e., if future generations are worse-off on average than the current generation). However, most IAMs assume that the future will be better-off on average despite the climate threat, thus inducing a lower ex-ante prioritarian SCC compared to the undiscounted utilitarian one.

Let us now compare prioritarianism and expected discounted utilitarianism. Like in the deterministic setting, ex-ante prioritarianism requires discounting future individuals' well-being if the future is expected to be better-off. In contrast, expected discounted utilitarianism discounts future well-being because of the time distance. Therefore, both frameworks tend to discount the well-being of future generations, although for different reasons. A priori we cannot say if the expected discounted utilitarian SCC is larger or smaller than the ex-ante prioritarian one, as the comparison depends on the relative size of the time discount rate ρ, the concavity of the priority function g, and the stream of expected well-being across generations.

Suppose that the prioritarian social welfare function belongs to the Atkinson family, $g(u) = \frac{u^{1-\gamma}}{1-\gamma}$, with γ representing aversion to inequality in (expected) well-being. An increase in the inequality aversion parameter γ reduces the ex-ante prioritarian SCC, since the social evaluator

[31] Simply put, there are more degrees of freedom in the prioritarian framework as we have two different functions.

attaches an even lower priority to future individuals' well-being. In contrast, an increase in risk aversion η has an ambiguous effect. On one hand, as risk aversion increases, concerns about the risk faced by the future generations gain more prominence. The future is considered relatively less better off than previously thought compared to the present, and, as a consequence, deserves more priority.[32] On the other hand, if there is economic growth, future generations will be richer, on average, than the current one, thereby reducing the incentives to invest in climate policies that increase the income of future generations. As usual, the strength of such a motive is captured by the parameter η.

In the ex-post prioritarian framework (8.4), the social evaluator is concerned about the distribution of realized well-being and attaches higher priority to individuals that end up in a bad state of nature (i.e., with very low consumption). The ex-post prioritarian social evaluator aims at preventing catastrophic climate consequences occurring. The higher the concavity of the priority function g, the higher the aversion to inequality in realized well-being, and, as a result, the higher the propensity to avoid catastrophic states. In particular, the ex-post prioritarian social evaluator is more concerned with catastrophic states than the expected utilitarian one. On the other hand, because of social and economic progress, the current generation is worse-off than future generations in most of cases (i.e., unless a devastating climate catastrophe occurs such that the consumption of future generations is lower than the consumption of the current generation). Therefore, an ex-post prioritarian social evaluator is more likely to protect the well-being of the current generation than a utilitarian one. And the larger the concavity of the priority function g, the more future individuals' well-being will be discounted. The comparison between ex-post prioritarianism and undiscounted utilitarianism is therefore ambiguous, and, once again, depends on which type of inequality is expected to be larger (whether across generations or across states of the world). The implications of ex-post prioritarianism are thus very similar to those of expected utilitarianism.

32 In addition, increasing η can reduce the ratio of the levels of future expected utility and current expected utility (due to marginal utility declining more quickly), which implies that with an Atkinson SWF the present takes less priority (see expression 8.A.10). See also Adler et al. 2017 for a similar result in the deterministic setting.

To better illustrate the previous point, consider an isoelastic utility function with $\eta < 1$ and an Atkinson social welfare function, and suppose that $c_{zero} = 0$. Thus, formula (8.4) becomes: $\sum_t N_t \sum_s \pi_s \frac{c_{st}^{(1-\eta)(1-\gamma)}}{(1-\eta)(1-\gamma)} = \sum_t N_t \sum_s \pi_s \frac{c_{st}^{1-\psi}}{1-\psi}$, with $\psi = \eta + \gamma(1-\eta) > \eta$. An ex-post prioritarian approach is mathematically equivalent to an undiscounted utilitarian with elasticity of marginal utility ψ instead of η. As $\psi > \eta$, the ex-post prioritarian social evaluator is more risk and inequality averse than the utilitarian one, as the parameters ψ and η capture both attitudes. However, as described earlier, an increase in the coefficient η does not necessarily induce an increase in the SCC. Rather, in most IAMs an increase in the risk/inequality aversion parameter lowers the SCC because the inequality in consumption across generations created by the prospects of economic growth is larger than the inequality within a generation created by the risk of negative climate outcomes. Therefore, under the typical assumptions about economic growth and climate risks made in IAMs, ex-post prioritarianism is likely to lead to a lower SCC than undiscounted utilitarianism.

Finally, let us consider the equally distributed equivalent prioritarian social welfare function (8.5). In the EDE-P case, the social evaluator cares about the distribution of realized well-being, like the ex-post prioritarian one. Moreover, she cares about the distribution of intergenerational welfare across states of the world, attaching a higher weight to states with high total inter-generational welfare through the convexity of g^{-1}. Let us define states with high intergenerational welfare "good" states, and states with low intergenerational welfare "bad" states. The EDE-prioritarian social evaluator attaches higher weight to well-being changes that affect the worse-off individuals living in good states of the world. Therefore, the SCC increases with respect to the undiscounted utilitarian one if the generations that suffer more from climate change are expected to suffer proportionally more in states where all the other generations are doing well rather than in states where the other generations are also doing poorly.

The EDE-prioritarian social evaluator aims to protect generations with a very bad fate compared to other generations. For instance, if climate change is expected to fall hard on a few generations, while future ones will recover, then the EDE-prioritarian SCC is likely to be larger than the undiscounted utilitarian one. If, instead, climate change hurts everyone indiscriminately, the opposite is likely to occur.[33] The reason is that the EDE-prioritarian social welfare function is, strictly speaking, catastrophe-prone, i.e., it gives higher value to situations with no ex-post inequality. Consider the following two lotteries, where rows stand for generations, columns for equally-probable states, and numbers represent well-being levels:

$$A : \begin{pmatrix} 2 & 0 \\ 0 & 2 \end{pmatrix} \qquad B : \begin{pmatrix} 2 & 0 \\ 2 & 0 \end{pmatrix}$$

For an EDE-prioritarian social welfare framework, lottery B is preferred to lottery A, because in B there is no ex-post inequality. However, lottery B is also riskier than lottery A, since we do not know the distribution of well-being that will obtain. In addition, lottery B includes a very bad state where everyone has a very low well-being (0 in this case).

It is unclear whether catastrophe seeking is a good ethical assumption. Rheinberger and Treich (2017) review the literature on catastrophe-sensitive behaviors, where a catastrophe is defined as the case when many people suffer a loss. They find that many studies support a catastrophe-seeking preference on behalf of individuals, especially when it comes to loss of life. It is an open question whether a social evaluator should also be catastrophe seeking.[34]

More work has to be done to fully understand the implications of prioritarianism for climate policy, and, in particular, its feasibility and practical differences from a utilitarian approach. To shed some light on the policy implications of a prioritarian social welfare function, we have performed some simulation exercises based on a very simple

[33] Ferranna (2020) defines some sufficient conditions under which the EDE-prioritarian social welfare function leads to a larger SCC with respect to the utilitarian case.

[34] While EDE-P is technically a catastrophe-prone prioritarian SWF, Ferranna (2020) discusses a variant based on the expected utility of the equally-distributed level of consumption (as opposed to the formula presented here, where expected value is taken of the equally distributed equivalent of vNM utility), which can incorporate catastrophe-averse attitudes (i.e., aversion to scenarios where there is coincidence of fates, and either many individuals suffer a loss or many individuals enjoy a gain). Variants also exist for both prioritarianism and utilitarianism, with suitable concave transformations; see, e.g., Adler and Treich (2015). We will not discuss these less common forms of prioritarianism and utilitarianism in the chapter.

climate-economy model inspired by Nordhaus' DICE model (see Appendix 8.A.1 for a full description of the model). We assume that the sensitivity of future consumption to increases in temperature is uncertain (damage risk), and we investigate the impact of varying the welfare framework on the SCC. The SCC has been computed along the business-as-usual emission path, i.e., under the assumption that no climate policy is introduced.

A standard feature of the DICE-family models is the assumption that future generations will be wealthier than the current one, despite the possibility of very large climate damages. As a consequence, the results presented here are based on the assumption that the current generation is the worse-off one. We assume that the uncertain damage parameter is distributed normally. Assuming more negatively skewed distributions will change the results quantitatively, but not qualitatively (i.e., the assumed economic growth is high enough that future generations will be relatively better-off even in the worst climate damage scenario).[35]

Figure 8.1 depicts the SCC in the expected utilitarian case as a function of risk aversion η (the elasticity of marginal utility of consumption of an isoelastic function) and utility discount rate ρ. As expected, the SCC is decreasing both in ρ and in η. The negative relation between the SCC and the coefficient η is due to the fact that η represents both aversion to risk and aversion to inequality. Although the extent of future damages is unknown, the expected economic growth overcompensates the risk, thereby reducing the SCC as η increases. In the calibration, we have considered a normal distribution of the damage coefficient. More skewed distributions could lead to different results.[36] However, Table 8.1 shows that the presence of risk

[35] In other words, to have a scenario where the current generation is not the worse-off one, we would need a model that explicitly considers consumption falling to subsistence level if a climate catastrophe is triggered. For the sake of simplicity, we do not model tipping points (e.g., Lemoine and Traeger 2014, Kent et al. 2019).

[36] If the probability distribution has a fat tail, it is possible that the certainty-equivalent consumption of future generations (i.e., future expected consumption adjusted for the risk) is below current consumption. Then, increasing η (the risk aversion parameter) decreases the certainty equivalent and raises the SCC. However, as previously noted, the models belonging to the DICE family are unlikely to support this result because of the assumption of sustained economic progress, unless we explicitly model tipping points and consumption falling to subsistence levels (see note 36).

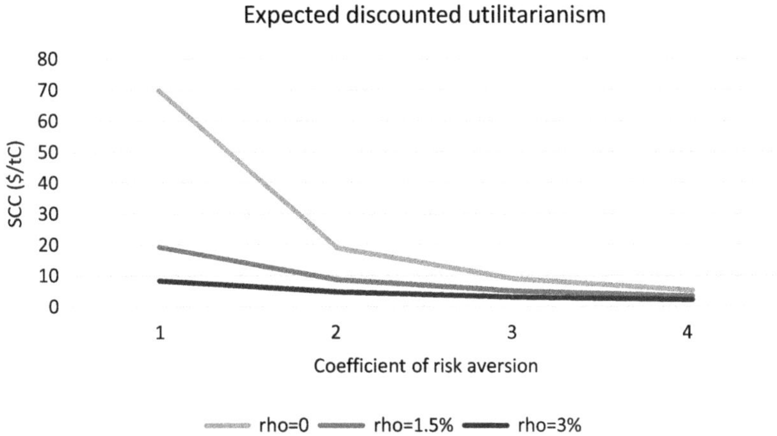

Figure 8.1 The Social Cost of Carbon under the expected discounted utilitarian approach, as a function of the utility discount rate ρ and of the coefficient of risk aversion η

does induce an increase in the SCC with respect to the deterministic scenario.

Figure 8.2 depicts the SCC in the ex-post prioritarian scenario, as a function of both the coefficient of risk aversion η and of the coefficient of inequality aversion γ of an Atkinson social welfare function. The SCC is decreasing both in risk aversion and in inequality aversion. The reason is that the ex-post prioritarian social evaluator attaches higher weight to consumption changes occurring to the worse-off generation, and, due to the economic growth assumption, the present generation is the worse-off one, despite the climate risk. The higher the aversion to inequality, the lower the incentive to reduce emissions for the sake of future generations. Risk aversion has a similar effect because the concavity of the function u is capturing both aversion to risk in consumption and aversion to inequality in consumption. Moreover, since the SCC is decreasing in γ, the ex-post prioritarian SCC is lower than the utilitarian one.

Table 8.1 shows that the results under the three prioritarian approaches under risk are very similar. All approaches favor a lower SCC than the undiscounted utilitarian case (although the reasons behind this result are different), and the higher the aversion to inequality in well-being (captured by the coefficient γ), the lower the SCC. This conclusion may not hold under a different calibration.

Table 8.1. ***The Social Cost of Carbon under different social welfare function approaches as a function of the coefficient of risk aversion η***

	Coefficient of risk aversion		
	$\eta = 1$	$\eta = 2$	$\eta = 3$
Undiscounted utilitarianism (no risk)	\$65.4	\$17.5	\$8.2
Undiscounted expected utilitarianism	\$69.7	\$18.8	\$8.9
Prioritarianism (no risk)	\$39.9	\$16.7	\$8.2
Ex-ante prioritarianism	\$42.6	\$17.9	\$8.8
Ex-post prioritarianism	\$42.7	\$17.9	\$8.8
Equally-distributed-equivalent prioritarianism	\$42.5	\$17.9	\$8.8

Notes: Assumptions for the prioritarian approaches: $c_{zero} = \$1000$, coefficient of inequality aversion $\gamma = 1$. In the chapter, η was also referred as the elasticity of marginal utility of consumption.

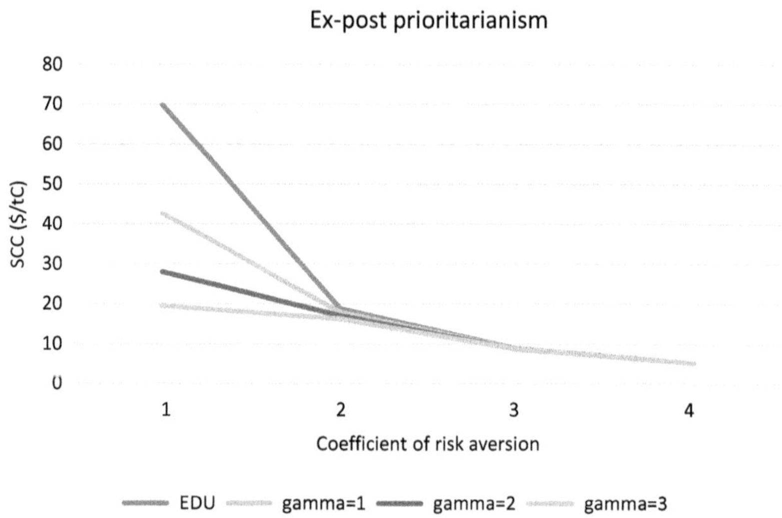

Figure 8.2. The Social Cost of Carbon under ex-post prioritarianism as a function of the coefficient of risk aversion η and of the coefficient of inequality aversion γ

Notes: When $\gamma = 0$, the ex-post prioritarian case coincides with undiscounted expected utilitarianism. Assumption: $c_{zero} = \$1000$.

One issue with the EDE-prioritarian framework is the non-separability assumption. In the SCC formula we have implicitly assumed that only present and future generations matter, although a faithful application of the framework would also include the past.

As previously pointed out, we have reason to believe that including the past will not dramatically affect the results. If anything, the inclusion of the past should induce more cautionary behaviors, because the social evaluator will aim at avoiding in particular those states where future generations are so badly hurt that they face a fate even worse than the past.

So far, we have focused on the impact of prioritarianism in a world with only intergenerational inequality. If intra-generational inequality is added, results become more blurry. As in the deterministic case, inter- and intra-generational inequality push in different directions. Take for instance the EAP framework, which allocates priority to the individuals that face the worst risk in terms of certainty equivalent. If these individuals are in the future, then EAP will recommend a higher SCC than undiscounted ant utilitarianism. The opposite occurs if those expected worse-off individuals are in the present. Similarly, the EDE-prioritarian framework will recommend giving priority to the individuals that, ex-post, do very badly compared to others. If these individuals live in the future, the SCC increases with respect to the utilitarian framework. More analysis has to be done to see which type of inequality predominates in a prioritarian world.

8.6 Extensions

8.6.1 Heterogeneous Preferences

As seen in Adler, Chapter 2 this volume, in a general framework allowing for preference heterogeneity and multiple attributes, the utilitarian formula would be $\sum_{tis}(1+\rho)^{-1}\pi_s N_{it} u_i(c_{sit})$, where u_i is the von Neumann-Morgenstern function of individual *i*. The difficulty when individuals have different vNM utility functions is that an appropriate scaling of the utility functions is needed to make them comparable. Indeed, the same preferences over risk can be represented with many vNM functions (each being an affine transform of the other), and there is no obvious choice of a single representation.

The literature has offered some interesting options for scaling vNM utility functions. The most popular one is the "0–1" scaling, which consists of assigning value 0 to the worst option and value 1 to the best option (Dhillon and Mertens 1999). In the case of consumption, there is no obvious choice for a "best" option, especially when looking at growth paths in which the average individual becomes ten times as wealthy as the current population. Another option, proposed by Adler (2012), picks a level of consumption below the highest for the utility value 1. Such choices have important consequences, because very risk averse individuals have much lower marginal utility under Adler's scaling (above the consumption level giving utility 1) than with the 0–1 scaling, and therefore receive much less priority in the allocation of resources.

Preference heterogeneity in the climate policy context is relevant especially when we think about the preferences of future generations. It is reasonable to assume that people living in the future might hold different values from ours, for example concerning the value of protecting environmental amenities or biodiversity, and the substitutability between preserving the environment and market activities (Beltratti et al. 1998; Ayong Le Kama 2001). Additionally, future preferences may be influenced by the policies enacted today (e.g., changes in mobility preferences induced by urban planning interventions), raising the question of whether and to what extent this endogeneity in preferences should be accounted for in the analysis (Mattauch and Hepburn 2016). The implication of variable preferences for climate policy is an area of research not yet well explored.

8.6.2 Equivalent Income

So far, we have focused on the case in which consumption is the only argument of the utility function. As a matter of fact, in the main IAMs, damages to consumption due to climate change include non-economic costs, such as mortality or morbidity. These costs are monetized, according to certain conventions, such as the value of a statistical life in the case of mortality.[37]

This way of monetizing non-monetary aspects of life can be understood with the concept of equivalent income, also called money-metric utility. Let $u_i(c_{sit}, d_{sit})$ denote the utility in group i that depends on both consumption c_{sit} and non-consumption attributes d_{sit}.[38] It is possible to

[37] See, for example, Scovronick et al. (2020) on how to monetize health impacts of climate change.

[38] See Sterner and Persson (2008) for one of the few attempts at explicitly considering a utility function that depends on both consumption and environmental quality. By using Nordhaus' DICE model, they find that the

convert all non-monetary dimensions of well-being (such as health, leisure, happiness, social inclusion or environmental amenities) into monetary terms, so as to build an "equivalent", or normalized, consumption index c_{sit}^{norm}. Let d^{ref} be some well-chosen reference level of non-consumption attributes. The equivalent consumption index for a given bundle of attributes (c_{sit}, d_{sit}) is determined using each individual's preferences, by solving the equation $u_i(c_{sit}, d_{sit}) = u_i\left(c_{sit}^{norm}, d^{ref}\right)$ for c_{sit}^{norm}. Once this is done, one can drop d^{ref} which is fixed, and simply write $u_i\left(c_{sit}^{norm}\right)$.

This normalization does not have any effect on the analysis if one trusts the utility values, as in the vNM approach, since utility of the normalized consumption is just equal to the original utility $u_i(c_{sit}, d_{sit})$.[39] But the equivalent consumption index c_{sit}^{norm} itself, which is a representation of the individual's preferences, can also be used as an index of well-being for a prioritarian approach, taking inspiration from resourcist approaches (such as Rawls' theory of justice) according to which inequality should be assessed in terms of resources or opportunities offered to individuals rather than in terms of subjective well-being such as the vNM utility. This alternative prioritarian approach can be applied through a variant of expression (8.5):

$$W^{EDE-P2} = N \sum_{s} \pi_s u \circ g^{-1} \left(\frac{1}{N} \sum_{t,i} N_{it} g\left(c_{sit}^{norm}\right) \right) \tag{8.6}$$

In this variant, the EDE is computed in terms of equivalent consumption, and risk aversion is brought by the function u which can either be a representation of risk aversion in the population (assuming it is uniform in the population), or the risk attitude of the social evaluator (Ferranna 2020). One advantage of this formula is that, depending on whether the degree of risk aversion in u is greater or smaller than the degree of inequality aversion in g, then $u \circ g^{-1}$ is a concave or convex function and the social welfare function is averse to catastrophes or not, which brings more flexibility about catastrophe avoidance than formula (8.5).

optimal emission path is very sensitive to the elasticity of substitution between the two attributes.

39 In the previous analysis we have assumed that utility depends only on consumption. But the same results hold if we interpret consumption as "normalized consumption."

8.6.3 Variable Population

Generally, climate policy analysis assumes that the present and future population is fixed and unaffected by climate change. However, climate change can change the size of a future population. For example, climate change can worsen health and lead to premature mortality. A higher degree of warming could cause a decline in reproduction either because of health-related effects or because of premature mortality (people that might have been borne are not borne because their potential parents have died prematurely). As an extreme scenario, climate change could cause human extinction. The opposite might occur as well, at least for the short term. Increased frequency of damages may slow down the current decline in fertility in some developing regions (such as sub-Saharan Africa) because of the increased risk to household income and the consequent increased opportunity cost of having a child.

IAMs rarely analyze the impact of population dynamics on the climate policy, and the possible endogeneity of population size in the climate context. Clearly, also in the standard discounted utilitarian model, we can see that population size matters. Assume for the time being that population is exogenous. The more people that live in the future, the larger their total well-being, and, as a consequence, their weight in the social evaluation. In the presence of population growth, we can assume that the social evaluator is more inclined to invest in a climate policy that will benefit the more numerous future people. For instance, Scovronick et al. (2017) show that in Nordhaus' DICE model, if the size of the population is exogenously predicted to be greater than previously assumed, then the SCC rises by so much that the optimal carbon tax policy induces lower emissions and a lower temperature profile over the future.

Standard IAMs (such as Nordhaus' DICE model) implicitly assume a "total" utilitarian approach to population ethics. In the case of total utilitarianism, outcomes are ranked according to the sum of individual well-being. In a deterministic setting, the total (discounted) utilitarian social welfare function is given by the formula $\sum_t \frac{1}{(1+\rho)^t} \sum_i N_{it} u(c_{it})$, which is exactly the one that was analyzed in Section 8.4.[40] Total

[40] Total utilitarianism is the view according to which adding someone to the population increases welfare if and only if the person's life is better than

utilitarianism leads to the so-called "repugnant conclusion," according to which policies that increase the population are ethically recommended even if the lives added are barely worth living (thus inducing a sharp decline in average quality of life), as long as the increase in population is sufficiently large. An alternative approach is "average" utilitarianism, where outcomes are ranked according to average well-being. The average (discounted) utilitarian social welfare function would be equal to $\frac{1}{\sum_{it}\frac{1}{(1+\rho)^t}N_{it}}\sum_{it}\frac{1}{(1+\rho)^t}N_{it}u(c_{it})$ (Dasgupta 2001).[41] Average utilitarianism violates the "negative expansion principle," according to which adding a life not worth living should never be ethically acceptable. A third classical approach is "critical-level" utilitarianism, according to which it is ethically acceptable to add an individual whose well-being is above a critical level. The corresponding social welfare function is given by $\sum_{it}\frac{1}{(1+\rho)^t}N_{it}(u(c_{it}) - u_{crit})$. If the critical level is chosen such that it is higher than the level making a life worth living, then critical-level utilitarianism satisfies the negative expansion principle and avoids the repugnant conclusion.[42]

The result, that faster population growth rises the SCC, holds under all forms of utilitarianism previously described (i.e., both total, average and critical- level). Indeed, they do not differ in how they estimate the SCC, and, as a consequence, in how the SCC reacts to an exogenous change in the projected population growth.[43] The main reason is that

non-existence. If u_{worth} is the well-being level such that a life is equal to not existing at all, then the total utilitarian formula would be $\sum_{it}\frac{1}{(1+\rho)^t}N_{it}(u(c_{it}) - u_{worth})$. To simplify, in the text we assume that $u_{worth} = 0$.

41 If there is time discounting $\rho > 0$, average utilitarianism requires to discount population number at the denominator. Otherwise, social welfare could be increased by making people live at earlier dates, along a path of constant individual well-being (Dasgupta 2001).

42 See also Adler, Chapter 2 this volume, for a discussion of total, average and critical-level prioritarianism.

43 In other words, since climate change is assumed to have no impact on population growth (but only impacts on consumption), the SCC formula under both average utilitarianism and critical-level utilitarianism is equivalent to the one under total utilitarianism. In average utilitarianism, the term $\frac{1}{\sum_{it}\frac{1}{(1+\rho)^t}N_{it}}$ is a constant multiplicative factor that cancels out when computing the SCC. In critical-level utilitarianism, the term -$\sum_{it}\frac{1}{(1+\rho)^t}N_{it}(u_{crit})$ is a constant additive factor which cancels out when computing the SCC. These terms cancel out because they do not depend on consumption, which is the only attribute that is affected by climate change in this context.

the size of the future population is assumed to be independent of climate change. Control of the future population is not included in the potential benefits of a climate policy, and, consequently, in the benefits included in the computation of the SCC.

The previous formulas can be extended to prioritarianism, allowing us to define total, average and critical-level prioritarianism as follows: $\sum_{it} N_{it} g(u(c_{it}))$, $\frac{1}{\sum_{it} N_{it}} \sum_{it} N_{it} g(u(c_{it}))$ and $\sum_{it} N_{it} [g(u(c_{it})) - g(u_{crit})]$. As in the utilitarian case, different forms of prioritarianism do not affect the computation of the SCC, as long as population growth is exogenous and we are in a deterministic setting. The extension to a risky setting raises additional complications.

Climate change may affect the size of the future human population, for example through a large disaster that changes the habitability of the planet for humans and causes human extinction or a drastic reduction in population size. If such a risk is large enough, then it should have a first-order effect on the SCC. In the case of endogenous population risk, population ethics will affect the computation of the SCC, and the value placed to policies that prevent human extinction. For example, under a total utilitarian social welfare function the risk of a reduction in the size of the future population is likely to increase the SCC compared to a situation with no risk, since, by construction, total utilitarianism cares about the total number of people. In contrast, under an average utilitarian social welfare function, the SCC with endogenous population risk may actually be lower than the one with exogenous population risk, as long as there is no consequence for average well-being. If climate change reduces population size, but the well-being of those surviving is sufficiently high, then the average utilitarian policy maker is not concerned about the population impact of a changing climate.

The issue of endogenous population size has not received much attention in the climate economics literature. One of the few examples is Méjean et al. (2020), who build an IAM that explicitly accounts for the risk of extinction of the human population due to climate change. Méjean et al. (2020) consider an entire family of population-sensitive utilitarian welfare functions, ranging from total utilitarianism to average utilitarianism, both with the possibility of a critical level. They show that, independently of the framework adopted, the risk of endogenous extinction calls for more mitigation at the expense of exacerbating intergenerational inequality. No study has investigated the implications of endogenous population risk under a prioritarian framework. It is unclear to what extent the results would differ with respect to the utilitarian setting.

8.6.4 Uncertainty

The deep uncertainty surrounding the climate change phenomenon questions the reliability of probabilistic calculus, since the likelihood of different scenarios is often based on subjective beliefs. Millner et al. (2013) have argued that uncertainty about probability distributions should be explicitly acknowledged when performing benefit-cost analysis. As a consequence, they suggest the use of ambiguity-averse approaches, where the social evaluator is averse to the uncertainty concerning the likelihood of different events. From a practical point of view, ambiguity aversion makes the social evaluator more cautious when evaluating policy options, by focusing on the less favorable probability distributions, and, as a result, by putting more weight on the worst scenarios. However, since ambiguity aversion violates expected utility axioms, the rationality of such an approach is, once again, under question.[44]

8.7 Conclusion

Most integrated climate-economy models adopt an expected discounted utilitarian (EDU) welfare function to evaluate climate policies. EDU is a flexible framework given the informational and computational constraints concerning the climate change problem (in particular, homogeneous preferences and normalized consumption as the only attribute). It takes account of inequalities both within and between generations, the granularity depending on available information. Moreover, it can capture different ethical stances by varying the values of the parameters of interest.

[44] A related topic is the impact of learning on the evaluation of climate policies. The arrival of new information will reduce the uncertainty over some key climate parameters, allowing for more targeted policies. A trade-off arises between postponing stringent climate policies to wait for more information and acting strongly immediately to prevent the occurrence of low-probability catastrophic scenarios (e.g., Kolstad 1996). For the sake of simplicity, we decided to leave this topic aside.

In this chapter, we have discussed the implications of prioritarian welfare functions in climate policy. Compared to the expected utilitarian case, prioritarianism attaches a higher weight to consumption changes affecting generations that are worse-off. As a consequence, it is more sensitive than utilitarianism to the occurrence of catastrophic events that induce a sharp reduction in the consumption possibilities of future generations. However, we have shown that in standard climate-economy models, a switch to a prioritarian welfare function often induces a lower incentive to reduce emissions for the sake of future generations due to the assumption of consistent economic growth. The result is not general, and speaks of the debatable assumptions that are often adopted in climate-economy models.

8.A Appendix: Simulation Exercise

This Appendix describes the simple climate-economy model used in the simulation exercise, and derives the expressions for the Social Cost of Carbon under the various ethical approaches analyzed in the chapter. For the sake of simplicity, we assume that there is no intra-generational inequality, i.e., consumption and climate damages are equally distributed within a generation.

8.A.1 The Climate-Economy Model

We consider a simple climate-economy model in the spirit of the DICE model by Nordhaus (2008). Let Y_t denote the total amount of consumption goods produced at time t. Carbon emissions $E_t = \lambda_t Y_t$ are generated during the production activities, where λ_t is the carbon intensity of production. As in Nordhaus (2017), carbon intensity falls over time according to the following law: $ln \frac{\lambda_t}{\lambda_{t-1}} = g_\lambda e^{\delta_\lambda t}$, where g_λ is the initial rate of decarbonization, and δ_λ the rate of decline of the rate of decarbonization.

Climate change is driven by the accumulation of CO2 in the atmosphere. The stock M_{t+1} of atmospheric carbon dioxide evolves according to (Traeger 2014):

$$M_{t+1} = M_{pre} + (1 - \delta_M)\big(M_t - M_{pre}\big) + E_t \tag{8.A.1}$$

where M_{pre} is the pre-industrial level of CO2, and $\delta_M \in (0, 1)$ the decay rate of the carbon stock exceeding pre-industrial levels. The accumulation of carbon dioxide leads to a gradual increase in atmospheric temperature:

$$T_{t+1} = (1 - \phi)T_t + \phi \frac{\chi}{ln\, 2}\, ln \frac{M_{t+1}}{M_{pre}} \tag{8.A.2}$$

where T_t is the increase in temperature in period t with respect to the pre-industrial level, ϕ the degree of inertia of the climate system, and

Table 8.2 *Parameters used in the climate-economy model*

Parameter	Definition	Value	Source
Y_0	GDP in 2018	\$85.91 trillion	World Bank
E_0	Emissions in 2018	10.04 GtC	Tollefson (2019)
g_λ	Rate of decarbonization	−0.0102	Dietz et al. (2018)
δ_λ	Rate of decline of rate of decarbonization	−0.001	Nordhaus (2017)
M_{pre}	Pre-industrial level of CO2	280ppm	
M_0	Carbon stock in 2018	409ppm	NOAA
δ_M	Decay rate of the carbon stock	0.0138	Lemoine and Rudik (2017)
χ	Climate sensitivity	3	Assumed
T_0	Temperature increase with respect to pre-industrial level in 2018	1.1°C	Hansen et al. (2019)
ϕ	Inertia of the climate system	0.032	Traeger (2014)
α	Damage coefficient	Mean=0.26% Standard Deviation=0.1616%	Tol (2014)
μ	Economic growth rate	2.06%	Assumed
N_0	Global population in 2018	7.5 billion	United Nations, World Population Prospects
g_N	Annual population growth rate	0.0268	Assumed
L_∞	Asymptotic population	11.5 billion	Assumed

χ the climate sensitivity, which measures the equilibrium warming that results from doubling the atmospheric concentration of CO2.

Warming produces economic damages through a reduction in consumption. Damages $D(T_t)$ have an exponential quadratic form:

$$D(T_t) = 1 - e^{-\alpha T_t^2} \tag{8.A.3}$$

where the damage coefficient α measures the sensitivity of consumption to warming. The damage coefficient α is subject to uncertainty. We assume that it is distributed normally. Climate damages reduce the total consumption in period t, $C_t = Y_t e^{-\alpha T_t^2}$, but have no effect on the economic growth rate: $Y_{t+1} = Y_t e^{\mu}$, with μ the growth rate of the economy.

As in DICE, population evolves over time according to: $N_t = N_{t-1}^{1-g_N} L_{\infty}^{g_N}$

Given the previous equations, the per capita climate damages at time t and state s from a small increase in emissions at time 0 (usually 1 ton) are equal to:

$$b_{st} = 2\frac{C_{st}}{N_t}\alpha T_t \frac{dT_t}{dE_0} \tag{8.A.4}$$

$$\frac{dT_t}{dE_0} = (1-\phi)\frac{dT_{t-1}}{dE_0} + \phi\chi\frac{(1-\delta_M)^t}{M_t\, ln\, 2} \tag{8.A.5}$$

8.A.2 Derivation of the Expressions For the SCC

The Social Cost of Carbon represents the present value of economic damages created by an additional ton of carbon released into the atmosphere. Estimating the SCC involves a four-step procedure: (i) given an emission path, projecting the impact of an additional ton of carbon on future temperature (the term $\frac{dT_t}{dE_0}$ in the previous expression, for all $t \geq 0$); (ii) identifying the impacts of the changing climate on the economy and society; (iii) evaluating those damages in monetary terms (i.e., computing b_{st} in the previous expression); and (iv) computing the net present value of the climate damages by using an appropriate formula. The formula depends on the specific welfare function that is adopted. In the following, we will state the various formulae, and compute the SCC associated to a 1 ton increase in carbon emissions at time 0 (year 2018).

Let c_{st} be the per capita amount consumed by individuals of generation t in state s, c_0 the sure amount consumed by people in the current generation, $u'(c)$ the marginal utility of consumption, and b_{st} the monetized benefits enjoyed by generation t in state s if current carbon emissions are reduced by a small amount (one ton). With the common isoelastic assumption about the utility function u, the SCC under expected discounted utilitarianism is equal to:

$$SCC^{EDU} = \sum_{t=0}^{T} \frac{1}{(1+\rho)^t} \frac{N_t}{N_0} \sum_{s \in S} \pi_s \frac{u'(c_{st}) b_{st}}{u'(c_0)} \equiv \sum_{t=0}^{T} \frac{1}{(1+\rho)^t} \frac{N_t}{N_0} \sum_{s \in S} \pi_s \left(\frac{c_{st}}{c_0}\right)^{-\eta} b_{st} \tag{8.A.6}$$

where ρ is the utility discount rate, while η represents risk aversion, and, by extension, also the social evaluator's aversion to inequality in consumption. From the previous expression, we can also recover the formula to determine the SCC in the deterministic scenario:

$$SCC^{DU} = \sum_{t=0}^{T} \frac{1}{(1+\rho)^t} \frac{N_t}{N_0} \left(\frac{c_t}{c_0}\right)^{-\eta} b_t \tag{8.A.7}$$

Assume that the priority function g also has an isoelastic form: $g(u) = \frac{u^{1-\gamma}}{1-\gamma}$ if $\gamma \neq 1$, and $g(u) = log(u)$ if $\gamma = 1$, where γ denotes the social evaluator's aversion to inequality in individual well-being. The utility function u has a zero point to guarantee a positive well-being level: $u(c) = \frac{c^{1-\eta}}{1-\eta} - \frac{c_{zero}^{1-\eta}}{1-\eta}$. Let $g'(u)$ represent the marginal priority of utility. In a deterministic context, the SCC under prioritarianism is given by:

$$SCC^{P} = \sum_{t=0}^{T} \frac{N_t}{N_0} \frac{g'(u(c_t))}{g'(u(c_0))} \frac{u'(c_t) b_t}{u'(c_0)} = \sum_{t=0}^{T} \frac{N_t}{N_0} \left(\frac{c_t^{1-\eta} - c_{zero}^{1-\eta}}{c_0^{1-\eta} - c_{zero}^{1-\eta}}\right)^{-\gamma} \left(\frac{c_t}{c_0}\right)^{-\eta} b_t \tag{8.A.8}$$

The previous expression can be easily extended to the ex-post prioritarian approach:

$$\begin{aligned} SCC^{EPP} &= \sum_{t=0}^{T} \frac{N_t}{N_0} \sum_{s \in S} \frac{g'(u(c_{st}))}{g'(u(c_0))} \frac{u'(c_{st}) b_{st}}{u'(c_0)} \\ &= \sum_{t=0}^{T} \frac{N_t}{N_0} \sum_{s \in S} \left(\frac{c_{st}^{1-\eta} - c_{zero}^{1-\eta}}{c_0^{1-\eta} - c_{zero}^{1-\eta}}\right)^{-\gamma} \left(\frac{c_{st}}{c_0}\right)^{-\eta} b_{st} \end{aligned} \tag{8.A.9}$$

It is similar to the EDU formula except for the fact that the utility discount rate ρ has been replaced by a "priority discount" term.

In the ex-ante prioritatian case, the policy evaluator cares about the distribution of expected utilities across generations. The SCC is equal to:

$$
\begin{aligned}
SCC^{EAP} &= \sum_{t=0}^{T} \frac{N_t}{N_0} \frac{g'\left(\sum_{s \in S} \pi_s u(c_{st})\right)}{g'(u(c_0))} \sum_{s \in S} \frac{u'(c_{st}) b_{st}}{u'(c_0)} \\
&= \sum_{t=0}^{T} \frac{N_t}{N_0} \left(\sum_{s \in S} \pi_s \frac{c_{st}^{1-\eta} - c_{zero}^{1-\eta}}{c_0^{1-\eta} - c_{zero}^{1-\eta}} \right)^{-\gamma} \sum_{s \in S} \pi_s \left(\frac{c_{st}}{c_0} \right)^{-\eta} b_{st}
\end{aligned}
\tag{8.A.10}
$$

Let $(g_s^{-1})'$ be the first derivative of the function $g_s^{-1} = g^{-1}\left(\frac{1}{N}\sum_{t=0}^{T} N_t g(u(c_{st}))\right)$. When using an Atkinson social welfare function, we get: $g_s^{-1} = \left(\frac{1}{N}\sum_{t=0}^{T} N_t \left(\frac{c_{st}^{1-\eta}}{1-\eta} - \frac{c_{zero}^{1-\eta}}{1-\eta}\right)^{1-\gamma}\right)^{\frac{1}{1-\gamma}}$, and its derivative is equal to: $(g_s^{-1})' = \frac{1}{1-\gamma}\left(\frac{1}{N}\sum_{t=0}^{T} N_t \left(\frac{c_{st}^{1-\eta}}{1-\eta} - \frac{c_{zero}^{1-\eta}}{1-\eta}\right)^{1-\gamma}\right)^{\frac{\gamma}{1-\gamma}}$. In the equally distributed equivalent ex-post prioritarian framework, the SCC is given by:

$$
\begin{aligned}
SCC^{EDE-P} &= \sum_{t=0}^{T} \frac{N_t}{N_0} \sum_{s \in S} \pi_s \frac{(g_s^{-1})'}{\sum_{s \in S} (g_s^{-1})'} \frac{g'(u(c_{st}))}{g'(u(c_0))} \frac{u'(c_{st}) b_{st}}{u'(c_0)} \\
&= \sum_{t=0}^{T} \frac{N_t}{N_0} \sum_{s \in S} \hat{\pi}_s \left(\frac{c_{st}}{c_0} \right)^{-\eta} b_{st}
\end{aligned}
\tag{8.A.11}
$$

with

$$
\hat{\pi}_s = \pi_s \frac{\left(\frac{1}{N}\sum_{t=0}^{T} N_t \left(\frac{c_{st}^{1-\eta}}{1-\eta} - \frac{c_{zero}^{1-\eta}}{1-\eta}\right)^{1-\gamma}\right)^{\frac{\gamma}{1-\gamma}}}{\sum_{s \in S} \pi_s \left(\frac{1}{N}\sum_{t=0}^{T} N_t \left(\frac{c_{st}^{1-\eta}}{1-\eta} - \frac{c_{zero}^{1-\eta}}{1-\eta}\right)^{1-\gamma}\right)^{\frac{\gamma}{1-\gamma}}} \left(\frac{c_{st}^{1-\eta} - c_{zero}^{1-\eta}}{c_0^{1-\eta} - c_{zero}^{1-\eta}} \right)^{-\gamma}
\tag{8.A.12}
$$

References

Ackerman, F., Stanton, E., and Bueno, R. (2013). "Epstein-Zin Utility in DICE: Is Risk Aversion Irrelevant to Climate Policy?" *Environmental and Resource Economics*, 56: 73–84. https://doi.org/10.1007/s10640–013-9645-z

Adler, M.D. (2012). *Well-Being and Fair Distribution: Beyond Cost-Benefit Analysis*, Oxford: Oxford University Press.

Adler, M.D., Anthoff, D., Bosetti, V., Garner, G., Keller, K., and Treich, N. (2017). "Priority for the Worse Off and the Social Cost of Carbon." *Nature Climate Change*, 7: 443–449. https://doi.org/10.1038/nclimate3298

Adler, M.D., and Treich, N. (2015). "Prioritarianism and Climate Change." *Environmental and Resource Economics*, 62: 279–308. https://doi.org/10.1007/s10640–015-9960-7

Anthoff D., Hepburn C., and Tol, R.S.J. (2009). "Equity Weighting and the Marginal Damage Costs of Climate Change." *Ecological Economics*, 68: 836–849. https://doi.org/10.1016/j.ecolecon.2008.06.017

Ayong Le Kama, A. (2001). "Preservation and Exogenous Uncertain Future Preferences." *Economic Theory*, 18: 745–752.

Beltratti, A., Chichilnisky, G., and Heal, G. (1998). "Uncertain Future Preferences and Conservation." In Chichilnisky, G., Heal, G., Vercelli, A. (eds.), *Sustainability: Dynamics and Uncertainty*. Amsterdam: Kluwer Academic Publishers. Chapter 3.4, pp. 257–275.

Budolfson, M.B., and Spears, D. (2018). "Incorporating Non-Anthropocentric Valuation of Ecosystems and Animal Welfare into Environmental Decision-Making Models." working paper.

Cline, W.R. (1992). *The Economics of Global Warming*. Washington, DC: Institute for International Economics.

Grainger, C.A., and Kolstad, C.D. (2010). "Who Pays a Price on Carbon?" *Environmental and Resource Economics*, 46: 359–376. https://doi.org/10.1007/s10640–010-9345-x

Dasgupta, P. (2001). *Human Well-Being and the Natural Environment*. Oxford: Oxford University Press.

(2008). "Discounting Climate Change." *Journal of Risk and Uncertainty*, 37:141–169. https://doi.org/10.1007/s11166–008-9049-6

Dasgupta, P., and Heal, G. (1979). *Economic Theory and Exhaustible Resource*, Cambridge: Cambridge University Press

Dennig, F., Budolfson, M.B., Fleurbaey, M., Siebert, A., and Socolow, R.H. (2015). "Inequality, Climate Impacts on the Future Poor, and Carbon Prices." *Proceedings of the National Academy of Sciences*, 112: 15827–15832. https://doi.org/10.1073/pnas.1513967112

Dhillon, A., and Mertens, J.-F. (1999). "Relative Utilitarianism: An Improved Axiomatization." *Econometrica*, 67: 471–498. https://doi.org/10.1111.1468-0262.00033

Dietz, S., and Asheim, G.B. (2012). "Climate Policy under Sustainable Discounted Utilitarianism." *Journal of Environmental Economics and Management*, 63: 321–335. https://doi.org/10.1016/j.jeem.2012.01.003

Dietz, S., Gollier, C., and Kessler, L. (2018). "The Climate Beta". *Journal of Environmental Economics and Management*, 87: 258–274. https://doi.org/10.1016/j.jeem.2017.07.005

Ferranna M. (2020). "Intergenerational Equity, Risk Aversion and the Social Cost of Carbon." working paper.

Fleurbaey, M. (2010). "Assessing Risky Social Situations." *Journal of Political Economy*, 118: 649–680. https://doi.org/10.1086/656513
Fleurbaey, M., Ferranna, M., Budolfson, M.B., et al. (2019). "The Social Cost of Carbon: Valuing Inequality, Risk, and Population for Climate Policy." *The Monist*, 102: 84–109. https://doi.org/10.1093/monist/ony023
Fleurbaey, M., and Zuber, S. (2013). "Inequality aversion and separability in risk evaluation." *Economic Theory*, 54: 675–692. https://doi.org/10.1007/s00199–012-0730-2
Gollier, C. (2002). "Discounting an Uncertain Future." *Journal of Public Economics,* 85: 149–166. https://doi.org/10.1016/S0047-2727(01)00079-2
(2012). *Pricing the Planet's Future*. Princeton: Princeton University Press.
Hansen, J., Sato, M., Ruedy, R., Schmidt, G.A., and Lo, K. (2019). "Global Temperature in 2018 and Beyond." www.columbia.edu/~jeh1/mailings/2019/20190206_Temperature2018.pdf.
Harsanyi, J.C. (1955). "Cardinal Welfare, Individualistic Ethics, and Interpersonal Comparisons of Utility." *The Journal of Political Economy*, 63: 309–321.
Hope, C. (2006). "The Marginal Impact of CO2 from PAGE 2002." *Integrated Assessment Journal*, 6: 9–56.
Kelleher, J.P. (2017). "Descriptive Versus Prescriptive Discounting in Climate Change Policy Analysis." *Georgetown Journal of Law & Public Policy*, 15: 957–977.
Kent, D., Litterman, R.B., and Wagner, G. (2019). "Declining CO2 Price Paths." *Proceedings of the National Academy of Sciences*, 116: 20886–20891. https://doi.org/10.1073/pnas.1905755116
Kolstad, C.D. (1996). "Learning and Stock Effects in Environmental Regulation: The Case of Greenhouse Gas Emissions." *Journal of Environmental Economics and Management*, 31: 1–18. https://doi.org/10.1006/jeem.1996.0028
Kornek, U., Klenert, D., Edenhofer, O., and Fleurbaey, M. (2021). "The Social Cost of Carbon and Inequality: When Local Redistribution Shapes Global Carbon Prices." *Journal of Environmental Economics and Management* 107: 102450. https://doi.org/10.1016/j.jeem.2021.102450.
Lemoine, D., and Rudik. I. (2017). "Steering the Climate System: Using Inertia to Lower the Cost of Policy." *American Economic Review*, 107: 2947–2957. https://doi.org/10.1257/aer.20150986
Lemoine, D., and Traeger, C. (2014). "Watch Your Step: Optimal Policy in a Tipping Climate." *American Economic Journal: Economic Policy*, 6: 137–166. https://doi.org/10.1257/pol.6.1.137
Levinson, A. (2019). "Energy Efficiency Standards are More Regressive than Energy Taxes: Theory and Evidence." *Journal of the Association of Environmental and Resource Economists*, 6: S7–S36. https://doi.org/10.1086/701186

Mattauch, L., and Hepburn, C. (2016). "Climate Policies When Preferences Are Endogenous – and Sometimes They Are." *Midwest Studies in Philosophy*, 40: 76–95. https://doi.org/10.1111/misp.12048

Méjean, A., Pottier, A., Fleurbaey, M. et al. Catastrophic climate change, population ethics and intergenerational equity. *Climatic Change* 163, 873–890 (2020). https://doi.org/10.1007/s10584-020-02899-9

Millner, A. (2013). "On Welfare Frameworks and Catastrophic Climate Risks." *Journal of Environmental Economics and Management*, 65: 310–325. https://doi.org/10.1016/j.jeem.2012.09.006

Millner, A., Dietz, S., and Heal, G. (2013). "Scientific Ambiguity and Climate Policy." *Environmental and Resource Economics*, 55: 21–46. https://doi.org/10.1007/s10640–012-9612-0

Nordhaus, W.D. (2007). "A Review of the Stern Review on the Economics of Climate Change." *Journal of Economic Literature*, 45: 686–702. https://doi.org/10.1257/jel.45.3.686

(2008). *A Question of Balance*. New Haven and London: Yale University Press

(2017). "Revisiting the Social Cost of Carbon." *Proceedings of the National Academy of Sciences*, 114: 1518–1523. https://doi.org/10.1073/pnas.1609244114

Pindyck, R. (2019). "The Social Cost of Carbon Revisited." *Journal of Environmental Economics and Management*, 94: 140–160. https://doi.org/10.1016/j.jeem.2019.02.003

Rabinowicz, W. (2002), "Prioritarianism for Prospects." *Utilitas*, 14: 2–21. https://doi.org/10.1017/S0953820800003368

Rheinberger, C., and Treich, N. (2017). "Attitudes Toward Catastrophe." *Environmental and Resource Economics*, 67: 609–636. https://doi.org/10.1007/s10640–016-0033-3

Schelling, T. (1995). "Intergenerational Discounting." *Energy Policy*, 23: 395–401. https://doi.org/10.1016/0301-4215(95)90164-3

Scovronick N., Budolfson, M.B., Dennig, F., et al. (2017). "Impact of Population Growth and Population Ethics on Climate Change Mitigation Policy." *Proceedings of the National Academy of Sciences*, 114(46): 12338–12343. https://doi.org/10.1073/pnas.1618308114

Scovronick, N., Ferranna, M., Dennig, F., and Budolfson, M.B. (2020). "Valuing Health Impacts in Climate Policy: Ethical Issues and Economic Challenges." *Health Affairs*, 39: 2105–2112. https://doi.org/10.1377/hlthaff.2020.01117

Schneider, M., Traeger, C., and Winkler, R. (2012). "Trading off Generations: Equity, Discounting, and Climate Change." *European Economic Review*, 56: 1621–1644. https://doi.org/10.1016/j.euroeconrev.2012.08.006

Schwerhoff, G., Dao, N.T., Edenhofer, O., et al. (2017). "Policy Options for a Socially Balanced Climate Policy." *Economics: The Open Access, Open Assessment E-Journal*, 11: 1–11.

Stern, N.H. (2007). *The Economics of Climate Change: The Stern Review.* Cambridge University Press, Cambridge.

Sterner, T., and Persson, M. (2008). "An Even Sterner Review: Introducing Relative Prices into the Discounting Debate." *Review of Environmental Economics and Policy*, 2: 61–76. https://doi.org/10.1093/reep/rem024

Tol, R.S.J. (2009). "The Economic Effects of Climate Change." *Journal of Economic Perspectives*, 23: 29–51.

Tollefson, J. (2019). "Can the World Slow Global Warming?" *Nature* 573: 324–327. www.nature.com/immersive/d41586-019-02711-4/public/pdf/d41586-019-02711-4.pdf

Traeger, C. (2009). "Recent Developments in the Intertemporal Modeling of Uncertainty." *Annual Review of Resource Economics*, 1: 261–285. https://doi.org/10.1146/annurev.resource.050708.144242

(2014). "A 4-Stated DICE: Quantitatively Addressing Uncertainty Effects in Climate Change." *Environmental and Resource Economics*, 59: 1–37. https://doi.org/10.1007/s10640–014-9776-x

Weitzman, M.L. (2007). "A Review of the Stern Review on the Economics of Climate Change." *Journal of Economic Literature*, 45: 703–724. https://doi.org/10.1257/jel.45.3.703

(2009). "On Modeling and Interpreting the Economics of Catastrophic Climate Change." *Review of Economics and Statistics*, 91: 1–19. https://doi.org/10.1162/rest.91.1.1

Zuber, S., and Asheim, G.B. (2012). "Justifying Social Discounting: The Rank-Discounted Utilitarian Approach." *Journal of Economic Theory*, 147: 1572–1601. https://doi.org/10.1016/j.jet.2011.08.001

9 *Prioritarianism and Education*

ERWIN OOGHE*

9.1 Introduction

Equity in education is a big topic in various disciplines (economics, philosophy, psychology, and sociology). Yet, *operational* normative views – i.e., views that provide a clear mathematical formulation of how to compare the goodness of different "social states" – turn out to be rare.[1] The first aim of this chapter is to summarize the normative views that are operational in the academic literature on education. This summary reveals that prioritarianism is compatible with the existing normative views.[2] Not the idea of priority as such, but "priority of what?" turns out to be the dividing line between the different normative views.

The answer to the question "priority of what?" leads to four normative views in the education literature, depending on (i) whether the relevant metric is educational (e.g., test scores and attitudes) or economic (e.g., future income and leisure) in nature and (ii) whether one wants to provide outcomes or opportunities in these metrics. The second aim of this chapter is to critically discuss these four normative views as applied to sufficiently young pupils. I do so by directly challenging the philosophical foundations underlying the different views. I complement this direct approach by assessing whether

* I would like to thank the editors, Matt Adler and Ole Norheim, and the participants at the PiP-network meetings in Duke (2017, 2018) and Bergen (2019, 2020) for valuable comments that, in the end, not only changed this chapter, but also some of my views on education.

[1] In the case of economics, Waltenberg (2010: 107) observes: "While the handbook of health economics [...] contains three chapters explicitly concerned with normative health economics, [...] the analogous handbook of economics of education [...] does not contain any chapter or part devoted exclusively to equity and education."

[2] Prioritarianism is explained at length by Adler (Chapter 2, this volume). For now it suffices to know that prioritarianism provides some middle ground between utilitarianism and Rawlsianism. We come back to it later.

counterintuitive policy recommendations result from adopting these views in the context of a simple human capital investment problem: whose education should we invest in if we have an extra euro to spend? Both critiques highlight that outcomes, rather than opportunities, should be prioritized.

While the previous critical discussion was based on a simple static setting, it is interesting to look at optimal human capital investment in a dynamic setting. The third aim of this chapter is to examine the policy recommendations derived in a dynamic model of skill formation from an outcome-prioritarian – rather than an outcome-utilitarian or an outcome-Rawlsian – point of view. The results show that some utilitarian or Rawlsian claims are not true for prioritarians. For example, the utilitarian recommendation to reinforce (rather than to compensate) the impact of background in later stages of education does not necessarily hold for prioritarians. And, as another example, also the Rawlsian recommendation to equally compensate for ability and background (over all stages together) does not hold for prioritarians.

In the aforementioned static and dynamic setting, I consider a *school team* in *basic education* that optimally *designs* its *resource* allocation over pupils based on a prioritarian objective defined over an *educational index*. The fourth and final aim of this chapter is to check whether the derived policy recommendations also hold if I change the italicized elements in the benchmark story. In particular, I will focus on a different decision-maker (*minister* versus *school team*), a different age of pupils (*higher* versus *basic education*), a different normative exercise (*evaluation* versus *design*), different policy tools (beyond simple *resources*), and multidimensional outcomes (*multiple skills* versus an *educational index*).[3]

This chapter is organized as follows. Section 9.2 summarizes the different normative views that are operational in the academic literature on education. Section 9.3 critically discusses these normative views as applied to sufficiently young pupils and argues that educational outcomes should be prioritized. Section 9.4 analyses outcome-prioritarian

[3] One extension that I do not discuss is how to deal with (historical) discrimination. In other words, I will assume that educational differences that are linked to differences in background are based only on differences in resources (such as time, skills, and money) that families can and want to invest in their children, and not on discrimination. See, e.g., Schouten (2012) for a discussion.

human capital investment in a dynamic model of skill formation. Section 9.5 briefly discusses several extensions. A final Section 9.6 concludes. Technical details are relegated to appendices 9.A.1–9.A.3.

9.2 Normative Views in Education

The aim of this section is to summarize the normative views adopted in the different disciplines that study education from an academic point of view. As this literature is huge, I use the following stringent selection principles. First, I focus on operational views, i.e., views for which there exists a clear mathematical formulation of how to compare the goodness of different social states in education.[4] Second, I focus on the broad methodological principles underlying the different research strands, not on their research findings. Third, references to publications will be limited, for obvious reasons, to a selection of key publications (with, admittedly, a bias towards research in economics).

In the remainder of this section, I first provide a brief overview of the literature. While this overview is quick and dirty, my hope is that the resulting classification encompasses the bulk of the literature.[5] Afterwards, I discuss in somewhat more detail whether prioritarianism is compatible with these approaches. In my view, the answer is clearly yes: not the idea of prioritarianism itself, but what should be prioritized, turns out to be the dividing line in the normative literature on education.

9.2.1 A Brief Overview

Table 9.1 classifies the academic literature on education on the basis of its research aim: evaluation or design.

A first strand wants to *evaluate* either policy interventions (e.g., based on experimental or quasi-experimental data) or educational systems (e.g., based on large-scale internationally comparable data). This strand encompasses all disciplines with a quantitative interest in

[4] This principle excludes most of the philosophical literature. However, we will come back to that literature in the next section to critically discuss the operational normative views adopted in other disciplines.

[5] I will briefly mention some exceptions that do not fit in the provided straitjacket.

Table 9.1. *A classification of the education literature*

Research aim	Evaluation	Design
Disciplines	Economics, psychology, sociology	Mainly economics
Research type	Data-driven (empirical)	Model-driven (theoretical)
Education level	Often (pre-)primary and secondary	Often not specified
Cardinalization	Educational opportunities Economic opportunities	Educational outcomes Economic outcomes
Aggregation	Dashboard, i.e., no aggregation	Welfarist, including prioritarian

education (economics, psychology, and sociology).[6] The research in this literature is data-driven and focuses mostly on (pre-)primary and secondary education, probably because data is more readily available for these education levels in many countries.

A second strand wants to optimally *design* educational policies (such as educational resources, accountability schemes, or vouchers). Especially economists are very active in this strand. The research in this literature is model-driven and the exact education level is often not specified, in which case it is meant to capture all levels in an abstract way.

I now turn to the normative views adopted in both strands, summarized in the second part of Table 9.1. I distinguish two steps: a cardinalization step (what is the appropriate metric?) and an aggregation step (how should these metrics be aggregated into an overall judgment of the goodness of social states?).

First, I discuss the cardinalization step.

In the *evaluation* literature, the (distributional) purpose of education is usually thought to be the provision of equal opportunities, defined as the same opportunities for all pupils independent of background characteristics (such as gender, race, ethnicity, family income, and parental education). Depending on whether equality of opportunity must hold for educational outcomes (e.g., skills and attitudes) or economic outcomes (e.g., future earnings and leisure), two sub-strands result: the

[6] Still, there are some small differences between the different disciplines. Economists focus more on policy evaluations, sociologists prefer system evaluations, and psychologists (including educational scientists) do both.

equality of educational opportunity literature (initiated by Coleman, 1966) and the equality of economic opportunity literature (initiated by Bowles, 1973).[7]

In the *design* literature, the purpose of education is usually thought to provide outcomes, rather than opportunities.[8] Depending again on the outcome of interest, two sub-strands emerge. One strand focuses on optimal investment in education (initiated by Arrow, 1971), while the optimal redistribution literature (initiated by Ulph, 1977) designs educational subsidies, alongside earnings taxes, to generate and redistribute earnings.[9] The optimal redistribution literature is the only sub-strand that introduces preferences over net earnings and effort (to study and/or work). In these cases, the metric is usually utility, rather than earnings.

Second, I discuss the aggregation step in both literatures.

The *evaluation* literature usually follows a dashboard approach. In such a dashboard approach, researchers report several indices in isolation and do not specify how to trade off the different reported indices to arrive at a global evaluation.[10] The dashboard typically includes the average outcome, the dispersion in outcomes, and the correlation (or, more generally, the association) between outcomes and background characteristics. The correlation is important in the evaluation literature as it measures to what extent equality of opportunity is realized, where a correlation closer to zero is considered as better.

The *design* literature is deeply rooted in economics and therefore welfarist in nature. In other words, the global evaluation of goodness is an

[7] I refer to Bowles (1973) as an example of seminal work because he focuses specifically on the role of education in explaining unequal economic opportunities. See Brunori, Ferreira, and Peragine (Chapter 11, this volume) for additional references on the equality of opportunity literature.

[8] There exists a small literature that focus on *designing* education policies from an equality-of-opportunity point of view; see, e.g., Betts and Roemer (2007) and Keane and Roemer (2009).

[9] Interested readers may also consult (i) Bruno (1976), de Fraja (2002), and Cunha and Heckman (2007) on optimal investment in education and (ii) Hare and Ulph (1979), Tuomala (1986), Fleurbaey, Gary-Bobo, and Maguain (2002), Brett and Weymark (2003), and Bovenberg and Jacobs (2005) on the joint design of education and taxation.

[10] The dashboard approach does not specify how to commensurate the different dashboard indicators and therefore, somewhat contrary to our definition of an operational normative view, it does not provide a complete mathematical formulation of how to judge the goodness of social states.

increasing function of the individual metric only. This welfarist approach often uses a prioritarian aggregation (to be defined in a more precise way later on), usually for pragmatic, rather than deep normative reasons.

9.2.2 *Compatibility with Prioritarianism*

In the previous subsection I made a rough classification of different normative views in the academic literature on education. While I initially started with two strands depending on research aim (evaluation or design), two sub-strands emerged within each strand, depending on the outcome of interest (educational or economic).

While prioritarianism as an aggregation device is often used in the "welfarist" design literature, and is thus clearly compatible with this strand, the remaining question is therefore whether prioritarianism is also compatible with the evaluation literature. Nevertheless, as it is interesting to see the implications of employing a prioritarian approach in each case, I will discuss all four sub-strands in the sequel.

I introduce a simple example that will be used, with some slight modifications, throughout the rest of this chapter. Educational achievement e is an increasing function of innate ability a, background b, and (class) resources c, so, I write $e = E(a, b, c)$.[11] Economic achievement y is an increasing function of ability, background, and education; I write $y = Y(a, b, e)$ and thus I also have $y = Y(a, b, E(a, b, c))$.[12]

Some quick remarks. First, educational and economic achievement are assumed to be cardinally measurable. Second, for simplicity, all variables are assumed to be unidimensional (for now).[13] Third, there is

[11] Ability, background, and resources are (assumed to be) good for educational achievement.

[12] Ability, background, and educational achievement are (assumed to be) also good for economic achievement. Note that ability and background have a direct and indirect effect on economic achievement. Controlling for educational achievement, the direct effect of background on economic achievement captures, e.g., parental network effects that give access to more/better job offers or parental gifts that affect income.

[13] So, educational achievement is an index based on, e.g., acquired skills and attitudes; economic achievement is an index capturing, e.g., earned and unearned income; innate ability captures the influence of inborn genetic endowments; background is an index based on, e.g., gender, race, ethnicity, and socio-economic characteristics of the family (including the resources they invest); and class resources capture all resources at class level, e.g., class size, teacher quality/time, and peers.

Table 9.2. *Four metrics underlying the different sub-strands*

	Opportunity	Outcome
Educational	$\mathbb{E}[e\|b] = \mathbb{E}[E(a,b,c)\|b]$	$e = E(a,b,c)$
Economic	$\mathbb{E}[y\|b] = \mathbb{E}[Y(a,b,E(a,b,c))\|b]$	$y = Y(a,b,E(a,b,c))$

no effort at this stage, an issue to which I return when I discuss higher, rather than basic, education.[14]

A common practice in the equality of educational opportunity literature is to measure opportunities by the expected (educational or economic) outcome, conditional on background.[15] These conditional expectations are denoted $\mathbb{E}[e|b]$ and $\mathbb{E}[y|b]$. According to opportunity-egalitarians, equality of this conditional expectation is, *ceteris paribus*, "ideal" because it means that all pupils can expect the same outcome irrespective of their background. The metrics used in the four different sub-strands are summarized in Table 9.2.

To aggregate these metrics over pupils, I define a prioritarian evaluation function. Let w be one of the four metrics defined in Table 9.2. The global prioritarian evaluation is essentially based on the average transformed metric, i.e., on

$$g^{-1}\left(\int g(w)f(w)dw\right), \tag{9.1}$$

where g is a strictly increasing and strictly concave transformation function and f is the density of the metric under consideration.[16] In particular, note that increasingness of the transformation function g guarantees that higher (expected) outcomes are better (no levelling down), while concavity ensures that increases in (expected) outcomes

[14] I do not claim that effort, as such, does not exist in basic education, but I will argue later on, that, contrary to higher education, effort does not require a different normative treatment compared to ability or background.

[15] This approach to equality of opportunity is called the ex ante (Van de gaer) approach, which differs from the ex post (Roemer) approach; see Brunori, Ferreira, and Peragine (Chapter 11, this volume) for a discussion of both approaches.

[16] See Adler (Chapter 2, this volume) for a detailed discussion of prioritarianism. Adding the inverse g^{-1} in Equation (9.1) does not change the ranking of social states (if there is no uncertainty) and allows for simple and clean decomposition results later on (in Table 9.3).

Table 9.3. *Four evaluations decomposed in key statistics and the degree of priority*

	Opportunity	Outcome
Educational	$\mu_e - \frac{\pi}{2} \cdot \rho_{be}^2 \cdot \sigma_e^2$	$\mu_e - \frac{\pi}{2} \cdot \sigma_e^2$
Economic	$\mu_y - \frac{\pi}{2} \cdot \rho_{by}^2 \cdot \sigma_y^2$	$\mu_y - \frac{\pi}{2} \cdot \sigma_y^2$

matter more for the worse off, being those with lower (expected) outcomes. How much more priority should be given to a worse off pupil is left open. Prioritarians lie in between utilitarians (all pupils have equal priority) and Rawlsians (the worst-off pupil has absolute priority over all other pupils).[17]

I add some auxiliary assumptions to simplify the analysis.[18] To be clear, these additional assumptions are introduced only in this subsection and for ease of exposition; results in later sections will hold more generally. Under these auxiliary assumptions, the evaluation in each of the four sub-strands reduces to a simple formula based on some key statistics – the mean (μ), the variance (σ^2), and the squared correlation (ρ^2) – and the degree of priority π, which lies in between utilitarians (with $\pi \to 0$) and Rawlsians (with $\pi \to \infty$).

Table 9.3 summarizes.

In both the opportunity-prioritarian and outcome-prioritarian approach, the mean is essentially corrected downwardly for inequalities. The correction depends on the degree of priority: the higher the

[17] Utilitarians and Rawlsians are defined in this chapter as limiting cases of prioritarians, with either an infinitely small or an infinitely large degree of priority. As the latter limit is not well-defined, a Rawlsian strictly prefers one state over another if the worst off is strictly better off in the former state. This is compatible with both maximin and leximin objectives.

[18] First, the transformation function g is of the Kolm-Pollak type. Second, there is a linear relation between either educational or economic achievement and background and this relation is estimated using standard regression techniques. Third, background and regression errors are independent and follow normal distributions. These assumptions, as well as the results, can be found in Appendix 9.A.1. I also show that if one starts from an Atkinson transformation function and adds log-linear relations and lognormal distributions, one ends up with a very similar, but multiplicative decomposition that does not change the main story line.

degree of priority assigned to the worse off, the higher the downward correction will be, *ceteris paribus*.

The measure of inequality is different, however, in both approaches. While outcome-prioritarians only care about the variance, being a measure of dispersion, opportunity-prioritarians also care about the squared correlation between background and outcome. In particular, being squared, a zero correlation between background and outcome is, *ceteris paribus*, optimal according to opportunity-prioritarians. Alternatively, opportunity-prioritarians only care about that part of the total variance that is morally objectionable in their view, i.e., the part that is correlated with background.[19]

9.2.3 A Brief Summary

While prioritarianism, as an aggregation device, is often used in the "welfarist" design literature, and thus clearly compatible with it, I investigated whether prioritarianism is also compatible with the evaluation literature.

If I apply prioritarianism to an opportunity metric, the resulting opportunity-prioritarian view turns out to evaluate social states based on those key statistics that are typically reported in the dashboard approach that underlies most of the evaluation literature. So, while prioritarianism turns out to be compatible with the evaluation literature, prioritarians go one step further in fact, as they trade off these different statistics in a specific way.

To conclude, not so much priority as such, but the metric over which prioritarianism should be defined – i.e., the question "priority of what?" – is the bone of contention, in my view. The next section will therefore critically discuss the four metrics of Table 9.2, while taking the prioritarian aggregation of Equation (9.1) for granted.

9.3 A Critical Discussion of the Four Metrics

In this section, I use a prioritarian aggregation procedure, i.e., Equation (9.1), and critically discuss the four metrics of Table 9.2 as

[19] Note that this correlation does not only capture the direct effect of background on the outcome under consideration, but also the indirect effect of background via its correlation with ability (caused, e.g., by genetic inheritance from the parents) and with available class resources (caused, e.g., by the school choice of parents).

applied to sufficiently young pupils (an assumption that will be made precise and relaxed later on in Section 9.5.2).

I will use two types of arguments to uncover whether a metric is reasonable or not. First, I use arguments from the philosophical literature on education that directly question the normative position underlying some of these metrics. Second, I use the Gospel of Matthew (7:16), "Ye shall know them by their fruits," and look at the policy consequences of adopting either approach in a simple human capital investment setting.[20] If counterintuitive results obtain in simple settings, then the underlying normative goal seems questionable. This strategy is what philosophers refer to as a reflective equilibrium.[21]

The analysis below is structured along two questions that directly relate to the four metrics discussed before. What is the value of education: intrinsic or instrumental (or both)? And what should education provide: outcomes or opportunities? I start with the latter question.

9.3.1. *Outcomes or Opportunities?*

Suppose that the aim of education is the provision of opportunities, as adopted in the bulk of the evaluation literature. From a distributional point of view the desire is that (educational and/or economic) outcomes do not depend on background characteristics. Two critical remarks can be made.

First, let us look at the philosophical literature on equality of opportunity. One normative reason underlying equality of opportunity is the idea that pupils are not (or cannot be held) responsible for their background. This seems a logical normative starting point in my view. Still, there exist many other traits – think, e.g., of variations in innate ability and perseverance for a given background – that also influence outcomes and that sufficiently young pupils cannot be held responsible for too.

The so-called luck-egalitarians have criticized the Rawlsian distinction between social contingencies (such as background) and natural contingencies (such as innate ability).[22] But if one endorses the position

[20] This citation of Matthew is borrowed from Samuelson (1977) and has been applied to education by, e.g., Jencks (1988). I will adapt Jencks' example of "teacher Higgins" later on.

[21] See, e.g., Adler (2019: 22-23) for a more detailed elaboration.

[22] Admittedly, Rawls recognizes this problem: "[t]here is no more reason to permit the distribution of income and wealth to be settled by the distribution of natural

that these natural contingencies are equally arbitrary from a moral point of view, then the next question is: what are the normative consequences of this stance?

Recall that if pupils are not responsible for their background, then a common operationalization is to focus on the expected outcome conditional on background. However, if sufficiently young pupils cannot be held responsible for anything, then one should condition over all traits. But this implies that opportunities, understood as expectations conditional on all factors for which a pupil cannot be held responsible, reduce to outcomes. In other words, promoting opportunities implies promoting outcomes.[23]

Second, let us investigate some of the policy consequences of equalizing opportunities. I use a teacher called Higgins, first introduced in Jencks (1988), to set up a simple story. Teacher Higgins is a third-grade teacher in a small town. During the school year he notices that two pupils start lagging behind, so he decides to devote some extra help to them right after each lunch break. According to teacher Higgins, both pupils have currently about the same educational achievement. Yet, both pupils are different in terms of innate ability and family background. The first pupil has limited abilities, but these are somewhat moderated by an advantageous family background. The second pupil has favorable abilities, but has a disadvantaged family background. Teacher Higgins knows that the same amount of extra time will lead to the same progress in educational achievement for both pupils: in the language of economists, there are no efficiency considerations to worry about.[24]

assets than by historical and social fortune [. . .] since social contingencies and natural abilities are 'equally arbitrary' from a moral point of view (Rawls, 1999: 64–65)." However, Rawls' view is that disadvantages caused by natural contingencies (e.g., innate ability) and disadvantages caused by social contingencies (e.g., social background) must be treated differently: the natural disadvantages in the final distribution of resources (regulated by the "difference principle") and the social disadvantages in education itself (regulated by the principle of "fair equality of opportunity").

23 Recall that the focus here is on sufficiently young pupils in basic education. We come back to older pupils, say at college level, in the extensions.

24 We focus here on educational opportunities, rather than economic opportunities. A similar story, with the same conclusions, can be told for economic opportunities.

Teacher Higgins wonders how he should divide his extra time over both pupils. For now, I assume that (only) education matters.[25] Suppose that teacher Higgins would adopt an opportunity-prioritarian view, i.e., Equation (9.1) defined over educational opportunities, i.e., $\mathbb{E}[e|b]$, as the appropriate metric. As a consequence, he will devote more time and effort to the pupil with the lowest opportunities, being the second pupil with a disadvantaged background. The reason for teacher Higgins – and for all those adopting an opportunity-prioritarian view – to devote more resources to the second pupil is not that this pupil needs it more than the first pupil, or that this pupil will progress more from the same help. Rather, the reason is group-based: devoting more resources to the second pupil helps the group of pupils who are, like the second pupil, disadvantaged in terms of background and who are expected to lag behind. Teacher Higgins must tell the parents of the first pupil that, while their child also needs extra time and would equally benefit from it, he still has decided to give less extra help because their child does not belong to a group that is considered to be disadvantaged. This seems a violation of the first pupil's right to equal treatment in an otherwise equal educational situation.

This violation would not have occurred if teacher Higgins used educational outcome e as the appropriate metric. In that case he would devote the same amount of extra resources to both pupils as they currently reach the same education level and as they would equally benefit from extra resources. The adoption of an outcome-prioritarian view implies therefore that teacher Higgins will give extra help to all pupils who lag behind, including pupils, like the first one, with learning difficulties, and pupils, like the second one, with a disadvantaged background.

I would like to stress several things.

First, to be clear, outcome-prioritarians, similar to opportunity-prioritarians, will on average assign more resources to pupils with a disadvantaged background. But, contrary to opportunity-prioritarians, outcome-prioritarians do not provide extra help to every pupil with a disadvantaged background. They provide it only to those pupils who need it, with needs defined on the basis of educational achievement rather than background. In other words, outcome-prioritarians also

[25] In the next subsection, I introduce well-being, a function of both education and economic achievement, as a broader currency of justice.

equalize opportunities to some extent. Somewhat related is the often heated discussion on (preferential) affirmative action. Opportunity-prioritarians would indeed assign more resources to the pupil with a disadvantaged background even if educational backlog and prospects for progress are identical. In other words, if education is the currency of justice, then they would provide an educational advantage to pupils with a disadvantaged background that is, in my view, preferential and thus hard to justify.[26]

Second, one could also wonder whether the choice of teacher Higgins, allocating his resources over pupils, is different from similar choices at higher levels, e.g., minister Higgins allocating her resources over schools. Jencks (1988: 519) writes "I believe, but will not try to prove, that all the principled claims about how [...] Higgins ought to allocate [...] time among [...] pupils recur in essentially the same form when we argue about how school principals, boards of education, or legislatures ought to allocate scarce resources." Indeed, if teachers and ministers agree that children cannot be held responsible for background and ability, then teachers and ministers should agree to focus on outcomes, rather than opportunities. But this does not imply that teachers and ministers should allocate resources over pupils in the same way.

I briefly mention two cases here that will be discussed in more detail later on. One: even if teachers and ministers have the same normative goal, they may have different information and instruments at their disposal such that they could make different choices in the end.[27] For example, it is plausible that minister Higgins, in contrast to teacher Higgins, can only observe background and must therefore allocate

[26] Two remarks. First, while (preferential) affirmative action is not desirable for young pupils, this can be different at later stages of education. In the context of college admissions, affirmative action can be justified if ability is thought to be (one of) the eligibility criteria. For example, mediocre high school results, caused by low abilities and an advantaged family background, could be a reason to refuse admission, while this is not necessarily true if these mediocre results are caused by high abilities and a disadvantaged background. Second, affirmative action can be justified if it is not preferential. Later on, we will discuss such a possibility when the currency of justice is more broadly defined (in terms of well-being based on both educational and economic achievement).

[27] In fact, Jencks (1988: 519) seems to allude to this possibility: "I recognize, however, that the practical arguments for various possible distributions of [...] Higgins's time are often quite different from those that come into play when a board of education or a legislature is allocating resources."

resources over schools based only on the background of the pupils at the different schools. Two: teachers and ministers may agree that outcomes, not opportunities, are the appropriate metric, but they may focus on different outcomes. For example, it could be argued that teachers should focus on educational outcomes, while ministers should adopt a broader definition of well-being, based, e.g., on both educational and economic outcomes.

To recapitulate, my first argument shows that the responsibility-logic underlying equality of opportunity, consistently applied to sufficiently young pupils who cannot be held responsible for ability, background, and other traits, leads to the promotion of outcomes. My second argument shows that policies that promote opportunities deny some pupils the right to receive equal help, even if they equally need help and would equally benefit from receiving help. The reason is that, based on their ability deficit, they do not belong to a group that is recognized as being disadvantaged. This problem does not occur if one focuses on outcomes, because it implies that all educational backlog, whether caused by ability or background, is considered to be a reason for help (at least in the absence of efficiency considerations). I conclude that not opportunities, but outcomes are the appropriate metric for sufficiently young pupils. I have indicated that outcome-prioritarians also equalize opportunities, albeit in a different way. I have also stressed that teachers and ministers should both focus on outcomes, but this does not imply that they allocate resources over pupils in the same way, an issue to which I return in the next section.

9.3.2 *Intrinsic or Instrumental?*

In the previous subsection, I have argued that it is appropriate to promote outcomes, not opportunities in the case of sufficiently young pupils. In this subsection, I adopt this focus on outcomes, but investigate what outcome one should promote: education as an intrinsic goal or education as an instrument to improve, e.g., future economic achievement.

The normative position that education has both intrinsic and instrumental value seems to be common ground in the philosophical literature on education.[28] Such a position immediately discards using only

[28] See, e.g., Rawls (1999: 87): "The value of education should not be assessed solely in terms of economic efficiency and social welfare. Equally if not more

economic achievement as the appropriate metric. Moreover, the position that only economic achievement should be the goal of education can also be criticized if one looks at its consequences. For example, in the (first-best) redistribution literature, leave out equity and efficiency considerations can be separated. As a consequence, one should organize educational systems efficiently and redistribute optimally afterwards. Such an efficient organization of education would imply that those who are not efficient in attaining education (e.g., because of a limited ability or a disadvantaged background) will get a far more limited education that will be compensated for by monetary transfers in later life.[29] Such a policy seems objectionable and can be avoided by assigning intrinsic value to education too.

While the use of *only* economic achievement is thus not reasonable, the question whether *only* educational achievement would be reasonable is less evident. Suppose that I would define well-being as a strictly increasing function of education e and economic achievement y, say, $w(e, y)$. Using the definition $y = Y(a, b, e)$ introduced before, well-being can be rewritten as

$$w(e, Y(a, b, e)), \tag{9.2}$$

which is a function of ability, background, and education. Contrary to the previous section, well-being is now the currency of justice, which is broader than education only. Education has a double impact on well-being: directly (intrinsically) and indirectly (instrumentally, via its impact on economic achievement).

Ability and background play a role in Equation (9.2) and I must investigate whether this is reasonable or not. To judge this, I look again at teacher Higgins and his two pupils. Recall that both pupils had the same educational achievement and would equally benefit from receiving extra help. The first pupil had limited abilities, but these were somewhat moderated by an advantageous family background.

important is the role of education in enabling a person to enjoy the culture of his society and to take part in its affairs, and in this way to provide for each individual a secure sense of his own worth." While this view is common, note that the distinction between intrinsic and instrumental is not always very clear; see, e.g., Kristjánsson (2017).

29 The same trade-off also holds in second-best settings, but to a lesser extent; see, e.g., Fleurbaey, Gary-Bobo, and Maguain (2002).

The second pupil had normal abilities, but had a disadvantaged family background.

Important additional information, for the current story, is that teacher Higgins correctly anticipates that the same amount of progress in *educational achievement* will also lead to the same amount of progress in the *well-being* of both pupils. So, to sum up, the same extra resources would not only lead to the same educational progress of both pupils (as before), but the same progress in education would, in turn, also lead to the same progress in the well-being of both pupils. This additional assumption ensures, again, that there are no efficiency considerations in the story and, as a consequence, the allocation problem of teacher Higgins is a matter of equity only.

Teacher Higgins thinks it is best to adopt a prioritarian view, i.e., Equation (9.1), but now defined over well-being, i.e., Equation (9.2). Who should get priority? One way to examine priority, is to compare the marginal social welfare weights of both pupils, obtained by differentiating (9.1) with respect to class resources. As both pupils currently have the same educational achievement (say, $e_1 = e_2 \equiv e$), the marginal social welfare weight is, up to a common efficiency factor, equal to[30]

$$\phi'\Big(w\big(e, Y(a_i, b_i, e)\big)\Big), \tag{9.3}$$

for pupil $i = 1, 2$. As a consequence, the pupil with a higher (expected) economic achievement, will get a lower priority (as ϕ' is strictly decreasing in w and w is strictly increasing in y).

Without loss of generality, I assume that, *given the same educational achievement*, background is (always) more valuable than ability for economic achievement, e.g., because parental network effects (to get a job) and parental gifts (to get started in adult life) are relatively more important for economic success. If true, then $Y(a_2, b_2, e) < Y(a_1, b_1, e)$ holds for the two pupils (for all education levels) and the marginal social welfare weight of the second pupil will be larger. This implies that the second pupil receives priority over the first pupil. As a consequence, teacher Higgins will devote more (extra) resources to the

[30] The efficiency factor captures the (direct and indirect) effect of resources on well-being and is, at the margin, equal to $[w'_e(e, y_i) + w'_y(e, y_i)Y'_e(a_i, b_i, e)]E'_c(a_i, b_i, c)$ for pupil $i = 1, 2$. This factor is, by assumption, equal for both pupils and therefore not relevant to assess their relative priority.

second pupil, but the reason is now that this second pupil can be expected to lag behind in future economic achievement. In other words, the second pupil receives priority in education, and will, in the end, be better educated than the first pupil, but only to compensate for a lower future economic success.[31]

Is this a reasonable outcome? Can teacher Higgins tell the parents of the less able pupil that he devotes less extra time to their child because he or she has better opportunities to succeed later in life anyway? In my view, he cannot justify this unequal treatment. Compensating pupils in education for having worse economic prospects in the future does not seem attractive, at least for a teacher.

While this conclusion is probably intuitive for teacher Higgins, it is, in the current setting, less obvious for minister Higgins. In the previous subsection, education was the only currency of justice. Assigning more educational resources to the second pupil would give that second pupil an advantage (a higher education level) that could not be justified. In the current setting, however, the currency of justice is well-being. So, assigning more educational resources to the second pupil will, of course, also imply a higher education level, but only to compensate for the fact that this pupil would, even with the same education level, still lag behind in future economic achievement and thus also in well-being.[32] While I think that such a compensation should not be pursued by teacher Higgins, it is a plausible policy for minister Higgins. Let us discuss the consequences for teacher Higgins and minister Higgins separately.

For teacher Higgins I must adjust the metric in Equation (9.2) to ensure that it no longer depends on ability and background. One possibility is to integrate out ability and background to arrive at an average well-being metric that depends only on education, i.e.,

$$\bar{w}(e) = \iint w(e, Y(a,b,e)) f(a,b) da db, \tag{9.4}$$

31 Vice versa, if background is (always) less valuable compared to ability, then the first pupil receives priority over the second pupil. It could also be that neither background nor ability are always less valuable; we do not discuss this possibility further.

32 While there is (preferential) treatment in education, this treatment is meant to compensate and therefore does not provide a final advantage in terms of well-being. So, if well-being is the currency of justice, I would not necessarily classify this treatment as (preferential) affirmative action.

where f denotes the joint density function of ability and background.[33] The new metric $\bar{w}$ only depends on education, but still captures, on average, the intrinsic and instrumental impact of education on well-being. The resulting average well-being metric will be country-specific (or even region-specific) if, e.g., the instrumental importance of education for future economic achievement is different between countries.[34] This may matter because, intuitively, the higher the instrumental value of education in a country, the more one should care about the educational backlog of pupils in that country.

For minister Higgins, there are two possible normative positions. Either the objective of minister Higgins coincides with the one of teacher Higgins: a prioritarian view, i.e., Equation (9.1), with well-being defined as in Equation (9.4). Minister Higgins will therefore not preferentially treat schools serving disadvantaged pupils to compensate for lower future economic success. This will be the benchmark case in the next section. Or minister Higgins adopts a prioritarian view, i.e., Equation (9.1), but now with well-being defined as in Equation (9.2). In such a case she allows for educational policies that preferentially treat schools serving disadvantaged pupils to compensate for lower economic success. I will discuss this case in Section 9.5.1.2.

9.3.3 A Brief Summary

I have argued that both teachers and ministers should focus on outcomes, rather than opportunities, in case of sufficiently young pupils.

For teachers, the relevant outcome is educational, but, still, it can accommodate for both the intrinsic and instrumental value of education, albeit only in some average way as in Equation (9.4).

For ministers, there are two possibilities. Either their outcome coincides with the one of teachers (Equation (9.4); the benchmark case) or their outcome is given by Equation (9.2) and thus deviates from teachers. In the latter case, ministers may preferentially treat pupils in education to compensate for lower future economic success. Whether

33 I use f throughout this chapter to denote a density function. While somewhat loose, confusion is not possible as it is always clear from the context which density is meant.

34 It is therefore not clear how one must compare educational systems across countries (as is often the purpose in the evaluation literature). We come back to it later on in Section 9.5.3.

pupils with a lower ability or pupils with a disadvantaged background should be preferentially treated depends on whether background or ability has a higher impact on economic success for the same education level. This is, in the end, an empirical question.

In the simple story of teacher and minister Higgins, I have up to now neglected at least two important considerations. First, to be sure that the discussion was about equity, I neglected efficiency considerations, assuming that the two pupils under consideration would equally benefit from an extra amount of help. Second, the model was static, while education is, in reality, a dynamic cumulative process with different stages. The next section will look at the allocation of resources while taking these considerations into account.

9.4 Resource Allocation and Skill Formation

The allocation of resources in education consists of at least two questions. How should one divide resources between the different stages of education (the vertical allocation question)? And how should one allocate resources over pupils with different characteristics at each stage (the horizontal allocation question)?

To answer both questions, I extend the previous static model to allow for different stages. In a first subsection I will therefore introduce a model of dynamic skill formation. In a second subsection I formulate the problem of an outcome-prioritarian school team that wants to optimally allocate resources over pupils in each stage. As mentioned before, ministers may allocate resources differently, because of different information or a different view on the relevant outcome; I discuss this extension, and other ones, later on.

9.4.1 A Simple Dynamic Model of Skill Formation

The simplest possible way to get insight in the dynamics of education is to allow for two stages only. I will refer to stage 1 as representing the early stages of education and stage 2 as the later stages of education. Using obvious notation, the production of education at the different stages is governed by a simple additive process:[35]

[35] It is best to think of this model as a growth model, i.e., E_1 and E_2 measure the change in skills (respectively from e_0=0 and e_1) in period 1 and 2. Without loss of generality, one could make the starting point e_0 non-zero (e.g., a function of ability and background only).

$$\begin{aligned} e_1 &= E_1(a, b, c_1), \\ e_2 &= e_1 + E_2(a, b, c_2). \end{aligned} \tag{9.5}$$

As a consequence, I can define the final education level as

$$e \equiv E(a, b, c_1, c_2) \equiv E_1(a, b, c_1) + E_2(a, b, c_2). \tag{9.6}$$

I assume, as before, that the functions E_1 and E_2, and thus also the function E, are strictly increasing in all arguments. In addition, the law of diminishing returns implies that the functions E_1 and E_2, and thus also the function E, are strictly concave in class resources. Moreover, the empirical literature tells us that some additional assumptions are plausible. I discuss these assumptions here in an informal way and refer to Appendix 9.A.2 for the formal details.

First, *everything else equal*, investment is more effective at earlier stages, a result that Cunha et al. (2006: 710) call "a major finding of an entire literature." I refer to this assumption as Assumption 1.[36]

Second, background and resources are substitutes in early stages, and complements in later stages, which is Assumption 2. It simply means that extra class resources have a higher impact on the education of pupils with a more disadvantaged background at early stages and vice versa at later stages. This is "in line" with the empirical literature. Cunha, Heckman, and Schennach (2010) observe that, especially for cognitive skills, the elasticity of substitution between background and resources decreases over time from substitutes to complements.[37] This makes intuitive sense, indeed. Suppose that background and class resources are proxies for the time and effort that, respectively, parents and teachers invest. Then it seems indeed plausible that background and class resources must be relatively good substitutes at early stages of education, while at later stages, requiring more specialized knowledge, this substitutability decreases and even turns into complementarity.

36 While it is called "a major finding," the technology of skill formation in this literature, based on nested production functions of the constant elasticity of substitution (CES) type, does not satisfy Assumption 1 if the elasticities of substitution are different at different stages. The latter seems to be true for cognitive skills in the United States; see, e.g., Cunha, Heckman, and Schennach (2010).

37 As this empirical literature focuses on background only, we do not impose a similar assumption for ability. We briefly come back to this issue later on.

Third, the empirical literature focuses on background and not so much on (innate) ability. So, the next assumption is more of a reasonable a priori, rather than a falsified statement about the real world. I split the assumption into two parts. First, I assume that, at each stage, class resources are better substitutes for background than for ability (Assumption 3a). This can again be related to the previous story, because class resources and background (as proxies for the invested time and effort of, respectively, teachers and parents) are quite close in nature and therefore probably better substitutes than class resources and innate ability. Second, while class resources remain a reasonable substitute for background over the different stages, this might be less the case for ability: class resources can compensate for ability at the early stages, but much less, or even not at all, at later stages (Assumption 3b).

While this dynamic model extends our previous simple static view on educational production, it is also worth looking at some limitations. Dynamic complementarity – the possibility that investment and educational skills reinforce each other – is not present in our additive model.[38] Yet, all known empirical results from the dynamic skill formation literature can be obtained in an additive model, which suggests that, while a limitation, dynamic complementarity is not important for the (empirical) story that we know up to now.[39] More important, skills are unidimensional in my model and must therefore capture both non-cognitive and cognitive skills. This is a clear limitation, because the dynamics, and thus also the resulting policy implications, can be quite different for both types of skills. I will come back to it in the extensions. Finally, because background is also a proxy for parental investment, and because parental investment is endogenous, parental investment may change as class resources change. This feedback effect is not captured in the main results, but could be important. For example, the assumption that class resources are better substitutes for background than for ability may no longer be true if the use of class

[38] Additivity implies $\partial^2 E/\partial e_1 \partial c_2 = 0$.

[39] The opposite might even be true. Figure 1 in Cunha, Heckman, and Schennach (2010: 889) shows that, in a simplified version of the model, the ratio of early to late optimal investment is larger than one if and only if the skill multiplier is larger than one-half. Actually, the larger the degree of complementarity, the lower this ratio becomes for a given skill multiplier, which suggests that complementarity reduces the case in favor of early over late investment. In any case, in Appendix 9.A.2 I also present the more general formula that allows for dynamic complementarity.

resources to compensate for background is counteracted by higher parental investment of resource-rich families.

9.4.2 The Problem of an Outcome-Prioritarian School Team

An outcome-prioritarian school team must decide how to allocate resources over their pupils at the different stages of the educational process. Let $C_1(a,b)$ and $C_2(a,b)$ denote the resources invested in a pupil with characteristics (a,b) at each of the two stages, $\bar{C}^S$ is the available amount of resources (expressed per pupil) that the school team received from the minister of education, and f^S is the density function over types at school S. So, the outcome-prioritarian problem of the school team is to choose the functions C_1 and C_2 to maximize an outcome-prioritarian evaluation function based on Equations (9.1) and (9.4), i.e.,

$$g^{-1}\left(\iint_{a,b} g\left(\bar{w}\left(E(a,b,C_1(a,b),C_2(a,b))\right)\right)f^S(a,b)dadb\right), \tag{9.7}$$

subject to the budget constraint of the school team (i.e., allocated resources cannot exceed available resources), which, neglecting discounting, is given by

$$\iint_{a,b} (C_1(a,b)+C_2(a,b))f^S(a,b)dadb \leq \bar{C}^S. \tag{9.8}$$

The current exercise is similar to Arrow (1971), but is now applied to a model of dynamic skill formation as popularized by Heckman (2006). The Arrow-Heckman model presented here extends both literatures, because the analysis in Arrow is essentially prioritarian, but static only, and the analysis in Heckman is dynamic, but utilitarian only.[40] Moreover, I introduce heterogeneity in both (innate) ability and background.[41] This additional extension allows to investigate, e.g., whether one should compensate more for background than for ability.

40 Admittedly, the title of Arrow's (1971) article is somewhat misleading in this respect because Arrow's approach is, in the notation of this chapter, essentially prioritarian. The work of Heckman and colleagues often focuses explicitly on maximizing average test scores, which is, in the notation of this chapter, utilitarian.

41 Arrow (1971: 410) focuses on ability, which he very broadly defines as the "capacity to benefit from the [educational] expenditures in question." This may include, e.g., parental education. Cunha, Heckman, and Schennach (2010: 886) mainly focus on the parental environment, but do recognize that "genetic factors may influence [...] initial conditions."

Table 9.4. *A comparison of different normative positions*

Question	Key Assumption	Utilitarian	Prioritarian	Rawlsian
Q1	A1	yes	yes	yes
Q2a	A2	yes	yes	yes
Q2b	A2	no	no/?	?
Q2c	A2	?	?/yes	yes
Q3a	A3	yes	yes/no	no
Q3b	A3	yes	yes	yes
Q3c	A3	yes	yes	=

Q1: Should a school team invest more resources in early education?
Q2a: Should a school team invest more in pupils from a more disadvantaged background in early education?
Q2b: Should a school team invest more in pupils from a more disadvantaged background in later education?
Q2c: Should a school team invest more in pupils from a more disadvantaged background *in total*?
Q3a: Should a school team compensate more for background than for ability in early education?
Q3b: Should a school team compensate more for background than for ability in later education?
Q3c: Should a school team compensate more for background than for ability *in total*?

I discuss all results in an informal way and refer to Appendix 9.A.2 for formal details. Table 9.4 summarizes the answers of a utilitarian, prioritarian, and Rawlsian school team to the questions listed below the table.[42]

Possible answers are "yes," "no," "?" (meaning that the answer is ambiguous without further assumptions), "=" (meaning that equality must hold), and "x"/ "y" (meaning that for low degrees of priority the answer is "x" and for high degrees of priority the answer is "y"). The prioritarian answers that are different from the utilitarian or Rawlsian answer are highlighted in Table 9.4.

[42] Note that the second question is not posed with respect to ability because little is empirically known about the interaction between resources and ability (as innate ability is difficult to observe). We will briefly come back to this later on.

9.4.2.1 Vertical Allocation

The first question deals with the vertical allocation problem, i.e., how to allocate resources over the different stages of education. The answer is that a school team should invest more in early stages than in later stages for each type of pupil (i.e., $C_1^S(a,b) > C_2^S(a,b)$ for all a, b).[43] This answer is well-known in the academic literature and follows directly from the empirical observation that investment matters more at earlier stages (Assumption 1). It holds for utilitarians, prioritarians, and Rawlsians alike as it is essentially an efficiency result.

9.4.2.2 Horizontal Allocation: Background

The second question deals with the horizontal allocation problem, i.e., how to allocate resources over different types of pupils. It asks whether a school team should invest more in pupils from a more disadvantaged background (i.e., *compensate* for background) or invest less in these pupils (i.e., *reinforce* background) at the different stages of education (questions 2a and 2b) as well as in total over both stages (question 2c).[44] Assumption 2 plays a crucial role here.[45]

In the early stages of education, utilitarians, prioritarians, and Rawlsians agree that background should be compensated (i.e., $\partial C_1^S(a,b)/\partial b < 0$ for all a, b). Again, this answer is well-known in the academic literature and follows from the fact that there seems to be no conflict between equity and efficiency in the early stages of education. To be more precise, it is not only equitable to compensate for background, but it is also more efficient to do so in stage 1 as resources have a larger impact on pupils from disadvantaged backgrounds.

In later stages, utilitarians, prioritarians, and Rawlsians no longer agree. Only the answer of utilitarians and prioritarians with a sufficiently low degree of priority is clear: background should be reinforced at later stages (i.e., $\partial C_2^S(a,b)/\partial b > 0$ for all a, b). The reason is simply because it is efficient to do so in stage 2 as extra resources now have a larger impact on advantaged pupils. The answer of prioritarians with

43 C_1^S and C_2^S denote the optimal solution of school S in both stages and $C^S = C_1^S + C_2^S$ is their sum.

44 I use compensation and reinforcement rather than Arrow's (1971) input-progressivity and input-regressivity.

45 Recall that, based on the existing empirical literature, we only made Assumption 2 with respect to background. If we would make the same assumption for ability, then all results for background would hold for ability too.

a sufficiently high degree of priority and Rawlsians is ambiguous as they trade off such efficiency gains against the equity losses.

Seen over both stages together, utilitarians, prioritarians, and Rawlsians also disagree. As utilitarians want to compensate for background in early stages, but reinforce it in later stages, their answer to the question whether to compensate for background in total is ambiguous. Rawlsians want to compensate for background over both stages together (i.e., $\partial C^S(a,b)/\partial b < 0$ for all a, b). This stands to reason, as Rawlsians actually want to fully compensate for background (as well as for ability).[46] Full compensation for background means that the opportunity-egalitarian ideal will be reached, i.e., that educational achievement will be independent of background. Yet, as we have seen before, Rawlsians will not necessarily fully compensate in each stage separately as they want to reach full total compensation in the most efficient way, which may require to be compensated differently in the different stages.[47] Prioritarians with a sufficiently high degree of priority will also compensate for background in total.[48]

9.4.2.3 Horizontal Allocation: Ability versus Background

The third question also deals with the horizontal allocation problem, but focuses on the degree of compensation for ability relative to the degree of compensation for background. The answers now depend on Assumption 3 or subparts of it.[49] For the interpretation, note two things.

[46] Arrow (1971) calls full compensation output-neutrality.

[47] While Rawlsians always fully compensate for background, an interesting question is under what additional assumptions also utilitarians and prioritarians would go for the opportunity-egalitarian ideal. It turns out that they would do so if, e.g., background and class resources are perfect substitutes in stage 1 and background plays no role in stage 2. So, opportunity-egalitarians and prioritarians might still agree if these stringent conditions on educational production were true (which is not in line with, e.g., the evidence for the United States).

[48] This is in line with Arrow's (1971) tentative conclusion that, in case of education, more resources should go to the less able (broadly defined) if the degree of priority is strong enough.

[49] Recall that assumption 3, especially 3b, is not based on empirical evidence. Alternatively, if one were to assume that the elasticity of background and resources decreases faster over time, then the answers to questions 3a and 3b must be switched, which has implications for prioritarians and Rawlsians, but not for utilitarians.

First, if I write that "X *compensates more* for background than for ability," with X being a utilitarian, prioritarian or Rawlsian, I mean that the educational gap caused by a more disadvantaged background is counteracted more by X than the gap caused by a lower ability. Somewhat loosely, it is probably best to think of it in a proportional way: "X *compensates more* for background than for ability," means that, e.g., 50 percent of the gap caused by a more disadvantaged background is eliminated via extra resources, while, e.g., only 40 percent of the gap caused by a lower ability is counteracted.[50] I stress, therefore, that compensating more for background than for ability does not necessarily mean that more resources are allocated to pupils with a more disadvantaged background compared to pupils of lower ability. The size of the gap, for example, plays a role as well.

Second, although I often write that "X wants to *compensate more* for background than for ability," note that this is only relative and could thus also mean that "X wants to *reinforce* background *less* than ability." In other words, and again somewhat loosely, "X wants to *compensate more* for background than for ability," could also mean that the gap caused by a more disadvantaged background is enlarged to, e.g., 120 percent by providing less resources to these pupils, while the gap caused by a lower ability is enlarged to, e.g., 140 percent.

In the early stages of education, utilitarians will compensate more for background than for ability. The reason is that class resources are better substitutes for background than for ability (Assumption 3a), so it is simply more efficient to compensate for background than ability. A Rawlsian proposes the exact opposite. A Rawlsian, recall, wants to fully compensate for both ability and background in total (over both stages together) and chooses to do so in the most efficient way. Because the possibility to compensate for lower abilities compared to compensating for a disadvantaged background declines over time (Assumption 3b), they will compensate more for ability differences in early stages and more for background differences in later stages. For prioritarians, it all depends on the degree of priority: if sufficiently small, they follow

[50] The comparison is based on a normalized degree of compensation, which is, in fact, a marginal concept. A normalized degree of compensation (for ability or background) equal to zero corresponds with no compensation and a normalized degree of compensation equal to one corresponds with full compensation; see Appendix 9.A.2 for more details.

the utilitarian recommendation, if sufficiently large, they follow the Rawlsian recommendation.

In later stages of education, utilitarians still compensate more for background as class resources are also better substitutes for background than for ability in stage 2 (Assumption 3a). Rawlsians, being concerned with full compensation, will also compensate more for background in stage 2 for the reason that I mentioned before. And prioritarians are again intermediate between both positions, but, as utilitarians and Rawlsians now agree, prioritarians will also compensate more for background in later stages.

In total, over both stages, utilitarians and prioritarians will compensate more for background than for ability. Rawlsians will compensate fully for both ability and background, so the degree of compensation will be exactly equal. The finding for prioritarians may seem to be in contrast with the story of teacher Higgins. Only if there were no efficiency considerations (as in the story of teacher Higgins) would the (total) degree of compensation for ability and background be the same for prioritarians. But, as resources are here assumed to compensate more effectively for background than for ability in both stages (Assumption 3a), the degree of compensation must be higher for background compared to ability according to a prioritarian. In other words, prioritarians might in the end agree with opportunity-egalitarians that, in total over both stages, more should be done for pupils having a disadvantaged background, but for efficiency reasons.

9.4.3 A Brief Summary

Prioritarian school teams may differ from utilitarian and Rawlsian ones in terms of policy recommendations. Contrary to Rawlsians, and in line with utilitarians, they are inconclusive whether background should, in total, be compensated or reinforced (question 2c) and they agree that background should, in total, be compensated more than ability (question 3c). Contrary to utilitarians, and in line with Rawlsians, they are inconclusive whether background should be compensated or reinforced in later stages of education (question 2b). Finally, whether background should be compensated more than ability in early stages, depends for outcome-prioritarians on the degree of priority: they are in line with utilitarians – who want to compensate more for background in early stages – if the degree of priority is sufficiently low and they are in line with Rawlsians – who want to compensate more for ability in early stages – if the degree of priority is sufficiently high.

9.5 Extensions

In the previous section, I analyzed a *school team* in *basic education* that optimally *designs* its *resource* allocation over pupils based on a prioritarian objective defined over an *educational index*. The question is whether the derived results also hold if I change some elements in the story.

In this section, I focus on a different decision-maker (*minister* versus *school team*), pupils at different ages (*higher* versus *basic education*), a different policy exercise (*evaluation* versus *design*), different policy tools (beyond *resources*), and different outcomes (*multiple skills* versus *educational index*).

The first extension is closely related to the previous section from an analytical viewpoint and therefore discussed in more detail. The other extensions are less related such that prioritarian recommendations are harder to derive without a detailed analysis. These other extensions should therefore best be read as caveats of the previous sections, useful after-thoughts, additional literature, or suggestions for future research.

9.5.1 Minister versus School Team

In this section I look at a higher decision level, i.e., a minister of education who allocates resources over schools.

First, I will focus on a minister who successfully convinced all school teams to pursue the same outcome-prioritarian goal based on Equation (9.4). However, the difference is informational: the school team can observe both the ability and background of each pupil, while the minister observes only the background of the pupils at the different schools. I call this case the "same goal, other information" case.

Second, I will look at the opposite case, called "other goal, same information." So, the minister has the same information about pupils as the school teams, but has a different goal. In particular, the minister and the school teams are both outcome-prioritarian, but the school teams focus on education only, i.e., Equation (9.4), while the minister focuses on a broader well-being concept, based on both education and economic success, i.e., Equation (9.2). Recall that in this case the minister, contrary to the school teams, allows for policies that treat disadvantaged pupils "preferentially" in education to compensate for lower future economic success.

9.5.1.1 Same Goal, Other Information

If the minister has the same goal, but only observes the background of the pupils at different schools, a paradox may occur. I discuss this paradox here informally and refer to Appendix 9.A.3 for the technical details.

Suppose that both the minister and the school teams have the same outcome-prioritarian goal based on education, i.e., Equation (9.4). Suppose also that school teams would find it optimal to compensate for background over both stages together and to reinforce ability over both stages. This position is consistent with Table 9.4 if the degree of priority is sufficiently large.

This position would also hold for the minister if she were able to observe ability and if she could directly allocate resources to pupils. Yet, while the minister would like to compensate for background if she did not face informational constraints, she will not necessarily allocate more resources (per pupil) to schools serving pupils with a more disadvantaged background if she cannot observe ability. So, the decision level, and in particular, the information available at the decision level, may matter.

To understand why, suppose first that there is no association (or, that there is a negative association) between ability and background. In this case the previous paradox cannot arise. In other words, the result at the pupil level ("give, as a school team, more resources to pupils with a more disadvantaged background") extends towards the school level ("give, as a minister, more resources per pupil to schools serving pupils with a more disadvantaged background").

However, if there is a positive association between ability and background, then this result does not necessarily hold anymore. On the one hand, the minister would like to compensate for a disadvantaged background. On the other hand, ability is not observable: so, given a positive association, a more advantaged background signals a higher ability, which is what the minister wants to reinforce. Both forces counteract each other. The final allocation is therefore not clear and depends, among other things, on the strength of the association between ability and background. Indeed, even if the minister agrees that school teams should compensate pupils for a disadvantaged background, she might somewhat paradoxically decide not to give more resources per pupil to schools serving pupils with a more disadvantaged background.

9.5.1.2 Other Goal, Same Information

I have argued before that it is not very compelling for teacher Higgins to preferentially treat some children in education to compensate for lower future economic success. However, minister Higgins could maybe adopt a more holistic view towards well-being, based on education and economic success, as defined in Equation (9.2). The problem becomes far more complex now as one obtains a so-called principal-agent problem, where the principal (the minister) has a different goal than the agents (the school teams). I therefore do not analyze this case in detail here, but discuss some intriguing questions.

First, is it inconsistent that the minister and the school teams have different objectives? Let us suppose that the holistic view of the minister towards well-being is the true goal in society. The fact that teachers are not allowed to preferentially treat some pupils then acts as a deontological constraint on their actions.[51] But if the holistic view is the true goal, then it is better, from a consequentialist point of view, that everyone works towards that same goal. The point is not that constraints are not allowed, but only that everyone should work towards the same goal, either with or without constraints. So, the penultimate question is, in my view, what position society should endorse toward the education of children. The positions of ministers, school teams, and teachers should then be aligned with this societal goal.

Second, I realize that the previous view is contentious or the alignment may not be feasible. So, what happens if the minister adopts a holistic view, but teachers are not allowed to preferentially treat pupils in education? Recall the story of the two pupils (with the same

[51] Note that a constraint on a shared goal (as discussed here) is in fact different from integrating out ability and background in the shared goal (as we did in Equation (9.4)). We do not discuss this difference further.

educational achievement, but pupil one has limited abilities and pupil two has a disadvantaged background) and teacher Higgins who must choose how to allocate resources over both pupils from an equity perspective, i.e., ignoring efficiency considerations. I look at two cases.

In the first case, pupil one and two go to school A led by teacher Higgins and two exact copies of both pupils go to school B led by an exact copy of teacher Higgins. For ease of exposition, no other pupil is involved. Because schools A and B are exact copies, the minister cannot, but allocate the same resources to both schools. The teachers in both schools are not allowed to preferentially treat one pupil over the other, so they will both allocate the same resources to both pupils. In other words, pupil one and two are treated the same in both schools.

In the second case, pupils are re-sorted over schools such that pupil one and his copy go to school A and pupil two and her copy go to school B, *ceteris paribus*. In this case, teachers cannot but allocate the same resources to both pupils in each school. But the minister can allocate different resources to the schools. If future economic success depends more on ability than background (for the same educational achievement), then the minister will allocate more resources to school A serving the pupils of limited ability. And if future economic success depends more on background than ability (for the same educational achievement), then the minister will allocate more resources to school B serving the disadvantaged pupils.[52]

Both cases also show that different allocations may arise depending on the sorting of pupils over schools. More diverse schools (case 1) imply that the goal of school teams will receive more weight in the final allocation and less diverse schools (case 2) imply that the goal of the minister receives more weight. But, as sorting can be linked to parental decisions, for which sufficiently young pupils are not held responsible, this dependency is puzzling.[53] In any case, such a dependency would not have occurred if ministers and teachers adopted the same normative position toward the relevant outcome.

[52] It could also be undefined, in fact, if, e.g., ability is, at some education levels, more important than background, but vice versa for other education levels. While plausible, we do not discuss it further for ease of exposition.

[53] Sorting can also be influenced by school teams and ministers. In any case, as sufficiently young pupils cannot be held responsible for anything, the same puzzling result obtains.

9.5.2 *Higher versus Basic Education*

In this section I look at a higher education level, i.e., tertiary rather than basic (pre-primary and primary) education. Up to now, I indeed focused on sufficiently young pupils, say basic education. This focus avoided the discussion of responsibility such that, in the end, priorities were defined over outcomes rather than opportunities.

While I do not know the exact age at which responsibility kicks in, it seems reasonable to allow outcomes to be ambition-sensitive in tertiary education. Indeed, individual ambitions may lead to different decisions about continuing studying after high school, the study field, the time and effort to devote to your studies, and so on. And ambitions do not only impact educational outcomes, but also future economic success, depending, e.g., on the type of job one chooses in later life and how hard one is willing to work. I again discuss some intriguing questions.

Suppose I indeed allow outcomes to be ambition-sensitive. For example, if two individuals are equally well-prepared for tertiary education, but one of them wants to study philosophy and the other prefers to become a surgeon, differences in future economic success could be considered legitimate to some extent. Or, as another example, if two individuals end up with the same tertiary degree, but one genuinely decides to work half-time and the other prefers to work full-time, then, again, the resulting differences in earnings could be justified.

A complication arises, however. These ambitions are also formed during previous education. Gintis (1972: 593), for example, writes "The fallacy, of course, is the basing of all recommendations concerning education on the postulate of fixed preferences, in a situation where the educational system is a central instrument in the formation of preferences." The question then is how to allow ambitions to play a role during tertiary education and in the labor market if these ambitions are formed during basic education. Is it plausible to be ambition-sensitive in later life if one pupil has learnt to work hard and the other not?

It is, in my view, not necessarily wrong to assign responsibility over ambitions at later ages even if these ambitions are formed (or even partly imposed) on pupils at earlier ages. Such ambitions are not under control, but one could still be held responsible as long as one identifies with one's own ambitions.[54] The key question then is how the allocation of resources would change.

Suppose that I introduce effort, besides ability and background, as a factor that determines (higher) education outcomes as well as economic success. Suppose also that I keep individuals responsible for their preferences that govern the choice of effort. The presence of effort probably implies that the extent to which one wants to compensate for ability and background in higher education will be smaller compared to basic education. Whether one wants to reinforce ability relatively more than background in higher education will now also depend on their complementarities with effort. For example, if effort and ability are more complementary than effort and background (i.e., extra effort has a stronger effect on educational outcomes at higher ability levels and this is not (or to a lesser extent) true for background), then this will favor reinforcing ability more in higher education.

9.5.3 *Evaluation versus Design*

In this section I look at a different normative exercise, i.e., the evaluation of educational systems rather than their design. Up to now, I indeed focused on the optimal allocation of resources over pupils and schools within a specific country. Recall that the goal was outcome-prioritarian and the outcome was country-specific, irrespective of whether Equation (9.2) or (9.4) was used.

As long as one sticks to policy design, country differences do not raise problems. Educational systems are designed within a country and must therefore take the specific context of a country into account. For example, in countries where educational differences matter less for future economic success (e.g., because of high levels of earnings redistribution), educational inequalities are also less problematic. Educational differences may therefore be mitigated less, resulting in higher levels of educational inequality in such countries.

However, if I switch from design to evaluation, an interesting question arises: how can one compare the educational systems of different countries? Because the evaluation is country-specific, it is possible that system A is best for country A and system B is best for country B. This

[54] The responsibility cut can indeed be based on what individuals "control" or on "preferences" with which individuals identify.

implies that, from the viewpoint of country A, system A is better than B, and from the viewpoint of country B, system B is better than system A. While this is, in my view, not problematic, it implies that the comparison of educational systems is a delicate exercise, far more delicate than simply comparing key educational statistics, which, as discussed before, is the common practice in the evaluation literature.

9.5.4 Beyond Resources

In this section I look beyond the allocation of resources. Up to now, resources were used as a catch-all word whose meaning depends, e.g., on the decision level. At the level of the minister one typically thinks of money to be allocated to schools. At the level of the school team, resources could refer to the money, time, and effort to run the school and, in particular, to educate the pupils. But, beyond resources, there exist many other ways to influence educational outcomes.[55]

One way to improve outcomes is to introduce school competition by, e.g., extending school choice (e.g., using school vouchers or charter schools) or introducing school accountability. Such school competition policies promise to be "a tide that lifts all boats" and are therefore, in theory, efficiency-improving policies that ensure that resources are used in their most productive way. If true, prioritarians would not oppose it.

In practice, however, such overall improvements are rather unlikely.[56] School accountability, for example, may lead to incentives for pupil selection. Such unproductive uses of resources by teachers and school teams may counteract potential efficiency gains of competition. But if overall improvements are not possible, equity comes in again. Depending on who wins and loses, prioritarians may or may not be in favor of school accountability. If school accountability leads to student retainment and the removal of low-achieving students, as observed in some empirical studies, then it is very likely to be discarded by prioritarians, especially if their degree of priority is high.

55 I will restrict attention to institutional features (at the decision level of ministers) rather than pedagogical features (at the decision level of school teams and teachers).

56 See, e.g., Epple, Romano, and Urquiola (2017) for a review of school vouchers, Epple, Romano, and Zimmer (2016) for a review of charter schools, and Figlio and Loeb (2011) for a review of school accountability schemes.

Another way to improve educational outcomes is to group pupils in different ways. Mixing, tracking, and streaming are examples of such policies.

Mixing refers to obtaining a sufficiently diverse mix of pupils at schools in terms of background. While the intrinsic argument is that schools should simply mirror society, there may also be instrumental reasons to mix pupils depending on the direction of so-called peer effects (i.e., cognitive and non-cognitive spillover effects between pupils). Such mixing may be enforced directly (e.g., via desegregation busing policies) or can be introduced in a more subtle way in school assignment policies.

Tracking and streaming refer to obtaining a less diverse mix of pupils in terms of ability.[57] Tracking is more popular in Europe and typically puts pupils with different abilities in different schools (i.e., between-school grouping); streaming is more popular in Anglo-Saxon countries (e.g., the United States) and puts pupils with different abilities either in different classes within schools (within-school grouping) or in different groups within classes (within-class grouping) for a selection of courses.

Little can be said about the outcome-prioritarian design of such alternative policies without explicit modeling. Moreover, as peer effects are highly non-linear and the underlying mechanisms not well-understood, such models will be fairly complex and clear policy recommendations cannot be guaranteed at all.[58] In any case, the core questions underlying Table 9.4 will definitely be influenced by diversity policies, which are therefore an intriguing topic for further research.

9.5.5 Multiple Skills versus Educational Index

In this final section I look at different outcomes, i.e., non-cognitive and cognitive skills as separate outcomes. Up to now, education was indeed measured by an index of different skills, including cognitive and non-cognitive skills, that is produced as a whole. However, cognitive and

[57] While mixing on the one hand and tracking and streaming on the other hand seem opposite, mixing and (especially) streaming are compatible as one can strive for a more diverse mix of pupils at schools in terms of background and still group these pupils, for one or more courses, in ability groups.

[58] While peer effects do exist in specific contexts, the mechanisms and policy consequences are not fully grasped yet; see Sacerdote (2014) for a review.

non-cognitive skills are produced in different ways; see, e.g., Kautz et al. (2014) for an overview. For example, non-cognitive skills remain relatively more plastic at later ages.[59] Moreover, there are also indications that non-cognitive skills improve cognitive skills, but not vice versa.

Splitting up our educational index in cognitive and non-cognitive skills is likely to change the prioritarian allocation of resources over pupils. Probably the best starting point for such an ambitious exercise is Cunha, Heckman, and Schennach (2010). They estimate the educational production of cognitive and non-cognitive skills and simulate optimal policies based on a utilitarian objective defined over either the number of schooling years or crime, which are both a function of cognitive and non-cognitive skills. I leave a prioritarian evaluation, eventually based on a less instrumental view of education, for future research.

9.6 Conclusion

The first aim of this chapter was to summarize the operational normative views that have been adopted in the academic literature on education. This summary reveals that while prioritarianism as an aggregation device is often used in the "welfarist" design literature, and thus clearly compatible with it, prioritarianism is also compatible with the dashboard approach used in the evaluation literature. Not prioritarianism as such, but the metric over which prioritarianism should be defined – the question "priority of what?" – turns out to be the real bone of contention.

The answer to the question "priority of what?" leads to four normative views in the education literature, depending on whether the metric is educational or economic and whether one should provide outcomes or opportunities in these metrics. The second aim of this chapter was to critically analyze these four existing normative views. I did so by directly engaging its philosophical foundations and by looking at its policy recommendations in a simplified setting. My analysis strongly suggests that outcomes – and not opportunities – should be the

[59] In the technical jargon we used before, the elasticity of substitution between resources and either background or ability decreases less rapidly over time for non-cognitive skills.

appropriate metric for sufficiently young pupils. In addition, the appropriate outcome should capture both the intrinsic and instrumental value of education, but the precise formulation may be different for school teams and ministers.

The third aim of this chapter was to introduce a dynamic model of skill formation and to analyze the policy recommendations from an outcome-prioritarian – rather than outcome-utilitarian or outcome-Rawlsian – point of view. It turns out that, whenever equity is at stake, prioritarian school teams may recommend different policies compared to utilitarians or Rawlsians.

The fourth and final aim was to discuss several extensions to see whether and how the derived policy recommendations would change if I changed the benchmark story. Some of these extensions were analyzed in detail and revealed paradoxical results. Some extensions were only dealt with briefly and can therefore best be seen as an invitation to further study the consequences of prioritarianism for educational policies.

9.A Appendix

9.A.1 Decomposing the Four Metrics

I start with formally defining the assumptions.

First, the transformation function g is of the Kolm-Pollak type, i.e., $g : w \mapsto \exp(-\pi w)$ with π the degree of priority in between utilitarian ($\pi \to 0$) and Rawlsian ($\pi \to \infty$).

Second, "reduced-form" linear regression techniques are used to regress either educational or economic achievement on background. So, these regression equations, including errors, are $e = \alpha_e + \beta_e b + \varepsilon_e$ and $y = \alpha_y + \beta_y b + \varepsilon_y$. I call it a reduced form, because the error terms capture, among other things, remaining differences associated with innate ability (after having corrected for background).

Third, background and regression errors are independent and follow normal distributions, so, I have $b \perp \varepsilon_e \perp \varepsilon_y$ and $b \sim \mathrm{N}(\mu_b, \sigma_b^2)$, $\varepsilon_e \sim \mathrm{N}(0, \sigma_{\varepsilon_e}^2)$, and $\varepsilon_y \sim \mathrm{N}(0, \sigma_{\varepsilon_y}^2)$.

The decomposition is based on two observations.

First, if a metric, say w, is normally distributed, say, $w \sim \mathrm{N}(\mu_w, \sigma_w^2)$ and if the transformation function g is of the Kolm-Pollak type (as defined before), then the evaluation in Equation (9.1) reduces to $-\frac{1}{\pi}\ln(\exp(-\pi\mu_w + \frac{1}{2}\pi^2\sigma_w^2)) = \mu_w - \frac{\pi}{2}\sigma_w^2$. So, given that also e and y follow normal distributions, I directly get $\mu_e - \frac{\pi}{2}\sigma_e^2$ (if $w = e$) and $\mu_y - \frac{\pi}{2}\sigma_y^2$ (if $w = y$) for the outcome-prioritarians (to the right of Table 9.2).

Second, the conditional expectations $\mathbb{E}[e|b] = \alpha_e + \beta_e b$ and $\mathbb{E}[y|b] = \alpha_y + \beta_y b$ also follow normal distributions. Replacing β_e and β_y by their best linear unbiased estimators, i.e., $\hat{\beta}_e = \rho_{be}\sigma_e/\sigma_b$ and $\hat{\beta}_y = \rho_{by}\sigma_y/\sigma_b$ respectively, I get for the opportunity-prioritarians (to the left of Table 9.2)

$$\mu_{\alpha_e+\hat{\beta}_e b} - \frac{\pi}{2}\cdot\sigma^2_{\alpha_e+\hat{\beta}_e b} = \mu_e - \frac{\pi}{2}\cdot\hat{\beta}_e^2\cdot\sigma_b^2 = \mu_e - \frac{\pi}{2}\cdot\rho_{be}^2\cdot\sigma_e^2,$$

and

$$\mu_{a_y+\hat{\beta}_y b} - \frac{\pi}{2} \cdot \sigma^2_{a_y+\hat{\beta}_y b} = \mu_y - \frac{\pi}{2} \cdot \hat{\beta}_y^2 \cdot \sigma_b^2 = \mu_y - \frac{\pi}{2} \cdot \rho_{by}^2 \cdot \sigma_y^2.$$

As a side note, one can also combine an Atkinson transformation function, i.e., $g : w \to w^{1-\pi}$, with log-linear relations (i.e., $\ln e = \ln \alpha_e + \beta_e \ln b + \ln \varepsilon_e$ and $\ln y = \ln \alpha_y + \beta_y \ln b + \ln \varepsilon_y$) and independent and lognormal distributions (i.e., $\ln b \perp \ln \varepsilon_e \perp \ln \varepsilon_y$ and $\ln b \sim N(\mu_{\ln b}, \sigma^2_{\ln b})$, $\ln \varepsilon_e \sim N(0, \sigma^2_{\ln \varepsilon_e})$, and $\ln \varepsilon_y \sim N(0, \sigma^2_{\ln \varepsilon_y})$). I show that it leads to a very similar (multiplicative) decomposition that does not change the main story line.

To see this, note first that if a metric w is lognormally distributed, say, $\ln w \sim N(\mu_{\ln w}, \sigma^2_{\ln w})$ and the transformation function g is of the Atkinson type (as defined before), then the evaluation in Equation (9.1) reduces to $\mu_w \exp(-\frac{\pi}{2} \cdot \sigma^2_{\ln w})$.[60] So, given that now e and y follow lognormal distributions, I directly get $\mu_e \exp(-\frac{\pi}{2} \cdot \sigma^2_{\ln e})$ and $\mu_y \exp(-\frac{\pi}{2} \cdot \sigma^2_{\ln y})$ for the outcome-prioritarians.

Second, given loglinear relations, the conditional expectations – being, $\mathbb{E}[e|b] = \alpha_e b^{\beta_e} \mathbb{E}[\varepsilon_e]$ and $\mathbb{E}[y|b] = \alpha_y b^{\beta_y} \mathbb{E}[\varepsilon_y]$ – also follow lognormal distributions and β_e and β_y can again be replaced by their best linear unbiased estimators, i.e., $\hat{\beta}_e = \rho_{\ln b \ln e} \sigma_{\ln e} / \sigma_{\ln b}$ and $\hat{\beta}_y = \rho_{\ln b \ln y} \sigma_{\ln y} / \sigma_{\ln b}$ respectively. So, for the opportunity-prioritarians I get

$$\mu_{\mathbb{E}[e|b]} \exp\left(-\frac{\pi}{2} \cdot \sigma^2_{\ln \mathbb{E}[e|b]}\right) = \mu_e \exp\left(-\frac{\pi}{2} \cdot \hat{\beta}_e^2 \sigma^2_{\ln b}\right) = \mu_e \exp\left(-\frac{\pi}{2} \cdot \rho^2_{\ln b \ln e} \cdot \sigma^2_{\ln e}\right),$$

and

$$\mu_{\mathbb{E}[y|b]} \exp\left(-\frac{\pi}{2} \cdot \sigma^2_{\ln \mathbb{E}[y|b]}\right) = \mu_y \exp\left(-\frac{\pi}{2} \cdot \hat{\beta}_y^2 \sigma^2_{\ln b}\right) = \mu_y \exp\left(-\frac{\pi}{2} \cdot \rho^2_{\ln b \ln y} \cdot \sigma^2_{\ln y}\right).$$

9.A.2 The Allocation of a School Team

In this appendix, I first discuss the assumptions of the dynamic model of skill formation in a formal way. Afterwards, I derive the optimal outcome-prioritarian allocation of resources of the school team over pupils.

9.A.2.1 *Assumptions*

I assume that (final) education is strictly increasing in all arguments and strictly concave in class resources, i.e.,

$$E_a' > 0, E_b' > 0, E_1' > 0, E_2' > 0, E_1'' < 0, E_2'' < 0,$$

[60] Note that we use $\mu_w = \exp(\mu_{\ln w} + \frac{1}{2} \cdot \sigma^2_{\ln w})$ here.

where subscripts 1 and 2 refer to the partial derivatives with respect to resources c_1 and c_2, respectively.

On top of these standard assumptions, I impose three additional assumptions.

First, *everything else equal*, investment is more effective at earlier stages. With two stages, I impose

Assumption 1. $E_1'(a,b,c,c) > E_2'(a,b,c,c)$ for all (a,b,c).

Note that, given additivity, assumption 1 implies $E_{1,1}'(a,b,c) > E_{2,2}'(a,b,c)$ for all (a,b,c).

Second, it is more effective to compensate for background at earlier stages, but this result turns around at later stages. With two stages, I get

Assumption 2. $E_{b1}''(a,b,c_1,c_2) < 0 < E_{b2}''(a,b,c_1,c_2)$ for all (a,b,c_1,c_2).

Define the "Hicksian" measure of complementarity as

$$\varsigma_{ij}(a,b,c_1,c_2) = \frac{E(a,b,c_1,c_2)E_{ij}''(a,b,c_1,c_2)}{E_i'(a,b,c_1,c_2)E_j'(a,b,c_1,c_2)},$$

where $i,j \in \{a,b,1,2\}$. For later use, note that Assumption 2 implies $\varsigma_{b1} < 0 < \varsigma_{b2}$.

The third assumption imposes that ability is more complementary to resources than background in all stages (Assumption 3a) and this difference in complementarity increases over time (Assumption 3b). As mentioned before, this assumption is a priori plausible, especially Assumption 3a, but there is no empirical evidence that supports it. With two stages, I impose:

Assumption 3. $\varsigma_{a1} - \varsigma_{b1} > 0$ and $\varsigma_{a2} - \varsigma_{b2} > 0$ (A3a) and $\varsigma_{a2} - \varsigma_{b2} > \varsigma_{a1} - \varsigma_{b1}$ (A3b).

9.A.2.2 *The Problem of the School Team*

Start from Equation (9.7), leave out the inverse g^{-1} (as strictly increasing transformations do not matter to derive the optimal solution), and define the composite function $\hat{g} = g \circ \bar{w}$. The system of first-order conditions with respect to resources in each stage is

$$\hat{g}'\left(E(a,b,C_1^S(a,b),C_2^S(a,b))\right)\cdot E_1'(a,b,C_1^S(a,b),C_2^S(a,b)) = \lambda^S,$$
$$\hat{g}'\left(E(a,b,C_1^S(a,b),C_2^S(a,b))\right)\cdot E_2'(a,b,C_1^S(a,b),C_2^S(a,b)) = \lambda^S, \tag{9.9}$$

for some λ^S, being the Lagrange multiplier of the budget constraint of school S. Dividing the first-order conditions and using additivity (i.e., $E_t' = E_{t,t}'$ holds at each stage t), one must have equal marginal productivities, i.e.,

$$E_{1,1}'(a,b,C_1^S(a,b)) = E_{2,2}'(a,b,C_2^S(a,b)), \tag{9.10}$$

at the optimum. Assigning equal class resources cannot be optimal because Assumption 1 implies $E_{1,1}'(a,b,c) > E_{2,2}'(a,b,c)$ everywhere. As both production functions are concave in resources, I must have $C_1^S(a,b) > C_2^S(a,b)$, which is the answer to question 1.

The system of first-order conditions (9.9) can be "abbreviated" as

$$\hat{g}'\cdot E_1' = \lambda^S,$$
$$\hat{g}'\cdot E_2' = \lambda^S. \tag{9.11}$$

Differentiating (9.11) with respect to either ability or background (denoted $z = a, b$), I get

$$\hat{g}''(E_z' + E_1'C_{1,z}^{S\prime} + E_2'C_{2,z}^{S\prime})E_1' + \hat{g}'(E_{z1}'' + E_{11}''C_{1,z}^{S\prime} + E_{12}''C_{2,z}^{S\prime}) = 0,$$
$$\hat{g}''(E_z' + E_1'C_{1,z}^{S\prime} + E_2'C_{2,z}^{S\prime})E_2' + \hat{g}'(E_{z2}'' + E_{12}''C_{1,z}^{S\prime} + E_{22}''C_{2,z}^{S\prime}) = 0, \tag{9.12}$$

for $z = a, b$, which can be written in matrix form as

$$\begin{bmatrix} \hat{g}'E_{11}'' + \hat{g}''(E_1')^2 & \hat{g}''E_1'E_2' + \hat{g}'E_{12}'' \\ \hat{g}''E_1'E_2' + \hat{g}'E_{12}'' & \hat{g}'E_{22}'' + \hat{g}''(E_2')^2 \end{bmatrix} \begin{bmatrix} C_{1,z}^{S\prime} \\ C_{2,z}^{S\prime} \end{bmatrix} = -\begin{bmatrix} \hat{g}'E_{z1}'' + \hat{g}''E_1'E_z' \\ \hat{g}'E_{z2}'' + \hat{g}''E_2'E_z' \end{bmatrix} \tag{9.13}$$

Using Cramer's rule, the solution is

$$C_{1,z}^{S\prime} = -\frac{E_z'}{E_1'}\frac{(\pi - \varsigma_{z1})(\pi - \varsigma_{22}) - (\pi - \varsigma_{z2})(\pi - \varsigma_{12})}{(\pi - \varsigma_{11})(\pi - \varsigma_{22}) - (\pi - \varsigma_{12})^2}, \tag{9.14}$$

and

$$C_{2,z}^{S\prime} = -\frac{E_z'}{E_2'}\frac{(\pi - \varsigma_{z2})(\pi - \varsigma_{11}) - (\pi - \varsigma_{z1})(\pi - \varsigma_{12})}{(\pi - \varsigma_{11})(\pi - \varsigma_{22}) - (\pi - \varsigma_{12})^2}, \tag{9.15}$$

with $\pi = -\frac{\hat{g}''(E)}{\hat{g}'(E)}E > 0$ the degree of priority and $\varsigma_{xy} = \frac{EE_{xy}''}{E_x'E_y'}$ the Hicksian complementarity measure that we defined before. I assume that the denominator is strictly positive, i.e., we have $(\pi - \varsigma_{11})(\pi - \varsigma_{22}) - (\pi - \varsigma_{12})^2 > 0$ (to satisfy the second-order conditions).

9.A.2.2.1 Background

Using additivity ($\varsigma_{12} = 0$) and focusing first on background ($z = b$), the comparative statics reduce to

$$C^{S\prime}_{1,b} = -\frac{E'_b}{E'_1}\frac{\varsigma_{b1}\varsigma_{22} + \pi(\varsigma_{b2} - \varsigma_{b1} - \varsigma_{22})}{\varsigma_{11}\varsigma_{22} - \pi(\varsigma_{11} + \varsigma_{22})}, \tag{9.16}$$

and

$$C^{S\prime}_{2,b} = -\frac{E'_b}{E'_2}\frac{\varsigma_{11}\varsigma_{b2} + \pi(\varsigma_{b1} - \varsigma_{b2} - \varsigma_{11})}{\varsigma_{11}\varsigma_{22} - \pi(\varsigma_{11} + \varsigma_{22})} \tag{9.17}$$

Several results can be deduced.

First, as Assumption 2 implies $\varsigma_{b1} < 0 < \varsigma_{b2}$ and as the standard assumptions imply $\varsigma_{11}, \varsigma_{22} < 0$, I must have $C^{S\prime}_{1,b} < 0$ because the numerator (and denominator) of the second fraction in (9.16) is always positive. This means that, irrespective of the degree of priority, the impact of background must be compensated in stage 1. This is the answer to question 2a.

Second, the sign of $C^{S\prime}_{2,b}$ is not clear in general. For utilitarians ($\pi \to 0$) the sign is positive, so they will reinforce the impact of background in stage 2. For prioritarians with a sufficiently low degree of priority, the sign must be positive too (using continuity). For Rawlsians ($\pi \to \infty$) the sign is not clear without further assumptions. This is the answer to question 2b.

As a side note (which is also mentioned in the main text), a special case arises if background and resources are perfect substitutes in stage 1 (i.e., $E_1(a, b, c_1) = f(a, b + \gamma c_1)$ everywhere for some function f and scalar γ) and if background has no impact on outcomes in period 2 (i.e., $E_2(a, b, c_2) = f(a, c_2)$ everywhere for some function f).[61]

[61] Actually, this result holds more generally. Consider a (not necessarily additive) educational production function in stage 2, say, $E_2(e, a, b, c_2)$. This implies that final educational achievement would be given by $E(a, b, c_1, c_2) = E_2(E_1(a, b, c_1), a, b, c_2)$. If this function can be written as $E(a, b, c_1, c_2) = f(a, b + \gamma c_1, c_2)$ everywhere, then $\varsigma_{b1} = \varsigma_{11}$ and $\varsigma_{b2} = \varsigma_{12}$ hold, which, plugged into Equations (9.16) and (9.17), lead to the same result (full compensation for background in period 1 and no compensation for it in period 2). An open

Both conditions lead to $\varsigma_{b1} = \varsigma_{11}$ and $\varsigma_{b2} = 0$, implying $C^{S\prime}_{1,b} = -\frac{E'_b}{E'_1} = -\frac{E'_{1,b}}{E'_{1,1}}$ and $C^{S\prime}_{2,b} = 0$. Because $-\frac{E'_b}{E'_1} = -\frac{E'_{1,b}}{E'_{1,1}}$ is the marginal rate of technical substitution between resources and background (in stage 1, using additivity), the interpretation is simple. In stage 1, the impact of background on outcomes must be fully compensated and thus equality of opportunity applies (as the outcome does not depend on background). In stage 2 there is no effect of background on education and resources therefore do not change with background. So, after the policy intervention, equality of opportunity applies also in the second stage.

9.A.2.2.2 Ability versus Background

Using additivity ($\varsigma_{12} = 0$) and focusing now on ability ($z = a$), the comparative statics are

$$C^{S\prime}_{1,a} = -\frac{E'_a}{E'_1}\frac{\varsigma_{a1}\varsigma_{22} + \pi(\varsigma_{a2} - \varsigma_{a1} - \varsigma_{22})}{\varsigma_{11}\varsigma_{22} - \pi(\varsigma_{11} + \varsigma_{22})}, \tag{9.18}$$

and

$$C^{S\prime}_{2,a} = -\frac{E'_a}{E'_2}\frac{\varsigma_{11}\varsigma_{a2} + \pi(\varsigma_{a1} - \varsigma_{a2} - \varsigma_{11})}{\varsigma_{11}\varsigma_{22} - \pi(\varsigma_{11} + \varsigma_{22})}. \tag{9.19}$$

First, the product $-\frac{E'_t}{E'_z} \cdot C^{S\prime}_{t,z}$ (for $z = a, b$) measures the normalized degree of compensation for characteristic z in stage t. To see this, note that the lower the second factor $C^{S\prime}_{t,z}$, the less reinforcement or the more compensation there is for ability or background and, as the first factor is negative, the higher the degree of compensation. Furthermore, the first factor is the (inverse of the) marginal rate of technical substitution. The marginal rate of technical substitution tells us how much extra resources in period t are needed to compensate for a small change in z. The first factor therefore is a normalization that guarantees that full compensation corresponds with a degree of compensation equal to one. As this normalization holds irrespective of whether I look at ability or background, it me allows to compare the degree of compensation for ability and background.

question is what other specifications, besides the additive one that I use, are made possible by this generalization.

So, whether ability should be compensated more or less compared to background in each stage depends on the sign of $\Delta_t = -\frac{E'_t}{E'_a} C^{S\prime}_{t,a} + \frac{E'_t}{E'_b} C^{S\prime}_{t,b}$. If negative, for example, then ability is, compared to background, compensated less (or reinforced more) in stage *t*. I get:

$$\Delta_1 = \frac{\varsigma_{22}(\varsigma_{a1} - \varsigma_{b1}) + \pi((\varsigma_{a2} - \varsigma_{b2}) - (\varsigma_{a1} - \varsigma_{b1}))}{\varsigma_{11}\varsigma_{22} - \pi(\varsigma_{11} + \varsigma_{22})}, \tag{9.20}$$

and

$$\Delta_2 = \frac{\varsigma_{11}(\varsigma_{a2} - \varsigma_{b2}) + \pi((\varsigma_{a1} - \varsigma_{b1}) - (\varsigma_{a2} - \varsigma_{b2}))}{\varsigma_{11}\varsigma_{22} - \pi(\varsigma_{11} + \varsigma_{22})}. \tag{9.21}$$

I can now use Assumption 3, being

$$\varsigma_{a2} - \varsigma_{b2} > \varsigma_{a1} - \varsigma_{b1} > 0, \tag{9.22}$$

to derive the answers to questions 3a and 3b.

For a utilitarian ($\pi \to 0$) both Δ_1 and Δ_2 turn out to be negative, i.e., always more compensation for background than for ability, indeed.

For a Rawlsian, I take the limit, leading to

$$\lim_{\pi \to \infty} \Delta_1 = \frac{(\varsigma_{a2} - \varsigma_{b2}) - (\varsigma_{a1} - \varsigma_{b1})}{-(\varsigma_{11} + \varsigma_{22})} > 0,$$

and

$$\lim_{\pi \to \infty} \Delta_2 = \frac{(\varsigma_{a1} - \varsigma_{b1}) - (\varsigma_{a2} - \varsigma_{b2})}{-(\varsigma_{11} + \varsigma_{22})} < 0,$$

as required.

For a prioritarian, Δ_2 is negative for sure, but the result for Δ_1 depends on the degree of priority. If sufficiently small, then the prioritarian agrees with the utilitarian to compensate more for background, and if sufficiently large, then the prioritarian agrees with the Rawlsian to compensate more for ability in stage 1.

9.A.2.2.3 Total Investment over Both Stages

Finally, I analyze total resources, i.e., $C^S(a,b) = C^S_1(a,b) + C^S_2(a,b)$. The comparative statics with respect to *z=a,b* are

$$C_z^{S\prime}(a,b) = C_{1,z}^{S\prime}(a,b) + C_{2,z}^{S\prime}(a,b),$$
$$= -\frac{E_z'}{E_{1/2}'}\frac{\varsigma_{z1}\varsigma_{22} + \varsigma_{11}\varsigma_{z2} - \pi(\varsigma_{11} + \varsigma_{22})}{\varsigma_{11}\varsigma_{22} - \pi(\varsigma_{11} + \varsigma_{22})}, \tag{9.23}$$

where I use (9.10) to define $E_{1/2}' = E_1' = E_2'$. This expression highlights four things.

First, for utilitarians with $\pi \to 0$, the sign depends on the sign of $\varsigma_{b1}\varsigma_{22} + \varsigma_{11}\varsigma_{b2}$, which is ambiguous. Taking the limit $\pi \to \infty$, the second fraction in Equation (9.23) is equal to one. So, an outcome-Rawlsian school team will fully compensate for both ability and background over both stages together. For prioritarians with a sufficiently high degree of priority the sign of the second fraction must be positive too (invoking continuity). These results together provide an answer to question 2c.

Second, the total degree of compensation, appropriately normalized, for characteristic z is $-\frac{E_z'}{E_{1/2}'}C_z^{S\prime}(a,b)$. The difference between the degree of compensation for ability and background is therefore

$$\Delta = -\frac{E_{1/2}'}{E_a'}C_a^{S\prime} + \frac{E_{1/2}'}{E_b'}C_b^{S\prime},$$
$$= \frac{(\varsigma_{a1} - \varsigma_{b1})\varsigma_{22} + \varsigma_{11}(\varsigma_{a2} - \varsigma_{b2})}{\varsigma_{11}\varsigma_{22} - \pi(\varsigma_{11} + \varsigma_{22})}. \tag{9.24}$$

Using Equation (9.22) this difference is always negative; in other words, irrespective of the degree of priority, background will always be compensated more than ability *in total*. But, as this difference becomes zero in the limit $\pi \to \infty$, the degree of compensation for ability and background is equal for Rawlsians. This is the answer to question 3c.

9.A.3 The Allocation of a Minister

I look at the optimal outcome-prioritarian allocation of resources by the minister over schools, where the minister can only observe the background of the pupils at each school.

First, it is useful to consider how the minister would allocate resources if he could (hypothetically) allocate directly over pupils (rather than over schools) and if both ability and background were observable (rather than only background). In this first hypothetical case, the minister would solve the same problem as a school team, given by Equations (9.7) and (9.8), but now replacing the school resources by the total resources (per pupil) in society, say $\bar{C}$, and replacing the school density by the overall density, say f. In other words, the problem of the minister would be to choose resource functions C_1 and C_2 to maximize

$$g^{-1}\left(\iint_{a,b} g\left(\bar{w}\left(E\left(a,b,C_1(a,b),C_2(a,b)\right)\right)\right)f(a,b)dadb\right), \tag{9.25}$$

subject to the budget constraint, being

$$\iint_{a,b} (C_1(a,b)+C_2(a,b))f(a,b)dadb \leq \bar{C}. \tag{9.26}$$

Define $\hat{g} = g \circ \bar{w}$. The optimal solution of the minister, denoted C_1^M and C_2^M, must satisfy the first-order conditions:

$$\begin{aligned} \hat{g}' \cdot E_1' &= \lambda, \\ \hat{g}' \cdot E_2' &= \lambda, \end{aligned} \tag{9.27}$$

for some λ, being the Lagrange multiplier of the minister. For later use, define $C^M = C_1^M + C_2^M$ as the total resources over both stages.

The problem is that the minister cannot directly allocate resources over pupils. She must allocate resources over schools, which are then (optimally) reallocated afterwards over pupils by each school team according to the functions C_1^S and C_2^S that I derived before.

Second, it is useful to consider now how the minister would allocate resources over schools, but still assuming that ability and background are observable to the minister. Let p^S be the fraction of pupils at school S. The problem of the minister is now to allocate resources $\bar{C}^S$ to the different schools to maximize[62]

$$g^{-1}\left(\sum_S p^S \iint_{a,b} g\left(\bar{w}\left(E\left(a,b,C_1^S(a,b),C_2^S(a,b)\right)\right)\right)f^S(a,b)dadb\right), \tag{9.28}$$

subject to the budget constraint

[62] Be aware that the superscript S in $C_1^S(a,b)$ and $C_2^S(a,b)$ indicates that in fact the school team solution also depends on the amount of resources allocated to school S ($\bar{C}^S$) and on the density of types at school S (f^S).

$$\sum_S p^S \bar{C}^S \leq \bar{C}. \tag{9.29}$$

The solution to this problem of the minister is relatively easy because the goals of the minister and school teams are fully aligned and the prioritarian evaluation is separable. In particular, the optimal solution of the minister can be decentralized by giving each school S an amount of resources per pupil equal to

$$\bar{C}^S = \iint_{a,b} C^M(a,b) f^S(a,b) da db. \tag{9.30}$$

This allocation is feasible at societal level as it satisfies the budget constraint (9.29) of the minister (note that, by definition, $\sum_S p^S f^S = f$ must hold). Moreover, because also the first-order conditions of the minister and the schools coincide (i.e., Equations (9.27) and (9.11), choosing $\lambda = \lambda^S$), each school will implement the optimal allocation of the minister (as if the latter could directly allocate resources over pupils).

Third, I now also drop the assumption that the minister can observe ability. As $f^S(a,b) = f^S_{a|b}(a|b) f^S_b(b)$ holds by definition, the allocation in Equation (9.30) can be rewritten as

$$\bar{C}^S = \iint_{a,b} C^M(a,b) f^S_{a|b}(a|b) f^S_b(b) da db. \tag{9.31}$$

If the minister assumes that the distribution of ability conditional on background is common over all schools (i.e., $f^S_{a|b} = f_{a|b}$ for each school S), then the per-pupil resources allocated to school S become[63]

$$\bar{C}^S = \int_b \tilde{C}^M(b) f^S_b(b) db, \tag{9.32}$$

with

$$\tilde{C}^M(b) = \int_a C^M(a,b) f_{a|b}(a|b) da, \tag{9.33}$$

63 This assumption is not entirely realistic. Implicitly, it assumes that schools do not select pupils on the basis of ability (for a given background), e.g., for status or for money depending on the school funding rules, and that parents (with a given background) do not sort over schools on the basis of ability, e.g., to enjoy peer effects. Even if not entirely realistic, it is plausible that, without information on ability, the minister will assume it.

the resources invested in a pupil with background b. The allocation of resources over schools in Equation (9.32) only depends on background, as required.

Suppose that f_b^S, the pupil background distribution at school S, changes, i.e., school S attracts more pupils with a disadvantaged background.[64] This may arise because there are new pupils in the system or because pupils move from one school to another. The question whether school S will receive more resources depends on the derivative of Equation (9.33) with respect to b. If the sign of this derivative is negative, then, using standard (first-order) stochastic dominance techniques, the school will for sure get extra resources; see, e.g., Lambert (2001).

The derivative $\tilde{C}^{M'}(b)$ is equal to

$$\tilde{C}^{M'}(b) = \int_a C_b^{M'}(a,b) f_{a|b}(a|b) da + \int_a C^M(a,b) \frac{\partial f_{a|b}(a|b)}{\partial b} da. \tag{9.34}$$

The second term can be rewritten as

$$\int_a C^M(a,b) d\left(\frac{\partial F_{a|b}(a|b)}{\partial b}\right), \tag{9.35}$$

with $F_{a|b}(a|b) = \int_{\underline{a}}^{a} f(t,b)dt / f_b(b)$ the distribution of ability conditional on background. To verify Equation (9.35), note that

$$\frac{\partial F_{a|b}(a|b)}{\partial b} = \frac{f_b(b) \int_{\underline{a}}^{a} \frac{\partial f(t,b)}{\partial b} dt - \frac{\partial f_b(b)}{\partial b} \int_{\underline{a}}^{a} f(t,b) dt}{f_b(b)^2}, \tag{9.36}$$

which indeed implies that

$$\begin{aligned} d\left(\frac{\partial F_{a|b}(a|b)}{\partial b}\right) &= \frac{f_b(b)\frac{\partial f(a,b)}{\partial b} - \frac{\partial f_b(b)}{\partial b} f(a,b)}{f_b(b)^2} da, \\ &= \frac{\partial}{\partial b}\left(\frac{f(a,b)}{f_b(b)}\right) da, \\ &= \frac{\partial f_{a|b}(a|b)}{\partial b} da, \end{aligned} \tag{9.37}$$

[64] In technical terms, the old distribution (first-order) dominates the new one.

as required. Now, using integration by parts, Equation (9.35) is equal to

$$C^M(a,b)\frac{\partial F_{a|b}(a|b)}{\partial b}\bigg|_{\underline{a}}^{\bar{a}} - \int_a C_a^{M\prime}(a,b)\frac{\partial F_{a|b}(a|b)}{\partial b}da, \tag{9.38}$$

where the first term is zero (as $\frac{\partial F_{a|b}(\bar{a}|b)}{\partial b} = \frac{\partial F_{a|b}(\bar{a}|b)}{\partial b} = 0$ and $C^M(a,b)$ finite at the boundaries). To sum up, Equation (9.34) can be written as

$$\tilde{C}^{M\prime}(b) = \int_a C_b^{M\prime}(a,b)f_{a|b}(a|b)da - \int_a C_a^{M\prime}(a,b)\frac{\partial F_{a|b}(a|b)}{\partial b}da. \tag{9.39}$$

What does this equation tells us? Consider an outcome-prioritarian minister with $C_a^{M\prime}(a,b) > 0$ and $C_b^{M\prime}(a,b) < 0$, a possible case as indicated in Table 9.4.

If there is no association between background and ability, then $\frac{\partial F_{a|b}(a|b)}{\partial b} = 0$ holds everywhere, and the second term drops out. In that peculiar case, the sign of the numerator depends on the sign of $C_b^{M\prime}(a,b)$, which was negative for the prioritarian minister under consideration. In this case, the result at the individual level extends towards the school level, i.e., with no association between background and ability, the minister will always provide more resources per pupil to schools serving pupils with a more disadvantaged background.[65]

If there is a positive association between background and ability, i.e., $\frac{\partial F_{a|b}(a|b)}{\partial b} < 0$ holds everywhere, then the second term no longer drops out and is negative (because $C_a^{M\prime}(a,b) > 0$). The sign of the derivative is no longer defined. So, while the minister would like to give more resources per pupil to schools serving pupils with a more disadvantaged background (the first term), being more disadvantaged also signals a lower ability, on average, which the minister does not want to reinforce (the second term). This may indeed lead to a paradox if the second term dominates: the minister would like to provide more resources to schools serving more disadvantaged pupils, but, not being able to observe ability and given a positive dependence between ability and background, she decides to give less resources to schools serving more disadvantaged pupils.

[65] If the association is negative, then the same result obtains.

References

Adler, M. (2019). "*Measuring Social Welfare: An Introduction.*" Oxford: Oxford University Press.

Arrow, K.J. (1971). "A utilitarian approach to the concept of equality in public expenditures." *The Quarterly Journal of Economics*, 85: 409–415.

Betts, J. and Roemer, J. (2007). "Equalizing opportunity for racial and socioeconomic groups in the United States through educational-finance reform." In L. Woessmann and P. Peterson, eds., *Schools and the Equal Opportunity Problem*, Cambridge, MA: MIT Press, pp. 209–238.

Bovenberg, L. and Jacobs, B. (2005). "Redistribution and education subsidies are Siamese twins." *Journal of Public Economics*, 89: 2005–2035.

Bowles, S. (1973). "Understanding unequal economic opportunity." *The American Economic Review Papers and Proceedings*, 63: 346–356.

Brett, C. and Weymark, J. (2003). "Financing education using optimal redistributive taxation." *Journal of Public Economics*, 87: 2549–2569.

Bruno, M. (1976). "Equality, complementarity and the incidence of public expenditures." *Journal of Public Economics*, 6: 395–407.

Coleman, J. (1966). "*The Concept of Equality of Educational Opportunity.*" Report, Washington, D.C., Government Printing Office.

Cunha, F. and Heckman, J. (2007). "The technology of skill formation." *American Economic Review*, 97: 31–47.

Cunha, F., Heckman, J., Lochner, L., and Masterov, D. (2006). "Interpreting the evidence on life cycle skill formation." In Hanushek, A. and Welch, F., eds., *Handbook of the Economics of Education*, Volume 1, North Holland: Elsevier, pp. 697–812.

Cunha, F., Heckman, J., and Schennach, S. (2010). "Estimating the technology of cognitive and non-cognitive skill formation." *Econometrica*, 78: 883–931.

de Fraja, G. (2002). "The design of optimal education policies." *The Review of Economic Studies*, 69: 437–466.

Epple, D., Romano, R., and Urquiola, M. (2017). "School vouchers: a survey of the economics literature." *Journal of Economic Literature*, 55: 441–492.

Epple, D., Romano, R., and Zimmer, R. (2016). "Charter schools: a survey of research on their characteristics and effectiveness." In E. Hanushek, S. Machin, and L. Woessmann, eds., *Handbooks in Economics of Education*, Volume 5, North Holland: Elsevier, 139–208.

Figlio, D. and Loeb, S. (2011). "School Accountability." In E. Hanushek, S. Machin, and L. Woessmann, eds., *Handbooks in Economics of Education*, Volume 3, North Holland: Elsevier, 383–421.

Fleurbaey, M., Gary-Bobo, R., and Maguain, D. (2002). "Education, distributive justice, and adverse selection." *Journal of Public Economics*, 84: 113–150.

Gintis, H. (1972). "A radical analysis of welfare economics and individual development." *The Quarterly Journal of Economics*, 86: 572–599.

Hare, P. and Ulph, D. (1979). "On education and distribution." *Journal of Political Economy*, 87: 193–212.

Heckman, J. (2006). "Skill formation and the economics of investing in disadvantaged children." *Science*, 312: 1900–1902.

Jencks, C. (1988). "Whom must we treat equally for educational opportunity to be equal?" *Ethics*, 98: 518–533.

Kautz, T., Heckman, J., Diris, R., ter Weel, B., and Borghans, L. (2014). "Fostering and measuring skills: Improving cognitive and non-cognitive skills to promote lifetime success." OECD Education Working Papers 110, OECD Publishing.

Keane, M. and Roemer J. (2009). "Assessing policies to equalize opportunity using an equilibrium model of educational and occupational choices." *Journal of Public Economics*, 93: 879–898.

Kristjánsson, K. (2017). "Recent work on flourishing as the aim of education: a critical review." *British Journal of Educational Studies*, 65: 87–107.

Lambert, P. (2001). "*The Distribution and Redistribution of Income.*" Third edition, Manchester: Manchester University Press.

Rawls, J. (1999). "*A Theory of Justice.*" Revised edition, Cambridge, MA: Harvard University Press.

Sacerdote, B. (2014). "Experimental and Quasi-Experimental Analysis of Peer Effects: Two Steps Forward?" *Annual Review of Economics*, 6: 253–272.

Samuelson, P. (1977). "Reaffirming the existence of "reasonable" Bergson-Samuelson social welfare functions." *Economica*, 44: 81–88.

Schouten, G. (2012). "Educational justice: closing gaps or paying debts?" *Journal of Applied Philosophy*, 29: 231–242.

Tuomala, M. (1986). "On the optimal income taxation and educational decisions." *Journal of Public Economics*, 30: 183–198.

Ulph, D. (1977). "On the optimal distribution of income and educational expenditure." *Journal of Public Economics*, 8: 341–356.

Waltenberg, F. (2010). "Essential educational achievements as the currency of educational justice." *Cuadernos de Economía*, 29: 103–126.

10 *Empirical Research on Ethical Preferences: How Popular is Prioritarianism?*

ERIK SCHOKKAERT AND BENOÎT TARROUX*

10.1 Introduction

There are two strands in the literature on distributive justice. The first strand is empirical and aims at getting a better understanding of the feelings and attitudes in society with respect to distributive justice and how these are linked to the individual and social characteristics of the respondents. The second one is normative and discusses which arguments are valid for defining a "just" situation or a "just" society. It is possible to keep these two approaches completely separate. Ethical theories are usually more subtle and complex than everyday opinions and a survey that would be based on the former runs the danger of being far removed from any relevant psychological reality of lay citizens. Moreover, a specific perspective on distributive justice does not become ethically acceptable, just because it is supported by a majority of the population.

Yet, in a political democracy it is nearly impossible to implement any theory of justice without sufficient support from the general public. This support will depend on the citizen's own values and preferences. As an example, if (as seems to be the case) for a majority of citizens the shape of the tax function matters independently of the resulting final outcomes, a prioritarian policy maker will have a hard time putting some of his specific policy proposals into practice. Even if one considers the majority opinions to be ethically unacceptable, one still has to convince a sufficient number of citizens if one wants to implement one's own supposedly superior conception of justice. A better understanding of the empirical structure of the uninformed opinions, that have "to be corrected," may then be extremely useful, even necessary.

* We thank the editors and participants at presentations at the University of Bergen for helpful comments.

One could even go further and also accept that knowledge of the empirical results can contribute to ethical reasoning[1]. Following the Rawlsian model of the reflective equilibrium, the challenge of normative thinking is to construe a consistent view of the world in which "relevant normative facts" concerning specific matters in the real world cohere with general principles. The former should perhaps not be restricted to the own intuitions of the ethical observer as in the traditional Rawlsian position. In fact, these intuitions may be strongly biased if that ethical observer is a white, highly educated, male, economics, philosophy or law professor with an income in the upper decile of the distribution. The quest for a reflective equilibrium becomes more challenging and relevant if we include among the relevant normative facts also the "judgments" of other people, i.e. the "common-sense" opinions in society (Miller, 1992) – and even real "justice related" behavior (Güth and Kliemt, 2010).

In this chapter we look at prioritarianism from this empirical perspective – and with the double purpose of getting a better insight into the societal feasibility of prioritarian policies and of collecting relevant findings that may challenge traditional ethical thinking. We first discuss some results that are derived from questionnaire studies. It would be inappropriate to derive any behavioral predictions from these studies, as the incentives in the real world are very different from those in a questionnaire environment. Actual behavior will normally not be driven primarily by normative considerations, but it will reflect a mixture of self-interest, norms, and the desire to make a good impression on other people. Yet, the aim of this research is to derive information about subjective norms and ethical convictions, and not to predict behavior. In a study about norms, we do not want the subjects to be guided by self-interested considerations, and questionnaire studies without monetary payments are then a natural approach. We will argue that these methods can (and perhaps should) exploit the possibilities of quasi-experimental designs. In Section 10.2 we summarize some relevant results that are obtained in large survey studies with representative samples of the population, while Section 10.3 is devoted to more structured quasi-experimental questionnaire studies. It will turn out that it is not easy to really test for the popular acceptance of

[1] See Gaertner and Schokkaert, 2012, for a more elaborate justification of this position

prioritarianism, but that it still can be safely concluded that some of its main ingredients (such as the Pigou-Dalton transfer principle) are put in question by respondents. We also give an overview of estimates of the degree of inequality aversion and show that the results are sensitive to the framing of the questions. Some more basic issues about the acceptance of the veil of ignorance as an intellectual device and about the traditional welfarist framework are discussed in Sections 10.3.4 and 10.3.5 respectively.

Section 10.4 summarizes the results from real behavioral experiments in which subjects are financially incentivized. These experiments are useful if we want to understand real behavior. Yet, the section also shows that cleverly designed experiments yield indeed normatively relevant facts. To get insights into ethical preferences, rather than e.g. into the degree of altruism or envy, we focus on experimental settings in which one subject takes the position of a social planner or in which subjects have to decide behind a veil of ignorance. As with the questionnaires, there are not many studies that aim directly at checking the relevance of prioritarianism, but we will see that there are relevant results on the trade-off between equity and efficiency and, more specifically, on the acceptance of the (crucial) transfer axiom. We will also discuss some findings on the choice between ex ante and ex post approaches in a context of risk.

In Section 10.5 we come back to the issue of the subtle relationship between the empirical work surveyed in this chapter and the normative debate about prioritarianism. Section 10.6 is a brief conclusion.

We focus in this chapter on questionnaire and experimental studies of the attitudes of the population. Other related questions are not treated. We do not discuss inverse optimum studies, that try to derive the underlying value judgments of decision makers from real-world policy decisions (some of this work is summarized in Chapter 4, this volume). We do not elaborate on the link between inequality and subjective well-being (see Clark and d'Ambrosio, 2015, for a survey on this topic). Finally, we focus on inequality aversion and not on risk aversion. There is a substantial literature on the similarities and differences between these two notions, and studies have investigated in some detail whether decisions under risk and redistributive decisions follow the same logic. We will comment on the issue when we discuss the results concerning the veil of ignorance, but a complete summary of this literature goes beyond the boundaries of this chapter.

10.2 Ethical Preferences as Measured in Large Surveys

Questionnaire studies on redistributive preferences or attitudes have always played a prominent role in the work of sociologists and political scientists, but in recent years they have also become more popular among economists. The resulting literature is huge and it is impossible to summarize it in this brief contribution. We will therefore limit ourselves to some basic findings from the economic literature that seem most relevant for prioritarianism. Yet we will argue that, while these findings are highly relevant to understand which redistributive policies are politically feasible in the real world, they do not really give a deeper insight into the specific normative questions relating to prioritarianism. For that purpose more focused approaches are necessary. These will be discussed in Section 10.3.

10.2.1 Many People Want Redistribution, but There Are Large Interindividual Differences in Distributive Preferences

Most often, the dependent variable in the survey studies is derived from the answers to simple questions such as:

> Some people think that the government in Washington should do everything to improve the standard of living of all poor Americans. (They are at point 1 on this card.) Other people think it is not the government's responsibility and that each person should take care of himself. (They are at point 5.) Where are you placing yourself in this scale?' (General Social Survey – GSS)
>
> It is the responsibility of the government to reduce the difference in income between people with high incomes to those with low incomes (International Social Survey Program – ISSP)
>
> The government should take measures to reduce differences in income levels (European Social Survey – ESS)

Figure 10.1 (taken from Kuziemko et al., 2015) gives a broad picture of the answers on these questions for the US. The results for other countries are sometimes slightly different, but the overall picture is rather robust. A majority of the population is in favor of redistribution, but (not surprisingly) support is more outspoken among low-income earners. However, support for redistribution did not increase in the last decades, despite the fact that there is near consensus that income inequality in the US did strongly increase in that period. We first

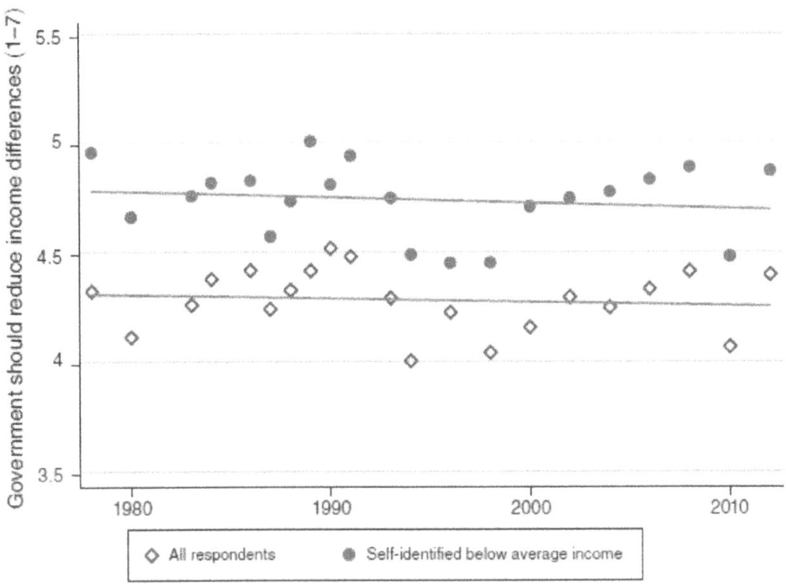

Figure 10.1 "Government should reduce income differences" (GSS) – average responses in the US over the last decades
(*Source*: Kuziemko et al., 2015, figure 1)

comment on the first finding and then on the second (in Section 10.2.2).

The general picture in Figure 10.1 hides a lot of interindividual variation. In their survey chapter, Alesina and Giuliano (2011) point to the importance of self-interest. This captures the direct effect of own income (as in Figure 10.1), but also the indirect effect of inequality on own income, e.g., through the increase in criminal behavior. Personal experiences also play a role. These include, for instance, misfortune in the past (growing up in a recession increases the willingness to redistribute, Giuliano and Spilimbergo, 2014), or the number of siblings and the position of the respondent in the order of children (younger children are more in favor of redistribution, Yamamura, 2015).

A second important factor is the belief in social mobility, which has become known as the "prospect of upward mobility" (POUM) hypothesis (Bénabou and Ok, 2001). This phenomenon has been further analyzed in Alesina et al. (2018). Respondents who believe that there is a substantial degree of social mobility in society are less in favor of income redistribution, as they believe that everybody (including themselves) has a fair chance to improve his own position. Perceptions of mobility are unrealistic, however. Americans overestimate the degree of mobility in their society, while Europeans overestimate the risk of getting trapped in poverty. We will come back to the importance of (mis)perception, but the empirical results on mobility clearly suggest that respondents take a lifetime perspective when evaluating distributions.

An essential finding in the literature is the overwhelming importance attached by respondents to the causes of income differences. At least since the work of Fong (2001), it has become generally accepted that respondents make a distinction between factors for which individuals should be held responsible (their "effort") and factors for which they should be compensated ("luck"). We will come back to the normative implications of this finding in Section 10.3.5, but it is certainly fair to state that there is consensus about the descriptive relevance of the distinction. This does not mean that everybody gives the same content to what is "effort" and what is "luck," or has the same estimate about the relative importance of effort and luck in the determination of incomes. Different opinions or perceptions in this regard seem to be among the main factors underlying differences in ethical preferences, e.g. between males and females or between different educational or ethnic groups (Schokkaert and Truyts, 2017).

In fact, Alesina and Angeletos (2005) point out that the interaction between ethical preferences and policy outcomes may be at the heart of intercountry differences in both. They show that there is a significant positive relationship at the cross-country level between the percentage of respondents who believe that income is mainly determined by luck rather than by effort, and social spending as a percentage of GDP. This positive relationship does not necessarily imply that attitudes "cause" policies. Causality also runs in the opposite direction, with the percentage of social spending influencing both the justice perceptions of individuals and the link between luck and income in the real world. This interaction can result in multiple equilibria, as illustrated in Figure 10.2. In the "American" equilibrium, low taxes make effort very important in the determination of incomes, inducing ethical preferences supporting low taxes. The "European" equilibrium is characterized by a high level of redistribution, undermining the importance of effort in income formation. Whether one accepts the specific model of

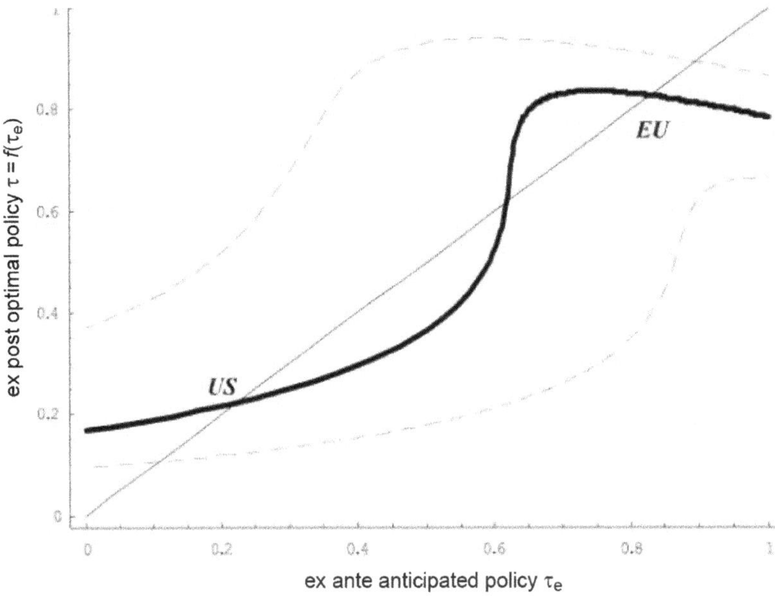

Figure 10.2 Preferences and policies: multiple equilibria
(*Source*: Alesina and Angeletos, 2005, figure 2)

Alesina and Angeletos or not,[2] it seems clear that attitudes of respondents are strongly influenced by the institutions in which they grow up. Intercultural differences in preferences even persist after people have moved to another country (Luttmer and Singhal, 2011).

As we have seen, perceptions of mobility or of the relative importance of effort and luck in the determination of incomes, are crucial to interpret correctly the answers of the respondents. In general, neglecting the basic (and almost trivial) insight that respondents start from their perception of the actual situation when evaluating the desirability of redistribution, may lead to completely mistaken conclusions about their true ethical preferences. A striking illustration is given by the

[2] In the Alesina-Angeletos model, perceptions of the relative importance of effort and luck are realistic. Bénabou and Tirole (2006) have an alternative model which gives a much greater role to misperceptions and biases in explaining the differences between Europe and the US. Moreover, Isaksson and Lindskog (2009) present some empirical evidence to question the starting point that different weights given to effort and luck would be the main driving force of intercountry differences in redistributive preferences.

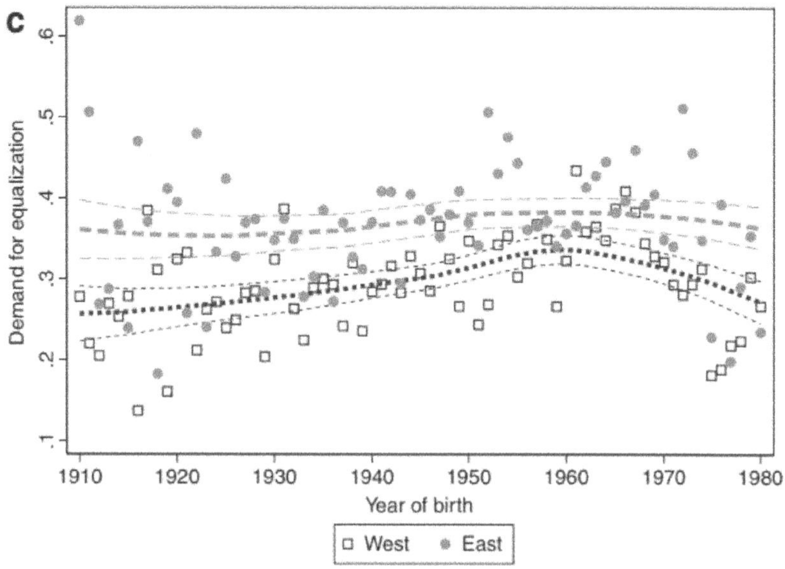

Figure 10.3 Willingness to redistribute by Eastern and Western Germans (*Source*: Kuhn, 2013, figure 1)

work of Kuhn (2013) on the differences in the willingness to redistribute of Eastern and Western Germans. Kuhn uses the ISSP-questions (of the waves 1992 and 1999) on the "estimated" and "ethically justified" wages of different occupations to calculate Gini inequality measures. Figure 10.3 shows the degree of redistribution, i.e. the reduction in the Gini, that is desired by his respondents. The results suggest that Eastern Germans are more in favor of redistribution at all possible ages. It is tempting to relate this finding to the fact that Eastern Germans have been influenced by the values of communism.

Yet, this conclusion should be interpreted cautiously, as illustrated in Figure 10.4. Panel a of that Figure shows the inequality as perceived by Eastern and Western Germans. The former clearly perceive more inequality. Panel b describes the desired inequality: there are no longer any differences between the two groups (again, whatever the age of the respondents)! The seemingly stronger willingness to redistribute, suggested by Figure 10.3, does not reflect any difference in inequality aversion, but only differences in the perception of actual wage differentials. Note that very many studies do not collect this information on

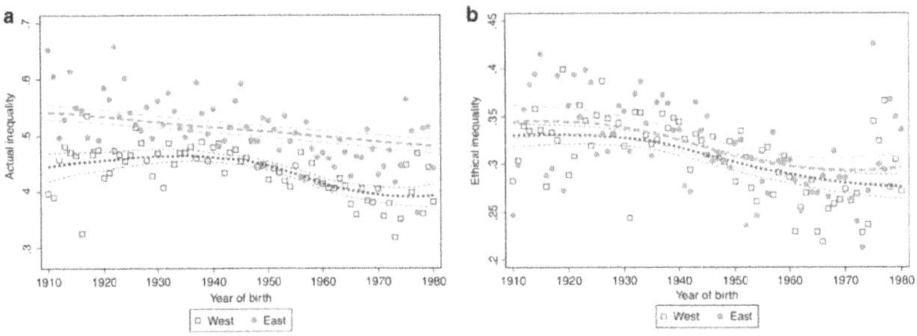

Figure 10.4 Actual and ethical inequality, as evaluated by Eastern and Western Germans
(*Source*: Kuhn, 2013, figure 1)

perceived inequality, and just ask about the willingness to redistribute (see the formulations of the questions at the beginning of this section).

10.2.2 Survey Experimental Designs

Almost all the results in the previous section are built on associations found in cross-sectional studies. It is difficult to draw conclusions about causal relationships from this kind of cross-sectional data. One of the most promising developments in the recent literature is therefore the growing use of experimental designs in large Internet-surveys. In such a design different groups of individuals are subjected to different treatments. The setup is very similar to some of the behavioral experiments that will be discussed in Section 10.4, but in the survey-experimental designs respondents do not always get financial incentives. We briefly discuss two examples.

Cruces et al. (2013) analyze (with a sample of 1,060 respondents in Buenos Aires) the importance of the perception of one's own position in the income distribution. Consistent information on that ranking was provided to a randomly selected treatment group, while perceptions of the control group were not corrected. The results suggest that respondents who overestimate their relative position are inclined to demand higher levels of redistribution after having been informed that they are in reality poorer than they initially thought. Such an experimental study offers more convincing evidence for the importance of the own relative income position than can be obtained with cross-sectional associations, as it can control for confounding factors.

Kuziemko et al. (2015) use a similar method to find an explanation for the puzzle that the desire to redistribute of US citizens apparently has remained stable in an era where inequality has grown considerably. A treatment group receives clear information about real-world developments, a control group does not receive that information. Kuziemko et al. (2015) find that giving information indeed changes the general attitude towards inequality, in the sense that respondents express a stronger desire to reduce inequality, but at the same time the information does not strongly change the degree of acceptance of redistributive government policies.[3] In a follow-up study, they try to find an explanation for this fascinating result. Two treatments have a significant effect on the acceptance of redistributive policies: priming respondents to think about the working of the government itself and giving information about specific policy measures. This suggests that the lack of popularity of redistributive policies is driven by the lack of trust in the government (which is more of a problem in the US than in Europe), but that this lack of trust can be partly overcome by drawing attention to the way in which specific policies can indeed be successful in reducing inequality. The political feasibility of redistributive policies clearly does not depend only on the normative attractiveness of prioritarian convictions.

10.2.3 What Did We Learn about the Acceptance of Prioritarianism?

The results summarized in this section are certainly relevant to understand the social reality of redistribution and to gauge the potential of redistributive policies. They offer us a better insight into the acceptance of such policies by the general public and contribute to a better understanding of the underlying differences in the ethical convictions and the factors explaining these differences. The questions are sufficiently simple to be understood by large fractions of the population and are not too far removed from the cognitions and emotions of the respondents. This is important, as it reduces the danger that the survey itself would induce specific answers from respondents who have never

[3] At least for income tax. The results for estate tax are different and further analyzed in great length in the paper.

thought deeply about the issue and are not familiar with a more abstract ethical reasoning.

Yet this approach also has its limitations and it certainly is not very informative with respect to the specific questions raised by prioritarianism. The simple questions that are analyzed in these surveys are not explicit about what it exactly means to "reduce inequality," as they do not specify a measure of inequality. Utilitarians, prioritarians and Rawlsians may all agree that "income differences should be reduced" and the same is true for approaches aiming at equalizing opportunities (in their different interpretations) or for adherents of some sort of capability theory. For a prioritarian who wants to get information about the acceptance of the assumptions underlying this well-defined framework, or about the views of the population on the values of crucial parameters such as the degree of inequality aversion, more detail is needed and the survey questions should be structured in line with welfare economic theory. Let us now turn to studies that make an attempt in this direction.

10.3 Questionnaire-Experimental Work: the Acceptance of Prioritarianism

The challenge for empirical research on prioritarianism is clear. On the one hand, general questions, such as the ones discussed in the previous section, may be close to the intuitions of the respondents, but they are not sufficiently specific to relate the answers to welfare economic theories. On the other hand, welfare economic theory is so abstract that it is nearly impossible to "test" its acceptance among the general population. One cannot ask general questions about the acceptance of prioritarianism versus utilitarianism to subjects who do not have the slightest idea about the meaning of these concepts – and who are likely to have ethical intuitions that are not welfarist. Explaining the relevant concepts before asking about them may induce strong framing effects, as individuals confronted with new information will be influenced by the way this new information is presented. We will first discuss this methodological challenge and then turn to the "testing" of the prioritarian axioms and the "measurement" of the degree of inequality aversion. We will mainly focus on issues related to income distribution, but also briefly discuss inequalities in health. In Section 10.3.4, we summarize some results on the relevance of the veil of ignorance and we end with some results on the limitations of welfarism in general.

10.3.1 Some Methodological Preliminaries

Some progress can be made by focusing on the acceptance not of broad theories, but of specific axioms.[4] As illustrated in Chapter 2 of this book, the axiomatic approach reduces the intricate reasoning of a complete ethical theory to its essential constitutive building blocks. As Luce and Raiffa (1957, p. 123) write: "By means of a (small) finite number of axioms, we are able to 'examine' the infinity of possible schemes, to throw away those which are unfair, and to characterize those which are acceptable." Focusing on the separate axioms allows empirical researchers to formulate questions which are theoretically meaningful and at the same time understandable for the population at large. It also allows them to focus on well-specified problems, rather than on generalities.

An obvious method to test for the empirical acceptance of theoretical ideas or axioms would be to formulate direct questions about them, e.g. "Does an income transfer from a rich to a poor person reduce inequality (or increase social welfare)?" Such direct questions force respondents to think in an abstract way about general principles concerning problems that are relatively new to them. To avoid framing effects, the largest part of the literature has followed another route. Respondents are then confronted with simple cases or with specific stories that are related to real-world situations, and are asked to give their opinion about what is an optimal (or just, or least unequal) allocation for that specific case. Usually they can choose from a set of precise, quantitatively formulated, options. This circumvents the perception distortions, which have been discussed earlier. Varying the background of the story allows researchers to "test" for context-dependency. Sometimes different variants of the same case are shown to all respondents (*within-respondents* design), in other studies different variants are shown to different randomly selected samples of respondents (*between-respondents* design). Some of the suggested options correspond to theoretical solutions, while others are unrelated to any theoretical concept. The relative acceptance of the various options then offers an indirect, quasi-experimental, way to test different axioms or solution concepts.

[4] Methodological issues with this approach are discussed in greater length in Gaertner and Schokkaert (2012)

Most (but not all) empirical studies use student samples. Although this choice is mainly explained by the easy availability of students, it has an obvious advantage. Students can be expected to understand complicated questions, which could not be introduced easily in a representative survey. This may be important if one wants to apply the questionnaire approach to discover new theoretical puzzles or to get a better insight into the trade-offs between different axioms. On the other hand, the lack of representativeness of the student samples is clearly problematic if one wants to check whether the theoretical approach is supported by different groups in society, or if one wants to get a better insight into social biases and intercultural differences. There is an obvious trade-off here, but it seems fair to say that future work should try to focus more on representative samples, the more so since the use of the Internet has made this practically feasible. There is no reason why one could not set up the type of survey experiments that have been described in Section 10.2.2 in order to test the acceptance of specific theoretical axioms. Quasi-experimental methods can be as easily implemented via the Internet as in a classroom.

We should be aware of the limitations of the simple quasi-experimental setup. It indeed allows us to remain close to the original ethical intuitions of the respondents – but these ethical intuitions may be very different from reasoned opinions. It would therefore be useful to design a dynamic study, in which respondents in a first round are asked simple questions, and in a second round are given additional information about the implications of their choices or about the position that different theories would take. Of course, if we force the respondents to think more explicitly, we will get more sophisticated answers. However, these answers may be influenced heavily by the setup of the questionnaire, and hence by the structure of the dominant theory. This is especially true if the respondents had no strong opinions before they were confronted with the questionnaire. The method to be followed will necessarily depend on what the main objectives of the study are.

10.3.2 Acceptance of the Prioritarian Axioms

The seminal work on the acceptance of the different axioms of inequality measurement has been done by Amiel and Cowell and most of this earlier work has been summarized in their 1999 monograph

(Amiel and Cowell, 1999). Their original aim was to "test" the popularity of the common axioms of inequality measurement, but in later work they extended their approach to social welfare, poverty, risk, mobility and polarization. We will focus on the results for social welfare, since these are most immediately relevant for this book. Amiel and Cowell investigate various axioms that are relevant for prioritarianism. Anonymity is not tested, but is implicitly assumed to hold. We will focus on the Pigou-Dalton transfer principle and on the monotonicity axiom, stating that an increase in the income of an individual leads to an increase in social welfare. As we will see, their results on the transfer principle also throw some light on the separability axiom.

Amiel and Cowell (1999) implement the methodology that we have described above. They focus on concrete cases, aiming at testing specific axioms. In testing the axioms they predominantly use a within-subjects design.[5] They go some way in the direction of the dynamic approach that has been suggested, by first asking respondents to evaluate numerical income vectors, and then confronting them with a verbal formulation of the relevant axioms. The numerical part comes first and after the verbal part, respondents can return and change their answers on the numerical questions if they want to. It turns out, however, that only a small minority of respondents wants to revise their original answers.

Let us illustrate their approach in some detail for the Pigou-Dalton transfer principle. Respondents were shown the following case description:

This questionnaire concerns peoples attitude to income distribution. We would be interested in your views, based on some hypothetical situations. Because it is about attitudes there are no "right" answers. Some of the suggested answers correspond to assumptions commonly made by economists; but these assumptions may not be good ones. Your responses will help to shed some light on this, and we would like to thank you for your participation. The questionnaire is anonymous.

In Alfaland two economic programs are proposed. It is known that both programs will have the same effect on the population except on their incomes and all the people are identical in every respect other than income. In each of the first ten questions there are given two alternative lists of incomes A and

[5] They opt for a between-subjects design to compare the acceptance of the axioms in different settings, e.g., in measuring inequality versus risk.

B (in Alfaland local currency) which result from these two programs respectively. Please state which program you consider would make the community of Alfaland better off by circling A or B. If you consider that each of the programs is just as good as the other then circle both A and B.

1) A = (1, 4, 7, 10, 13); B = (1, 5, 6, 10, 13).

In the questionnaire, this case (1) was only the first in a list of more than 10 choices. It is a "test" of the transfer axiom. Respondents who accept the latter should prefer society B. Other numerical cases are used to investigate the acceptance of other axioms.

The verbal formulation for the transfer axiom runs as follows:

Suppose there are two economic programs A and B which have only the following difference: The income of person i in program A is x units higher than his income in program B while the income of person j in program A is x units lower than his income in program B. In both programs the income of person i is higher than the income of person j. The incomes of all other people are unaffected by the choice of program A or program B.

a) Program A would make the community better off.
b) Program B would make the community better off.
c) The relative position of other people is also different by A and B. Therefore we cannot say which program would make the community better off.
d) None of the above.

In the light of the above, would you want to change your answer to question 1?[6]

The approach for the other basic axioms is similar (see Amiel and Cowell, 1999, for more details). Some results are summarized in Table 10.1. These are based on a sample of 620 students, located in Bonn, Koblenz, Stockholm, London, and Tel Aviv. The first column gives agreement with the basic axioms in the numerical formulation of the case, the second column shows agreement with the basic axioms if they are formulated verbally. The degree of rejection of the axioms is striking. This result is not only found in the work of Amiel and Cowell. Similar results are found in a number of other studies (Ballano and Ruiz-Castillo, 1993, Harrison and Seidl, 1994, Leibler et al., 2009, Jancewicz, 2016). The finding that the most basic axioms of

[6] "Question 1" was the numerical question given above.

Table 10.1. *Agreement with basic axioms on social welfare*

	Numerical	Verbal
Monotonicity	54	55
Transfer principle	47	33

Note: Adapted from Amiel and Cowell, 1999.

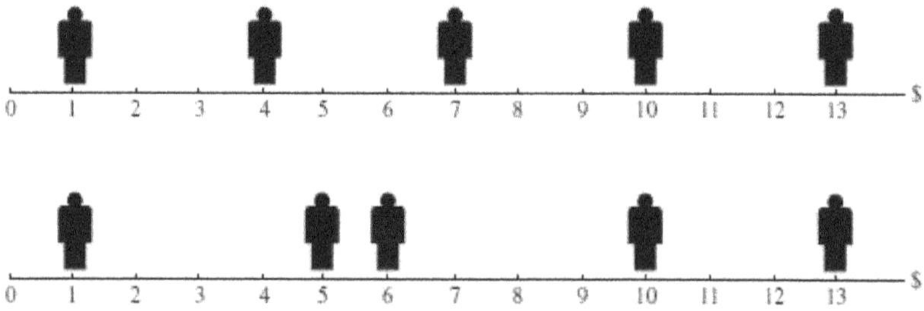

Figure 10.5 Transfer principle
(*Source*: Amiel and Cowell, 1999, figure 7.11)

prioritarianism are not supported by a large fraction of the population is very robust.

Let us first focus on the transfer principle. In the whole series of studies by Amiel and Cowell, the transfer principle is tested in many different numerical cases. Its rejection is not universal. For instance, a transfer from the highest income to the lowest income in the income vector, is almost generally accepted as welfare improving. The transfer (from A to B) as described in case 1 is one which large groups of respondents (more females than males) do not see as a welfare improvement. Note that this is not necessarily irrational. The psychological mechanism at work is nicely illustrated in Figure 10.5, which is also taken from Amiel and Cowell (1999). The transfer in case 1 lowers the distance between the second and the third individual in the row, but it increases the distance between the worst-off and the second worst-off. Respondents who focus on that distance may (and apparently do) see the transfer as welfare-decreasing. These respondents appear (a) to focus on the situation of the worst-off, and (b) to have the intuition that the welfare of the worst-off decreases if the income distance with the second worst-off increases, despite the fact that his/her own income remains the same. It is interesting to notice that these results suggest that respondents do not consider the pair of individuals who are involved in the transfer in isolation, but evaluate the transfer taking into account the income of other individuals. This amounts to a rejection of the separability axiom that is essential for prioritarianism.

Let us now turn to the interpretation of the rejection of monotonicity. Respondents are asked to evaluate an income increase for one individual and the questionnaire does not make explicit the relationship between income and individual well-being. Monotonicity is mainly rejected when an income in the upper part of the income vector increases. A natural interpretation of this result is again that respondents believe that a deterioration of the relative position of the poor leads to a decrease in their well-being. That the relative income influences individual well-being is also found in other questionnaire studies (see, e.g., Konow, 2001, Johansson-Stenman et al., 2002).[7] Rejecting monotonicity in the space of incomes therefore does not necessarily imply that the Pareto principle in the space of individual well-being is also rejected (see Amiel and Cowell, 1994). On the other hand, other questionnaire studies that have formulated the question explicitly in utility terms also have found limited support for the Pareto principle (Mc Clelland and Rohrbaugh, 1978).

This discussion on the interpretation of the axioms points to a more general issue. Although focused on social welfare evaluation, the questions in the work of Amiel and Cowell and in related work are about income redistribution, not about welfare redistribution. Hence, this work does not allow us to compare the acceptance of, e.g. utilitarianism and prioritarianism, since redistributive transfers will also be desirable for a utilitarian (if individual well-being is concave in income). We will come back to this point in Section 10.5.

10.3.3 *The Degree of Inequality Aversion*

Some authors have (implicitly or explicitly) taken the utilitarian or prioritarian framework as given and have focused on estimating the

[7] We are referring here to studies that explicitly focus on the *normative* evaluation of income distributions. Of course, the happiness literature contains an overwhelming amount of *positive* evidence that the relative position of individuals in the distribution of income (or well-being) matters for their own subjective well-being (see, e.g., the survey by Clark and d'Ambrosio, 2015).

degree of inequality aversion within that framework. Contrary to the prioritarian approach advocated in this book, this literature does not aim at measuring inequality aversion in the space of individual levels of well-being, but focuses on specific components of well-being. We first summarize some findings on the income distribution and then raise the issue of health inequalities.

10.3.3.1 Income Inequality

An early example of this work is by Glejser et al. (1977) who let students choose between different allocations of scholarships. Broadly speaking, in the more recent literature this question has been tackled in two ways: either through the idea of a leaky bucket (e.g., Amiel et al., 1999) or through a straightforward comparison of two distributions (e.g., Carlsson et al., 2005). Pirttilä and Uusitalo (2010) compare the results obtained with the two methods for a representative survey of the Finnish population. We present their formulation of the questions in some detail. The other studies follow a similar approach, although the specific formulation and the underlying formal model are different.

Pirttilä and Uusitalo (2010) assume that social welfare can be represented by an Atkinson-type social welfare function[8]

$$S = \sum_i \frac{y_i^{1-e}}{1-e} \text{ for } e \neq 1, \tag{10.1}$$

$$S = \sum_i \ln y_i \text{ for } e = 1. \tag{10.2}$$

They implement the leaky-bucket method by asking each respondent one question, corresponding to one value of e. For $e = 1$, the question goes as follows:

What is your opinion of the following reform proposal?

The taxation of all high-income earners, whose disposable income exceeds €3300 per month, is increased. The money is spent for the benefit of those low-income earners whose disposable income is less than €800 per month. The high-income earners can, however, react to the tax increase by reducing their work effort, and part of the money goes to administrative expenses.

[8] To avoid confusion with the other chapters, we use the symbol e to measure the degree of aversion to income inequality, rather than γ that is used to denote the degree of aversion to inequality in well-being.

Therefore, for each 100 paid by the high-income earners, only 25 can be spent for the benefit of low-income earners.

Are you, nevertheless, in favor of this proposal?

1. Yes 2. No 3. Cannot say.

The incomes of €3,300 and €800 correspond respectively to the average income in the highest and the lowest decile of the Finnish income distribution of 2003, inflated to 2006 values. A respondent with a personal value of $e > 1$ should be in favor of the proposal, someone with $e < 1$ should reject it. Similar questions, corresponding to $e = 0.5$, 2 and 3 are asked to other respondents. Pooling all the answers makes it possible to estimate the distribution of e in the population. Since a majority of respondents reject the proposal in the case $e = 0.5$, it appears that the median inequality aversion of the respondents lies below 0.5.[9]

In the second approach, the respondents get a choice between two distributions. Again, each respondent is asked one question, corresponding with the same value of e as was implemented in his/her leaky-bucket question. The income distributions are again calibrated on the real Finnish situation and for $e = 1$ the question then becomes:

Let us imagine that in wage negotiations two different alternatives are considered. Which of the following do you prefer?

1. If all employees are ordered from the lowest-income earner to the highest-income earner, someone belonging to the lowest decile earns 1,570 in a month, a person with average income earns 2,340 and a person belonging to the highest decile earns 3,480.
2. Income differences rise and the average income is increased, so that the low income earner gets 1,280 per month, the person with average income gets 2,580 and the high-income earner 5,190.
3. Cannot say.

A respondent with $e = 1$ should be indifferent between the two distributions, someone with $e > 1$ should prefer distribution 1 and someone with $e < 1$ should prefer distribution 2, since for the latter the increase in average income is large enough to compensate for the increased inequality. In this case, the more equal distribution is preferred by all

[9] The fraction of the sample rejecting the proposal for values of e larger than 0.5 is even larger, as it should be if the answers are consistent with the underlying theory.

respondents, suggesting that the median inequality aversion is larger than 3.

The difference between the results obtained with the two methods is surprisingly large, and this is even more striking because similar differences are found in other studies. Several explanations can be proposed for this difference. First, the reference points in the two questions of Pirttilä and Uusitalo are different. The leaky-bucket question describes a tax increase from an actual situation that is more unequal, the formulation of the comparison question suggests that the less unequal distribution is the starting point. The different answers could then just reflect status quo bias. This raises the question whether this status quo bias is a genuine psychological phenomenon that also would manifest itself in real-world decisions or just a framing effect, due to the questionnaire setting. If the former holds true, it is still another question whether this status quo bias has normative significance, e.g., in a libertarian setting with respect for property rights, or whether it should just be seen as a normatively irrelevant "true bias."

While the different reference points may contribute to the explanation for the different results obtained with the two methods in the setting of Pirttilä and Uusitalo, this is not sufficient to explain why a similar difference is found in the other studies with different formulations. Pirttilä and Uusitalo themselves propose an alternative explanation. They suggest that the degree of inequality aversion may be context-dependent – and different in a tax setting drawing attention to the cost induced by reducing work effort compared to a setting with two apparently pre-tax income distributions. Intuitions in the former case may be driven by the conviction that effort should be rewarded, while the different distributions in the latter story may be interpreted as a matter of bargaining. In fact, this explanation is closely related to the hypothesis about the lack of trust in the government that we have described in Section 10.2.2. Of course, all these explanations suggest that the ethical intuitions of respondents cannot be fully captured within an outcome-related approach. We will return to this point in Section 10.3.5.

10.3.3.2 Health Inequality

Until now we focused on the inequality aversion with respect to incomes. There is also a literature on inequality aversion in the space of health. This inequality aversion is crucial in a prioritarian approach to health care priority setting. The dominant approach in cost-effectiveness studies on health implements an objective function which is an unweighted sum of so-called “QALYS,” quality-adjusted life years. It is not always clear whether QALYS should be seen as a measure of health or as a measure of utility (see Hausman, 2015, for a critical discussion), but this issue goes beyond the topic of this chapter. What is relevant for our purpose, however, is the near consensus among the respondents in survey studies that this generally applied “unweighted” (quasi-utilitarian) objective function is not acceptable and that some (prioritarian) distributional weighting should be introduced (see Gaertner and Schokkaert, 2012, and Costa-Font and Cowell, 2019, for overviews of this literature).

A limited number of studies (e.g. Edlin et al., 2012; Ottersen et al, 2014) present measures of the inequality aversion in this health setting. These studies (with a design similar to the comparison method described in the previous subsection) find values of health inequality aversion that are in the same range as those of the income inequality aversion found with the same method, i.e. larger than 1 but smaller than 10.

Yet the majority of the studies do not focus on pure health inequality but rather on income (or socioeconomic status)-related health inequality (e.g. Dolan and Tsuchiya, 2011, Robson et al., 2017, Cookson et al., 2018, Lal et al., 2019). In this setting, Robson et al. (2017) write the social welfare function (for $\varepsilon \neq 1$) as[10]

$$S = \frac{1}{1-\varepsilon}\sum_{k} f(x_k)H_k^{1-\varepsilon} \tag{10.3}$$

where H_k is the health level of income group k, and $f(x_k)$ the proportion of the population in that group. In this framework the estimated degree of inequality aversion varies but is usually much larger than in the “pure” health inequality case. Dolan and Tsuchyia (2011) report a value of 29, and in other studies the degree of inequality aversion cannot even be estimated because preferences are no longer monotonic (Abasolo and Tsuchiya, 2004, 2013). This income-related inequality aversion is a different concept than the pure health inequality aversion,

[10] We focus on the Atkinson-type of social welfare function, since this yields results that are comparable between the different studies and domains. Robson et al. (2017) also show results for a Kolm-type social welfare function.

however. The way the questions are formulated draws attention to the issue of cumulative deprivation: respondents have to compare (changes in the) distributions of health in which the worse off are not only less healthy, but also have a lower income. It is not really surprising that they then show a more outspoken preference for redistribution.[11]

Robson et al. (2017) and Cookson et al. (2018) offer an interesting example of the dynamic approach that we advocated above. In their study (with admittedly a small number of respondents) they design two feedback procedures: one in which respondents receive more information on the implications of their choices in the first round, and a second one in which respondents are shown a video in which different characters introduce relevant arguments concerning the trade-off between total health and its distribution. Their hypothesis is that the simple questionnaire setting induces a pro-egalitarian attitude among respondents and that they are likely to become less inequality averse if they receive more information. This hypothesis is corroborated in their study in which the income-related health inequality aversion is around 10. Of course, compared to the traditional values in a pure income (or health) setting, this is still very large.

10.3.4 The Veil of Ignorance, Ex Ante and Ex Post

At least since Harsanyi (1953, 1955) and Rawls (1958, 1971) the concept of the "veil of ignorance" (VOI) has played a prominent role in the philosophical literature on distributive justice. It is built on the assumption that individuals would be free of any personal bias when they are put in the hypothetical situation in which they do not know their own relative position in society. Choices behind the veil would therefore yield an acceptable theory of justice and of social welfare. Different philosophers, notably Harsanyi and Rawls, make different assumptions about the "thickness" of the veil, i.e. the nature and the amount of information that is hidden, and derive different conclusions from it. For Rawls, decision makers under "his" VOI would choose the maximin criterion, for Harsanyi a rational decision maker behind the VOI would necessarily opt for utilitarianism, and not for

[11] The issue of the correlation between income and health has also been tackled in the context of inequality measurement, with special focus on the relevance of the concentration index; see, e.g., Bleichrodt et al. (2012) and Tarroux (2015).

prioritarianism. It is therefore relevant to check if the VOI is accepted by respondents as an intellectual device to arrive at a theory of social welfare. In fact, as we will see in Section 10.4, the VOI has often been used in laboratory experiments precisely for that purpose. It is less common in the questionnaire literature however.

The most relevant study on the topic has been conducted by Amiel et al. (2009). They reformulate the Alfaland-type question described above and introduce the idea that there are five regions in Alfaland, each with a different income. Respondents are again asked to indicate which of two situations (income vectors) would result in a better situation for Alfaland. There are two versions of the questionnaire. In the first, respondents are asked to put themselves in the shoes of an outside observer. In the second, they are asked to imagine that they themselves are assigned to one of the regions of Alfaland, with equal probability of finding themselves in one of the five regions. This second option is of course the VOI-treatment. The results are mixed (because students in Israel do not follow the general pattern), but in broad lines the authors find that the standard prioritarian axioms, and more specifically the Pigou-Dalton transfer principle, are followed to a larger extent in the "ethical observer" treatment than in the VOI-treatment.

Bosmans and Schokkaert (2004) find similar results in a different setting. Students are asked to evaluate the situation of two firms that each plan to employ 100 recently graduated students. In each firm there are three types of jobs, corresponding with different incomes. Bosmans and Schokkaert have a number of different treatments but two of them correspond to those proposed by Amiel et al. (2009): the "impartial and sympathetic observer" and the "rational individual behind the veil of ignorance." Only between 10 and 13 percent of the respondents respect the axioms of expected utility theory, which in the VOI-treatment is the basic justification of utilitarianism by Harsanyi (1953, 1955). Moreover, as in Amiel et al. (2009), the response patterns are significantly different between the observer- and the VOI-treatments. Similar results are reported by Bernasconi (2002).

While the previous studies were set in a setting with incomes, Pinto-Prades and Abellán-Perpiñán (2005) implement the VOI to derive the social values attached to different health states, and compare the obtained results with those from a so-called "person trade-off" approach (Nord, 1995), which focuses on the trade-off between the numbers of individuals treated and the severity of their disease. This is a typical "ex post" approach, in which the respondent is put in the position of a decision maker who has to take allocation decisions in front of the veil of ignorance. The survey was administered to a stratified random sample of 300 respondents, drawn from the general population of the Barcelona area. The two treatments again lead to very different results. The "outside observer" in the person trade-off case finds it more important to avoid that people die. Again, the large differences between the person trade-off and the VOI confirm that it is not acceptable to suppose that decisions behind a veil of ignorance would coincide with the decisions taken by an ethically motivated outside observer. This important finding seems to be quite robust in a large variety of settings.

10.3.5 A Broader Set of Questions: Welfarism, Desert and Taxation

The results described until now suggest that the prioritarian framework is not generally accepted by the population. A strong indication of this is the large degree of rejection of the transfer principle. In this section we collect some challenges raised by the questionnaire studies that are even more basic, because they put in doubt the traditional welfarist assumptions underlying prioritarianism.

First, there is by now overwhelming evidence that for (almost all) respondents the causes of income differences play an essential role in the evaluation of their legitimacy. As a clear example, there is near consensus that effort should be rewarded, and that income differences due to brute luck should be compensated. We mentioned already that this is a quasi-universal finding in the large survey studies. It is also found in the questionnaire-experimental work.[12] Surveys of these results can be found in Konow (2003) and Gaertner and Schokkaert (2012, chapter 4). In fact, already in the seminal study in this line of research, Yaari and Bar-Hillel (1984) found that Israeli students made a distinction between welfare differences due to needs and to tastes, and considered redistribution to be more legitimate in the former than

[12] And Section 10.4.5 will illustrate that it is also an important element in behavioral experiments.

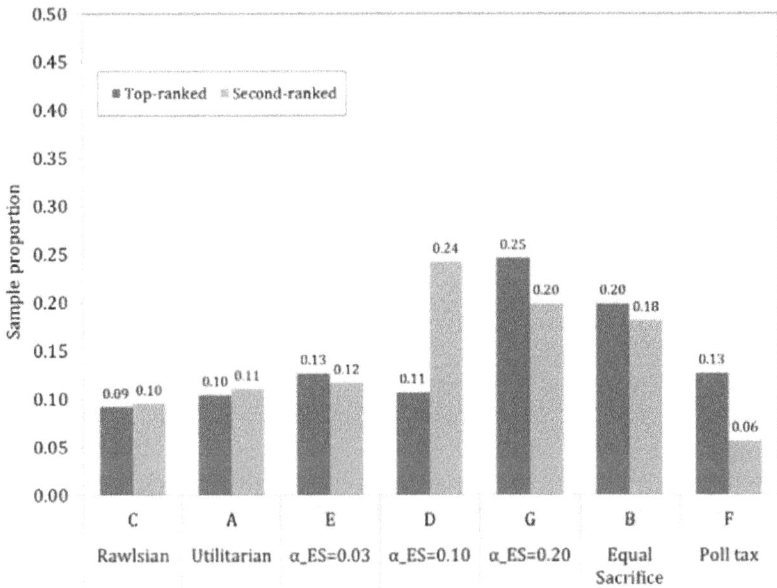

Figure 10.6 Utilitarian versus equal sacrifice taxation
(*Source*: Weinzierl, 2014, figure 2)

in the latter case. All these results can be seen as a clear rejection of welfarism and as supportive evidence for the popularity of the notion of equality of opportunity. The relationship between this notion and prioritarianism should be further explored. One interesting avenue is suggested by the theory of fair allocation, that integrates ideas about responsibility and compensation in its normative approach to individual well-being (see, e.g. Fleurbaey and Maniquet, 2011, 2018).

Second, when thinking about taxation, many (or even most) respondents go beyond the simple ideas underlying the optimization of a traditional social welfare function. This is convincingly shown by the work of Weinzierl, with Internet samples of US respondents. Weinzierl (2014) asks the respondents to rank different tax policies (see Figure 10.6). The equal sacrifice policy (in his case boiling down to proportional taxation) is more popular than either the Rawlsian or the utilitarian policy. Even more popular is a mixed approach with α_ES (the weight given to equal sacrifice) equal to 0.2. In another paper, Weinzierl (2017a) shows that respondents resist the fully egalitarian solution, even if there are no incentive problems and the initial income

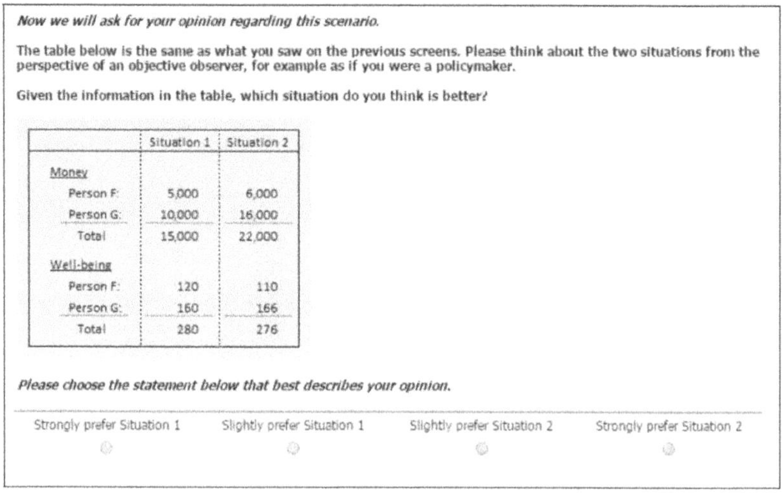

Now we will ask for your opinion regarding this scenario.

The table below is the same as what you saw on the previous screens. Please think about the two situations from the perspective of an objective observer, for example as if you were a policymaker.

Given the information in the table, which situation do you think is better?

	Situation 1	Situation 2
Money		
Person F:	5,000	6,000
Person G:	10,000	16,000
Total	15,000	22,000
Well-being		
Person F:	120	110
Person G:	160	166
Total	280	276

Please choose the statement below that best describes your opinion.

Strongly prefer Situation 1 | Slightly prefer Situation 1 | Slightly prefer Situation 2 | Strongly prefer Situation 2

Figure 10.7 Choice between income/well-being bundles
(*Source*: Weinzierl, 2017b, figure 3)

difference is due to brute luck.[13] Moreover, a large share of respondents prefer a classical benefit-based logic over the prioritarian logic of diminishing marginal social welfare. These two views are linked: respondents who more strongly resist equalization are more likely to prefer the classical benefit-based principle. As a last example, Weinzierl (2017b) asks respondents to choose between situations with explicit information about monetary income and well-being (see Figure 10.7). He suggests that the loss in well-being of person F in situation 2 is due to envy. About half of his respondents do not accept this as a legitimate reason to compensate person F. This study is one of the few examples where well-being is explicitly introduced in the formulation of the questions. Note that the finding that the negative effect of growing inequality on the well-being of the worse-off should not be compensated clashes with some of the findings that we discussed in Section 10.3.2. All of Weinzierl's results are obtained with US respondents and surely when questions are asked about specific policies, such as income taxation, respondents may be strongly influenced by the institutions in which they are living. This is illustrated by comparing

[13] This case is analyzed theoretically in Saez and Stantcheva (2013), and they show survey results that go in the same direction as those of Weinzierl (2017a).

Weinzierl's results to those of Tarroux (2019). In his French sample, respondents are first asked to rank final income distributions. When they are, in a second stage, informed about the average tax rates leading to these final distributions, the majority change their mind and opt for a progressive taxation policy. This means that not only the final outcomes matter, but also the shape of the tax function itself. Again, this finding cannot immediately be taken up in the simple prioritarian framework.

10.4 Ethical Preferences in the Lab

We now turn to an overview of the findings obtained from lab experiments. We will cover the same topics as in the previous section. After some methodological considerations (Section 10.4.1), we first discuss the acceptance of the basic prioritarian axioms (Section 10.4.2) and the estimation of the degree of inequality aversion (Section 10.4.3). We then show the results of recent work on the choice between ex ante and ex post perspectives in a context of risk and uncertainty (Section 10.4.4) and finally turn to some broader questions concerning the popularity of welfarism (Section 10.4.5).

10.4.1 Methodological Considerations

While there is a huge experimental economic literature on social preferences (altruism, reciprocity, envy, etc.),[14] ethical preferences have received less attention. Two methods, that we already have introduced in Section 10.3.4 on questionnaire studies, have been investigated in the literature.[15] The first method puts a subject in a position to choose a payoff allocation for *other* subjects in the lab. That is, subjects are grouped by $(n+1)$ and one of them, called the *social planner*[16] is asked to allocate a certain amount of money among the n others, called *stakeholders*. That *real* stakeholders are affected by the choice made by

[14] See for instance Andreoni and Miller (2002), Charness and Rabin (2002), Engelmann and Strobel (2004), Fehr et al. (2006) and Cooper and Kagel (2015) for a survey.

[15] See Aguiar et al. (2013) for a comparison between different methods.

[16] Subjects are not told whether their role is that of a social planner or stakeholder. Experimentalists are used to adopt a neutral language in order to avoid any demand effect.

the social planner should make her aware of her responsibilities and works as an incentive mechanism.[17] The subjects playing the role of social planner receive a payoff that is not affected by their choices. It can then be assumed that the social planner's choices reveal her view about how a resource should be shared among people.[18]

According to the second method, the subject is involved in the situation, i.e., she is a member of the group for which she is asked to choose an allocation of payoffs, but her decision is made *under a veil of ignorance*. Almost all the experiments on which we will report use a design in which subjects know the probability of each position. For instance, the subject is grouped with $(n-1)$ other subjects and she is asked to choose between $(x_1, \ldots, x_n)$ and $(y_1, \ldots, y_n)$ knowing that the probability of receiving x_i is equal to $\frac{1}{n}$. An alternative is to impose uncertainty; that is, subjects know the possible levels of payoff that they can receive but do not know the probability of each of them. Even if one accepts such a device as a way of determining what is fair or not, an open question is to know if such a framework works in the lab. As we have seen, it is not certain that a veiled choice of a group allocation really reflects ethical preferences.

Some papers in political science use a variant of the veil of ignorance approach in which groups deliberate about the principles of justice and next make a decision (Frohlich et al., 1987a, 1987b, Frohlich and Oppenheimer, 1990). Their aim is to test the Rawlsian "original position" and its implications: do people under the condition of a veil of ignorance converge to a consensus about what is fair, and do people agree to maximize the well-being of the worst-off?

10.4.2 Acceptance of the Prioritarian Axioms

Only few experimental papers aim at testing prioritarian axioms, even though there are a number of studies that investigate people's views of distributive justice. It seems there is no clear consensus in the literature. Some papers, like Frohlich et al. (1987a,1987b), Herne and Suojanen (2004) or Traub et al. (2005), find a rejection of maximin or leximin views and a support for maximizing the average income with a floor

[17] In Traub et al. (2005) and Traub et al. (2009), the social planner is pushed to the fore in order to increase her sense of responsibility.

[18] This assumption seems to be empirically valid: see for instance Capellen et al. (2013).

income guarantee. For instance, in Frohlich et al. (1987b), subjects are invited to discuss four alternative views: maximin, maximizing the average income, maximizing the average income while guaranteeing everybody a floor income and maximizing the average income with a range constraint. Their main results are that all the groups reach a consensus and that the most preferred option is to maximize the average income with a floor income (25 over 27 groups, 109 over 149 individuals). Yet other studies have found that respondents express a strong desire to redistribute income (e.g., Dickinson and Tiefenthaler, 2002; Becker and Miller, 2009; Muller and Renes, 2021). Based on a large and heterogeneous pool of German respondents, Muller and Renes (2021) found that the egalitarian allocation is the most popular allocation (50 percent of subjects opt for this allocation) but the maximin solution also remains attractive (40 percent of subjects). Only a low proportion of subjects (10 percent) seek to maximize total income.

Even if such studies are informative, they do not test the prioritarian axioms. To the best of our knowledge, the only lab experiments that are relevant for this purpose are reported by Beckman et al. (2002) and Traub et al. (2009). The former propose a test of the Pareto axiom while the goal of the latter is to study the popular support for the axioms of Pareto and Pigou-Dalton transfer and for the Lorenz and Generalized Lorenz dominance criteria. None of them are trying to test the axioms of anonymity, separability and continuity.

Beckman et al. (2002) test the acceptability of the Pareto axiom according to which social welfare increases if the income of at least one person increases while that of others remains at least unchanged.[19] In their experiment, subjects are grouped by five and are asked to vote between two payoff allocations (one obtained from the other by an increment of payoff of one or several individuals) without and with knowledge of their position in the group. Using a pool of subjects in different countries (the United States, Russia, Taiwan, and China), the authors found that the Pareto axiom is well supported by subjects under the veil of ignorance: on average, the Pareto axiom is rejected in only 10 percent of the relevant comparisons. This rejection rate varies from 5.4 percent in Taiwan to 20 percent in Russia. In the

[19] This axiom was called "monotonicity" in the previous section. We follow here the terminology of Beckman et al. (2002).

treatment in which positions are known, the rejection is higher: from 6.8 percent in the USA to 28 percent in China.

Traub et al. (2009) report the results of an experiment which aims at testing the usual dominance criteria for comparing income distributions. More precisely, they investigate the support for the axioms of Pareto, Pigou-Dalton, Lorenz and Generalized Lorenz dominance in the domain of income. The Lorenz criterion states that an income vector **v** is preferred to a distribution **w** if the share of total income belonging to the $p\%$ poorest individuals in **v** is at least equal to that in **w** for any $p \in [1, 100]$, and strictly larger for at least one $p \in [1, 100]$. The Generalized Lorenz dominance criterion works the same way, except that the share of total income is replaced by the amount of income. That is, **v** is preferred to **w** if the total income belonging to the $p\%$ poorest individuals in **v** is at least equal to that in **w** for any $p \in [1, 100]$, and strictly larger for at least one $p \in [1, 100]$. It can be shown that: (i) acceptance of Pareto and Pigou-Dalton implies acceptance of Generalized Lorenz dominance;[20] (ii) acceptance of Pigou-Dalton implies acceptance of Lorenz dominance.

Subjects are asked to give a complete and strict preference ordering of 12 income distributions. The authors run four treatments varying in terms of the subject's position. We choose here to focus on the two of them that are most relevant to investigate ethical preferences: when the subjects rank distributions under a veil of ignorance (*individual choice* treatment) and when they play the role of a social planner (*social planner* treatment).[21]

[20] More precisely, for two *income* vectors with the same number of individuals, the following conditions are *equivalent*: (i) **v** dominates **w** according to the Generalized Lorenz dominance; (ii) **v** can be obtained from **w** by a series of Pigou-Dalton transfers of income and/or increments of income (Pareto) and/or permutation of individuals; (iii) $\sum_i \phi(v_i) \geq \sum_i \phi(w_i)$ for all ϕ such that $\phi' \geq 0$ and $\phi'' \leq 0$ and $\sum_i \phi(v_i) > \sum_i \phi(w_i)$ for at least one ϕ in this class of functions.

[21] In the two other treatments, subjects are asked to rank lotteries without any reference to an income distribution or are put in the position of a group dictator evaluating distributions in which she is involved. The incentive mechanism in the experiment works as follows. First, in the individual choice treatment, five subjects in the room are randomly selected for payment; in the social planner treatment, six subjects are randomly selected: one for being the social planner (who is visible to all other subjects) and five for payment. Second, two distributions are randomly chosen from the set of the 12 available distributions and the preference ranking over these two distributions is applied for payment.

Table 10.2. *Distributions and their Borda score*

		Individual choice		Social planner	
No	Vector of incomes	Mean	Median	Mean	Median
1	(30, 30, 30, 30, 30)	5.5	6	5.3	6
2	(25, 27.5, 30, 32.5, 35)	6.38	7	5.88	6
3	(20, 25, 30, 35, 40)	6.45	6	6.03	6
4	(20, 20, 30, 40, 40)	5.32	5.5	5.48	5
5	(20, 30, 30, 30, 40)	5.02	5	5.89	7
6	(5, 10, 30, 50, 55)	3.52	2	3.38	2
7	(5, 30, 30, 30, 55)	3.03	2.5	3.62	2.5
8	(35, 35, 50, 55, 60)	9.40	10	8.65	10
9	(35, 35, 35, 45, 90)	9.67	10	8.8	10
10	(7.5, 7.5, 50, 55, 60)	4.05	3.5	4.06	3
11	(7.5, 7.5, 35, 45, 90)	4.28	4	4.88	4.5
12	(0, 30, 40, 125, 125)	3.37	1	4.02	2

Note: Adapted from Traub et al., 2009.
Note: This table reports the payoff distributions and the mean and median Borda counts for individual choice and social planner treatments. Note that the subjects are presented with distributions of ×1000 income.

The second column of Table 10.2 displays the distributions the subjects are asked to rank. Distributions 1–7 have the same mean income and distributions 2-7 can be obtained from distribution 1 by a Pigou-Dalton transfer of incomes. Distributions 8–12 have a higher mean income than distributions 1–7 but a higher level of (relative) inequality. Note that distributions 8 and 9 are the minimal income maximizing distributions. The second column of Table 10.3 reports the number of dominance relationships for each criterion. Interestingly, the authors study how people arbitrate between efficiency and equity. There are 25 cases in which a distribution dominates another one according to the Lorenz criterion but not according to the Generalized Lorenz one (e.g., distribution 8 Lorenz-dominates distribution 9 whereas the Generalized Lorenz criterion is silent). Among the Generalized Lorenz dominance relationships, 13 of them are in conflict with inequality; e.g., inequality is higher in distribution 8 than in distribution 2 according to relative Lorenz dominance but the former dominates the latter according to Generalized Lorenz dominance.

Table 10.3. *Acceptance rates of basic axioms*

Dominance criteria	Nb of cases	Acceptance rate (%) Individual choice	Social planner
Pareto-rank dominance	15	91.8	82.5
Progressive transfer dominance	17	57.8	61.6
Lorenz dominance	53	64.4	61.9
... with trade-off between efficiency and equity	25	59.1	55.2
... with no trade-off	28	75	67.9
Generalized Lorenz dominance	41	75.1	71.8
... with trade-off (no Lorenz dominance)	13	88.2	80.1

Note: Adapted from Traub et al., 2009. The acceptance rate is defined as the mean proportion of responses corresponding to a given dominance criterion.

The experiments were conducted at the University of Hannover with 252 students (between 60 and 66 subjects per treatment). Table 10.2 provides the mean and median Borda counts of each distribution and Table 10.3 summarizes the support of the basic dominance criteria in the two treatments. First, it is found that the Pareto principle is largely accepted by the subjects put in the position of social planner: the subject's choices respect Pareto dominance in 80 percent of the 15 comparisons.[22] This confirms the finding of the Beckman et al. (2002) study, but conflicts with the dominant findings in the questionnaire studies (see Section 10.3.2).

Second, and better in line with the questionnaire studies, the Pigou-Dalton axiom receives relatively low support. The acceptance rate is about 60 percent in both treatments. Considering distributions 1–7 (with the same mean), the aggregate ranking based on (mean) Borda counts is at odds with the ranking according to the Pigou-Dalton axiom: $3 \succ 2 \succ 1 \succ 4 \succ 5 \succ 6 \succ 7$ for the individual choice treatment and $3 \succ 5 \succ 2 \succ 4 \succ 1 \succ 7 \succ 6$ for the social planner treatment

[22] Since this proportion is similar irrespective of the potential conflict with inequity, the authors argue that the non-respect of the principle is due to errors.

against $1 \succ 2 \succ 5 \succ 3 \succ 4 \succ 7 \succ 6$ according to the Pigou-Dalton criterion.

Third, Lorenz dominance also receives low support but is more accepted when there is no conflict between efficiency and inequality. At the same time, Generalized Lorenz dominance is well supported.

The last observation pushes the authors to suggest that subjects have a strong preference for efficiency. However, one could as well argue that subjects (also) put a greater weight on the worst-off members. Indeed, the mean and median Borda counts indicate that the minimal income maximizing distributions (distributions 8 and 9) are the most preferred. Moreover, when comparing distributions 10–11 with distributions 1–5, the latter seem to be preferred to the former although the former have higher average earnings and the Generalized Lorenz dominance criterion is silent.

All in all, these two papers tend to reject one of the main axioms of prioritarianism, namely the Pigou-Dalton axiom applied to income distributions. This is in line with the questionnaire findings. More surprisingly, the Pareto principle seems to be well accepted in the laboratory.

10.4.3 *The Degree of Inequality Aversion*

Some papers studied more deeply how people arbitrate between equity (viewed as maximin) and efficiency (viewed as total income). Schildberg-Hörisch (2010), Frignani and Ponti (2012) and Heufer et al. (2018) try to disentangle the role of ethical and risk preferences behind a veil of ignorance and provide an estimate of inequality aversion. The general framework is a dictator game with uncertainty, i.e. subjects are asked to make a choice of a pair of payoffs within various budget sets:[23]

$$z = qy_1 + y_2 \text{ with } q \geq 1 \text{ and } z > 0 \tag{10.4}$$

where y_1 and y_2 are the low and high payoffs, z the total expenditure and q the cost of averaging payoffs. Three types of choice problem can be introduced. In a *risk problem*, the pair (y_1, y_2) is defined as a pair of payoffs in a bad and high state, the probability of each state being 50

[23] This experimental design was introduced by Andreoni and Miller (2002) and Fisman et al. (2007) to study individual social preferences.

percent. In a *choice under a veil of ignorance*, (y_1, y_2) is the sharing of the total payoff between two persons given that positions have the same probability. Schildberg-Hörisch (2010) and Frignani and Ponti (2012) also run a *standard dictator* treatment where the subjects know their position (as introduced by Andreoni and Miller, 2002).

In Schildberg-Hörisch (2010) the dictator has an endowment of 12 experimental units and has the opportunity to transfer money to the receiver knowing that the transfer is costly (1 unit transferred has a cost of 0.5). Using a pool of 167 subjects from the University of Mannheim, the author found that only 14 percent of subjects exhibit maximin preferences. On average, subjects send 3.5 points from the dictator to the receiver (i.e. 30 percent of the total payoff) entailing a decrease in total payoff from 12 to 10.25 points. Interestingly, she also reported that choices under the veil of ignorance are not (only) explained by risk aversion since subjects send 3.1 points from the good to the bad state in the risk problem. While 44 percent of the subjects transfer the same amount in the two types of decision problem, 35 percent of subjects transfer more in the allocation choice under the veil of ignorance. Finally, in the standard dictator game, subjects transfer 1.6 points, significantly less than when positions are uncertain.

In the experiment conducted by Frignani and Ponti (2012), subjects face 24 decision problems in one of the three conditions described above. Based on a pool of 192 students of Universidad de Alicante, they estimate a simple mean-variance utility function:

$$u_i = \bar{y} - \delta\sigma(y) \tag{10.5}$$

The estimated values of δ are: 0.267 in the standard dictator game, 0.347 under the veil of ignorance,[24] and 0.316 in the risk problem. Importantly, they found that there is no statistically significant difference between the values of δ based on allocation decisions under the veil of ignorance and in the risk problem. That suggests that, on average, decisions made under the veil of ignorance are mainly explained by risk aversion. However, the average values may hide individual heterogeneity, as was found by Schildberg-Hörisch (2010).

Heufer et al. (2018) report an experiment where subjects face 40 decision risk problems and 40 allocation problems under a veil of

[24] For the sake of illustration, with this degree of inequality aversion, (70, 32) is preferred to (44, 44).

ignorance. The use of a within-subject design allows them to take choices in the risk problems as a benchmark to evaluate ethical trade-offs. For instance, if the chosen payoff of the poor is higher (lower) than the one of the bad state, the decision-maker reveals a preference for equality (efficiency). The experiment was conducted in Xiamen University with 92 subjects. We present here some results that may be of interest for the evaluation of prioritarianism.

First, the authors found that the mean transfer to the poor/bad state amounts to 27–28 percent of the total payoff in both types of decision problem. However there is strong heterogeneity between subjects: for 51 of the 92 subjects, the authors cannot reject that they sent the same amount to the low payoff in both treatments. These subjects are classified as socially agnostic. Twenty-four subjects can be classified as equity-preferring in the sense that the amount sent to the poor is higher than the one sent to the bad state. The other seventeen subjects are efficiency-preferring.

Second, the authors estimate the demand functions for the low payoff (see Table 10.4). A rather surprising result is that in the VOI-treatment the demand of the equity-preferring subjects is more sensitive to price than that of the efficiency-preferring subjects. But, as the authors point out, an increase in the expenditure level z (i.e., the total amount to share between qy_1 and y_2) increases the low payoff by a higher amount for the equity-preferring subjects than for the others. Following an increase in z by 10 units, an equity-preferring subject increases the low payoff by 2.4 units, while a subject focusing on efficiency increases it by 1.4 units.

Third, the authors estimate a structural model assuming that a decision maker maximizes the following subjective utility function:[25]

$$V(y_1, y_2) = \alpha \frac{(y_1)^{1-e}}{1-e} + \frac{(y_2)^{1-e}}{1-e} \tag{10.6}$$

where e reflects subject's inequality or risk aversion and α is the ratio between the subjective probability of receiving the low payoff and that of receiving the high payoff ($\alpha > 0$). A value of α larger than 1 means

[25] Note that subjects are fairly rational: there are only 3 violations of the Generalized Axiom of Revealed Preferences (GARP) in risk decision problems and 4 in decisions under the veil of ignorance. The mean value of the critical cost efficiency index (CCEI) is equal to 0.95.

Table 10.4. *Demand for the low payoff*

	Types of subjects		
	Equity	Agnostic	Efficiency
Constant	28.32**	29.79**	28.45**
Price q	−9.57**	−10.06**	−10.24**
Expenditure z	0.20**	0.20**	0.21**
Constant × VOI	5.13**	0.08	−9.06**
Price $q\times$ VOI	−1.93**	0.11	3.71**
Expenditure $z\times$ VOI	0.04**	−0.004	−0.07**
Obs.	1920	4080	1360
R^2	0.72	0.62	0.58

Note: Adapted from Heufer et al., 2018, table 2. Dependent variable: payoff of the poor/bad state. Ordinary Least Squares(OLS) regressions with robust standard errors clustered at the individual level.

that the probability of the low payoff is larger than that of the high payoff.[26] The case where $\alpha = 1$ corresponds to the expected utility criterion. In a risk problem, e may be interpreted as the degree of risk aversion. In an allocation decision under a veil of ignorance, it may capture risk and inequality aversion. The authors estimate equation (10.6) for each subject. Table 10.5 reports the mean and median values of e and α. The level of e is higher in the allocation problem under a veil of ignorance than in the risk problem. Again they found a quite large heterogeneity between subjects, in particular under the veil of ignorance. The comparison of individual estimates of e in the two contexts allows the authors to identify the importance of their three types of preferences. Using the subjective expected utility model, only 20 of 64 subjects are not socially agnostic and, among them eleven are equity-preferring.[27]

26 This is the author's interpretation. However, it seems that in an allocation task under VOI, α can be interpreted as the relative weight one puts on the low payoff (the poor). If this is true, the results seem strange since the estimated mean value of α is about 0.5, suggesting that the rich get a larger weight. Maybe α is not so easy to interpret, in that it captures both the subjective probabilities ratio and the relative weight of the poor.

27 For the other subjects, we can not reject that they are socially agnostic. This inconclusive result may be due to noise.

Table 10.5. ***Estimates of e* and α** for both treatments

	EU: $\alpha = 1$		Subjective utility: $\alpha > 0$		
	e value			*e* value	
	VOI	Risk	α	VOI	Risk
Mean	1.61	1.16	0.53	3.81	2.77
Variance	4.46	3.34	0.25	40.25	8.69
Median	1.16	1.04	0.46	1.82	1.80
p25	0.72	0.73	0.09	1.15	1.09
p75	1.67	1.49	0.76	4.20	3.17

Note: Adapted from Heufer et al. 2018, table 5. Estimates using nonlinear least squares.

While Schildberg-Hörisch (2010), Frignani and Ponti (2012) and Heufer et al. (2018) aim at eliciting distributive preferences of involved decision makers under a veil of ignorance, Hong et al. (2015) use a similar methodology to identify distributive preferences of people put in the position of a social planner. Subjects had to choose an allocation between two other subjects given that $z = qy_1 + y_2$. They face 20 different budget sets varying in z and q. Their results might be summarized in two points. First, as expected, the average share of the poorest decreases with q but the subjects were less sensitive to a change in larger prices. An increase in q from 1 to 5 decreases *B*'s share from 0.47 to 0.22, a further increase from 5 to 10 decreases the share to 0.17.[28] Second, they estimate a Constant-Elasticity-of-Substitution-utility function:[29]

$$V(y_1, y_2) = [\alpha(y_1)^\rho + (1-\alpha)(y_2)^\rho]^{\frac{1}{\rho}} \tag{10.7}$$

Figure 10.8 reports the distribution of the estimates of α and of the elasticity of substitution, i.e., $\sigma = \frac{1}{\rho - 1}$. The median value of σ is found to be equal to -1.20 and σ is lower than -1 for a large part of subjects; that is, they value efficiency more than equity. Only about 20 percent of them have a preference for equity, i.e., σ higher than -1.

[28] However, the use of elasticities may provide a slightly different picture: One obtains arc elasticities of -0.54 and -0.38 and discrete elasticities of -0.13 and -0.23.

[29] The authors found that 56.9 percent of the subjects made choices that satisfied GARP but only 5 percent of them present a CCEI score lower than 0.97; that is, almost all subjects are almost GARP-consistent.

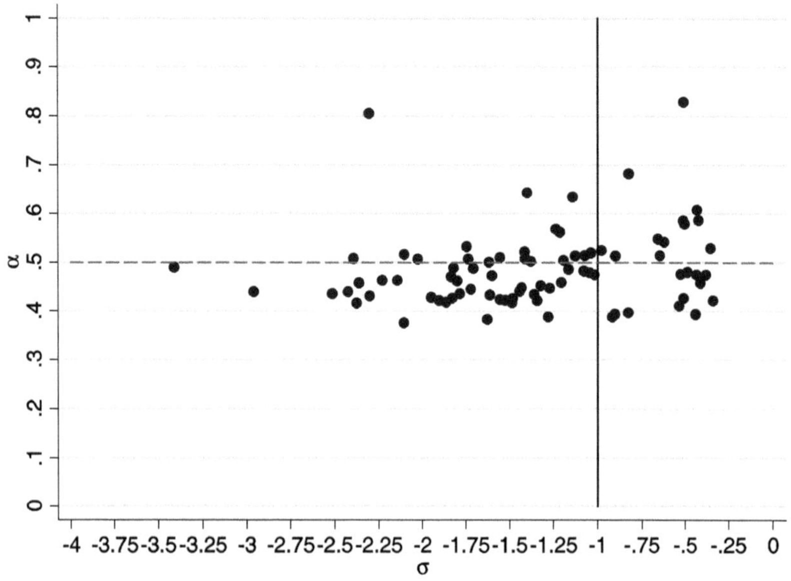

Figure 10.8 Estimates of σ and α
(*Source*: Hong et al., 2015, figure 6)

This experimental research offers valuable insights, even though the case of two-person groups might be considered to be restrictive. The extension of the framework to a setting with more than two stakeholders. raises a rather tricky theoretical question. Typically, the utility functions that are assumed in this research are representations of a social ordering respecting some desirable properties such as the principle of progressive transfer. In a two-person environment, this may be acceptable, but when there are more than two stakeholders, previous research, including the experimental and questionnaire studies described in Sections 10.4.2 and 10.3.2 respectively, has shown that this principle is far from being generally supported.

10.4.4 *Ex Ante versus Ex Post Views*

When we try to integrate risk and uncertainty in the normative evaluation of social situations, one of the most important questions is to determine whether we should adopt an ex ante or an ex post perspective. Within the prioritarian framework, the former approach asserts that **v** is preferred to **w** if the sum of individual's transformed expected well-being is larger in **v** than in **w** while, according to the latter, the comparison is based on the expected sum of individual's transformed well-being. In an Atkinson setting with n individuals and S states, the two approaches can be written formally:

$$W^{EAP} = \sum_{i=1}^{n} g\left(\sum_{s=1}^{S} \pi_s u(z_{is})\right)$$

$$W^{EPP} = \sum_{s=1}^{S} \pi_s \sum_{i=1}^{n} g(u(z_{is}))$$

$$\text{with } g(u) = \frac{u^{1-e}}{1-e}$$

where z_{is} is the payoff of i in state s, π_s the probability of state s, $u(.)$ an individual utility function (with $u' > 0$ and $u'' < 0$ in case of risk aversion) and $g(.)$ a transformation function (with $g' > 0$ and $g'' < 0$ in case of well-being inequality aversion). The ex ante perspective gives priority to the ex ante Pareto principle but violates a Dominance axiom, asserting that **v** should be preferred to **w** if **v** is better than **w** for *every* state of nature. On the contrary, the ex post approach respects Dominance but violates ex ante Pareto.

The papers that we report in this section aim at evaluating whether people adopt an ex ante or ex post view. Rohde and Rohde (2015) propose an experiment in which subjects in the position of a social planner have to rank different allocation of risks between ten stakeholders in a series of pairwise comparisons. The risky allocations to compare are the following:

- Independent lotteries (**I**): Each stakeholder independently faces the lottery $(p : \bar{y}; 1 - p : \underline{y})$, i.e., each stakeholder can be in one of the two states (she receives $\bar{y}$ or $\underline{y}$).
- Common Lottery (**CL**): All the stakeholders face the common lottery $(p : \bar{y}, 1 - p : \underline{y})$; i.e., there are only two social states (all receive $\bar{y}$ or all receive $\underline{y}$).
- Random Distribution (**R**): Five randomly drawn stakeholders receive $\bar{y}$ and the others receive $\underline{y}$.
- ID-based Distribution (**Id**): Five stakeholders receive $\bar{y}$ and the others receive $\underline{y}$ based on the student ID-number.
- Common Outcome (**CO**): All receive $(\bar{y} + \underline{y})/2$.

In the experiment, three sets of parameters are tested: $\left(p, \bar{y}, \underline{y}\right) = (0.5, 10, 5)$, $(0.2, 11.5, 6.5)$, and $(0.7, 9, 3)$.

Let us focus on the two first risk allocations. The authors describe the choice between them as follows. If one seeks to minimize the *expected* standard deviation of incomes ("pure" ex post inequality minimizing choice), then CL should be preferred. If the objective is to minimize the standard deviation of expected incomes (ex ante inequality minimizing choice), then one should be indifferent between CL and I. However note that collective risk is smaller for the independent lotteries than for the common lottery. Thus if a social planner prefers CL to I, she reveals a strong preference for ex post equality (despite the increase in the collective risk) or for collective risk seeking. The overall ranking allows the authors to disentangle attitudes with respect to ex ante and ex-post inequality and with respect to individual and collective risk.

The experiment was run at the Erasmus University of Rotterdam with 55 subjects. The aggregate ranking turns out to be: $\mathbf{CO} \sim \mathbf{I} \succsim \mathbf{CL} \succ \mathbf{R} \succ \mathbf{Id}$, and a large majority of subjects are consistent with this overall ranking. To better understand this result, the authors estimate a logit econometric model in which the value of an allocation depends on ex ante and ex post inequality and individual and collective risk (both measured by the variance of payoffs). The subjects are found to be ex ante inequality averse, individual risk averse, ex-post inequality seeking and collective risk seeking.

Another relevant experiment is conducted by Cettolin and Riedl (2016). Their subjects play the role of a social planner and are asked to allocate an amount of money, say z, between two *other* stakeholders, denoted C and U: $z = z_U + z_C$. The amount sent to C is certain, i.e. the amount of money allocated to C by the social planner is the one C receives. The amount received by U, denoted $\tilde{z}_U$, is not certain: U will receive $k^H z_U$ with probability p and $k^L z_U$ with probability $(1-p)$, where k^H and k^L are two multipliers such that $k^H > 1$ and $1 > k^L \geq 0$. The constraint imposed in the experiment is that the amount allocated to U is the expected payoff of U (then the expected total payoff remains constant). Formally:

$$z_U = E(\tilde{z}_U) = pk^H z_U + (1-p)k^L z_U.$$

Table 10.6. ***Amount given to U***

	Value of parameters			Amount given to ***U***	
Allocation problem	p	k^H	k^L	Mean	Std dev
1-Certainty	1	1	.	8.39	1.59
2-Risk	0.5	1.5	0.5	8.50	1.43
3-Risk	0.8	1.25	0	8.13	1.69
4-Risk	0.5	2	0	7.33	2.10
5-Risk	0.2	5	0	5.10	2.84

Note: Adapted from Cettolin and Riedl, 2016, table 3.

The amount of z is determined in a preliminary production phase (in which the productivity levels are similar between the two stakeholders).[30] Five types of allocation problems (i.e., sets of parameters) are displayed in Table 10.6.

The authors test whether the choices made by their subjects can be rationalized by the following views of justice:

- equality of expected payoffs (z_U should be always equal to 8);
- equality of expected utilities when utility is defined as $u(z) = z^\alpha$;
- ex post equality when equality is measured by the absolute difference between payoffs;
- utilitarianism, again with the utility function $u(z) = z^\alpha$.[31]

Table 10.7 reports the optimal choices according to the last three views (in the three last columns) given that $\alpha = 0.72$.[32] The first columns of Table 10.7 report some predictions of choices of z_U according to ex ante and ex post prioritarianism (EAP and EPP) for

[30] The subjects performed a very simple "slider task." Each group of stakeholders could earn a maximum of 16 euros and almost all groups earned 16 euros.

[31] The optimal choices are then:

Equality of expected utilities: $z_U^{EEU} = \frac{z}{K^{\frac{1}{\alpha}}+1}$ with $K = p\left(k^H\right)^\alpha + (1-p)\left(k^L\right)^\alpha$

Ex post equality: $z_U^{EPE} = \frac{1}{k^H+1} z$ if $k^H > \frac{1-p}{p}$ (always true in the experiment)

Utilitarianism: $z_U^U = \frac{z}{K^{\frac{1}{\alpha-1}}+1}$

[32] The authors elicited in a pre-experimental task the subject's belief about the others' risk preference. The subject's mean level of α is 0.72.

Table 10.7. *Some predictions – choice of* Z_U

	EAP	EPP	EAP	EPP	EAP	EPP	Utilitarian		
	$\gamma = 0.1$		$\gamma = 0.5$		$\gamma = 0.9$		$\gamma = 0$	EU equality	Ex Post equality
2-Risk	7.72	7.64	7.91	7.80	7.99	7.96	7.61	8.15	6.4
3-Risk	7.36	7.11	7.80	7.11	7.97	7.11	7.11	8.35	7.11
4-Risk	6.05	5.33	7.39	5.33	7.92	5.33	5.33	9.07	5.33
5-Risk	3.84	2.67	6.61	2.67	7.81	2.67	2.67	10.42	2.67

different levels of e.[33] First, the EAP and EPP optimal choices are quite similar in a low-risk situation but can be better distinguished when riskiness is larger. Second, due to the specific structure of the decision problem and the values of the parameters, a utilitarian planner and an ex post prioritarian one will choose the same level of z_U. Third, ex post equality and ex post prioritarianism also have similar predictions.

The authors ran the experiment with a pool of 90 subjects from the Maastricht University School of Business and Economics. Their results are quite different from the ones obtained by Rohde and Rohde (2015). The two last columns of Table 10.6 indicate the mean value and standard deviation of the amount sent to U. First, the amount sent to U is decreasing with riskiness for a rather high level of riskiness. There is no clear difference in the mean value of z_U between certainty and 2-Risk/3-Risk problems while it seems significantly lower in 4-Risk/5-Risk problems. Second, the dispersion becomes larger with riskiness, suggesting that there exists a strong heterogeneity across subjects. The authors then estimate for each social planner the view of justice that best fits her choices.[34] They find that 43 percent of the subjects equalize expected payoffs, 36 percent act as if they are utilitarian, 14 percent seek ex post equality, and 7 percent seek equality of expected utilities.

Finally, Andreoni et al. (2020) study the problem of allocating lottery tickets. Twenty lottery tickets have to be allocated between two poor (and equally-deserving) Kenyan households, denoted A and B. Ten of these tickets are randomly allocated by a computer and the problem of a social planner is to allocate the 10 remaining tickets. Next, one ticket is randomly drawn and the household to which the ticket is assigned receives \$10. Three classes of decision problems are studied. In a first class of problems (called *ex ante decision*), the decision of the social planner comes after learning the allocation of

[33] The optimal choices of ex ante and ex post prioritarianism are:

$$z_U^{EAP} = \frac{z}{K^{\frac{1-e}{\alpha(1-e)-1}} + 1} \text{ with } K = p\left(k^H\right)^{\alpha} + (1-p)\left(k^L\right)^{\alpha}$$

$$z_U^{EPP} = \frac{z}{M^{\frac{1}{\alpha(1-e)-1}} + 1} \text{ with } M = p\left(k^H\right)^{\alpha(1-e)} + (1-p)\left(k^L\right)^{\alpha(1-e)}$$

[34] As for the level of α, the authors use the social planner's belief about the risk aversion of others, elicited in a pre-experimental task.

the computer. In a second class (called *ex post decision*), the decision is made *after* learning whether the winning ticket is one of the computer's tickets or one of hers. A third one (called *ex ante decision with revision*) is similar to the *ex ante decision* frame except that, after her decision, the social planner is given the information about whether the winning ticket is one of the computer's tickets or one of hers and she can change her initial decision.

Suppose that the computer assigned six tickets to A. Let us first focus on an ex ante prioritarian social planner. The pattern of choices should be as follows: (i) she allocates four tickets to A in an *ex ante decision* frame; (ii) five tickets to A in an *ex post decision* frame; and (iii) revises her allocation in *ex ante decision with revision*. Andreoni et al. (2020) consider such a pattern of choices as time-inconsistent since the social planner fails to stick to her initial plan.[35] Then a fair ex ante consequentialist should commit herself against any change in choices. On the contrary, if one seeks to minimize ex post inequality of *earnings*, all the allocations of tickets are equivalent in terms of desirability since the same allocation, i.e., $(0, 10)$, is reached.[36]

Based on a pool of subjects from the University of California, San Diego, the authors report that most subjects equalize the chances of having the winning tickets in *ex ante decision* (more than 60 percent of choices) and *ex post decision* (about 45 percent of choices) settings. Moreover, when subjects have the opportunity to change their allocation after knowing the computer's allocations of its tickets (*ex ante decision with revision*), they tend to switch to the ex post equalizing choice, i.e., five tickets for both households.[37] Moreover, in an additional treatment in which subjects are free to make a contingent plan, they tend to plan to switch an ex ante equalizing choice to an ex post equalizing choice.

The authors also present a variant of this experiment in which subjects are invited to allocate \$10 between the two households in the same frames, given that there is a 50 percent probability that their

[35] However, one could also think that it is rational to change one's mind after receiving new (and relevant) information.

[36] Note that Andreoni et al. (2020) classifies as ex post equalizing choice a choice that gives five tickets to both potential recipients.

[37] The findings of additional treatments indicate that such a preference is strict and can not be explained by the resolution of indifference. That is, their choices are not consistent with ex post consequentialism.

choice is selected for payment and a 50 percent probability that the computer's choice is selected. Note that, according to an ex post inequality-averse view, one should always choose the allocation (5, 5). As for a social planner with a sufficiently large ex ante inequality aversion, she will choose an allocation that permits the equalization of expected utilities and may therefore change her choice once it is revealed whether it is the computer or her allocation that is selected for payment. The subjects are found to have a preference for equalizing expected utilities in *ex ante decision* (about 50 percent) even though the choice of equalizing the ex post distribution of payoffs represents a substantial part of choices (about 20 percent). When it is revealed that the subject's allocation is used for payment, subjects revise their choice and opt for an egalitarian allocation, i.e., $5 for each household (about 50 percent of choices).

All in all, according to the author's interpretation, this result contradicts fair (ex ante or ex post) consequentialism and indicates that subjects exhibit a time-consistent preference for applying a naive deontological principle (here equality).

These three papers give very different pictures of what could be people's ethical preferences in a risky or uncertain world. It is difficult to reconcile all these findings without any further research. Andreoni et al. (2020) stress an important (methodological) issue. Subjects probably have some difficulties grasping the decision of allocating uncertain resources (or chances) among people. The decision framing might thus play an important role. For instance, in the Rohde and Rohde (2015) experiment, allocations are displayed in such a way that subjects consider the problem in an ex ante perspective and do not pay attention to the possible ex post inequalities. As Andreoni et al. (2020) emphasize, lowering the cognitive overload associated with such a task may be an important challenge if we want to understand people's preferences. This brings us back to one of the basic insights of this chapter. It is not easy to "test" sophisticated ethical theories, such as prioritarianism, on the basis of the answers and/or the behavior of unsophisticated agents. On the other hand, in the real world people also take their decisions in framed situations. Understanding how the frame influences their distributive preferences may therefore be an interesting research question. Finally, it can be pointed out that these papers aim at studying what choices made by subjects in an allocation problem reveal about their underlying subjective social welfare function. Instead, it would be interesting to test directly the empirical support for basic principles such as the Dominance axiom and the ex ante Pareto principle.

10.4.5 A Broader Set of Questions: Welfarism, Desert and Taxation

We have described in Section 10.3.5 how questionnaire studies have found over and over again that the source of income differences is a crucial factor in distributive judgments. This finding is corroborated by the growing literature in experimental economics studying the role of effort and choices influencing the initial inequalities or the total income (Frohlich and Oppenheimer, 1990, Konow, 2000, Dickinson and Tiefenthaler, 2002, Capelen et al., 2013, Durante et al., 2014, Almas et al, 2010).[38] The method used in these papers consists of adding a *production phase* to the game: that might be an effort task like a quiz (Dickinson and Tiefenthaler, 2002, Durante et al., 2014), a computer game (Tetris in Durante et al., 2014), preparing letters for mailing (Konow, 2000) or risk-taking choice (Cappelen et al., 2013, Akbas et al., 2019, Mollerstrom et al., 2015). In all these studies, people are found to be less willing to redistribute when income differences are due to effort.

In a recent paper, Almas et al. (2020) report an experiment in which a social planner has the opportunity to redistribute income between two workers, that are recruited from the platform Amazon Mechanical Turk to complete small tasks. They are paired by groups. One worker is initially assigned $6 and the other $0 for completing the task. In the *luck treatment*, the assignment is randomly determined; in the *merit treatment*, the assignment is made according to the productivity level. The social planner then has the choice between seven allocations, from (6,0) to (0,6), and there is no cost of redistribution.[39] The experiment was run online with Norwegian and US subjects. When income

[38] We report here the experiments that aim to identify the ethical preferences of the social planner. There is also a growing literature studying how the sources of inequality affect ethical preferences or preferences for redistribution. See Cappelen et al. (2007), Cappelen et al. (2010), Almas et al. (2010), Balafoutas et al. (2013), Durante et al. (2014).

[39] They also ran an additional treatment where transferring earnings to the poorest worker is costly.

differences reflect luck, about 80 percent of Norwegian social planners and 55 percent of US social planners choose the equal distribution (3,3). In the merit treatment, social planners accept a higher level of inequality. Allocation (4,2) is the preferred option in Norway (more than 40 percent of Norwegian social planners) and (3,3) is chosen by 35 percent of them. Among the US social planners, allocations (4,2) and (6,0) are the most attractive (with about 40 percent of US social planners). This echoes the findings of intercultural differences that were reported in Section 10.2.

Some papers tackle the role of brute and option luck. In an experiment conducted by Cappelen et al. (2013), social planners can distribute a total amount of money between two subjects given that the total amount is determined by a choice between lotteries (a risky lottery versus a safe lottery). The authors found that social planners are willing to compensate inequality due to luck between two risk takers, but do not make transfers from a safer to an unlucky risk-taker (see also Akbas et al., 2019). Further, responsibility seems to be considered by social planners in a complex way. In an experiment where subjects face risk but have the opportunity to insure against it, Mollerstrom et al. (2015) report that social planners are less willing to compensate inequality due to bad brute luck when stakeholders do not make effort to control randomness. As mentioned already in Section 10.3.5, this almost universal finding that the source of income differences matters, raises an important challenge for prioritarian welfarism.

Few experimental papers study ethical preferences over taxation. In Durante et al. (2014), subjects are invited to choose a tax and redistribution scheme that consists of a proportional tax rate with a demogrant. The authors study preferences for redistribution in different contexts: position (involved behind a veil of ignorance or not), efficiency cost, sources of income. However, they use taxation as a frame to elicit ethical and social preferences but do not study whether people's ethical preferences are different in the specific context of taxation. In a recent paper, Charité et al. (2015) show that subjects in a position of redistributing unequal and unearned initial endowments between two recipients do not make the same choice whether the recipients know their initial endowment or not. It is found that allocators tend to be less willing to redistribute when initial endowments are known. The authors explain their result by the fact that allocators anticipate loss aversion, initial endowment being the reference point.

Again, this result seems to contradict prioritarian consequentialism according to which pre-tax incomes should not matter for the evaluation of the taxation scheme.

10.5 "Testing" Prioritarianism?

Let us now take stock and ask how relevant this empirical work is to better understand the popular acceptance of prioritarianism, or to get an estimate of the value of the crucial parameters, as perceived by the population. Let us start with the questionnaire studies. Traditionally, economists have been rather reluctant to take unincentivized answers by respondents seriously, but this attitude is recently changing. And rightly so. Answers on questionnaires should indeed not be trusted if we want to predict behavior, but they are very useful for gaining a better insight into ethical preferences. Ethical preferences are only one of the determinants of behavior, but they are worth investigating for their own sake, e.g., to check whether a given normative framework, such as prioritarianism, is popular among the population.

We have already mentioned the main limitation of the questionnaire studies on prioritarianism: the respondents are asked to evaluate income (or health) distributions, not distributions of well-being. This makes it impossible to interpret the results directly within a prioritarian framework. More specifically, it is not possible to rigorously distinguish utilitarianism and prioritarianism, as a utilitarian would also advocate income redistribution under the assumption of concave individual well-being functions. Analogously, the empirical estimates of the degree of inequality aversion relate to income or health levels, or to income-related health inequalities, not to individual well-being levels, and therefore do not yield an estimate of the inequality aversion η in the general prioritarian social welfare function analyzed in this book.

This does not mean, of course, that the results are not informative. The opposition to the basic axioms underlying prioritarianism, such as the Pigou-Dalton transfer principle or the axiom of monotonicity, remains relevant even when we take into account that they are formulated in the space of incomes. The rejection of monotonicity suggests that income externalities play some role in the ethical preferences of the respondents. Rejection of the transfer principle is even more fundamental, as one would certainly expect this principle to be satisfied within a prioritarian framework. Here, externalities may also play a role. As we have seen, the transfer principle is most often rejected when the income transfer tends to "isolate" the poor, which suggests that respondents imagine that the growing income gap between the poorest and the second-poorest decreases the well-being of the poorest even if their income does not change. More research is needed to better understand the rationale for the rejection of the transfer principle in the space of incomes.

The partial results on inequality aversion may also be useful inputs if the aim is to get a better insight into the structure of the prioritarian social welfare function. Sticking as before to the Atkinson framework, we can write this function as

$$S = \frac{1}{1-e}\sum_i w(y_i, H_i)^{1-e}, \tag{10.8}$$

which can be directly compared to the simpler forms (10.1)–(10.3). Studies such as those described in Section 10.3.3 (yielding estimates for e and ε) should be helpful to think about the specification of $w(.)$ and to estimate the parameter e. In fact, in a von Neumann-Morgenstern setting this work could be combined with other empirical work aiming at estimating the degree of risk aversion in the function $w(.)$. Interesting examples of this approach are Johansson-Stenman et al. (2002) and Carlsson et al. (2005), but they focus on relative incomes and interpret inequality as affecting individual well-being rather than as a normative parameter which does not necessarily depend on individual self-interested preferences.

The pros and cons of laboratory experiments to some extent mirror the pros and cons of questionnaire studies. Basically, they investigate how individuals in a lab share wealth within a small group. To be relevant for a discussion of prioritarianism, we need to make the crucial assumption that the choices made by subjects reveal their true ethical preferences. In a significant part of these experiments, subjects in the position of a social planner are asked to share an amount of money between other subjects. Some could argue that such experiments do not provide any informative insights because of the lack of incentives. This criticism is similar to the traditional criticism on questionnaire studies. In another set of experiments, participants are put behind a veil of ignorance. Although this procedure is suggested by (a part of) the philosophical literature, one can argue that participants behind a VOI are likely to reveal their risk preferences rather than their ethical ones. Second, even if the lab experiments correctly reveal the participant's ethical preferences, these can only be the preferences on (re)distribution within a small group. Does this say anything about their ethical preferences in a large society? One might think that these two contexts (a small group of students in a lab and a large and diverse society) imply different types of ethical reasoning. First, it is difficult to capture in a lab all relevant dimensions that may play a role in larger groups. For instance, transferring wealth between two persons might be differently evaluated depending on the presence of others. This echoes the findings about Pigou-Dalton in the questionnaires. Second, a laboratory is a small artificial society in which the norm is generally to earn as much money as possible.[40] A society is a set of people sharing values, norms, friendship, solidarity and identity that we fail to capture in the lab. For instance, persons may attach more importance to efficiency than to equity when sharing a resource in the lab than they would outside – even though they are not involved.

Yet, despite these problems, lab experiments remain very useful. First, we believe that one can be confident that what is revealed in a lab are the participant's ethical preferences. Assume, for instance, that a participant's preferences are represented by a utility function such as $v(x) = u(x_i) + \alpha w(x)$ where $x_i = (x_1, \ldots, x_i, \ldots)$ is the social state, x_j the payment of individual j, u is the self-centered utility function, w is the social welfare function and α is the weight put on the social welfare relative to her own self-centered utility. Then, in a position of a non-involved spectator, x_i is constant and her choice of a distribution of payoffs should reveal her ethical ranking. Moreover, the empirical work tends to show that, at least in the experiments using the spectator framework, participants reveal their ethical preferences rather than making only random choices (e.g., Cettolin and Riedl, 2016).

Second, eliciting ethical preferences in the field is almost impossible. It is very rare that people have to allocate resources within a group and, if this is the case (e.g. a manager who sets wages of her employees), decisions are not determined only by ethical preferences. Lab-experimental work may then helpfully complement questionnaire-experimental studies. In particular, it might inform whether stated

[40] The relative acceptance of the Pareto axiom in lab experiments might be explained by such a norm.

ethical preferences are consistent with allocative choices when there is a *real* stake. Moreover, placing individuals in the position of allocating a resource within a small group can be a good way to remove any external disturbances, such as those described in Section 10.2. A prime example is the biased perception of the actual situation. As we argued earlier, in a reflective equilibrium setting, we confront general principles with "relevant normative facts," and behavior in the lab can certainly be seen as normatively relevant information.

Finally, a significant part of the empirical studies we reported put the respondent in a position of choosing a wealth/health distribution behind the Harsanyi or Rawlsian veil of ignorance. There may indeed be doubts whether the veil of ignorance is the appropriate standpoint for determining what is fair or unfair. Harsanyi has argued that an agent behind the veil of ignorance should behave as a utilitarian social planner, reinforcing the view that it is not *rational* to be prioritarian. However, some authors argue that such a result is questionable on the ground that it is not obvious that his representation theorem justifies utilitarianism (see Roemer (1996) for a summary of the debate).[41] Moreover, it is not clear that society's preferences over social states should be derived from preferences behind a veil of ignorance (see Sen, 2009, for a deeper discussion). The finding, both in the questionnaire studies and in the lab experiments, that subjects in the role of external observer (or social planner) take different decisions than behind a veil of ignorance, is certainly relevant in this whole discussion. Moreover, even if we do believe that the uninvolved spectator is the *most* appropriate view for judging the fairness of a situation, decisions made by individuals facing lotteries of social states might still contribute to our understanding of people's ethical preferences.

10.6 Conclusion

The results summarized in this chapter are useful to assess the political feasibility of prioritarian policy evaluation in a democratic society. Another question is whether they can be used directly to guide

[41] Indeed, Harsanyi (1955) shows that the sum of individual vNM utilities is the only function that represents a social ordering over a lottery of social states when the social preference and individual's preference over social states respect the vNM axioms. It is not clear that the summation can be interpreted as the sum of individual "utilities."

normative tax analysis (as is suggested, e.g. by Weinzierl, 2014). This seems premature, as most of the questions raised in the representative questionnaire studies are rather simplistic, and the setting of the behavioral experiments is highly stylized. We first have to understand better the underlying structure of the ethical attitudes and their robustness. As we have seen, individuals change their views when they receive more information. Moreover, while we sometimes have seen strong majorities on some issues, there is almost never a full social consensus. A large degree of preference heterogeneity is found both in the survey studies and in the lab. Society therefore still has to devise an acceptable procedure to aggregate conflicting attitudes. It is tempting for social researchers to just take the average (or the median, or the majority) answers to specific questions, but it remains to be investigated if and under which circumstances these simple procedures yield socially desirable outcomes.

The relevance of these results from a normative point of view raises similar questions. The fact that welfarism in general, and more specifically prioritarianism, do not seem to be the dominant ethical views among the population of our societies is not an argument against them as a chosen ethical framework. It still raises two challenges, however. From a sociopolitical point of view, it gives us a good idea of the difficult task that lies ahead of us if we want to foster sufficient democratic support for the prioritarian policies that are described in the other chapters of this volume. From an academic point of view, it invites us to confront explicitly the deviating opinions. Is the Pigou-Dalton transfer principle indeed a crucial building block of our social welfare function – or is there some truth in the widely held view that it becomes problematic in a society with more than two individuals? Does the fact that preferences of respondents behind a veil of ignorance are different from their preferences as a social planner indicate that the veil of ignorance is a misleading device to recover social welfare judgments? Are ideas like "equal sacrifice" or "progressive taxation as a value in itself" ethically attractive? If they are, should they be integrated into prioritarian thinking? Or should they be seen as independent principles? But then, how to think about the trade-off between respecting these principles and optimizing a social welfare function? How to handle the dominant view that individuals should be held responsible for part of their outcomes? Is the normative definition of well-being that is explored in theories of fair allocation an attractive way out, or does this approach remove us too far from the basic intuition that individual well-being is not only normative, but has necessarily some underlying psychological basis? The empirical research on distributive preferences cannot answer these questions, but it has the merit to put them on the table.

References

Abasolo, I. and Tsuchiya, A. (2004). "Exploring social welfare functions and violations of monotonicity: an example from inequalities in health." *Journal of Health Economics*, 23: 313–329.

(2013) "Is more health always better for society? Exploring public preferences that violate monotonicity." *Theory and Decision*, 74: 539–563.

Aguiar, F., Becker, A. and Miller, L. (2013). "Whose impartiality? An experimental study of veiled stakeholders, involved spectators and detached observers." *Economics and Philosophy*, 29: 155–174.

Akbas, M., Ariely, D. and Yuksel, S. (2019). "When is inequality fair? An experiment on the effect of procedural justice and agency." *Journal of Economic Behavior and Organization*, 161: 114–127.

Alesina, A. and Angeletos, G.-M. (2005). "Fairness and redistribution." *American Economic Review*, 95: 960–980.

Alesina, A. and Giuliano, P. (2011). "Preferences for redistribution." In Benhabib, J., Bisin, A. and Jackson, M., eds., *Handbook of Social Economics, Vol. 1A*. New York: Elsevier, pp. 93–131.

Alesina, A., Stantcheva, S. and Teso, E. (2018). "Intergenerational mobility and support for redistribution." *American Economic Review*, 108: 521–554.

Almas, I., Cappelen, A.W., Sorensen, E., and Tungodden, B. (2010). "Fairness and the development of inequality acceptance." *Science*, 328: 1176–1178.

Almas, I., Cappelen, A.W. and Tungodden, B. (2020). "Cutthroat capitalism versus cuddly socialism: Are Americans more meritocratic and efficiency-seeking than Scandinavians?" *Journal of Political Economy*, 128: 1753–1788.

Amiel, Y. and Cowell, F. (1994). "Monotonicity, dominance and the Pareto principle." *Economics Letters*, 45: 447–450.

(1999). *Thinking about Inequality*. Cambridge: Cambridge University Press.

Amiel, Y., Cowell, F. and Gaertner, W. (2009). "To be or not to be involved: a questionnaire-experimental view on Harsanyi's utilitarian ethics." *Social Choice and Welfare*, 32: 253–274.

Amiel, Y., Creedy, J. and Hurn, D. (1999). "Attitudes towards inequality." *Scandinavian Journal of Economics*, 101: 83–96.

Andreoni, J., Aydin, D., Barton, B., Bernheim, B.D., and Naecker, J. (2020). "When fair isn't fair: Understanding choice reversals involving social preferences." *Journal of Political Economy*, 128: 1673–1711.

Andreoni, J. and Miller, J. (2002). "Giving according to garp: An experimental test of the consistency of preferences for altruism." *Econometrica*, 70: 737–753.

Balafoutas, L., Kocher, M.G., Putterman, L. and Sutter, M. (2013). "Equality, equity and incentives: an experiment." *European Economic Review*, 60: 32–51.

Ballano, C. and Ruiz-Castillo, J. (1993). "Searching by questionnaire for the meaning of income inequality." *Revista Espanola de Economia*, 10: 233–259.

Becker, A. and Miller, L.M. (2009). "Promoting justice by treating people unequally: an experimental study." *Experimental Economics*, 12: 437–449.

Beckman, S.R., Formby, J.P., Smith, W.J. and Zheng, B. (2002). "Envy, malice and pareto efficiency: an experimental examination." *Social Choice and Welfare*, 19: 349–367.

Bénabou, R. and Ok, E. (2001). "Social mobility and the demand for redistribution: the POUM hypothesis." *Quarterly Journal of Economics*, 116: 447–487.

Bénabou, R. and Tirole, J. (2006). "Belief in a just world and redistributive politics." *Quarterly Journal of Economics*, 121: 699–746.

Bernasconi, M. (2002). "How should income be divided? Questionnaire evidence from the theory of " impartial preferences." *Journal of Economics Supplement*, 9: 163–195.

Bleichrodt, H., Rohde, K. and Van Ourti, T. (2012). "An experimental test of the concentration index." *Journal of Health Economics*, 31: 86–98.

Bosmans, K. and Schokkaert, E. (2004). "Social welfare, the veil of ignorance and purely individual risk: an empirical examination." *Research on Economic Inequality*, 11: 85–114.

Cappelen, A.W., Hole, A.D., Sorensen, E. and Tungodden, B. (2007). "The pluralism of fairness ideals: an experimental approach." *American Economic Review*, 97: 818–827.

Cappelen, A.W., Konow, J., Sorensen, E. and Tungodden, B. (2013). "Just luck: An experimental study of risk-taking and fairness." *American Economic Review*, 103: 1398–1413.

Cappelen, A.W., Sorensen, E. and Tungodden, B. (2010). "Responsibility for what? Fairness and individual responsibility." *European Economic Review*, 54: 429–441.

Carlsson, F., Daruvala, D. and Johansson-Stenman, O. (2005). "Are people inequality averse or just risk averse?" *Economica*, 72: 375–396.

Cettolin, E. and Riedl, A. (2016). "Justice under uncertainty." *Management Science*, 63: 3739–3759.

Charité, J., Fisman, R. and Kuziemko, I. (2015). "Reference points and redistributive preferences: Experimental evidence." *NBER Working Paper* No. 21009.

Charness, G. and Rabin, M. (2002). "Understanding social preferences with simple tests." *Quarterly Journal of Economics*, 117: 817–869.

Clark, A. and d'Ambrosio, C. (2015). "Attitudes to income inequality: experimental and survey evidence." In Atkinson, A. and Bourguignon, F., eds., *Handbook of Income Distribution, Vol. 2A*. New York: Elsevier, pp. 1147–1208.

Cookson, R., Ali, S., Tsuchiya, A. and Asaria, M. (2018). "E-learning and health inequality aversion: a questionnaire experiment." *Health Economics*, 27: 754–1771.

Cooper, D. and Kagel, J.H. (2015). "Other-regarding preferences: A selective survey of experimental results." In Kagel, J. H. and Roth, A. E., eds., *Handbook of Experimental Economics, Vol. 2*. Princeton: Princeton University Press, pp. 217–289.

Costa-Font, J. and Cowell, F. (2019). "Incorporating inequality aversion in health-care priority setting." *Social Justice Research*, 32: 172–185.

Cruces, G., Perez-Truglia, R. and Tetaz, M. (2013). "Biased perceptions of income distribution and preferences for redistribution: evidence from a survey experiment." *Journal of Public Economics*, 98: 100–112.

Dickinson, D.L. and Tiefenthaler, J. (2002). "What Is Fair? Experimental Evidence." *Southern Economic Journal*, 69: 414–428.

Dolan, P. and Tsuchiya, A. (2011). "Determining the parameters in a social welfare function using stated preference data: an application to health." *Applied Economics*, 43: 2241–2250.

Durante, R., Putterman, L. and van der Weele, J. (2014). "Preferences for redistribution and perception of fairness: an experimental study." *Journal of the European Economic Association*, 12: 1059–1086.

Edlin, R., Tsuchiya, A. and Dolan, P. (2012). "Public preferences for responsibility versus public preferences for reducing inequalities." *Health Economics*, 21: 1416–1426.

Engelmann, D. and Strobel, M. (2004). "Inequality aversion, efficiency, and maximin preferences in simple distribution experiments." *American Economic Review*, 94: 857–869.

Fehr, E., Naef, M. and Schmidt, K.M. (2006). "Inequality aversion, efficiency, and maximin preferences in simple distribution experiments: comment." *American Economic Review*, 96: 1912–1917.

Fisman, R., Kariv, S. and Markovits, D. (2007). "Individual preferences for giving." *American Economic Review*, 97: 1858–1876.

Fleurbaey, M. and Maniquet, F. (2018). "Optimal income taxation theory and principles of fairness." *Journal of Economic Literature*, 56: 1029–1079.

(2011). *A Theory of Fairness and Social Welfare*. Cambridge: Cambridge University Press.

Fong, C. (2001). "Social preferences, self-interest, and the demand for redistribution." *Journal of Public Economics*, 82: 225–246.

Frignani, N. and Ponti, G. (2012). "Risk versus social preferences under the veil of ignorance." *Economics Letters*, 116: 143–146.

Frohlich, N. and Oppenheimer, J.A. (1990). "Choosing justice in experimental democracies with production." *American Political Science Review*, 84: 461–477.

Frohlich, N., Oppenheimer, J.A., and Eavey, C.L. (1987a). "Choices of principles of distributive justice in experimental groups." *American Journal of Political Science*, 31: 606–636.

(1987b). "Laboratory results on Rawls's distributive justice." *British Journal of Political Science*, 17: 1–21.

Gaertner, W. and Schokkaert, E. (2012). *Empirical social choice*. Cambridge: Cambridge University Press.

Giuliano, P. and Spilimbergo, A. (2014). "Growing up in a recession." *Review of Economic Studies*, 81: 787–817.

Glejser, H., Gevers, L., Lambot, P. and Morales, J. (1977). "An econometric study of the variables determining inequality aversion among students." *European Economic Review*, 10: 173–188.

Güth, W. and Kliemt, H. (2010). "What ethics can learn from experimental economics - if anything." *European Journal of Political Economy*, 26: 302–310.

Harrison, E. and Seidl, C. (1994). "Acceptance of distributional axioms: experimental findings." In Eichhorn, W., ed., *Models and measurement of welfare and inequality*. Berlin: Springer-Verlag, pp. 67–99.

Harsanyi, J. (1953). "Cardinal utility in welfare economics and the theory of risk-taking." *Journal of Political Economy*, 61: 434–435.

(1955). "Cardinal welfare, individualistic ethics and interpersonal comparisons of utility." *Journal of Political Economy*, 63: 309–321.

Hausman, D. (2015). *Valuing Health: Well-being, Freedom, and Suffering*. Oxford: Oxford University Press.

Herne, K. and Suojanen, M. (2004). "The role of information in choices over income distributions." *Journal of Conflict Resolution*, 48: 173–193.

Heufer, J., Shachat, J. and Xu, Y. (2018). "Measuring tastes for equity and aggregate wealth behind the veil of ignorance." *Tinbergen Institute Discussion Paper*, TI 2018-087/I.

Hong, H., Ding, J. and Yao, Y. (2015). "Individual social welfare preferences: an experimental study." *Journal of Behavioral and Experimental Economics*, 57: 89–97.

Isaksson, A.-S. and Lindskog, A. (2009). "Preferences for redistribution – a country comparison of fairness judgements." *Journal of Economic Behavior and Organization*, 72: 884–902.

Jancewicz, B. (2016). "Income inequalities: axioms of income inequality measures and people's perceptions." *Decyzje*, 5: 21–42.

Johansson-Stenman, O., Carlsson, F. and Daruvala, D. (2002). "Measuring future grandparents' preferences for equality and relative standing." *Economic Journal*, 112: 363–383.

Konow, J. (2000). "Fair shares: Accountability and cognitive dissonance in allocation decisions." *American Economic Review*, 90: 1072–1091.

(2001). "Fair and square: the four sides of distributive justice." *Journal of Economic Behavior and Organization*, 46: 137–164.

(2003). "Which is the fairest one of all? A positive analysis of justice theories." *Journal of Economic Literature*, 41: 1188–1239.

Kuhn, A. (2013). "Inequality perceptions, distributional norms, and redistributive preferences in East and West Germany." *German Economic Review*, 14: 483–499.

Kuziemko, I., Norton, M., Saez, E. and Stantcheva, S. (2015). "How elastic are preferences for redistribution? Evidence from randomized survey experiments." *American Economic Review*, 105: 1478–1508.

Lal, A., Mohebi, M., Sweeney, R., Moodie, M., Peeters, A. and Carter, R. (2019). "Equity weights for socioeconomic position: two methods – survey of stated preferences and epidemiological data." *Value in Health*, 22: 247–253.

Leibler, J., Zwack, L. and Levy, J. (2009). "Agreement with inequality axioms and perceptions of inequality among environmental justice and risk assessment professionals." *Health, Risk & Society*, 11: 55–69.

Luce, R. and Raiffa, H. (1957). *Games and Decisions*. New York: Wiley.

Luttmer, E. and Singhal, M. (2011). "Culture, context, and the taste for redistribution." *American Economic Journal: Economic Policy*, 3: 157–179.

McClelland, G. and Rohrbaugh, J. (1978). "Who accepts the Pareto axiom? The role of utility and equity in arbitration decisions." *Behavioral Science*, 23: 446–456.

Miller, D. (1992). "Distributive justice: what the people think." *Ethics*, 102: 555–593.

Mollerstrom, J., Reme, B.-A. and Sorensen, E. (2015). "Luck, choice and responsibility. An experimental study of fairness views." *Journal of Public Economics*, 131: 33–40.

Muller, D. and Renes, S. (2021). "Fairness views and political preferences: evidence from a large and heterogeneous sample." *Social Choice and Welfare*, 56: 679-711.

Nord, E. (1995). "The person-trade-off approach to valuing health care programs." *Medical Decision Making*, 15: 201–208.

Ottersen, T., Maestad, O. and Norheim, O. (2014). "Lifetime QALY prioritarianism in priority setting: quantification of the inherent trade-off." *Cost Effectiveness and Resource Allocation*, 12.

Pinto-Prades, J.-L. and Abellán-Perpiñán (2005). "Measuring the health of populations: the veil of ignorance approach." *Health Economics*, 14: 69–82.

Pirttilä, J. and Uusitalo, R. (2010). "A 'leaky bucket' in the real world: estimating inequality aversion using survey data." *Economica*, 77: 60–76.

Rawls, J. (1958). "Justice as fairness." *Philosophical Review*, 67: 164–194.

(1971). *A Theory of Justice*. Cambridge, MA.: Harvard University Press.

Robson, M., Asaria, M., Cookson, R., Tsuchiya, A. and Ali, S. (2017). "Eliciting the level of health inequality aversion in England." *Health Economics*, 26: 1328–1334.

Roemer, J. (1996). *Theories of Distributive Justice*. Cambridge, Ma.: Harvard University Press.

Rohde, I.M. and Rohde, K.I. (2015). "Managing social risks – tradeoffs between risks and inequalities." *Journal of Risk and Uncertainty*, 51: 103–124.

Saez, E. and Stantcheva, S. (2013). "Generalized social marginal welfare weights for optimal tax theory." *NBER: Working Paper* 18835.

Schildberg-Hörisch, H. (2010). "Is the veil of ignorance only a concept about risk? An experiment." *Journal of Public Economics*, 94: 1062–1066.

Schokkaert, E. and Truyts, T. (2017). "Preferences for redistribution and social structure." *Social Choice and Welfare*, 49: 545–576.

Sen, A. (2009).*The Idea of Justice*. London: Allen Lane.

Tarroux, B. (2015). "Comparing two-dimensional distributions: a questionnaire-experimental approach." *Social Choice and Welfare*, 44: 87–108.

(2019). "The value of tax progressivity: evidence from survey experiments." *Journal of Public Economics*, 179: Article 104068.

Traub, S., Seidl, C. and Schmidt, U. (2009). "An experimental study on individual choice, social welfare, and social preferences." *European Economic Review*, 53: 385–400.

Traub, S., Seidl, C., Schmidt, U., and Levati, M.V. (2005). "Friedman, Harsanyi, Rawls, Boulding – or somebody else? An experimental investigation of distributive justice." *Social Choice and Welfare*, 24: 283–309.

Weinzierl, M. (2014). "The promise of positive optimal taxation: normative diversity and a role of equal sacrifice." *Journal of Public Economics*, 118: 128–142.

(2017a). "Popular acceptance of inequality due to innate brute luck and support for classical benefit-based taxation." *Journal of Public Economics*, 155: 54–63.

(2017b). "A welfarist role for nonwelfarist rules: an example with envy." *Harvard Business School: Working Paper* 17-021.

Yaari, M. and Bar-Hillel, M. (1984). "On dividing justly." *Social Choice and Welfare*, 1: 1–24.

Yamamura, E. (2015). "Effects of siblings and birth order on income redistribution preferences: evidence based on Japanese General Social Survey." *Social Indicators Research*, 121: 589–606.

11 Prioritarianism and Equality of Opportunity

PAOLO BRUNORI, FRANCISCO H. G. FERREIRA AND VITO PERAGINE*

11.1 Introduction

What objective, if any, should society – or the State as its collective agent – seek to pursue for its own betterment? What social objective function – again, if any – should well-intentioned policymakers seek to maximize, as they choose among multiple possible outcomes?[1] For about two centuries, one single (and surprisingly simple) answer to this question has been supremely dominant across the social sciences, namely utilitarianism. Normally attributed to Jeremy Bentham (1789), the modern formulation of utilitarianism posits that society is made up of a collection of individuals, each of whom has a well-defined level of well-being $w_i(x)$, which depends on outcome x. Society's objective, then, is to choose the feasible outcome x where the sum of the individual levels of well-being over the population is greatest.

The influence of utilitarianism over generations of philosophers and social scientists cannot be overstated. Speaking of economists, Sen (2000) writes: "in many respects, utilitarianism serves as the 'default program' in welfare-economic analysis: the theory that is implicitly summoned when no others are explicitly invoked" (p. 64).

Yet in the late twentieth century, the unrivalled dominance of utilitarianism began to be questioned, often from very different perspectives. Libertarians argued that society would be better served by ensuring that certain fundamental individual rights were respected, rather than by seeking to maximize some notion of utility or well-being. Rawls (1971) suggested his famous two principles of justice, which included an Equal Opportunity Principle. Sen (1980, 1985)

* We are grateful to Matt Adler, Ole Norheim, and participants at the PiP Network workshops at Duke University and in Bergen for helpful discussions. We are solely responsible for any errors.

[1] The word "outcome" is used here to denote alternative worlds, or model representations thereof, as defined in Adler, Chapter 2 this volume.

himself argued for a broader view of people's capabilities as the basal space for his concept of social justice. And so on.

Many of these perspectives have been extensively reviewed elsewhere (e.g., Roemer, 1993 and Sen, 2000) and we do not dwell further on them here. Our narrower focus is on two among these alternative approaches that were critical of utilitarianism in its pure form, namely (what is now known as) prioritarianism and the equality of opportunity approach. Prioritarianism is the name given by philosophers to an approach that incorporates the idea that inequality in the distribution of well-being is costly in terms of social welfare. That is to say: merely summing across individual well-being levels ignores an important dimension of the social objective. If two outcomes, x and y, yield the same sum of well-being across society, but well-being in y is distributed more unequally than in x, then prioritarianism would rank x as preferable to y. (See Adler, Chapter 2 this volume.)

As we will briefly discuss in the next section, when a few other desiderata are taken into account, this implies that instead of summing across individual levels of well-being, one ought to sum across strictly concave transformations of well-being – so that an extra unit of well-being earned by a less well-off person contributes more to the total than if that unit had accrued to a better-off person. Formally introduced to philosophers by Derek Parfit (2000), this view corresponds directly to the notion of strictly concave and additive social welfare functions (SWFs), which were familiar to economists since at least the late 1960s and early 1970s.[2]

The normative theory of equality of opportunity (E.Op. for short), on the other hand, is driven by the idea that not all differences in well-being are normatively equivalent. Proponents postulate that inequality in well-being can arise because of circumstances beyond the control of individuals (such as a person's race, gender, parents, or birthplace) or because of the exercise of individual responsibility and effort.[3] They argue that the first kind of inequality is ethically unacceptable and should be compensated, whereas the second kind is permissible and

[2] See, for example, Atkinson (1970).

[3] Seminal contributions to this literature were made by Arneson (1989), Cohen (1989) and Dworkin (1981a, 1981b) among philosophers, and by Fleurbaey (1994, 1995), Roemer (1993, 1998) and van de Gaer (1993) among economists.

does not warrant compensation from society.[4] This is perhaps a more substantive departure from utilitarianism, in that it questions not only the aggregation procedure (across individual levels of well-being), but also the very "basal space" (Sen, 2000) upon which normative judgments should be made. The argument is that society should promote greater (and less unequal) amounts of *opportunity for welfare* among the population, rather than focusing on the distribution of welfare itself.

While both of these normative approaches to social justice constitute departures from pure-form utilitarianism, they are clearly different from each other. Prioritarianism still relies exclusively on the space of well-being to assess and rank different potential social outcomes and, in this sense, it is still "welfarist". But it does so while incorporating an aversion to inequality in well-being. Equality of opportunity also incorporates a form of inequality aversion but, critically, that aversion applies only to some forms of inequality and not to others. The space of well-being is no longer sufficient for assessing and ranking social outcomes: E.Op. requires additional information on the *sources* of well-being, and the role of individual responsibility among those sources. In this sense, it is a "non-welfarist" approach to social justice.

The question we ask in this chapter is whether these two non-utilitarian approaches to social justice are – or can be made – mutually compatible. A priori, it may seem obvious that the answer is "no". Indeed, Adler (2018), who considered a very similar question before us, comments: "The reader might observe that Conflict is obvious. *Of course* it's true that introducing a non-well-being element into the goodness ranking will be inconsistent with the focus on well-being that the well-being Pareto principles embody – or so the reader might think." (p. 26) But he goes on to argue that "the inconsistency is not [in fact] obvious," and to describe conditions under which it might not hold.

We follow a different path from Adler's and arrive at somewhat different results, but they are similar in one key respect: there are clear inconsistencies between the two approaches – as one would expect. As we will see, the inconsistencies are driven primarily by two of the

4 In this chapter, we will mostly gloss over the longstanding debate about how "luck" should be treated in this framework. At the risk of simplifying excessively, one may think of "brute luck" as being a stochastic component of the set of circumstances, and "option luck" as having at least some responsibility component.

fundamental axioms of prioritarianism: *Anonymity* (also known as symmetry) and the *Pigou-Dalton transfer principle*. Yet we also show, drawing on earlier results in the literature, that suitable restrictions on the domain of those two axioms (along with some strengthening of the Separability axiom) can make modified versions of prioritarianism consistent with the principles of equality of opportunity. Because there are different versions of those principles in the E.Op. literature, the nature of the ethical compromise differs according to which approach one subscribes to, and the empirical requirements differ substantially among them.

In what follows, we examine six different axiomatic "definitions" of equality of opportunity – arising from *two* alternative versions of the principle that inequalities due to circumstances (e.g. race, sex, family background, etc.) should be compensated, and *three* different attitudes to how individual effort and responsibility can be rewarded.[5] For each of the six definitions, we present a set of axioms that jointly define a *family* of social welfare functions embodying certain prioritarian properties. These families admit versions of the Atkinson SWF (or of Kolm-Pollack SWFs) which are discussed in earlier chapters. Rather than focusing on one or two specific SWFs, however, we follow an alternative approach: for each family of SWFs defined by the different sets of axioms, we present *the conditions under which a pair of distributions will be ranked unanimously by all members of that SWF family*. This approach uses stochastic dominance relationships between two distributions (or functionals[6] thereof) to provide robust welfare rankings: if those conditions hold, then all members of the family of welfare functions will rank the two distributions the same way. It goes back to Atkinson's (1970) results about the link between Lorenz dominance and welfare dominance, and various generalizations thereof (e.g., Shorrocks, 1983). The approach is standard in welfare economics, but we briefly summarize it below and provide references for the unfamiliar reader.

The chapter is organized as follows. The next section lays out a basic analytical framework for thinking about this question and provides a brief overview of prioritarianism and the theory of equality of opportunity, including the distinction between ex-ante and ex-post

[5] One of these six "cells" has been approached in two different ways in the literature, so a seventh empirical comparison is discussed in Appendix 11 A.2.

[6] A functional is simply a "function of a function," that is a functional relationship whose arguments may include other functions.

approaches to E.Op. Section 11.3 describes the conflict between prioritarianism and ex-ante E.Op., as well as the conditions under which the two can be reconciled by suitable axiomatic compromises. It presents the relevant dominance relationships allowing for robust rankings in each case. Section 11.4 does the same for ex-post E.Op., and Section 11.5 provides an empirical illustration using five waves of a panel household survey for South Africa, likely the most unequal country in the world today. Section 11.6 concludes. While some basic mathematical notation and a few key results are included in the main text, the chapter is written informally. Formal statements are consigned to footnotes or to Appendices 11.A.1 and 11.A.2.

11.2 The Basic Framework

In this section we introduce the canonical theoretical equality of opportunity framework.[7] Parts of this consider a discrete population of fixed and finite size N, with individuals indexed by l. Denote individual well-being in outcome x by $w_l(x)$, and the population distribution of well-being by the N-dimensional vector $\boldsymbol{w}(x)$. Suppose $w_l(x)$ is a function of multiple personal attributes $\boldsymbol{a}_l(x)$, and that this $(p+1)$-dimensional vector $\boldsymbol{a}$, which fully determines $w_l(x)$, can be unambiguously divided into two kinds of attributes: those that are given exogenously to the individual, in the sense that they are beyond her control, $C_l(x)$, and those over which she can exert at least a modicum of control, $e_l(x)$. Let $C_l(x)$ be a p-dimensional vector of circumstances that characterize each individual and $e_l(x)$ be a one-dimensional scalar index for effort or responsibility. Furthermore, denote $\varphi(x)$ as the set of tools ("policies") available to the policymaker in state x with which to influence well-being – say, by taxing some people and making transfers to others. Note that policies are chosen for society as a whole. They may vary among outcomes but, in each outcome, they are common to all.

We can then write individual well-being as:

$$w_l = w(C_l, e_l, \varphi) \tag{11.1}$$

[7] Parts of this section draw on Ferreira and Peragine (2016), who discuss the "canonical" model of equality of opportunity in greater detail. The reader unfamiliar with the E.Op. literature is directed to that survey for a lengthier exposition.

where each argument of the function $w(.)$ is itself a function of state x, omitted to simplify notation.[8] For expositional simplicity, let $e(x)$ and all elements of $\mathbf{C}(x)$ be discrete variables.[9]

Given C and e, the population can be partitioned in two ways. It can be divided into mutually exclusive groups of people who share identical circumstance vectors, C_i. In the literature, each of these circumstance-homogeneous groups is called a *type* (indexed by i and denoted T_i). Alternatively, we can partition the population into mutually exclusive groups of people who exert the same level of effort, e_j. These groups are called *tranches* (indexed by j and denoted T^j). Equation (11.1) can then be re-written as:

$$w_{ij} = w\left(C_i, e_j, \varphi\right) \tag{11.1'}$$

Since each individual l must belong to a single type and a single tranche, (11.1') merely rewrites the individual well-being function by indexing individuals by the type (i) and tranche (j) each one belongs to. If, without loss of generality, there are n types and m tranches then the population can be represented by a matrix $\left[W_{ij}\right]$, as in Figure 11.1. In this matrix, each row denotes the support of the well-being distribution of a type, whereas each column denotes the support of the well-being distribution of a tranche.[10] It will prove convenient to define effort $e(x)$ so that well-being is always (weakly) increasing in effort within each type.[11]

[8] In this chapter we write $w_{ij}(x) = w\left(C_i(x), e_j(x), \varphi(x)\right)$ to indicate that individual well-being depends on a person's circumstances and efforts, as well as on the set of policies in place in outcome x. We also abstract from uncertainty, so that each outcome corresponds to a single state of nature. Our setup is fully consistent with that of Adler, Chapter 2 in this volume, in which a policy maps each state of nature onto an outcome.

[9] In this discrete case, the well-being function is a mapping $w : \Omega \times \Theta \times \Phi \rightarrow \mathbb{R}$, where $\Omega \subseteq \mathbb{Z}^p$, $\Theta \subseteq \mathbb{Z}$ and $\Phi \subseteq \mathbb{R}$. Note that $w \in \mathbb{R}$, so differentiable functions of w can be defined. Discreteness of the circumstance and effort variables is not important for the analysis, but simplifies exposition.

[10] Distributions, like other functions, are mappings from a domain to a range. The support of a distribution is simply its domain: the set of all possible values that the variable being distributed can take. In this case, the distributions themselves are vectors where each w_{ij} value is entered p_{ij} times (see below).

[11] That is, the effort variable is *defined* so that $w_{ij} = w\left(C_i, e_j, \varphi\right) \leq w_{ij+1} = w\left(C_i, e_{j+1}, \varphi\right)$. An example illustrates: suppose Janet's well-being is increasing in the result of a school exam. If studying for twelve hours for the test and not sleeping leads to a worse exam result than studying six hours and sleeping for six hours, all else equal, then the second strategy involves the higher effort level.

	e_1	e_2	e_3	...	e_m
C_1	w_{11}	w_{12}	w_{13}	...	w_{1m}
C_2	w_{21}	w_{22}	w_{23}	...	w_{2m}
C_3	w_{31}	w_{32}	w_{33}	...	w_{3m}
...	...	...	...	...	...
C_n	w_{n1}	w_{n2}	w_{n3}	...	w_{nm}

Figure 11.1 Circumstances, effort and well-being

In general, there may of course be more than one person of type T_i in tranche T^j (that is, in each cell in the $[W_{ij}]$ matrix), so that a full description of the population would require defining a population size matrix $[P_{ij}]$, which is also $n \ x \ m$, and whose elements p_{ij} give the number of people with circumstances C_i and effort e_j. Naturally, $\sum_{1=1}^{n}\sum_{j=1}^{m}p_{ij} = N$.

This simple "model" of a society contains all the elements we will need to investigate the inconsistencies between prioritarianism and E.Op.. In particular, the introduction of a vector of circumstances, C(x), and an effort index, *e(x),* will allow us to treat differences in well-being differently, depending on whether they are driven by each. The matrix representation of society in Figure 11.1 is only a little richer than the vector representation familiar from welfarism (where all the information required for a social evaluation is contained in the distribution of well-being itself). But it will allow us to compare the two approaches. We begin with prioritarianism.

11.2.1 Prioritarianism

A Benthamite utilitarian would view the sum of individual levels of well-being in society,

$$S^U = \sum_{l=1}^{N} w_l = \sum_{i=1}^{n}\sum_{j=1}^{m} p_{ij}w_{ij} \tag{11.2}$$

as the appropriate social objective function. For her, this should be the maximand – the object a benign social planner should choose policies φ to maximize. A prioritarian, on the other hand, rejects (11.2) on the ground that it is insensitive to the distribution of well-being. She would prefer to maximize:

$$S^P = \sum_{l=1}^{N} g(w_l) = \sum_{i=1}^{n} \sum_{j=1}^{m} p_{ij} g(w_{ij}) \tag{11.3}$$

with $g'(w) > 0, g''(w) < 0$.[12] The strict concavity of the transformation function $g(w)$ ensures that a gain in well-being of Δw to a poorer person (in terms of well-being) makes a greater contribution to social welfare than an identical gain to a richer person. Indeed, Adler (2018) shows that if (and only if) a social planner holds to five key principles (plus a few more technical properties), then her social rankings across outcomes will be mirrored by some member of the class of social welfare functions described by (11.3). The five principles, or axioms, are as follows:[13,14]

I. *Anonymity (or symmetry):* If an outcome y is obtained from another outcome x merely by re-arranging well-being levels w_l among individuals (so that $\boldsymbol{w}(y)$ is a permutation of $\boldsymbol{w}(x)$), then one should be indifferent between x and y.
II. *Strong monotonicity (or strong Pareto):* If an outcome y is obtained from another outcome x by raising the well-being level of at least one person, and lowering no one's, then y is preferred to x.
III. *Pigou-Dalton transfer principle*: Suppose well-being levels are the same across outcomes x and y for all but two people. If y is

[12] For presentational purposes we assume twice-differentiability of the transformation functions $g(w)$, even though this property is not in fact required for any of the results reviewed in this chapter (and thus not one of the axioms listed).

[13] These axioms are standard in welfare economics and we state them informally here. Formal statements can be found in many different sources, e.g., Peragine (2004) or Adler (2019). See Adler, Chapter 2 in this volume, for a comprehensive discussion of the axiomatic foundation of prioritarianism.

[14] Our earlier assumption that the population size is fixed at N across all possible outcomes implies that we can dispense with the Population Replication Invariance axiom, which would otherwise be needed. If N were variable and that axiom were imposed, then (11.2) and (11.3) would involve a division by N, yielding the more frequent "per capita" interpretation.

obtained from x by means of a mean-preserving spread – that is a pure (non-leaky) transfer from the poorer to the richer person – then x is preferred to y. Equivalently, if y is obtained from x by means of a progressive rank-preserving pure (non-leaky) transfer – that is, from the richer to the poorer person, without switching their ranks – then y is preferred to x.

IV. *Separability*: The contribution of any individual to social well-being is independent from the contributions of others.[15]

V. *Continuity*: If state x is preferred to y given the two N-dimensional vectors $w(x)$ and $w(y)$, then there exists a N-dimensional vector $\varepsilon \neq 0$ such that $w(x) \pm \varepsilon$ is also preferred to y.

Although these axioms are well-known to readers familiar with welfare economics or political philosophy, it is worthwhile commenting briefly on each. Anonymity ensures the policymaker's impartiality: All else equal, she is indifferent between a world where Anne has a well-being of 5 while Paul has 10, and another where Anne has 10 and Paul has 5. This axiom requires that w be the only argument of the transformation function, $g(w)$. The Pareto principle (or strong monotonicity) rules out levelling down: social welfare improves if well-being rises for some while remaining unchanged for all others. It mandates the positive first derivative of the transformation function.

The Pigou-Dalton transfer principle is the locus of inequality aversion in the prioritarian social welfare formulation: it requires that a mean-preserving spread – a transfer from a poorer to a richer person – reduces social welfare. Equivalently it requires that a rank-preserving transfer from a richer to a poorer person increases social welfare: so long as the total amount of well-being is unchanged, a less unequal distribution is always preferred. This axiom mandates the negative second derivative – that is, the strict concavity – of the transformation function. Separability requires that the change in a person's well-being level affects social welfare only directly, and not through the well-being of others. A mathematical formulation says that the cross-partial derivative of S^P with respect to the individual wellbeing of two distinct individuals, w_l and w_k, is zero. This is by no means a trivial requirement, and it is not invulnerable to criticism. The reason it is ubiquitous

[15] More formally, if $K < N$ people have the same levels of well-being in outcomes x and y, then the ranking between x and y depends only on the well-being levels of the other N-K people. This holds for any $K < N$.

in welfare economics is that it mandates the additive formulation of (11.3), which makes analysis more tractable. Continuity is in a sense a more technical requirement, but it plays the important role of preventing very small changes in a person's well-being from having a disproportionately large effect on social welfare. It mandates the continuity of the transformation function.

Since all prioritarian social welfare functions satisfy these five axioms, this also holds for the two main SWF families used in this volume, namely those using the Atkinson and the Kolm-Pollak transformation functions. Let $g(w_{ij}) = \frac{w_{ij}^{1-\gamma}}{1-\gamma}$, where $\gamma > 0$ indicates the degree of inequality aversion (or priority for the worse-off), in Equation (11.3), and we have an Atkinson SWF. If, instead, we let $g(w_{ij}) = -e^{-\beta w_{ij}}$, with $\beta > 0$, we would have a Kolm-Pollak SWF, where β captures the degree of priority for the worse-off. These are well-established families of welfare functions, which can productively be applied to inform policy choices in a number of different domains, as documented in earlier chapters.

It is perfectly possible, however, for two different social welfare functions satisfying the above axioms to rank two distributions, x and y, in opposite ways. Even within a given SWF family, it is perfectly possible that one member of the family (say, an Atkinson function with $\gamma = 1$) will rank x as preferable to y, whereas another (say, an Atkinson function with $\gamma = 4$) will rank y as preferable to x. The same can be said of different members of the Kolm-Pollak family, and indeed of other functional forms satisfying Equation (11.3). This is not a problem, per se. As described by Adler (Chapter 2, this volume), an observer or policymaker follows her own process of ethical deliberation in choosing a SWF, and that includes the choice of the inequality aversion parameter (e.g. γ, β). Given those preferences, it is perfectly appropriate for one such observer to prefer x to y, while another prefers y to x.

Yet the fact that rankings are in general dependent on specific choices of functional forms or parameter values is somewhat problematic when the objective at hand is to investigate whether prioritarianism as a broad approach to social justice is consistent or inconsistent with equality of opportunity as another broad approach to social justice. This is why we follow the robust rankings approach described in the Introduction: we search for conditions (about the relationship between the two distributions, $\boldsymbol{w}(x)$ and $\boldsymbol{w}(y)$) under which *all* SWFs in a given family will rank x and y the same way. As is standard in the welfare economics literature, this is achieved through theorems that establish the mathematical equivalence between (i) a unanimous ranking among all members of a family of social welfare functions and (ii) a dominance condition, typically expressed in terms of cumulative distribution functions, that can be tested empirically.

Two equivalence results are particularly interesting as they characterize dominance conditions that will be frequently used in this chapter. The first is the equivalence between unanimous ranking in the broad family of SWFs defined by axioms I, II, IV and V above, without imposing the Pigou-Dalton transfer axiom (III), on the one hand, and first-order stochastic dominance (FOSD) on the other. A distribution $\boldsymbol{w}(x)$ is said to first-order stochastically dominate another, $\boldsymbol{w}(y)$, if at each and every rank, the element in $\boldsymbol{w}(x)$ is greater (or at least no less) than the corresponding element in $\boldsymbol{w}(y)$. That is, for all k, $w_k(x) \geq w_k(y)$. If this relationship holds between outcomes x and y, then Saposnik (1981) has shown that all SWFs in that broad family (which encompasses all prioritarian, as well as utilitarian and even various inequality-loving SWFs) will unambiguously rank x above y. Figure 11.2.A illustrates such a dominance result for two different types in South Africa in 2008.[16] Each of the two curves plots $w_k(x)$ as a function of k, for the respective type. Such curves are known as quantile functions and, as statistically minded readers will know, they are inverse functions of the cumulative distribution function (c.d.f.) of a distribution. As noted in Appendix 11.A.1, FOSD can also be – and indeed typically is – defined in terms of relationships between c.d.fs.

Even more important for this chapter is the equivalence between unanimous rankings in the family of prioritarian SWFs defined by axioms I–V above (now including axiom III: Pigou-Dalton) and second-order stochastic dominance (SOSD). A distribution $\boldsymbol{w}(x)$ is said to second-order stochastically dominate another, $\boldsymbol{w}(y)$ if, at each and every rank, the sum of all elements up until that rank is greater in $\boldsymbol{w}(x)$ than in $\boldsymbol{w}(y)$.[17] If this relationship holds between outcomes x and y, then Shorrocks (1983) has shown that all prioritarian SWFs will

[16] The empirical significance of the result is discussed in Section 11.5. The purpose of Figure 11.1 is merely to illustrate the concept.

[17] In general, this result is about the partial mean up to each rank: that is, the sum is divided by N. In our setting, N is fixed and finite, so the result can be expressed as above.

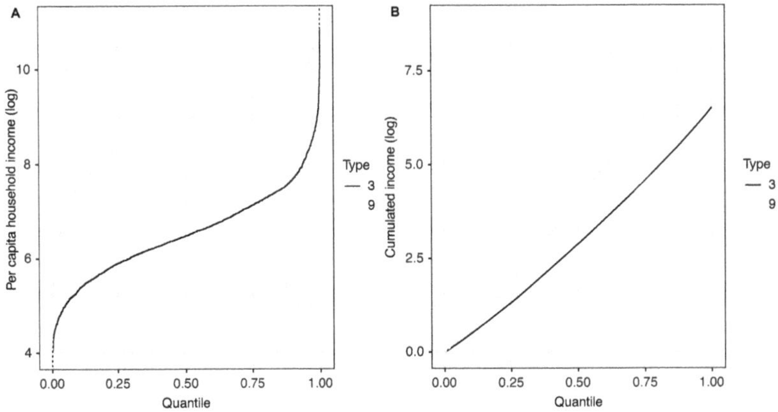

Figure 11.2 Illustrations of first- and second-order stochastic dominance (*Source*: NIDS Wave 1. Note: Panel A displays the quantile functions for two groups of people in South Africa. The curve lying everywhere above the other is said to first-order stochastically dominate it. Panel B displays Generalized Lorenz Curves for the same two groups. The curve lying everywhere above the other is said to second-order stochastically dominate it)

unambiguously rank x above y. Figure 11.2.B illustrates such a dominance result for the same two South African-type distributions shown in Panel A. In this case, each of the two curves plots cumulative well-being, $\frac{1}{N}\sum_{l=1}^{k} w_l(x)$ as a function of k, for the respective type (with income levels proxying for well-being). These curves are known as Generalized Lorenz Curves, written as $GL(k, x, N) = \frac{1}{N}\sum_{l=1}^{k} w_l(x), k = 1, \ldots, N$. To simplify notation, in this chapter we will denote the Generalized Lorenz Curve for any particular distribution *v(x)* simply as $GL(v(x), N)$, omitting the fact that the curve is a function of the rank k. When a distribution *v(x)* displays SOSD (or Generalized Lorenz Dominance) over *v(y)*, we write $GL(v(x), N) > GL(v(y), N)$. Appendix 11.A.1 contains the formal definitions of FOSD and SOSD, as well as a more formal statement of these two equivalence results.

11.2.2 Equality of Opportunity

The above discussion of prioritarianism made no reference to people's efforts or circumstances. It could have been written without using any i or j subscripts: all that mattered for assessing social welfare in an outcome x was the distribution of individual well-being, $w(x)$. How that distribution is generated and whether differences in well-being are due to differences in people's responsibility or effort choices (on the one hand), or merely to how rich their parents were (on the other), mattered not in the least.

That is not true in the normative theory of equality of opportunity (E. Op.), mentioned in the Introduction (and note 4). Under E.Op., whether differences in well-being are due to differences in a person's circumstances or efforts – i.e. to differences between rows or columns of Figure 11.1 – matters a great deal.[18] That is why a vector – $w(x)$ – no longer contains all the information sufficient for ranking social outcomes. A matrix $\left[W_{ij}\right]$ is needed. There are different versions of the theory, but all share two key principles, namely:

A. *Principle of Compensation*: Differences in "circumstances" beyond the control of the individuals warrant compensation, as they generate unfair inequalities in well-being.
B. *Principle of Reward*: "Efforts" should be rewarded, and the resulting inequalities in well-being should be preserved.

Although they can be stated in deceptively simple terms, and at first glance appear consistent with each other, these two principles can be defined in different ways and, in some cases, they are not actually mutually compatible. A substantial literature has now explored these differences and we will not dwell much on them here. The reader is referred to Fleurbaey and Peragine (2013) for some original results and to Ferreira and Peragine (2016) for a more general discussion. For our purposes it will suffice to distinguish between two different interpretations of the principle of compensation, and three alternative formulations of the reward principle.

[18] Because of the richer basal space in their approach, proponents of E.Op. see the theory as inherently non-welfarist and often describe it without using the words "well-being". Authors such as Roemer (1998) will speak of an "advantage" variable as the one that should be represented in Figure 11.1. An advantage has to be something that people value without strong satiation: more of it is never a bad thing. Empirical applications have used incomes, consumption expenditures, and measures of educational or health status as examples of advantage. Here we use "well-being" as the advantage in order to more easily integrate the discussion of E.Op. and prioritarianism. Furthermore, we remain agnostic as to the specific concept of "well-being": whether hedonic, preference-based, objective-good, etc. See Adler and Decanq, Chapter 3, this volume.

In its *ex-ante* version, the principle of compensation is about compensating for inequalities between types (the rows in $[W_{ij}]$). Specifically, the approach requires (i) defining the opportunity set faced by each type, and (ii) specifying a manner for evaluating those sets. In most empirical applications, the ith row of the matrix in Figure 11.1, which is the support of the well-being distribution for type T_i, is used to represent the opportunity set of that type. Naturally, any number of summary statistics could be used to summarize each such vector, thereby evaluating the opportunity set: its mode or median for example. Historically, most authors have used the mean, $\mu(T_i) = \sum_j p_{ij}w_{ij} / \sum_j p_{ij}$.

The *ex-post* version of compensation, on the other hand, looks at inequality in well-being between individuals at each and every level of effort.[19] In other words, it focuses on inequality within tranches (the columns in $[W_{ij}]$). These two versions of the compensation principle have implications that are quite different. In fact, as established by Fleurbaey and Peragine (2013), the two versions are mutually inconsistent in general, meaning that the policies (φ) chosen under one version might not be the same as those chosen under the other.

The reward principle is concerned with differences in well-being due to the exercise of personal responsibility. Since all individuals in each type share identical circumstances, the only thing that differs among them are the effort (or responsibility) levels e_j, so a reward principle is essentially about how to apportion different levels of well-being to different levels of effort, and so how to evaluate inequality in well-being within types and between tranches. This can be understood in a number of slightly different ways, of which we consider the following three.

The so-called *utilitarian reward* principle requires neutrality with respect to inequality in well-being within types: existing inequalities in well-being among individuals in the same type are a matter of social indifference. Alternatively, one could impose some degree of inequality aversion even within types – presumably to a lesser degree than between types. This view would correspond to a version of E.Op.

[19] In the E.Op. literature, it has become established for the terms *ex-ante* and *ex-post* to be used to refer to "before" and "after" the realization of effort levels, rather than to before and after the resolution of uncertainty as, for example, in ex-ante and ex-post prioritarianism. On the latter use of the terms, see Adler, Chapter 2 this volume.

where all inequalities are objectionable, but those due to differences in responsibility are less so. This is referred to as *inequality-averse reward*. Many different arguments can be used to motivate it. One practical argument is that, in empirical analysis, the researcher or policymaker can never expect to fully observe all elements of the vector of circumstances. To the extent that some circumstances remain unobserved, they "contaminate" $e(x)$, justifying some aversion to effort-driven inequality.[20] Finally, one can simply be agnostic about the degree of inequality aversion that should apply within types, perhaps because of the uncertainty just discussed. This approach is called, self-evidently, *agnostic reward*.

While these two versions of the compensation principle and three versions of the reward principle do not exhaust the variants proposed in the literature, they are varied enough to provide a solid basis for our discussion of whether E.Op. may be made consistent with simple prioritarianism, of the form given by Equation (11.3). If we restrict our attention to them, we can represent the variants of E.Op theory by a 2x3 matrix such as the one in Table 11.1.

The next two sections explore the nature of the clash between Prioritarianism and E.Op. under each of these six possible versions of the equality of opportunity approach. Section 11.3 considers the ex-ante approach to compensation: the first row of the matrix in Table 11.1. Section 11.4 turns to the bottom row and looks at the ex-post approach. We first show that Prioritarianism (as defined by the five axioms I–V above) is *in general* inconsistent with E.Op. Then for each cell in Table 11.1, we propose adjustments to two of the axioms of prioritarianism, namely Anonymity and Pigou-Dalton, that can accommodate the relevant E.Op. principles. Adjustments are also needed to strengthen Separability, although these are more technical in nature and less substantive from a normative point of view. Under the modified – and more restrictive – social welfare functions implied by the new axioms, we show that a compromise between E.Op. and

[20] It has been argued – against the E.Op. approach – that all differences are ultimately driven by circumstances, genetic, social or otherwise. In that view, inequality aversion within and between types becomes identical, and we are back to pure prioritarianism. In principle, the degree of aversion to inequality within types might reflect the relative weight one places on "unobserved circumstances" relative to "free will" as driving the within-type differences in well-being.

Table 11.1. *Variants of E.Op theory*

	Utilitarian reward	Inequality-averse reward	Agnostic reward
Ex-ante compensation			
Ex-post compensation			

prioritarianism *is* possible. Finally, drawing on earlier results in the literature, we state dominance conditions – variants of the first- and second-order stochastic dominance conditions discussed above – for classes of social welfare functions defined by the revised axioms. In Section 11.5, we illustrate these dominance results empirically for South Africa, demonstrating the existence of these compromises between prioritarianism and E.Op. in a real-world context.

11.3 Prioritarianism and Equality of Opportunity: The Ex-Ante Case

As noted above, the ex-ante version of the compensation principle requires an evaluation of the opportunity set faced by each type, which is used to rank types. In practice, this is often accomplished by relying on a summary statistic (such as the type mean) to represent the value of the opportunity set of each type. The principle then requires policies to reduce the inequality among these values.

Returning to the matrix $[W_{ij}]$, represented by Figure 11.1, let us order the types such that mean well-being rises as we move down the table.[21] Recall that effort is defined so that well-being rises within each type as we move to the right along each row of Figure 11.1.[22] Then in general it is clearly possible that there exist two individuals, A and B, such that A is worse-off than B even though A belongs to a better-off type – that is to a type with a higher mean.[23] B is better-off than

[21] That is: $\mu(T_{i+1}) \geq \mu(T_i), i \in [1, \ldots, n-1]$. In this discussion we use the type's mean to represent the value of each individual's opportunity set to simplify the presentation, but the conclusions would hold for any other scalar valuation of the sets.

[22] That is: $w_{ij} \leq w_{ij+1}, j \in [1, \ldots, m-1]$. See also note 12.

[23] A has well-being w_{ij}, B has well-being $w_{i-b,j+k}$. It is possible that $w_{ij} < w_{i-b,j+k}, b > 0, k > 0$.

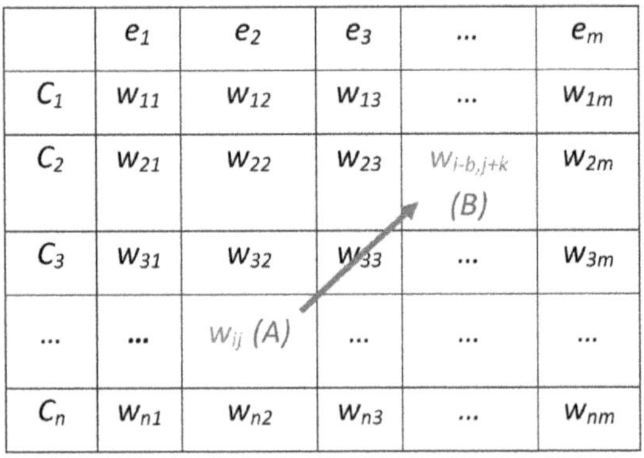

Figure 11.3 A stylized representation of the ex-ante E.Op. – prioritarianism clash

A because the rewards to her greater effort or responsibility more than compensate for the fact that she belongs to a lower-ranked type.

But therein lies a clash: According to the Pigou-Dalton transfer principle, if an outcome y (that is: a given matrix of well-being levels) is obtained from another outcome x exclusively by means of a transfer from A to B, with all other entries unchanged, then x should be preferred to y. This is a regressive transfer, from a poorer person (A) to a richer one (B). However, B belongs to a "poorer" (i.e. lower-ranked) *type* than A. The ex-ante principle of compensation therefore requires that we prefer outcome y to x, since inequality of opportunity (i.e. well-being differences due to circumstances) is lower in y. Inequality among type means is lower in y. This situation is represented in Figure 11.3: the transfer from A to B is regressive in terms of individuals, but progressive in terms of types. The Pigou-Dalton axiom of prioritarianism and the ex-ante compensation principle of E.Op. therefore clash. As stated so far, these two normative views are inconsistent: not all prioritarian social welfare functions S^P are consistent with the ex-ante principle of compensation.

When, as in this case, two desirable properties or principles clash, compromises can be sought by restricting the domains of one or more of them. We therefore ask: are there sub-classes of social welfare functions, that are prioritarian "in spirit" but satisfy slightly different axioms, which might be consistent with ex-ante E.Op.? It turns out that the answer is yes. Consider replacing the Anonymity axiom (I) from Section 11.2, with two different versions. The first is a partial symmetry property that applies only within types, while the second requires symmetry *of* (or among) types:

IA. *Anonymity (or symmetry) within types:* If an outcome y is obtained from another outcome x merely by re-arranging well-being levels w_{ij} among individuals *within types*, (so that a type distribution $\boldsymbol{w}_i(y)$ is a permutation of $\boldsymbol{w}_i(x)$, for all (i), then one should be indifferent between x and y.

IB. *Anonymity (or symmetry) of types:* If an outcome y is obtained from another outcome x merely by re-arranging types (without changing the well-being levels w_{ij} of individuals *within types)*, then one should be indifferent between x and y.

Furthermore, similarly restrict the domain of the Pigou-Dalton transfer principle, as follows:

IIIA. *Pigou-Dalton transfer between types*: Consider two types, i and k, with different means. If outcome y is obtained from outcome x by means of a finite sequence of pure (non-leaky) transfers exclusively between individuals in these two types (leaving all individuals in all other types unaffected), the net effect of which is that the richer type becomes even richer and the poorer type even poorer in y, then x is preferred to y.

These two new axioms simply re-define Anonymity and Pigou-Dalton so that they hold not over the full domain of the distribution of well-being, but in more restricted domains. Axiom IA, for example, implies that swapping the well-being levels of Paul and Peter (while everyone else's well-being is unchanged, as in our earlier example) must leave aggregate social welfare unchanged if Paul and Peter share the same circumstances, but *may not leave it unchanged if they do not*. Axiom IB implies that social preferences depend not on the specific identity of each type (e.g. "Black men with highly educated parents", or "Asian women with parents with low education"), but on the type's relative rank. Axiom IIIA requires that a net transfer from a lower-ranked type to a higher-ranked type must lower social welfare, regardless of whether the particular individuals making the transfer are better or worse-off than those receiving it. Importantly, the axiom says nothing about transfers within a type.

Finally, replace the separability axiom (IV) with a two-part *Additivity axiom*, which explicitly imposes an additive aggregation of well-being both within and between types:

IVA: Additivity

(i) *Between types*: the social value of an outcome is equal to the sum of some (type specific) function of the well-being of each type.
(ii) *Within types*: the well-being of a type is equal to the sum of some (individual specific) function of the well-being of individuals in that type.

It turns out that replacing axioms I, III and IV from the characterization of a prioritarian social welfare function in Section 11.2 with axioms IA, IB, IIIA and IVA can be used to define different classes of social welfare functions which *are* consistent with the ex-ante compensation principle.

To make further progress in specifying these classes and in stating the corresponding dominance conditions, we must distinguish among the three kinds of reward principle discussed earlier. Since this principle is concerned with rewarding effort or responsibility, and that is the only thing that differs among individuals within any given type, it is quite intuitive that one's attitude to reward is just a mirror image of one's attitude to inequality *within* types. If one is completely neutral with respect to inequality within types, then that implies that one subscribes to the utilitarian version of the reward principle. If one is still averse to inequality within types, although perhaps to a different extent than to inequality between types, then one subscribes to inequality-averse reward. Finally, one may decline to take either one of those ethical positions and choose to remain agnostic about inequality within types, a view corresponding to the agnostic reward principle. In this latter case, one does not impose any specific axiom.

These give rise to three *alternative* versions of the reward principle, governing aversion to inequality within types, as follows:

VIA: *Inequality neutrality within types:* Suppose well-being levels are the same across outcomes x and y for all but two people, A and B, both of whom belong to type i, and respectively to tranches j and k, $j>k$. Suppose, furthermore, that y is obtained from x by means of a transfer from the poorer individual (B) to the richer one (A).[24] Then one is indifferent between x and y.

[24] That is: $w_{ij}^{A}(x) > w_{ik}^{B}(x)$ and $w_{ij}^{A}(y) = w_{ij}^{A}(x) + \delta$ and $w_{ik}^{B}(y) = w_{ik}^{B}(x) - \delta$.

VIB: *Inequality aversion within types:* Suppose well-being levels are the same across outcomes x and y for all but two people, A and B, both of whom belong to type i, any i, and respectively to tranche j and k, $j<k$. Suppose that – as before – y is obtained from x by means of a transfer from the poorer individual (A) to the richer one (B). Then x is preferred to y.

VIC: *Inequality agnosticism within types:* No axiom is imposed.

Combining Axioms IA, IB, II, IIIA, IVA, V, and VIA yields a class of welfare functions given by:

$$S^N = \sum_{i=1}^{n} \sum_{j=1}^{m} p_{ij} g_i(w_{ij}) \tag{11.4}$$

where the functions $g_i(w_{ij})$, which may now vary across types, are all linear and become progressively less steep as types get "richer," or better-off.[25] (Peragine, 2004).

In other words, consider a person whose views on social justice are such that they value an increment in well-being for any person positively if no one else loses (monotonicity); they believe well-being should be aggregated additively both within and across types (additivity); they believe that people who share the same set of circumstances should be treated impartially (Anonymity within types), just as types themselves should also be treated symmetrically (Anonymity between types: what matters is a type's income vector, which determines its rank; not its "identity"); and that compensation should be made for inequality between types but not for any inequality within types (Pigou-Dalton between types and inequality neutrality within types). Such a person would rank outcomes in ways consistent with a SWF given by (11.4). Let's call all such people "Strict Opportunity Egalitarians," or SOEs.

Three key properties of (11.4) – in contrast to (11.3) – are worth noting. First, the transformation function $g(w)$ is now type-specific, rather than being identical for everyone in society. Second, each such type-specific transformation function is linear – and thus insensitive to redistribution within types. But third, its slope is lower as types become richer, meaning that transfers from a richer type to a poorer type

[25] More formally, $g_i(w)$ satisfy three properties. Within any type T_i, $g_i'(w) > 0, g_i''(w) = 0$. And $g_i'(w) > g_{i+1}'(w) > 0, \forall i \in [1, \ldots, n-1]$. Recall that types are ordered by their means; see footnote 22.

increase overall social welfare. A specific – and quite intuitive – member of S^N would be a weighted sum of type means, where the weights decline with the type mean.[26] This would be the discrete-setting equivalent of a sum (across types) of "concave" transformations of type means.

Having defined our first class of "opportunity-prioritarian" SWFs, we are now ready to state our first equivalence result. To do so, let's define the distribution of type well-being, $M(x)$, as the *n x 1* vector the elements of which are the sums of well-being levels accruing to all individuals in each type, in outcome x.[27] An important result due to Peragine (2004) is that if (and only if) a person's ethical views can be represented by *any* social welfare function in the S^N class, then this person will always prefer an outcome x over another outcome y if the distribution of total type well-being in x displays Generalized Lorenz Dominance over that in y, that is:

$$S^N(x) > S^N(y) \Leftrightarrow GL(M(x), n) > GL(M(y), n) \qquad (11.5)$$

This statement is analogous to Shorrocks's (1983) theorem reproduced in Appendix 11.A.1. That theorem established that if a distribution of *individual* well-being, $w(x)$, Generalized Lorenz dominated another, $w(y)$, then all prioritarian social welfare functions would rank x higher than y (and vice versa). Peragine's (2004) theorem 1 says that if a distribution of *type* well-being $M(x)$ Generalized Lorenz dominates another, $M(y)$, then all SOEs will rank x higher than y (and vice-versa). This gives us a result to fill in the first cell in Figure 11.2: a comparison of Prioritarianism and E.Op. when the latter adopts the ex-ante version of the compensation principle and the utilitarian version of the reward principle.[28]

If, instead, one subscribes to the inequality-averse reward principle, then it is axiom VIB that one wants to combine with axioms IA, IB, II, IIIA, IVA and V. This combination yields a slightly different class of

[26] For example: $g_i(w_{ij}) = n_i^{-1}\alpha^{n+1-i}\sum_{j|i} w_{ij}, \alpha > 1$.

[27] That is, each element of $M(x)$ is given by: $M_i = \sum_{j=1}^{m} p_{ij} w_{ij}(x)$.

[28] It is worth noting that if one takes aversion to inequality between types to an extreme, then $g_1'(w) > 0$ and $g_i'(w) \to 0, \forall i > 1$. Then all that matters is the poorest type, and the dominance conditions on $M(x)$ collapse to the first element of that vector of total incomes: $n_1\mu(T_1, x) > n_1\mu(T_1, y)$. This is the partial ordering equivalent to van de Gaer's allocation rule under the ex-ante compensation principle of E.Op., namely, to maximize the mean well-being of the poorest type – but here those means and population are weighted.

social welfare functions: it is still given by (4) and $g_i(w_{ij})$ continues to vary across types and to become progressively less steep as types get "richer," or better-off. But with axiom VIB, the transformation functions within each type are no longer linear; they are strictly concave instead.[29] We call this class S^V, and those who subscribe to it the "Inequality-Averse Opportunity Egalitarians" or IOEs. The only difference between S^V and S^N is, of course, that the second derivative of the type-specific transformation function is negative: $g_i''(w) < 0$. This imposes inequality aversion within types.

Now let $n_i = \sum_{j=1}^{m} p_{ij}$ denote the population of type T_i and the type-specific Generalized Lorenz Curve for T_i as $GL_i(w_i(x), n_i)$.[30] It turns out that a theorem due to Atkinson and Bourguignon (1987), which was stated and proved in a different context, can be straightforwardly re-interpreted to establish the dominance conditions analogous to (11.5) which apply for social welfare functions in S^V. The theorem establishes that:

$$S^V(x) > S^V(y) \Leftrightarrow \sum_{i=1}^{k} GL_i(w_i(x), n_i) \geq \sum_{i=1}^{k} GL_i(w_i(x), n_i), k = 1, \ldots, n \tag{11.6}$$

In other words: Shorrocks's (1983) theorem stated that Generalized Lorenz Dominance in the full distribution (across the entire population) of x over y implied that all prioritarian social welfare functions (i.e. all members of the S^P class) would rank x as preferred to y. Peragine's theorem in (11.5) told us that, if instead of being a prioritarian, you were a Strict Opportunity Egalitarian, whose welfare functions were of the form S^N, then the relevant condition was Generalized Lorenz Dominance not of the full distribution of individuals, but of the type's well-being distribution. Now we learn from the Atkinson-Bourguignon (1987) Theorem, re-stated in (11.6), that if you reject inequality neutrality within types (that is, utilitarian reward), but require instead some degree of inequality aversion within types, then

29 In this case within any type T_i, $g_i'(w) > 0, g_i''(w) < 0$. Although strict concavity is now permitted, it must be the case that $\inf g_i'(w) > \sup g_{i+1}'(w) > 0, \forall i \in [1, \ldots, n-1]$, so as to avoid a potential clash with axiom IIIA.

30 Specifically, $GL_i(w_i(x), n_i) = \frac{1}{n_i}\sum_{j=1}^{q} w_{ij}(x)$.

the relevant condition is sequentially additive second-order dominance of the type-specific Generalized Lorenz Curves.

A similar result exists also for the combination of ex-ante compensation and agnostic reward. Here we combine axioms IA, IB, II, IIIA, IVA and V only, without imposing any reward axiom; that is without imposing any restrictions on our attitude to inequality within types. This generates a class of social welfare functions still given by (11.4), but where the functions $g_i(w_{ij})$ satisfy only two properties: (i) within any type T_i, $g_i'(w) > 0$. And across types, (ii) $\mathit{inf}\, g_i'(w) > \mathit{sup}\, g_{i+1}'(w) > 0, \mathit{for\ all}\ i \in [1, \ldots, n-1]$. We call this class S^A, and those who hold such preferences "Agnostic Opportunity Egalitarians" (AOEs). The difference between this class and the two considered earlier is the absence of any restriction on the second derivative of the type-specific transformation functions $g_i(w_{ij})$: agnosticism with respect to inequality within types means that the transformation function within each type has to be upward-sloping, but it can be strictly concave, linear, or even strictly convex. Naturally, this yields a larger set of welfare functions, of which the two disjoint sets of S^N and S^V are both strict subsets. The dominance criterion for S^A will therefore be correspondingly stronger.

Indeed, Peragine and Serlenga (2008) find that a unanimous ranking of outcome x over outcome y among all social welfare functions in the S^A class requires a sequential first-order stochastic dominance of population-weighted type distributions between outcomes x and y:

$$S^A(x) > S^A(y) \Leftrightarrow \sum_{i=1}^{k} n_i F_i(w_{ij}(x)|T_i) < \sum_{i=1}^{k} n_i F_i(w_{ij}(y)|T_i), \mathit{for}\ k = 1, \ldots, n \tag{11.7}$$

In (11.7), $F_i(w_{ij}(x)|T_i)$ denotes the (discrete) cumulative distribution function of well-being in Type T_i, under outcome x.[31] The algorithm to check dominance is as follows: one first compares the distributions of the poorest type, in outcomes x and y. The c.d.f. in x must lie everywhere below that in y.[32] Then one adds the distribution of the second-poorest

[31] In general, we use the mathematical notation $(a|b)$ to denote "*a* conditional on *b*."

[32] More precisely, the c.d.f. in x must lie nowhere above and at least somewhere below that in y.

type, thereby creating a mixture of the distributions of the two lowest types under each outcome. Again, that mixture in x must first-order dominate the same mixture in y. Carry on creating mixtures of distributions by sequentially bringing in the next poorest type. If first-order dominance holds n times, then all SWFs of the S^A form will rank x higher than y.

The foregoing discussion allows us to fill in the axioms and results for the first row of Table 11.1, which we do below in Table 11.2:

11.3.1 Discussion

There is a clear analogy between these three dominance results and their well-known antecedents in welfare economics. For outcome x to be preferred to outcome y according to *any* SWF that satisfies Anonymity, Monotonicity, Continuity, and Separability (but not necessarily Pigou-Dalton), one needs first-order dominance of the distribution in x over y. If we add an inequality-aversion requirement – the Pigou-Dalton axiom – this makes the SWFs not only increasing but also strictly concave. That is a smaller set of functions, so it is "easier" to obtain dominance: instead of first-order stochastic dominance, only second-order is needed. That is, instead of the cumulative distribution function in x lying everywhere below that for y, we need the Generalized Lorenz Curve for x lying everywhere above that for y. And if we are strictly neutral with respect to inequality, then a comparison of means or sums is sufficient to rank x and y.

When we try to make social welfare rankings of that kind consistent with the two fundamental principles of equality of opportunity (compensation and reward), we face a clash: those two principles are generally inconsistent with two of the axioms used earlier in welfare rankings: Anonymity and Pigou-Dalton. As we have seen in this section, it is possible to reconcile the two principles with social welfare functions, but only if one is prepared to limit their domains. In the ex-ante case that we have seen so far, Anonymity must apply only partially: among people in the same type, and among the types themselves – but not among all people. Pigou-Dalton must apply only between types. With those restrictions, a compromise between welfarism (prioritarianism) and E.Op. can be obtained. Its exact nature depends on one's specific views on the reward principle.

If we choose to take the notion that all inequality within types is ethically acceptable and not to be compensated – that is: if we are Strict

Table 11.2. *Ex-ante compensation: axioms and results*

	Utilitarian reward	Inequality-averse reward	Agnostic reward
Ex-ante Compensation	**Axioms:** anonymity within types; anonymity of types; monotonicity; P-D between types; additivity; continuity; inequality neutrality within types. **Dominance condition:** Generalized Lorenz Dominance of the total type well-being distribution	**Axioms:** anonymity within types; anonymity of types; monotonicity; P-D between types; additivity; continuity; inequality aversion within types. **Dominance condition:** Sequential second-order dominance of the type-specific Generalized Lorenz Curves.	**Axioms:** anonymity within types; anonymity of types; monotonicity; P-D between types; additivity; continuity. **Dominance condition:** Sequential first-order dominance of population-weighted type-distributions.
Ex-post Compensation			

Opportunity Egalitarians – then we are neutral to inequality within types, and we can define a set of SWFs (those with the form and properties of W_N), all members of which will agree in their rankings across outcomes x and y if and only if we observe Generalized Lorenz Dominance of the total type well-being distributions between x and y. The total type well-being distribution is just a vector of the total type well-being accruing to each type, for all types. Total well-being is, of course, mean well-being in a type multiplied by the type's population.

If, on the other hand, we are not quite so convinced that all inequality within types should be accepted, then we are averse to inequality within types. Agreement among all SWFs with the form and properties of S^V will obtain if and only if a sequence of Generalized Dominances is observed for the type distributions (rather than just their means). This more demanding condition reflects the inequality aversion within types: if we don't care about this distribution within types, all that matters are the type means, or total sums. But if we do, we need the kind of second-order dominance we saw in Shorrocks's theorem, but now applied to each type (and then aggregated sequentially across types, from the lowest to the highest-ranked).

As always, dominance conditions become more demanding if we are seeking agreement across a larger set of SWFs. So, if we insist on being completely agnostic about inequality within types – allowing that second derivative to be anything from negative to positive infinity – then sequential second-order dominance of type distribution is no longer enough: first-order dominance is needed, for each step in the sequential summation of types (mixtures of distributions), from the poorest on upwards, until you have the full distribution.

We now turn to a discussion of the clash between Prioritarianism and E.Op. – and of possible axiomatic compromises to reconcile them – under an ex-post version of the compensation principle.

11.4 Prioritarianism and Equality of Opportunity: The Ex-Post Case

The ex-post compensation principle requires reducing the inequality in well-being among individuals exerting the same level of effort. The literature has proposed different versions of this principle and, in addition, different social criteria have been formulated which combine ex-post compensation and the different versions of the reward principle. In this section we briefly review this literature, focusing on the contributions that have adopted a social welfare approach to rank distributions. In general, much as for the ex-ante case discussed in the previous section, the features that distinguish the opportunity-egalitarian social welfare orderings from the prioritarian are the social evaluations of inequality-reducing operations (such as the Pigou-Dalton transfer) and permutations of individuals (expressed by the Symmetry axiom).

While in the prioritarian approach any inequality-reducing transfer has a positive impact on social welfare, in the ex-post opportunity egalitarian approach the social welfare judgment on such operations will be conditioned on the effort level exerted by the individuals involved in the transfer (the tranche). This is in contrast to the ex-ante approach, where such judgment is conditioned on the circumstances (the type) of the individuals involved. Similarly, while in the prioritarian approach no permutation of individuals has any effect on social welfare – meaning precisely that only individual well-being matters for social welfare – in the ex-post opportunity egalitarian approach the social welfare judgment on permutations will once again be conditioned on the effort level of the individuals involved. We now turn to the main criteria consistent with this view.

In his seminal contribution, Roemer (1993) proposes two different ex-post equality of opportunity criteria. According to the first criterion, the social objective should be to maximize the minimum welfare level for each degree of effort: that is to say, the social objective is the maximization of the minimum of each tranche distribution. This criterion clearly expresses extreme inequality aversion within tranches combined with an agnostic view on the inequality between tranches, i.e. an agnostic version of the reward principle. Roemer's original proposal was formulated in a context of optimal taxation, where the objective was to find the tax rate which maximizes the social welfare. Interpreted in the current context of social rankings, Roemer's first criterion can be defined as follows: one distribution x is preferred to another distribution y if, at each tranche j, the minimum in x is higher than the minimum in y. Formally:[33]

[33] Equivalently:
$S(x) > S(y) \Leftrightarrow min_i \left[w_{ij}(x)|e_j\right] > min_i \left[w_{ij}(y)|e_j\right], for\ all\ j = 1, \ldots, m$

$$S(x) > S(y) \Leftrightarrow min\left(T^j(x)\right) > min\left(T^j(y)\right), for\ all\ j = 1, \ldots, m \tag{11.8}$$

Peragine (2004) generalizes Roemer's first criterion by weakening the property of extreme inequality aversion within tranches and proposing instead a less-extreme view of ex-post compensation, based on a revised version of the Pigou-Dalton transfer principle. The property he proposes, *within tranches Pigou Dalton,* requires that any reduction of inequality among individuals in the same tranche should be welfare improving:

Within Tranches Pigou Dalton: Consider outcomes x and y, and assume they differ only for tranche j. If outcome y is obtained from outcome x by means of a finite sequence of pure (non-leaky) rank preserving progressive transfers between individuals in tranche j, then y is preferred to x.

This latter property is combined with the following properties:

- *anonymity within tranches:* any permutation within tranches does not change the social welfare);
- *additivity between tranches:* the social value of an outcome is equal to the sum of some (tranche-specific) function of the well-being of each tranche;
- *monotonicity:* any increment to individual income is welfare improving.

The axioms above yield the characterization of the following family of social welfare functions:

$$S^T(x) = \sum_{j=1}^{m} v_j\left(w_{ij}(x)\middle|e_j\right) \tag{11.9}$$

where the functions v_j, which may vary across tranches, satisfy two properties: within any tranche T^j, $v_j' > 0, v_j'' < 0$ (Peragine, 2004). Hence, social welfare is given by an additive aggregation of the welfare across tranches, where each tranche is evaluated by an increasing, symmetric and strictly concave function. Although in this general form, (11.9) continues to impose no restrictions on inequality between tranches – that is, it remains agnostic about reward – one can easily conceive of specific members of S^T that would introduce a specific reward scheme. The v_j function might, for example, use a single strictly concave transformation function for all tranches, but multiply the sum of transformed well-being within each tranche by some factor increasing in effort.[34]

Based on the above family of social welfare functions Peragine (2004) obtains a suitable dominance condition, according to which an outcome x is preferred to another outcome y if and only if, at each tranche, the distribution in x, $w_j(x)$, Generalized Lorenz dominates the distribution in y, $w_j(y)$. Formally, let $n_j = \sum_{i=1}^{n} p_{ij}$ denote the population of tranche T^j, and $GL_j(w_j(x), n_j)$ denote the tranche-specific Generalized Lorenz Curve for $T^j(x)$.[35] Peragine (2004)'s theorem establishes that:

$$S^T(x) > S^T(y) \Leftrightarrow GL_j(w_j(x), n_j) > GL_j(w_j(y), n_j), \textit{for all } j = 1, \ldots, m \tag{11.10}$$

This result is the "ex-post opportunity egalitarian" counterpart of Shorrocks' (1983) characterization of the Generalized Lorenz Dominance based on the family of (generalized) utilitarian social welfare functions.

Let us turn now to Roemer's (1993) second criterion. Keeping the extreme inequality aversion within tranches, Roemer's second proposed solution was to maximize the average of the minimal values of the tranche distributions. That is to say, the social planner should first identify the minimum of each tranche; then, she should take the mean of these minimal values. This quantity becomes the social objective: the "mean of (tranche) mins" criterion. This criterion endorses extreme inequality aversion within tranches and a utilitarian version of the reward principle. Formally:

$$\begin{aligned} S(x) > S(y) \Leftrightarrow & \frac{1}{m}\sum_{i=1}^{m} min\left(T^j(x)\right) \\ & > \frac{1}{m}\sum_{i=1}^{m} min\left(T^j(y)\right) \end{aligned} \tag{11.11}$$

Clearly this is a much less demanding criterion than Roemer's first condition: only one dominance test is required, instead of the m tests for Roemer's first condition. In a recent paper, Fleurbaey, Peragine and

[34] For example, $v_j(w_{ij}(x)|e_j) = a^j \sum_{i=1}^{n} g(w_{ij}(x)|e_j), g' > 0, g'' < 0, \alpha > 1$.

[35] Specifically: $GL_j(w_j(x), n_j) = \frac{1}{n_j}\sum_{i=1}^{q} w_{ij}(x)$.

Ramos (2017 – henceforth FPR) generalize both of Roemer's criteria by weakening the extreme within-tranche inequality aversion and focusing on the concept of the envelope of the type distributions. As seen above, Roemer (1993) proposes to look only at the worst-off individuals in each tranche. FPR's contribution is close in spirit to Roemer's proposal. However, in their approach not only the worst off, but also the second worst-off, and the third worst-off and so on are taken into account. More precisely, they define a *class* as a set of individuals that sit at the same position in their respective tranche distributions. The first class is exactly Roemer's maximand, but FPR consider all classes. Members of the same class are in the same position in their respective tranche distribution, meaning that the impact of circumstances is similar for all of them, when this impact is evaluated by their well-being ranking in their tranche. The FPR ex-post criteria are then based on the idea of reducing the inequality between classes.

Their proposal works as follows. Starting from the original matrix, first re-arrange the values within each tranche until all tranches contain rank-ordered welfare levels, from the lowest to the highest. In this way, we obtain a transformed matrix, whose rows are now labeled "classes."[36] The focus now becomes the reduction of inequality between classes. The authors then impose the crucial property of *Pigou Dalton Transfer between Classes*, which states that any progressive transfer between two classes improves social welfare:

Pigou Dalton Transfer between Classes: Consider two classes, *i* and *k*, with different means. If outcome *y* is obtained from outcome *x* by means of a finite sequence of pure (non-leaky) transfers exclusively between individuals in these two classes (leaving all individuals in all other classes unaffected), the net effect of which is that the richer class becomes even richer and the poorer class even poorer in *y*, then *x* is preferred to *y*.

This property, inspired by ex-post compensation, is then combined with *Monotonicity, Anonymity within Classes (requiring that any permutation within a class leaves social welfare unchanged)*, and three different versions of the reward principle: *Utilitarian, Agnostic* and *Inequality Averse Reward* within classes. Correspondingly, they obtain

[36] Note that, in general, classes are not the same as types because type distributions may cross: one type may "lie below" another over a given set of tranches, but above it for a different set of tranches. In the special case when there are no "type crossings," types and classes are the same.

three different dominance conditions, all expressed as sequential dominances of the class distributions.[37]

When Utilitarian Reward is used, a unanimous ranking $S(x) > S(y)$ requires Generalized Lorenz Dominance of the distribution of class means, defined analogously to the distribution of type well-being discussed in Section 11.3 (see Equation 11.5), but with the means taken over the rows of the re-organized class matrix, as opposed to the original matrix where rows were types.[38] When Agnostic Reward is used instead, unanimous rankings require an additive sequence of first-order dominance among class distributions, analogous to that between types, described in Equation (11.7). Finally, when inequality-averse reward within class is imposed, unanimity requires an additive sequence of Generalized Lorenz Dominance among class distributions, analogous to that described in Equation (11.6). Formal statements of these conditions are consigned to Appendix 11.A.2.

As noted in note 37, if the type distributions are characterized by sequential first-order dominance – that is, if for each level of effort, being in a higher type implies having higher level of well-being – then the classes correspond to the types. In this case, the ex-post dominance conditions characterized by FPR correspond to the ex-ante dominance conditions discussed in the previous section. More precisely, condition (i) in Appendix 11.A.2 corresponds to the ex-ante dominance characterized by Peragine (2004); condition (ii) to the condition in Peragine and Serlenga (2008); and condition (iii) to the sequential generalized Lorenz Dominance of Atkinson and Bourguignon (1987).

This review allows us to complete our comparison of axioms and results embodied in Tables 11.1 and 11.2, which we do in Table 11.3.

Just as in Section 11.3, note 29 noted that van de Gaer's "min of means" allocation rule corresponded to a special, extreme case of the combination of ex-ante compensation and utilitarian reward (cell 1,1 in Table 11.3), the foregoing discussion in this section has indicated that Roemer's "mean of mins" allocation rule (described above as his second criterion) is an extreme case of the combination of ex-post compensation and utilitarian reward (cell 2,1). In both cases, taking inequality aversion to an extreme leads to an exclusive focus on the

[37] Note that FPR do not impose *Continuity*.

[38] Recall, once again, that in our setup with N constant, these conditions can be expressed interchangeably in terms of sums or means.

Table 11.3. *Ex-ante and ex-post compensation: axioms and results*

	Utilitarian reward	Inequality-averse reward	Agnostic reward
Ex-ante Compensation	**Axioms:** anonymity within types; anonymity of types; monotonicity; P-D between types; additivity; continuity; inequality neutrality within types. **Dominance condition:** Generalized Lorenz Dominance of the total type well-being distribution.	**Axioms:** anonymity within types; anonymity of types; monotonicity; P-D between types; additivity; continuity; inequality aversion within types. **Dominance condition:** Sequential second-order dominance of the type-specific Generalized Lorenz Curves.	**Axioms:** anonymity within types; anonymity of types; monotonicity; P-D between types; additivity; continuity. **Dominance condition:** Sequential first-order dominance of population-weighted type distributions.
Ex-post Compensation (using Classes)	**Axioms:** anonymity within classes; monotonicity; P-D between classes; inequality neutrality within classes. **Dominance condition:** Generalized Lorenz Dominance of the distribution of class means.	**Axioms:** anonymity within classes; monotonicity; P-D between classes; inequality aversion within classes. **Dominance condition:** Sequential second-order dominance of the class-specific Generalized Lorenz Curves.	**Axioms:** anonymity within classes; monotonicity; P-D between classes. **Dominance condition:** Sequential first-order dominance of class distributions.
Ex-post Compensation (using Tranches)			**Axioms:** anonymity within tranches; monotonicity; p-d within tranches; additivity between tranches; continuity. **Dominance condition:** Generalized Lorenz Dominance within all tranches.

mean of the lowest-ranked type (in one case) or class (in the other). The use of the mean arises from the utilitarian version of the reward principle, which mandates inequality neutrality within the relevant group (type or class).

Analogously, a special case of Roemer's first criterion – which focuses on the full lower envelope of tranches – can be obtained by taking inequality aversion between envelopes (i.e. classes) to an extreme in a combination of ex-post compensation and agnostic reward (cell 2,3 in Table 11.3). Agnostic reward is extremely demanding, requiring first-order dominance among the relevant groups (classes, in this case). With extreme inequality aversion, all that matters is the lowest class, i.e. the lower envelope of tranches. Finally, in cell (3,3), Peragine (2004) shows that Generalized Lorenz Dominance within each and every tranche yields the same result as sequential first-order dominance of class distributions – as should be intuitively clear.

The discussion in Sections 11.3 and 11.4, drawing on various existing results from the literature, has enabled us to summarize the kinds of desiderata (axioms) that can be imposed on social orderings (or welfare functions) to combine the central features of prioritarianism (inequality aversion) and E.Op. theory (compensation for circumstances; reward to effort). We first established that the standard axioms of prioritarianism, in their pure form, clash with the compensation principle – whether in its ex-ante or ex-post forms. In essence, this is because prioritarianism is a welfarist criterion: the distribution of well-being contains all the information needed to rank societies (outcomes). In contrast, the normative theory of equality of opportunity is non-welfarist: the distribution of well-being does *not* contain all the information needed to rank societies; additional information is needed.

However, we then went on to note that suitable restrictions on two key axioms underpinning prioritarianism – namely Anonymity and the Pigou-Dalton transfer principle – could yield narrower classes of welfare functions that still satisfied (more limited versions of) impartiality and inequality aversion, while also allowing for differential roles for circumstances and efforts in assessing distributions of well-being.

The complexity, if any, arose from the fact that the principles of compensation and reward in the normative theory of equality of opportunity can be, and have been, formally defined in different ways. Table 11.3 summarizes seven such combinations of these principles which, while not exhaustive of the literature, cover a meaningful span of the normative choices one must make.

For each such combination of compensation and reward principle, we noted which axioms characterize the relevant classes of social orderings and described the dominance criteria between distributions that would be required to establish rankings that are robust to changes in functional form within each class. These requirements vary substantially: from comparing vectors of type or class means, to elaborate sequences of first-order dominance results. In practice, do these differences also imply widely different results – so that comparisons across distributions are highly sensitive to which particular combination of compensation and Loo reward principles (i.e., which cell in Table 11.3) one happens to choose? Although it is impossible to answer this question comprehensively here, the next section sheds some light on it by turning to one empirical example: an application of the comparisons just outlined to a ten-year period in the recent history of South Africa, possibly the world's most unequal country today.

11.5 An Empirical Application: The Case of South Africa

To investigate the various opportunity-prioritarian criteria for comparing social welfare that were proposed above, we use data from all waves of the South Africa National Income Dynamics Study (NIDS). There are five such waves, recording information from 2008, 2010/11, 2012, 2014/15 and 2017. NIDS was designed to follow the original sample of households over time. However, using suitable weights, each wave can also be treated as a cross-sectional survey representative of the South African population. Like most household surveys, the NIDS does not contain a measure that would truly correspond to the concept of "individual well-being," discussed in the foregoing sections. In common with most of the empirical literature, in this section we approximate well-being by monthly per capita household income. That variable includes all regular income received by the household on a monthly basis, net of taxes, as well as imputed rental income from owner-occupied housing.[39] Besides income, the NIDS also contains

[39] There is a large literature on the fraught and incomplete nature of income or consumption expenditure variables as proxies for well-being. The limitations are clearly important, but we do not discuss them further here.

information about a number of circumstances beyond individual control, notably: parental education, parental occupation, ethnicity, and area of birth.

In our analysis, we restrict the sample to adult individuals aged 18–65. Missing information further limits the sample that can be used to estimate distributions: for example, we exclude the circumstance "area of birth" because of the extremely high share of missing values (above 50 percent in four waves). We keep in the sample only observations with non-missing information for all the other circumstances, in at least one period.[40] Additional information about missing data is reported in Appendix 11.A.3.

We exploit the longitudinal nature of the survey, which includes probability weights calibrated to keep the samples representative of the population interviewed in Wave 1 over time (Brophy et al., 2018). Panel weights are set to zero for households that entered the survey in later waves, including the 2017 top-up sample introduced to improve the representativeness of top incomes in the survey. As a consequence, our empirical exercise does not assess the evolution of well-being or inequality of opportunity in South Africa over time. What it does evaluate is the dynamics of social welfare for the population originally sampled in 2008.[41]

Descriptive statistics for the samples used in our analysis are reported in Table 11.4. Average disposable income fell between 2008 and 2010/11, but gradually rose thereafter. By 2017, mean per capita income was 17 percent above its initial 2008 level. Income inequality was extremely high by international standards during the whole period but declined markedly over the period, particularly after 2010.

To compare the various alternative opportunity-prioritarian criteria discussed above, we first need to partition the sample into types and tranches, as in Figure 11.1. Selecting a type partition is not a trivial

[40] Following individuals over time, whenever information on a circumstance is missing in a given wave, but not missing in other waves, we impute the latest non-missing value.

[41] For the same reason and because the two re-rankings of types' mean income (in 2010/11 and 2014/15) are not statistically significant, the ranking of types is fixed in 2008 and subsequently preserved. The use of weights allows us to correct for attrition. Brophy et al., (2018) report an attrition rate of between 22 percent and 14 percent, depending on the waves, and involving especially white, Indian/Asian and high-income respondents.

Table 11.4. ***Descriptive statistics for the samples included in the analysis***

Wave	Sample size	Age	Income	Gini
2008	7,353	39.09	3,467.75	0.6879
2010/11	4,815	40.66	3,224.56	0.6844
2012	5,896	41.03	3,591.67	0.6574
2014/15	6,443	40.81	3,747.47	0.6262
2017	4,397	43.37	4,065.30	0.6283

Note: Adapted from NIDS W1–W5. Monthly disposable per capita incomes are in RAND 2015.

matter, since there is an empirical trade-off between comprehensiveness (seeking to limit the downward biases arising from the partial observability of circumstances) and precision (that arises from limiting the risk of overfitting the model, which can in principle bias estimates upward); see Brunori et al. (2019). We follow Brunori et al. (2018) and use a conditional inference regression tree to obtain our optimal type partition. This particular machine-learning algorithm has been shown to perform well when estimating inequality of opportunity on survey data (Hothorn et al., 2006; Brunori et al., 2018).[42]

[42] In order to obtain a robust type partition we control the growth of the tree by setting two rather conservative requirements: first we set the confidence level $(1-\alpha) = 0.99$; second we impose a minimum number of observations per type across all waves (100). The algorithm then obtains the partition in types iterating the following six steps:

1. The algorithm first tests the degree of correlation between the dependent variable (per capita income) and all the observable independent variables (circumstances).
2. If all tests have a Bonferroni-adjusted p-value higher than α the algorithm stops,
3. If one or more regressors have an adjusted p-value lower than α the algorithm selects the regressor with the lowest p-value.
4. Then the algorithm considers all values of such regressor as possible splitting points, that is the value used to partition the population into two subgroups. For each value and resulting subgroups, the algorithm tests whether the means of the dependent variable in the two subgroups are significantly different from each other;
5. The splitting value selected is again the value producing the lowest p-value of the test,
6. Steps 1 to 5 are repeated for all resulting subgroups.

The algorithm eventually stops at step 2 and the resulting partition can be represented as an upside-down tree.

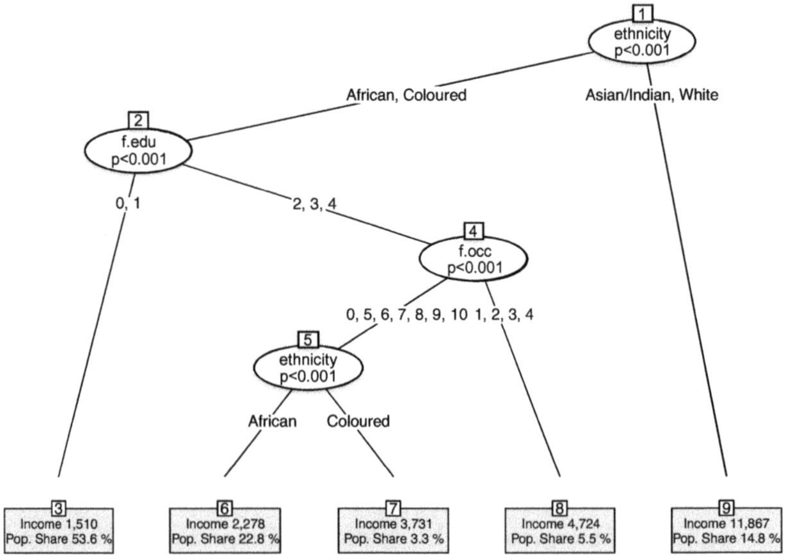

Figure 11.4 The partition of South Africa into five Roemerian types
(*Source*: Own elaboration from NIDS Wave 1)

Note: monthly disposable per capita income is in RAND 2015. Race is coded in four categories: African, Asian/Indian, Coloured, White. Parental occupation (f.occ, m.occ) is 1 digit ISCO code (10 = "never worked"). Parental education (f.edu, m.edu): 0 = no education, 1 = foundation phase, 2 = intermediate phase, 3 = senior phase, 4 = higher education.

Figure 11.4 shows the opportunity tree obtained for South Africa in 2008. Independent variables used to split the sample into types are the circumstances beyond individual control already mentioned: race (four categories), father's and mother's education (five ordinal values each), father's and mother's occupation (eleven categories each). Alongside the name of the variable, each splitting point reports the Bonferroni-adjusted *p*-value of the correlation test. Terminal nodes describe the partition in five types and report expected incomes and population shares. Types' empirical cumulative distribution functions are shown in Figure 11.A.2 in Appendix 11.A.3.

Given the significance test and other restrictions imposed (and described above), the regression tree arguably yields a partition of the population into the most salient types. The five selected types, corresponding to the terminal nodes in Figure 11.4, are: Type "3": Africans and "Coloured" people whose fathers had low levels of education (54 percent

Table 11.5. ***Type income means, population shares and sample sizes, over time***

	2008				2010/11		
Type	Income	Share	N	Type	Income	Share	N
3	1,510	53.6	4,582	3	1,573	56.5	3,160
6	2,278	22.8	1,521	6	2,543	24.4	1,022
7	3,731	3.3	340	8	3,838	3.6	149
8	4,724	5.5	298	7	4,040	3.9	255
9	11,867	14.8	612	9	12,140	11.7	229
	2012				2014/15		
Type	Income	Share	N	Type	Income	Share	N
3	1,936	57	3,839	3	2,126	53.5	3,924
6	2,743	22.6	1,185	7	3,124	4.1	358
7	2,946	3.5	304	6	3,194	26.5	1,576
8	4,457	4.8	242	8	6,765	5.5	300
9	12,797	12.1	326	9	12,063	10.5	285
	2017						
Type	Income	Share	N				
3	2,164	54.5	2,752				
6	3,658	25.3	1,009				
7	4,723	3.8	243				
8	8,364	5.7	210				
9	12,218	10.6	183				

Note: Adapted from NIDS Wave 1–Wave 5. Types' number correspond to terminal nodes in Figure 11.4. Population shares are in percent; monthly disposable per capita incomes are in RAND 2015.

of the population): Type "6": Africans whose fathers had better levels of education, but were employed in lower-ranked occupations; Type "7": "Coloured" people whose fathers had better levels of education, but were employed in lower-ranked occupations; Type "8": Africans and "Coloured" people whose fathers had better levels of education and were employed in higher-ranked occupations; and Type "9": Whites and people reporting Asian/Indian ethnicity. Table 11.5 reports opportunity profiles, that is population share and average outcome in each type.

Table 11.6. *Population-wide Generalized Lorenz Dominance*

	2008	2010/11	2012	2014/15	2017
2008	.	.	$<^{***}$	$<^{***}$	$<^{***}$
2010/11	.	.	$<^{***}$	$<^{***}$	$<^{***}$
2012	$>^{***}$	$>^{***}$	.	$<^{***}$	$<^{***}$
2014/15	$>^{***}$	$>^{***}$	$>^{***}$	.	.
2017	$>^{***}$	$>^{***}$	$>^{***}$	.	.

Note: Adapted from NIDS Wave 1–Wave 5. Confidence levels are calculated based on the percentile distribution of 500 bootstrap replications of the statistics: $^{*} = 0.9$, $^{**} = 0.95$, $^{***} = 0.99$.

We define ten tranches as the tenths in the income distribution within each type (following Roemer, 1998). Based on this partition we check the dominance conditions summarized in Table 11.3. Each dominance is tested for each pair of waves, in a discrete number of points (ten), and the result reported in one entry of a 5x5 matrix. If at all ten points distribution *i* dominates distribution *j*, we report ">" in cell *i,j* (row *i*, column *j*). In addition, if at all points we can reject the null hypothesis that distribution *j* dominates distribution *i* and, at least in one point we cannot reject the null hypothesis that distribution *i* dominates distribution *j*, we consistently report the confidence level. Table 11.6 reports results for simple Generalized Lorenz Dominance of the overall distribution in year $i(w(x))$ over year $j(w(y)) : GL(w(x), N) > GL(w(y), N)$. These correspond to pure prioritarian rankings, with unanimity in the class of social welfare functions S^P.

Table 11.6 indicates that social welfare in 2008 and 2010/11 cannot be unambiguously ranked in this class, as there is no second-order dominance. Neither can 2014/15 and 2017 be ranked. Aside from those two, every other pairwise comparison yields unambiguous welfare rankings: 2012 dominates both 2008 and 2010/11. The year 2014/15 dominates all three previous waves; and 2017 does the same, except for 2014/15. Overall, this is a tale of consistent improvements in social welfare over time (aside from a blip in 2010/11, and an inconclusive comparison between the last two waves), consistent with a rising mean and declining inequality.

As noted in Section 11.3, the comparisons in Table 11.6 are based purely on the well-being (here: income) vector and take no account of differences in circumstances and efforts. Table 11.7 presents results for

Table 11.7. ***Six versions of opportunity-prioritarian dominance results for South Africa: 2008–2017***

(a) Generalized Lorenz Dominance of the total type well-being distribution

	2008	2010/11	2012	2014/15	2017
2008	.	.	<***	<***	<***
2010/11	.	.	<***	<***	<***
2012	>***	>***	.	<***	<***
2014/15	>***	>***	>***	.	<*
2017	>***	>***	>***	>*	.

(b) Sequential second-order dominance of the type-specific Generalized Lorenz Curves

	2008	2010/11	2012	2014/15	2017
2008	.	.	<***	<***	<***
2010/11	.	.	<***	<***	<***
2012	>***	>***	.	<***	<***
2014/15	>***	>***	>***	.	.
2017	>***	>***	>***	.	.

(c) Sequential first-order dominance of population-weighted type distributions

	2008	2010/11	2012	2014/15	2017
2008	.	.			<***
2010/11	.	.	<***	<***	<***
2012	.	>***	.	.	.
2014/15	.	>***	.	.	.
2017	>***	>***	.	.	.

(d) Generalized Lorenz Dominance of the distribution of class means

	2008	2010/11	2012	2014/15	2017
2008	.	.	<***	<***	<***
2010/11	.	.	<***	<***	<***
2012	>***	>***	.	.	<***
2014/15	>***	>***	.	.	<***
2017	>***	>***	>***	>***	.

Table 11.7. (*cont.*)

(e) Sequential second-order dominance of the class-specific Generalized Lorenz Curves

	2008	2010/11	2012	2014/15	2017
2008	.	.	.	<***	<***
2010/11	.	.	<***	<***	<***
2012	.	>***	.	<***	<***
2014/15	>***	>***	>***	.	.
2017	>***	>***	>***	.	.

(f) Sequential first-order dominance of class distributions

	2008	2010/11	2012	2014/15	2017
2008	.	.			<***
2010/11	.	.	<***	<***	<***
2012	.	>***	.	.	.
2014/15	.	>***	.	.	.
2017	>***	>***	.	.	.

Note: Adapted from NIDS Wave 1–Wave 5. Confidence levels are calculated based on the percentile distribution of 500 bootstrap replications of the statistics: * = 0.9, ** = 0.95, *** = 0.99.

the six different opportunity-prioritarian dominance criteria summarized in Table 11.3.[43]

Table 11.7 contains the key empirical results of the chapter. There is a one-to-one correspondence between its six panels and the six main panels of Table 11.3: Panels (a), (b) and (c) in Table 11.7 test the dominance conditions described in the first row of Table 11.3, for the combination of the ex-ante version of the compensation principle with the three different versions of the reward principle (utilitarian, inequality averse and agnostic). Panels (d), (e) and (f) test the dominance conditions from the second row of Table 11.3, for the combination of ex-post compensation with the three different versions of the

[43] Note that Table 11.7 does not present the combination of ex-post compensation using tranches and agnostic reward.

reward principle.[44] As noted earlier, the type-based results in the first three panels and the class-based results in the last three would be identical if the quantile functions (or c.d.fs) of the five types did not ever cross in our data. Figure 11.A.3 in the Appendix 11.A.3 shows (for 2012) that there are type crossings in the data – for example, belonging to Type 7 (Colored, with an educated father working in low occupations) is an advantage for individuals in the lowest tranches, but not so much an advantage for individuals in the highest tranches – so the ex-ante and ex-post compensation results can differ in principle. As we see below, they do differ in practice as well, although not very substantially.

How do the "opportunity-prioritarian" dominance results under these various combinations of compensation and reward principles compare among themselves, and with the pure prioritarian rankings in Table 11.6? Overall, there is remarkable consistency in the number and identity of rankings among the results consistent with utilitarian and inequality-averse reward, regardless of the compensation principle. These results are also generally similar to those in Table 11.6. The rankings in panel (b) – ex-ante compensation and inequality-averse reward – are identical to those in Table 11.6 (pure prioritarianism). Panel (a) – ex-ante compensation and utilitarian reward – has the same results, and adds dominance of 2017 over 2014/15, albeit only at the 10 percent significance level. Compared to Table 11.6, panel (d) – ex-post compensation and utilitarian reward – also adds dominance of 2017 over 2014/15 but loses dominance of 2014/15 over 2012. Panel (e) – ex-post compensation and inequality-averse reward – loses the dominance of 2012 over 2008.

Results are much less similar if we wish to remain agnostic about reward. In this case, the classes of social welfare functions over which we demand unanimity are much larger, so dominance is harder to obtain. In particular, first-order – rather than second-order – dominance is required: sequentially among type distributions in the ex-ante case, and sequentially among class distributions in the ex-post case. It is unsurprising, then, that panels (c) and (f) display many fewer instances where rankings are unanimous for the relevant class of

[44] For the combination of ex-post compensation and agnostic reward, Section 11.4 had also presented a dominance result using tranche distributions, rather than classes. The empirical results for that exercise are presented in Table 11.A.2 in the Appendix 11.A.3.

SWFs. Nonetheless, dominance is still found for 2017 over 2008; and for 2017, 2014/15 and 2012 over 2010/11. Interestingly, the results are identical in the ex-ante and ex-post cases.

Taken together, the empirical results suggest that prioritarians (that is, folks with SWFs in S^P) would have a generally positive assessment of income dynamics in South Africa over those ten years. Changes in welfare between the first two waves were ambiguous. But after that, 2012 dominated both previous waves; 2014/15 dominated all three waves that preceded it; and 2017 dominated three of the four preceding waves.

More interestingly from the point of view of this chapter, modifying the tenets of prioritarianism to normatively differentiate inequalities arising from personal responsibility from those arising from exogenous circumstances makes relatively little difference – unless one is prepared to accept social welfare functions in which *greater* inequality within types or classes is regarded as a social improvement. Ruling out that degree of agnosticism about the reward principle – that is, confining our attention to the utilitarian and inequality-averse versions in panels (a), (b), (d), and (e) – it turns out that, at least in this particular application, incorporating personal responsibility considerations into prioritarianism makes little difference in terms of robust rankings, regardless of which specific versions of the compensation and reward principles one happens to favor.

11.6 Conclusions

This chapter sought to address the question of whether prioritarianism – the view that social welfare judgments should incorporate an explicit preference for the worst-off – can be made consistent with the normative theory of equality of opportunity – the view that differences in well-being arising from differences in the exercise of personal responsibility may be acceptable, whereas those arising through circumstances beyond the control of the individual must be compensated. We found that the two views, in their pure forms, are inconsistent: if a person is better-off despite humble beginnings and great disadvantage, whereas someone else is worse-off despite very favorable circumstances, largely because of lack of effort or irresponsible behavior, the two normative views might recommend different policies or interventions.

However, we also found that the two views could be combined provided one accepted two main kinds of adjustments to the principles (axioms) underpinning prioritarianism. First, the notion of impartiality, or symmetry of treatment, which is universal under prioritarianism, needs to be restricted to specific subsets of the population; for example: to those who share the same circumstances, or to those who exert similar degrees of personal effort. Second, the notion of progressive (Pigou-Dalton) transfers must also be restricted. They should no longer be required to represent improvements over the entire domain of the population but only, once again, within smaller subsets, defined either in terms of circumstances or efforts. A strengthening of the Separability axiom – to an Additivity one – is also needed.

Because there are differences in the specific approaches the literature has taken to the E.Op. principles of compensation and reward, we explored six main different combinations and, in each case, identified the set of axioms that would define an appropriate class of social welfare functions.[45] Furthermore, we noted – drawing on established results in the literature – the specific conditions that must hold when comparing two distributions for it to be the case that all social welfare functions in the relevant class would rank them unanimously. It turns out that all these conditions are variants of first- or second-order stochastic dominance conditions, defined over different population subgroups and/or distributions, according to the specific combination of E.Op. principles.

Finally, in an empirical application to South Africa during the 2008–2017 period, we compared the stochastic dominance results obtained empirically for the pure prioritarianism version with those for the various different versions of what we call "opportunity-prioritarianism." Despite the a priori risk that the differences in approaches might yield very different rankings, it turns out that, *in this particular application*, there was remarkable agreement among the various criteria, with the exception of the more demanding conditions associated with a fully agnostic attitude to the reward principle. We hope to have provided a useful toolkit of criteria for distributional comparisons for use by analysts whose social judgments incorporate two different kinds of ethical priority: a priority for the worst-off; and a priority for combating inequalities arising from circumstances for which individuals are not responsible.

[45] The six main combinations are those arising from crossing two versions of the compensation principle (ex-ante and ex-post) with three versions of the reward principle (utilitarian, inequality-averse, and agnostic). One combination – of ex-post compensation and agnostic reward – has been approached using tranches or classes, leading to the seventh cell in Table 11.3.

Appendix 11.A.1 Stochastic Dominance and Welfare Comparison Results

Definition of First Order Stochastic Dominance: *For any ordered distributions* $\boldsymbol{w}(x) = (w_1(x), \ldots, w_N(x))$ *and* $\boldsymbol{w}(y) = (w_1(y), \ldots, w_N(y))$ *with population N, distribution* $\boldsymbol{w}(x)$ *First Order Dominates distribution* $\boldsymbol{w}(y)$ *if and only if:*

$$w_k(x) \geq w_k(y), k = 1, \ldots, N \textit{ and a strict inequality for some } k \tag{A.1.1}$$

Equivalently, first-order dominance can be expressed in terms of cumulative distribution functions: for any distributions F(x) and G(x), F first-order stochastically dominates G if and only if F (x) $\leq$ G (x) (for all x, and strictly for some x).

Denote by $\boldsymbol{S}^I$ the family of all social welfare functions satisfying the axioms of Strong monotonicity, Anonymity and Separability. Saposnik (1981) demonstrates the following equivalence result:

Theorem: *For any ordered distributions* $\boldsymbol{w}(x) = (w_1(x), \ldots, w_N(x))$ *and* $\boldsymbol{w}(y) = (w_1(y), \ldots, w_N(y))$ *with population N,* $S(x) > S(y)$ *for all S in the family* $\boldsymbol{S}^I \Leftrightarrow w_k(x) \geq w_k(y), k = 1, \ldots, N$ *and* $w_k(x) > w_k(y)$*, for some k.*

Definition of the Generalized Lorenz Curve: *For any ordered distributions* $X = (w_1(x), \ldots, w_N(x))$ *with population N, the Generalized Lorenz Curve of X is defined as:*

$$GL(k, x, N) = \frac{1}{N}\sum_{l=1}^{k} w_l(x), k = 1, \ldots, N \tag{A.1.2}$$

Definition of Generalized Lorenz Dominance: For any ordered distributions $\mathbf{w}(x) = (w_1(x), \ldots, w_N(x))$ and $\mathbf{w}(y) = (w_1(y), \ldots, w_N(y))$ with population N, distribution $\mathbf{w}(x)$ Generalized Lorenz

Dominates distribution **w**(y) $(GL(w(x), N) > GL(w(y), N))$ *if and only if:*

$$\frac{1}{N}\sum_{l=1}^{k} w_l(x) \geq \frac{1}{N}\sum_{l=1}^{k} w_l(y), \textit{for } k = 1, \ldots, N \textit{ and a strict inequality for some } k \qquad \text{(A.1.3)}$$

Denote by S^S the family of all social welfare functions satisfying the axioms of Strong monotonicity, Anonymity, Separability and Strong Pigou Dalton Transfer. A corollary of theorem 2 in Shorrocks (1983) states that all S in S^S will rank $w(x)$ as preferable to $w(y)$ if and only if the distribution $w(x)$ displays generalized Lorenz dominance over $w(y)$:

Shorrocks Theorem: *For any ordered distributions* $w(x) = (w_1(x), \ldots, w_N(x))$ *and* $w(y) = (w_1(y), \ldots, w_N(y))$ *with population N,*

$$S(x) > S(y) \text{ for all } S \text{ in the family } S^S \Leftrightarrow GL(w(x), N) > GL(w(y), N) \qquad \text{(A.1.4)}$$

Appendix 11.A.2 Summary of results in Fleurbaey, Peragine and Ramos (2017)

Formally, given a distribution x, let us denote the class i by $C_i(x)$, $i = 1, \ldots, n$, with corresponding mean $\mu(C_i(x))$, population $n(C_i(x))$, cumulative distribution function $F_i(w_{ij}(x)|C_i)$ and Generalized Lorenz Curve $GL(C_i, x)$. Fleurbaey et al. (2017) obtain the following set of results:

i. FPR (2017) first criterion, based on utilitarian reward, implies a sequential procedure of comparison of the class distributions, where, at each step, the distributions are simply ranked by their means. This condition can also be interpreted as Generalized Lorenz dominance of the distributions of the class means. Formally, $S(x) > S(y)$ if and only if

$$\sum_{i=1}^{k} \mu(C_i(x)) > \sum_{i=1}^{k} \mu(C_i(y)), \textit{for } k = 1, \ldots, n \qquad \text{(A.2.1)}$$

ii. FPR (2017) second criterion, based on agnostic reward, implies a sequential procedure of comparison of the class distributions, where, at each step, the distributions are ranked by first order dominance. Formally, $S(x) > S(y)$ if and only if

$$\sum_{i=1}^{k} \left[F_i(w_{ij}(x)|C_i)\right] > \sum_{i=1}^{k} \left[F_i(w_{ij}(y)|C_i)\right], \textit{for } k = 1, \ldots, n \qquad \text{(A.2.2)}$$

iii. FPR (2017) third criterion, based on inequality-averse reward, implies a sequential procedure of comparison of the class distributions, where, at each step, the distributions are ranked by Generalized Lorenz Dominance. Formally, $S(x) > S(y)$ if and only if

$$\sum_{i=1}^{k} [GL(x, C_i)] > \sum_{i=1}^{k} [GL(y, C_i)], \textit{for } k = 1, \ldots, n \qquad \text{(A.2.3)}$$

Appendix 11.A.3 Empirical analysis: Descriptive statistics and illustrations

As discussed in Section 11.5, the National Income Dynamics Study (NIDS) Panel Survey contains information on various individual characteristics that can be confidently treated as circumstances, in an E.Op. sense. Unfortunately, however, information on these variables is frequently missing, as documented in Table 11.A.1.

As might be expected, missing observations are not randomly distributed: there is selection in item non-response. In particular, there is a positive correlation between the outcome variable of interest, namely household per capita income, and the probability that an observation has missing information on a circumstance. Figure 11.A. 1 plots the difference between average household disposable income for observations with and without missing information circumstances. The difference is statistically significant for all circumstances in 2008 and never statistically significant in 2017. The particularly alarming correlation detected for race in 2008 involves a relatively small number of observations (4 percent).

Table 11.A.1. *Distribution of missing information*

Wave	Father occupation (f.occ)	Mother occupation (m.occ)	Father education (f.edu)	Mother education (m.edu)	Ethnicity
2008	22%	24%	31%	33%	4%
2010	29%	29%	42%	36%	0%
2012	23%	25%	30%	32%	0%
2014	27%	29%	29%	33%	0%
2017	36%	38%	41%	45%	0%

Note: Adapted from NIDS Wave 1–Wave 5.

Table 11.A.2. *Tranches Generalized Lorenz Dominance*

	2008	2010/11	2012	2014/15	2017
2008	.	.	.	.	$<^{***}$
2010/11	.	.	$<^{***}$	$<^{***}$	$<^{***}$
2012	.	$>^{***}$	.	$<^{***}$	$<^{***}$
2014/15	.	$>^{***}$	$>^{***}$	.	.
2017	$>^{***}$	$>^{***}$	$>^{***}$	.	.

Note: Adapted from NIDS Wave 1–Wave 5. Confidence levels are calculated based on the percentile distribution of 500 bootstrap replications of the statistics: * = 0.9, ** = 0.95, *** = 0.99.

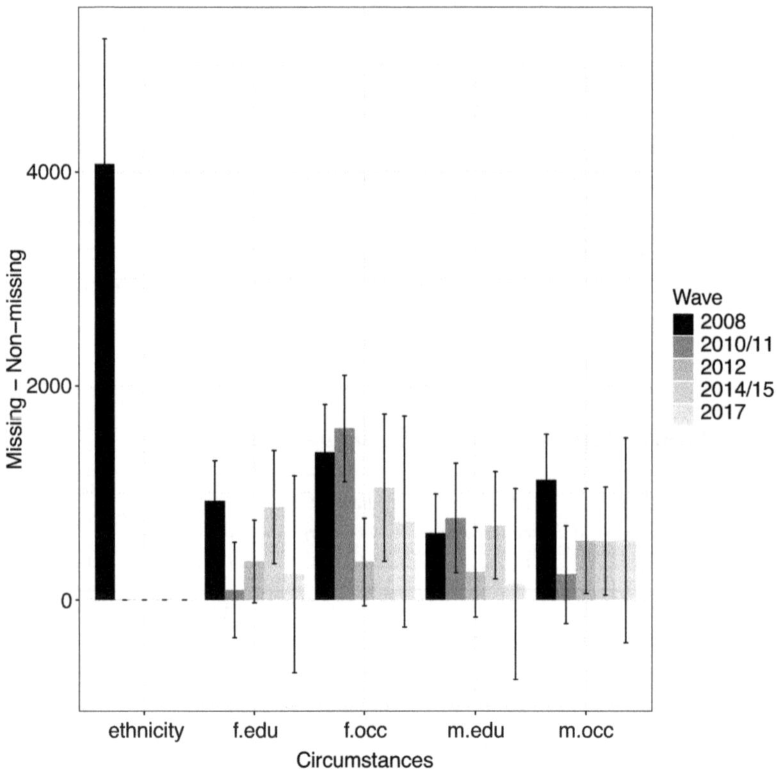

Figure 11.A.1 Income differences between observations with missing and non-missing circumstances

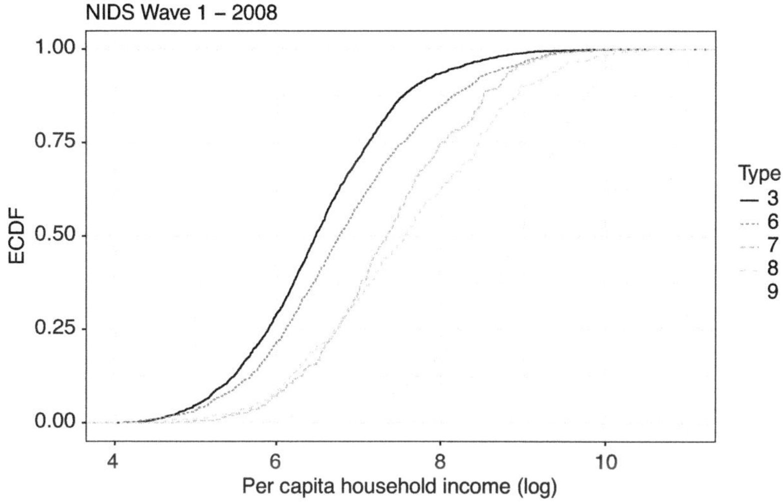

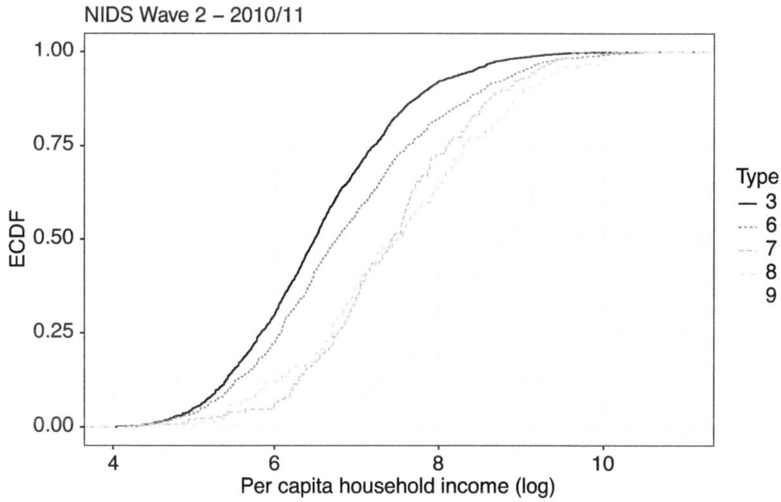

Figures 11.A.2 through 11.A.6 Empirical cumulative distribution functions for five types in South Africa: 2008–2017
(*Source*: NIDS Wave 1–Wave 5)

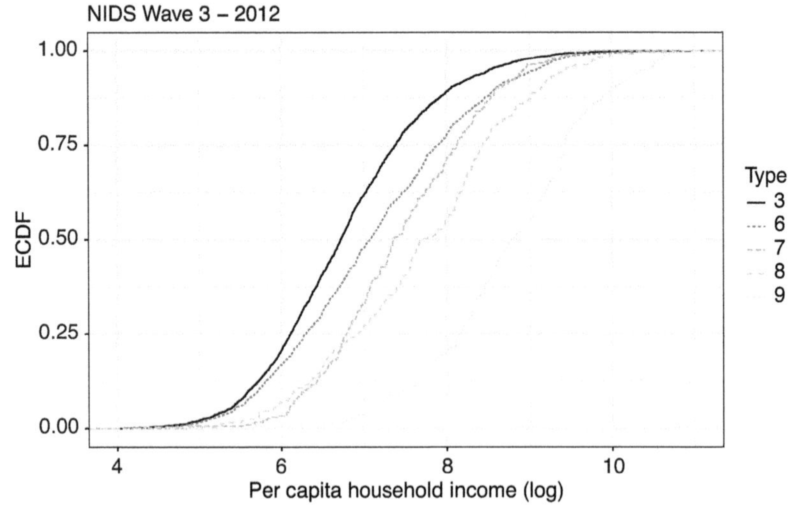

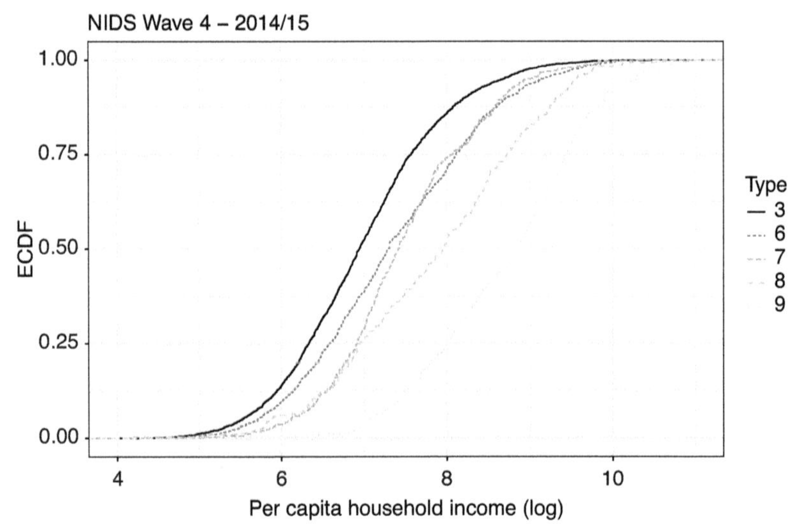

Figures 11.A.2 through 11.A.6 *(cont.)*

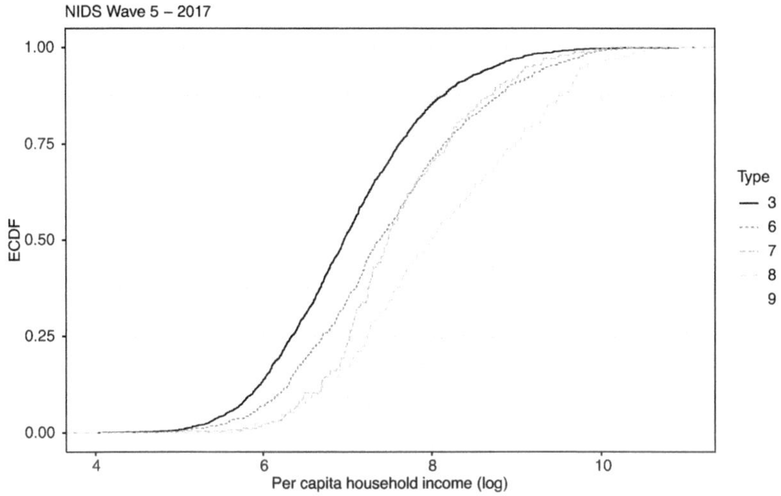

Figures 11.A.2 through 11.A.6 (*cont.*)

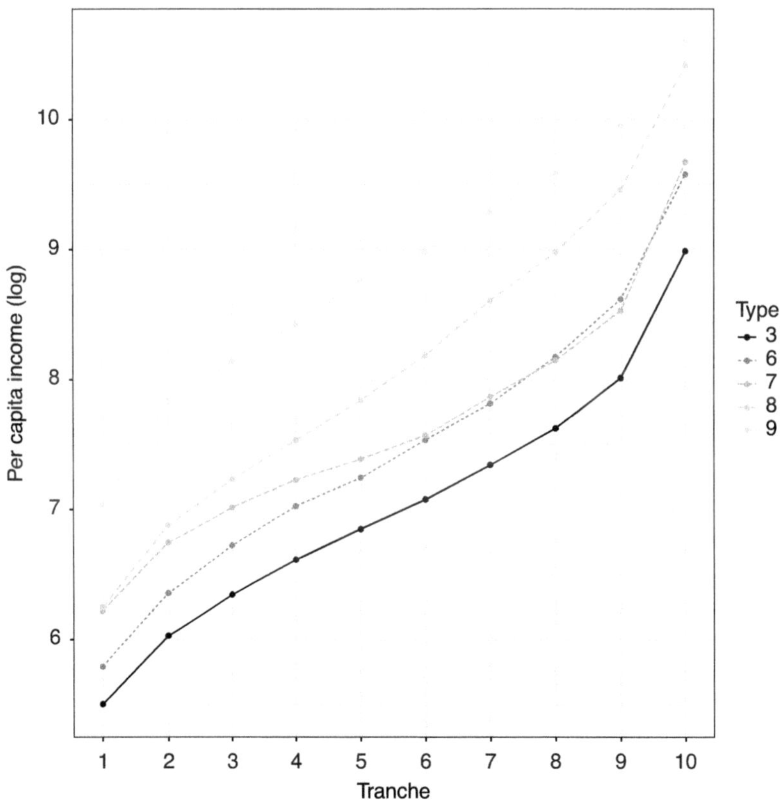

Figure 11.A.7 Re-ranking of types across tranches in 2012
(*Source*: NIDS Wave 3)

References

Adler, M. (2018). "Prioritarianism: Room for Desert?" *Utilitas*, 30: 172–197.

(2019). *Measuring Social Welfare: An Introduction*. Oxford: Oxford University Press.

Arneson, R. (1989). "Equality of Opportunity for Welfare." *Philosophical Studies*, 56: 77–93.

Atkinson, A.B. (1970). "On the measurement of inequality." *Journal of Economic Theory*, 2: 244–263.

Atkinson, A.B. and Bourguignon, F. (1987). "Income Distribution and Differences in Need." In G. F. Feiwel, ed., *Arrow and the Foundation of the Theory of Economic Policy*. London: Macmillan, pp. 350–370.

Bentham, J. (1789). *An Introduction to the Principles of Morals and Legislation*. London: T. Payne and Son.

Brophy T., Branson, N., Daniels, R.C., Leibbrandt, M., Mlatsheni, C. and Woolard, I. (2018). *National Income Dynamics Study Panel User Manual*. Release 2018 Version 1. www.datafirst.uct.ac.za

Brunori, P., Hufe, P. and D. Mahler. (2018). "The Roots of Inequality: Estimating Inequality of Opportunity from Regression Trees and Random Forests", Ifo Working Paper, No. 252, Ifo Institute - Leibniz Institute for Economic Research at the University of Munich, Munich.

Brunori, P., Peragine, V. and Serlenga, L. (2019). "Upward and downward bias when measuring inequality of opportunity." *Social Choice and Welfare*, 52: 635–661.

Cohen, G.A. (1989). "On the Currency of Egalitarian Justice." *Ethics*, 99: 906–944.

Dworkin, R. (1981a). "What is equality? Part 1: Equality of welfare." *Philosophy & Public Affairs*, 10: 185–246.

(1981b). "What is equality? Part 2: Equality of resources." *Philosophy & Public Affairs*, 10: 283–345.

Ferreira, F.H.G. and Peragine, V. (2016). "Individual Responsibility and Equality of Opportunity". In M. Adler and M. Fleurbaey, eds., *Oxford Handbook of Well-Being and Public Policy*. Oxford: Oxford University Press, pp. 746–784.

Fleurbaey, M. (1994). "On fair compensation." *Theory and Decision*, 36: 277–307.

(1995). "Three solutions for the compensation problem." *Journal of Economic Theory*, 65: 505–521.

Fleurbaey, M. and Peragine, V. (2013). "Ex ante versus ex post equality of opportunity." *Economica,* 80: 118–130.

Fleurbaey, M., Peragine, V. and Ramos, X. (2017). "Ex-Post Inequality of Opportunity Comparisons." *Social Choice and Welfare,* 49: 577–603.

Hothorn T., Hornik, K. and Zeileis, A. (2006). "Unbiased recursive partitioning: A conditional inference framework." *Journal of Computational and Graphical Statistics*, 15: 651–674.

Parfit, D. (2000). "Equality or Priority?" In M. Clayton and A. Williams, eds., *The Ideal of Equality*. Houndmills: Palgrave, pp. 81–125.

Peragine, V. (2004). "Ranking income distributions according to equality of opportunity." *Journal of Economic Inequality*, 2: 11–30.

Peragine, V. and Serlenga, L. (2008). "Higher education and equality of opportunity in Italy." In J. Bishop and B. Zheng, eds., *Research on Economic Inequality*, 16: 67–97.

Rawls, J. (1971). *A Theory of Justice*. Cambridge, MA: Harvard University Press.

Roemer, J. (1993). "A pragmatic theory of responsibility for the egalitarian Planner." *Philosophy & Public Affairs*, 10: 146–166.

(1998). *Equality of Opportunity*. Cambridge, MA: Harvard University Press.

Saposnik, R. (1981). "Rank-dominance in Income Distributions." *Public Choice*, 36: 147–151

Sen, A.K. (1980). "Equality of what?" In S. McMurrin, ed., *The Tanner Lectures on Human Values*. Salt Lake City: University of Utah Press, pp. 197–220.

(1985). *Commodities and Capabilities*. Amsterdam: North-Holland.

(2000). "Social Justice and Distribution of Income." In Atkinson, A.B. and F. Bourguignon, eds., *Handbook of Income Distribution: Vol.1*. Amsterdam: North Holland, chapter 1.

Shorrocks, A. (1983). "Ranking Income Distributions." *Economica*, 50: 3–17.

Van de Gaer, D. (1993). "*Equality of opportunity and investment in human capital*." Ph.D. Dissertation, Katholieke Universiteit Leuven.

12 *Prioritarianism and the COVID-19 Pandemic*

MADDALENA FERRANNA,
J.P. SEVILLA AND DAVID E. BLOOM*

This chapter was drafted in December 2020. The following discussion of COVID-19 summarizes what was known about the virus, its impacts, and the steps taken to control it, as of that date.

12.1 Introduction

Coronavirus disease 2019 (COVID-19), which is caused by severe acute respiratory syndrome coronavirus 2 (SARS-CoV-2), was first reported in Wuhan, China, in December 2019. Since then, COVID-19 has spread explosively around the world, with catastrophic health, social, and economic effects. By mid-December 2020, roughly 72 million cases had been detected worldwide, including nearly 1.7 million deaths.[1] The socioeconomic costs of the COVID-19 pandemic (and of the nonpharmaceutical interventions adopted to control its spread) are staggering.[2] The International Monetary Fund estimates that COVID-19 is associated with an expected 4.4 percent contraction of the world economy in 2020 (IMF 2020). By comparison, the 2009 global financial crisis caused a 0.1 percent contraction of the world economy (Gopinath 2020).

Several factors underlie the dramatic consequences of COVID-19. SARS-CoV-2 is a novel virus with many features that remain substantially unknown. However, it appears to be very infectious, lethal, and geographically unconstrained. In comparison, the World Health

* We thank the editors, James Hammitt, Nicolas Treich, and participants at the "Prioritarianism in Practice" meeting on May 21–22, 2020 for useful comments. This work was supported by the Value of Vaccination Research Network (VoVRN) through a grant from the Bill & Melinda Gates Foundation (Grant OPP1158136). The content is solely the responsibility of the authors and does not necessarily reflect the views of the VoVRN or the foundation.

[1] https://coronavirus.jhu.edu/map.html

[2] The World Health Organization declared COVID-19 a pandemic on March 11, 2020.

Organization reports that the seasonal flu has an infection fatality rate (i.e., the proportion of deaths among all infected individuals) of 0.1 percent (WHO 2020), whereas the infection fatality rate of COVID-19 is estimated to be in the range of 0.5%–1% (Levin et al. 2020; Perez-Saez et al. 2020; Streek et al. 2020; Yang et al. 2020), although much uncertainty remains (Ioannidis 2020). Lack of adequate health sector responses (i.e., testing, treatment, and vaccination) has undermined effective efforts to contain the pandemic. However, the pandemic has also spurred an unprecedented innovations race (Bloom et al. 2021). For example, more than 270 vaccines against COVID-19 are under development around the world, with more than 60 already in the clinical testing phase, and eight already approved for full or emergency use in several countries.[3] Absent effective treatments and a vaccine, countries have implemented social and physical distancing policies to curb the infections (e.g., quarantine, masks, staying 6 feet apart, and economic shutdowns), which have proven to be socially, culturally, economically, and politically severe and burdensome and which have required a drastic and perhaps permanent reorganization of large segments of society (e.g., social norms about handshakes, hugging, and kissing; patterns of working from home; virtual instead of in-person meetings; air travel; and building planning).

The COVID-19 pandemic has exacerbated existing inequalities through patterns of infections, sickness, and deaths that disproportionately affect disadvantaged populations; socioeconomic differences in healthcare access and in ability to invest in resources to tackle the pandemic; and inadequate redistribution mechanisms to equitably share the economic burden of the pandemic and nonpharmaceutical interventions to control it (Avent 2020). Lack of global leadership, coupled with rising nationalism and populism, has hampered a timely, effective, and globally fair solution to the COVID-19 crisis (Hafner et al. 2020).

Management of the pandemic raises many policy questions, the answers to which depend on the ethical framework that is used to evaluate reductions in deaths and morbidity against socioeconomic costs. For example, to what extent and for how long should we restrict social interactions and limit economic activities? When is it safe to reopen schools and businesses? How much should countries spend on

[3] www.nytimes.com/interactive/2020/science/coronavirus-vaccine-tracker.html

research and development (R&D) for a vaccine against COVID-19? How should the financing burden be divided among countries and stakeholders? How should scarce healthcare resources such as ventilators, intensive care unit beds, vaccine doses, or drugs be allocated among the population?

This chapter explores how utilitarian and prioritarian social welfare function (SWF) frameworks can help answer some of these questions. In particular, we will focus on two issues: disease control and vaccine allocation. We discuss these value frameworks in the context of simplified and stylized examples, which aim to demonstrate how pandemic response requires addressing distributional issues of the kind that SWF frameworks can inform rather than to generate real-world policy conclusions. Section 12.2 describes some of the core pieces of the analytical frameworks and discusses the main issues at stake in the COVID-19 crisis. We will focus on the value of policies to control the spread of the pandemic (e.g., economic lockdowns) and of prioritizing different groups in allocating scarce vaccine supplies. Section 12.3 qualitatively discusses the main differences among benefit-cost analysis (BCA), utilitarianism, and prioritarianism. Section 12.4 presents a stylized example of control interventions, and Section 12.5 a stylized example of vaccine prioritization strategies supported by the three value frameworks. Section 12.6 concludes. Although we focus on the COVID-19 pandemic, the lessons we draw generalize to other epidemics and to any intervention with health and non-health impacts.

The analysis draws two main sets of conclusions. When deciding the strength of the control policy, what counts is the relative regressivity of COVID-19 burdens and policy costs. The more regressive the burdens of COVID-19 are, the more the distribution sensitivity of the value framework raises the value of strict control policies (i.e., increased regressivity increases the value of control for prioritarianism more than it does for utilitarianism, and for utilitarianism more than it does for BCA). The more regressive the costs of strict control policies are, the more the distribution sensitivity of the value framework will lower the value of strict control policies. Thus, the net impact of the value framework's distribution sensitivity on the value of control depends on the relative strength of the two patterns of regressivity. The sensitivity of utilitarianism and prioritarianism to the distribution of policy costs implies that they will strongly support income redistribution mechanisms (e.g., unemployment benefits).

The second set of conclusions concerns vaccine allocation. None among BCA, utilitarianism, and prioritarianism prioritizes specific groups based solely on the size of the risk of severe health outcomes from COVID-19 that they face. BCA tends to favor the wealthy because they have the larger ability to pay and thus the larger willingness to pay (although, in practice, benefit-cost analysts often use unit values that are invariant to income). Utilitarianism and prioritarianism skew the allocation toward the poor because they bear a disproportionate burden of COVID-19. Because the young and the poor are among the worse-off in the population, prioritarianism is more likely to target young, socioeconomically disadvantaged populations in allocating COVID-19 vaccines than are utilitarianism and BCA. However, because the difference in COVID-19 mortality risks between the old and the young is so high, even prioritarianism will rank the socioeconomically disadvantaged elderly at the top of the vaccine priority list (even though the wealthy elderly may be ranked lower than the socioeconomically disadvantaged young).

A note of caution before we proceed. As mentioned, the current chapter was completed in December 2020. Although the evaluation tools discussed herein have enduring relevance, their application to COVID-19 is based on the information available as of December 2020 and should be read and understood in that light.

12.2 Background

12.2.1 Concept of Well-Being

The main goal of the chapter is to discuss the evaluation of COVID-19 interventions through the lens of SWFs, specifically utilitarian and prioritarian ones. Under the SWF approach, assessing the value of an intervention involves two steps: (i) estimating the intervention's impacts on all the attributes of individual well-being and (ii) aggregating individuals' well-being gains and losses to assess the intervention's impact on overall social welfare. The specific aggregation rule depends on the adopted SWF (Adler 2019).

We start by specifying a measure of individual well-being. We assume individual well-being depends on attributes including consumption/income, longevity, and health status. Specifying a well-being measure and its dependence on its attributes can be done in several ways. Adler and Decancq, Chapter 3 of this volume, review the most common methods. We rely on utility functions that represent individuals' preferences and risk attitudes regarding alternative probability distributions of attributes over a lifetime. We interpret the period and lifetime utility functions of microeconomic theory as interpersonally comparable ratio-scale indices of individual well-being (with meaningful zeros and defined up to a common multiplicative constant). We therefore treat "well-being" and "utility" interchangeably.

We assess policy impact on lifetime rather than sub-lifetime utility, which is standard in the literature and in this volume. We assume that lifetime utility is additive in period (e.g., annual) utility, there is no time discounting, and the marginal utility of income (or consumption) is diminishing so that a dollar raises the utility of the poor more than it does that of the rich. The time additivity and zero discounting assumptions jointly imply that marginal utility is linear in (expected or realized) longevity. Therefore, all else equal, longevity increments have the same positive effect on lifetime utility independently of the age of the individual.[4] The time additivity assumption, although standard in the literature, bears on the comparison between utilitarianism and prioritarianism and, in particular, on the weight given to the young in policy evaluation.[5]

12.2.2 *Impact of COVID-19 on Well-Being*

The COVID-19 pandemic has health and non-health negative impacts on individuals' well-being. The health burden includes the probability and severity of infections, which can lead to death, temporary and

[4] Suppose that a 20-year-old and a 70-year-old are going to die soon, but they can both live five more years if they take an experimental treatment. The quality of life of those additional five years is the same for both individuals. Time additivity and zero discounting imply that the two individuals attach the same value to the life-extension treatment. If marginal utility were decreasing in longevity, then the value of the treatment for the 20-year-old would be larger than the value of the treatment for the 70-year-old on the grounds that the life of the former is shorter.

[5] As discussed later, if we retain the time additivity and zero discounting assumptions, under utilitarianism a given increase in longevity for the young has the same value as an equal increase in longevity for the old, while that is not true for prioritarianism. If we remove the time additivity and zero discounting assumptions, both utilitarianism and prioritarianism would give greater priority to increases in longevity for the young, although more for the latter than for the former.

long-term physical disability, and temporary or long-term mental health burdens in patients and in friends and family. Health-system-related burdens include treatment and other costs; congestion of intensive care units and other resources leading to rationing, delay, and disruption of medical and public health services (including immunization programs critical to the health and the cognitive and physical development of children around the world, especially in developing countries); and out-of-pocket expenditures on health. The non-health impacts of COVID-19 include the potential loss of income due to work stoppage, unemployment, furlough, or sickness.

The health impacts of COVID-19 are strongly associated with pre-existing health and socioeconomic status. Some demographic groups seem to be disproportionately exposed to risks of COVID-19 complications and deaths, particularly the elderly, those with underlying health conditions, and males (e.g., Guan et al. 2020; Zhou et al. 2020; Chow et al. 2020). Risk of infection seems higher for low-socioeconomic (SES) individuals and communities due to their over-representation in essential jobs and service jobs requiring physical presence (and disallowing working from home), more crowded living arrangements, higher probability of using public transportation, and lower financial ability to stockpile food (Blundell et al. 2020; Brown and Ravallion 2020). Risk of infection also seems to be higher in polluted neighborhoods (Wu et al. 2020) and in areas with less access to healthcare resources. In the United States, COVID-19 deaths are overrepresented among African Americans, Hispanics, and Native Americans (Subbaraman 2020).

COVID-19 can have direct negative economic impacts on infected individuals and their families, e.g., through medical bills, salary losses due to sick days or to taking care of sick family members, and decreased productivity due to the onset of a long-term disability. Social distancing to control infections or reduce exposure, whether mandated or voluntary, creates profound macroeconomic costs. People who can afford to do so will spend more work and leisure time at home, which can shift the pattern of demand (e.g., from restaurant meals to online groceries, or from office space to home office supplies). Overall levels of consumption and demand may also fall if income is reduced (e.g., among the unemployed) or if people are saving for precautionary reasons or in anticipation of spending more after the pandemic. In turn, such reduced demand can lead to unemployment or furloughs, particularly in some contact-intensive sectors (e.g., restaurants); bankruptcy and business closures; and increased exposure to socioeconomic strains and the risk of poverty among the most vulnerable groups. Moreover, outbreaks in the workplace will prevent normal functioning of the locale, possibly threatening its own existence and the health and well-being of its employees. In addition, outbreak-induced interruptions in global supply chains can have worldwide negative effects, even in regions not directly affected by the outbreak (UNIDO 2020).

12.2.3 Control Policies

12.2.3.1 Flattening the Curve, Suppression, and Mitigation: Disease Control Basics

Since the worldwide outbreaks of COVID-19 began in winter 2019/2020, epidemiologists have warned that the best immediate course of action to reduce the burden of COVID-19 is to "flatten the infection curve" through social and physical distancing (Roberts 2020). Figure 12.1 depicts the idea. The steep curve represents the projected number of infections over time without any measure to control the spread of the disease (e.g., handwashing or economic lockdown), while the flat curve represents the projected number of infections over time when social and physical distancing measures are enforced. Absent any intervention, existing epidemiological models predict a steep surge of infections well beyond countries' healthcare system capacity for treatment, represented by the thick horizontal line (e.g., Ferguson et al. 2020, Giordano et al. 2020, Kissler et al. 2020). Measures to control the spread of the disease aim to reduce this surge and thereby contain the demand for scarce healthcare resources. Implementing these measures results in a curve with a flatter slope, denoting a slower rate of infection extended over a longer time.

Flattening the curve achieves three main goals. First, it reduces the daily number of positive cases, thereby preventing the healthcare system from being overwhelmed with cases; allowing more people to get treatment; and, hopefully, reducing the number of deaths. Second, flattening the curve diminishes the total number of cases and deaths throughout the pandemic by allowing more people to get treated daily and by reducing the probability of spreading the disease. Therefore, not only will fewer cases and deaths occur per day, but the total number of cases and deaths is also expected to reduce, despite the longer time that the

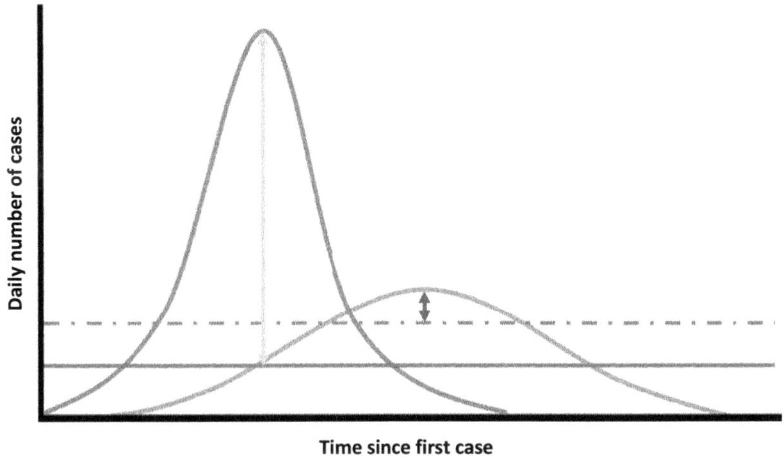

Figure 12.1 Number of COVID-19 cases over time with and without non-pharmaceutical interventions and projected rationing

Note: The steep curve represents the projected number of cases over time without nonpharmaceutical intervention to control the spread of the disease (such as handwashing or economic lockdown); the flat curve represents the projected number of cases over time with those measures. The horizontal lines represent the healthcare system capacity constraints, and the arrows represent the peak rationing of healthcare resources (i.e., the number of cases that cannot receive treatment). Implementing nonpharmaceutical interventions and relaxing the healthcare system capacity constraint are both useful strategies to reduce the required rationing.[6]

epidemic takes to be resolved. Finally, flattening the curve buys some time to develop and test a vaccine or new therapeutic drugs. Expanding the supply of scarce healthcare resources (i.e., moving from the thick horizontal line to the dotted one) is a complementary strategy to flattening the curve. Interventions to relax the healthcare system capacity constraint include, for example, developing faster and more accurate tests for COVID-19 and for COVID-19 antibodies, postponing elective procedures, and easing supply chain bottlenecks and financial constraints to improve the distribution of resources.

Strategies to control the course of the pandemic can be divided into two broad categories: suppression and mitigation (Yglesias 2020). Suppression aims at keeping the number of infections as close to zero as possible. Mitigation allows a controlled outbreak to occur, with the aim of keeping the number of cases within the healthcare system

[6] We thank Daniel Cadarette for creating the picture.

capacity. Stay-at-home orders and economic lockdowns suppress the infection as long as they are in place. Contact tracing, quarantine of positive cases, and social distancing of the elderly are examples of measures to mitigate the infection without completely suppressing it. A useful reference point for delineating the control strategy has been the so-called reproduction number, labeled R, which measures the expected number of infections that one case directly generates (Adam 2020). When $R < 1$, the outbreak is shrinking. Mitigation strategies that aim at slowing down transmission without necessarily ending it may have $R > 1$; suppression strategies always result in $R < 1$.

Suppression measures could delay the outbreak, spare many lives, and buy time until a vaccine or treatment is developed. However, suppression strategies are also very costly, potentially triggering massive unemployment, business closures, educational setbacks, and worsening mental health. In addition, if suitable mitigation policies do not follow once they are lifted, a new surge of cases is likely to occur as herd protection has typically not yet been achieved.[7] Mitigation strategies, which may be used with or instead of suppression, are less invasive as they do not rely on complete economic shutdown. However, they require extensive testing and contact tracing to control the pandemic successfully and the political and technological capacity to quickly revert to more aggressive suppression strategies if the outbreak gets out of control.

After the initial outbreak of COVID-19, most countries around the world implemented economic shutdowns and placed strict limitations on individuals' mobility to suppress the pandemic and ease overloaded healthcare systems.[8] Once the outbreak was considered under control, countries started lifting stay-at-home orders and slowly reopening their economies, with the underlying goal of moving from a suppression to a mitigation phase. Sweden is the famous outlier, with its decision to not suppress the outbreak through school and business closures, instead relying on social distancing and non-mandatory guidance to reach

[7] Herd protection occurs when the number of immune individuals in a population is sufficiently large that nonimmune individuals are also protected from infection thanks to reduced likelihood of transmission. For COVID-19, the herd protection threshold is estimated to be at least 60 percent in the absence of any intervention (Fontanet and Cauchemez 2020).

[8] www.imf.org/en/Topics/imf-and-covid19/Policy-Responses-to-COVID-19

herd protection in a controlled way (Vogel 2020). As we write this chapter, the relative success of these alternative strategies is unclear.

12.2.3.2 Health–Income Trade-Offs

Some argue that a critical issue in COVID-19 control is how to trade off health and income, while others argue that effectively no such trade-off exists (Mahoney 2020). Under the trade-off view, societies must choose between a "low-health, high-income" state achieved with less aggressive control and a "high-health, low-income" state achieved with more aggressive control. The preferred state depends on the distribution of gains and losses in health and income produced by the control policies required to get to those states.

In contrast, under the no-trade-off view, an uncontrolled pandemic will ultimately lead to economic unravelling, so the surest way to protect income is to protect health first. In such a case, the only two states to choose from are a "high-health, high-income" state brought about by aggressive control and a "low-health, low-income state" from less aggressive control. The plausibility of the no-trade-off view rises if the economic costs of inaction are high, if individuals stringently self-protect, and if the policy horizon is long.

The experience in the first few months of the pandemic showed that control measures can meaningfully reduce the number of infections and deaths due to COVID-19, often at the expense of staggering social and economic costs. The more aggressive the control is, the higher the costs seem to be, suggesting a trade-off.

However, this appearance of a trade-off can be misleading for several reasons. First, it fails to recognize that the "do nothing" scenario (i.e., a policy of uncontrolled spread of the virus) can also have huge negative economic impacts beyond the dreadful burden of many fatalities. As described earlier, these costs relate to the endogenous social distancing implemented by individuals for fear of infection and the disruptions in global supply chains. If we account for the economic costs of inaction, the stark trade-off between health and income (or between "saving lives" and "saving livelihoods") is mitigated, if not completely gone.

The length of the policy horizon matters as well. A stringent control policy enacted at the beginning of the pandemic (e.g., with school and business closures and shelter-at-home orders) allows countries to gain quick control over the spread of the virus and to transition to more lenient mitigation policies in the medium run (based, e.g., on extensive testing, contact tracing and quarantine, physical distancing, and adoption of protective behaviors like wearing masks and washing hands) while keeping the economy open. Such a policy scenario entails staggering economic losses in the short run when the economy shuts down, but much lower costs in the medium to long term when the economy is open and the pandemic is under control. Specifically, the overall costs are likely to be lower than in a no-action scenario with a lot of fatalities and a recession triggered by the panic and the burden of disease. The overall costs are also likely to be lower than in a scenario where virus spread is initially left uncontrolled, panic spreads, and aggressive policies are later introduced to stop the virus and to control the economic downturn. A short-sighted policy maker will focus only on the short-run stark trade-off between lives and livelihoods. However, for any reasonably long policy horizon, saving lives is also good for the economy and for preserving individuals' livelihoods.

The effectiveness of such a narrative depends on many factors. The virus can be kept under control without resorting to lockdowns (or limiting economic lockdowns to short periods of time) only if a country has an efficient testing, contact tracing, and quarantine system; constraints on healthcare system capacity have been relaxed (e.g., the number of hospital beds); and access to healthcare resources is constant and equitably shared (e.g., easy and affordable access to testing). The compliant behavior of the population matters as well, particularly the spread of precautionary measures such as handwashing and wearing a mask. Additionally, complementary redistributive measures such as higher unemployment benefits and recovery grants for businesses can relieve the economic burden of control strategies on individuals and businesses and ensure that no effective trade-off between saving lives and saving livelihoods occurs.

In particular, as the burden of COVID-19 is likely to exacerbate preexisting inequities in health, income, and education, so do the policies to control its spread. Younger workers, women, and low-SES individuals have primarily felt the costs of economic lockdowns and social distancing because they are more likely to work in the high-contact sectors that the policies mainly affect (Dingel and Neiman 2020). Women tend also to bear the brunt of childcare and home schooling. In many places, school closures are likely to widen the educational gap between high- and low-SES pupils, due to the difficulties in effective online learning that the latter face (Andrew et al. 2020). Retired people may have been protected from the economic hardships of control policies, but they suffer from social isolation and deteriorating physical and mental health (Armitage and Nellums 2020). These inequities are going to be even more apparent in low-resource settings.

Thus, context also matters. How best to handle the pandemic and its health and economic costs has no single recipe. The best compromise between saving lives and saving livelihoods depends, among other factors, on the amount of healthcare resources available to a country, its capacity to provide economic relief, overall access to sanitation, and the ability to practice social and physical distancing effectively (e.g., the state of living arrangements).[9] Aggressive lockdown policies coupled with a poorly equipped social security system and overcrowded living arrangements may have moderate effects on the number of infections, shrink the economy, cause extreme food insecurity, and prevent people from accessing basic healthcare services, threatening not only the livelihoods but also the lives of the poorest populations. In this case, saving livelihoods seems to be a precondition for saving lives (e.g., Brown et al. 2020; Cash and Patel 2020).

12.2.4 The Value of Vaccines

The staggering health and non-health burdens of COVID-19 and of the interventions to control its spread highlight the broad benefits of having a vaccine for COVID-19 (Bloom et al. 2021). The vaccine will reduce the morbidity and mortality impacts of the disease. It will also avert the implementation of control measures and their associated costs, e.g., massive unemployment, business closures, disruptions in global supply chains, and increased learning gaps between rich and poor children.

As of December 2020, more than 270 R&D efforts have been undertaken around the world to find a vaccine against SARS-CoV-2, with more than 60 vaccines in human trials and eight candidate vaccines approved for full or limited use in several countries, including Canada, China, Russia, Singapore, the United Kingdom, and the United States.[10] Such a race raises several issues, from the trade-off

[9] As well as the evaluation framework, of course.

[10] www.nytimes.com/interactive/2020/science/coronavirus-vaccine-tracker.html Two of these vaccines (the Pfizer-BioNTech one and the Moderna one) use novel technologies that have never been approved for use in humans before

between safety and speed to the most efficient and fair way of organizing the development, manufacture, and distribution of vaccines (Bloom et al. 2021).

An important topic concerns the allocation of vaccine doses among the population, given that manufacturing capacity constraints will make it a scarce resource, at least at the beginning of the distribution process. The COVID-19 crisis has seen growing "vaccine nationalism," in which countries take a "my nation first" approach to developing, manufacturing, and distributing a vaccine and other treatments against COVID-19. Against that has been a surge of appeals to overcome nationalistic forces and to make the vaccine available everywhere in the world and to all socioeconomic groups, independently of countries' and individuals' ability to pay for it (Emanuel et al. 2020a).[11]

Several guidelines for COVID-19 vaccine prioritization strategies within countries have been proposed (e.g., JCVI 2020; NASEM 2020; Toner et al. 2020).[12] These guidelines share the ethical objective of maximizing some kind of overall good (e.g., individuals' aggregate well-being, or cumulative health and non-health benefits), while accounting for the specific epidemiological characteristics of COVID-19 (e.g., age differences in severity and risk). Most guidelines seek also to be sensitive to equity concerns, in particular to pre-existing health and economic inequities and to the apparent correlation between burdens of COVID-19 and structural inequalities (Schmidt et al. 2020).

One hotly debated issue is whether essential workers within the healthcare sector and service industries should be prioritized over older adults and individuals with serious medical conditions, despite the fact that the latter face a considerably higher risk of severe health consequences (Goodnough and Hoffman 2020). Epidemiological, economic,

(messenger RNA). Several of the other most promising vaccines are also using methods that are at the technological innovation frontier (e.g., viral vector vaccines).

[11] For instance, more than 140 world leaders and experts called for a "people's vaccine" on May 14, 2020, demanding that COVID-19 vaccines, diagnostics, tests, and treatments be provided free of charge to everyone and everywhere in the world: www.unaids.org/en/resources/presscentre/featurestories/2020/may/20200514_covid19-vaccine-open-letter

[12] Debates about the allocation of other scarce medical resources within countries have occurred as well, especially at the beginning of the pandemic, when the explosive pace of infections overwhelmed hospitals in some locales, forcing hard choices of whom to treat and how to allocate resources such as ICU beds and ventilators (e.g., Emanuel et al. 2020b; Bloom et al. 2020).

and ethical reasons have been suggested to support this argument (Ferranna et al. 2021). Essential workers are at highest risk of exposure and transmission of the virus because their work often involves unavoidable high-frequency indoor proximity or interaction with others. If the vaccine can block transmission from vaccinated individuals (an uncertain feature of the approved vaccines as we write this chapter, see, e.g., Peiris and Leung 2020), then vaccinating essential workers first may be more beneficial. Economic reasons for prioritizing essential workers refer to their instrumental value in keeping essential services in the economy open (in addition to the instrumental value in saving other people's lives). Ethical reasons appeal to reciprocity and compensation for the work done by these workers in keeping the economy open while overexposing themselves to the risk of infection. Social justice arguments have also been raised highlighting the fact that many essential workers belong to disadvantaged racial and ethnic minorities and socioeconomically vulnerable groups.

12.3 Value Frameworks to Evaluate Control and Vaccine Allocation Strategies

An emergent and rapidly growing economic literature assesses the value of various measures to control the spread of COVID-19 and to determine the best course of action. Some of the questions this literature addresses are the optimal extent and length of economic shutdowns (how many sectors of the economy to close and for how long), the timing and process of reopening the economy, and the opportunity for age-targeted interventions.[13] In terms of evaluation methods, two main approaches have emerged: BCA, using value-of-statistical-life measures (see, e.g., Acemoglu et al. 2020, Alvarez et al. 2020, Favero et al. 2020, Gollier 2020), and utilitarian SWFs (see, e.g., Eichenbaum et al. 2020, Glover et al. 2020, Jones et al. 2020, Quaas et al. 2020). Only a couple of papers adopt a prioritarian perspective in evaluating COVID-19 control policies (Adler et al. 2020 and Adler 2020).[14]

[13] See, for instance, Bloom, Kuhn, and Prettner (forthcoming 2022) for a review of the literature on the macroeconomic costs of COVID-19 and policies to control its spread.

[14] Adler et al. (2020) is based on the COVID-19 simulator created by Marc Fleurbaey and co-authors (https://sites.google.com/site/marcfleurbaey/Home/covid).

The literature on vaccine allocation, instead, is based mainly on health metrics. While ethical guidelines for vaccine prioritization recommend also considering non-health outcomes and being sensitive to the burden of COVID-19 impacts among socioeconomically vulnerable groups, most modeling exercises focus on strategies that maximize some health benefits, e.g., deaths averted or years of life lost averted (e.g., Bubar et al. 2021; Buckner et al. 2020; Rodríguez et al. 2020). Note that maximizing (quality-adjusted) years of life is tantamount to a utilitarian approach where well-being is assumed to depend only on (quality-adjusted) longevity (see also Cookson, Norheim, and Skarda, Chapter 6 this volume).

In broad terms, the main difference among BCA, utilitarianism, and prioritarianism concerns the relative weight attached to the policy impacts experienced by different individuals.[15] BCA relies on the principle that "a dollar is a dollar is a dollar." BCA evaluates a given policy by converting all its health and economic impacts into monetary equivalents based on individuals' willingness to pay (WTP) to avoid these impacts and then summing up these equivalents. Consequently, the method is unconcerned with the distribution of willingness to pay in the population: health and economic impacts experienced by low-income individuals have the same moral importance as impacts experienced by wealthy individuals, where impacts are measured by individuals' willingness to pay.

The "dollar is a dollar is a dollar" principle has two main consequences. First, because willingness-to-pay measures are inextricably linked to individuals' ability to pay, the interests of the better-off count more than the interests of the less well-off. Wealthy individuals are likely to offer more to reduce the risk of COVID-19 infection and death than their less-wealthy counterparts not because they value life more, but because they have more resources and are thereby more inclined to trade wealth for a given change in health. BCA might value saving 100 rich lives more than saving 100 poor lives because the total willingness to pay of the former is considerably larger than the total willingness to pay of the latter. As an extreme case, BCA might condone a control policy that saves 100 rich lives from COVID-19 while condemning 100 poor lives to starvation and death.

[15] See also Adler (2019), chapter 5, and Hammitt and Treich, Chapter 7 this volume, for a comparison of BCA, utilitarianism, and prioritarianism.

Additionally, BCA would allocate scarce medical resources (including vaccines) to wealthy individuals first, on the grounds that they have a larger willingness to pay than poorer individuals for the same expected improvement in health through immunization.

Note that, to avoid these ethically objectionable results, benefit-cost analysts in practice often use a constant willingness to pay throughout the population, independent of individuals' characteristics such as income or age (Robinson 2007). The analysis in the chapter focuses on "textbook" BCA, which allows for heterogeneous willingness to pay across the population.

Second, because BCA attaches the same value to dollars paid by the rich and dollars paid by the poor (according to the "a dollar is a dollar is a dollar" rule), the distribution of the (net) policy costs plays no role in the evaluation process. Willingness-to-pay measures express how much individuals are ready to pay to reduce their own risk of contracting the virus and suffering the pandemic costs. But, if the policy is implemented, some individuals might end up paying more than their willingness-to-pay threshold, while supporting the risk reduction of other individuals. In particular, absent adequate support policies (e.g., unemployment benefits, paid sick leave, and support for virtual learning), disadvantaged populations, like ethnic minorities and low socioeconomic groups, will mainly feel the costs both of COVID-19 and of the nonpharmaceutical interventions to control it. It is reasonable to assume that a control policy that saves lives while condemning thousands to poverty should rank lower than another control policy that saves the same number of lives, costs the same amount of money in aggregate, but whose burden is felt mainly by the wealthy. However, BCA would be indifferent between the two policies. The same principle holds for the financing of alternative vaccine allocation strategies. BCA is indifferent about who pays for the vaccine doses, whether they are privately paid by single individuals or paid through tax revenues (i.e., sharing the costs collectively).

In contrast, utilitarianism relies on the principle that "a util is a util is a util," where "util" is a quantum of well-being. The utilitarian SWF evaluates policies based on their impacts on individuals' total expected well-being. A known criticism of utilitarianism is its indifference to the distribution of well-being across the population. Consequently, the utilitarian approach is indifferent to whether policy benefits go mainly to the well-off or the worse-off, as long as it leads to an increase in the sum of individuals' well-being.

Although the utilitarian approach is insensitive to inequalities in individual well-being levels, it is sensitive to inequalities in individual income because of the diminishing marginal utility of money assumption. Thus, policies that reduce the income of the poor are valued less than similar policies that induce an identical reduction in the income of the rich. Applied to COVID-19, control policies whose costs are paid mainly by the high-income quintiles are considered better than identical policies (in terms of infection and fatality reductions) whose costs are paid mainly by the low-income quintiles. In contrast, BCA is indifferent to the distribution of the policy costs. Concerns about the incidence and distribution of policy costs have arisen, for instance, in some developing countries, where lack of suitable redistribution mechanisms (e.g., unemployment benefits) make policy costs fall harder on the economically worse-off.[16]

Additionally, because utilitarianism values policy changes in terms of their impact on individual well-being rather than in terms of the individuals' willingness to pay for those changes, ability to pay is implicitly accounted for (in other words, utilitarianism can be thought of as a form of WTP-driven assessment where willingness to pay is adjusted to reflect differential abilities to pay). As a result, the approach does not inflate the policy benefits accruing to the well-off relative to the worse-off merely because money has relatively lower marginal value for the well-off.

A further consequence is that the utilitarian optimal allocation of vaccines is only sensitive to differences in well-being impacts of the vaccine; individual differences in the marginal utility of money (which reflect differences in their ability to pay) do not, as such, change the optimal allocation. In other words, the framework prioritizes individuals that benefit more in well-being terms from being vaccinated. This will typically include those that face the higher burden of COVID-19 (e.g., those with a high COVID-19 fatality risk). However, the framework is sensitive also to life expectancy (the larger the number of years one is expected to live if vaccinated, the larger the increase in well-being) and to the quality of life preserved.

Finally, prioritarianism relies on the principle that "a priority-weighted util is a priority-weighted util is a priority-weighted util"; i.e., unlike utilitarianism, the method is concerned with the distribution

[16] See, for instance, Cash and Patel (2020).

of the individual well-being impacts of the pandemic, attaching higher value to well-being increments that accrue to the worse-off than to identical well-being impacts that accrue to the better-off. Applied to the evaluation of COVID-19 control and vaccine allocation strategies, the prioritarian approach favors interventions with the overall effect of benefiting mainly the worse-off in the population.

Two main forms of prioritarianism can be considered, which differ in the definition of the "worse-off" (Adler, Chapter 2, this volume). *Ex-ante prioritarianism* is concerned with the distribution of *expected* lifetime well-being across the population. From an ex-ante point of view, the worse-off individuals are those who in expectation have poor lifetime prospects. For example, individuals with low expected longevity, individuals who are expected to have low income, and individuals with high chances of suffering from illness. In contrast, *ex-post prioritarianism* is concerned with the expected distribution of *realized* lifetime well-being. From an ex-post point of view, the worse-off individuals are those who have experienced some hardship during their life, expressed in a low lifetime well-being. For example, individuals who die prematurely, individuals who have low lifetime income, and disabled individuals who suffer from poor health and lack access to many lifetime opportunities.

Compared with utilitarianism, the concern for the worse-off has two consequences. First, prioritarianism is even less likely than utilitarianism to support situations where low-income groups bear the brunt of COVID-19 (net) control policy costs. Equivalently, a prioritarian approach to control policy evaluation is likely to support more redistributive transfers favoring unemployed and essential workers because they bear the greatest economic and health burdens, respectively, of the COVID-19 pandemic and thus are among the worse-off in the population. Second, while utilitarianism is indifferent between saving the life of a well-off individual or the life of a worse-off individual, provided they enjoy the same increase in well-being if saved, prioritarianism prefers the latter. Because young individuals are among the worse-off in lifetime terms (because they have not yet had the opportunity to live a full life), prioritarian SWFs attach higher value than utilitarianism to interventions that benefit mostly the young. One consequence of this is that prioritarianism is more likely than utilitarianism to prioritize the young in the allocation of vaccine doses, despite the fact that they might have lower overall benefits from being vaccinated.

Note that all three methods eventually support the introduction of control policies over an uncontrolled spread of the virus because of the death toll imposed by the pandemic and the positive economic feedback from controlling the virus (e.g., the poor can only go back to work when the pandemic is under control). However, the three methods will differ in the specific characteristics of the recommended control policy (e.g., when to start the lockdown and when to start reopening, whether to have age-specific policies, how to allocate tests and healthcare resources, and so on). In particular, if the trade-off between saving lives and saving livelihoods exists, BCA, utilitarianism, and prioritarianism are, in that order, increasingly sensitive to distribution and so could differ in the choice between more or less aggressive control. If the net costs of control are regressively distributed, for example, aggressive control may be more optimal under BCA than under utilitarianism or prioritarianism. In contrast, if the trade-off between health and the economy does not exist, aggressive control may be optimal under all three views However, the three views will support providing different levels of income assistance to the worse off during the control period, depending on their relative sensitivity to distributional concerns (with prioritiarianism and utilitarianism supporting greater assistance than BCA).

12.4 Example 1: The Value of COVID-19 Control Policies in the United States

This section considers a simple example to illustrate the differences among BCA, utilitarianism, and prioritarianism when it comes to evaluating COVID-19 control policies. The example applies to the U.S. economy. Here, we discuss the main features of the example, while Appendix 12.A describes the model in full. The example is not intended to provide policy recommendations, but to clarify the implications of different evaluation methods.

Suppose that, at the beginning of the pandemic, the policy maker must choose between a no intervention strategy (i.e., letting the virus spread in an uncontrolled way) and a strict control strategy that prevents all deaths and is maintained until a vaccine or an effective treatment is found. Further suppose that the vaccine and/or treatment is expected to be available in one year. What is the maximum socially acceptable Gross Domestic Product (GDP) loss from the intervention to consider the control strategy better than no intervention at all? If the actual cost of the policy is lower than the maximum socially acceptable GDP loss, then the policy maker will implement the policy. In contrast, if the actual cost of the policy is larger than the maximum acceptable GDP loss, then no intervention is better than the control strategy. What is regarded as "socially acceptable" depends on the chosen evaluation method. Obviously, no real-world policy maker faces a stark choice between strict control and doing nothing. But the lessons from this simple example generalize to more realistic settings in which the optimal degree of strictness of the control can be set in a manner more or less sensitive to the distributional implications of such control.

In sum, this example shows that, all else equal: (i) the more regressive the burdens of COVID-19 (i.e., the more concentrated these burdens are on the worse-off), the higher the value of control to distribution-sensitive value frameworks (i.e., as regressivity increases, the value of control increases more for prioritarianism than it does for utilitarianism, and more for utilitarianism than it does for BCA); (ii) the more regressive the economic costs of control (net of any redistribution of such costs), the lower the value of control to distribution-sensitive value frameworks; (iii) thus, whether the value of control rises with the distribution-sensitivity of the value framework depends on the relative magnitude of these two regressive patterns.

12.4.1 Setup

We assume that the population is divided into five income quintiles and two age groups, the "young" (<65 years old) and the "old" (65+). The young constitute 84 percent of the population. Individuals remain in the same quintile all their life. We use the U.S. lifetable to construct the survival function of the two age groups in a non-COVID-19 situation (see Appendix 12.A for more details). Ample evidence indicates that life expectancies are lower for individuals in low-income groups. To account for the socioeconomic gradient of health, we assume that the survival curve derived from the U.S. lifetable applies to individuals with median income, and we scale up and down the survival chances of the other income quintiles.

We introduce heterogeneity across ages and income quintiles in COVID-19 mortality. To simplify, we assume that, absent any intervention, all age and income groups have the same probability of being infected and of spreading the infection.[17] However, conditional on being infected, older people have a higher risk of being hospitalized and of dying. Based on the estimates of infection fatality risk by age in Verity et al. (2020) and on the 2019 U.S. population structure (U.S. Census Bureau 2020), the average infection fatality rate is 0.95 percent. However, the infection fatality rate of the young is 0.28 percent, while the infection fatality rate of the old is 4.36 percent. Assuming that, absent any intervention, 70 percent of the population will be infected, 0.67 percent of the population will die of COVID-19 on average. From this it follows that the COVID-19 mortality rate of the young is 0.2 percent, while the mortality rate of the old is 3.05 percent (i.e., 0.2 percent of the young and 3.05 percent of the old die of COVID-19).

Additionally, we assume that the fatality rate may be a decreasing function of income to capture the socioeconomic gradient of health (Seligman et al. 2021). Low socioeconomic groups often face constraints in accessing healthcare (e.g., because they have access to lower-quality healthcare, or because they wait to see a doctor, even if ill, to avoid losing their job), thereby exposing them to a higher fatality risk. The presence of comorbidities such as hypertension and diabetes has also been found to be correlated with the risk of death from COVID-19, and low socioeconomic groups disproportionately suffer from these conditions. In the benchmark scenario, we assume that low-income quintiles bear a disproportionate number of deaths, and we compare it with the case in which all income quintiles suffer the same number of deaths (i.e., independently of income, 0.2 percent of the young die of COVID-19 vs 3.05 percent of the old). Table 12.1 summarizes the COVID-19 mortality rates by age and income group if low-income quintiles bear a disproportionate number of deaths.

We introduce heterogeneities across age and income quintile in the economic costs of control. COVID-19 control policies reduce economic activity and, as a result, induce a GDP contraction. The costs of this contraction are heterogeneously distributed across the population. Lower socioeconomic groups are more likely to bear the brunt of the costs, but adopting relief programs (such as extending

[17] In reality, members of low-income groups tend to face higher probabilities of infection because they are often essential workers or otherwise more likely to be exposed to the virus. To simplify, we abstract from this.

Table 12.1. *COVID-19 mortality rates by age and income group*

	1st quintile	2nd quintile	3rd quintile	4th quintile	5th quintile
Young	0.32%	0.23%	0.18%	0.15%	0.10%
Old	4.96%	3.51%	2.87%	2.31%	1.62%

Note: We assume that 70 percent of the population is infected, the infection fatality rate for the young is 0.28 percent, the infection fatality rate for the old is 4.36 percent. COVID-19 deaths occur disproportionately in low-income groups, with an income elasticity of the mortality rate equal to −0.5 (see Appendix 12.A). The 1st income quintile is the poorest, and the 5th is the richest. The numbers are rounded to the second significant digit.

unemployment benefits) can substantially redistribute the costs away from low-income groups. As noted earlier, the pandemic itself can induce an economic contraction because of spontaneous reductions in economic activity brought about by fear of infection (e.g., working from home, avoiding crowded places, etc.), job and income loss, and asset depreciation, but in the example we ignore that. In other words, we assume a trade-off between saving lives and saving livelihoods, i.e., avoiding COVID-19 deaths induces a GDP contraction relative to the no intervention scenario. Stated differently, we assume that GDP with an uncontrolled COVID-19 pandemic and no intervention is the same as pre-pandemic GDP. We consider two cases: one in which the monetary costs of the policy are borne by individuals in proportion to their income, and one in which they are disproportionately borne by lower-income individuals. Additionally, young individuals may be more exposed to the negative economic effects of control policies, and so we account for the age distribution of policy costs as well.

We assume that individual well-being depends on two attributes: income and longevity. COVID-19 reduces expected longevity (and possibly income). COVID-19 control policies shrink the longevity reduction at the expense of a larger income contraction. To simplify, we assume that other individual attributes (e.g., physical and mental health status, the ability to interact socially, human capital, etc.) do not affect well-being. We also assume that the income contraction brought about by the control policy has only short-term effects (i.e., once the pandemic is over, the economy goes back to pre-COVID-19 levels), and we do not consider increased mortality due, for instance, to overburdened healthcare systems. The short-term effects assumption implies that the policy-induced GDP contraction lasts only one year, i.e., the time until the vaccine or treatment is available.

12.4.2 WTP Calculations

Before determining the maximum GDP loss triggered by the intervention that the policy maker would find socially acceptable (based on the chosen evaluation method) such that the intervention is better than no intervention, let us compute the maximum income loss that each individual would find acceptable for the same intervention. This is defined as the maximum percentage of current *own* income the individual is willing to sacrifice to eliminate the COVID-19 mortality risk she faces. In other words, the individual is indifferent between, on the one hand, suffering the COVID-19 mortality risk and, on the other hand, losing income equal to the willingness to pay while suffering no COVID-19 mortality risk (the individual is indifferent in the sense that her well-being is constant in the two situations). This willingness to pay is the backbone of BCA. Because the intervention we are considering eliminates all COVID-19-related fatalities, such a willingness to pay can also be interpreted as the individual burden of the pandemic, absent any intervention (and no economic loss triggered by the pandemic itself).

Table 12.2 summarizes individuals' willingness to pay for the intervention assuming that low-income quintiles bear a disproportionate number of deaths, i.e., adopting the mortality rates displayed in

Table 12.2. ***Individuals' willingness to pay as a percentage of own income for a policy that eliminates the risk of death from COVID-19, by age and income quintile***

	1st quintile	2nd quintile	3rd quintile	4th quintile	5th quintile
Young	9.1%	17.7%	23%	28.6%	38.3%
Old	38.2%	56.4%	63.7%	69.9%	77.9%

Note: COVID-19 fatalities occur disproportionately in low-income groups (COVID-19 mortality rates by age and income quintile are taken from Table 12.1); there is no income loss associated to an uncontrolled pandemic.

Table 12.1. We derive this willingness to pay through a modeling exercise that posits a reasonable functional form for individual expected well-being, and that relies on the distribution of income and longevity across the population and on existing information about individuals' risk attitudes and individuals' incentives to trade off income and longevity. Appendix 12.A more formally describes our computations.

Because of the higher COVID-19 fatality risk, the old age group attaches a much higher value to policies that eliminate the risk of COVID-19 than the young age group. Moreover, even though the low-income quintiles face a larger fatality risk, they are willing to sacrifice much less than the top quintiles to eliminate the risk of COVID-19. This is a direct result of the lower ability to pay of individuals at the bottom of the income distribution. For example, although an old individual in the 1st income quintile has three times the mortality risk of an old individual in the 5th income quintile, the difference in income implies that the former is willing to pay only a third of her income to avoid the risk of a COVID-19 death, while the latter is willing to pay more than two-thirds of her (much higher) income to avoid a relatively lower risk of death.[18] Table 12.A.1 in Appendix 12.A.1 shows individuals' willingness to pay when the distribution of fatalities is independent of income. The same pattern of income-related differences applies, although high-income individuals have higher willingness to pay than the values reported in Table 12.2 due to the higher risk they face, while low-income individuals have lower willingness to pay than the values in Table 12.2 due to the lower risk they face.

12.4.3 Comparison of BCA, Utilitarianism, and Prioritarianism: Increasing Sensitivity to the Distribution of the Costs of Control

BCA evaluates an intervention by summing the amounts individuals are willing to sacrifice to implement the intervention. Using the values of Table 12.2 and the share of each age-income group in the

[18] In absolute terms, and assuming that the 1st quintile income is $16,250, while the 5th quintile income is $152,750, the old individual in the 1st quintile is willing to pay $6,200 and the old individual in the 5th income quintile $118,978.

population, BCA implies that the maximum socially acceptable cost of an intervention that avoids all COVID-19 deaths equals 36.8 percent of annual aggregate GDP. Therefore, the policy maker adopting a BCA approach is ready to sacrifice up to 36.8 percent of GDP to eliminate the pandemic, independently of who bears the brunt of those policy costs. In this case, if the policy costs are proportional to income, all individuals pay 36.8 percent of their own income to finance the intervention. But if the policy costs are regressive (i.e., the low-income quintiles pay a disproportionate amount of them), the individuals in the lowest income quintile would end up sacrificing much more than 36.8 percent of their income, while the top-income quintile would sacrifice much less than that.[19] However, BCA would find the two situations equally valuable, and would recommend any control policy to eliminate the pandemic as long as, on average, it costs less than 36.8 percent of GDP. Such a result occurs because BCA is insensitive to the distribution of costs, thereby overemphasizing the interests of the wealthy individuals.

Table 12.3 shows the maximum percentage reduction in aggregate GDP that utilitarian and prioritarian policy makers find acceptable to finance an intervention that eliminates the COVID-19 mortality risk. In other words, the maximum acceptable GDP loss is defined such that the policy maker finds a situation where no COVID-19 deaths occur but individuals bear that GDP loss socially equivalent to a situation where individuals die of COVID-19 but bear no policy-related income loss (i.e., the two situations yield the same social welfare). Because the intervention under consideration eliminates all COVID-19 deaths, the maximum acceptable GDP loss can be interpreted as the societal burden of the pandemic, absent any intervention. We compute the societal burden of the pandemic for the three SWFs discussed: utilitarianism, ex-ante prioritarianism, and ex-post prioritarianism. We assume an Atkinson prioritarian SWF of the form $g(w) = \frac{w^{1-\gamma}}{1-\gamma}$, where the parameter γ represents the degree of priority to the worse-off in

[19] For example, if the income elasticity of policy costs is equal to 0.5 (distribution of policy costs is mildly regressive), the 1st income quintile pays 11 percent of the total costs, the 2nd 15 percent, the 3rd 19 percent, the 4th 23 percent, and the 5th 33 percent (see Appendix 12.A.1). As a percentage of their own income, individuals in the 1st income group have to sacrifice 79 percent of their own income, while the other income groups scarifice, respectively, 56 percent, 45 percent, 37 percent, and 26 percent of their own income.

Table 12.3. ***Maximum percentage GDP loss that is considered socially acceptable to pay for an intervention that eliminates the COVID-19 mortality risk***

Scenario	BCA (%)	Utilitarianism (%)	Ex-ante prioritarianism (%)		Ex-post prioritarianism (%)	
			$\gamma = 1$	$\gamma = 2$	$\gamma = 1$	$\gamma = 2$
Scenario 1: Regressive distribution of deaths Regressive distribution of costs Only the young pay the costs	36.8	15.3	12.7	10.6	13.1	11.1
Scenario 2: Regressive distribution of deaths Distribution of costs proportional to income Only the young pay the costs	36.8	26.4	23.2	20.3	24	21.3
Scenario 3: Regressive distribution of deaths Progressive distribution of costs Only the young pay the costs	36.8	40.9	39.7	38.2	41	40
Scenario 4: Regressive distribution of deaths Regressive distribution of costs All age groups pay the costs	36.8	16.2	13.5	11.2	14	11.9
Scenario 5: Distribution of deaths independent of income Regressive distribution of costs Only the young pay the costs	44.7	16.1	12.7	9.9	13.2	10.5

Note: there is no income loss associated with an uncontrolled pandemic; Scenarios 1 through 4 adopt the age- and income-specific mortality rates due to COVID-19 from Table 12.1, while Scenario 5 adopts the mortality rates from Table 12.A.1.

(expected or realized) lifetime well-being w.[20] We consider two different degrees of priority $\gamma = \{1, 2\}$.[21]

To determine the sensitivity of the utilitarian and prioritarian societal burden of the pandemic to the distribution of policy costs and COVID-19 fatalities, we consider five scenarios: (1) The distribution of COVID-19 deaths is regressive (i.e., a disproportionate number of COVID-19 fatalities occur among low-income groups), the distribution of policy costs is also regressive (i.e., low-income groups bear the brunt of the policy costs), and only the young population suffers an income loss due to the intervention. (2) The distribution of COVID-19 deaths is regressive, the distribution of policy costs is proportional to income, and only the young population suffers an income loss due to the intervention. (3) The distribution of COVID-19 deaths is regressive, the distribution of policy costs is progressive (i.e., high-income groups bear the brunt of the policy costs), and only the young population suffers an income loss due to the intervention. (4) The distribution of COVID-19 deaths is regressive, the distribution of policy costs is also regressive, and all age groups suffer an income loss due to the intervention. (5) The distribution of COVID-19 deaths is independent

[20] See Adler, Chapter 2, this volume for a description of Atkinson SWFs. Note that if the priority parameter $\gamma = 1$, then the Atkinson SWF is of the form: $g(w) = \ln w$.

[21] Suppose that individual utility has the form $u(c) = \frac{c^{1-\lambda}}{1-\lambda} - k$, with $\lambda = 2$ the coefficient of relative risk aversion, and $k = -0.000125288$ the utility at subsistence consumption level (see Appendix 12.A.1 for the calibration details). Take two individuals, one in the 1st income quintile (income = \$16,250) and one in the 5th income quintile (income = \$152,750). The former has about 10 percent of the income of the latter. Based on the example (in particular, coefficient of relative risk aversion equal to 2), a utilitarian decision maker (for which the priority parameter $\gamma = 0$) would be indifferent between donating \$100 to the high-income person and \$1.13 to the low-income person, with $\frac{u'(c_5)}{u'(c_1)} * \$100 = \left(\frac{16{,}250}{152{,}750}\right)^2 * \$100 = \$1.13$, and $u'(c) = c^{-2}$ the marginal utility of consumption (i.e., donating \$1.13 to the low-income person is as valuable as donating \$100 to the high-income person – thus, donations to low-income individuals create much more value than equal donations to high-income individuals). A prioritarian decision maker with priority parameter equal to 1 is indifferent between donating \$100 to the high-income person and \$0.6 to the low-income person, with $\frac{g'(c_5)}{g'(c_1)} * \$100 = \left(\frac{u_1}{u_5}\right)^\gamma \left(\frac{16{,}250}{152{,}750}\right)^2 * \$100 = \$0.6$. A prioritarian decision maker with priority parameter equal to 2 is indifferent between donating \$100 to the high-income person and \$0.3 to the low-income person.

of income (i.e., COVID-19 mortality risk depends only on age), the distribution of policy costs is regressive, and only the young population suffers an income loss due to the intervention.

We have already commented on the fact that the value determined through BCA is independent of the distribution of policy costs, based on the principle that "a dollar is a dollar is a dollar." Note that if the COVID-19 mortality risk is independent of income (Scenario 5), the maximum socially acceptable cost is larger, at 44.7 percent of GDP, due to the relatively higher burden of deaths suffered by high-income quintiles in this scenario (see Table 12.A.1 in Appendix 12.A.1). Because BCA values the mortality risk reductions of wealthy individuals more than those of low-income ones, the value of an intervention that saves wealthy lives is larger than the value of an intervention that saves the same number of lives, but mainly poor lives. This is because willingness to pay depends on ability to pay (thus wealthy people value a 1 percentage point reduction in mortality risk considerably more than low-income ones), and BCA takes the unweighted sum of individuals' willingness to pay, i.e., without adjusting for differences in abilities to pay.

A striking result from Table 12.3 is that, for most scenarios, BCA condones more expensive policies to eliminate the risk of COVID-19 than does utilitarianism or prioritarianism. Only when the distribution of policy costs is progressive (Scenario 3), i.e., when high-income groups pay proportionately more of the policy costs than low-income groups, do both utilitarianism and prioritarianism attach higher values to COVID-19 risk suppression policies than BCA. For example, if the intervention to suppress COVID-19 triggers a 30 percent reduction in yearly GDP, BCA would find such an intervention better than no intervention at all; utilitarianism and prioritarianism, in contrast, would recommend against implementing such a control strategy, unless the distribution of policy costs is highly progressive.

Unlike BCA, utilitarianism and prioritarianism are sensitive to the distribution of policy costs. Moving from Scenario 1 to Scenario 3, as the distribution of costs becomes more progressive (i.e., as the economic burden of the control policy shifts from low- to high-income groups), the maximum socially acceptable GDP loss associated with the intervention increases. In other words, the more likely the utilitarian or prioritarian policy maker will rank the control policy over no intervention. Consequently, if income-support policies are in place (e.g., unemployment benefits) to redistribute policy costs from low- to high-income quintiles, the societal value of eliminating COVID-19 risk increases.

The sensitivity of utilitarianism and prioritarianism to the distribution of policy costs reflects a shared assumption about the decreasing value of money, and in the prioritarian case an extra concern for the worse off. The decreasing value of money assumption implies that dollars paid by low-income quintiles decrease their well-being and total utilitarian welfare more than an equal number of dollars paid mainly by high-income quintiles. Therefore, for a given total reduction in COVID-19 deaths, progressive distributions of costs lead to a lower decrease in welfare. In the prioritarian case, the sensitivity to policy costs reflects the additional prioritarian concern for preserving the (expected or realized) well-being of the worse-off. Because low-income individuals are among the worse-off, less regressive distributions of costs are even more valuable under prioritarianism than under utilitarianism. For instance, the maximum utilitarian socially acceptable GDP loss is 2.7 times larger with a progressive rather than regressive distribution of policy costs (40.9 percent in Scenario 3 vs 15.3 percent in Scenario 1). In the ex-ante and ex-post prioritarian cases the ratio between the two scenarios is even higher: The maximum socially acceptable prioritarian GDP loss is more than three times larger with a progressive rather than regressive loss, and the higher the priority parameter, the larger the ratio.

As a consequence, the more regressive the costs of controlling COVID-19, the more the distribution sensitivity of the value framework lowers the value attached to suppressing the pandemic. Increasing the regressivity of the distribution of policy costs reduces the maximum socially acceptable GDP loss, and such a reduction is larger under prioritarianism than under utilitarianism, and is in turn larger under utilitarianism than under BCA (where there is effectively no reduction at all). Analogous results would hold if the pandemic itself caused financial losses. The more regressive the financial burdens of COVID-19, the larger the increment in the socially acceptable GDP loss from suppression for both utilitarianism and prioritarianism. And this increment is larger under prioritarianism than it is under utilitarianism, which in turn is larger than the increment under BCA, this latter equaling zero given BCA's distribution insensitivity. What ultimately matters is the distribution of policy costs net of the COVID-19 costs: the more regressive the net burden, the more the distribution sensitivity of the value framework lowers the value attached to suppression.

Consider again Scenario 1, where the distribution of costs is regressive. Compared with utilitarianism, ex-ante prioritarianism places a lower value on policies aimed at eliminating the risk of COVID-19 (i.e., the ex-ante prioritarian maximum acceptable GDP loss is lower than the utilitarian one). Additionally, the higher the priority conferred to the worse-off in expected well-being (i.e., the higher the parameter γ), the lower the maximum reduction in GDP that an ex-ante prioritarian policy maker would find acceptable to fund an intervention that completely suppresses the pandemic and its death toll. In Scenario 1, older individuals are most at risk of COVID-19 death, while only young and mainly less wealthy individuals bear the costs of the policy. From an ex-ante point of view, the poor and the young are among the worse-off in the population: the poor because they have less access to resources and opportunities and have lower living standards overall, and the young because they have lived for fewer years and have not yet had a chance to live a full life. Thus, ex-ante prioritarianism is less likely to support eliminating COVID-19 risk because doing so hurts the prospects of those who will certainly pay the costs of the policy but who are unlikely to die from COVID-19. Note that the difference between ex-ante prioritarianism and utilitarianism declines once the distribution of costs becomes more progressive (moving from Scenario 1 to Scenario 2 to Scenario 3) because of the reduced burden on low-income quintiles and the associated reduced need to protect the worse-off.

The ex-post prioritarian maximum acceptable GDP loss for eliminating COVID-19 also tends to be smaller than the utilitarian one, and decreases as the degree of priority to the worse-off increases. Moreover, in the example the ex-post prioritarian acceptable loss is larger than the ex-ante prioritarian one. Undoubtedly, from an ex-post point of view, those who die poor and prematurely are the worst-off in the population, especially if they die young. Young, low-income individuals are also the worst-off ex-ante because they face a larger lifetime mortality risk and have lower expected well-being. But they are the worst-off only in expectation, i.e., the situation might get rosier. That is likely one reason why ex-post prioritarianism values COVID-19 elimination more than ex-ante prioritiarianism does. Everyone bears the costs of the policy (both those who survive and those who die), and many individuals face a risk of dying of COVID-19 ex-ante, but only a few will be dead because of COVID-19 ex-post. Protecting their interests is thus a priority.

Note that as the degree of priority increases, the maximum acceptable GDP loss associated with the policy reduces. The reason is that, from an ex-post point of view, the worse-off includes not only those who die prematurely of COVID-19, but also those who die prematurely of other causes (not necessarily related to COVID-19 or indirectly triggered by COVID-19). In other words, the ex-post prioritarian policy maker must trade off the interests of those who die of COVID-19 (who are better-off with the policy), those who die prematurely from other causes but still bear the costs of a COVID-19 policy (who are worse-off with the policy), and those who do not die but pay the costs (who are worse-off with the policy). Because the second group represents the majority among those who die prematurely (after all, they are more likely to die of other causes than of COVID-19), protecting their interests means not investing in the control policy. The larger the priority parameter, the larger the concern for protecting their livelihood, because preventing their death is not possible. However, the ex-post prioritarian concern for protecting the interests of those who die of COVID-19 is sufficient for accepting larger policy-induced income losses than utilitarianism does.

BCA highly values policies that reduce the fatality risk of high-income groups, as shown by a comparison of Scenario 5 with Scenario 1. In contrast, the distribution of fatalities by income group has only a marginal effect on the evaluation under the utilitarian and prioritarian approaches. Utilitarianism attaches a slightly higher value to preventing COVID-19 if fatalities were independent of income rather than disproportionally falling on low-income quintiles. This is because well-being increases with income in the model; that is, high-income groups have larger expected well-being than low-income groups. Consequently, for a utilitarian policy maker, saving a wealthy life is more valuable than saving a less well-off life because differences in income are associated with differences in quality of life.

Ex-ante prioritarianism finds COVID-19 more burdensome if fatalities disproportionately affect low-income quintiles because that increases well-being inequality among individuals.[22] Individuals in

[22] With $\gamma = 1$, the two values are pretty close: 12.697 percent when the distribution of deaths is regressive, 12.685 percent when the distribution of deaths is independent of income.

low-income quintiles are the worst-off in expectation because they have lower income and lower life expectancy; the risk of COVID-19 further erodes their lifetime well-being, particularly if they face a higher fatality rate than the top-income quintiles. Ex-post prioritarianism also values interventions against COVID-19 more if the fatalities occur disproportionately in the low-income quintiles as long as the priority parameter is sufficiently high.[23] Dying young and poor is the worst-off situation from an ex-post point of view, thereby increasing the value of policies aimed at preventing that.

Note that distributing the policy costs among all age groups rather than only the young (Scenario 4) does not seem to have a sizable impact on the value of the control policy relative to Scenario 1. If the costs are divided among all age groups, the societal burden of COVID-19 increases slightly under both utilitarianism and prioritarianism as compared with Scenario 1. A more equal distribution of costs across the age groups explains the increase in the maximum socially acceptable GDP loss.

This example shows that: (i) the more regressive the burdens of COVID-19, the more the distribution sensitivity of the value framework raises the value of control[24]; (ii) regardless of the SWF approach, the value of controlling COVID-19 decreases if doing so hurts the poor; prioritarianism reinforces this result with respect to utilitarianism; (iii) the net impact of distribution sensitivity on the value of control depends on the relative strength of the two patterns of regressivity.

Note that, no matter the evaluation method, the simplified model analyzed here suggests that the societal burden of uncontrolled COVID-19 is likely to be substantial; "do nothing" is unlikely to be the best policy option compared with a control policy, i.e., the actual costs of the control policy are likely to be lower than the maximum acceptable economic losses computed in Table 12.3.

The example also illustrated that ex-ante prioritarianism and ex-post prioritarianism evaluate policies to eliminate the risk of COVID-

[23] When the priority parameter is close to zero, the ex-post prioritarian socially acceptable GDP loss is smaller with a regressive distribution of deaths than with a distribution independent of income. This resembles the utilitarian case.

[24] The more regressive the health burdens of COVID-19, the more prioritarianism values control policies, while that does not necessarily hold for utilitarianism and BCA. However, if we add also non-health burdens of COVID-19, then, by parallel with the effects of regressive policy costs, we get that the more regressive the total burdens of COVID-19, the more the value of control increases going from BCA, to utilitarianism, to prioritarianism.

19 quite differently, with the latter attaching more value to such policies than the former. The difference in perspective explains the last result. Even if some individuals face a substantial risk of infection and death from COVID-19, that is just one of many possible outcomes – after all, they might survive COVID-19. Ex-post, some individuals have died of COVID-19 and were definitely victims of the pandemic. Their fate is worse than the fate of someone who might die because of the pandemic, but who has not yet died. Thus, the ex-post prioritarianism societal burden of COVID-19 is higher than the ex-ante prioritarian one. Adler, Chapter 2, this volume discusses the pros and cons of the two approaches. One reason why the ex-post perspective may be more appropriate for evaluating COVID-19 policies is that, at the population level, there is no risk. Some people will definitely die of COVID-19; we just do not know their identity. In contrast, at the individual level, death from COVID-19 occurs only with some (small) probability. Focusing on the relatively small individual risk discounts the negative fate of those who die due to COVID-19.

The model we have considered so far has several limitations. Addressing them changes the societal burden of COVID-19 and possibly the comparison between BCA, utilitarianism and the various forms of prioritarianism. For instance, we have neglected the morbidity effects of COVID-19 – for example, pain and suffering when ill, or the long-term health effects of the disease; adding them would make COVID-19 even more costly. Even absent governmental interventions, people might change their behavior for fear of infection, for example, deciding to work from home if possible or avoiding crowded places like restaurants and bars. Accounting for this endogenous social distancing reduces the value of policies to control the spread of COVID-19 (see, e.g., Farboodi et al. 2020, Toxvaerd 2020).

Moreover, the example assumes that all financial impacts caused by the control policy are borne in the current period (i.e., while the pandemic ravages and we wait for a vaccine or better treatment). This is a strong assumption, because governments often increase their debt in the face of a crisis, thereby shifting some of the burden to future periods or future generations. The impact of such smoothing on the societal burden of COVID-19 and on the differences across evaluation methods is likely to depend on the regressivity of the resulting distribution of costs across individuals and across time.

Additionally, because we do not account for behavioral changes in the absence of intervention, we underestimate the economic losses of the pandemic. But the "do nothing" strategy might end up being far more costly than eliminating the COVID-19 risk, thereby leading to no effective trade-off between saving the economy and saving lives. In other words, the actual costs of the control policy may be lower than the economic loss triggered by the pandemic itself. If the pandemic causes deaths *and* threatens individuals' livelihoods, the maximum reduction in pre-pandemic GDP triggered by the control intervention that the policy maker would find socially acceptable will be even larger than the values computed so far. This result holds independently of the evaluation method and is because the pandemic is bad both for the economy and for population health. Because the threshold for acceptability has increased, the control policy is more likely to be the optimal strategy.

Policy evaluations based on BCA require a methodology to determine individuals' willingness to pay. The standard methodology is to employ value-of-statistical-life (VSL) measures to monetize the value of avoiding a death (Hammitt 2000; Kniesner and Viscusi 2019). VSL represents the monetary equivalent of saving one (unidentified) life among a group of identical people and derives from the rate at which individuals are willing to substitute a small change in their income (or wealth) for a small change in their survival probability. This rate is estimated either through revealed preference data from observing individuals' choices that affect both income and mortality risk (e.g., purchases of protective equipment or decisions to select a safer job) or through stated preference methods such as surveying people about their hypothetical choices regarding income and mortality risk. For example, if individuals are willing to pay $10 to reduce their risk of premature death by 1 in a million, then the monetary value of saving one statistical life is $10,000,000. In a group of 10 million identical people, one death is avoided for sure, and if everyone is willing to pay $10, the total value of saving one life is exactly $10 million.

There is an extensive literature providing VSL estimates for the population of interest (Viscusi 2018). In the example, we used those estimates to infer individuals' preferences between income and longevity, and to calibrate the functional form of individual well-being. We then calculate individuals' willingness to pay through a modeling exercise.

Although the calibration relies on VSL estimates from the literature, we did not directly adopt those estimates to measure individuals' WTP for two reasons. First, although VSL is not constant across the population, reflecting the preferences and circumstances of different individuals (e.g., their life expectancy or their wealth), in practice it is often assumed to be uniform across the population. This avoids the ethically objectionable result that saving the life of a wealthy individual is more valuable than saving the life of a less well-off individual because of differences in abilities to pay. However, assuming a constant VSL also implies that life expectancy differences do not matter, i.e., saving the life of a young or of an old person is equally valuable, even though the young person will live more years if saved. To account for differences in life expectancy, value-of-statistical-life years (VSLY) measures are often employed (Hammitt 2007). VSLY is computed by dividing the constant VSL by the average life expectancy in the population. The value of extending the life of an individual is then equal to the product of VSLY and the number of life years gained if the person is saved, thereby accounting for age and life expectancy differences.

The second issue with VSL (and VSLY) is the marginality assumption. VSL is the *marginal* rate of substitution between wealth and survival probability, but COVID-19 may represent a *nonmarginal* risk of death. Standard theory implies that the individual's willingness to pay for a nonmarginal increase in survival probability is an increasing, concave function of the change in survival probability (Hammitt 2020). In other words, the higher the increment in survival probability, the larger the individual's willingness to pay, but as the increment grows larger, the rate at which the individual is willing to trade wealth for incremental increases in survival probability decreases.[25] For example, Adler (2020) shows that, for fatality rates of 1 percent of the population (a nonmarginal risk and close to the estimated mortality rate of COVID-19), the individual's willingness to pay to eliminate

[25] For example, the individual might be willing to pay $1,000 for increasing her chances of survival by 0.1 percentage points, but she might be ready to pay at most $1,800 for increasing her chances of survival by 0.2 percentage points. The concavity of individual willingness to pay with respect to the size of the increment in survival probability is due to the constraints on the individual's ability to spend and the fact that the opportunity cost of spending increases the more the individual has already reduced her mortality risk.

such a risk is only half the amount associated with VSL.[26] Therefore, for large probabilities of preventing death, the VSL is likely to overestimate the value that individuals place on saving lives.

12.5 Example 2: Vaccine Allocation

Manufacturing and delivery constraints make vaccine against SARS-CoV-2 a scarce and valuable resource, at least initially. The questions in this initial phase include how to distribute the scarce vaccine doses and who should get them first. Different approaches have been proposed to allocate vaccines among the population. For instance, they could be allocated randomly through a lottery, based on the principle that everyone should be treated equally – although not necessarily fairly, because individuals may have different needs. Or a vaccine could be allocated based on a first-come, first-served principle, thereby potentially favoring those with easier access to healthcare resources or with better information. Or they could be allocated based on need by giving them first to those who are at higher risk, e.g., the elderly in the case of COVID-19 or essential workers. Alternatively, they could be allocated based on the size of expected health benefits, thereby favoring not only high-risk individuals, but also those who will have a long and healthy life if saved (thus, according to this view, a younger person may receive the vaccine before an older person, even if the latter is at greater risk).[27] Or they could be allocated based on the size of both health and non-health benefits, e.g., prioritizing those who cannot earn labor income unless they prove they have been vaccinated. Or they could be allocated based on the instrumental value created by the immunized, e.g., prioritizing essential workers within the healthcare

[26] Adler (2020) assumes a VSL of more than $9 million, which, in a population of 100 people, corresponds to an individual willingness to pay to marginally reduce the fatality risk of about $90,000. In contrast, the individual willingness to pay to eliminate the 1 percent fatality risk (a nonmarginal reduction) is only $46,000, half the value implied by VSL. Thus, VSL tend to overestimate the value individuals place on reducing the risk.

See also Cutler and Summers (2020), Greenstone and Nigam (2020), and Thunström et al. (2020) for analyses using the VSL framework that suggest that policies to reduce fatalities from COVID-19 are worth trillions of dollars.

[27] We say "may" but not "will." If fatality risk is much higher for the older adults, and the vaccine is effective at reducing their risk, expected health gains are maximized by prioritizing older adults even though they have lower healthy life expectancy.

sector and service industries given that keeping them healthy is instrumental in saving other people's lives or keeping essential services open. Another approach is to allocate resources based on ability to pay, thus favoring the wealthy. Or, in contrast, priority could be given to the worse-off to compensate for pre-existing injustices.

Adapting the example of Section 12.4, we comment now on the best approach to allocate vaccines through the lenses of utilitarian and prioritarian SWFs and BCA. Although the example is better suited to illustrate vaccine allocation within a country, similar considerations can also guide vaccine allocation among countries.

Individuals are divided into five income quintiles and two age groups, the "young" (<65) and the "old" (65+). Individuals' well-being depends on income and longevity; the risk of COVID-19 threatens both. Suppose that a limited number of vaccine doses is administered. Who should receive the first dose of vaccine? Should we allocate it to a young person or an old one, a person in the bottom of the income distribution or someone in the high-income quintiles? Appendix 12.B presents the model more formally.

Vaccines can provide both direct protection to the vaccinated individual and indirect protection to others who are at reduced risk of infection from the vaccinated individual.[28] The example focuses on the direct social value of protecting the vaccinated person from COVID-19, leaving aside the indirect social value created by reduced community transmission (e.g., reduced risk of death for unvaccinated persons, increased social and economic activity by nonvaccinated members of society, increased nonmarket productive activities such as childcare or volunteering). Our goal is to determine who in the population has the largest direct social value of being vaccinated. This individual will be the first to get the vaccine.

The general conclusions are that BCA allocates vaccines based on individuals' WTP for vaccination, while the utilitarian and prioritarian allocations are based, respectively, on well-being gains and priority-adjusted well-being gains. In our example, the groups that tend to have larger WTP for vaccination are the old (because of higher fatality risk

[28] Many vaccines block the symptoms of a disease, but do not prevent infection or onward transmission of the pathogen (Warfel et al. 2014; Hodgson et al. 2020). As we write this chapter (December 2020), whether the COVID-19 candidate vaccines will be effective at reducing the risk of transmission is unclear (Peiris and Leung 2020).

from COVID-19) and the wealthy (because of higher ability to pay). Larger well-being gains from vaccination are, instead, experienced by the old (because of higher fatality risk from COVID-19) and by the less wealthy (because COVID-19 disproportionately affects low-income individuals), although not the poorest (because in the model quality of life, and thus well-being, increases in income). Because the groups that tend to be worse-off are the young and the poor, the prioritarian allocation will account for the size of the well-being gains but skew the prioritization strategy toward the young and poor. Depending on the relative strength of empirical facts and priority concerns, young poor populations might be vaccinated before some of the older adults, especially older wealthy adults.

Interestingly, a prioritarian approach seems to substantiate the argument that essential workers should be among the first to be vaccinated for social justice reasons. Many essential workers belong to disadvantaged racial and ethnic minorities and socioeconomically vulnerable groups. Therefore, a prioritarian approach to vaccine allocation suggests that essential workers should be prioritized not only because they face a high risk of exposure to COVID-19 and of transmission of the virus, but also because of their social and economic vulnerability.

12.5.1 *Epidemiological Considerations in Vaccine Allocation*

Given that our simplified model focused only on longevity and income impacts, the direct social value of vaccinating an individual in a given group depends on (i) the clinical effectiveness and safety of the vaccine for the individual; (ii) the individual's pre-vaccination probability of suffering from COVID-19; (iii) the individual's infection fatality rate; (iv) the potential non-health benefits of being vaccinated, e.g., the income gains if proof of vaccination is required to work; and (v) the social value of a given reduction in mortality risk and a given increase in income for the individual. This last value depends on the ethical framework adopted for the analysis, i.e., BCA, utilitarianism, or prioritarianism (or any other approach not considered in this chapter).[29]

[29] An often-debated issue is whether vaccine allocation strategies should depend only on number of deaths or also on life years gained, and potentially on other metrics (Emanuel and Wertheimer 2006). These questions pertain to the ethical framework that is adopted in the analysis, and the extent to which the ethical framework values those outcomes.

Individuals' infection fatality rates (iii) for COVID-19 vary by age and socioeconomic status, with older individuals and individuals in low socioeconomic groups more likely to suffer severe health consequences, e.g., due to the higher incidence of comorbidities, more frequent use of public transit, and reduced access to high-quality healthcare (O'Driscoll et al. 2021; McLaren 2020). This heterogeneity in fatality risks may call for vaccinating older people first, especially older people in low-SES groups. However, the safety and effectiveness of a vaccine (i) usually vary across individuals. Vaccines (e.g., flu vaccines) are frequently less effective in older adults because the immune system weakens with age (Bridle and Sharif 2020).[30] Additionally, early clinical trials rarely include older populations to test the safety and efficacy of vaccines. Pressure to release a vaccine as soon as possible implies that the first vaccines may not be proven effective and safe for older people, thereby raising the question of how to balance effectiveness and mortality risk. If effectiveness reduces with age, vaccinating the younger population first may be better, even if they face a lower risk of dying from COVID-19.

Moreover, infection fatality rates may depend on the existence of an economically viable and effective treatment and on the effectiveness of this treatment by age, comorbid status, etc. Therefore, what matters for vaccine allocation is not just the individuals' infection fatality risk, but rather the infection fatality risk net of the potential protection conferred by the treatment. For example, if a treatment is forthcoming soon that is more effective for older people than the vaccine, vaccinating the young generations and letting the older generation wait for the treatment may be better (even if that wait will cause some deaths among the elderly).

The probability of being infected with COVID-19 (ii) depends on individuals' characteristics; for example, older people may be more susceptible to infection (i.e., conditional on a contact with an infected person, they are more likely to catch the virus), and individuals with many social contacts are more likely to be infected (Ferguson et al. 2020; Viner et al. 2021). However, this probability depends also on the social and economic context wherein the vaccine is introduced, e.g., the number and characteristics of the people still susceptible (assuming

[30] As of December 2020, there is some evidence suggesting that leading COVID-19 vaccines work well also among the elderly (Mandavilli 2020).

that the once infected have acquired permanent or temporary immunity), the presence of nonpharmaceutical interventions (those interventions will likely remain in place in the initial phases if the number of vaccine doses is limited), and individuals' behavior and compliance with social-distancing norms. For example, if we are in a hypothetical society where populations at higher fatality risk can be safely and perfectly isolated from the rest of the population, and where such an isolation is not burdensome for them and their families, vaccinating first the individuals with high contacts, but low fatality risk, rather than the individuals with low contacts, but high fatality risk, may be better. Likewise, the non-health benefits of being vaccinated (iv) depend on the economic burden of the counterfactual scenario and how this burden is distributed across the population. For instance, if months of economic lockdown have strained young generations economically and mentally, vaccinating them first rather than the elderly may be more valuable if employability requires proof of vaccination, even if the latter are more at risk.

Another factor to consider is the quantity of vaccine supplied and the timing of its availability. If individuals are not vaccinated today, will they be vaccinated before a new surge of cases and deaths? For example, if the next stock of vaccine doses will be distributed only in six months, the argument for prioritizing the high-fatality-risk individuals gains strength, because those individuals are likely to die while waiting for the next stock.

The discussion and the example focus on the direct value of vaccination. However, note that if the vaccine could stop the transmission of the virus, vaccinating the super-spreaders first (i.e., those individuals with many contacts), rather than the high-fatality-risk individuals, might be better (Medlock and Galvani 2009).

To abstract from many of these considerations, while keeping the main trade-offs, we will make the following assumptions. A limited stock of vaccine doses is distributed at the beginning of the pandemic; no more doses will be distributed in the foreseeable future (or at least in the relevant time horizon of the analysis). Vaccination reduces mortality risk, but has no impact on income; except for the vaccine, no other intervention is implemented, in particular, there is no social or physical distancing policy and no treatment is discovered. Vaccination reduces the mortality rate of the vaccinated, but has no impact on the mortality rate of the unvaccinated (i.e., we neglect the disease transmission channels). Therefore, we assume that the unvaccinated individuals face the same mortality risk as in the benchmark uncontrolled outbreak scenario analyzed in Section 12.4. Table 12.1 summarized the probability of dying from COVID-19 for each age and income group, under the assumption that deaths over-proportionately occur in low-income groups.

12.5.2 Prioritization Groups under BCA, Utilitarianism and Prioritarianism

Benefit-cost analysis. Consider first the allocation rule that a benefit-cost approach would support. BCA evaluates policies (i.e., ways of allocating vaccine doses) by estimating individuals' willingness to pay and summing up those monetary amounts. A safe and 100 percent effective vaccine eliminates the risk of COVID-19-related death for the individual. Table 12.2, which measured individuals' willingness to pay to eliminate the risk of COVID-19, is then informative of the monetary value that individuals place on being vaccinated. The table shows that individuals' willingness to pay is larger for the old than for the young because the former are expected to benefit more from being vaccinated (as they face a much higher fatality risk). Additionally, the monetary values are larger for top-income quintiles than for bottom-income quintiles because the former have a greater ability to pay. Therefore, the allocation rule supported by a benefit-cost approach is sensitive to the size of the expected benefits and to differences in abilities to pay, and thus, the vaccine dose will be given to an old individual in the top income quintile. We have already commented on the ethically objectionable discrimination of BCA toward the interests of the wealthy.

Utilitarian SWF. Consider now the utilitarian framework. The utilitarian SWF evaluates policies based on the change in the sum of individuals' expected well-being compared with the status quo. The optimal allocation rule of vaccine doses is that which confers the greatest increase in the sum of individuals' well-being. In other words, the first vaccine dose will be given to the individual who is expected to gain most in terms of an increase in well-being. The first consequence is that the vaccine is likely to be given to individuals who will experience a larger reduction in their COVID-19-related fatality risk thanks to vaccination, i.e., individuals with high baseline COVID-19 fatality risk and/or individuals with high vaccine effectiveness. The second consequence is that the size of the mortality risk reduction is insufficient to determine who gets the vaccine first, because changes in well-being are more than just changes in health.

To determine which demographic group gains the most well-being from COVID-19 vaccination, let us first introduce the concept of social value of mortality risk reduction (SVRR).[31] The $SVRR_{ia}$ is defined as the change in social welfare induced by a small reduction (e.g., a 1 in 100,000 probability reduction) in the mortality risk of an individual in age group a and income group i. If $SVRR_{ia} \geq SVRR_{jb}$, then reducing the mortality risk of an individual in age group a and income group i generates more social welfare than reducing the mortality risk of an individual in age group b and income group j by the exact same amount. The SVRR is the moral weight associated with a given reduction in fatality risk.

The *utilitarian* $SVRR_{ia}^{U}$ is the change in *utilitarian* social welfare (i.e., the change in individual lifetime expected well-being) induced by a small reduction in the mortality risk of an individual in age group a and income group i. Suppose that vaccination reduces the COVID-19 fatality risk of an individual in age group a and income group i by x_{ia}, while reducing the fatality risk of an individual in age group b and income group j by x_{jb}. The utilitarian vaccine allocation rule prioritizes the individual in age group a and income group i over the individual in age group b and income group j if and only if $SVRR_{ia}^{U}x_{ia} \geq SVRR_{jb}^{U}x_{jb}$. Suppose that $x_{ia} > x_{jb}$, i.e., the fatality risk reduction an individual in age group a and income group i experiences thanks to the COVID-19 vaccine is larger than the fatality risk reduction an individual in age group b and income group j experiences. If reducing the fatality risk of the former is considered more valuable from a utilitarian point of view than reducing the fatality risk of the latter (i.e., $SVRR_{ia}^{U} \geq SVRR_{jb}^{U}$), the individual experiencing the larger fatality risk reduction obtains the vaccine first. However, if reducing the fatality risk of an individual in age group a and income group i is considered less valuable from a utilitarian point of view than reducing the fatality risk of an individual in age group b and income group j (i.e., $SVRR_{jb}^{U} > SVRR_{ia}^{U}$), then the vaccine is allocated to the former first only if the associated COVID-19 fatality risk reduction is large enough, $x_{ia} \geq \frac{SVRR_{jb}^{U}}{SVRR_{ia}^{U}}x_{jb}$.

[31] See also Hammitt and Treich, Chapter 7, this volume, and Adler et al. (2021) for a definition and some properties of social value of mortality risk reduction.

Table 12.4. ***Utilitarian SVRR compared with the corresponding utilitarian SVRR attached to an older person in the 1st income quintile, by age and income group***

	1st quintile	2nd quintile	3rd quintile	4th quintile	5th quintile
Young	2.51	3.85	4.36	4.71	5.11
Old	1	1.48	1.64	1.76	1.86

Table 12.1 indicates that older individuals in the lowest-income quintile face the largest COVID-19 mortality risk. Additionally, for each income quintile, the COVID-19 mortality rate of the older population is about 15 times larger than the corresponding mortality rate of the younger population. Unless the age difference in vaccine effectiveness is very large (i.e., the vaccine is at least 15 times more effective for the young than for the old), the older people in low-income groups are likely to benefit the most from a vaccine with any average vaccine effectiveness in terms of mortality risk reduction (i.e., they have the larger x). However, they will be allocated the vaccine first only if the SVRR attached to a given reduction in their mortality risk is large enough.

Table 12.4 shows the ratio of the utilitarian SVRR for each age and income group to the corresponding utilitarian SVRR of an old individual in the 1st income quintile. For each age group a and income group i, we divided $SVRR_{ia}^{U}$ by the corresponding SVRR attached to mortality risk reductions an old individual in the 1st income quintile enjoys ($SVRR_{1o}^{U}$). Values greater than 1 in age group a and income group i mean that, from a utilitarian perspective, reducing the mortality risk of an individual in age group a and income group i by a given amount is more valuable than reducing the mortality risk of an old individual in the 1st income quintile by the same amount.

Although older people in the 1st income quintile are expected to experience the largest risk-reduction benefit from the vaccine (Table 12.1), they have the lowest utilitarian SVRR, while young wealthy individuals have the highest value. For example, a small reduction in mortality risk is valued almost five times more for a young individual in the 4th income quintile than an old individual in the 1st income quintile. More generally, the utilitarian SVRR decreases in age and increases in income. This is because younger individuals have longer remaining life expectancies if saved (i.e., a higher number of life years gained). Also, in the simplified model used in this chapter, income buys happiness, i.e., utility increases in income. Thus, reducing the mortality risk of an individual with a better quality of life is more valuable from a utilitarian perspective.

Let $\frac{SVRR_{ia}}{SVRR_{1o}} x_{ia}$ be the "utilitarian-adjusted" COVID-19 mortality risk reduction that an individual in age group *a* and income group *i* experiences if vaccinated, and x_{1o} the vaccine-induced COVID-19 mortality risk reduction experienced by an older individual in the 1st income quintile. Even though older individuals in the 1st income quintile have the lowest utilitarian SVRR, they should still receive the vaccine first if their mortality risk reduction is larger than the "utilitarian-adjusted" mortality risk reduction any other group would experience, i.e., $x_{1o} > \frac{SVRR_{ia}}{SVRR_{1o}} x_{ia}$, for any $ia \neq 1o$.

For example, suppose the vaccine is 100 percent effective for all age groups. Then, Table 12.1 implies that such a vaccine reduces the COVID-19 mortality risk of an old individual in the 1st income quintile by 4.96 percentage points. The same vaccine reduces the mortality risk of a young individual in the 4th income quintile by only 0.15 percentage points. However, any given reduction in mortality risk is valued 4.71 times more if it occurs to a young individual in the 4th income quintile rather than an old one in the 1st income quintile. Therefore, the 0.15 percentage point reduction accruing to the young is as valuable as a 0.7 percentage point reduction (4.71×0.15) accruing to the old. In other words, a vaccine that saves 0.15 percent of the young people in the 4th income quintile is as valuable, from a utilitarian point of view, as a vaccine that saves 0.7 percent of the old people in the 1st income quintile (if the two groups have the same number of members).

Table 12.5 shows the utilitarian-adjusted reductions in COVID-19 mortality risk induced by a vaccine that is 100 percent effective for all age groups (where the numbers in Table 12.5 are derived by multiplying the SVRRs in Table 12.4 by the COVID-19 mortality rates in Table 12.1). Elderly individuals in the 2nd income quintile have the largest utilitarian-adjusted mortality risk reduction if vaccinated, i.e., vaccinating them creates the largest increase in utilitarian social welfare. Indeed, vaccinating an elderly individual in the 2nd income quintile – which reduces their mortality risk by 3.51 percentage points –

Table 12.5. ***Utilitarian-adjusted reduction in COVID-19 mortality risk if the vaccine is 100 percent effective for all age groups, by age and income group***

	1st quintile	2nd quintile	3rd quintile	4th quintile	5th quintile
Young	0.8%	0.87 %	0.8%	0.7%	0.53%
Old	4.96%	5.2%	4.71%	4.06%	3.01%

Note: COVID-19 deaths occur disproportionately in low income groups, with COVID-19 mortality rates displayed in Table 12.1. If the vaccine is less than 100 percent effective, the values in the table should be multiplied by the reduced effectiveness (e.g., if effectiveness is 60 percent, the utilitarian-adjusted reduction for a young individual in the 1st income quintile is 0.6×0.8 percent).

raises utilitarian social welfare as much as reducing the mortality risk of an older individual in the 1st income quintile by 5.2 percentage points. Vaccinating the elderly in the 2nd income quintile therefore yields more utilitarian welfare than vaccinating those in the 1st income quintile, which would only reduce the latter's mortality risk by 4.96 percentage points.

Therefore, the utilitarian allocation rule will prioritize elderly individuals in low-income quintiles, though not necessarily the poorest ones. Differences in length and quality of life by income explain this result: individuals in the 2nd quintile face a relatively high COVID-19 mortality rate and, if saved from death can expect a longer life and higher income than those in the 1st quintile. More generally, our assumptions imply that for any age invariant vaccine effectiveness, the mortality risks faced by the poor elderly are large enough to ensure that the utilitarian allocation rule will prioritize them (although not the poorest ones), despite the lower relative social value attached to extending their life.

If vaccine effectiveness decreases with age, the likelihood of prioritizing the young individual increases. Earlier, we pointed out that vaccinating the young in our example could produce larger mortality risk reductions than vaccinating the elderly if vaccine effectiveness in the young were at least 15 times that for the old. However, the lower utilitarian value of mortality risk reductions in the elderly implies that smaller age differences in vaccine efficacy are required to prioritize the young. Indeed, vaccine efficacy in the young that is six times higher than that in the old suffices to prioritize the young. (We divide the utilitarian-adjusted risk reduction of an old person in the 2nd income quintile by the utilitarian-adjusted risk reduction of a young person in the 2nd income quintile[32].) For example, if the vaccine is 50 percent effective for the young and only 8 percent effective for the old, the young get priority.

Ex-ante prioritarian SWF. Ex-ante prioritarianism evaluates policies based on changes in the sum of strictly increasing and strictly concave transformations of individuals' expected lifetime well-being compared with the status quo. The concave transformation guarantees that, for a given increase in individuals' well-being, the worst-off in expected lifetime well-being are prioritized. The ex-ante prioritarian allocation rule then depends on the change in an individual's expected well-being if vaccinated (i.e., the rule should consider who gains more from the vaccine in terms of well-being, as in the utilitarian rule) and on the identity of the vaccinated person, with a preference for the most disadvantaged in expected well-being. Individuals with low expected well-being are typically people in low socioeconomic groups, people with short life expectancies (i.e., the sick and disabled), and the young because they have lived for fewer years and face a higher lifetime risk of dying prematurely than the individuals who have already reached an old age.

To determine the ex-ante prioritarian allocation strategy, define the ex-ante prioritarian social value of mortality risk reduction $SVRR_{ia}^{EA}$ as the change in ex-ante prioritarian social welfare induced by a small mortality risk reduction of an individual in age group a and income group i. If $SVRR_{ia}^{EA} \geq SVRR_{jb}^{EA}$, then reducing the mortality risk of an individual in age group a and income group i is more valuable from an ex-ante prioritarian point of view than reducing the mortality risk of an individual in age group b and income group j by the same amount. Let x_{ia} and x_{jb} be the COVID-19 mortality risk reductions induced by vaccination; individuals in age group a and income group i get priority over individuals in age group b and income group j if and only if $SVRR_{ia}^{EA} x_{ia} \geq SVRR_{jb}^{EA} x_{jb}$, or equivalently, $x_{ia} \geq \frac{SVRR_{jb}^{EA}}{SVRR_{ia}^{EA}} x_{jb}$.

Table 12.6 shows the ratio of the ex-ante prioritarian SVRR for each age and income group to the corresponding ex-ante prioritarian SVRR of the elderly in the 1st income quintile. It is the ex-ante prioritarian

32 We chose the 2nd income quintile because it represents the largest value of vaccination, from Table 12.5.

Table 12.6. *Ex-ante prioritarian SVRR compared with the corresponding ex-ante prioritarian SVRR attached to an older person belonging to the 1st income quintile, by age and income group*

	1st quintile	2nd quintile	3rd quintile	4th quintile	5th quintile
Young	2.87	1.91	1.69	1.58	1.47
Old	1	0.66	0.58	0.54	0.5

Note: Atkinson SWF with priority parameter equal to 2.

counterpart of Table 12.4 for the utilitarian case. To compute the values in Table 12.6, we assume an Atkinson SWF of the form $g(w) = \frac{w^{1-\gamma}}{1-\gamma}$, with priority parameter γ equal to 2. Table 12.6 shows that given our assumptions, from an ex-ante prioritarian perspective, a 1 percentage point reduction in the mortality risk of a young individual in the 1st income quintile is valued 2.87 times more than a 1 percentage point reduction in the mortality risk of an old individual in the 1st income quintile.

As in the utilitarian case, reducing the mortality risk of young people is valued more than reducing the mortality risk of older people by the same amount. This priority to the young is even stronger than in the utilitarian case: the young are prioritized because they are expected to live longer if saved (as in the utilitarian case) and because they are among the worse-off in lifetime terms (they have not yet lived a full life). For instance, if we take the first income quintile, the ex-ante prioritarian SVRR of a young individual is 2.87 times the value of an older one, while the utilitarian value is 2.51 times the value of an older one: reducing the mortality risk of the young rather than the old is more valuable under ex-ante prioritarianism than utilitarianism. A similar comparison holds for the other income quintiles.[33]

Unlike in the utilitarian case, our assumptions imply that the ex-ante prioritarian SVRR decreases in income. For a given age, a 1 percentage point reduction in the mortality risk of a low-income individual is more

[33] For each income quintile, we can divide the value for the young by the value for the old to determine how much more valuable it is to prioritize the young. In the utilitarian case, we find 2.51 (1st), 2.59 (2nd), 2.65 (3rd), 2.68 (4th), and 2.74 (5th). In the ex-ante prioritarian case, we find 2.87 (1st), 2.91 (2nd), 2.92 (3rd), 2.93 (4th), and 2.96 (5th). For each income quintile, the value is higher in the ex-ante prioritarian case than in the utilitarian one.

Table 12.7. ***Ex-ante-prioritarian-adjusted reduction in COVID-19 mortality risk if the vaccine is 100 percent effective for all age groups, by age and income group***

	1st quintile	2nd quintile	3rd quintile	4th quintile	5th quintile
Young	0.92%	0.43%	0.31%	0.23%	0.15%
Old	4.96%	2.3%	1.66%	1.24%	0.8%

Note: Atkinson SWF with priority parameter equal to 2. If the vaccine is less than 100 percent effective, the values in the table should be multiplied by the reduced effectiveness (e.g., if effectiveness is 60 percent, the ex-ante-prioritarian-adjusted reduction for a young individual in the 1st income quintile is 0.6×0.92 percent).

valuable than the equivalent reduction in that of a wealthier one. For example, the ex-ante prioritarian SVRR of an old individual in the 5th quintile is only half that of an old individual in the 1st quintile. This is because low-income individuals are among the worse-off, both because of their poorer economic conditions and because of their shorter life expectancy due to the income gradient in health and the larger COVID-19 mortality risk if not vaccinated. Note that this result of SVRR declining in income is specific to our model assumptions and not generalizable. Table 12.B.1 in Appendix 12.B.1 reports the ex-ante prioritarian SVRR when the priority parameter is equal to 1 (i.e., giving less priority to the worse-off than when the parameter equals 2). While reducing the mortality risk of the young remains more valuable than reducing that of the old, reducing the risk of a rich young person is now more valuable than reducing that of a poor one. Although low-income individuals are among the worse-off, they also expect to gain less from having their life saved because of their shorter life expectancies and lower incomes.

Consider again Table 12.6. Poor young individuals have the largest ex-ante prioritarian social value of mortality risk reduction. Will they receive the vaccine first? As before, we can compute the "ex-ante-prioritarian-adjusted" mortality risk reductions to determine which age and income group has the largest ex-ante prioritarian value of vaccination. The ex-ante prioritarian-adjusted mortality risk reduction of an individual in age group a and income group i is defined as $\frac{SVRR^{EA}_{ia}}{SVRR^{EA}_{1o}} x_{ia}$. Table 12.7 displays the results for a vaccine that is 100 percent effective for all age groups.

Table 12.7 indicates that if the vaccine is 100 percent effective for everyone, it will be allocated first to elderly in the 1st quintile because of the high expected reduction in mortality risk despite the low ex-ante prioritarian SVRR of a given reduction in such risk (see Table 12.6). For example, the vaccine reduces the mortality risk of the old in the 1st quintile by 4.96 percentage points, while the ex-ante-prioritarian-adjusted reduction in the mortality risk of the young in the 1st quintile is only 0.92 percentage points. In other words, vaccinating a young individual in the 1st quintile is equivalent, from an ex-ante prioritarian perspective, to reducing the mortality risk of an old individual in the 1st quintile by 0.92 percentage points, a lesser reduction than that from vaccinating an old person in the 1st quintile (who would experience a 4.96 percentage point reduction in mortality risk). These numbers account for the lower ex-ante prioritarian social value associated with reductions in mortality risk experienced by the young compared with those experienced by old.

These results differ from those of the utilitarian case in two respects. First, the ex-ante prioritarian rule prioritizes individuals in the 1st income quintile over people in higher income quintiles, which was not always the case with a utilitarian SWF. Second, the rule prioritizes poor young individuals over rich older ones. A strong priority for the worse-off implies that young low-income individuals get priority over older wealthy people because of their young age and despite the lower expected death rate from COVID-19. For example, vaccinating a young person in the 1st income quintile is more valuable than vaccinating an old one in the 5th income quintile: vaccinating the former is equivalent to achieving a 0.92 percentage point reduction in mortality risk of an old individual in the 1st income quintile, while vaccinating the latter is equivalent to achieving only a 0.8 percentage point reduction. Note that a policy maker with less concerns for the worse-off (priority parameter equal to 1 instead of 2) will also prioritize the old poor individuals in allocating the vaccine, but not the poor young over the wealthy old (Table 12.B.2 in Appendix 12.B.2).

If the vaccine effectiveness reduces with age, will a young low-income individual get the vaccine before an old low-income one? The answer is positive if the effectiveness for the young is at least 5.4 times the effectiveness for the old (where the figure has been computed by dividing the ex-ante-prioritarian-adjusted mortality risk reduction of the old in the 1st income quintile from Table 12.7 by the corresponding value of a young person). Therefore, young individuals get priority despite the lower gain in mortality if the vaccine is sufficiently more effective for them than it is for old people. Note that the "excess" effectiveness for prioritizing the young is lower than in the utilitarian case. Once again, that is because, compared with utilitarianism, ex-ante prioritarianism attaches higher moral importance to preserving the life of a young person than the life of an older one.

Ex-post prioritarian SWF. Ex-post prioritarianism evaluates policies based on the expected sum of concave transformations of individuals' realized well-being. The concave transformation implies that, for a given increase in realized well-being, priority is given to those with lower realized lifetime well-being. From an ex-post point of view, the worse-off are those who die prematurely, the individuals in low-income groups, and the young (because dying prematurely while young is considered worse than dying prematurely while old).

Let $SVRR_{ia}^{EP}$ represent the ex-post prioritarian social value of reducing the mortality risk of an individual in age group a and income group i. Such a value is defined as the change in ex-post prioritarian social welfare induced by a small mortality risk reduction of an individual in age group a and income group i. If $SVRR_{ia}^{EP} \geq SVRR_{jb}^{EP}$, then reducing the mortality risk of an individual in age group a and income group i is considered more valuable from an ex-post prioritarian point of view than reducing the mortality risk of an individual in age group b and income group j by the exact same amount. Moreover, let x_{ia} and x_{jb} be the COVID-19 mortality risk reductions induced by vaccination in these two individuals. The ex-post prioritarian policy maker allocates the vaccine to the individual in age group a and income group i before the individual in age group b and income group j if and only if $SVRR_{ia}^{EP} x_{ia} \geq SVRR_{jb}^{EP} x_{jb}$, or equivalently, $x_{ia} \geq \frac{SVRR_{jb}^{EP}}{SVRR_{ia}^{EP}} x_{jb}$.

Table 12.8 shows the ratio of the ex-post prioritarian SVRR for each age and income group to the corresponding ex-post prioritarian SVRR for an old individual in the 1st quintile, assuming an Atkinson SWF with priority parameter equal to 2. For example, from an ex-post prioritarian perspective, a 1 percentage point reduction in the mortality risk of a young individual in the 1st income quintile is valued 5.58 times more than a 1 percentage point reduction in the mortality risk of an old individual in the 1st income quintile.

As in the ex-ante prioritarian case, the value of reducing mortality risk by a fixed amount decreases in income. Additionally, as in the

Table 12.8. *Ex-post prioritarian SVRR compared with the corresponding ex-post prioritarian SVRR attached to an older person belonging to the 1st income quintile, by age and income group*

	1st quintile	2nd quintile	3rd quintile	4th quintile	5th quintile
Young	5.58	3.89	3.59	3.39	3.27
Old	1	0.67	0.61	0.57	0.54

Note: Atkinson SWF with priority parameter equal to 2.

utilitarian and ex-ante prioritarian cases, reducing the mortality risk of a young individual is more valuable than reducing the mortality risk of an older individual by the same amount. Note that the priority conferred to the young is considerably higher than in both the utilitarian and ex-ante prioritarian cases. Consider, for example, the 1st income quintile. The ex-post prioritarian SWF values risk reductions accruing to the young 5.58 times more than comparable risk reductions accruing to the old; the corresponding values in the utilitarian and ex-ante prioritarian cases are, respectively, 2.51 and 2.87. Comparable differences hold for the other income quintiles.

All three SWFs prioritize the young because they are expected to experience a bigger gain in lifetime well-being if saved from COVID-19 (i.e., a larger number of life years gained). On top of that, ex-ante and ex-post prioritarianism prioritize the young because they rank among the worse-off in well-being terms since they have lived for fewer years. However, this "fair innings" argument[34] is stronger under ex-post prioritarianism than under ex-ante prioritarianism. This difference depends on the fact that the ex-post prioritarian favors the young because they are definitely the worst-off if they die prematurely; the ex-ante prioritarian favors them because they face a higher risk, that is, they are the worst-off in expectation. Table 12.8 assumes a relatively high degree of priority to the worse-off. Table 12.B.3 in Appendix 12.B.3 shows that, with a lower degree of priority, differences in income

[34] The "fair innings" argument refers to the idea that mortality risk reduction policies benefiting younger people should be counted more because the young have not yet had a fair innings in their life, i.e., they have not had a chance to live for a normal lifespan (Hammitt and Treich, Chapter 7, this volume; Adler et al. 2021).

Table 12.9. ***Ex-post-prioritarian-adjusted reduction in COVID-19 mortality risk if the vaccine is 100 percent effective for all age groups, by age and income group***

	1st quintile	2nd quintile	3rd quintile	4th quintile	5th quintile
Young	1.78%	0.88%	0.66%	0.5%	0.34%
Old	4.96%	2.37%	1.74%	1.32%	0.87%

Note: Atkinson SWF with priority parameter equal to 2. If the vaccine is less than 100 percent effective, the values in the table should be multiplied by the reduced effectiveness (e.g., if effectiveness is 60 percent, the ex-post-prioritarian-adjusted reduction for a young individual in the 1st income quintile is 0.6×1.78 percent).

do not matter any longer, i.e., for a given age, a 1 percentage point reduction in mortality risk has approximately a constant value independently of whether it occurs to a poor or a rich individual. In contrast, differences in age still matter considerably, with higher values attached to interventions that benefit primarily the young.

Multiplying the COVID-19 mortality risk each demographic group faces (Table 12.1) and the ex-post prioritarian SVRRs of Table 12.8, we can determine to whom the ex-post prioritarian policy maker will allocate a 100 percent uniformly effective vaccine first. Table 12.9 presents the "ex-post-prioritarian–adjusted" mortality risk reductions achieved by such a vaccine, where the ex-post prioritarian-adjusted mortality risk reduction of an individual in age group a and income group i is defined as $\frac{SVRR^{EP}_{ia}}{SVRR^{EP}_{1o}} x_{ia}$. The age and income group with the largest ex-post-prioritarian-adjusted mortality risk reduction receives the vaccine first.

Once again, an old individual in the 1st income quintile will receive the vaccine first because the achievable reduction in COVID-19 mortality risk outweighs the lower ex-post prioritarian value attached to interventions that benefit the old. For example, vaccinating an old person in the 1st income quintile reduces her probability of death by 4.96 percentage points. Vaccinating a young person in the 1st income quintile is equivalent, from an ex-post prioritarian perspective, to reducing the probability of death of an old person in the 1st income quintile by only 1.78 percentage points. Clearly, vaccinating the old produces more value.

Additionally, as with the ex-ante prioritarian SWF, the priority conferred to the young is so high that a young, low-income individual will get the vaccine before an old, high-income one. Specifically, vaccinating a young individual in the 1st income quintile produces more value than vaccinating an old individual is the 3rd (or higher) income quintile. This result hinges on the relatively high priority parameter, and it disappears if the policy maker has a low concern for the worse-off (Table 12.B.4 in Appendix 12.B.4).

If vaccine effectiveness decreases with age, under which conditions will it be given first to a young individual? Fix, for instance, the 1st income quintile. If the vaccine is at least 2.8 times more effective for a young than for an old person, the ex-post prioritarian rule will allocate it to a young person first, regardless of the lower risk faced by the young (where the 2.8 figure has been computed by dividing the ex-post-prioritarian-adjusted mortality risk reduction of the old in the 1st income quintile from Table 12.9 by the corresponding value of a young person). For example, if the vaccine is 50 percent effective for the young, and only 20 percent effective for the old, the higher ex-post prioritarian value conferred to saving a young life implies that a young person in the 1st income quintile will get the vaccine first.

One clear conclusion from this discussion is that age matters in allocating vaccine doses and that both ex-ante and ex-post prioritarian SWFs are more likely than utilitarianism to allocate the vaccine to young people first (or at least to some poor young people over wealthier older people), despite their lower COVID-19 mortality risk. Note that this "ageist" feature of prioritarian SWFs is likely to be softened if we recognize that current young generations have higher standards of living than previous young generations (i.e., those who are currently old). Even if the young have not yet had a chance to live a full life, the quality of their life (both the one already lived and the expected one) might be, all things considered, higher than that of the current older generations. Accounting for that is likely to reduce the higher priority attached to interventions that benefit primarily the young.

The discussion so far has completely neglected the costs of different allocation rules. Logistical and political constraints may make it infeasible or expensive to distribute the vaccine in some areas, even if the populations in those areas would benefit most from it. Feasibility constraints are also linked to the properties of the vaccine. For example, widely distributing vaccines that need to be stored at very cold temperatures is more difficult. Vaccine hesitancy also interferes with the optimal vaccine allocation mechanism. If complementary interventions are required to persuade people to get the vaccine, the optimal vaccine allocation may be tilted toward nonhesitant individuals independent of the expected benefits. Additionally, we have so far assumed that only one vaccine will be allocated. Competition among multiple vaccines with different properties may result in a vaccine being allocated first to individuals who will benefit less from it.

12.6 Discussion and Conclusions

This chapter discusses the use of utilitarian and prioritarian SWFs in assessing COVID-19 control and prevention policies, as compared with more standard BCA. We show that SWF analysis is a rich and flexible evaluation framework; unlike BCA, it is sensitive to the distribution of policy costs and benefits among the population, and it does not have the ethically objectionable result that the interests of the rich count more than the interests of the poor in the evaluation process. One key implication is that, all else equal, if the net costs of control are regressively distributed, aggressive control may be more optimal under BCA than under utilitarianism or prioritarianism. (Though if the burdens of COVID-19 are regressive, then all else equal, both utilitarianism and prioritarianism will recommend more stringent control policies than BCA). BCA prioritizes vaccinating the wealthy based on their higher ability to pay. In contrast, SWF analysis (whether prioritarian or utilitarian), values policies not in terms of people's willingness to pay for their effects but rather in terms of those policies' effects on well-being, thus doing away with any priority the rich may get from their greater ability to pay.

The main difference between utilitarianism and prioritarianism is that the former is only concerned with maximizing the aggregate well-being gains from policy while the latter will accept lower aggregate gains for a better distribution of such gains toward the worse-off. One example where such a difference plays out is in the allocation of vaccine doses. Young individuals are among the worse-off in the population because they have not yet had the opportunity to live a full life. So both forms of prioritarianism prioritize vaccinating low-income young individuals before wealthy older adults, even though the latter face a higher COVID-19 mortality risk and could enjoy larger utility benefits from being saved. In the utilitarian case, all older adults should receive priority over younger populations independently of their relative income. However, note that all three SWFs agree in ranking low-income older individuals at the top of the vaccine prioritization strategy.

Both BCA and SWF analysis are likely to support policies that control the pandemic over an uncontrolled spread, although the optimal degree of stringency may vary. Both context and policy horizon matter. In a country where the trade-off between saving lives and saving livelihoods is stark (e.g., if the control policy causes widespread unemployment, depletion of savings, fall into poverty, and associated increase in mortality) and the distribution of policy costs is regressive, BCA might support more aggressive control policies than utilitarianism or prioritarianism if the burdens of COVID-19 are not too regressive. If instead there is no trade-off between health and the economy (e.g., if the economic losses from an uncontrolled pandemic are staggering) and the only way to save the economy is through suppression, then all three methods will support suppression and mainly differ on the magnitude of the income support to the worse-off. The policy horizon plays a role as well. Excessive attention to short-run economic costs of suppression leads to less aggressive policies, independently of the chosen method.

One important topic concerning COVID-19 that we have not discussed is the role of uncertainty. Great uncertainty surrounds the transmission mechanisms of SARS-CoV-2, the severity of its effects, and the timing and effectiveness of treatments and vaccines. Countries must make decisions about the best control strategy based on uncertain and evolving scientific evidence. Prudential considerations suggest employing aggressive control strategies to avoid worst-case scenarios with unknown probability and/or magnitude, regardless of the high policy costs.[35]

[35] However, an argument may exist that learning about the virus occurs only as the pandemic unfolds. The effects of the virus have been found to be more severe among the elderly because we have observed more deaths in this age group. The presence of endogenous learning implies that, from a purely informational perspective, it is better not to completely suppress the virus. This suggests a trade-off between the value of information and the value of being precautious, although, in practice, the former is likely to be small in the face of an unfolding pandemic.

Another issue the COVID-19 pandemic raises is that of aversion to catastrophic outcomes. From a population-level perspective, a catastrophic outcome refers to a situation in which many people die or face a loss together. Thus, not only the eventual magnitude, but also the coincidence or bunching together of deaths and losses might affect policy evaluation. Many COVID-19 deaths occur among old people who would likely have died from other causes soon. Yet, instead of having those deaths spread over a few months or years, they occurred all at the same time. Images of rooms and trucks filled with coffins have been frequently broadcast during the pandemic. Aversion to such a dreadful situation calls for stringent control policies even if they impose high costs on the economy.[36]

The chapter focuses on COVID-19 policies. However, the evaluation tools described can be applied to other epidemics, and, more generally, to the evaluation of health technologies and health interventions. One area in which SWF analysis can be useful is in determining the value of vaccines. Traditional economic evaluations of vaccines adopt a narrowly defined health-centric perspective, focusing on two types of benefits: (i) the direct health benefits for the immunized (e.g., the reduction in the number of fatalities or the number of quality-adjusted life years gained) and (ii) the savings in the healthcare system due to a reduced need for alternative treatments. This perspective implies that developing, manufacturing, and distributing a new vaccine is valuable only insofar as it avoids deaths and disabilities and saves health sector costs.[37] A rapidly growing body of evidence suggests that vaccination yields sizable health, economic, and social benefits far beyond the narrow health-centric benefits traditionally captured in economic evaluations (see, e.g., Bloom et al. 2018; Jit et al. 2015; Nandi et al. 2019). These benefits include, e.g., protection against nosocomial infections (i.e., infections acquired in hospitals or in healthcare-associated locales), and herd protection; increasing labor force participation and labor productivity among the working-age

[36] See Rheinberger and Treich (2017) for an exact definition of catastrophe aversion and whether catastrophe aversion is a common sentiment. Hammitt and Treich, Chapter 7 this volume, also discusses the notion of catastrophe aversion.

[37] Note, in particular, that traditional economic evaluation of vaccines often does not incorporate the vaccine-induced decrease in transmission of the pathogen and the resulting herd protection.

population; protection against catastrophic health spending and the risk of falling into poverty traps; better cognitive functioning, higher school attendance, and higher educational attainment among vaccinated children; increases in tax revenues; and promotion of social equity insofar as the vaccine-preventable disease disproportionately affects low-income groups, minorities, and disadvantaged populations in general.

SWF analysis, with its focus on the overall well-being impact of health technologies and its concern for distributions, can easily accommodate all the relevant dimensions of vaccine evaluation.[38] Drawing from the analysis in the chapter, when assessing the value of vaccines through a SWF approach, what counts are not just the distributional aspects of the disease burden and the distributional aspects of disease-control interventions, but also the distributional aspects of financing vaccines. A vaccine paid for by rich countries and distributed free of charge throughout the world contributes more to social welfare than an equally effective vaccine whose costs are shared by all countries, also developing ones.

[38] Note that the framework can also encompass the potential adverse effects of vaccination.

Appendix 12.A The Value Of COVID-19 Control Policies in the United States

12.A.1 Distribution of Costs and Fatalities

The population is divided into two age groups, the "young" (age less than 65) and the "old" (65+), and five income groups, corresponding to the quintiles of the income distribution; based on the 2019 U.S. population age structure (U.S. Census Bureau 2020), 84 percent of the population is young. Let q_i be the proportion of aggregate GDP that individuals in income group i own, with $\sum_{i=1}^{5} q_i = 1$. The income distribution is given by $q_i = \{5\%, 10\%, 15\%, 23\%, 47\%\}$. We follow the COVID-19 simulator created by Fleurbaey and co-authors in representing the distribution of fatalities and costs by income quintiles.[39]

Let σ_{ia} be the proportion of the total income loss caused by the control policy or by the pandemic that an individual belonging to income group $i = \{1, 2, 3, 4, 5\}$ and age group $a = \{y, o\}$ bears:

$$\sigma_{ia} = \frac{5}{N} \frac{q_i^{\omega}}{\sum_i q_i^{\omega}} \frac{\sigma_a}{n_a} \tag{12.A.1}$$

where ω is the elasticity of costs to income, σ_a the proportion of costs paid by age group a, n_a the proportion of individuals in age group a, N the total population, and $\frac{N}{5}$ the size of each income group.[40] If $\omega = 1$, individuals pay proportionally to their income; if $\omega < 1$, lower-income quintiles bear a disproportionate amount of the costs. If $\frac{\sigma_a}{n_a} = 1$, all ages suffer an economic loss; if only the young pay the costs of the pandemic, then $\sigma_o = 0$ and $\frac{\sigma_y}{n_y} = \frac{1}{n_y}$, where n_y is the share of young in the

39 https://sites.google.com/site/marcfleurbaey/Home/covid

40 There are ten age-income combinations in the example. The proportion of costs paid by each age-income group is $\frac{q_i^{\omega}}{\sum_i q_i^{\omega}} \sigma_a$. Since the size of an age-income group is $0.2\, n_a N$, each individual in age group a and income group i pays $\sigma_{ia} = \frac{q_i^{\omega}}{\sum_i q_i^{\omega}} \sigma_a \frac{1}{0.2\, n_a\, N} = \frac{5}{N} \frac{q_i^{\omega}}{\sum_i q_i^{\omega}} \frac{\sigma_a}{n_a}$.

population. If the pandemic reduces aggregate income by the amount ΔGDP, each individual in age group a and income group i pays $\sigma_{ia}\Delta GDP$.

Let δ_{ia} be the proportion of individuals in age group a and income group i that die of COVID-19:

$$\delta_{ia} = \frac{5}{N}\frac{q_i^{\xi}}{\sum_i q_i^{\xi}}\frac{\delta_a}{n_a}D \tag{12.A.2}$$

where D is the total number of COVID-19 fatalities, ξ is the elasticity of fatalities to income and δ_a the share of deaths experienced by individuals in age group a.If there are D total COVID-19 fatalities, $D_{ia} = \frac{q_i^{\xi}}{\sum_i q_i^{\xi}}\delta_a D$ denotes the number of deaths accruing to individuals in age group a and income group i, and $\delta_{ia} = \frac{D_{ia}}{0.2n_a N}$ the mortality rate of individuals in age group a and income group i (i.e., the share of individuals in age group a and income group i that die of COVID-19). If $\xi = 0$, mortality risk is independent of socioeconomic status (i.e., every income group bears the same number of COVID-19 fatalities). If $\xi < 0$, individuals in low socioeconomic groups bear a disproportionate number of deaths due to COVID-19. If $\frac{\delta_a}{n_a} = 1$, then the mortality rate would be the same in all age groups. Based on the estimates of infection fatality rate by age in Verity et al. (2020) and on the 2019 U.S. population structure (U.S. Census Bureau 2020), the infection fatality rate (i.e., the percentage of fatalities among the infected) of the young is equal to 0.28 percent and the infection fatality rate of the old is equal to 4.36 percent. If both age groups have the same probability of getting infected, 25 percent of COVID-19 fatalities occur among the young. As a consequence, $\delta_y = 0.25$ and $\delta_o = 0.75$.

Per capita annual GDP in the pre-COVID-19 situation is set equal to \$65,000. The per capita income distribution across quintiles is given by \$16,250; \$32,500; \$48,750; \$74,750; and \$152,750.[41] We also assume that, absent any control policy, the pandemic will cause 70 percent of the population to be infected, resulting in a mortality rate equal to 0.67 percent of the population. More specifically, 0.2 percent of the young will die from COVID-19, while the mortality rate of the old is 3.05

[41] Per capita income of individuals in income group i is given by: $\frac{q_i N}{0.2\,N}$ \$65,000, where N is total population size and $0.2N$ the size of the income group.

percent. Regarding the distribution of fatalities across income quintiles, we consider two scenarios:

(i) Elasticity of fatalities to income ξ equals -0.5, i.e., low-income quintiles bear a disproportionate number of deaths. The corresponding percentages of fatalities accruing to the 1st, 2nd, 3rd, 4th, and 5th income quintiles are, respectively, 33 percent, 23 percent, 19 percent, 15 percent, and 11 percent. Table 12.1 presents the resulting mortality rates δ_{ia} per income and age group.[42]

(ii) Elasticity of fatalities to income ξ equals 0, i.e., the distribution of fatalities is independent of income. Consequently, all young individuals have a COVID-19 mortality risk of 0.2 percent, and all old individuals a mortality risk equal to 3.05 percent.

Likewise, we consider three different cases for the distribution of policy costs:

(i) Elasticity of policy costs to income $\omega = 1$, i.e., the distribution of costs is proportional to income. The percentages of policy costs paid by the 1st, 2nd, 3rd, 4th, and 5th income quintiles are equal to the income distribution q_i.

(ii) Elasticity of policy costs to income $\omega = 0.5$, i.e., the distribution of costs is regressive, or low-income groups bear a higher proportion of economic losses. The percentages of policy costs paid by the 1st, 2nd, 3rd, 4th, and 5th income quintiles are, respectively, 11 percent, 15 percent, 19 percent, 23 percent, and 33 percent (while their income share is 5 percent, 10 percent, 15 percent, 23 percent, 47 percent).

(iii) Elasticity of policy costs to income $\omega = 1.5$, i.e., the distribution of costs is progressive, or high-income groups bear the brunt of economic losses. The percentages of policy costs paid by the 1st, 2nd, 3rd, 4th, and 5th income quintiles are, respectively, 2 percent, 6 percent, 11 percent, 21 percent, and 60 percent (while their income share is 5 percent, 10 percent, 15 percent, 23 percent, 47 percent).

42 The mortality rates are computed by multiplying the age-specific mortality rates, $\frac{\delta_a}{n_a}\frac{D}{N}$ (0.2 percent for the young and 3.05 percent for the old), by five times the quintile-specific proportion of deaths, $5\frac{q_i^{\xi}}{\sum_i q_i^{\xi}}$. For example, the mortality rate of young individuals in the 1st income quintile is equal to 0.2*5*0.33 percent.

12.A.2 Individual Well-Being

Individual well-being depends on consumption and longevity. Lifetime well-being is time separable, and the period utility is $u(c_{ia}) = \frac{c_{ia}^{1-\lambda}}{1-\lambda} - k$, where λ is the coefficient of relative risk aversion, c_{ia} the consumption of an individual in age group a and income group i, and k the utility at the subsistence consumption level. We assume that in the pre-COVID-19 situation, consumption was constant across ages and equal to the income of the associated quintile: $c_{ia} = c_i = \frac{5}{N} q_i GDP$, where GDP denotes aggregate income. If the pandemic (or the nonpharmaceutical intervention to control it) causes a GDP contraction of X, consumption is equal to $c_{ia} = c_i - \sigma_{ia} X$, where σ_{ia} is the proportion of total loss borne by an individual in age group a and income group i, and its expression is given by (12.A.1). To simplify, we assume that all costs occur in one year.

Let μ_{iy} be the pre-COVID-19 fraction of young individuals who die prematurely, that is, before reaching an old age, and μ_{io} the fraction of old individuals who die prematurely in the pre-COVID-19 setting, i.e., before reaching a reasonable length of life, set at 85. Both probabilities depend on the income group, with low-income quintiles facing a higher risk of dying prematurely. Based on the 2017 U.S. lifetable (NCHS 2019), and averaging across all ages in an age group, we find that 13 percent of the young die before reaching age 65 and 43 percent of the old die prematurely, i.e., before reaching age 85. The average age of the young who do not live past 65 is 51, and of the old who do not live past 85 is 76; the life expectancy of the old who do live past age 85 (the assumed desirable longevity) is 88. We assume that the derived fractions of premature deaths apply to individuals in the 3rd income quintile, and we scale them to compute the probabilities of the other income quintiles. Based on Chetty et al. (2016) and following Adler et al. (2021), we assume that the annual probabilities of dying for individuals in the 1st, 2nd, 4th, and 5th quintiles are, respectively, 1.5, 1.3, 0.9, and 0.75 times the annual probability of dying of individuals with median income. As a result, the fractions of young and old that die prematurely for each income quintile are (19 percent, 57 percent), (16 percent, 49 percent), (13 percent, 43 percent), (12 percent, 40 percent), and (10 percent, 34 percent).

COVID-19 increases the number of individuals who die prematurely. Let μ_{ia}^* be the total fraction of individuals in age group a and income group i who die prematurely, with

$$\mu_{ia}^* = \mu_{ia} + \delta_{ia} \tag{12.A.3}$$

and δ_{ia} the fraction of individuals in age group a and income group i who die of COVID-19, whose expression is given in (12.A.2).

Let V_{ia} be the expected lifetime utility of individuals in age group a and income group i. For the "old" we have

$$V_{io} = 75u(c_i) + u(c_i - \sigma_{io}X) + (1 - \mu_{io}^*)12u(c_i).$$

The "old" individual has already lived for 75 years, sustains a consumption loss in the 76th year of age (the average age of the "old"), and is expected to live for an additional 12 years (until age 88) if she does not die prematurely of COVID-19 or of other causes (i.e., $1 - \mu_{io}^*$ of the "old" reach at least the desirable longevity of 85 years).

For the "young" we have

$$V_{iy} = 50u(c_i) + u(c_i - \sigma_{iy}X) + (1 - \mu_{iy}^*)[\mu_{io}25u(c_i) + (1 - \mu_{io})37u(c_i)].$$

The "young" individual has lived for 50 years and sustains a consumption loss in the 51st year of age (the average age of the young). A proportion μ_{iy}^* dies before the old age (i.e., at age 51) for either COVID-19 or other causes. Among those that survive the old age, a proportion $1 - \mu_{io}$ reaches the desirable length of life and dies at age 88, thereby living for an additional 37 years; the remaining individuals die at age 76 before reaching the desirable length of life, thereby living for an additional 25 years.

Moreover, let $U_{ia}(t)$ be the realized lifetime utility of an individual in age group a and income group i who dies exactly at $t = \{51, 76, 88\}$:

$$U_{ia}(t) = (t - 1)u(c_i) + u(c_i - \sigma_{ia}X).$$

For example, a young individual who survives the young age, but dies prematurely when old, will have a lifetime realized well-being equal to $U_{iy}(76) = 75u(c_i) + u(c_i - \sigma_{iy}X)$. The second term denotes the fact that, when young, he had to pay the costs of the pandemic for one year.

To calibrate the utility function, we set $\lambda = 2$ (a standard assumption in the literature), and the parameter k is set such that the value of a statistical life of an individual with median income at age 40 is equal to 10 million.[43]

[43] Consider a marginal change in the baseline probability of dying young. Assuming consumption is constant through life, the formula for the VSL is $VSL = \frac{u(c)}{u'(c)} LE_{40}$, where LE_{40} is the remaining life expectancy of a 40-year-old individual (set at 40.16) and $u'(c)$ the marginal utility of consumption. We set

12.A.3 Individual Willingness to Pay to Eliminate Pandemic Risks

Given the definition of expected individual lifetime utility, we can compute the amount of own income each individual is willing to sacrifice to get rid of COVID-19, that is, to eliminate the COVID-19-related mortality risk and income losses absent any intervention.

Consider an old individual and let ΔGDP be the aggregate income loss associated with no control over COVID-19. The individual willingness to pay wtp_{io} of an old individual in income group i is defined as

$$\begin{aligned} V_{io}(\mu_{io}, wtp_{io}) &\equiv 75u(c_i) + u(c_i - wtp_{io}) + (1-\mu_{io})12u(c_i) \\ &= 75u(c_i) + u(c_i - \sigma_{io}\Delta GDP) + \left(1-\mu_{io}^*\right)12u(c_i) \\ &\equiv V_{io}\left(\mu_{io}^*, \Delta GDP\right) \end{aligned} \tag{12.A.4}$$

Similarly, the willingness to pay of a young individual in income group i is defined as

$$\begin{aligned} V_{iy}\left(\mu_{iy}, wtp_{iy}\right) &\equiv 50u(c_i) + u\left(c_i - wtp_{iy}\right) \\ &\quad + \left(1-\mu_{iy}\right)[\mu_{io}25u(c_i) + (1-\mu_{io})37u(c_i)] \\ &= 50u(c_i) + u\left(c_i - \sigma_{iy}\Delta GDP\right) \\ &\quad + \left(1-\mu_{iy}^*\right)[\mu_{io}25u(c_i) + (1-\mu_{io})37u(c_i)] \\ &\equiv V_{iy}\left(\mu_{iy}^*, \Delta GDP\right) \end{aligned} \tag{12.A.5}$$

Table 12.2 summarizes the individuals' willingness to pay to eliminate the pandemic risk by income and age group, under the assumption that an uncontrolled pandemic does not cause any income loss (i.e., $\Delta GDP = 0$).[44]

consumption at \$48,750 (the consumption value of an individual with median income) and solve the expression to derive k. We find that $k = -0.000125288$.

44 Applying the definitions of willingness to pay in (12.A.4) and (12.A.5), and given that $u(c_i) = \frac{c_i^{1-\lambda}}{1-\lambda} + k$ and $\lambda = 2$, the willingness to pay of an individual in age group a and income group i solves the following equation:

$$wtp_{ia} = c_i - \left[k - \left(k - \frac{1}{c_i}\right)\Delta L_{ia}\right]^{-1}$$

with $\Delta L_{iy} = 1 - \delta_{iy}(37 - 12\mu_{io})$ and $\Delta L_{io} = 1 - \delta_{io}12$.

12.A.4 Evaluation Methods

Under BCA, the value of a policy to eliminate the risk of COVID-19 is equal to the unweighted sum of individuals' willingness to pay to eliminate COVID-19. Let wtp_{ia} be the willingness to pay of an individual in age group a and income group i. Under BCA, the total value X^{BCA} of the intervention is given by:

$$X^{BCA} = N\frac{1}{5}\sum_{i=1}^{5}\left(n_y wtp_{iy} + n_o wtp_{io}\right),$$

where n_y is the proportion of young people in the population, $n_o = 1 - n_y$ the proportion of old people, and N the total (pre-pandemic) population.

We consider three alternative SWFs:

1. Utilitarianism. The utilitarian SWF is the sum of expected individual lifetime well-being:

$$S^U = N\frac{1}{5}\sum_{i=1}^{5}\left(n_y V_{iy} + (1 - n_y) V_{io}\right).$$

2. Ex-ante prioritarianism. The ex-ante prioritarian SWF is the sum of a concave transformation of expected individual lifetime well-being:

$$S^{EA} = N\frac{1}{5}\sum_{i=1}^{5}\left(n_y g(V_{iy}) + (1 - n_y) g(V_{io})\right),$$

   where g is a strictly increasing and strictly concave function, denoting the degree of priority to the worse-off in (expected) lifetime well-being.

3. Ex-post prioritarianism. The ex-post prioritarian SWF is the expected sum of a strictly increasing and strictly concave transformation of realized individual lifetime well-being:

$$S^{EP} = N\frac{1}{5}n_y\sum_{i=1}^{5}\Big[\mu_{iy}^* g(U_{iy}(51)) + \left(1 - \mu_{iy}^*\right)\mu_{io} g(U_{iy}(76)) + \left(1 - \mu_{iy}^*\right)(1 - \mu_{io}) g(U_{iy}(88))\Big] + N\frac{1}{5}(1 - n_y)\sum_{i=1}^{5}\left[\mu_{io}^* g(U_{io}(76)) + (1 - \mu_{io}^*) g(U_{io}(88))\right].$$

We assume that the function g belongs to the Atkinson family, with γ the priority parameter: $g(w) = \frac{w^{1-\gamma}}{1-\gamma}$.

The maximum GDP loss X associated with the policy that the policy maker finds acceptable is defined as the reduction in current aggregate GDP that society is willing to suffer to eliminate the pandemic. Let $S^U\left(\mu_{iy}^*, \mu_{io}^*, \Delta GDP\right)$, $S^{EA}\left(\mu_{iy}^*, \mu_{io}^*, \Delta GDP\right)$, and $S^{EP}\left(\mu_{iy}^*, \mu_{io}^*, \Delta, GDP\right)$ be the utilitarian, ex-ante prioritarian, and ex-post prioritarian social welfare levels with COVID-19 and no control policy, where ΔGDP is the potential income loss associated with an uncontrolled policy (note that in the examples considered in the text ΔGDP is set to zero). The utilitarian societal burden X^U is defined as

$$\begin{aligned} S^U\left(\mu_{iy}, \mu_{io}, X^U\right) &\equiv N\frac{1}{5}\sum_{i=1}^{5}\left(n_y V_{iy}\left(\mu_{iy}, X^U\right) + (1-n_y)V_{io}\left(\mu_{io}, X^U\right)\right) \\ &= S^U\left(\mu_{iy}^*, \mu_{io}^*, \Delta GDP\right), \end{aligned}$$

with
$V_{iy}\left(\mu_{iy}, X^U\right) = 50u(c_i) + u\left(c_i - \sigma_{iy}X^U\right) + \left(1-\mu_{iy}\right)[25u(c_i) + (1-\mu_{io})$ $12u(c_i)]$ and $V_{io}\left(\mu_{io}, X^U\right) = 75u(c_i) + u\left(c_i - \sigma_{io}X^U\right) + (1-\mu_{io})12u(c_i)$.

The ex-ante prioritarian societal burden X^{EA} is defined as

$$\begin{aligned} S^{EA}\left(\mu_{iy}, \mu_{io}, X^{EA}\right) &\equiv N\frac{1}{5}\sum_{i=1}^{5}\left(n_y g\left(V_{iy}\left(\mu_{iy}, X^{EA}\right)\right) + (1-n_y)g\left(V_{io}\left(\mu_{io}, X^{EA}\right)\right)\right) \\ &= S^{EA}\left(\mu_{iy}^*, \mu_{io}^*, \Delta GDP\right). \end{aligned}$$

Finally, the ex-post prioritarian societal burden X^{EP} is defined as

$$\begin{aligned} S^{EP}\left(\mu_{iy}, \mu_{io}, X^{EP}\right) \equiv\; & N\frac{1}{5}n_y\sum_{i=1}^{5}\Big[\mu_{iy}g\left(U_{iy}(51; X^{EP})\right) \\ & +\left(1-\mu_{iy}\right)\mu_{io}g\left(U_{iy}(76; X^{EP})\right) \\ & +\left(1-\mu_{iy}\right)(1-\mu_{io})g\left(U_{iy}(88; X^{EP})\right)\Big] \\ & +N\frac{1}{5}(1-n_y)\sum_{i=1}^{5}\Big[\mu_{io}g\left(U_{io}(76; X^{EP})\right) \\ & +(1-\mu_{io})g\left(U_{io}(88; X^{EP})\right)\Big] \\ =\; & S^{EP}\left(\mu_{iy}^*, \mu_{io}^*, \Delta GDP\right), \end{aligned}$$

with $U_{ia}(t; X^{EP}) = (t-1)u(c_i) + u(c_i - \sigma_{ia}X^{EP})$.

The results in Table 12.3 correspond to the value X^U, X^{EA}, X^{EP} computed by solving the previous expressions.

12.A.5 Additional Tables

Table 12.A.1. ***Individuals' willingness to pay as a percentage of own income for a policy that eliminates the risk of death from COVID-19, by age group and income quintile***

	1st quintile	2nd quintile	3rd quintile	4th quintile	5th quintile
Young	5.8%	15.8%	24.2%	34.6%	54%
Old	27.5%	53%	65.2%	75.4%	86.9%

Note: COVID-19 fatality risk is independent of income; the young die of COVID-19 with probability 0.2 percent, the old with probability 3.05 percent; there is no income loss associated with an uncontrolled pandemic.

Appendix 12.B. The Allocation of Vaccine Doses

Consider again the example in Section 12.4. Individuals are divided into five income and two age groups, and life expectancies depend on the income quintile. We denoted δ_{ia} the probability that an individual in income quintile i and age group a dies because of COVID-19. If the individual is vaccinated, her COVID-19 mortality rate decreases to $\delta_{ia}(1 - e_a)$, where e_a is the effectiveness of the vaccine for individuals of age a. We consider the case where low-income quintiles are overburdened with deaths. The COVID-19 mortality rates by income and age group are given in Table 12.1.

Consider an old person in income group i and suppose for simplicity that COVID-19 does not entail any income loss, only the risk of premature mortality. If the individual is not vaccinated, her expected well-being is $V_{io}^{no\ vax} = 76u(c_i) + (1 - \mu_{io} - \delta_{io})12u(c_i)$. If the individual is vaccinated, her well-being becomes $V_{io}^{vax} = 76u(c_i) + (1 - \mu_{io} - \delta_{io}(1 - e_o))12u(c_i)$. The well-being gain from being vaccinated then equals

$$\Delta V_{io} = 12u(c_i)e_o\delta_{io}.$$

Consider now a young person in income group i. If the individual is not vaccinated, her expected well-being is $V_{iy}^{no\ vax} = 51u(c_i) + \left(1 - \mu_{iy} - \delta_{iy}\right)[25u(c_i) + (1 - \mu_{io})12u(c_i)]$. If the individual is vaccinated, her well-being becomes $V_{iy}^{vax} = 51u(c_i) + \left(1 - \mu_{iy} - \delta_{iy}(1 - e_y)\right)[25u(c_i) + (1 - \mu_{io})12u(c_i)]$. The well-being gain from being vaccinated then equals

$$\Delta V_{iy} = [37 - \mu_{io}12]u(c_i)e_y\delta_{iy}.$$

In the utilitarian case, social welfare is the sum of individuals' expected lifetime well-being, $S^U = \frac{N}{5}\sum_i \left(n_y V_{iy} + \left(1 - n_y\right)V_{io}\right)$. Therefore, one dose of vaccine to allocate will be given to the individual who gains more in terms of increase in expected well-being.

Let ΔV_{1o} be the utilitarian value of vaccinating an old individual in the 1st income quintile. We can compute the utilitarian value of vaccinating an individual at age a and income group i as a proportion of the utilitarian value of vaccinating an old individual in the 1st income quintile:

$$\frac{\Delta V_{iy}}{\Delta V_{1o}} = \frac{[37 - \mu_{io}12]u(c_i)}{12u(c_1)} \frac{e_y \delta_{iy}}{e_o \delta_{1o}}$$

$$\frac{\Delta V_{io}}{\Delta V_{1o}} = \frac{12u(c_i)}{12u(c_1)} \frac{e_o \delta_{io}}{e_o \delta_{1o}}$$

In both expressions, the first term represents the utilitarian social value of a given reduction in mortality risk $SVRR^U_{ia}$ (e.g., a 1 percentage point reduction) experienced by an individual at age a and in income group i as a proportion of the utilitarian value $SVRR^U_{1o}$ attached to a comparable reduction accruing to an old individual in the 1st income quintile (Table 12.4). The second term is the health benefit of vaccination, as compared with the health benefit enjoyed by an old person in the 1st income quintile. The terms $\frac{\Delta V_{iy}}{\Delta V_{1o}} e_o \delta_{1o}$ and $\frac{\Delta V_{io}}{\Delta V_{1o}} e_o \delta_{1o}$ are the utilitarian-adjusted mortality risk reductions achieved by vaccinating an individual (Table 12.5). For example, vaccinating a young individual in the 1st income quintile is equivalent, from a utilitarian point of view, to reducing the mortality risk of an old individual in the 1st income quintile by $\frac{\Delta V_{1y}}{\Delta V_{1o}} e_o \delta_{1o}$.

In the ex-ante prioritarian case, social welfare is the sum of strictly increasing and strictly concave transformations of individual expected well-being: $S^{EA} = \frac{N}{5} \sum_i (n_y g(V_{iy}) + (1 - n_y) g(V_{io}))$, with g strictly increasing and strictly concave. The ex-ante prioritarian welfare gain from vaccinating a young person in income group i is given by

$$\Delta S^{EA}_{iy} = g\left(V^{vax}_{iy}\right) - g\left(V^{no\ vax}_{iy}\right) \simeq g'\left(V^{no\ vax}_{iy}\right) \Delta V_{iy}.$$

The second expression derives from approximating the g function around the no vaccination case. Note that the approximation is good only if the change in expected well-being is sufficiently small (an assumption that, for the sake of simplicity, we make here). Similarly, the ex-ante prioritarian welfare gain from vaccinating an old person in income group i is given by

$$\Delta S^{EA}_{io} = g(V^{vax}_{io}) - g(V^{no\ vax}_{io}) \simeq g'(V^{no\ vax}_{io}) \Delta V_{io}.$$

The ex-ante prioritarian value of vaccinating an individual at age a and in income group i as a proportion of the ex-ante prioritarian value of vaccinating an old individual in the 1st income quintile is

$$\frac{\Delta S_{iy}^{EA}}{\Delta S_{1o}^{EA}} = \frac{g'\left(V_{iy}^{no\ vax}\right)[37 - \mu_{io}12]u(c_i)}{g'\left(V_{1o}^{no\ vax}\right)12u(c_1)}\frac{e_y\delta_{iy}}{e_o\delta_{1o}}$$

$$\frac{\Delta S_{io}^{EA}}{\Delta S_{1o}^{EA}} = \frac{g'\left(V_{io}^{no\ vax}\right)12u(c_i)}{g'\left(V_{1o}^{no\ vax}\right)12u(c_1)}\frac{e_o\delta_{io}}{e_o\delta_{1o}}$$

where, in both expressions, the first term is the ex-ante prioritarian social value $SVRR_{ia}^{EA}$ attached to a given reduction in mortality risk experienced by an individual at age a and in income group i as a proportion of the ex-ante prioritarian value $SVRR_{1o}^{EA}$ of a comparable risk reduction accruing to an old individual in the 1st income quintile (Tables 12.6 and 12.B.1). The results in Tables 12.7 and 12.B.2 are determined by multiplying the previous expressions by $e_o\delta_{1o}$.

In the ex-post prioritarian case, social welfare is the expected sum of concave transformations of individual realized well-being: $S^{EP} = N\frac{1}{5}n_y\sum_{i=1}^{5}\left[\left(\mu_{iy} + \delta_{iy}\right)g(U_i(51)) + \left(1 - \mu_{iy} - \delta_{iy}\right)\mu_{io}g(U_i(76)) + \left(1 - \mu_{iy} - \delta_{iy}\right)(1 - \mu_{io})g(U_i(88))\right] + N\frac{1}{5}(1 - n_y)\sum_{i=1}^{5}[(\mu_{io} + \delta_{io})g(U_i(76)) + (1 - \mu_{io} - \delta_{io})g(U_i(88))]$, with $U_i(a) = u(c_i)a$. The ex-post prioritarian welfare gain from vaccinating an old person in income group i is given by

$$\Delta S_{io}^{EP} = \delta_{io}[g(U_i(88)) - g(U_i(76))] \simeq \delta_{io}g'(U_i(76))12u(c_i) = g'(U_i(76))\Delta V_{io}.$$

Once again, we implicitly assume that the change in realized well-being is small enough such that the approximation is good.

The ex-post prioritarian welfare gain from vaccinating a young person in income group i is given by

$$\begin{aligned}\Delta S_{iy}^{EP} &= \delta_{iy}[g(U_i(88)) - g(U_i(51)) - \mu_{io}(g(U_i(88)) - g(U_i(76)))] \\ &\simeq \delta_{iy}[g'(U_i(51))37u(c_i) - \mu_{io}g'(U_i(76))12u(c_i)] \\ &= g'(U_i(51))\Delta V_{iy} + \delta_{iy}\mu_{io}12u(c_i)[g'(U_i(51)) - g'(U_i(76))].\end{aligned}$$

The ex-post prioritarian value of vaccinating an individual at age a and in income group i as a proportion of the ex-post prioritarian value of vaccinating an old individual in the 1st income quintile is

$$\frac{\Delta S_{iy}^{EP}}{\Delta S_{1o}^{EP}} = \frac{g'(U_i(51))37u(c_i) - \mu_{io}g'(U_i(76))12u(c_i)}{g'(U_1(76))12u(c_1)} \frac{e_y\delta_{iy}}{e_o\delta_{1o}}$$

$$\frac{\Delta S_{io}^{EP}}{\Delta S_{1o}^{EP}} = \frac{g'(U_i(76))12u(c_i)}{g'(U_1(76))12u(c_1)} \frac{e_o\delta_{io}}{e_o\delta_{1o}}$$

where, in both expressions, the first term is the ex-post prioritarian value $SVRR_{ia}^{EP}$ attached to a given reduction in mortality risk experienced by an individual at age a and in income group i as a proportion of the ex-post prioritarian value $SVRR_{1o}^{EP}$ of a comparable risk reduction accruing to an old individual in the 1st income quintile (Tables 12.8 and 12.B.3). The results in Tables 12.9 and 12.B.4 are determined by multiplying the previous expressions by $e_o\delta_{1o}$.

12.B.1 Additional Tables

Table 12.B.1. *Ex-ante prioritarian SVRR compared with the ex-ante prioritarian SVRR attached to an older person belonging to the 1st income quintile, by age and income group*

	1st quintile	2nd quintile	3rd quintile	4th quintile	5th quintile
Young	2.69	2.71	2.72	2.73	2.74
Old	1	0.99	0.98	0.97	0.96

Note: Atkinson SWF with priority parameter equal to 1.

Table 12.B.2. *Ex-ante-prioritarian-adjusted reduction in COVID-19 mortality risk if the vaccine is 100 percent effective for all age groups, by age and income group*

	1st quintile	2nd quintile	3rd quintile	4th quintile	5th quintile
Young	0.86%	0.61%	0.5%	0.41%	0.29%
Old	4.96%	3.46%	2.8%	2.25%	1.56%

Note: Atkinson SWF with priority parameter equal to 1. If the vaccine is less than 100 percent effective, the values in the table should be multiplied by the reduced effectiveness (e.g., if effectiveness is 60 percent, the ex-ante-prioritarian-adjusted reduction for a young individual in the 1st income quintile is 0.6×0.86 percent).

Table 12.B.3. *Ex-post prioritarian SVRR compared with the ex-post prioritarian SVRR attached to an older person belonging to the 1st income quintile, by age and income group*

	1st quintile	2nd quintile	3rd quintile	4th quintile	5th quintile
Young	3.75	3.87	3.95	4	4.09
Old	1	1	1	1	1

Note: Atkinson SWF with priority parameter equal to 1. When the priority parameter is equal to 1, the approximated formula of the ex-post prioritarian SVRR for an old person is $g'(U_i(76))\Delta V_{io} = [76u(c_i)]^{-1}12u(c_i) = \frac{12}{76}$, which is constant across income groups.

Table 12.B.4. *Ex-post-prioritarian-adjusted reduction in COVID-19 mortality risk if the vaccine is 100 percent effective for all age groups, by age and income group*

	1st quintile	2nd quintile	3rd quintile	4th quintile	5th quintile
Young	1.19%	0.87%	0.73%	0.59%	0.43%
Old	4.96%	3.51%	2.87%	2.31%	1.62%

Note: Atkinson SWF with priority parameter equal to 1. If the vaccine is less than 100 percent effective, the values in the table should be multiplied by the reduced effectiveness (e.g., if effectiveness is 60 percent, the ex-post-prioritarian-adjusted reduction for a young individual in the 1st income quintile is 0.6×1.19 percent).

References

Acemoglu, D., Chernozhukov, V., Werning, I., and Whinston, M.D. (2020). "Optimal Targeted Lockdowns in a Multi-Group SIR Model." *NBER Working Paper* n. 27102. Available at www.nber.org/papers/w27102.pdf

Adam, D. (2020). "The Limits of R." *Nature*, 583: 346–348. Available at www.nature.com/articles/d41586-020-02009-w

Adler, M.D. (2019). *Measuring Social Welfare. An Introduction.* Oxford: Oxford University Press.

(2020). "What Should We Spend to Save Lives in a Pandemic? A Critique of the Value of Statistical Life." *Duke Law School Public Law and Legal Theory Series* No. 2020-40. Available at https://papers.ssrn.com/sol3/papers.cfm?abstract_id=3636550

Adler, M.D., Bradley, R., Ferranna, M., Fleurbaey, M., Hammitt, J.K., and Voorhoeve, A. (2020). Assessing the Well-Being Impacts of the COVID-19 Pandemic and Three Policy Types: Suppression, Control, and Uncontrolled Spread." *T20 Policy Brief*. Available at www.g20-insights.org/wp-content/uploads/2020/11/assessing-the-wellbeing-impacts-of-the-covid-19-pandemic-and-three-policy-types-suppression-control-and-uncontrolled-spread-1606214930.pdf

Adler, M.D., Ferranna, M., Hammitt, J.K., and Treich, N. (2021). "Fair Innings? The Utilitarian and Prioritarian Value of Risk Reduction Over a Whole Lifetime." *Journal of Health Economics*, 75: 102412. Available at https://doi.org/10.1016/j.jhealeco.2020.102412.

Alvarez, F., Argente, D., Lippi, F. (2020). "A Simple Planning Problem for COVID-19 Lockdown." *NBER Working Paper* n. 26981. Available at www.nber.org/papers/w26981.pdf

Andrew, A., Cattan, A., Costa Dias, M., et al.(2020). "Inequalities in Children's Experiences of Home Learning during the COVID-19 Lockdown in England." *Fiscal Studies*, 41: 653–683. Available at https://doi.org/10.1111/1475-5890.12240

Armitage, R., and Nellums, L.B. (2020). "COVID-19 and the Consequences of Isolating the Elderly." *The Lancet, Public Health*, 5: E256. Available at https://doi.org/10.1016/S2468–2667(20)30061-X

Avent, R. (2020). "COVID-19 Leaves a Legacy of Increased Inequality." *The Economist*, November 17, 2020.

Bloom, D.E., Cadarette, D., and Ferranna, M. (2021). "The Value of Vaccination in the Age of COVID-19." *American Journal of Public Health*, 111: 1049–1054. Available at https://doi.org/10.2105/AJPH.2020.306114

Bloom, D.E., Cadarette, D., Ferranna, M., Hyer, R.N., and Tortorice, D.L. (2021). "How New Models of Vaccine Development for COVID-19 Have Helped Address an Epic Public Health Crisis." *Health Affairs*, 40: 1–8. Available at https://doi.org/10.1377/hlthaff.2020.02012

Bloom, D.E., Cadarette, D., Ferranna, M., and Seligman, B. (2020). "A Matter of Life and Death." *Finance and Development*. Available at https://www.imf.org/external/pubs/ft/fandd/2020/04/allocating-scarce-medical-resources-during-the-COVID19-pandemic-bloom.htm

Bloom, D.E., Fan, V.Y., and Sevilla, JP. (2018). "The Broad Socioeconomic Benefits of Vaccination." *Science Translational Medicine*, 10: eaaj2345. Available at and https://doi.org/10.1126/scitranslmed.aaj2345

Bloom, D.E., Kuhn, M., and Prettner, K. (forthcoming 2022). "Modern Infectious Diseases: Macroeconomic Impacts and Policy Responses." Journal of Economic Literature.

Blundell, R., Costa Dias, M., Joyce, R., and Xu, X. (2020). "COVID-19 and Inequalities." *Fiscal Studies*, 41: 291–319. Available at https://doi.org/10.1111/1475-5890/12232.

Bridle, B.W., and Sharif, S. (2020). "Why Vaccines Are Less Effective in the Elderly, and What It Means for COVID-19." *The Conversation*. Available at https://theconversation.com/why-vaccines-are-less-effective-in-the-elderly-and-what-it-means-for-covid-19-141971

Brown, C.S., and Ravallion, M. (2020). "Inequality and the Coronavirus: Socioeconomic Covariates of Behavioral Responses and Viral Outcomes Across US Counties." *NBER Working Paper* n. 27549. Available at https://doi.org/10.3386/w27549

Brown, C.S., Ravallion, M., van de Walle, D. (2020). "Can the World's Poor Protect Themselves from the New Coronavirus?" *NBER Working Paper* n. 27200. Available at www.nber.org/papers/w27200.pdf

Bubar, K.M., Kissler, S.M., Lipsitch, M., Cobey, S., Grad, Y.H., and Larremore, D.B. (2021). "Model-Informed COVID-19 Vaccine Prioritization Strategies by Age and Serostatus." *Science*, eabe6959. Available at https://doi.org/10.1126/science.abe6959

Buckner, J.H., Chowell, G., and Springborn, M.R. (2020). "Dynamic Prioritization of COVID-19 Vaccines When Social Distancing Is Limited for Essential Workers." *medRxiv*. Available at https://doi.org/10.1101/2020.09.22.20199174

Cash, R., and Patel, V. (2020). "Has COVID-19 Subverted Global Health?" *The Lancet,* 395: 1687–1688. Available at https://doi.org/10.1016/S0140-6736(20)31089-8

Chetty, R., Stepner, M., Abraham, S., et al. (2016). "The Association between Income and Life Expectancy in the United States, 2001–2014." *Journal of the American Medical Association,* 315: 1750–1766. Available at https://doi.org/10.1001/jama.2016.4226

Chow, N., Fleming-Dutra, K., Gierke, R., et al. (2020). "Preliminary Estimates of the Prevalence of Selected Underlying Health Conditions among Patients with Coronavirus Disease 2019—United States, February 12–March 28, 2020." *Morbidity and Mortality Weekly Report, Centers for Disease Control and Prevention* 69: 382–386. Available at https://doi.org/10.15585/mmwr.mm6913e2

Cutler, D.M., and Summers, L.H. (2020). "The COVID-19 Pandemic and the $16 Trillion Virus." *Journal of the American Medical Association*, 324: 1495-1496. Available at https://doi.org/10.1001/jama.2020.19759

Dingel, J.I., Neiman, B. (2020) How many jobs can be done at home?, Journal of Public Economics, 189: 104235, https://doi.org/10.1016/j.jpubeco.2020.104235.

Eichenbaum, M.S., Rebelo, S., and Trabandt, M. (2020). "The Macroeconomics of Epidemics." *NBER Working Paper* n. 26882. Available at www.nber.org/papers/w26882.pdf

Emanuel, E.J., Persad, G., Kern, A., et al. (2020a). "An Ethical Framework for Global Vaccine Allocation." *Science*, 369: 1309–1312. Available at https://doi.org/10.1126/science.abe2803

Emanuel, E.J., Persad, G., Upshur, R., et al. (2020b). "Fair Allocation of Scarce Medical Resources in the Time of COVID-19." *New England Journal of Medicine*, 382: 2049–2055. Available at https://doi.org/10.1056/NEJMsb2005114

Emanuel, E.J., and Wertheimer, A. (2006). "Who Should Get Influenza Vaccine When Not All Can?" *Science*, 312: 854–855. Available at https://doi.org/10.1126/science.1125347

Farboodi, M., Jarosch, G., and Shimer, R. (2020). "Internal and External Effects of Social Distancing in a Pandemic." *NBER Working Paper* n. 27059. Available at www.nber.org/papers/w27059.pdf

Favero, C.A., Ichino, A., and Rustichini, A. (2020). "Restarting the Economy while Saving Lives under COVID-19." Available at https://papers.ssrn.com/sol3/papers.cfm?abstract_id=3580626

Ferguson, N.M., Laydon, and D., Nedjati-Gilani, G., et al. (2020). "Impact of Non-Pharmaceutical Interventions (NPIs) to Reduce COVID-19 Mortality and Healthcare Demand." Imperial College, London, Working Paper. Available at https://doi.org/10.25561/77482

Ferranna, M., Cadarette, D., and Bloom, D.E. (2021). "COVID-19 Vaccine Allocation: Modeling Health Outcomes and Equity Implications of Alternative Strategies." *Engineering* 7(7): 924–935. Available at https://doi.org/10.1016/j.eng.2021.03.014

Fontanet, A., and Cauchemez, S. (2020). "COVID-19 Herd Immunity: Where Are We?" *Nature Reviews Immunology*, 20: 583–584. Available at https://doi.org/10.1038/s41577-020-00451-5

Giordano, G., Blanchini, F., and Bruno, R., et al. (2020). "Modelling the COVID-19 Epidemic and Implementation of Population-Wide Interventions in Italy." *Nature Medicine*, 26: 855–860. Available at https://doi.org/10.1038/s41591-020-0883-7

Glover, A., Heathcote, J., Krueger, D., and Ríos-Rull, J.-V. (2020). "Health versus Wealth: On the Distributional Effects of Controlling a Pandemic." *NBER Working Paper* No. 27046. Available at www.nber.org/papers/w27046.pdf

Gollier, C. (2020). "Cost-Benefit Analysis of Age-Specific Deconfinement Strategies." *COVID Economics*, 24: 1–31.

Goodnough, A., and Hoffman, J. (2020). "The Elderly vs. Essential Workers: Who Should Get the Coronavirus Vaccine First?" *The New*

York Times, December 05, 2020. Available at www.nytimes.com/2020/12/05/health/covid-vaccine-first.html

Gopinath, G. (2020). "The Great Lockdown: Worst Economic Downturn Since the Great Depression." Available at https://blogs.imf.org/2020/04/14/the-great-lockdown-worst-economic-downturn-since-the-great-depression/

Greenstone, M., and Nigam, V. (2020). "Does Social Distancing Matter?" *COVID Economics*, 7: 1–23. Available at https://bfi.uchicago.edu/wp-content/uploads/BFI_WP_202026.pdf

Guan, W., Liang, W., Zhao, Y., et al. (2020). "Comorbidity and Its Impact on 1590 Patients with COVID-19 in China: A Nationwide Analysis." *European Respiratory Journal*, 55: 20000547. Available at https://doi.org/10.1183/13993003.00547-2020

Hafner, M., Yerushalmi, E., Fays, C., Dufresne, E., and Van Stolk, C. (2020). "COVID-19 and the Cost of Vaccine Nationalism." *RAND Europe Report*. Available at https://doi.org/10.7249/RRA769-1

Hammitt, J.K. (2000). "Valuing Mortality Risk: Theory and Practice." *Environmental Science and Technology*, 34: 1396–1400. Available at https://doi.org/10.1021/es990733n

(2007). "Valuing Changes in Mortality Risk: Lives Saved versus Life Years Saved." *Review of Environmental Economics and Policy*, 1: 228–240. Available at https://doi.org/10.1093/reep/rem015

(2020). "Valuing Mortality Risk in the Time of COVID-19." *Journal of Risk and Uncertainty*, 11: 1–26. Available at https://doi.org/10.1007/s11166-020-09338-1

Hodgson, S.H., Mansatta, K., Mallett, G., Harris, V., Emary, K.R.W., and Pollard, A.J. (2020). "What Defines an Efficacious COVID-19 Vaccine? A Review of the Challenges Assessing the Clinical Efficacy of Vaccines against SARS-CoV-2". *The Lancet, Infectious Diseases* 21: E26–E35. Available at https://doi.org/10.1016/S1473–3099(20)30773-8

IMF (International Monetary Fund). (2020). *World Economic Outlook, October 2020: A Long and Difficult Ascent*. Available at www.imf.org/en/Publications/WEO/Issues/2020/09/30/world-economic-outlook-october-2020

Ioannidis, J. (2020). "The Infection Fatality Rate of COVID-19 Inferred from Seroprevalence Data." *Bulletin of the World Health Organization* (published online October 14, 2020). Available at www.who.int/bulletin/online_first/BLT.20.265892.pdf

Jit, M., Hutubessy, R., Png, M.E., et al. (2015). "The Broader Economic Impact of Vaccination: Reviewing and Appraising the Strength of Evidence." *BMC Medicine*, 13: 209. Available at https://doi.org/10.1186/s12916-015-0446-9

JCVI (Joint Committee on Vaccination and Immunisation). (2020). "Priority Groups for Coronavirus (COVID-19) Vaccination: Advice from the JCVI. 2 December 2020." Available at www.gov.uk/government/publications/priority-groups-for-coronavirus-covid-19-vaccination-advice-from-the-jcvi-2-december-2020/priority-groups-for-coronavirus-covid-19-vaccination-advice-from-the-jcvi-2-december-2020

Jones, C.J., Philippon, T., and Venkateswaran, V. (2020). "Optimal Mitigation Policies in a Pandemic: Social Distancing and Working from Home." *NBER Working Paper* No. 26984. Available at www.nber.org/papers/w26984.pdf

Kissler, S.M., Tedijanto, C., Goldstein, E., Grad, Y.H., and Lipsitch, M. (2020). "Projecting the Transmission Dynamics of SARS-CoV-2 through the Postpandemic Period." *Science*, 368: 860–868. Available at https://doi.org/10.1126/science.abb5793

Kniesner, T.J., and Viscusi, W.K. (2019). "The Value of a Statistical Life." Oxford Research Encyclopedia of Economics and Finance. Available at https://doi.org/10.1093/acrefore/9780190625979.013.138

Levin, A.T., Hanage, W.P., Owusu-Boaitey, N., Cochran, K.B., Walsh, A.P., and Meyerowitz-Katz, G. (2020). "Assessing the Age Specificity of Infection Fatality Rates for COVID-19: Systematic Review, Meta-Analysis, and Public Policy Implications." *European Journal of Epidemiology* 35: 1123–1138. Available at https://doi.org/10.1007/s10654–020-00698-1

Mahoney, N. (2020). "Don't Fall for the False Trade-offs of COVID-19 Policy." *Chicago Booth Review,* (published online March 26, 2020). Available at https://review.chicagobooth.edu/economics/2020/article/don-t-fall-false-trade-offs-covid-19-policy

Mandavilli, A. (2020). "The Next Vaccine Challenge: Reassuring Older Americans." The New York Times, December, 14, 2020. Available at www.nytimes.com/2020/12/14/health/coronavirus-vaccine-elderly.html

McLaren, J. (2020). "Racial Disparity in COVID-19 Deaths: Seeking Economic Roots with Census data." *NBER Working Paper* No. 27407. Available at https://doi.org/10.3386/w27407

Medlock, J., and Galvani, A.P. (2009). "Optimizing Influenza Vaccine Distribution." *Science*, 325: 1705–1708. Available at https://doi.org/10.1126/science.1175570

Nandi, A., Shet, A., Behrman, J.R., Black, M.M., Bloom, D.E., and Laxminarayan, R. (2019). "Anthropometric, Cognitive, and Schooling Benefits of Measles Vaccination: Longitudinal Cohort Analysis in Ethiopia, India, and Vietnam." *Vaccine*, 37: 4336–4343. Available at https://doi.org/10.1016/j.vaccine.2019.06.025

NASEM (National Academy of Sciences Engineering and Medicine) (2020). *Framework for Equitable Allocation of COVID-19 Vaccine*. Washington, DC: The National Academy Press.

NCHS (National Center for Health Statistics) (2019). *National Vital Statistics Reports*, 68: 7. Available at: www.cdc.gov/nchs/data/nvsr/nvsr68/nvsr68_07-508.pdf

O'Driscoll, M., Ribeiro Dos Santos, G., Wang, L., et al. (2021). "Age-Specific Mortality and Immunity Patterns of SARS-CoV-2." *Nature*, 590: 140–145. Available at https://doi.org/10.1038/s41586-020-2918-0

Peiris, M., Leung, G.M. (2020). "What Can We Expect from First-Generation COVID-19 Vaccines?" *The Lancet*, 396: 1467–1469. Available at https://doi.org/10.1016/S0140-6736(20)31976-0

Perez-Saez, J., Lauer, S.A., Kaiser, L., et al. (2020). "Serology-Informed Estimates of SARS-CoV-2 Infection Fatality Risk in Geneva, Switzerland." *The Lancet Infectious Diseases* (published online July 14, 2020). Available at https://doi/org/10.1016/S1473-3099(20)30584-3

Quaas, M.F., Meya, J.N., Schenk, H., Bos, B., Drupp, M.A., and Requate, T. (2020). "The Social Cost of Contacts: Theory and Evidence for the COVID-19 Pandemic in Germany." *CESifo Working Paper* No. 8347. Available at www.cesifo.org/DocDL/cesifo1_wp8347.pdf

Rheinberger, C.M., and Treich, N. (2017). "Attitudes Toward Catastrophe." *Environmental and Resource Economics*, 67: 609–636. Available at https://doi.org/10.1007/s10640-016-0033-3

Roberts, S. (2020). "Flattening the Coronavirus Curve." *The New York Times*, March 27, 2020. Available at www.nytimes.com/article/flatten-curve-coronavirus.html

Robinson, L. (2007). "How U.S. Government Agencies Value Mortality Risk Reductions." *Review of Environmental Economics and Policy*, 1: 283–299. https://doi.org/10.1093/reep/rem018

Rodríguez, J., Patón, M., and Acuña, J.M. (2020). "Prioritisation of Population Groups with the Most Interactions for COVID-19 Vaccination Can Substantially Reduce Total Fatalities." *medRxiv*. Available at https://doi.org/10.1101/2020.10.12.20211094

Schmidt, H., Gostin, L.O., and Williams, M.A. (2020). "Is It Lawful and Ethical to Prioritize Racial Minorities for COVID-19 Vaccines?" *Journal of American Medical Association*, 324: 2023–2024. Available at https://doi.org/10.1001/jama.2020.20571

Seligman, B., Ferranna, M., and Bloom, D.E. (2021). "Social Determinants of Mortality from COVID-19: A Simulation Study Using NHANES." *PLOS Medicine*, 18: e1003490. Available at https://doi.org/10.1371/journal.pmed.1003490

Streek, H., Schulte, B., and Kümmerer, B.M., et al. (2020). "Infection Fatality Rate of SARS-CoV-2 in a Super-Spreading Event in Germany." *Nature Communications*, 11: 5829. Available at https://doi.org/10.1038/s41467-020-19509-y

Subbaraman, N. (2020). "How to Address the Coronavirus's Outsized Toll of People of Colour." *Nature*, 581: 366–367. Available at https://doi.org/10.1038/d41586-020-01470-x

Thunström, L., Newbold, S.C., Finnoff, D., Ashworth, M., and Shogren, J.F. (2020). "The Benefits and Costs of Using Social Distancing to Flatten the Curve for COVID-19." *Journal of Benefit-Cost Analysis*, 11: 179–195. Available at https://doi.org/10.1017/bca.2020.12

Toner, E., Barnill, A., Krubiner, C., and Bernstein, J. (2020). "Interim Framework for COVID-19 Allocation and Distribution in the United States." The Johns Hopkins Center for Health Security, Baltimore, MD. Available at www.centerforhealthsecurity.org/our-work/pubs_archive/pubs-pdfs/2020/200819-vaccine-allocation.pdf.

Toxvaerd, F. (2020). "Equilibrium Social Distancing." *Cambridge Working Papers in Economics*, 2021. Available at www.econ.cam.ac.uk/research-files/repec/cam/pdf/cwpe2021.pdf

UNIDO (United Nations Industrial Development Organization). (2020). "Managing COVID-19: How the Pandemic Disrupts Global Value Chains." Available at https://iap.unido.org/articles/managing-covid-19-how-pandemic-disrupts-global-value-chains

U.S. Census Bureau, Population Division (2020). "Annual Estimates of the Resident Population for Selected Age Groups by Sex for the United States: April 1, 2010 to July 1, 2019 (NC-EST2019-AGESEX)." Available at: https://www.census.gov/newsroom/press-kits/2020/population-estimates-detailed.html

Verity, R., Okell, L.C., Dorigatti, I., et al. (2020). "Estimates of the Severity of Coronavirus Disease 2019: A Model-Based Analysis." *The Lancet, Infectious Diseases,* 20: 669–677. Available at https://doi.org/10.1016/S1473-3099(20)30243-7

Viner, R.M., Mytton, O.T., Bonell, C., et al. (2021). "Susceptibility to SARS-CoV-2 Infection Among Children and Adolescents Compared with Adults: A Systematic Review and Meta-Analysis." *Journal of American Medical Association, Pediatrics*, 175: 143–156. Available athttps://doi.org/10.1001/jamapediatrics.2020.4573

Viscusi, W.K. (2018). *Pricing Lives: Guideposts for a Safer Society.* Princeton: Princeton University Press.

Vogel, G. (2020). "Sweden's Gamble." Science, 370: 159–163. Available at https://doi.org//10.1126/science.370.6513.159

Warfel, J.M., Zimmerman, L.I., and Merkel, T.J. (2014). "Acellular Pertussis Vaccines Protect Against Disease but Fail to Prevent Infection and Transmission in a Nonhuman Primate Model." *Proceedings of the National Academy of Science*, 111: 787–792. Available at https://doi.org/10.1073/pnas.13146888110

WHO (World Health Organization). (2020). "Coronavirus Disease 2019 (COVID-19): Situation Report, 46." Available at www.who.int/docs/default-source/coronaviruse/situation-reports/20200306-sitrep-46-covid-19.pdf?sfvrsn%3d96b04adf_4

Wu, X., Nethery, R.C., Sabath, B.M., Braun, D., Dominici, F. (2020). "Exposure to Air Pollution and COVID-19 Mortality in the United States: A Nationwide Cross-Sectional Study." *Science Advances*, 6: eabd4049. Available at https://doi.org/10.1126/sciadv.adb4049

Yang, W., Kandula, S., Huynh, M., et al. (2020). "Estimating the Infection-Fatality Risk of SARS-CoV-2 in New York City During the Spring 2020 Pandemic Wave: A Model-Based Analysis." *The Lancet, Infectious Diseases*, 21: 203–212. Available at https://doi.org/10.1016/S1473–3099(20)30769-6

Yglesias, M. (2020). "Flattening the Curve isn't Good Enough." *Vox* (published online May 6, 2020). Available at www.vox.com/2020/5/6/21241058/coronavirus-mitigation-suppression-flatten-the-curve

Zhou, F., Yu, T., Du, R., et al. (2020). "Clinical Course and Risk Factors for Mortality of Adult Inpatients with COVID-19 in Wuhan, China: A Retrospective Cohort Study." *Lancet*, 395: 1054–1062. Available at https://doi.org/10.1016/s0140-6736(20)30566-3

Index

For EU product safety concerns, contact us at Calle de José Abascal, 56–1°,
28003 Madrid, Spain or eugpsr@cambridge.org.

www.ingramcontent.com/pod-product-compliance
Ingram Content Group UK Ltd.
Pitfield, Milton Keynes, MK11 3LW, UK
UKHW022338190325
456511UK00017B/308
* 9 7 8 1 1 0 8 7 0 3 6 0 4 *